TEACHING
the BOOK *of*
MORMON

PART ONE

I NEPHI - ALMA 18

THANKS FOR YOUR
SUPPORT !
HAPPY TEACHING !

John Marris

TEACHING
the BOOK *of*
MORMON

PART ONE

1 NEPHI - ALMA 18

JOHN S. BUSHMAN, REED ROMNEY,
JOHN R. MANIS & CURT R. WAKEFIELD

CFI

An Imprint of Cedar Fort, Inc,

Springville, Utah

This is not an official publication of The Church of Jesus Christ of Latter-day Saints. The opinions and views expressed herein belong solely to the author and do not necessarily represent the opinions or views of Cedar Fort, Inc. Permission for the use of sources, graphics, and photos is also solely the responsibility of the author.

ISBN 13: 978-1-4621-1217-3

Published by CFI, an imprint of Cedar Fort, Inc., 2373 W. 700 S., Springville, UT 84663
Distributed by Cedar Fort, Inc., www.cedarfort.com

LIBRARY OF CONGRESS CATALOGING-IN-PUBLICATION DATA

Bushman, John S. (John Sanford), 1971- author.
Teaching the Book of Mormon / John S. Bushman, Reed Romney, John R. Manis, Curt R. Wakefield.
  pages cm
Includes bibliographical references and index.
Summary: Designed specifically for teachers of the Book of Mormon.
ISBN 978-1-4621-1217-3 (alk. paper)
1. Book of Mormon--Study and teaching. I. Romney, Reed, 1980- author. II. Manis, John R., author. III. Wakefield, Curt Ryan, author. IV. Title.

BX8627.B87 2013
289.3'22071--dc23

2013007035

Cover design by Rebecca J. Greenwood and Shawnda T. Craig
Cover design © 2013 Lyle Mortimer
Edited by Summer Romney and Michelle Stoll
Typeset by Emily S. Chambers
Printed in the United States of America

10 9 8 7 6 5 4 3 2 1

Printed on acid-free paper

To the dedicated teachers and students
of scripture everywhere.

CONTENTS

INTRODUCTION

"Remember the New Covenant, Even the Book of Mormon"

In September 1832, several missionaries returned from their fields of labor to Kirtland, Ohio. They had been preaching the message of the restored gospel of Jesus Christ as they had been commissioned by revelation through the Prophet Joseph Smith. After reporting their missionary labors, the Lord gave another revelation to the Prophet Joseph, now recorded as Section 84 of the Doctrine and Covenants. Speaking to the group of elders, the Lord explained that the elders' "minds in times past have been darkened because of unbelief, . . . and [the whole church] shall remain under this condemnation until they repent and remember the new covenant, even the Book of Mormon." (See Doctrine and Covenants 84:54–57.)

While these missionaries had not been completely unsuccessful in their preaching, it seemed they had not achieved all the success possible or expected. The Lord indicates that this "darkness" was because of their indifference toward a former commandment given to all teachers of the Church in Doctrine and Covenants 42:12, "And again, the elders, priests and teachers of this church shall teach the principles of my gospel, which are in the Bible and the Book of Mormon, in the which is the fulness of the gospel."

Since the beginning of this dispensation, the Lord has emphasized the importance of the Book of Mormon in gospel teaching. Ezra Taft Benson famously reiterated the same message in a general conference of the Church when he taught, "If the early Saints were rebuked for treating the Book of Mormon lightly, are we under any less condemnation if we do the same? The Lord Himself bears testimony that it is of eternal significance" (Ezra Taft Benson, "The Book of Mormon—The Keystone of Our Religion," *Ensign,* November 1986).

As Latter-day Saints, we must make the effort to utilize the Book of Mormon in our personal gospel study and while teaching gospel principles to others. Since many publications assist with personal Book of Mormon study, the purpose of this book is to help overcome obstacles inhibiting the latter effort—teaching others the principles of the gospel. *Teaching the Book of Mormon* provides several major advantages to Latter-day Saint teachers.

An All-in-One Resource

As many teachers know, instruction materials can be cumbersome. Scriptures, manuals, magazines, references, lesson outlines, and other materials can quickly become a disorganized mess. *Teaching the Book of Mormon* provides lesson plans, supporting quotations, explanatory references, and the scriptural text in one easy-to-view volume.

Lesson Plans for Complete Book of Mormon Courses. Many teachers are assigned to sequentially teach the entire content of the Book of Mormon. Official Church curriculum is generally provided to these teachers and should be used as the primary resources for lesson plans.

However, as many teachers understand, some lesson ideas don't seem to be the right approach for a certain class. *Teaching the Book of Mormon* provides strong additional resources for useful lesson plans and ideas. A teacher may choose to utilize an entire lesson plan from this book or may simply glean questions, object lessons, or activities to enhance plus adapt Church curriculum.

Teaching Ideas for Using the Book of Mormon in Topical Instruction. While some courses focus solely on the Book of Mormon, Latter-day Saint teachers are also frequently involved in topical instruction. Seminary courses excluded, much of the primary and youth-oriented curriculum approaches gospel teaching in this manner. Topical teaching also occurs in priesthood and Relief Society meetings, family home evenings, and informally throughout the Church. The Lord expects us to continue to utilize the Book of Mormon in this type of teaching. For this purpose, *Teaching the Book of Mormon* contains a topical index. If a lesson centers on the topic of faith, for example, a teacher may use the index to find ideas on how to teach the doctrine of faith as it is found within the Book of Mormon.

Use for Personal Study. *Teaching the Book of Mormon* may also be an excellent study aid for personal scripture study. Members of the Church will find the ideas, questions, insights, and invitations found within this book an engaging way to study the scriptures on their own.

As Latter-day Saint teachers endeavor to teach the principles of the gospel from the Book of Mormon, they will find greater success in their classes, experience the enlightenment of the Holy Ghost, and bring the gospel into the hearts of their class members. *Teaching the Book of Mormon* is an attempt to help teachers fulfill this commission.

How to Use This Book

Principles and Doctrines. You must have a clear understanding of *what* you want to teach before you can decide *how* you want to teach it. Principles and doctrines are short statements of truth that encapsulate the main lesson you

want your class to learn. In *Teaching the Book of Mormon*, the principles and doctrines are in bold text and indicate the verse(s) they are derived from. Principles generally 1) describe an action, 2) are personal, and 3) have a result. Some examples of how a principle might be written at the beginning of a lesson idea are:

v. 10 When I make righteous choices, I will be happier.

v. 3 Studying the scriptures will give me guidance.

Doctrines generally are statements of belief that you would want your class to understand and have a testimony of. In this book, they look like this:

vv. 25–26 The Fall was necessary for our growth and happiness.

vv. 24–28 God loves His children and wants every one of them to be saved.

⚡ **Lesson Starter.** When you start teaching a lesson or a different set of verses, you will want to do something to get or regain the class's attention and help them prepare to learn. Teachers sometimes call this a "starter." The lesson starter will grab class members' interest so that they will want to turn to their scriptures and learn more. It also prepares the class members' hearts and minds so that they may learn by the Holy Ghost. Often a starter is an object lesson or a compelling question that shows the relevancy of what you will be studying. In this book, the lesson starter icon will show you the starter you might want to use to help stimulate interest in what you will be teaching.

🔎 **Look For.** Once you have captured class members' interest with a starter, you will want to direct them to the scriptures. Before asking someone to read, you will want to give them something to **look for** in those verses so that they will be engaged and focused. The look for icon will also be used before a long quote is read or sometimes even before watching a video. Italicized text indicates questions or statements that you may choose to use word for word.

? **Questions.** Effective teaching is most often centered around powerful discussion questions. Again, italicized phrases indicate that you could ask those questions of your class exactly as they appear in the book. In addition, there are different types of questions to be used at different points during a discussion. This book outlines two types of questions: analyze and apply. Analyze questions are designed to help the learner analyze and ponder the scriptures being discussed. Once the doctrine or principle has been effectively analyzed and understood, the teacher can ask the apply questions, which helps the learners apply the analyzed doctrines and principles.

✋ **Group Work.** Class members often enjoy getting into smaller groups and working with each other on a task you have given them. This provides variety in teaching methods and also allows more class members the opportunity to share their thoughts.

👥 **Participation Activities.** Similar to group work, participation activities get the class members participating in more ways than just a class discussion.

🖊 **Writing Activities.** Here the class members have the opportunity to either write in a journal or annotate their scriptures.

To assist with understanding the content of each scripture chapter, this book also provides Insights and Quotations.

💡 **Insights.** This icon adds historical and contextual information that may add depth to the understanding of a chapter.

💬 **Quotations.** Often a quote by a prophet or Church leader can greatly enhance a lesson.

❤ **Deep into Their hearts.** Henry B. Eyring taught, "The pure gospel of Jesus Christ must go down into the hearts of students by the power of the Holy Ghost" (*We Must Raise Our Sights*, CES Conference on the Book of Mormon, August 14, 2001, Brigham Young University). These icons help the learner feel the promptings of the Holy Ghost, make applications to their lives, and commit to live those principles.

Topical Index. The Book of Mormon "contains the fulness of the everlasting gospel" (introduction to the Book of Mormon) and can be used in any teaching situation. *Teaching the Book of Mormon* offers teaching ideas and suggestions to be used in various settings—from a seminary or church classroom to a family home evening lesson, or even for personal study. This book provides a topical index to aid in your lesson preparation. If you are preparing a lesson on the Godhead, for example, refer to the index for references to the Godhead taught in the Book of Mormon. You can then turn to that scripture and have a lesson outline ready to teach from.

Teaching Tips from Prophets' Lips Teaching tips will be found within various chapters of the book to give both general and specific principles of teaching and learning. Though not every quote will be from a prophet, all sources come from Church publications. Additionally, these quotes will be tied to the specific lesson to enhance your ability to teach with power and understanding.

Combined Chapter Lesson Plans. While having enough time to focus on every chapter of the Book of Mormon in detail is ideal, often a teacher must pace himself or herself in such a way that will allow the class to cover the most material. For this reason, in addition to the chapter-by-chapter lesson ideas, *Teaching the Book of Mormon* contains a few lesson plans that combine multiple chapters into one lesson. These lesson ideas are broad and will allow a teacher to summarize the key ideas of several chapters in a single lesson, while still clearly presenting one or two principles.

THE FIRST BOOK OF NEPHI

1 NEPHI SUMMARY

Time Period: 600–587 BC (13 years)

Contributors: Nephi, Lehi, Isaiah

Source: Small plates of Nephi

Synopsis:

Chapters 1–7: Lehi's and Ishmael's families depart from Jerusalem and obtain the plates of brass.

Chapter 8: Lehi's dream.

Chapter 9: Explanation of the two records of Nephi.

Chapter 10: Teachings of Lehi to his family.

Chapters 11–15: Nephi's vision of Lehi's dream and more.

Chapters 16–18: Their travels to the promise land.

Chapters 19–22: Nephi speaks about his record, Isaiah (Isaiah 48–49), the Gentiles, and Israel's destiny in the last days.

The First Book of Nephi: His Reign and Ministry

An account of Lehi and his wife Sariah, and his four sons, being called, (beginning at the eldest) Laman, Lemuel, Sam, and Nephi. The Lord warns Lehi to depart out of the land of Jerusalem, because he prophesieth unto the people concerning their iniquity and they seek to destroy his life. He taketh three days' journey into the wilderness with his family. Nephi taketh his brethren and returneth to the land of Jerusalem after the record of the Jews. The account of their sufferings. They take the daughters of Ishmael to wife. They take their families and depart into the wilderness. Their sufferings and afflictions in the wilderness. The course of their travels. They come to the large waters. Nephi's brethren rebel against him. He confoundeth them, and buildeth a ship. They call the name of the place Bountiful. They cross the large waters into the promised land, and so forth. This is according to the account of Nephi; or in other words, I, Nephi, wrote this record.

💡 The above heading was part of the original translation.

🔎 While reading, look for a clue as to who wrote it and is the youngest son of the four.

Notes

1 NEPHI 1

Nephi Writes of Lehi's Calling
About 600 BC

1–3, Nephi introduces himself; 4–17, The manifestations of God to Lehi; 18–20, The prophet Lehi ministers in Jerusalem.

I, Nephi, having been born of goodly parents, therefore I was taught somewhat in all the learning of my father; and having seen many afflictions in the course of my days, nevertheless, having been highly favored of the Lord in all my days; yea, having had a great knowledge of the goodness and the mysteries of God, therefore I make a record of my proceedings in my days.

v. 1 Goodly parents are always teaching their children.

⚡ Invite class members to share a time when they learned something valuable from their parents. Have your class list attributes of a good parent.

🔍 *Look for what Nephi's parents taught him.*

❓ Analyze:
  • *What kinds of lessons do parents teach their children?*
  • *Why shouldn't parents leave teaching their children to the schools or people at church?*
  • *When are opportune times parents can teach their children?*

💬 See M. Russell Ballard's General Conference talks "Mothers and Daughters," *Ensign,* May 2010, and "Fathers and Sons: A Remarkable Relationship," *Ensign,* November 2009 for suggestions on how to learn from your parents.

❤ Challenge class members to find opportunities to teach in their families.

2 Yea, I make a record in the language of my father, which consists of the learning of the Jews and the language of the Egyptians.

🔍 *In verse 2, search for the language the Book of Mormon was written in.*

✏ *Write Mormon 9:32–33 in the margin.*

💡 This document is believed to be part of the "Anthon Transcript" containing characters from the Book of Mormon translation. See Joseph Smith—History 1:63–65.

💡 In the years prior to Lehi leaving Jerusalem, the Kingdom of Judah was a vassal state to Egypt, meaning the Jews were subservient to Egyptian law and customs. It was very likely, therefore, that Lehi would have known how to write Egyptian (see 2 Kings 23:32–37).

3 And I know that the record which I make is true; and I make it with mine own hand; and I make it according to my knowledge.

4 For it came to pass in the commencement of the first year of the reign of Zedekiah, king of Judah, (my father, Lehi, having dwelt at Jerusalem in all his days); and in that same year there came many prophets, prophesying unto the people that they must repent, or the great city Jerusalem must be destroyed.

💡 Some of the contemporary Old Testament prophets during Lehi's time were Jeremiah, Habakkuk, Zephaniah, Obadiah, and Nahum.

5 Wherefore it came to pass that my father, Lehi, as he went forth prayed unto the Lord, yea, even with all his heart, in behalf of his people.

6 And it came to pass as he prayed unto the Lord,

Notes

there came a pillar of fire and dwelt upon a rock before him; and he saw and heard much; and because of the things which he saw and heard he did quake and tremble exceedingly.

7 And it came to pass that he returned to his own house at Jerusalem; and he cast himself upon his bed, being overcome with the Spirit and the things which he had seen.

8 And being thus overcome with the Spirit, he was carried away in a vision, even that he saw the heavens open, and he thought he saw God sitting upon his throne, surrounded with numberless concourses of angels in the attitude of singing and praising their God.

9 And it came to pass that he saw One descending out of the midst of heaven, and he beheld that his luster was above that of the sun at noon-day.

10 And he also saw twelve others following him, and their brightness did exceed that of the stars in the firmament.

11 And they came down and went forth upon the face of the earth; and the first came and stood before my father, and gave unto him a book, and bade him that he should read.

12 And it came to pass that as he read, he was filled with the Spirit of the Lord.

13 And he read, saying: Wo, wo, unto Jerusalem, for I have seen thine abominations! Yea, and many things did my father read concerning Jerusalem— that it should be destroyed, and the inhabitants thereof; many should perish by the sword, and many should be carried away captive into Babylon.

🔎 *Look for the first mention of Jesus Christ in the Book of Mormon (v. 9). Explain that Christ becomes the focus of discussion within the first nine verses. Ask, What does this tell you about the emphasis of the Book of Mormon?*

💡 On average, the Book of Mormon references Jesus Christ every 1.7 verses (Susan Ward Easton, "Name of Christ in the Book of Mormon," *Ensign*, June 1978).

14 And it came to pass that when my father had read and seen many great and marvelous things, he did exclaim many things unto the Lord; such as: Great and marvelous are thy works, O Lord God Almighty! Thy throne is high in the heavens, and thy power, and goodness, and mercy are over all the inhabitants of the earth; and, because thou art merciful, thou wilt not suffer those who come unto thee that they shall perish!

15 And after this manner was the language of my father in the praising of his God; for his soul did rejoice, and his whole heart was filled, because of the things which he had seen, yea, which the Lord had shown unto him.

vv. 14–15 Praising the Lord helps us to rejoice in Him.

⚡ *How does someone praise the Lord in prayer? How is praising different than thanking the Lord? When you are praising another person, what are you doing?*

🔎 *Look for how Lehi praises the Lord in 14–15.*

❓ Analyze: *Why should we praise God? How did praising the Lord affect Lehi in verse 14?*

❓ Apply: *How often is praising God part of your prayers?*

♥ Challenge class members to include praise to God in their prayers for one week. Later, follow up and ask how it is making a difference in their prayers.

16 And now I, Nephi, do not make a full account of the things which my father hath written, for he hath written many things which he saw in visions and in dreams; and he also hath written many things which he prophesied and spake unto his children, of which I shall not make a full account.

17 But I shall make an account of my proceedings in my days. Behold, I make an abridgment of the record of my father, upon plates which I have made with mine own hands; wherefore, after I

Notes

have abridged the record of my father then will I make an account of mine own life.

18 Therefore, I would that ye should know, that after the Lord had shown so many marvelous things unto my father, Lehi, yea, concerning the destruction of Jerusalem, behold he went forth among the people, and began to prophesy and to declare unto them concerning the things which he had both seen and heard.

v. 18 We should be missionaries everyday by sharing the gospel with those we know.

⚡ *Would it be easier to share the gospel with people you already know or with strangers? Why? How could sharing with people you know be hard?*

🔍 *Look for what Lehi began to do after his great spiritual experiences.* Show the picture "Lehi Prophesying to the People of Jerusalem" from the church library.

✋ Invite a few class members to tell of an experience when they were able to share what they believed with people they know.

❤ Invite them to share their beliefs with others often.

19 And it came to pass that the Jews did mock him because of the things which he testified of them; for he truly testified of their wickedness and their abominations; and he testified that the things which he saw and heard, and also the things which he read in the book, manifested plainly of the coming of a Messiah, and also the redemption of the world.

20 And when the Jews heard these things they were angry with him; yea, even as with the prophets of old, whom they had cast out, and stoned, and slain; and they also sought his life, that they might take it away. But behold, I, Nephi, will show unto you that the tender mercies of the Lord are over all those whom he hath chosen, because of their faith, to make them mighty even unto the power of deliverance.

Notes

v. 20 As we recognize the Lord's "tender mercies," we will see how blessed we are.

✏ Have class members write down a time when the Lord blessed them in a difficult situation.

🔍 *Look for what that has to do with verse 20.*

💬 See David A. Bednar's, "The Tender Mercies of the Lord" (*Ensign*, May 2005, 99–100).

❤ Challenge your class to look for how the Lord extends his tender mercies each day.

Teaching Tips from Prophets' Lips "There is a hunger in the land, and a genuine thirst—a great hunger for the word of the Lord and an unsatisfied thirst for things of the Spirit. . . . The world is starved for spiritual food. Ours is the obligation and the opportunity to nourish the soul." (Gordon B. Hinckley "Feed the Spirit, Nourish the Soul," *Ensign*, Oct. 1998, 2)

1 NEPHI 2

Lehi's Family Leaves Jerusalem
About 600–592 BC

1–5, Lehi's family leaves Jerusalem; 6–15, Lehi counsels Laman and Lemuel to be righteous despite their murmurings; 16–24, Nephi prays to the Lord and gains his own testimony.

Overarching Principle: In order to gain a personal testimony I need to take correct action.

⚡ To help teach the importance of individual action, invite two class members to the front and ask one (class member A) if she is ready to do some push-ups. Ask the other person (class member B) to do five push-ups. Once he is finished, ask class member A if she is tired. After a "no" response, have class member B do five more push-ups. Once completed, ask class member A if she is tired yet. You can repeat this process as many times as you want. Finally ask class member

A why she is not tired and use her answer to define the purpose of this activity. (Answer could be as simple as "If I want the benefit, I need to do the work.")

1 For behold, it came to pass that the Lord spake unto my father, yea, even in a dream, and said unto him: Blessed art thou Lehi, because of the things which thou hast done; and because thou hast been faithful and declared unto this people the things which I commanded thee, behold, they seek to take away thy life.

2 And it came to pass that the Lord commanded my father, even in a dream, that he should take his family and depart into the wilderness.

3 And it came to pass that he was obedient unto the word of the Lord, wherefore he did as the Lord commanded him.

4 And it came to pass that he departed into the wilderness. And he left his house, and the land of his inheritance, and his gold, and his silver, and his precious things, and took nothing with him, save it were his family, and provisions, and tents, and departed into the wilderness.

5 And he came down by the borders near the shore of the Red Sea; and he traveled in the wilderness in the borders which are nearer the Red Sea; and he did travel in the wilderness with his family, which consisted of my mother, Sariah, and my elder brothers, who were Laman, Lemuel, and Sam.

vv. 1–5 "Going through the motions" of gospel living might not be enough to gain a sustained testimony.

🔍 *Look for who leaves Jerusalem and what they leave behind.*

💡 Note with the class that Laman and Lemuel fulfilled some of the same obligations as Nephi and Sam—namely, they retrieved the brass plates, returned to Jerusalem to recruit Ishmael's family, built a boat, and sailed across the ocean.

❓ Analyze: *If all the brothers did the same*

things, what makes Nephi and Sam different from Laman and Lemuel?

vv. 1–4 We need to be willing to sacrifice anything and everything to follow God.

⚡ Before class, write on the board, "Sacrifice is giving up something good for something better." Invite class members to give an example of this.

🔍 *Look for the "something good for something better" in verses 1–4.*

❓ Analyze: *Which verse shows that Lehi's family was giving up a lot of wealth?*

✏️ *Write 1 Nephi 3:25 in the margin and look for evidence of how wealthy he was.*

❓ Apply: *Would you be willing to sacrifice today in the very same way? What are things the Lord asks us to give up for something better?*

❤ Have class members write down one thing the Lord would want them to sacrifice now. Challenge them to give that up and trust that God has something better for them.

6 And it came to pass that when he had traveled three days in the wilderness, he pitched his tent in a valley by the side of a river of water.

7 And it came to pass that he built an altar of stones, and made an offering unto the Lord, and gave thanks unto the Lord our God.

8 And it came to pass that he called the name of the river, Laman, and it emptied into the Red Sea; and the valley was in the borders near the mouth thereof.

9 And when my father saw that the waters of the river emptied into the fountain of the Red Sea, he spake unto Laman, saying: O that thou mightest be like unto this river, continually running into the fountain of all righteousness!

10 And he also spake unto Lemuel: O that thou mightest be like unto this valley, firm and steadfast, and immovable in keeping the commandments of the Lord!

Notes

11 Now this he spake because of the stiffnecked-ness of Laman and Lemuel; for behold they did murmur in many things against their father, because he was a visionary man, and had led them out of the land of Jerusalem, to leave the land of their inheritance, and their gold, and their silver, and their precious things, to perish in the wilderness. And this they said he had done because of the foolish imaginations of his heart.

12 And thus Laman and Lemuel, being the eldest, did murmur against their father. And they did murmur because they knew not the dealings of that God who had created them.

13 Neither did they believe that Jerusalem, that great city, could be destroyed according to the words of the prophets. And they were like unto the Jews who were at Jerusalem, who sought to take away the life of my father.

14 And it came to pass that my father did speak unto them in the valley of Lemuel, with power, being filled with the Spirit, until their frames did shake before him. And he did confound them, that they durst not utter against him; wherefore, they did as he commanded them.

15 And my father dwelt in a tent.

♀ 1 Nephi 2:15 is the shortest verse in the Book of Mormon. *What does this verse teach about Lehi's consecration to God?*

16 And it came to pass that I, Nephi, being exceed-ingly young, nevertheless being large in stature, and also having great desires to know of the mys-teries of God, wherefore, I did cry unto the Lord; and behold he did visit me, and did soften my heart that I did believe all the words which had been spoken by my father; wherefore, I did not rebel against him like unto my brothers.

17 And I spake unto Sam, making known unto him the things which the Lord had manifested unto me by his Holy Spirit. And it came to pass that he believed in my words.

18 But, behold, Laman and Lemuel would not

hearken unto my words; and being grieved because of the hardness of their hearts I cried unto the Lord for them.

vv. 11–13, 16–18 Murmuring led Laman and Lemuel to reject the Spirit of the Lord, while praying allowed Nephi to find out the truth for himself. We should follow Nephi's example.

🔎 *In verses 11–13 and 16–18, look for the dif-ference between Laman and Lemuel, and Nephi and Sam.* You may want to have a class member serve as scribe as the class discusses the differences between the brothers.

❓ Analyze:
- *If the Lord did "soften" Nephi's heart, how was it originally?*
- *What did Nephi do in the verse that led it to be softened?*
- *How is this different than what his oldest brothers did in verses 11–13?*
- *What did Nephi's seeking lead to?*
- *Why do you think prayer helped soften Nephi's heart?*
- *Why do you think murmuring gave Laman and Lemuel a negative attitude?* (Continue to ask your own questions that lead class mem-bers to understand the differences between the brothers. Before applying this principle with class members, be sure they under-stand the differences between the brothers.)

💬 "Simply saying prayers is quite a different thing from engaging in meaningful prayer . . . [which is] to not only express but to do. . . . I testify that prayer becomes meaningful as we ask in faith and act" (David A. Bednar "Ask in Faith," *Ensign*, May 2008, 94–97).

♥ *How is Nephi applying the push-up lesson dis-cussed in the beginning of the class? What can you do to be like Nephi?* (You may want to allow class members time to write their thoughts down before they answer.) Invite class members to pray to God for under-standing and to not murmur when they are in times of doubt or difficulties.

Notes

vv. 17–18 Sharing our own testimonies with family members may inspire their faith.

🔍 *Look for what Nephi did after the Lord helped him understand.*

❓ Analyze: *How did this bless Sam's life? Why didn't it bless his oldest brothers' lives?*

✋ Invite a class member to share when a family member's faith blessed him or her.

❤ Challenge them to look for opportunities to share their faith with family members.

19 And it came to pass that the Lord spake unto me, saying: Blessed art thou, Nephi, because of thy faith, for thou hast sought me diligently, with lowliness of heart.

20 And inasmuch as ye shall keep my commandments, ye shall prosper, and shall be led to a land of promise; yea, even a land which I have prepared for you; yea, a land which is choice above all other lands.

21 And inasmuch as thy brethren shall rebel against thee, they shall be cut off from the presence of the Lord.

22 And inasmuch as thou shalt keep my commandments, thou shalt be made a ruler and a teacher over thy brethren.

23 For behold, in that day that they shall rebel against me, I will curse them even with a sore curse, and they shall have no power over thy seed except they shall rebel against me also.

24 And if it so be that they rebel against me, they shall be a scourge unto thy seed, to stir them up in the ways of remembrance.

vv. 19–24 The Lord blesses us if we seek Him on our own.

🔍 *Look for the blessings that come to Nephi because of his prayer in verse 16 and the consequences that come to Laman and Lemuel because they do not pray.*

❤ Discuss with class members the future

blessings that would come to them if they were to follow Nephi's example in the way he gained a testimony. Ask some class members to either share their testimonies or experiences on how they gained one.

1 NEPHI 3

Seeking the Brass Plates
About 600–592 BC

1–9, Nephi and his brothers return to Jerusalem to obtain the brass plates from Laban; 10–14, First Attempt: Laman's attempt to obtain the plates from Laban fails; 15–26, Second Attempt: The brothers' attempt to buy the plates fails; 27–31, Laman and Lemuel beat Nephi and Sam.

1 And it came to pass that I, Nephi, returned from speaking with the Lord, to the tent of my father.

2 And it came to pass that he spake unto me, saying: Behold I have dreamed a dream, in the which the Lord hath commanded me that thou and thy brethren shall return to Jerusalem.

3 For behold, Laban hath the record of the Jews and also a genealogy of my forefathers, and they are engraven upon plates of brass.

4 Wherefore, the Lord hath commanded me that thou and thy brothers should go unto the house of Laban, and seek the records, and bring them down hither into the wilderness.

vv. 1–4 We should make searching and learning about the genealogy of our forefathers a priority.

🔍 Refer to Bible Map 9 "The World of the Old Testament" and find the approximate miles from Jerusalem to the Red Sea. Cross reference verse 2 with 1 Nephi 2:5–6. Ask, *At least how many days have they traveled from Jerusalem?* (Three days from the Red Sea, plus the amount of time to travel from Jerusalem to the Red Sea.)

Notes

? Analyze:
- *Why do you think the Lord wanted Lehi to have his genealogy?*
- *What message is the Lord teaching Lehi about genealogy?*
- *Why should we care about our genealogy?*

5 And now, behold thy brothers murmur, saying it is a hard thing which I have required of them; but behold I have not required it of them, but it is a commandment of the Lord.

6 Therefore go, my son, and thou shalt be favored of the Lord, because thou hast not murmured.

7 And it came to pass that I, Nephi, said unto my father: I will go and do the things which the Lord hath commanded, for I know that the Lord giveth no commandments unto the children of men, save he shall prepare a way for them that they may accomplish the thing which he commandeth them.

8 And it came to pass that when my father had heard these words he was exceedingly glad, for he knew that I had been blessed of the Lord.

Chapters 3–4 Overarching Principle: Doing the Lord's work "our own way" fails. Since the Lord prepares a way for us, we should include Him in our lives.

⚡ Chapters 3–4 are one continuous story and would best be taught together. To contrast the Lord providing a way for us versus doing things our way, bring a piece of wood, a screw, a hammer, and a screwdriver to class (keep the screwdriver hidden). Instruct a volunteer to get the screw into the block of wood using the hammer, and then allow the person a few moments to try. Ask the class what would be more effective than a hammer; then allow the volunteer a few moments to use a screwdriver. The object lesson represents our dependence on the Lord; the instructions of getting the screw into the wood represent God asking us to do His work; the hammer represents us doing His work our way, and the screwdriver represents Him providing a way for us. At this point in the lesson, you may choose to explain what the object lesson means or you can explain to the class that they will discover how this applies to Nephi as you continue with the lesson.

⚡ To keep track of each person's reactions in the scripture story, before class, write the names of the people on the board: Laman, Lemuel, Nephi, Sam, Laban, and Zoram. (You may consider even drawing pictures of each of them above their names. Don't worry about your artistic skills, sometimes the worse the drawing is, the more memorable and fun the lesson is.) As you teach 1 Nephi 3–4, write each person's ideas and reactions to their situation.

🔎 Read verses 5–7 and look for each of the sons' reaction to their father's request.

🔎 Mark phrases showing Nephi's faith that God would provide a way for him to accomplish this task in verse 7.

? Analyze:
- *Why did you select that phrase?*
- *What does that phrase mean?*
- *How does that phrase show faith?*

? Apply: *In what situations would Nephi's example apply today?*

💬 Richard G. Scott stated, "Spirituality yields two fruits. The first is inspiration to know what to do. The second is power, or the capacity to do it. These two capacities come together. That is why Nephi could say, 'I will go and do the things which the Lord hath commanded.' . . . Yes, God answers prayers and gives us spiritual direction when we live obediently and exercise the required faith in Him" (Richard G. Scott, "To Acquire Spiritual Guidance," *Ensign,* November 2009, 6).

9 And I, Nephi, and my brethren took our journey in the wilderness, with our tents, to go up to the land of Jerusalem.

Notes

_____

_____

_____

10 And it came to pass that when we had gone up to the land of Jerusalem, I and my brethren did consult one with another.

11 And we cast lots—who of us should go in unto the house of Laban. And it came to pass that the lot fell upon Laman; and Laman went in unto the house of Laban, and he talked with him as he sat in his house.

12 And he desired of Laban the records which were engraven upon the plates of brass, which contained the genealogy of my father.

13 And behold, it came to pass that Laban was angry, and thrust him out from his presence; and he would not that he should have the records. Wherefore, he said unto him: Behold thou art a robber, and I will slay thee.

14 But Laman fled out of his presence, and told the things which Laban had done, unto us. And we began to be exceedingly sorrowful, and my brethren were about to return unto my father in the wilderness.

vv. 9–14 First attempt to obtain the plates.

🖊 Have a class member be a scribe and write about each character's reaction during the first attempt on the board. Invite class members to mark the attempts in their scriptures and label "First attempt" in the margins.

🔍 Look for the following questions during each attempt and write the answers on the board:

1. *Did they include the Lord in the decision process?*

2. *What was the result of each attempt?*

3. *What is each person's reaction?*

Your chart could look like this:

Nephi Sam Laman Lemuel Laban

Include the Lord?

Result

Reaction

15 But behold I said unto them that: As the Lord liveth, and as we live, we will not go down unto our father in the wilderness until we have accomplished the thing which the Lord hath commanded us.

16 Wherefore, let us be faithful in keeping the commandments of the Lord; therefore let us go down to the land of our father's inheritance, for behold he left gold and silver, and all manner of riches. And all this he hath done because of the commandments of the Lord.

17 For he knew that Jerusalem must be destroyed, because of the wickedness of the people.

18 For behold, they have rejected the words of the prophets. Wherefore, if my father should dwell in the land after he hath been commanded to flee out of the land, behold, he would also perish. Wherefore, it must needs be that he flee out of the land.

19 And behold, it is wisdom in God that we should obtain these records, that we may preserve unto our children the language of our fathers;

20 And also that we may preserve unto them the words which have been spoken by the mouth of all the holy prophets, which have been delivered unto them by the Spirit and power of God, since the world began, even down unto this present time.

Notes

🔍 *Despite the brothers' failure in their first attempt, look for an indication of Nephi's faith in verses 15–20.*

❓ Analyze: *How easy would it have been for Nephi to give up hope in obtaining the plates? What in verses 19–20 motivates him to continue?*

21 And it came to pass that after this manner of language did I persuade my brethren, that they might be faithful in keeping the commandments of God.

22 And it came to pass that we went down to the land of our inheritance, and we did gather together our gold, and our silver, and our precious things.

23 And after we had gathered these things together, we went up again unto the house of Laban.

24 And it came to pass that we went in unto Laban, and desired him that he would give unto us the records which were engraven upon the plates of brass, for which we would give unto him our gold, and our silver, and all our precious things.

25 And it came to pass that when Laban saw our property, and that it was exceedingly great, he did lust after it, insomuch that he thrust us out, and sent his servants to slay us, that he might obtain our property.

26 And it came to pass that we did flee before the servants of Laban, and we were obliged to leave behind our property, and it fell into the hands of Laban.

27 And it came to pass that we fled into the wilderness, and the servants of Laban did not overtake us, and we hid ourselves in the cavity of a rock.

28 And it came to pass that Laman was angry with me, and also with my father; and also was Lemuel, for he hearkened unto the words of Laman. Wherefore Laman and Lemuel did speak many hard words unto us, their younger brothers, and they did smite us even with a rod.

vv. 21–28 Second attempt to obtain the plates.

🔍 Have class members look for the same things as above during their second attempt.

✏️ Continue with your scribe writing each of the person's reactions on the board.

👥 Throughout the class, partner two or three class members together and have them briefly discuss what ways Nephi's story is like the screwdriver object lesson. Ask one or two partnerships to share.

❓ Analyze:
- *Nephi has clearly exercised faith twice—why hasn't it worked? (Refer back to the screw and hammer.)*
- *What is Nephi doing that applies to the object lesson?*
- *Consider Laman and Lemuel's reaction to the second failed attempt. Why are they so angry? After two failed attempts, how easy would it have been for Nephi to give up?*

❓ Apply:
- *When things do not work out the way people plan, why do you think they get upset?*
- *How does getting upset about our situation show a lack of faith in God?*
- *How do some people today "give up" after perceived failed attempts of praying, paying tithing, gaining a testimony, etc.?*

❤️ Refer back to the object lesson and ask, *Since Nephi has been using a hammer (doing things his own way), should he give up?* Help class members discover that, like Nephi, we need to turn to the Lord for a better way. Note: Nephi's third attempt is in chapter 4. Refer to the teaching ideas there to complete the story.

29 And it came to pass as they smote us with a rod, behold, an angel of the Lord came and stood before them, and he spake unto them, saying: Why do ye smite your younger brother with a rod? Know ye not that the Lord hath chosen him to be a ruler over you, and this because of your iniquities? Behold ye shall go up to Jerusalem

Notes

again, and the Lord will deliver Laban into your hands.

30 And after the angel had spoken unto us, he departed.

31 And after the angel had departed, Laman and Lemuel again began to murmur, saying: How is it possible that the Lord will deliver Laban into our hands? Behold, he is a mighty man, and he can command fifty, yea, even he can slay fifty; then why not us?

> **Teaching Tips from Prophets' Lips** "A good beginning is very important. It is half the battle. If the teacher employs discipline constantly, from the beginning, the class will be successful" (Boyd K. Packer, *Teach Ye Diligently*, 131).

1 NEPHI 4

Finally Obtaining the Brass Plates
About 600–592 BC

1–3, Nephi encourages his brethren to try again; 4–18, The brothers' third attempt to retrieve the plates; Lord guides Nephi to slay Laban; 19–29, Nephi poses as Laban to obtain the brass plates; 30–38, Nephi persuades Zoram to join them.

Overarching Principle: Great faith is doing what is right, even when everything is going wrong—not when everything is going right. Note: You can use 1 Nephi 3:28–31 and 1 Nephi 5:1–3 as further evidence of this principle.

1 And it came to pass that I spake unto my brethren, saying: Let us go up again unto Jerusalem, and let us be faithful in keeping the commandments of the Lord; for behold he is mightier than all the earth, then why not mightier than Laban and his fifty, yea, or even than his tens of thousands?

2 Therefore let us go up; let us be strong like unto Moses; for he truly spake unto the waters of the Red Sea and they divided hither and thither, and our fathers came through, out of captivity, on dry ground, and the armies of Pharaoh did follow and were drowned in the waters of the Red Sea.

3 Now behold ye know that this is true; and ye also know that an angel hath spoken unto you; wherefore can ye doubt? Let us go up; the Lord is able to deliver us, even as our fathers, and to destroy Laban, even as the Egyptians.

vv. 1–3 If we have faith, God can perform miracles for us just as He did anciently.

⚡ *Is the Lord less likely to do great miracles today as He did anciently? Why or why not?*

🔎 *Look for what that question has to do with verses 1–3.*

❓ Analyze: *Why would Nephi mention Moses to try and convince his brothers to endure? If the Lord allowed miracles for people anciently, why not now?*

✎ Invite your class to write Moroni 7:35–37 in their margins and then read those verses.

♥ Share with the class (or invite a class member to share) a time when God helped you to accomplish something hard. Testify to your class that if miracles have ceased, it is because of a lack of faith. God can do miracles for us just as He did for people anciently.

4 Now when I had spoken these words, they were yet wroth, and did still continue to murmur; nevertheless they did follow me up until we came without the walls of Jerusalem.

5 And it was by night; and I caused that they should hide themselves without the walls. And after they had hid themselves, I, Nephi, crept into the city and went forth towards the house of Laban.

6 And I was led by the Spirit, not knowing beforehand the things which I should do.

7 Nevertheless I went forth, and as I came near

Notes

unto the house of Laban I beheld a man, and he had fallen to the earth before me, for he was drunken with wine.

8 And when I came to him I found that it was Laban.

9 And I beheld his sword, and I drew it forth from the sheath thereof; and the hilt thereof was of pure gold, and the workmanship thereof was exceedingly fine, and I saw that the blade thereof was of the most precious steel.

v. 6 Often we need to start moving forward the best we are able to before we can expect direction from God.

✐ Invite class members to write by verse 6, "Third attempt".

🔍 *In verses 4–6, look for whether or not Nephi knew what God wanted him to do.*

❓ Analyze: *Why didn't God lay out the whole plan to Nephi before he started to move toward the city? What does this teach us about how God teaches us?*

♥ *Has there been a time in your life when you were like Nephi, having to rely on God for direction?* Challenge class members to move forward in faith, even if they are unsure what the outcome will be. You could have them write in their margins, "God can't steer a parked car."

10 And it came to pass that I was constrained by the Spirit that I should kill Laban; but I said in my heart: Never at any time have I shed the blood of man. And I shrunk and would that I might not slay him.

11 And the Spirit said unto me again: Behold the Lord hath delivered him into thy hands. Yea, and I also knew that he had sought to take away mine own life; yea, and he would not hearken unto the commandments of the Lord; and he also had taken away our property.

12 And it came to pass that the Spirit said unto me

again: Slay him, for the Lord hath delivered him into thy hands;

13 Behold the Lord slayeth the wicked to bring forth his righteous purposes. It is better that one man should perish than that a nation should dwindle and perish in unbelief.

14 And now, when I, Nephi, had heard these words, I remembered the words of the Lord which he spake unto me in the wilderness, saying that: Inasmuch as thy seed shall keep my commandments, they shall prosper in the land of promise.

15 Yea, and I also thought that they could not keep the commandments of the Lord according to the law of Moses, save they should have the law.

16 And I also knew that the law was engraven upon the plates of brass.

17 And again, I knew that the Lord had delivered Laban into my hands for this cause—that I might obtain the records according to his commandments.

18 Therefore I did obey the voice of the Spirit, and took Laban by the hair of the head, and I smote off his head with his own sword.

vv. 10–18 Whatever God commands is right; therefore, we should obey even when the commandment doesn't completely make sense.

⚡ *Did the Lord ask Nephi to do something wrong when he told Nephi to slay Laban? Why would God tell Nephi to break a commandment?*

💬 Joseph Smith stated the following: "God said, 'Thou shalt not kill;' at another time He said 'Thou shalt utterly destroy.' This is the principle on which the government of heaven is conducted—by revelation adapted to the circumstances in which the children of the kingdom are placed. Whatever God requires is right, no matter what it is, although we may not see the reason thereof till long after the events transpire" (*Teachings of the Prophet Joseph Smith*, 256–57).

🔍 *Look for what reasons the angel gives for the unusual instruction.*

Notes

❓ Analyze: *Why do you think Nephi hesitates with the instruction? Why does Nephi finally kill Laban?*

❓ Apply: *How is this story relevant today?*

💡 Long ago, the Lord made some conditions for when a person could slay another and not be guilty before God. Invite class members to write Exodus 21:30 in their margins and have them see if Nephi met all the requirements outlined to slay Laban without being guilty of murder.

19 And after I had smitten off his head with his own sword, I took the garments of Laban and put them upon mine own body; yea, even every whit; and I did gird on his armor about my loins.

20 And after I had done this, I went forth unto the treasury of Laban. And as I went forth towards the treasury of Laban, behold, I saw the servant of Laban who had the keys of the treasury. And I commanded him in the voice of Laban, that he should go with me into the treasury.

21 And he supposed me to be his master, Laban, for he beheld the garments and also the sword girded about my loins.

22 And he spake unto me concerning the elders of the Jews, he knowing that his master, Laban, had been out by night among them.

23 And I spake unto him as if it had been Laban.

24 And I also spake unto him that I should carry the engravings, which were upon the plates of brass, to my elder brethren, who were without the walls.

25 And I also bade him that he should follow me.

26 And he, supposing that I spake of the brethren of the church, and that I was truly that Laban whom I had slain, wherefore he did follow me.

27 And he spake unto me many times concerning the elders of the Jews, as I went forth unto my brethren, who were without the walls.

28 And it came to pass that when Laman saw me he was exceedingly frightened, and also Lemuel and Sam. And they fled from before my presence; for they supposed it was Laban, and that he had slain me and had sought to take away their lives also.

29 And it came to pass that I called after them, and they did hear me; wherefore they did cease to flee from my presence.

30 And it came to pass that when the servant of Laban beheld my brethren he began to tremble, and was about to flee from before me and return to the city of Jerusalem.

31 And now I, Nephi, being a man large in stature, and also having received much strength of the Lord, therefore I did seize upon the servant of Laban, and held him, that he should not flee.

32 And it came to pass that I spake with him, that if he would hearken unto my words, as the Lord liveth, and as I live, even so that if he would hearken unto our words, we would spare his life.

33 And I spake unto him, even with an oath, that he need not fear; that he should be a free man like unto us if he would go down in the wilderness with us.

34 And I also spake unto him, saying: Surely the Lord hath commanded us to do this thing; and shall we not be diligent in keeping the commandments of the Lord? Therefore, if thou wilt go down into the wilderness to my father thou shalt have place with us.

35 And it came to pass that Zoram did take courage at the words which I spake. Now Zoram was the name of the servant; and he promised that he would go down into the wilderness unto our father. Yea, and he also made an oath unto us that he would tarry with us from that time forth.

36 Now we were desirous that he should tarry with us for this cause, that the Jews might not know concerning our flight into the wilderness, lest they should pursue us and destroy us.

37 And it came to pass that when Zoram had made an oath unto us, our fears did cease concerning him.

Notes

38 And it came to pass that we took the plates of brass and the servant of Laban, and departed into the wilderness, and journeyed unto the tent of our father.

v. 38 Just because God provides a way for us to do His will doesn't mean it will be easy. Great faith is doing what is right, even when it is very difficult.

🔍 *Look for ways God helped Nephi in verse 19–38. Have class members list and discuss what they found.*

❓ Analyze: Note with the class that Nephi had just as much faith on his first attempt as he did on the third attempt. Ask,
 • *Why did the third attempt work, while the first two did not?*
 • *What does this whole story in chapters 3 and 4 teach us about how God will "prepare a way" for us to do the things he has commanded?*
 • *If God prepares a way to do what He asks* (1 Nephi 3:7), *why didn't things work out right the first time they tried to retrieve the plates?*
 • *What does this teach about faithfulness and endurance?*

✋ Have class members think of a great person of faith and have them raise their hands when they have thought of someone. Ask if everything worked right for them all of the time because of their great faith? Why?

❤ Ask class members to share what person of faith they were thinking of and how that person kept doing what was right, even when things were difficult. Challenge them to do likewise. Explain that God will prepare a way for us, but we have to be willing to fail a few times, change plans a few times, have people turn against us, and possibly even get physically hurt, but if we are faithful, we can endure.

1 NEPHI 5

The Sons Return
About 600–592 BC

1–9, Lehi and Sariah welcome their sons' and Sariah's faith is strengthened; 10–16, The family learns from the brass plates and their own ancestry; 17–19, Lehi prophesies; 20–22, Nephi summarizes their journey.

1 And it came to pass that after we had come down into the wilderness unto our father, behold, he was filled with joy, and also my mother, Sariah, was exceedingly glad, for she truly had mourned because of us.

2 For she had supposed that we had perished in the wilderness; and she also had complained against my father, telling him that he was a visionary man; saying: Behold thou hast led us forth from the land of our inheritance, and my sons are no more, and we perish in the wilderness.

3 And after this manner of language had my mother complained against my father.

4 And it had come to pass that my father spake unto her, saying: I know that I am a visionary man; for if I had not seen the things of God in a vision I should not have known the goodness of God, but had tarried at Jerusalem, and had perished with my brethren.

5 But behold, I have obtained a land of promise, in the which things I do rejoice; yea, and I know that the Lord will deliver my sons out of the hands of Laban, and bring them down again unto us in the wilderness.

6 And after this manner of language did my father, Lehi, comfort my mother, Sariah, concerning us, while we journeyed in the wilderness up to the land of Jerusalem, to obtain the record of the Jews.

7 And when we had returned to the tent of my father, behold their joy was full, and my mother was comforted.

Notes

vv. 1–8 Fear removes our faith, and faith will remove fear.

⚡ Ask class members to think of a time when they experienced great fear. Discuss with them how difficult it was to have faith during that time and why.

🔍 In verses 1–3, underline and list the fears that Sariah was struggling with.

❓ Analyze: *Would you be scared in the same situation? Why?*

🔍 In verses 4–6, underline and list why Lehi had faith.

❓ Analyze: *How did Sariah's fears hinder her faith? How did Lehi's faith overcome his fears?*

❓ Apply: *When we are in a trying situation, how can we overcome our fears?*

💬 George A. Smith once related that Joseph Smith had told him at a time of great difficulty: "I should never get discouraged, whatever difficulties might surround me. If I was sunk in the lowest pit of Nova Scotia and all the Rocky Mountains piled on top of me, I ought not to be discouraged but hang on, exercise faith, and keep up good courage and I should come out on the top of the heap at last" (George A. Smith, "History of George Albert Smith by Himself," 49, George Albert Smith, Papers, 1834–75, Church Archives).

✏️ Write on the board, and invite your class to write in their margins: "Am I led by fear or faith?"

❤️ Challenge class members to not let their fear lead them, but rather let their faith guide them.

8 And she spake, saying: Now I know of a surety that the Lord hath commanded my husband to flee into the wilderness; yea, and I also know of a surety that the Lord hath protected my sons, and delivered them out of the hands of Laban, and given them power whereby they could accomplish the thing which the Lord hath commanded

them. And after this manner of language did she speak.

9 And it came to pass that they did rejoice exceedingly, and did offer sacrifice and burnt offerings unto the Lord; and they gave thanks unto the God of Israel.

vv. 8–9 To endure the trials of life, we must have our own testimony that is independent from others.

⚡ Invite class members to think of someone they know personally who they think has a very strong testimony. Ask, *If that person were to lose their testimony, would it affect yours? Do you feel your testimony is somewhat dependent on others? If everyone in your family left the Church, would you remain faithful?*

🔍 Look for how Sariah's testimony grew in verses 8–9.

💬 Write on the board, "The time will come when no man nor woman will be able to endure on borrowed light. Each will have to be guided by the light within himself. If you do not have it, how can you stand?" (See Orson F. Whitney, *Life of Heber C. Kimball*, 449–50).

❓ Apply:
• *Is there ever a time when borrowed light is a good thing?*
• *How is your testimony strengthened by others sharing their testimonies?*
• *What is Elder Kimball suggesting?*
• *What can a person do to obtain this kind of testimony that is independent of others?*

❤️ Invite class members to start now by doing the things required to receive a solid testimony so that they will be strong enough to face the challenges of life.

10 And after they had given thanks unto the God of Israel, my father, Lehi, took the records which were engraven upon the plates of brass, and he did search them from the beginning.

11 And he beheld that they did contain the five

Notes

books of Moses, which gave an account of the creation of the world, and also of Adam and Eve, who were our first parents;

12 And also a record of the Jews from the beginning, even down to the commencement of the reign of Zedekiah, king of Judah;

13 And also the prophecies of the holy prophets, from the beginning, even down to the commencement of the reign of Zedekiah; and also many prophecies which have been spoken by the mouth of Jeremiah.

14 And it came to pass that my father, Lehi, also found upon the plates of brass a genealogy of his fathers; wherefore he knew that he was a descendant of Joseph; yea, even that Joseph who was the son of Jacob, who was sold into Egypt, and who was preserved by the hand of the Lord, that he might preserve his father, Jacob, and all his household from perishing with famine.

15 And they were also led out of captivity and out of the land of Egypt, by that same God who had preserved them.

16 And thus my father, Lehi, did discover the genealogy of his fathers. And Laban also was a descendant of Joseph, wherefore he and his fathers had kept the records.

💡 *Look for what great biblical person Lehi descends from.* The tribes from Joseph are Ephraim and Manasseh. *Which tribe was Lehi from?* Have your class write *Alma 10:3* in their margins and look it up for the answer. See also Genesis 49:22–26.

17 And now when my father saw all these things, he was filled with the Spirit, and began to prophesy concerning his seed—

18 That these plates of brass should go forth unto all nations, kindreds, tongues, and people who were of his seed.

19 Wherefore, he said that these plates of brass should never perish; neither should they be dimmed any more by time. And he prophesied many things concerning his seed.

20 And it came to pass that thus far I and my father had kept the commandments wherewith the Lord had commanded us.

21 And we had obtained the records which the Lord had commanded us, and searched them and found that they were desirable; yea, even of great worth unto us, insomuch that we could preserve the commandments of the Lord unto our children.

22 Wherefore, it was wisdom in the Lord that we should carry them with us, as we journeyed in the wilderness towards the land of promise.

vv. 19–22 We show the Lord that we value the scriptures by how often we use them.

⚡ Display an older set of scriptures that have been lightly sprinkled with flour. Ask, *How valuable do you think these scriptures have been to the owner?* Blow off the flour to make it look like a cloud of dust you are blowing away.

🔍 *Look for how these scriptures relate to verse 19.*

❓ Analyze: *What did Lehi mean when he said that now the brass plates wouldn't get dimmed by time? What do you think would cause the plates to get "dimmed" by time?*

✏️ Invite class members to underline words in verses 21–22 that show Lehi and his family would make good use of the scriptures. Discuss what class members found.

❤️ Invite class members to show that they value the scriptures by using them, rather than allowing them to collect dust.

Teaching Tips from Prophets' Lips "An unrushed atmosphere is absolutely essential if you are to have the Spirit of the Lord present in your class" (Jeffrey R. Holland, "Teaching and Learning in the Church", *Ensign*, June 2007, 88–105).

Notes

1 NEPHI 6

Nephi's Intent in Writing
About 600–592 BC

1–3, Nephi's record will not be a complete history or have much genealogy; 4–6, The things written on the plates will be those things which bring people to God.

1 And now I, Nephi, do not give the genealogy of my fathers in this part of my record; neither at any time shall I give it after upon these plates which I am writing; for it is given in the record which has been kept by my father; wherefore, I do not write it in this work.

2 For it sufficeth me to say that we are descendants of Joseph.

3 And it mattereth not to me that I am particular to give a full account of all the things of my father, for they cannot be written upon these plates, for I desire the room that I may write of the things of God.

4 For the fulness of mine intent is that I may persuade men to come unto the God of Abraham, and the God of Isaac, and the God of Jacob, and be saved.

5 Wherefore, the things which are pleasing unto the world I do not write, but the things which are pleasing unto God and unto those who are not of the world.

6 Wherefore, I shall give commandment unto my seed, that they shall not occupy these plates with things which are not of worth unto the children of men.

vv. 1–6 When we write spiritual experiences in our journals, we will help those who read it come closer to the Lord.

⚡ Show a journal to the class and discuss with them what things people might include in their journal entries.

🔍 Have class members look for what Nephi said he would *not* include in great detail on the plates in verses 1–3. Then look in verses 4–6 for what he said he *would* include.

❓ Analyze: *Why would Nephi choose to include the most worthwhile details in his record? What does that teach about the value of the scriptures?*

❓ Apply: Note with the class that some people consider Nephi's writings to be a journal. Ask, *What could Nephi's example in this chapter teach about keeping a personal journal?*

🗨 Spencer W. Kimball stated, "Get a good notebook, a good book that will last through time and into eternity for the angels to look upon. Begin today and write in it your goings and your comings, your deeper thoughts, your achievements, and your failures, your associations and your triumphs, your impressions and your testimonies" (Spencer W. Kimball, "President Kimball Speaks Out on Personal Journals," *New Era*, December 1980, 26).

1 NEPHI 7

Returning for the Family of Ishmael
About 600–592 BC

1–5, Lehi's sons return to Jerusalem to bring Ishmael's family into the wilderness; 6–15, Some desire to return but Nephi exhorts them to faithfulness; 16–18, Nephi is bound by his brothers and freed according to his faith; 19–22, The brothers ask forgiveness of Nephi and he frankly forgives them.

Note: You may want to continue to contrast the two sets of brothers as these stories unfold throughout 1 Nephi.

1 And now I would that ye might know, that after my father, Lehi, had made an end of prophesying concerning his seed, it came to pass that the Lord spake unto him again, saying that it was not meet for him, Lehi, that he should take his family into the wilderness alone; but that his

Notes

sons should take daughters to wife, that they might raise up seed unto the Lord in the land of promise.

2 And it came to pass that the Lord commanded him that I, Nephi, and my brethren, should again return unto the land of Jerusalem, and bring down Ishmael and his family into the wilderness.

vv. 1–5 Marriage is an essential part of the plan of salvation.

🔍 *Search for why the brothers return again to Jerusalem, in verses 1–2.*

💡 Notice that when the brothers return to Jerusalem to get female companions, there is no murmuring from Laman and Lemuel!

💬 "The family is ordained of God. Marriage between man and woman is essential to His eternal plan" ("The Family: A Proclamation to the World").

❤ Testify about the importance of family and eternal marriage in the temple.

3 And it came to pass that I, Nephi, did again, with my brethren, go forth into the wilderness to go up to Jerusalem.

💡 Notice when traveling to Jerusalem, Nephi refers to Jerusalem as "up," and when traveling away from Jerusalem Nephi uses the word "down." Refer to Map 14 ("Holy Land Elevations in Bible Times") to find out why.

4 And it came to pass that we went up unto the house of Ishmael, and we did gain favor in the sight of Ishmael, insomuch that we did speak unto him the words of the Lord.

5 And it came to pass that the Lord did soften the heart of Ishmael, and also his household, insomuch that they took their journey with us down into the wilderness to the tent of our father.

6 And it came to pass that as we journeyed in the wilderness, behold Laman and Lemuel, and two of the daughters of Ishmael, and the two sons of Ishmael and their families, did rebel against us; yea, against me, Nephi, and Sam, and their father, Ishmael, and his wife, and his three other daughters.

7 And it came to pass in the which rebellion, they were desirous to return unto the land of Jerusalem.

8 And now I, Nephi, being grieved for the hardness of their hearts, therefore I spake unto them, saying, yea, even unto Laman and unto Lemuel: Behold ye are mine elder brethren, and how is it that ye are so hard in your hearts, and so blind in your minds, that ye have need that I, your younger brother, should speak unto you, yea, and set an example for you?

9 How is it that ye have not hearkened unto the word of the Lord?

10 How is it that ye have forgotten that ye have seen an angel of the Lord?

11 Yea, and how is it that ye have forgotten what great things the Lord hath done for us, in delivering us out of the hands of Laban, and also that we should obtain the record?

12 Yea, and how is it that ye have forgotten that the Lord is able to do all things according to his will, for the children of men, if it so be that they exercise faith in him? Wherefore, let us be faithful to him.

13 And if it so be that we are faithful to him, we shall obtain the land of promise; and ye shall know at some future period that the word of the Lord shall be fulfilled concerning the destruction of Jerusalem; for all things which the Lord hath spoken concerning the destruction of Jerusalem must be fulfilled.

14 For behold, the Spirit of the Lord ceaseth soon to strive with them; for behold, they have rejected the prophets, and Jeremiah have they cast into prison. And they have sought to take away the life of my father, insomuch that they have driven him out of the land.

Notes

15 Now behold, I say unto you that if ye will return unto Jerusalem ye shall also perish with them. And now, if ye have choice, go up to the land, and remember the words which I speak unto you, that if ye go ye will also perish; for thus the Spirit of the Lord constraineth me that I should speak.

vv. 6–12 The Lord is able to do all things, therefore be faithful unto Him.

⚡ To help the class members understand that confidence leads to faithful action, ask a class member who has a well-known talent what it means to have confidence in their abilities. Also ask, *What has given you that confidence?* Explain that *faithful* practice leads to confidence.

🔎 *In verses 6–7, after leaving Jerusalem with Ishmael's family what do Laman, Lemuel, and a few others desire while in the wilderness?*

✏️ Invite class members to make a list of the six "How Is It" questions Nephi asks his brothers (vv. 8–12). You may want to make the same list on the board.

🔎 *In verse 12, look for what Nephi's concluding invitation to his brothers is.*

❓ Analyze:
- *What does Nephi mean by saying they have not hearkened unto the Lord?*
- *How are Laman and Lemuel blind in their minds?*
- *How is it that Laman and Lemuel could forget the Lord's deliverance from Laban so quickly?*

❓ Apply:
- *How does this apply to us today?*
- *How can we make sure we are not blind in our minds?*
- *How can we make sure we are faithful to God?*

♥ Note with class members the phrase in verse 15 "if ye have a choice." Remind class members that we always have a choice, so we should choose to be faithful to the Lord. Refer

back to the conversation with the talented student: *faithful* practice yields confidence.

💡 To learn more about the political climate in Jerusalem during the year that Lehi leaves, refer to 2 Kings 24:11–20, see also 1 Nephi 1:4.

16 And it came to pass that when I, Nephi, had spoken these words unto my brethren, they were angry with me. And it came to pass that they did lay their hands upon me, for behold, they were exceedingly wroth, and they did bind me with cords, for they sought to take away my life, that they might leave me in the wilderness to be devoured by wild beasts.

17 But it came to pass that I prayed unto the Lord, saying: O Lord, according to my faith which is in thee, wilt thou deliver me from the hands of my brethren; yea, even give me strength that I may burst these bands with which I am bound.

18 And it came to pass that when I had said these words, behold, the bands were loosed from off my hands and feet, and I stood before my brethren, and I spake unto them again.

vv. 16–18 Our faith-building experiences from the past can strengthen faith for present challenges and can give us more confidence in the Lord.

🔎 *In verse 16, look for the rebellious brothers' reaction to Nephi's instructions to continue traveling in the wilderness.*

✋ To help visualize the story and principle, bring a rope to class and ask for a volunteer to come to the front of class. Have one or two class members tie the person up as tight as they can. Ask the tied up person to read Nephi's prayer in verse 17.

❓ Analyze: *How much faith would it take Nephi to burst the bands? How did Nephi acquire this kind of faith?* (List his previous experiences.)

✋ Ask the tied-up class member to loosen the ropes. After a failed attempt, allow him to return to their seat.

Notes

❓ Apply: *Why does Nephi have such great faith? What does this story teach us about faith?*

♥ Ask a class member to share an experience when their faith was strengthened, or share one of your personal experiences.

19 And it came to pass that they were angry with me again, and sought to lay hands upon me; but behold, one of the daughters of Ishmael, yea, and also her mother, and one of the sons of Ishmael, did plead with my brethren, insomuch that they did soften their hearts; and they did cease striving to take away my life.

20 And it came to pass that they were sorrowful, because of their wickedness, insomuch that they did bow down before me, and did plead with me that I would forgive them of the thing that they had done against me.

21 And it came to pass that I did frankly forgive them all that they had done, and I did exhort them that they would pray unto the Lord their God for forgiveness. And it came to pass that they did so. And after they had done praying unto the Lord we did again travel on our journey towards the tent of our father.

22 And it came to pass that we did come down unto the tent of our father. And after I and my brethren and all the house of Ishmael had come down unto the tent of my father, they did give thanks unto the Lord their God; and they did offer sacrifice and burnt offerings unto him.

vv. 19–21 We should frankly forgive those who have wronged us.

⚡ Discuss with class members if they or a family member have ever been intentionally hurt, wronged, or offended. Ask, *Why is it sometimes difficult to forgive?*

🔎 *Look for what Nephi's response is to his brothers asking forgiveness.*

✏ Possible synonyms for *frankly* include "openly," "sincerely," or "outright." Invite class members to write some synonyms of *frankly* in their scriptures.

✋ Ask a class member to explain verses 20–21 in their own words.

♥ Apply: *In what ways can we frankly forgive those who hurt us?* Invite a class member (if it isn't too personal) to share an experience of family members frankly forgiving each other.

Teaching Tips from Prophets' Lips "Oh, if I could teach you this one principle: a testimony is to be found in the bearing of it" (Boyd K. Packer, *Mine Errand from the Lord: Selections from the Sermons and Writings of Boyd K. Packer*, ed. Clyde J. Williams [Salt Lake City: Deseret Book, 2008] 118).

1 NEPHI 8

Lehi's Dream
About 600–592 BC

1–16, Lehi partakes of the fruit and desires his family to also partake; 17–20, Lehi sees the iron rod and the straight and narrow path; 21–23, 1st group loses way; 24–29, 2nd group is ashamed and falls away; 30, 3rd group stays at the tree; 31–33, 4th group seeks the spacious building; 34–38, Lehi exhorts his children.

Overarching Principle: I need to continually hold fast to the word of God in order to come to the tree of life.

1 And it came to pass that we had gathered together all manner of seeds of every kind, both of grain of every kind, and also of the seeds of fruit of every kind.

2 And it came to pass that while my father tarried in the wilderness he spake unto us, saying: Behold, I have dreamed a dream; or, in other words, I have seen a vision.

✏ Explain that Lehi has a dream and invite class

Notes

members to write "Lehi's Dream" next to verse 2 or by the chapter heading.

3 And behold, because of the thing which I have seen, I have reason to rejoice in the Lord because of Nephi and also of Sam; for I have reason to suppose that they, and also many of their seed, will be saved.

4 But behold, Laman and Lemuel, I fear exceedingly because of you; for behold, methought I saw in my dream, a dark and dreary wilderness.

5 And it came to pass that I saw a man, and he was dressed in a white robe; and he came and stood before me.

6 And it came to pass that he spake unto me, and bade me follow him.

7 And it came to pass that as I followed him I beheld myself that I was in a dark and dreary waste.

8 And after I had traveled for the space of many hours in darkness, I began to pray unto the Lord that he would have mercy on me, according to the multitude of his tender mercies.

9 And it came to pass after I had prayed unto the Lord I beheld a large and spacious field.

10 And it came to pass that I beheld a tree, whose fruit was desirable to make one happy.

11 And it came to pass that I did go forth and partake of the fruit thereof; and I beheld that it was most sweet, above all that I ever before tasted. Yea, and I beheld that the fruit thereof was white, to exceed all the whiteness that I had ever seen.

12 And as I partook of the fruit thereof it filled my soul with exceedingly great joy; wherefore, I began to be desirous that my family should partake of it also; for I knew that it was desirable above all other fruit.

13 And as I cast my eyes round about, that perhaps I might discover my family also, I beheld a river of water; and it ran along, and it was near the tree of which I was partaking the fruit.

14 And I looked to behold from whence it came; and I saw the head thereof a little way off; and at the head thereof I beheld your mother Sariah, and Sam, and Nephi; and they stood as if they knew not whither they should go.

15 And it came to pass that I beckoned unto them; and I also did say unto them with a loud voice that they should come unto me, and partake of the fruit, which was desirable above all other fruit.

16 And it came to pass that they did come unto me and partake of the fruit also.

17 And it came to pass that I was desirous that Laman and Lemuel should come and partake of the fruit also; wherefore, I cast mine eyes towards the head of the river, that perhaps I might see them.

18 And it came to pass that I saw them, but they would not come unto me and partake of the fruit.

19 And I beheld a rod of iron, and it extended along the bank of the river, and led to the tree by which I stood.

20 And I also beheld a strait and narrow path, which came along by the rod of iron, even to the tree by which I stood; and it also led by the head of the fountain, unto a large and spacious field, as if it had been a world.

⚡ (Idea 1) Distribute a piece of paper to each class member and have them draw each element of Lehi's dream (see 🔑 below). Once the drawings are completed allow class members to "show and tell."

⚡ (Idea 2) Break the class members into groups and assign each group to draw one element of Lehi's dream on the board so the class can visualize the dream in its entirety (see 🔑 below). Invite class members to explain their pictures.

⚡ (Idea 3) Before class, draw your own version

Notes

of Lehi's dream on the board with each element labeled so class members can look for them during the lesson (see 🔍 below).

🔍 Identify the elements of Lehi's dream in the following verses: A) 4–7; B) 9; C) 10–11; D) 12; E) 13; F) 15–18; G) 19; H) 20; I) 26–27; J) 32–34.

❓ Analyze: *What seems to be the central symbol in Lehi's dream? What leads the people to the tree?*

🔍 *Look for what the tree and the iron rod represent.* Invite class members to write 1 Nephi 11:25 in their scriptures, then turn there.

❓ Analyze: *What is the word of God?* (There can be many answers to this question, but "scriptures" would be the most basic.) *How does the iron rod, or the word of God, lead people to the tree of life in Lehi's vision?*

❓ Apply: *In our day, how can the scriptures (iron rod) help people feel the love of God (the tree)? How can we hold steadfastly to the word of God?*

♥ To help solidify this principle in the hearts of the class members, ask for a volunteer to come to the front of the room. Select an object to represent the iron rod (a chair, desk, whiteboard) and ask the class, *In order for this person to get the most out of scripture study, she has to be holding to the rod herself, right?* You, or another volunteer, then hold the iron rod. Then hold the hand of the volunteer who would now not be holding the rod directly. Ask, *Why is this not a good idea for her?* Share your testimony about the importance of holding to the rod yourself.

21 And I saw numberless concourses of people, many of whom were pressing forward, that they might obtain the path which led unto the tree by which I stood.

22 And it came to pass that they did come forth, and commence in the path which led to the tree.

23 And it came to pass that there arose a mist of

darkness; yea, even an exceedingly great mist of darkness, insomuch that they who had commenced in the path did lose their way, that they wandered off and were lost.

24 And it came to pass that I beheld others pressing forward, and they came forth and caught hold of the end of the rod of iron; and they did press forward through the mist of darkness, clinging to the rod of iron, even until they did come forth and partake of the fruit of the tree.

25 And after they had partaken of the fruit of the tree they did cast their eyes about as if they were ashamed.

vv. 21–30 Three groups of people in Lehi's dream teach us how to hold to the rod. We need to develop habits of daily scripture study in order to have the strength to resist temptations.

✎ Invite a class member to be a scribe. Have the scribe make three columns on the board and label each column Group 1, Group 2, and Group 3, respectively. To the left of the columns, have the class member create two rows, one labeled "How they used the rod" and the other "What happens to them in the end." As a class, fill the in chart on the board from the following verses: Group 1, vv. 21–23; Group 2, vv. 24–28; Group 3, v. 30. Also invite class members to mark these groups in their scriptures. Use the questions that follow to help class members analyze what they found.

	Group 1 vv. 21–23	Group 2 vv. 24–28	Group 3 v. 30
How they used the rod			
What happened to them in the end			

Notes

❓ Analyze:
- *Why did Group 1 wander off?* Note with the class that they never grasped the iron rod, which guaranteed they would become lost.
- *Why does Group 2 arrive at the tree?*
- *Why is it good to cling to the rod?* (It is apparently insufficient, however, because this group later becomes lost)
- *What does it mean to cling to something?*

💬 David A. Bednar stated: "Clinging to the rod of iron suggests to me only occasional 'bursts' of study or irregular dipping rather than consistent, ongoing immersion in the word of God" (CES Fireside for Young Adults, February 4, 2007).

🔍 *In verse 24, when does Group 2 cling?*

❓ Apply: *Based on what Elder Bednar is saying, in what ways do people only cling to the rod of iron today?*

❓ Analyze:
- *How does Group 3 use the iron rod?*
- *What does it mean to continually hold fast to the iron rod?*
- *What does it mean if we are continually holding fast to the scriptures?*

❓ Apply: *When have you felt the scriptures were a benefit in your life?*

❤️ Testify of the power of the word of God and invite the class members to be part of Group 3. This can be a great moment for you to challenge the class to read their scriptures every day for a certain amount of time—for instance a seven-day consecutive reading program—to help encourage them to continually hold fast to the rod of iron.

💬 "The third group also pressed forward with faith and conviction. . . . Perhaps this third group of people *consistently* read *and* studied *and* searched the words of Christ. . . . This is the group you and I should strive to join" (David A. Bednar, CES Fireside for Young Adults February 4, 2007).

26 And I also cast my eyes round about, and beheld, on the other side of the river of water, a great and spacious building; and it stood as it were in the air, high above the earth.

27 And it was filled with people, both old and young, both male and female; and their manner of dress was exceedingly fine; and they were in the attitude of mocking and pointing their fingers towards those who had come at and were partaking of the fruit.

28 And after they had tasted of the fruit they were ashamed, because of those that were scoffing at them; and they fell away into forbidden paths and were lost.

29 And now I, Nephi, do not speak all the words of my father.

30 But, to be short in writing, behold, he saw other multitudes pressing forward; and they came and caught hold of the end of the rod of iron; and they did press their way forward, continually holding fast to the rod of iron, until they came forth and fell down and partook of the fruit of the tree.

💡 The iron rod is defined as the word of God by Nephi. One of Jesus' titles is The Word (John 1:1, 14). What additional insights can come to this lesson if we were to continually hold fast to Christ?

31 And he also saw other multitudes feeling their way towards that great and spacious building.

32 And it came to pass that many were drowned in the depths of the fountain; and many were lost from his view, wandering in strange roads.

33 And great was the multitude that did enter into that strange building. And after they did enter into that building they did point the finger of scorn at me and those that were partaking of the fruit also; but we heeded them not.

34 These are the words of my father: For as many as heeded them, had fallen away.

Notes

_____

_____

_____

vv. 31–34 The temptations of the world lure us away from the path, therefore *heed them not!*

Due to probable time constraints in teaching 1 Nephi 8, the lesson outline for this principle is found in 1 Nephi 12:16–20. You can teach this principle at this point or wait until 1 Nephi 12.

35 And Laman and Lemuel partook not of the fruit, said my father.

36 And it came to pass after my father had spoken all the words of his dream or vision, which were many, he said unto us, because of these things which he saw in a vision, he exceedingly feared for Laman and Lemuel; yea, he feared lest they should be cast off from the presence of the Lord.

37 And he did exhort them then with all the feeling of a tender parent, that they would hearken to his words, that perhaps the Lord would be merciful to them, and not cast them off; yea, my father did preach unto them.

38 And after he had preached unto them, and also prophesied unto them of many things, he bade them to keep the commandments of the Lord; and he did cease speaking unto them.

vv. 35–37 Loving parents are concerned about their children.

🔍 *In verses 36, Laman and Lemuel do not partake of the fruit of the tree of life. What is Lehi's reaction to that? (v. 37) What does he do as a result?*

❓ Analyze: *What does this teach us about parents' concern for their children?*

💜 Invite class members to listen when their parents are teaching them. Assure them that their parents love them.

1 NEPHI 9

"For a Wise Purpose"
About 600–592 BC

1–4, Nephi makes two sets of plates: one for secular history and the other for spiritual teachings; 5–6, Nephi does not know why the Lord wants him to make two sets, but he trusts that God has a reason.

1 And all these things did my father see, and hear, and speak, as he dwelt in a tent, in the valley of Lemuel, and also a great many more things, which cannot be written upon these plates.

2 And now, as I have spoken concerning these plates, behold they are not the plates upon which I make a full account of the history of my people; for the plates upon which I make a full account of my people I have given the name of Nephi; wherefore, they are called the plates of Nephi, after mine own name; and these plates also are called the plates of Nephi.

3 Nevertheless, I have received a commandment of the Lord that I should make these plates, for the special purpose that there should be an account engraven of the ministry of my people.

4 Upon the other plates should be engraven an account of the reign of the kings, and the wars and contentions of my people; wherefore these plates are for the more part of the ministry; and the other plates are for the more part of the reign of the kings and the wars and contentions of my people.

Notes

The Book of Mormon Plates as Given to Joseph Smith

Book of Lehi – The 116 lost pages
(Doctrine and Covenants 10)
*Abridged by Mormon

Small plates – The writings of 9 men being the books of 1st Nephi through Omni

Words of Mormon

Large Plates – The books of Mosiah through Mormon chapter 7
* Abridged by Mormon

Mormon 8–9 written by Moroni

Book of Ether – The history of the Jaredites
*Abridged by Moroni

Book of Moroni

The Sealed Plates

Although it is confusing in this chapter, we call the two sets of plates the *large plates of Nephi* and the *small plates of Nephi*. The *large plates* give a "full account" of things and the *small plates* consist of his ministry and things of a spiritual nature. First Nephi through Omni come from the *small plates of Nephi*.

With your class, write an "**S**" in the margin when Nephi is talking about the *small plates* (Nephi refers to them as "these plates") and an "**L**" when he is talking about the *large plates* (Nephi refers to them as "the other plates".)

5 Wherefore, the Lord hath commanded me to make these plates for a wise purpose in him, which purpose I know not.

6 But the Lord knoweth all things from the beginning; wherefore, he prepareth a way to accomplish all his works among the children of men; for behold, he hath all power unto the fulfilling of all his words. And thus it is. Amen.

vv. 5–6 We should do what God wants us to, even when we don't fully understand.

Have the class search for why Nephi wrote his history in two places.

Analyze: *What did God know would happen in the future that Nephi knew nothing about?*

Ask a class member to share what happened to Joseph Smith and the lost 116 pages of the translation of the Book of Mormon.

Invite class members to write "Words of Mormon 1:7, Doctrine and Covenants 3:19, and Doctrine and Covenants 10:45" in their margins.

Ask a class member to share a time they followed a prompting that they didn't understand, but later found out why.

Testify of the trust we can put in God because He "knoweth all things" (2 Nephi 9:20). Challenge them to trust in God's promptings, even when they don't understand the purpose behind it.

Teaching Tips from Prophets' Lips "Many topics are interesting, important, and even relevant to life and yet not nourishing to the soul. It is not our commission to teach such topics. Instead, we are to edify others and teach them principles that pertain to the kingdom of God and the salvation of mankind" (*Teaching, No Greater Call* [Deseret Book: Salt Lake City, 1999], 5).

Notes

1 NEPHI 10

Lehi Prophecies of the Messiah
About 600–592 BC

1–12, Lehi prophesies concerning the Jews, John the Baptist, Jesus's ministry, and the Gentiles; 13–16, The scattering and gathering of Israel; 17–22, Nephi desires personal revelation concerning all that his father taught.

1 And now I, Nephi, proceed to give an account upon these plates of my proceedings, and my reign and ministry; wherefore, to proceed with mine account, I must speak somewhat of the things of my father, and also of my brethren.

2 For behold, it came to pass after my father had made an end of speaking the words of his dream, and also of exhorting them to all diligence, he spake unto them concerning the Jews—

3 That after they should be destroyed, even that great city Jerusalem, and many be carried away captive into Babylon, according to the own due time of the Lord, they should return again, yea, even be brought back out of captivity; and after they should be brought back out of captivity they should possess again the land of their inheritance.

💡 Jeremiah had prophesied that the Jews would be captive in Babylon for seventy years (Jeremiah 25:11–12). Miraculously, after the Jews had been captive for seventy years, King Cyrus freed them and charged them to return and rebuild Jerusalem and the temple that had been destroyed (Ezra 1:1–4).

4 Yea, even six hundred years from the time that my father left Jerusalem, a prophet would the Lord God raise up among the Jews—even a Messiah, or, in other words, a Savior of the world.

5 And he also spake concerning the prophets, how great a number had testified of these things, concerning this Messiah, of whom he had spoken, or this Redeemer of the world.

6 Wherefore, all mankind were in a lost and in a fallen state, and ever would be save they should rely on this Redeemer.

vv. 4–6 We are all fallen. To return to God, we must rely on and follow the Savior.

⚡ Have class members discuss the requirements to enter the celestial kingdom. Read 1 Nephi 10:21 and ask, *What chances do we have of being able to save ourselves?*

🔍 Invite class members to search for our current spiritual state in verse 6.

❓ Analyze: *What does it mean that we are fallen or lost? How can we be redeemed from that lost and fallen state?*

💡 Explain that any sin makes us unclean (verse 21), and doing what is right does not remove sin, but rather keeps us from slipping further from the standard. We remain unclean until we allow Christ to remove sin through His Atonement.

🗨 Ezra Taft Benson taught, "Just as a man does not really desire food until he is hungry, so he does not desire the salvation of Christ until he knows why he needs Christ. No one adequately and properly knows why he needs Christ until he understands and accepts the doctrine of the Fall and its effect upon all mankind" ("The Book of Mormon and the Doctrine and Covenants," *Ensign*, May 1987, 83–87).

❤ Testify of your knowledge of the Fall, and our absolute need for and dependence on our Redeemer.

7 And he spake also concerning a prophet who should come before the Messiah, to prepare the way of the Lord—

8 Yea, even he should go forth and cry in the wilderness: Prepare ye the way of the Lord, and make his paths straight; for there standeth one among you whom ye know not; and he is mightier than I, whose shoe's latchet I am not worthy

Notes

to unloose. And much spake my father concerning this thing.

9 And my father said he should baptize in Bethabara, beyond Jordan; and he also said he should baptize with water; even that he should baptize the Messiah with water.

10 And after he had baptized the Messiah with water, he should behold and bear record that he had baptized the Lamb of God, who should take away the sins of the world.

11 And it came to pass after my father had spoken these words he spake unto my brethren concerning the gospel which should be preached among the Jews, and also concerning the dwindling of the Jews in unbelief. And after they had slain the Messiah, who should come, and after he had been slain he should rise from the dead, and should make himself manifest, by the Holy Ghost, unto the Gentiles.

🔍 Have class members mark in the margin every time there is a prophecy that has been fulfilled in verses 7–11.

12 Yea, even my father spake much concerning the Gentiles, and also concerning the house of Israel, that they should be compared like unto an olive tree, whose branches should be broken off and should be scattered upon all the face of the earth.

13 Wherefore, he said it must needs be that we should be led with one accord into the land of promise, unto the fulfilling of the word of the Lord, that we should be scattered upon all the face of the earth.

14 And after the house of Israel should be scattered they should be gathered together again; or, in fine, after the Gentiles had received the fulness of the Gospel, the natural branches of the olive tree, or the remnants of the house of Israel, should be grafted in, or come to the knowledge of the true Messiah, their Lord and their Redeemer.

💡 For more about the scattering and gathering of Israel, see the lesson ideas in Jacob 5.

15 And after this manner of language did my father prophesy and speak unto my brethren, and also many more things which I do not write in this book; for I have written as many of them as were expedient for me in mine other book.

16 And all these things, of which I have spoken, were done as my father dwelt in a tent, in the valley of Lemuel.

17 And it came to pass after I, Nephi, having heard all the words of my father, concerning the things which he saw in a vision, and also the things which he spake by the power of the Holy Ghost, which power he received by faith on the Son of God—and the Son of God was the Messiah who should come—I, Nephi, was desirous also that I might see, and hear, and know of these things, by the power of the Holy Ghost, which is the gift of God unto all those who diligently seek him, as well in times of old as in the time that he should manifest himself unto the children of men.

18 For he is the same yesterday, today, and forever; and the way is prepared for all men from the foundation of the world, if it so be that they repent and come unto him.

19 For he that diligently seeketh shall find; and the mysteries of God shall be unfolded unto them, by the power of the Holy Ghost, as well in these times as in times of old, and as well in times of old as in times to come; wherefore, the course of the Lord is one eternal round.

vv. 17–19 We can receive revelations just like people in the scriptures.

Note that it might be best to teach these verses when you also teach 1 Nephi 11:1–5 about personal revelation.

⚡ Discuss the following questions with class members. *Would it be appropriate for you*

Notes

to pray and ask God to let you experience Lehi's Dream or Joseph Smith's vision of the degrees of glory? Why or why not?

🔍 Have class members look for what Nephi prays for in verse 17.

💡 Note with the class that the Lord grants his request in 1 Nephi chapters 11–14.

🔍 Have a scribe come to the board and have the class search verses 17–19 and list what we must do or believe in order to also have our own personal revelations.

💬 Joseph Smith said: "God hath not revealed anything to Joseph, but what he will make known unto the Twelve, and even the least Saint may know all things as fast as he is able to bear them" (*Teachings of the Prophet Joseph Smith,* 149).

❤ Challenge class members to seek personal revelation in their lives.

20 Therefore remember, O man, for all thy doings thou shalt be brought into judgment.

21 Wherefore, if ye have sought to do wickedly in the days of your probation, then ye are found unclean before the judgment-seat of God; and no unclean thing can dwell with God; wherefore, ye must be cast off forever.

22 And the Holy Ghost giveth authority that I should speak these things, and deny them not.

1 NEPHI 11

Nephi's Vision of Christ's Life and the Early Church
About 600–592 BC

1–7, Nephi desires to know the visions of his father; 8–23, He sees the tree and that it represents the love of God, also learns of the condescension of God; 24–33, Nephi sees the mortal ministry of Jesus including His crucifixion; 34–36, He learns more about the large and spacious building.

Notes

1 For it came to pass after I had desired to know the things that my father had seen, and believing that the Lord was able to make them known unto me, as I sat pondering in mine heart I was caught away in the Spirit of the Lord, yea, into an exceedingly high mountain, which I never had before seen, and upon which I never had before set my foot.

2 And the Spirit said unto me: Behold, what desirest thou?

3 And I said: I desire to behold the things which my father saw.

4 And the Spirit said unto me: Believest thou that thy father saw the tree of which he hath spoken?

5 And I said: Yea, thou knowest that I believe all the words of my father.

vv. 1–5 Nephi teaches us a formula for how to receive personal revelation: Desire + Belief + Pondering scriptures = Personal Revelation.

⚡ Put up a simple formula on the board like R*T=D (Rate * Time = Distance). Ask, *Why are formulas useful? Is there a formula for things like personal revelation?* Write "_____ + _____ + _____ = Personal Revelation" on the board. Have class members read verse one and look for the formula. Have someone come to the board and fill in the blanks based on verse 1.

🔍 Have class members look for what Nephi does next in 1 Nephi 11:2–5.

❓ Analyze: *Why would God expect Nephi to express what he desired? Doesn't God already know what Nephi wants?*

❓ Apply: *How would Nephi's example apply to someone who wants to know whether the Book of Mormon is true? When have you expressed a desire to God in prayer, and how was it answered?*

❤ Encourage class members to express their desires to God in prayer. Explain to them that they will now see the result of Nephi's request in the next few chapters (1 Nephi 11–14).

6 And when I had spoken these words, the Spirit cried with a loud voice, saying: Hosanna to the Lord, the most high God; for he is God over all the earth, yea, even above all. And blessed art thou, Nephi, because thou believest in the Son of the most high God; wherefore, thou shalt behold the things which thou hast desired.

7 And behold this thing shall be given unto thee for a sign, that after thou hast beheld the tree which bore the fruit which thy father tasted, thou shalt also behold a man descending out of heaven, and him shall ye witness; and after ye have witnessed him ye shall bear record that it is the Son of God.

8 And it came to pass that the Spirit said unto me: Look! And I looked and beheld a tree; and it was like unto the tree which my father had seen; and the beauty thereof was far beyond, yea, exceeding of all beauty; and the whiteness thereof did exceed the whiteness of the driven snow.

9 And it came to pass after I had seen the tree, I said unto the Spirit: I behold thou hast shown unto me the tree which is precious above all.

10 And he said unto me: What desirest thou?

11 And I said unto him: To know the interpretation thereof—for I spake unto him as a man speaketh; for I beheld that he was in the form of a man; yet nevertheless, I knew that it was the Spirit of the Lord; and he spake unto me as a man speaketh with another.

12 And it came to pass that he said unto me: Look! And I looked as if to look upon him, and I saw him not; for he had gone from before my presence.

13 And it came to pass that I looked and beheld the great city of Jerusalem, and also other cities. And I beheld the city of Nazareth; and in the city of Nazareth I beheld a virgin, and she was exceedingly fair and white.

14 And it came to pass that I saw the heavens open; and an angel came down and stood before me; and he said unto me: Nephi, what beholdest thou?

15 And I said unto him: A virgin, most beautiful and fair above all other virgins.

16 And he said unto me: Knowest thou the condescension of God?

17 And I said unto him: I know that he loveth his children; nevertheless, I do not know the meaning of all things.

18 And he said unto me: Behold, the virgin whom thou seest is the mother of the Son of God, after the manner of the flesh.

19 And it came to pass that I beheld that she was carried away in the Spirit; and after she had been carried away in the Spirit for the space of a time the angel spake unto me, saying: Look!

20 And I looked and beheld the virgin again, bearing a child in her arms.

21 And the angel said unto me: Behold the Lamb of God, yea, even the Son of the Eternal Father! Knowest thou the meaning of the tree which thy father saw?

22 And I answered him, saying: Yea, it is the love of God, which sheddeth itself abroad in the hearts of the children of men; wherefore, it is the most desirable above all things.

23 And he spake unto me, saying: Yea, and the most joyous to the soul.

24 And after he had said these words, he said unto me: Look! And I looked, and I beheld the Son of God going forth among the children of men; and I saw many fall down at his feet and worship him.

25 And it came to pass that I beheld that the rod of iron, which my father had seen, was the word of God, which led to the fountain of living waters, or to the tree of life; which waters are a representation of the love of God; and I also beheld that the tree of life was a representation of the love of God.

26 And the angel said unto me again: Look and behold the condescension of God!

27 And I looked and beheld the Redeemer of the

Notes

world, of whom my father had spoken; and I also beheld the prophet who should prepare the way before him. And the Lamb of God went forth and was baptized of him; and after he was baptized, I beheld the heavens open, and the Holy Ghost come down out of heaven and abide upon him in the form of a dove.

28 And I beheld that he went forth ministering unto the people, in power and great glory; and the multitudes were gathered together to hear him; and I beheld that they cast him out from among them.

29 And I also beheld twelve others following him. And it came to pass that they were carried away in the Spirit from before my face, and I saw them not.

30 And it came to pass that the angel spake unto me again, saying: Look! And I looked, and I beheld the heavens open again, and I saw angels descending upon the children of men; and they did minister unto them.

31 And he spake unto me again, saying: Look! And I looked, and I beheld the Lamb of God going forth among the children of men. And I beheld multitudes of people who were sick, and who were afflicted with all manner of diseases, and with devils and unclean spirits; and the angel spake and showed all these things unto me. And they were healed by the power of the Lamb of God; and the devils and the unclean spirits were cast out.

32 And it came to pass that the angel spake unto me again, saying: Look! And I looked and beheld the Lamb of God, that he was taken by the people; yea, the Son of the everlasting God was judged of the world; and I saw and bear record.

33 And I, Nephi, saw that he was lifted up upon the cross and slain for the sins of the world.

vv. 8–33 God loves all His children, therefore come unto Him and partake of His love.

⚡ Before class write, "God loves His children.

How do you prove it?" on the board so class members can see it when they walk in. Role-play by pretending you are a non-member who does not believe in God and allow the class to discuss that question with you.

🔎 *Look in verse 16 and see how Nephi is going to prove to us that God loves us.*

✏️ Invite class members to write the following definition in their scriptures: *The term condescension of God refers to Christ leaving his throne of glory to come to earth and live as a mortal man.*

🔎 In a column, write the following verses on the board to help the class look for what Nephi sees in vision as the condescension of God. 8–11, 12–18, 19–23, 24, 26–28, 31–33.

❓ Analyze:
- *Based on what Nephi has seen, what is the condescension of God?*
- *How does the crucifixion prove God's love for His children?*
- *Based on what Nephi is being shown, what do you think is the meaning of the tree which his father saw? (vv. 21–23.)*
- *Why do you think that the fruit of the tree of life tastes as good as it does?*

❓ Apply: *Which verse from what you have studied is most meaningful to you and why?*

❤️ Explain that Nephi experiences the love of God for himself because of what he did in verse 1. Invite class members to share a time when they have experienced the love of God, or share one yourself.

34 And after he was slain I saw the multitudes of the earth, that they were gathered together to fight against the apostles of the Lamb; for thus were the twelve called by the angel of the Lord.

35 And the multitude of the earth was gathered together; and I beheld that they were in a large and spacious building, like unto the building which my father saw. And the angel of the Lord spake unto me again, saying: Behold the world

Notes

_____

_____

_____

and the wisdom thereof; yea, behold the house of Israel hath gathered together to fight against the twelve apostles of the Lamb.

36 And it came to pass that I saw and bear record, that the great and spacious building was the pride of the world; and it fell, and the fall thereof was exceedingly great. And the angel of the Lord spake unto me again, saying: Thus shall be the destruction of all nations, kindreds, tongues, and people, that shall fight against the twelve apostles of the Lamb.

vv. 34–36 Pride makes people reject Jesus Christ.

🔍 Nephi sees the large and spacious building. Ask, *In verses 34–36, What are the people in the building doing against the twelve apostles of the Lamb?*

❓ Analyze:
 • *What does the large and spacious building represent?*
 • *How does pride cause people to fight against and reject God?*
 • *What happens to the large and spacious building?*

❓ Apply: *How can pride be destructive to us? If we are being prideful, how can we become humble?*

❤ "Pride is the universal sin, the great vice. Yes, pride is the universal sin, the great vice. The antidote for pride is humility—meekness, submissiveness" (Ezra Taft Benson, "Beware of Pride," *Ensign,* May 1989, 4).

Teaching Tips from Prophets' Lips "If we have the Spirit of the Lord to guide us, we can teach any person, no matter how well educated, any place in the world. The Lord knows more than any of us, and if we are his servants, acting under his Spirit, He can deliver his message of salvation to each and every soul" (Dallin H. Oaks, "Teaching and Learning by the Spirit," *Ensign,* March 1997, 7).

1 NEPHI 12

Nephi's Vision of Lehi's Descendants
About 600–592 BC

1–5, Nephi's vision continues, he sees many generations of his descendants on the land of promise; 6–10, Jesus Christ ministers to the Nephites and chooses twelve ministers; 11–23, The destruction of the Nephites and the degeneration of the Lamanites.

1 And it came to pass that the angel said unto me: Look, and behold thy seed, and also the seed of thy brethren. And I looked and beheld the land of promise; and I beheld multitudes of people, yea, even as it were in number as many as the sand of the sea.

2 And it came to pass that I beheld multitudes gathered together to battle, one against the other; and I beheld wars, and rumors of wars, and great slaughters with the sword among my people.

3 And it came to pass that I beheld many generations pass away, after the manner of wars and contentions in the land; and I beheld many cities, yea, even that I did not number them.

4 And it came to pass that I saw a mist of darkness on the face of the land of promise; and I saw lightnings, and I heard thunderings, and earthquakes, and all manner of tumultuous noises; and I saw the earth and the rocks, that they rent; and I saw mountains tumbling into pieces; and I saw the plains of the earth, that they were broken up; and I saw many cities that they were sunk; and I saw many that they were burned with fire; and I saw many that did tumble to the earth, because of the quaking thereof.

5 And it came to pass after I saw these things, I saw the vapor of darkness, that it passed from off the face of the earth; and behold, I saw multitudes who had not fallen because of the great and terrible judgments of the Lord.

6 And I saw the heavens open, and the Lamb of

Notes

God descending out of heaven; and he came down and showed himself unto them.

7 And I also saw and bear record that the Holy Ghost fell upon twelve others; and they were ordained of God, and chosen.

8 And the angel spake unto me, saying: Behold the twelve disciples of the Lamb, who are chosen to minister unto thy seed.

9 And he said unto me: Thou rememberest the twelve apostles of the Lamb? Behold they are they who shall judge the twelve tribes of Israel; wherefore, the twelve ministers of thy seed shall be judged of them; for ye are of the house of Israel.

10 And these twelve ministers whom thou beholdest shall judge thy seed. And, behold, they are righteous forever; for because of their faith in the Lamb of God their garments are made white in his blood.

11 And the angel said unto me: Look! And I looked, and beheld three generations pass away in righteousness; and their garments were white even like unto the Lamb of God. And the angel said unto me: These are made white in the blood of the Lamb, because of their faith in him.

12 And I, Nephi, also saw many of the fourth generation who passed away in righteousness.

13 And it came to pass that I saw the multitudes of the earth gathered together.

14 And the angel said unto me: Behold thy seed, and also the seed of thy brethren.

15 And it came to pass that I looked and beheld the people of my seed gathered together in multitudes against the seed of my brethren; and they were gathered together to battle.

vv. 1–15 A future prophesy of the Nephites and Lamanites.

🔍 Look for the future Lamanite/Nephite event Nephi is prophesying of in verses 1–7 and 11–15.

✏️ Have class members write the fulfillment of these events in their scriptures: (verse 4) 3 Nephi 8; (verse 5) 3 Nephi 8:20; (verse 6) 3 Nephi 11:8–11; (verse 7) 3 Nephi 12:1; (verse 11) 4 Nephi; (verse 15) Mormon 6. You can read these scriptures with class members, or you can explain them in your own words.

16 And the angel spake unto me, saying: Behold the fountain of filthy water which thy father saw; yea, even the river of which he spake; and the depths thereof are the depths of hell.

17 And the mists of darkness are the temptations of the devil, which blindeth the eyes, and hardeneth the hearts of the children of men, and leadeth them away into broad roads, that they perish and are lost.

18 And the large and spacious building, which thy father saw, is vain imaginations and the pride of the children of men. And a great and a terrible gulf divideth them; yea, even the word of the justice of the Eternal God, and the Messiah who is the Lamb of God, of whom the Holy Ghost beareth record, from the beginning of the world until this time, and from this time henceforth and forever.

19 And while the angel spake these words, I beheld and saw that the seed of my brethren did contend against my seed, according to the word of the angel; and because of the pride of my seed, and the temptations of the devil, I beheld that the seed of my brethren did overpower the people of my seed.

vv. 18–19 The temptations of the world lure us away from the path, therefore *heed them not!*

⚡ Display various caution signs as well as the *For the Strength of Youth* pamphlet and ask, *What do these have in common? How is the* For the Strength of Youth *Pamphlet a warning sign?*

🔍 In verse 18, if Nephi could post a warning sign in front of a building, which building would he choose?

Notes

✋ Give class members the following verses, ask them to read the verses, and invite them to write on the board everything they know about the great and spacious building. 1 Nephi 8:26–27, 31–33; 11:35–36; 12:17–18.

❓ Analyze:
- *Why is the great and spacious building so enticing?*
- *What effect does it have on followers of Christ as they journey on the path to the tree?*
- *Why is it so bad to be in the great and spacious building?*

❓ Apply: *What could the great and spacious building represent today? In what ways do the people inside the great and spacious building target members of the Church?*

💬 "To those of you who are inching your way closer and closer to that great and spacious building, let me make it completely clear that the people in that building have absolutely nothing to offer except instant, short-term gratification inescapably connected to long-term sorrow and suffering" (Bishop Glenn L. Pace, "They're Not Really Happy," *Ensign*, November 1987).

🔍 In 1 Nephi 8:33–34, look for how we can guarantee to never get caught up in the great and spacious building.

❓ Apply: *What could be considered modern-day scoffing? What can you do to ignore the great and spacious building?*

20 And it came to pass that I beheld, and saw the people of the seed of my brethren that they had overcome my seed; and they went forth in multitudes upon the face of the land.

21 And I saw them gathered together in multitudes; and I saw wars and rumors of wars among them; and in wars and rumors of wars I saw many generations pass away.

22 And the angel said unto me: Behold these shall dwindle in unbelief.

23 And it came to pass that I beheld, after they had

dwindled in unbelief they became a dark, and loathsome, and a filthy people, full of idleness and all manner of abominations.

1 NEPHI 13

Nephi's Vision of the Gentiles in the Americas
About 600–592 BC

1–9, Nephi sees many nations and the formation of an abominable church; 10–19, Gentiles discovering and colonizing the Americas; 20–29, Plain and precious truths lost from the Bible and brought to America; 30–42, Judgments upon those in the Americas, the restoration of the gospel, and more scripture brought forth.

1 And it came to pass that the angel spake unto me, saying: Look! And I looked and beheld many nations and kingdoms.

2 And the angel said unto me: What beholdest thou? And I said: I behold many nations and kingdoms.

3 And he said unto me: These are the nations and kingdoms of the Gentiles.

4 And it came to pass that I saw among the nations of the Gentiles the formation of a great church.

5 And the angel said unto me: Behold the formation of a church which is most abominable above all other churches, which slayeth the saints of God, yea, and tortureth them and bindeth them down, and yoketh them with a yoke of iron, and bringeth them down into captivity.

6 And it came to pass that I beheld this great and abominable church; and I saw the devil that he was the founder of it.

7 And I also saw gold, and silver, and silks, and scarlets, and fine-twined linen, and all manner of precious clothing; and I saw many harlots.

8 And the angel spake unto me, saying: Behold the

gold, and the silver, and the silks, and the scarlets, and the fine-twined linen, and the precious clothing, and the harlots, are the desires of this great and abominable church.

9 And also for the praise of the world do they destroy the saints of God, and bring them down into captivity.

vv. 4–9 The "great and abominable church" is any organization that keeps people from the Lord and His gospel.

⚡ Discuss with class members what they know about the "great and abominable church"?

💡 Note that the "great and abominable church" is not one particular church or denomination.

✏ Have class members write "1 Nephi 14:10" in their scriptures and find the answer.

💬 "The titles church of the devil and great and abominable church are used to identify all churches or organizations of whatever name or nature—whether political, philosophical, educational, economic, social, fraternal, civic, or religious—which are designed to take men on a course that leads away from God and his laws and thus from salvation in the kingdom of God" (Bruce R. McConkie, "Church of the Devil," *Mormon Doctrine,* 137).

✋ Have a scribe come to the board and have the class list organizations that try to take people away from their faith in God. You may need to look at the broad categories that Elder McConkie listed.

❤ Challenge class members to avoid anything that minimizes one's faith in God.

10 And it came to pass that I looked and beheld many waters; and they divided the Gentiles from the seed of my brethren.

11 And it came to pass that the angel said unto me: Behold the wrath of God is upon the seed of thy brethren.

12 And I looked and beheld a man among the Gentiles, who was separated from the seed of my brethren by the many waters; and I beheld the Spirit of God, that it came down and wrought upon the man; and he went forth upon the many waters, even unto the seed of my brethren, who were in the promised land.

13 And it came to pass that I beheld the Spirit of God, that it wrought upon other Gentiles; and they went forth out of captivity, upon the many waters.

14 And it came to pass that I beheld many multitudes of the Gentiles upon the land of promise; and I beheld the wrath of God, that it was upon the seed of my brethren; and they were scattered before the Gentiles and were smitten.

15 And I beheld the Spirit of the Lord, that it was upon the Gentiles, and they did prosper and obtain the land for their inheritance; and I beheld that they were white, and exceedingly fair and beautiful, like unto my people before they were slain.

16 And it came to pass that I, Nephi, beheld that the Gentiles who had gone forth out of captivity did humble themselves before the Lord; and the power of the Lord was with them.

17 And I beheld that their mother Gentiles were gathered together upon the waters, and upon the land also, to battle against them.

18 And I beheld that the power of God was with them, and also that the wrath of God was upon all those that were gathered together against them to battle.

19 And I, Nephi, beheld that the Gentiles that had gone out of captivity were delivered by the power of God out of the hands of all other nations.

20 And it came to pass that I, Nephi, beheld that they did prosper in the land; and I beheld a book, and it was carried forth among them.

21 And the angel said unto me: Knowest thou the meaning of the book?

22 And I said unto him: I know not.

Notes

23 And he said: Behold it proceedeth out of the mouth of a Jew. And I, Nephi, beheld it; and he said unto me: The book that thou beholdest is a record of the Jews, which contains the covenants of the Lord, which he hath made unto the house of Israel; and it also containeth many of the prophecies of the holy prophets; and it is a record like unto the engravings which are upon the plates of brass, save there are not so many; nevertheless, they contain the covenants of the Lord, which he hath made unto the house of Israel; wherefore, they are of great worth unto the Gentiles.

vv. 10–23 God will sometimes prophesy of future events in great detail.

✋ Before class, prepare a matching activity by making two columns like the ones you see below. Read the verses as a class and as class members discover what the verse is describing, have someone draw a line between the two to make a match.

Prophecy	Fulfillment
13:10	Christopher Columbus
13:11	American Revolutionary War
13:12	American Indians
13:13–16	Holy Bible
13:17	Atlantic Ocean
13:18–19	Pilgrims
13:20–23	England

✏ In the margins of their scriptures, have the class write the fulfillment of each prophecy next to the verse it appears in.

🔎 *In verse 12, look for how Christopher Columbus was guided.*

💬 Christopher Columbus stated, "The Lord was well disposed to my desire, and He bestowed upon me courage and understanding; . . . our Lord unlocked my mind, sent me upon the sea, and gave me, fire for the deed. Those who heard of my enterprise called it foolish, mocked me, and laughed. But who can doubt that the Holy Ghost inspired me?" (Jacob Wasserman, *Columbus: Don Quixote of the Seas* [Little, Brown, 1930], 1920).

24 And the angel of the Lord said unto me: Thou hast beheld that the book proceeded forth from the mouth of a Jew; and when it proceeded forth from the mouth of a Jew it contained the fulness of the gospel of the Lord, of whom the twelve apostles bear record; and they bear record according to the truth which is in the Lamb of God.

25 Wherefore, these things go forth from the Jews in purity unto the Gentiles, according to the truth which is in God.

26 And after they go forth by the hand of the twelve apostles of the Lamb, from the Jews unto the Gentiles, thou seest the formation of that great and abominable church, which is most abominable above all other churches; for behold, they have taken away from the gospel of the Lamb many parts which are plain and most precious; and also many covenants of the Lord have they taken away.

27 And all this have they done that they might pervert the right ways of the Lord, that they might blind the eyes and harden the hearts of the children of men.

28 Wherefore, thou seest that after the book hath gone forth through the hands of the great and abominable church, that there are many plain and precious things taken away from the book, which is the book of the Lamb of God.

29 And after these plain and precious things were taken away it goeth forth unto all the nations of the Gentiles; and after it goeth forth unto all the nations of the Gentiles, yea, even across the many waters which thou hast seen with the Gentiles which have gone forth out of captivity, thou seest—because of the many plain and precious things which have been taken out of the book, which were plain unto the understanding of the children of men, according to the plainness

Notes

which is in the Lamb of God—because of these things which are taken away out of the gospel of the Lamb, an exceedingly great many do stumble, yea, insomuch that Satan hath great power over them.

vv. 24–29 Some plain and precious parts of the Bible have been taken out. There are also other errors which cause people to misunderstand God's word.

✋ Have class members try to put verses 25–26 in their own words and then share how they summarized the verses.

❓ Analyze: *Why do you think Satan would want to change the Bible?*

🔎 *Search for what effect the corruption of the Bible has on people in verse 29.*

💬 Joseph Smith stated, "I believe the Bible as it read when it came from the pen of the original writers. Ignorant translators, careless transcribers, or designing and corrupt priests have committed many errors" (*Teachings of the Prophet Joseph Smith*, 327).

❓ Analyze: *If a corrupt Bible is giving great power to Satan and causing people to stumble, what do you think God can do about it?* (Read verse 29 for the answer.) *What has the Lord done to help correct these errors?*

💡 In the remainder of 1 Nephi 13, Nephi sees what God's solution is to a Bible that has had plain and precious parts removed.

30 Nevertheless, thou beholdest that the Gentiles who have gone forth out of captivity, and have been lifted up by the power of God above all other nations, upon the face of the land which is choice above all other lands, which is the land that the Lord God hath covenanted with thy father that his seed should have for the land of their inheritance; wherefore, thou seest that the Lord God will not suffer that the Gentiles will utterly destroy the mixture of thy seed, which are among thy brethren.

31 Neither will he suffer that the Gentiles shall destroy the seed of thy brethren.

32 Neither will the Lord God suffer that the Gentiles shall forever remain in that awful state of blindness, which thou beholdest they are in, because of the plain and most precious parts of the gospel of the Lamb which have been kept back by that abominable church, whose formation thou hast seen.

33 Wherefore saith the Lamb of God: I will be merciful unto the Gentiles, unto the visiting of the remnant of the house of Israel in great judgment.

34 And it came to pass that the angel of the Lord spake unto me, saying: Behold, saith the Lamb of God, after I have visited the remnant of the house of Israel—and this remnant of whom I speak is the seed of thy father—wherefore, after I have visited them in judgment, and smitten them by the hand of the Gentiles, and after the Gentiles do stumble exceedingly, because of the most plain and precious parts of the gospel of the Lamb which have been kept back by that abominable church, which is the mother of harlots, saith the Lamb—I will be merciful unto the Gentiles in that day, insomuch that I will bring forth unto them, in mine own power, much of my gospel, which shall be plain and precious, saith the Lamb.

35 For, behold, saith the Lamb: I will manifest myself unto thy seed, that they shall write many things which I shall minister unto them, which shall be plain and precious; and after thy seed shall be destroyed, and dwindle in unbelief, and also the seed of thy brethren, behold, these things shall be hid up, to come forth unto the Gentiles, by the gift and power of the Lamb.

36 And in them shall be written my gospel, saith the Lamb, and my rock and my salvation.

37 And blessed are they who shall seek to bring forth my Zion at that day, for they shall have the gift and the power of the Holy Ghost; and if they endure unto the end they shall be lifted up at the last day, and shall be saved in the everlasting

Notes

kingdom of the Lamb; and whoso shall publish peace, yea, tidings of great joy, how beautiful upon the mountains shall they be.

38 And it came to pass that I beheld the remnant of the seed of my brethren, and also the book of the Lamb of God, which had proceeded forth from the mouth of the Jew, that it came forth from the Gentiles unto the remnant of the seed of my brethren.

39 And after it had come forth unto them I beheld other books, which came forth by the power of the Lamb, from the Gentiles unto them, unto the convincing of the Gentiles and the remnant of the seed of my brethren, and also the Jews who were scattered upon all the face of the earth, that the records of the prophets and of the twelve apostles of the Lamb are true.

40 And the angel spake unto me, saying: These last records, which thou hast seen among the Gentiles, shall establish the truth of the first, which are of the twelve apostles of the Lamb, and shall make known the plain and precious things which have been taken away from them; and shall make known to all kindreds, tongues, and people, that the Lamb of God is the Son of the Eternal Father, and the Savior of the world; and that all men must come unto him, or they cannot be saved.

✋ This activity is similar to the one with verses 10–23. After the verses have been read and matched, have the class mark the elements in the right column in their scriptures.

Prophecy	Fulfillment
13:34	Missionaries
13:35	Restoration of the Gospel
13:37	Book of Mormon
13:39	Doctrine and Covenants and Pearl of Great Price

🔍 In verse 40, look for what effect the restoration and the Book of Mormon have had on the Bible.

❤ Testify of how the Book of Mormon has helped you see truth easier.

41 And they must come according to the words which shall be established by the mouth of the Lamb; and the words of the Lamb shall be made known in the records of thy seed, as well as in the records of the twelve apostles of the Lamb; wherefore they both shall be established in one; for there is one God and one Shepherd over all the earth.

42 And the time cometh that he shall manifest himself unto all nations, both unto the Jews and also unto the Gentiles; and after he has manifested himself unto the Jews and also unto the Gentiles, then he shall manifest himself unto the Gentiles and also unto the Jews, and the last shall be first, and the first shall be last.

Teaching Tips from Prophets' Lips "If they (the writers) saw our day and chose those things which would be of greatest worth to us, is not that how we should study the Book of Mormon? We should constantly ask ourselves, 'Why did the Lord inspire Mormon (or Moroni or Alma) to include that in his record? What lesson can I learn from that to help me live in this day and age?'" (Ezra Taft Benson, *Ensign*, November 1986, 6).

1 NEPHI 14

Nephi's Vision of the Latter-day Church
About 600–592 BC

1–7, Blessings and curses on the Gentiles are dependent on how the restoration of the gospel is received; 8–17, Latter-day conflict between the church of the lamb and the church of the devil; 18–30, John the Revelator is given the commission to write concerning what was revealed to Nephi.

Notes

⚡ Before class, write on the board, "Would you rather study prophecy of things that have already happened, or study prophecy about today and what is perhaps in our near future?" Once you are at this point in class, ask class members what they think about the question and why. Explain that prior to this, Nephi has been sharing about what is already history to us. But now Nephi is going to prophesy about the latter days.

1 And it shall come to pass, that if the Gentiles shall hearken unto the Lamb of God in that day that he shall manifest himself unto them in word, and also in power, in very deed, unto the taking away of their stumbling blocks—

2 And harden not their hearts against the Lamb of God, they shall be numbered among the seed of thy father; yea, they shall be numbered among the house of Israel; and they shall be a blessed people upon the promised land forever; they shall be no more brought down into captivity; and the house of Israel shall no more be confounded.

3 And that great pit, which hath been digged for them by that great and abominable church, which was founded by the devil and his children, that he might lead away the souls of men down to hell—yea, that great pit which hath been digged for the destruction of men shall be filled by those who digged it, unto their utter destruction, saith the Lamb of God; not the destruction of the soul, save it be the casting of it into that hell which hath no end.

4 For behold, this is according to the captivity of the devil, and also according to the justice of God, upon all those who will work wickedness and abomination before him.

5 And it came to pass that the angel spake unto me, Nephi, saying: Thou hast beheld that if the Gentiles repent it shall be well with them; and thou also knowest concerning the covenants of the Lord unto the house of Israel; and thou also hast heard that whoso repenteth not must perish.

6 Therefore, wo be unto the Gentiles if it so be that they harden their hearts against the Lamb of God.

7 For the time cometh, saith the Lamb of God, that I will work a great and a marvelous work among the children of men; a work which shall be everlasting, either on the one hand or on the other—either to the convincing of them unto peace and life eternal, or unto the deliverance of them to the hardness of their hearts and the blindness of their minds unto their being brought down into captivity, and also into destruction, both temporally and spiritually, according to the captivity of the devil, of which I have spoken.

vv. 1–7 Righteousness brings positive consequences; wickedness brings negative consequences.

👥 On the board write down the following verses on the side, and then "Condition" and "Blessing/Curse" as show below. Break your class into groups of three and assign each group one of the sets of verses. (Depending on the size of your class, multiple groups might have the same verses.) Explain that each group will need to determine what the condition is in their verse(s), and the resulting blessing or curse that comes from it. Once completed, ask the groups to teach what they have learned.

Verses	Condition	Blessing/Curse
14:1		
14:2–4		
14:5		
14:6–7		

❤ After all the groups have shared, ask, *What does this teach us about consequences? How can we make sure we have good consequences in our lives?* Invite class members to live so they can have the positive consequences of a righteous life.

Notes

8 And it came to pass that when the angel had spoken these words, he said unto me: Rememberest thou the covenants of the Father unto the house of Israel? I said unto him, Yea.

9 And it came to pass that he said unto me: Look, and behold that great and abominable church, which is the mother of abominations, whose founder is the devil.

10 And he said unto me: Behold there are save two churches only; the one is the church of the Lamb of God, and the other is the church of the devil; wherefore, whoso belongeth not to the church of the Lamb of God belongeth to that great church, which is the mother of abominations; and she is the whore of all the earth.

11 And it came to pass that I looked and beheld the whore of all the earth, and she sat upon many waters; and she had dominion over all the earth, among all nations, kindreds, tongues, and people.

12 And it came to pass that I beheld the church of the Lamb of God, and its numbers were few, because of the wickedness and abominations of the whore who sat upon many waters; nevertheless, I beheld that the church of the Lamb, who were the saints of God, were also upon all the face of the earth; and their dominions upon the face of the earth were small, because of the wickedness of the great whore whom I saw.

13 And it came to pass that I beheld that the great mother of abominations did gather together multitudes upon the face of all the earth, among all the nations of the Gentiles, to fight against the Lamb of God.

14 And it came to pass that I, Nephi, beheld the power of the Lamb of God, that it descended upon the saints of the church of the Lamb, and upon the covenant people of the Lord, who were scattered upon all the face of the earth; and they were armed with righteousness and with the power of God in great glory.

15 And it came to pass that I beheld that the wrath of God was poured out upon that great and abominable church, insomuch that there were wars and rumors of wars among all the nations and kindreds of the earth.

16 And as there began to be wars and rumors of wars among all the nations which belonged to the mother of abominations, the angel spake unto me, saying: Behold, the wrath of God is upon the mother of harlots; and behold, thou seest all these things—

17 And when the day cometh that the wrath of God is poured out upon the mother of harlots, which is the great and abominable church of all the earth, whose founder is the devil, then, at that day, the work of the Father shall commence, in preparing the way for the fulfilling of his covenants, which he hath made to his people who are of the house of Israel.

vv. 9–17 God will give us power to stand strong as we follow Him and His prophets.

⚡ Show a picture of soldiers in battle to your class. Ask, *How many of you feel you might have to someday fight in a war? How are you already like these soldiers?*

🔎 *Look for who the conflict is between in verses 9–10. Make sure class members understand that the conflict isn't against any particular religion; rather, it is against the devil. Share the quote from Bruce R. McConkie from the lesson idea in 1 Nephi 13:4–9 if you haven't already.*

🔎 *Look for attributes of the church of the lamb of God in the last days according to verse 12.*

❓ Analyze: *In what ways are members of the Church "few"?*

💡 Before class, look up the approximate world population and compare that with the Church's current membership. Have a class member divide the world population into the Church population and then multiply it by 100, and they will determine that about 0.2% of the world's population is LDS.

🔎 *Despite its comparatively small numbers, look*

Notes

for how the Church is to survive the conflicts against it in verses 13–17.

❓ Apply: *What can we do so that power will descend on upon us? How can we be armed with righteousness?*

♥ Testify to your class that we will always have God's power to help us as we are following Him and his prophets.

18 And it came to pass that the angel spake unto me, saying: Look!

19 And I looked and beheld a man, and he was dressed in a white robe.

20 And the angel said unto me: Behold one of the twelve apostles of the Lamb.

21 Behold, he shall see and write the remainder of these things; yea, and also many things which have been.

22 And he shall also write concerning the end of the world.

23 Wherefore, the things which he shall write are just and true; and behold they are written in the book which thou beheld proceeding out of the mouth of the Jew; and at the time they proceeded out of the mouth of the Jew, or, at the time the book proceeded out of the mouth of the Jew, the things which were written were plain and pure, and most precious and easy to the understanding of all men.

24 And behold, the things which this apostle of the Lamb shall write are many things which thou hast seen; and behold, the remainder shalt thou see.

25 But the things which thou shalt see hereafter thou shalt not write; for the Lord God hath ordained the apostle of the Lamb of God that he should write them.

26 And also others who have been, to them hath he shown all things, and they have written them; and they are sealed up to come forth in their purity, according to the truth which is in the Lamb, in the own due time of the Lord, unto the house of Israel.

27 And I, Nephi, heard and bear record, that the name of the apostle of the Lamb was John, according to the word of the angel.

28 And behold, I, Nephi, am forbidden that I should write the remainder of the things which I saw and heard; wherefore the things which I have written sufficeth me; and I have written but a small part of the things which I saw.

vv. 18–28 John the Revelator is given a special responsibility to write about some of the events preceding the Second Coming.

⚡ *Have you ever been told by a non-member that the Bible should not be added to? Where do they get that idea?* Have class members turn to Revelation 22:18–19 and read the verses. Explain that the Bible was not compiled until hundreds of years later, and John was writing about his special message, which is now referred to as the book of Revelation.

🔎 Nephi sees all the events that preceded the Second Coming but was forbidden to write them. Have class members look for why Nephi was forbidden to write these things as you read together verses 18–22 and 24–28. Explain to class members that the words at the end of the book of Revelation were given because, like Nephi said, John was given this special responsibility to write about those aspects of the Second Coming.

29 And I bear record that I saw the things which my father saw, and the angel of the Lord did make them known unto me.

30 And now I make an end of speaking concerning the things which I saw while I was carried away in the spirit; and if all the things which I saw are not written, the things which I have written are true. And thus it is. Amen.

Notes

1 NEPHI 15

Helps for Understanding
the Scriptures
About 600–592 BC

1–11, Nephi discusses the need for personal revelation with his brethren; 12–20, The scattering and gathering of Israel is compared to an olive tree; 21–36, The symbols in Lehi's dream are discussed.

1 And it came to pass that after I, Nephi, had been carried away in the spirit, and seen all these things, I returned to the tent of my father.

2 And it came to pass that I beheld my brethren, and they were disputing one with another concerning the things which my father had spoken unto them.

3 For he truly spake many great things unto them, which were hard to be understood, save a man should inquire of the Lord; and they being hard in their hearts, therefore they did not look unto the Lord as they ought.

4 And now I, Nephi, was grieved because of the hardness of their hearts, and also, because of the things which I had seen, and knew they must unavoidably come to pass because of the great wickedness of the children of men.

5 And it came to pass that I was overcome because of my afflictions, for I considered that mine afflictions were great above all, because of the destruction of my people, for I had beheld their fall.

6 And it came to pass that after I had received strength I spake unto my brethren, desiring to know of them the cause of their disputations.

7 And they said: Behold, we cannot understand the words which our father hath spoken concerning the natural branches of the olive tree, and also concerning the Gentiles.

8 And I said unto them: Have ye inquired of the Lord?

9 And they said unto me: We have not; for the Lord maketh no such thing known unto us.

10 Behold, I said unto them: How is it that ye do not keep the commandments of the Lord? How is it that ye will perish, because of the hardness of your hearts?

11 Do ye not remember the things which the Lord hath said?—If ye will not harden your hearts, and ask me in faith, believing that ye shall receive, with diligence in keeping my commandments, surely these things shall be made known unto you.

vv. 1–11 God will lead us to understanding as we ask for His guidance.

⚡ Ask class members to think of a gospel-centered question they have been wondering or are confused about. Ask them to raise their hands when they have something in mind. Ask a few class members to share if the comments are not too personal. Then ask, *Have you asked God about it?* If some answer no, ask them why not. If some answer yes, ask them about the experience if they are willing to share.

🔍 *Search for how this discussion relates to 1 Nephi 15:6–9.*

❓ Analyze: *Why do you think Laman and Lemuel feel this way?* Read verses 3 and 10 and ask, *Why is it difficult to have things revealed unto us when we have a "hardness of heart"?*

❓ Apply: *What could cause someone feel this way today?*

♥ Invite class members to ask the Lord about whatever it is that has been on their mind that they raised their hands about. Remind the class that sometimes the way God reveals things to us is by directing us to people who will be able to help us or by discovering the answers ourselves as we study and seek confirmation.

12 Behold, I say unto you, that the house of Israel was compared unto an olive tree, by the Spirit of

Notes

the Lord which was in our father; and behold are we not broken off from the house of Israel, and are we not a branch of the house of Israel?

13 And now, the thing which our father meaneth concerning the grafting in of the natural branches through the fulness of the Gentiles, is, that in the latter days, when our seed shall have dwindled in unbelief, yea, for the space of many years, and many generations after the Messiah shall be manifested in body unto the children of men, then shall the fulness of the gospel of the Messiah come unto the Gentiles, and from the Gentiles unto the remnant of our seed—

14 And at that day shall the remnant of our seed know that they are of the house of Israel, and that they are the covenant people of the Lord; and then shall they know and come to the knowledge of their forefathers, and also to the knowledge of the gospel of their Redeemer, which was ministered unto their fathers by him; wherefore, they shall come to the knowledge of their Redeemer and the very points of his doctrine, that they may know how to come unto him and be saved.

15 And then at that day will they not rejoice and give praise unto their everlasting God, their rock and their salvation? Yea, at that day, will they not receive the strength and nourishment from the true vine? Yea, will they not come unto the true fold of God?

16 Behold, I say unto you, Yea; they shall be remembered again among the house of Israel; they shall be grafted in, being a natural branch of the olive tree, into the true olive tree.

17 And this is what our father meaneth; and he meaneth that it will not come to pass until after they are scattered by the Gentiles; and he meaneth that it shall come by way of the Gentiles, that the Lord may show his power unto the Gentiles, for the very cause that he shall be rejected of the Jews, or of the house of Israel.

18 Wherefore, our father hath not spoken of our seed alone, but also of all the house of Israel, pointing to the covenant which should be fulfilled in the latter days; which covenant the Lord made to our father Abraham, saying: In thy seed shall all the kindreds of the earth be blessed.

19 And it came to pass that I, Nephi, spake much unto them concerning these things; yea, I spake unto them concerning the restoration of the Jews in the latter days.

20 And I did rehearse unto them the words of Isaiah, who spake concerning the restoration of the Jews, or of the house of Israel; and after they were restored they should no more be confounded, neither should they be scattered again. And it came to pass that I did speak many words unto my brethren, that they were pacified and did humble themselves before the Lord.

vv. 12–20 The Lord will gather Israel through the Restoration and the Book of Mormon. Note that these teaching ideas can easily be used to teach Jacob 5 also. If you feel you don't have time at this point in the lesson, you can save this teaching idea or principle for when you teach Jacob 5.

⚡ Before class, layer a baking pan with a quarter inch of sand. Then take a magnet and slowly gather out the black iron ore (already in most sand) and save it for later. During class, gather class members around the pan and lay out a small line of the iron ore on the top of the sand. Explain that this line represents Israel. Ask class members what happened to Israel over time. (They have been scattered throughout the earth.) With a spoon, sprinkle the iron throughout the sand in the pan. As you are slowly spreading, you might want to bring up topics such as Lehi's group leaving Jerusalem, lost ten tribes, and other events which first separated the Israelites, and eventually scattered them. Once the iron ore is spread, discuss what can be done to gather Israel back. (Use the magnet.) Ask, *As God is gathering Israel in our day, what do you think is the equivalent of the magnet?*

Notes

🔍 *Look for what will gather scattered Israel in verse 14.*

💬 Ezra Taft Benson stated, "The Book of Mormon is the instrument that God designed to 'sweep the earth as with a flood, to gather out [His] elect.' This sacred volume of scripture needs to become more central in our preaching, our teaching, and our missionary work" ("Flooding the Earth with the Book of Mormon," *Ensign*, November 1988).

❤ Have the class rub the magnet(s) around and "gather" Israel. Testify of the importance of spreading the gospel by sharing the Book of Mormon with people.

21 And it came to pass that they did speak unto me again, saying: What meaneth this thing which our father saw in a dream? What meaneth the tree which he saw?

22 And I said unto them: It was a representation of the tree of life.

23 And they said unto me: What meaneth the rod of iron which our father saw, that led to the tree?

24 And I said unto them that it was the word of God; and whoso would hearken unto the word of God, and would hold fast unto it, they would never perish; neither could the temptations and the fiery darts of the adversary overpower them unto blindness, to lead them away to destruction.

25 Wherefore, I, Nephi, did exhort them to give heed unto the word of the Lord; yea, I did exhort them with all the energies of my soul, and with all the faculty which I possessed, that they would give heed to the word of God and remember to keep his commandments always in all things.

v. 24 Satan will entice with little temptations at first. Studying the scriptures helps us to resist those temptations.

⚡ Display pictures of various weapons to the class and discuss what the purpose is of weapons.

🔍 *Look for what weapons Satan uses in verse 24.*

❓ Analyze: *Of all the possible weapons for Satan to use, why a dart? Why wouldn't Satan's weapon of choice be a more deadly weapon?*

❓ Apply: *What does that teach us about Satan's tactics today? What could be examples of modern-day "darts" that Satan uses?*

❤ Conclude by challenging class members to resist the little temptations that Satan tries to tempt us with. Encourage them to remain faithful by studying the scriptures each day.

26 And they said unto me: What meaneth the river of water which our father saw?

27 And I said unto them that the water which my father saw was filthiness; and so much was his mind swallowed up in other things that he beheld not the filthiness of the water.

28 And I said unto them that it was an awful gulf, which separated the wicked from the tree of life, and also from the saints of God.

29 And I said unto them that it was a representation of that awful hell, which the angel said unto me was prepared for the wicked.

30 And I said unto them that our father also saw that the justice of God did also divide the wicked from the righteous; and the brightness thereof was like unto the brightness of a flaming fire, which ascendeth up unto God forever and ever, and hath no end.

31 And they said unto me: Doth this thing mean the torment of the body in the days of probation, or doth it mean the final state of the soul after the death of the temporal body, or doth it speak of the things which are temporal?

32 And it came to pass that I said unto them that it was a representation of things both temporal and spiritual; for the day should come that they must be judged of their works, yea, even the works which were done by the temporal body in their days of probation.

Notes

33 Wherefore, if they should die in their wickedness they must be cast off also, as to the things which are spiritual, which are pertaining to righteousness; wherefore, they must be brought to stand before God, to be judged of their works; and if their works have been filthiness they must needs be filthy; and if they be filthy it must needs be that they cannot dwell in the kingdom of God; if so, the kingdom of God must be filthy also.

34 But behold, I say unto you, the kingdom of God is not filthy, and there cannot any unclean thing enter into the kingdom of God; wherefore there must needs be a place of filthiness prepared for that which is filthy.

35 And there is a place prepared, yea, even that awful hell of which I have spoken, and the devil is the preparator of it; wherefore the final state of the souls of men is to dwell in the kingdom of God, or to be cast out because of that justice of which I have spoken.

36 Wherefore, the wicked are rejected from the righteous, and also from that tree of life, whose fruit is most precious and most desirable above all other fruits; yea, and it is the greatest of all the gifts of God. And thus I spake unto my brethren. Amen.

v. 36 We can enjoy the promise of eternal life while in mortality.

⚡ Quiz your class on what the various symbols in Lehi's dream represent such as the rod, the path, and the mist of darkness. Ask, *What does the tree represent? What does the fruit of the tree represent?*

🔑 *Try to determine the answer by studying verse 36.* (You may have to guide class members to their footnotes. Through this verse and Doctrine and Covenants 14:7, it is evident that the fruit is eternal life. Encourage them to mark that footnote.)

❓ Analyze: *Can we partake of eternal life while we are still mortals?*

💬 Brigham Young stated: "It is present salvation and the present influence of the Holy Ghost that we need every day to keep us on saving ground. . . . I want present salvation. . . . Life is for us, and it is for us to receive it to-day, and not wait for the Millennium. Let us take a course to be saved to-day" (Young, in JD, 8:124–25).

❤ Share Doctrine and Covenants 88:4 with your class. Testify that as we are living with the Lord's Spirit in our lives, we can be assured of God's promise of eternal life. It is possible to walk away from this blessing like the people in Lehi's dream did, but as we are living in a way to have the Lord's Spirit, salvation is ours to enjoy.

Teaching Tips from Prophets' Lips "Faith promoting incidents occur in teaching when students take a role in teaching and testifying to their peers" (Robert D. Hales, "Teaching by Faith," 4).

1 NEPHI 16

The Liahona and Nephi's Bow
About 600–592 BC

1–5, The wicked take the truth to be hard; 6–17, Lehi finds the Liahona and it helps guide them through the wilderness; 18–27, Nephi's bow breaks and the family complains for want of food; 28–33, The Liahona works according to faith and diligence; 34, Ishmael dies; 35–39, Some desire to rebel and kill Lehi and Nephi.

Overarching Principle: In our day, the gift of the Holy Ghost can guide us as the Liahona guided Lehi's family in the wilderness. Nephi teaches us three principles on how to be guided by God.

⚡ Before class, sporadically place pieces of masking tape on the floor in the walking path of class members. On the tape write phrases like, "Do you know where you are going?" "Are we there yet?" and "Where are we?"

Notes

Once class starts, discuss with the class if they think Lehi was ever asked these same questions on the floor by his family, or if Lehi ever wondered those questions himself? Try to help the class members relate with the anxiety of these travelers. Ask, *Since God asked Lehi to take this journey, what should He ideally give him?*

1 And now it came to pass that after I, Nephi, had made an end of speaking to my brethren, behold they said unto me: Thou hast declared unto us hard things, more than we are able to bear.

2 And it came to pass that I said unto them that I knew that I had spoken hard things against the wicked, according to the truth; and the righteous have I justified, and testified that they should be lifted up at the last day; wherefore, the guilty taketh the truth to be hard, for it cutteth them to the very center.

3 And now my brethren, if ye were righteous and were willing to hearken to the truth, and give heed unto it, that ye might walk uprightly before God, then ye would not murmur because of the truth, and say: Thou speakest hard things against us.

4 And it came to pass that I, Nephi, did exhort my brethren, with all diligence, to keep the commandments of the Lord.

vv. 1–2 The truth cuts the wicked to the very center.

⚡ *Have you ever been proven wrong? What did it feel like?*

🔎 Nephi's teachings in 1 Nephi 15 have a serious impact on Laman and Lemuel. Have class members look in verse 1 to find out what the impact is and in verse 2 to find out why Laman and Lemuel are affected the way they are.

❓ Analyze: *Why do you think the wicked take the truth to be hard? How does truth cut someone to the very center?*

❓ Apply: *In what ways do people today take the truth to be hard? In what ways do the responsibilities of bishops or branch presidents relate to what Nephi is doing right now with his brothers—that is, cutting them to the very center by telling them what they are doing wrong?*

❤ Explain that one of the roles of Church leaders is to help members keep the commandments, which means that they have to offer correction if needed. Read and discuss the following quote from Spencer W. Kimball: "I am sure Peter, James, and Paul found it unpleasant business to constantly be calling people to repentance and warning them of dangers, but they continued unflinchingly. So we, your leaders, must be everlastingly at it; if young people do not understand, then the fault may be partly ours. But if we make the true way clear to you, then we are blameless" ("Love Versus Lust," *Brigham Young Speeches of the Year*, Provo, Utah, 5 January 1965, 6).

5 And it came to pass that they did humble themselves before the Lord; insomuch that I had joy and great hopes of them, that they would walk in the paths of righteousness.

6 Now, all these things were said and done as my father dwelt in a tent in the valley which he called Lemuel.

7 And it came to pass that I, Nephi, took one of the daughters of Ishmael to wife; and also, my brethren took of the daughters of Ishmael to wife; and also Zoram took the eldest daughter of Ishmael to wife.

8 And thus my father had fulfilled all the commandments of the Lord which had been given unto him. And also, I, Nephi, had been blessed of the Lord exceedingly.

9 And it came to pass that the voice of the Lord spake unto my father by night, and commanded him that on the morrow he should take his journey into the wilderness.

Notes

10 And it came to pass that as my father arose in the morning, and went forth to the tent door, to his great astonishment he beheld upon the ground a round ball of curious workmanship; and it was of fine brass. And within the ball were two spindles; and the one pointed the way whither we should go into the wilderness.

11 And it came to pass that we did gather together whatsoever things we should carry into the wilderness, and all the remainder of our provisions which the Lord had given unto us; and we did take seed of every kind that we might carry into the wilderness.

12 And it came to pass that we did take our tents and depart into the wilderness, across the river Laman.

13 And it came to pass that we traveled for the space of four days, nearly a south-southeast direction, and we did pitch our tents again; and we did call the name of the place Shazer.

14 And it came to pass that we did take our bows and our arrows, and go forth into the wilderness to slay food for our families; and after we had slain food for our families we did return again to our families in the wilderness, to the place of Shazer. And we did go forth again in the wilderness, following the same direction, keeping in the most fertile parts of the wilderness, which were in the borders near the Red Sea.

15 And it came to pass that we did travel for the space of many days, slaying food by the way, with our bows and our arrows and our stones and our slings.

16 And we did follow the directions of the ball, which led us in the more fertile parts of the wilderness.

vv. 10–16 To be guided by God—Principle 1: God guides us through various external means.

⚡ There are three different principles in this chapter on how to be guided by God. You may want to bring objects with you to help class members visualize each of these stories. For this first principle, you can bring a compass, a small golden ball (you can make one from Styrofoam and gold spray paint), or a replica of the Liahona.

🔍 In verses 10 and 16, *look for what Lehi receives from God and how it helps him.*

✏️ Consider keeping track of each of the three principles found later in this chapter on the board and invite class members to write them down either in their scriptures or journals.

❓ Analyze: *Why do you think God gives Lehi an external object to help guide him? Couldn't God just speak to Lehi? Why or why not?*

❓ Apply:
  • *What could we call the first principle of being guided by God?* (God uses external means to guide us. Write the class members' response on the board, even if it doesn't match what is in parenthesis here.)
  • *How are we guided today by external means?*
  • *Why doesn't God just communicate directly to us? Why do it through these external means?*

❤️ *Has there been a time when you felt you were guided by God through one of these ways? Consider sharing a personal experience.*

17 And after we had traveled for the space of many days, we did pitch our tents for the space of a time, that we might again rest ourselves and obtain food for our families.

18 And it came to pass that as I, Nephi, went forth to slay food, behold, I did break my bow, which was made of fine steel; and after I did break my bow, behold, my brethren were angry with me because of the loss of my bow, for we did obtain no food.

19 And it came to pass that we did return without food to our families, and being much fatigued, because of their journeying, they did suffer much for the want of food.

Notes

20 And it came to pass that Laman and Lemuel and the sons of Ishmael did begin to murmur exceedingly, because of their sufferings and afflictions in the wilderness; and also my father began to murmur against the Lord his God; yea, and they were all exceedingly sorrowful, even that they did murmur against the Lord.

21 Now it came to pass that I, Nephi, having been afflicted with my brethren because of the loss of my bow, and their bows having lost their springs, it began to be exceedingly difficult, yea, insomuch that we could obtain no food.

22 And it came to pass that I, Nephi, did speak much unto my brethren, because they had hardened their hearts again, even unto complaining against the Lord their God.

23 And it came to pass that I, Nephi, did make out of wood a bow, and out of a straight stick, an arrow; wherefore, I did arm myself with a bow and an arrow, with a sling and with stones. And I said unto my father: Whither shall I go to obtain food?

24 And it came to pass that he did inquire of the Lord, for they had humbled themselves because of my words; for I did say many things unto them in the energy of my soul.

25 And it came to pass that the voice of the Lord came unto my father; and he was truly chastened because of his murmuring against the Lord, insomuch that he was brought down into the depths of sorrow.

26 And it came to pass that the voice of the Lord said unto him: Look upon the ball, and behold the things which are written.

vv. 17–26 To be guided by God—Principle 2. Bad things may happen to us in life. God can guide us through those challenges depending on how we react in those situations.

⚡ For this principle you may consider bringing a bow and arrow. If you do not have access to one, you can probably find one at a dollar store or show a picture of one.

🔎 Invite the class to read verse 18 and look for what happens to Nephi's bow as they were hunting in the wilderness.

❓ Analyze: *If Nephi was being obedient, why did God allow his bow to break? If God is guiding them, why wouldn't He help them?*

🔎 In verses 19–21, look for everyone's reaction to the breaking of the bow, except Nephi's. Discuss the different reactions. In verses 22–23 look for Nephi's reaction.

❓ Analyze:
- *Instead of complaining and doing nothing, what does Nephi do?*
- *How would Nephi making his own bow allow God to give him guidance?*
- *Why would doing nothing and complaining interfere with receiving direction from God?*

🔎 *In verses 24–26, look for what happens to Lehi as a result of Nephi's example.*

✎ *Based on what we have just read, what is being taught regarding receiving direction from God?*

❓ Apply: *In what ways does Nephi's example apply to us today as we are seeking guidance from God?*

27 And it came to pass that when my father beheld the things which were written upon the ball, he did fear and tremble exceedingly, and also my brethren and the sons of Ishmael and our wives.

28 And it came to pass that I, Nephi, beheld the pointers which were in the ball, that they did work according to the faith and diligence and heed which we did give unto them.

29 And there was also written upon them a new writing, which was plain to be read, which did give us understanding concerning the ways of the Lord; and it was written and changed from time to time, according to the faith and diligence which we gave unto it. And thus we see that by small means the Lord can bring about great things.

Notes

30 And it came to pass that I, Nephi, did go forth up into the top of the mountain, according to the directions which were given upon the ball.

31 And it came to pass that I did slay wild beasts, insomuch that I did obtain food for our families.

32 And it came to pass that I did return to our tents, bearing the beasts which I had slain; and now when they beheld that I had obtained food, how great was their joy! And it came to pass that they did humble themselves before the Lord, and did give thanks unto him.

33 And it came to pass that we did again take our journey, traveling nearly the same course as in the beginning; and after we had traveled for the space of many days we did pitch our tents again, that we might tarry for the space of a time.

vv. 27–29 To be guided by God—Principle 3. We must exercise faith and diligence to receive God's guidance.

⚡ For this principle you can refer back to your Liahona object.

🔍 Look in verses 28–29 and consider what Lehi and his family had to do or have in order for the Liahona to work.

❓ Analyze:
- *Why do you think God would require faith and diligence for the Liahona to work?*
- *What do you think Nephi and the others had to have faith in?*
- *What did they have to exercise diligence with?*
- *What do you think Nephi means by the phrase "by small means the Lord can bring about great things"?*

❓ Apply:
- *In order to be guided by God today, what do you have to be diligent with?*
- *How do we exercise faith to be guided?*
- *What role does the Holy Ghost play in our being guided by God?*
- *How does faith and diligence relate to our use of the gift of the Holy Ghost?*

💬 "As we strive to align our attitudes and actions with righteousness, then the Holy Ghost becomes for us today what the Liahona was for Lehi and his family in their day. The very factors that caused the Liahona to work for Lehi will likewise invite the Holy Ghost into our lives. And the very factors that caused the Liahona not to work anciently will likewise cause us to withdraw ourselves from the Holy Ghost today" (David A Bednar "That We May Always Have His Spirit to Be with Us," *Ensign,* May, 2006, 28).

❤ *We are given the gift of the Holy Ghost so we can be guided by God. Why do you think righteousness is a requirement, as Elder Bednar has indicated?* Encourage class members to seek guidance from God by continually using the gift of the Holy Ghost. Consider sharing a personal experience when you felt you were being guided by God. Encourage class members to share personal experiences of their own or of someone they know.

34 And it came to pass that Ishmael died, and was buried in the place which was called Nahom.

v. 34 Ishmael dies.

💡 There are many LDS scholars who think they have located a probable site for the place Lehi calls Nahom. To learn more about this archeological site, perform an internet search with "Nahom" as your keyword.

35 And it came to pass that the daughters of Ishmael did mourn exceedingly, because of the loss of their father, and because of their afflictions in the wilderness; and they did murmur against my father, because he had brought them out of the land of Jerusalem, saying: Our father is dead; yea, and we have wandered much in the wilderness, and we have suffered much affliction, hunger, thirst, and fatigue; and after all these sufferings we must perish in the wilderness with hunger.

36 And thus they did murmur against my father,

Notes

and also against me; and they were desirous to return again to Jerusalem.

37 And Laman said unto Lemuel and also unto the sons of Ishmael: Behold, let us slay our father, and also our brother Nephi, who has taken it upon him to be our ruler and our teacher, who are his elder brethren.

38 Now, he says that the Lord has talked with him, and also that angels have ministered unto him. But behold, we know that he lies unto us; and he tells us these things, and he worketh many things by his cunning arts, that he may deceive our eyes, thinking, perhaps, that he may lead us away into some strange wilderness; and after he has led us away, he has thought to make himself a king and a ruler over us, that he may do with us according to his will and pleasure. And after this manner did my brother Laman stir up their hearts to anger.

39 And it came to pass that the Lord was with us, yea, even the voice of the Lord came and did speak many words unto them, and did chasten them exceedingly; and after they were chastened by the voice of the Lord they did turn away their anger, and did repent of their sins, insomuch that the Lord did bless us again with food, that we did not perish.

CHAPTER 17

Nephi Builds a Ship
About 592 BC

1–7, For 8 years they journey till they reach Bountiful; 7–16, Nephi starts to build a ship as directed by the Lord; 17–22, His brothers mock him; 23–44, Nephi relates Israelite history to his brothers; 45, Laman and Lemuel are past feeling; 46–55, Nephi reproves Laman and Lemuel and the Lord shocks them and they repent.

Overarching Principle: Keeping the commandments of God leads us to be confident while

murmuring against God causes us to become hardened against the spirit to a point of being past feeling.

⚡ Before class, draw and write on your board a picture similar to the one below. As you read and discuss each of the items listed, fill in the answers on the board. You may want to invite the class members to copy a similar chart for reference.

Nephi's Command

Nephi's Reaction   Laman and Lemuel's Reaction

Nephi's Lesson Learned   Laman and Lemuel's Lesson Learned

Lesson for Me

🔍 Find the following and write them on the board: Nephi's Command (vv. 7–8); Nephi's Reaction (vv. 9–11, 15); Laman and Lemuel's Reaction (vv. 17–22).

1 And it came to pass that we did again take our journey in the wilderness; and we did travel nearly eastward from that time forth. And we did travel and wade through much affliction in the wilderness; and our women did bear children in the wilderness.

2 And so great were the blessings of the Lord upon us, that while we did live upon raw meat in the wilderness, our women did give plenty of suck for their children, and were strong, yea, even like unto the men; and they began to bear their journeyings without murmurings.

3 And thus we see that the commandments of God must be fulfilled. And if it so be that the children of men keep the commandments of God he doth nourish them, and strengthen them, and provide means whereby they can accomplish the thing which he has commanded them; wherefore, he did provide means for us while we did sojourn in the wilderness.

Notes

4 And we did sojourn for the space of many years, yea, even eight years in the wilderness.

5 And we did come to the land which we called Bountiful, because of its much fruit and also wild honey; and all these things were prepared of the Lord that we might not perish. And we beheld the sea, which we called Irreantum, which, being interpreted, is many waters.

6 And it came to pass that we did pitch our tents by the seashore; and notwithstanding we had suffered many afflictions and much difficulty, yea, even so much that we cannot write them all, we were exceedingly rejoiced when we came to the seashore; and we called the place Bountiful, because of its much fruit.

7 And it came to pass that after I, Nephi, had been in the land of Bountiful for the space of many days, the voice of the Lord came unto me, saying: Arise, and get thee into the mountain. And it came to pass that I arose and went up into the mountain, and cried unto the Lord.

8 And it came to pass that the Lord spake unto me, saying: Thou shalt construct a ship, after the manner which I shall show thee, that I may carry thy people across these waters.

9 And I said: Lord, whither shall I go that I may find ore to molten, that I may make tools to construct the ship after the manner which thou hast shown unto me?

10 And it came to pass that the Lord told me whither I should go to find ore, that I might make tools.

11 And it came to pass that I, Nephi, did make a bellows wherewith to blow the fire, of the skins of beasts; and after I had made a bellows, that I might have wherewith to blow the fire, I did smite two stones together that I might make fire.

12 For the Lord had not hitherto suffered that we should make much fire, as we journeyed in the wilderness; for he said: I will make thy food become sweet, that ye cook it not;

13 And I will also be your light in the wilderness;

and I will prepare the way before you, if it so be that ye shall keep my commandments; wherefore, inasmuch as ye shall keep my commandments ye shall be led towards the promised land; and ye shall know that it is by me that ye are led.

14 Yea, and the Lord said also that: After ye have arrived in the promised land, ye shall know that I, the Lord, am God; and that I, the Lord, did deliver you from destruction; yea, that I did bring you out of the land of Jerusalem.

15 Wherefore, I, Nephi, did strive to keep the commandments of the Lord, and I did exhort my brethren to faithfulness and diligence.

16 And it came to pass that I did make tools of the ore which I did molten out of the rock.

17 And when my brethren saw that I was about to build a ship, they began to murmur against me, saying: Our brother is a fool, for he thinketh that he can build a ship; yea, and he also thinketh that he can cross these great waters.

18 And thus my brethren did complain against me, and were desirous that they might not labor, for they did not believe that I could build a ship; neither would they believe that I was instructed of the Lord.

19 And now it came to pass that I, Nephi, was exceedingly sorrowful because of the hardness of their hearts; and now when they saw that I began to be sorrowful they were glad in their hearts, insomuch that they did rejoice over me, saying: We knew that ye could not construct a ship, for we knew that ye were lacking in judgment; wherefore, thou canst not accomplish so great a work.

20 And thou art like unto our father, led away by the foolish imaginations of his heart; yea, he hath led us out of the land of Jerusalem, and we have wandered in the wilderness for these many years; and our women have toiled, being big with child; and they have borne children in the wilderness and suffered all things, save it were death; and it would have been better that they had died before they came out of Jerusalem than to have suffered these afflictions.

Notes

21 Behold, these many years we have suffered in the wilderness, which time we might have enjoyed our possessions and the land of our inheritance; yea, and we might have been happy.

22 And we know that the people who were in the land of Jerusalem were a righteous people; for they kept the statutes and judgments of the Lord, and all his commandments, according to the law of Moses; wherefore, we know that they are a righteous people; and our father hath judged them, and hath led us away because we would hearken unto his words; yea, and our brother is like unto him. And after this manner of language did my brethren murmur and complain against us.

23 And it came to pass that I, Nephi, spake unto them, saying: Do ye believe that our fathers, who were the children of Israel, would have been led away out of the hands of the Egyptians if they had not hearkened unto the words of the Lord?

24 Yea, do ye suppose that they would have been led out of bondage, if the Lord had not commanded Moses that he should lead them out of bondage?

25 Now ye know that the children of Israel were in bondage; and ye know that they were laden with tasks, which were grievous to be borne; wherefore, ye know that it must needs be a good thing for them, that they should be brought out of bondage.

26 Now ye know that Moses was commanded of the Lord to do that great work; and ye know that by his word the waters of the Red Sea were divided hither and thither, and they passed through on dry ground.

27 But ye know that the Egyptians were drowned in the Red Sea, who were the armies of Pharaoh.

28 And ye also know that they were fed with manna in the wilderness.

29 Yea, and ye also know that Moses, by his word according to the power of God which was in him, smote the rock, and there came forth water, that the children of Israel might quench their thirst.

30 And notwithstanding they being led, the Lord their God, their Redeemer, going before them, leading them by day and giving light unto them by night, and doing all things for them which were expedient for man to receive, they hardened their hearts and blinded their minds, and reviled against Moses and against the true and living God.

31 And it came to pass that according to his word he did destroy them; and according to his word he did lead them; and according to his word he did do all things for them; and there was not any thing done save it were by his word.

32 And after they had crossed the river Jordan he did make them mighty unto the driving out of the children of the land, yea, unto the scattering them to destruction.

33 And now, do ye suppose that the children of this land, who were in the land of promise, who were driven out by our fathers, do ye suppose that they were righteous? Behold, I say unto you, Nay.

34 Do ye suppose that our fathers would have been more choice than they if they had been righteous? I say unto you, Nay.

35 Behold, the Lord esteemeth all flesh in one; he that is righteous is favored of God. But behold, this people had rejected every word of God, and they were ripe in iniquity; and the fulness of the wrath of God was upon them; and the Lord did curse the land against them, and bless it unto our fathers; yea, he did curse it against them unto their destruction, and he did bless it unto our fathers unto their obtaining power over it.

36 Behold, the Lord hath created the earth that it should be inhabited; and he hath created his children that they should possess it.

37 And he raiseth up a righteous nation, and destroyeth the nations of the wicked.

38 And he leadeth away the righteous into precious lands, and the wicked he destroyeth, and curseth the land unto them for their sakes.

Notes

39 He ruleth high in the heavens, for it is his throne, and this earth is his footstool.

40 And he loveth those who will have him to be their God. Behold, he loved our fathers, and he covenanted with them, yea, even Abraham, Isaac, and Jacob; and he remembered the covenants which he had made; wherefore, he did bring them out of the land of Egypt.

41 And he did straiten them in the wilderness with his rod; for they hardened their hearts, even as ye have; and the Lord straitened them because of their iniquity. He sent fiery flying serpents among them; and after they were bitten he prepared a way that they might be healed; and the labor which they had to perform was to look; and because of the simpleness of the way, or the easiness of it, there were many who perished.

42 And they did harden their hearts from time to time, and they did revile against Moses, and also against God; nevertheless, ye know that they were led forth by his matchless power into the land of promise.

43 And now, after all these things, the time has come that they have become wicked, yea, nearly unto ripeness; and I know not but they are at this day about to be destroyed; for I know that the day must surely come that they must be destroyed, save a few only, who shall be led away into captivity.

44 Wherefore, the Lord commanded my father that he should depart into the wilderness; and the Jews also sought to take away his life; yea, and ye also have sought to take away his life; wherefore, ye are murderers in your hearts and ye are like unto them.

45 Ye are swift to do iniquity but slow to remember the Lord your God. Ye have seen an angel, and he spake unto you; yea, ye have heard his voice from time to time; and he hath spoken unto you in a still small voice, but ye were past feeling, that ye could not feel his words; wherefore, he has spoken unto you like unto the voice of thunder, which did cause the earth to shake as if it were to divide asunder.

46 And ye also know that by the power of his almighty word he can cause the earth that it shall pass away; yea, and ye know that by his word he can cause the rough places to be made smooth, and smooth places shall be broken up. O, then, why is it, that ye can be so hard in your hearts?

47 Behold, my soul is rent with anguish because of you, and my heart is pained; I fear lest ye shall be cast off forever. Behold, I am full of the Spirit of God, insomuch that my frame has no strength.

48 And now it came to pass that when I had spoken these words they were angry with me, and were desirous to throw me into the depths of the sea; and as they came forth to lay their hands upon me I spake unto them, saying: In the name of the Almighty God, I command you that ye touch me not, for I am filled with the power of God, even unto the consuming of my flesh; and whoso shall lay his hands upon me shall wither even as a dried reed; and he shall be as naught before the power of God, for God shall smite him.

49 And it came to pass that I, Nephi, said unto them that they should murmur no more against their father; neither should they withhold their labor from me, for God had commanded me that I should build a ship.

50 And I said unto them: If God had commanded me to do all things I could do them. If he should command me that I should say unto this water, be thou earth, it should be earth; and if I should say it, it would be done.

51 And now, if the Lord has such great power, and has wrought so many miracles among the children of men, how is it that he cannot instruct me, that I should build a ship?

52 And it came to pass that I, Nephi, said many things unto my brethren, insomuch that they were confounded and could not contend against me; neither durst they lay their hands upon me nor touch me with their fingers, even for the space of many days. Now they durst not do this

Notes

lest they should wither before me, so powerful was the Spirit of God; and thus it had wrought upon them.

53 And it came to pass that the Lord said unto me: Stretch forth thine hand again unto thy brethren, and they shall not wither before thee, but I will shock them, saith the Lord, and this will I do, that they may know that I am the Lord their God.

54 And it came to pass that I stretched forth my hand unto my brethren, and they did not wither before me; but the Lord did shake them, even according to the word which he had spoken.

55 And now, they said: We know of a surety that the Lord is with thee, for we know that it is the power of the Lord that has shaken us. And they fell down before me, and were about to worship me, but I would not suffer them, saying: I am thy brother, yea, even thy younger brother; wherefore, worship the Lord thy God, and honor thy father and thy mother, that thy days may be long in the land which the Lord thy God shall give thee.

vv. 45, 48, 53–55 Lessons learned for Laman and Lemuel.

🔍 Nephi explains to Laman and Lemuel that he can build a boat. You can quickly summarize in your own words what Nephi says in verses 23–43, then ask your class to look for Laman and Lemuel's reaction to Nephi's explanation in verse 48.

🔍 In verse 45, look for what Nephi says causes their reaction.

❓ Analyze: What do you think it means to be "swift to do iniquity but slow to remember the Lord your God"? What are some examples from Laman and Lemuel's lives that demonstrate that they are swift to do iniquity and slow to remember the Lord?

❓ Apply: What does it look like today for someone to be swift to do iniquity and slow to remember God? How can members of the Church be like this sometimes?

❓ Analyze: What do you think Nephi means when he says that Laman and Lemuel were past feeling? Why do you think God speaks in a way that we have to feel rather than hear?

💬 "Perhaps the single greatest thing I learned from reading the Book of Mormon is that the voice of the Spirit comes as a *feeling* rather than a sound. You will learn, as I have learned, to 'listen' for that voice that is *felt* rather than *heard*" (Boyd K. Packer, "Counsel to Youth," *Ensign,* November 2011, 16).

❓ Apply:
- *Since the Spirit often communicates through feelings, what does it feel like?* Consider spending some time on this question trying to encourage class members to share experiences they have had with the Holy Ghost. Be sure to emphasize that the Spirit may feel different to different people. That is why President Packer says that you have to "learn . . . to listen"—it takes practice and experience.
- *What causes someone to reach the point of being "past feeling" with the Holy Ghost?*
- *What role does murmuring and complaining play in the inability to feel the Holy Ghost?*
- *How would someone know if they are "past feeling"?*

🔍 Laman and Lemuel finally learn their lesson and feel something from the Lord. Have your class read verses 53–55 and look for what God does to ensure that they learn a lesson.

❤ *What is the lesson learned for Laman and Lemuel?* Write class members' responses on the board.

vv. 48–51 Lesson learned for Nephi.

🔍 Contrast Laman and Lemuel with Nephi. *In verses 48–51, look for what lesson Nephi learns from this experience.* Write the class members' responses on the board.

❓ Analyze: What do you know about Nephi's life that would have led him to have that confidence?

Notes

❓ Apply: *How does keeping the commandments give us confidence in God's ability to help us?*

♥ Invite one or two class members to share a "Lesson for Me" based on what they learned today. You may want to write their responses on the board.

> **Teaching Tips from Prophets' Lips** "Teach the doctrines of salvation; supply spiritual food; bear testimony of our Lord's divine Sonship—anything short of such a course is unworthy of a true minister who has been called by revelation. Only when the Church is fed the bread of life are its members kept in paths of righteousness" (Bruce R. McConkie, *Doctrinal New Testament Commentary,* 3 vols. [1966–73], 2:178).

1 NEPHI 18

Sailing to the Promised Land
About 591–589 BC

1–4, The ship is completed; 5–10, Their journey begins and Nephi cautions them in their behavior; 11–14, Nephi is tied up and a storm ensues; 15–21, Out of fear of destruction, they untie Nephi and the storm ceases; 22–25, They continue to sail, reach the promise land, and praise the Lord for its abundance.

1 And it came to pass that they did worship the Lord, and did go forth with me; and we did work timbers of curious workmanship. And the Lord did show me from time to time after what manner I should work the timbers of the ship.

2 Now I, Nephi, did not work the timbers after the manner which was learned by men, neither did I build the ship after the manner of men; but I did build it after the manner which the Lord had shown unto me; wherefore, it was not after the manner of men.

3 And I, Nephi, did go into the mount oft, and I did pray oft unto the Lord; wherefore the Lord showed unto me great things.

4 And it came to pass that after I had finished the ship, according to the word of the Lord, my brethren beheld that it was good, and that the workmanship thereof was exceedingly fine; wherefore, they did humble themselves again before the Lord.

vv. 1–4 Revelation does not come all at once so we can learn to grow and rely on God.

⚡ *If someone wanted you to build a house, what would you need first and why?*

🔍 *As you read verses 1–2, look for whether or not Nephi was given a full set of plans at the beginning.*

❓ Analyze: *Why didn't the Lord give Nephi everything he needed all at once? What did this teach Nephi?*

🔍 *Look for what Nephi needed to do in verse 3. Why is that a good thing?*

✏ Invite class members to write "Isaiah 28:13" in their margins and look up what lesson this verse teaches.

♥ Challenge class members to follow Nephi's example and seek the Lord often in order to be directed by Him.

5 And it came to pass that the voice of the Lord came unto my father, that we should arise and go down into the ship.

6 And it came to pass that on the morrow, after we had prepared all things, much fruits and meat from the wilderness, and honey in abundance, and provisions according to that which the Lord had commanded us, we did go down into the ship, with all our loading and our seeds, and whatsoever thing we had brought with us, every one according to his age; wherefore, we did all go down into the ship, with our wives and our children.

7 And now, my father had begat two sons in the wilderness; the elder was called Jacob and the younger Joseph.

Notes

8 And it came to pass after we had all gone down into the ship, and had taken with us our provisions and things which had been commanded us, we did put forth into the sea and were driven forth before the wind towards the promised land.

9 And after we had been driven forth before the wind for the space of many days, behold, my brethren and the sons of Ishmael and also their wives began to make themselves merry, insomuch that they began to dance, and to sing, and to speak with much rudeness, yea, even that they did forget by what power they had been brought thither; yea, they were lifted up unto exceeding rudeness.

10 And I, Nephi, began to fear exceedingly lest the Lord should be angry with us, and smite us because of our iniquity, that we should be swallowed up in the depths of the sea; wherefore, I, Nephi, began to speak to them with much soberness; but behold they were angry with me, saying: We will not that our younger brother shall be a ruler over us.

11 And it came to pass that Laman and Lemuel did take me and bind me with cords, and they did treat me with much harshness; nevertheless, the Lord did suffer it that he might show forth his power, unto the fulfilling of his word which he had spoken concerning the wicked.

12 And it came to pass that after they had bound me insomuch that I could not move, the compass, which had been prepared of the Lord, did cease to work.

13 Wherefore, they knew not whither they should steer the ship, insomuch that there arose a great storm, yea, a great and terrible tempest, and we were driven back upon the waters for the space of three days; and they began to be frightened exceedingly lest they should be drowned in the sea; nevertheless they did not loose me.

14 And on the fourth day, which we had been driven back, the tempest began to be exceedingly sore.

15 And it came to pass that we were about to be swallowed up in the depths of the sea. And after we had been driven back upon the waters for the space of four days, my brethren began to see that the judgments of God were upon them, and that they must perish save that they should repent of their iniquities; wherefore, they came unto me, and loosed the bands which were upon my wrists, and behold they had swollen exceedingly; and also mine ankles were much swollen, and great was the soreness thereof.

vv. 5–15 High-Low Game.

✋ To prepare to play the High-Low Game, fill a cup with a small candy. Count the exact amount of candy within the cup and keep that number secretly written on the bottom of the cup. Break the class into two or three teams and explain that after they study a set of verses, you will ask the team questions. When a person answers a question correctly, they and their team can try to guess the exact number of candies in the cup, and you will tell them either "Higher" or "Lower." Then the next team will be given a question to try to answer and guess at the number in the cup. Thus each guess narrows it down until they can guess the exact amount of candy in the cup. The team that guesses the correct number wins the cup to share with their team. Give class members a few minutes to study verses 5–15 and be ready to answer any questions you will give them. Some possible questions you could ask are:

- *What word is used to describe the Liahona?* (v. 12)
- *What is the name of the youngest brother of Laman?* (v. 7)
- *Who was directed to tell everyone it was time to leave?* (v. 5)
- *In what order did they get into the ship?* (v. 6)
- *What did their light-mindedness lead to?* (v. 9)
- *How many days was Nephi tied up?* (v. 14)
- *What finally convinced them to untie Nephi?* (v. 15)

Notes

16 Nevertheless, I did look unto my God, and I did praise him all the day long; and I did not murmur against the Lord because of mine afflictions.

v. 16 We should trust and praise God.

⚡ Discuss the following with the class:
- *Which is more frustrating: bad things happening after you have not been righteous, or bad things happening after you have been trying to be faithful?*
- *Why are trials you experience when you are trying to do what is right more frustrating?*
- *Have you ever been tempted to be angry at God when you are trying to do what is right but things are not working out?*

✋ Invite class members to choose and share one word that describes how their attitude might be after being tied up for four days.

🔍 *Look for Nephi's attitude in verse 16.*

❓ Analyze: *What is a word that would describe Nephi's attitude? What does this teach about Nephi?*

❓ Apply: *What is the lesson for us?*

♥ Challenge class members that, although bad things happen to good people, they should trust in God and not murmur.

17 Now my father, Lehi, had said many things unto them, and also unto the sons of Ishmael; but, behold, they did breathe out much threatenings against anyone that should speak for me; and my parents being stricken in years, and having suffered much grief because of their children, they were brought down, yea, even upon their sick-beds.

18 Because of their grief and much sorrow, and the iniquity of my brethren, they were brought near even to be carried out of this time to meet their God; yea, their grey hairs were about to be brought down to lie low in the dust; yea, even they were near to be cast with sorrow into a watery grave.

19 And Jacob and Joseph also, being young, having need of much nourishment, were grieved because of the afflictions of their mother; and also my wife with her tears and prayers, and also my children, did not soften the hearts of my brethren that they would loose me.

20 And there was nothing save it were the power of God, which threatened them with destruction, could soften their hearts; wherefore, when they saw that they were about to be swallowed up in the depths of the sea they repented of the thing which they had done, insomuch that they loosed me.

21 And it came to pass after they had loosed me, behold, I took the compass, and it did work whither I desired it. And it came to pass that I prayed unto the Lord; and after I had prayed the winds did cease, and the storm did cease, and there was a great calm.

22 And it came to pass that I, Nephi, did guide the ship, that we sailed again towards the promised land.

23 And it came to pass that after we had sailed for the space of many days we did arrive at the promised land; and we went forth upon the land, and did pitch our tents; and we did call it the promised land.

24 And it came to pass that we did begin to till the earth, and we began to plant seeds; yea, we did put all our seeds into the earth, which we had brought from the land of Jerusalem. And it came to pass that they did grow exceedingly; wherefore, we were blessed in abundance.

25 And it came to pass that we did find upon the land of promise, as we journeyed in the wilderness, that there were beasts in the forests of every kind, both the cow and the ox, and the ass and the horse, and the goat and the wild goat, and all manner of wild animals, which were for the use of men. And we did find all manner of ore, both of gold, and of silver, and of copper.

Notes

vv. 17–25 High-Low Game (continued).

✋ Continue the High-Low Game by having class members read verses 17–25 and prepare for your questions. Some questions you might ask could be:

- *Name at least two types of animals they found in the promise land.* (v. 25)
- *What did Nephi mention about his wife?* (v. 19)
- *What was Lehi and Sariah's health like during the voyage?* (vv. 17–18)
- *What portion of their provision of seeds did they not plant?* (v. 24)
- *What was the last thing done before the storm ceased?* (v. 21)

1 NEPHI 19

Prophecies of Christ
About 588–570 BC

1–6, Nephi speaks concerning recording on the plates; 7–12, Nephi, Zenock, Neum, and Zenos write about Christ's sufferings; 13–17, The Jews crucify the Savior and are scourged, despised, and hated because of it; 18–24, Nephi speaks of prophesying and introduces Isaiah's prophecies and a means to teach and testify of Christ.

1 And it came to pass that the Lord commanded me, wherefore I did make plates of ore that I might engraven upon them the record of my people. And upon the plates which I made I did engraven the record of my father, and also our journeyings in the wilderness, and the prophecies of my father; and also many of mine own prophecies have I engraven upon them.

2 And I knew not at the time when I made them that I should be commanded of the Lord to make these plates; wherefore, the record of my father, and the genealogy of his fathers, and the more part of all our proceedings in the wilderness are engraven upon those first plates of which I have spoken; wherefore, the things which transpired before I made these plates are, of a truth, more particularly made mention upon the first plates.

3 And after I had made these plates by way of commandment, I, Nephi, received a commandment that the ministry and the prophecies, the more plain and precious parts of them, should be written upon these plates; and that the things which were written should be kept for the instruction of my people, who should possess the land, and also for other wise purposes, which purposes are known unto the Lord.

4 Wherefore, I, Nephi, did make a record upon the other plates, which gives an account, or which gives a greater account of the wars and contentions and destructions of my people. And this have I done, and commanded my people what they should do after I was gone; and that these plates should be handed down from one generation to another, or from one prophet to another, until further commandments of the Lord.

5 And an account of my making these plates shall be given hereafter; and then, behold, I proceed according to that which I have spoken; and this I do that the more sacred things may be kept for the knowledge of my people.

6 Nevertheless, I do not write anything upon plates save it be that I think it be sacred. And now, if I do err, even did they err of old; not that I would excuse myself because of other men, but because of the weakness which is in me, according to the flesh, I would excuse myself.

💡 1 Nephi chapters 6 and 9 also cover in detail what Nephi is discussing here.

💡 In 1 Nephi 19:4, Nephi shares his intention that the small plates be handed down, not from father to son, but from prophet to prophet. The plates were passed down within the same family until the book of Omni when Amaleki gives them to King Benjamin (see Omni 1:25).

Notes

7 For the things which some men esteem to be of great worth, both to the body and soul, others set at naught and trample under their feet. Yea, even the very God of Israel do men trample under their feet; I say, trample under their feet but I would speak in other words—they set him at naught, and hearken not to the voice of his counsels.

v. 7 We are trampling upon God when we disregard His council.

⚡ Hold up a picture of Christ and some tape and discuss with the class how they would feel if someone taped this picture of Christ to the floor where people would walk. Caution: Out of respect and reverence, do not actually place the picture of the Savior on the floor.

🔍 *Look for one way people figuratively trample on God in verse 7.* After the verse is read, ask someone to explain how it is possible to trample God under our feet.

❓ Analyze:
  • *What does the phrase to "set at naught" mean?* (A good adjective for the word "naught" is "worthless".)
  • *What does it mean then to set Jesus "at naught"?*
  • *How would "hearkening not" to God's counsels show Him that His word is not of great worth to us?*

❓ Apply: *How do some people trample God under their feet today? What does this teach about how we should hearken to the words of the prophets today?* You may want to cross-reference Doctrine and Covenants 1:38.

👥 Break class members into groups of three and give each group a *For the Strength of Youth* pamphlet. Assign each group a topic in the pamphlet and have them prepare to share with the class a way a particular point addressed in the pamphlet is often trampled on by some people. After each group shares, have them explain how they can more fully live the counsel.

♥ *How can we demonstrate that the words of prophets are of great worth to us?* Challenge class members to follow the counsel of God that He gives through His prophets. You may feel impressed to testify of a particular counsel that was discussed earlier.

8 And behold he cometh, according to the words of the angel, in six hundred years from the time my father left Jerusalem.

9 And the world, because of their iniquity, shall judge him to be a thing of naught; wherefore they scourge him, and he suffereth it; and they smite him, and he suffereth it. Yea, they spit upon him, and he suffereth it, because of his loving kindness and his long-suffering towards the children of men.

v. 9 Christ allowed Himself to suffer, bleed, and die because of His love for us.

⚡ Draw the accompanying image on the board (both the uncompleted and completed puzzles are provided following). When read, tell the class you have a puzzle for them to solve. Reveal the image and inform them that they can find the answer to the puzzle in 1 Nephi 19:9.

1 Nephi 19:9	
They...	And He...
S_____ →	S_____
S_____ →	S_____
S_____ →	S_____

1 Nephi 19:9	
They...	And He...
Scourge →	Suffereth
Smite →	Suffereth
Spit →	Suffereth

Notes

❓ Analyze:
- *What does the word "suffereth" mean?*
- *In what other scriptural contexts have you heard it used?* Explain that the word "suffereth" can mean to suffer in pain or discomfort, but it also means to allow or let happen. As an example, you may share the Savior's words to John the Baptist in Matthew 3:15, "Suffer it to be so now . . ."
- *How does that definition change the meaning of the verse for you?*
- *According to the verse, why did the Savior allow such difficult things to happen to Him?*

10 And the God of our fathers, who were led out of Egypt, out of bondage, and also were preserved in the wilderness by him, yea, the God of Abraham, and of Isaac, and the God of Jacob, yieldeth himself, according to the words of the angel, as a man, into the hands of wicked men, to be lifted up, according to the words of Zenock, and to be crucified, according to the words of Neum, and to be buried in a sepulchre, according to the words of Zenos, which he spake concerning the three days of darkness, which should be a sign given of his death unto those who should inhabit the isles of the sea, more especially given unto those who are of the house of Israel.

v. 10 There are prophets whose writings should have been, but were not, included in the Bible we have today. Not all of God's word is found in the Bible.

🔑 *Underline the names of prophets who are mentioned in verse 10, but are not found in the Bible.*

💡 Have class members mark the footnote for 10g and reference "Lost Books" in the Bible Dictionary to learn more. Note with the class that there are Old Testament prophets whose writings are not found in the Bible.

11 For thus spake the prophet: The Lord God surely shall visit all the house of Israel at that day, some with his voice, because of their righteousness, unto their great joy and salvation, and others with the thunderings and the lightnings of his power, by tempest, by fire, and by smoke, and vapor of darkness, and by the opening of the earth, and by mountains which shall be carried up.

12 And all these things must surely come, saith the prophet Zenos. And the rocks of the earth must rend; and because of the groanings of the earth, many of the kings of the isles of the sea shall be wrought upon by the Spirit of God, to exclaim: The God of nature suffers.

💡 Concerning verse 12, Dionysius, a historian who lived at Heliopolis in Egypt at the time Jesus was crucified, took notice of the darkness and said, "Either the God of nature is suffering, or the machine of the world is tumbling into ruin."

13 And as for those who are at Jerusalem, saith the prophet, they shall be scourged by all people, because they crucify the God of Israel, and turn their hearts aside, rejecting signs and wonders, and the power and glory of the God of Israel.

14 And because they turn their hearts aside, saith the prophet, and have despised the Holy One of Israel, they shall wander in the flesh, and perish, and become a hiss and a byword, and be hated among all nations.

15 Nevertheless, when that day cometh, saith the prophet, that they no more turn aside their hearts against the Holy One of Israel, then will he remember the covenants which he made to their fathers.

16 Yea, then will he remember the isles of the sea; yea, and all the people who are of the house of Israel, will I gather in, saith the Lord, according to the words of the prophet Zenos, from the four quarters of the earth.

17 Yea, and all the earth shall see the salvation of the Lord, saith the prophet; every nation,

Notes

kindred, tongue and people shall be blessed.

18 And I, Nephi, have written these things unto my people, that perhaps I might persuade them that they would remember the Lord their Redeemer.

19 Wherefore, I speak unto all the house of Israel, if it so be that they should obtain these things.

20 For behold, I have workings in the spirit, which doth weary me even that all my joints are weak, for those who are at Jerusalem; for had not the Lord been merciful, to show unto me concerning them, even as he had prophets of old, I should have perished also.

💡 V. 20: Sometimes the workings of the spirit will cause people to become weak afterward. Cross reference 1 Nephi 14:47; Joseph Smith—History 1:48; Moses 1:9–10; Alma 27:17.

21 And he surely did show unto the prophets of old all things concerning them; and also he did show unto many concerning us; wherefore, it must needs be that we know concerning them for they are written upon the plates of brass.

22 Now it came to pass that I, Nephi, did teach my brethren these things; and it came to pass that I did read many things to them, which were engraven upon the plates of brass, that they might know concerning the doings of the Lord in other lands, among people of old.

23 And I did read many things unto them which were written in the books of Moses; but that I might more fully persuade them to believe in the Lord their Redeemer I did read unto them that which was written by the prophet Isaiah; for I did liken all scriptures unto us, that it might be for our profit and learning.

v. 23 We will profit from our scripture study as we liken the scriptures to ourselves.

⚡ Write the words "Prophet" and "Profit" on the board and ask the class what the definition is of each word. Write the following formula on the board: Profit = Revenue −Expenses. Give class members the following formula and ask them to determine profit: *If you sell 10 donuts for 50 cents each, and it costs you 40 cents to make each donut, what is your profit?*

🔍 Look for how the word profit is used in verse 23.

❓ Analyze: *What does profit mean in this sense?*

❓ Apply:
  • *What is this verse teaching about scripture study?*
  • *What particular tip for scripture study does Nephi give in verse 19?*
  • *What does it mean to "liken" the scriptures?*
  • *How does likening the scriptures to our lives become profitable to us?*

❤ Refer the class back to the formula on the board. Under the word Revenue write, "Liken Scriptures" and under the word Expenses write, "the time it takes to study the scriptures". Ask class members what you should write under the word Profit. Challenge them in their own personal scripture study to look for a lesson on each page of scripture and write down how it applies to them.

24 Wherefore I spake unto them, saying: Hear ye the words of the prophet, ye who are a remnant of the house of Israel, a branch who have been broken off; hear ye the words of the prophet, which were written unto all the house of Israel, and liken them unto yourselves, that ye may have hope as well as your brethren from whom ye have been broken off; for after this manner has the prophet written.

Teaching Tips from Prophets' Lips "If any brother or sister feels unprepared—even incapable—of responding to a call to serve, to sacrifice, to bless the lives of others, remember this truth: 'Whom God calls, God qualifies.' He who notes the sparrow's fall will not abandon the servant's need" (Thomas S. Monson, "Tears, Trials, Trust, Testimony," *Ensign*, September 1997, 5).

Notes

1 NEPHI 20

Nephi Quotes Isaiah 48
About 600–592 BC

1–8, The wickedness and hypocrisy of Israel; 9–19, The forgiving nature of God; 20–22, "Go ye out of Babylon."

1 Hearken and hear this, O house of Jacob, who are called by the name of Israel, and are come forth out of the waters of Judah, or out of the waters of baptism, who swear by the name of the Lord, and make mention of the God of Israel, yet they swear not in truth nor in righteousness.

2 Nevertheless, they call themselves of the holy city, but they do not stay themselves upon the God of Israel, who is the Lord of Hosts; yea, the Lord of Hosts is his name.

3 Behold, I have declared the former things from the beginning; and they went forth out of my mouth, and I showed them. I did show them suddenly.

4 And I did it because I knew that thou art obstinate, and thy neck is an iron sinew, and thy brow brass;

5 And I have even from the beginning declared to thee; before it came to pass I showed them thee; and I showed them for fear lest thou shouldst say—Mine idol hath done them, and my graven image, and my molten image hath commanded them.

vv. 1–4 Isaiah defines hypocrisy as making covenants with God, but not in righteousness, and calling ourselves holy while being unfaithful to Him.

🔍 *Isaiah spoke to very wicked people. Search for what the people are doing in verses 1, 2, and 4 that makes them so wicked.*

❓ Analyze:
- *In verse 1 the people are being baptized and swearing, or covenanting, in the name of the*

Lord; is that good or bad? (It is good.)
- *In verse 2 they swear not in righteousness; is that good or bad? (It is bad.)*
- *In verse 2 they call themselves the holy city; is it good or bad to call yourself righteous? (It is good.)*
- *In verse 2 they do not stay themselves on the Lord, in other words, they are not righteous; is that good or bad? (It is bad)*
- *How is Isaiah describing hypocrisy in these two verses?*

❓ Apply: *How can members of the Church today be hypocritical in these same ways?*

💬 Explain that hypocrisy can happen to any of us. Share the following quote by Dieter F. Uchtdorf; "My dear brothers and sisters, consider the following questions as a self-test: Do you harbor a grudge against someone else? Do you gossip, even when what you say may be true? Do you exclude, push away, or punish others because of something they have done? Do you secretly envy another? Do you wish to cause harm to someone? If you answered yes to any of these questions, you may want to apply the two-word sermon from earlier: stop it!"

Pause from reading the quote and ask, *If we are participating in the kinds of things President Uchtdorf asks, how would they lead to hypocrisy?*

Continue his quote: "In a world of accusations and unfriendliness, it is easy to gather and cast stones. But before we do so, let us remember the words of the One who is our Master and model: 'He that is without sin among you, let him first cast a stone.' Brothers and sisters, let us put down our stones. Let us be kind. Let us forgive. Let us talk peacefully with each other. Let the love of God fill our hearts. 'Let us do good unto all men'" ("The Merciful Obtain Mercy," *Ensign*, May 2012, 76).

❓ Apply: *How can engaging ourselves in the activities President Uchtdorf describes help us to be less hypocritical?*

Notes

5 And I have even from the beginning declared to thee; before it came to pass I showed them thee; and I showed them for fear lest thou shouldst say—Mine idol hath done them, and my graven image, and my molten image hath commanded them.

6 Thou hast seen and heard all this; and will ye not declare them? And that I have showed thee new things from this time, even hidden things, and thou didst not know them.

7 They are created now, and not from the beginning, even before the day when thou heardest them not they were declared unto thee, lest thou shouldst say—Behold I knew them.

8 Yea, and thou heardest not; yea, thou knewest not; yea, from that time thine ear was not opened; for I knew that thou wouldst deal very treacherously, and wast called a transgressor from the womb.

9 Nevertheless, for my name's sake will I defer mine anger, and for my praise will I refrain from thee, that I cut thee not off.

10 For, behold, I have refined thee, I have chosen thee in the furnace of affliction.

11 For mine own sake, yea, for mine own sake will I do this, for I will not suffer my name to be polluted, and I will not give my glory unto another.

vv. 5–11 Because God is so loving, He will defer His anger from us.

🔍 *Despite Israel's hypocrisy, and our own at times, look for what Isaiah teaches us in verse 9. (He will defer His anger for His sake.)*

❓ Analyze: Note with the class that He defers His anger for His sake. *What do you think He means by that? What does this teach us about the nature of God?*

🔍 All of us have imperfections and weaknesses that lead us to sin. If we allow God to help us, these imperfections will become strengths. *Read verses 10–11 and look for how Isaiah describes this process.*

✎ As the class members respond, write their responses on the board. Label a title on the board that reads, "Today's Principle". Have class members cross reference Isaiah 20:10 with Ether 12:27. Read the scripture in Ether as a class and ask someone to explain in their own words how Ether 12:27 relates to "Today's Principle".

❓ Analyze:
- *Why does a loving God allow us to experience trials?*
- *Why does a loving God allow us to sin and make mistakes?*
- *How can making mistakes and experiencing trials make us better?*
- *What do you think God means when he says "for mine own sake do I [allow my children to go through trials]"? (v. 11)*

💬 Dallin H. Oaks stated, "Most of us experience some measure of what the scriptures call the 'furnace of affliction.' . . . [Some] suffer the death of a loved one. . . . Others struggle with personal impairments or with feelings of rejection, inadequacy, or depression. Through the justice and mercy of a loving Father in Heaven, the refinement and sanctification possible through such experiences can help us achieve what God desires us to become" (Dallin H. Oaks, "The Challenge to Become," *Ensign*, November 2000, 32).

❓ Apply: *How does this quote relate to the lesson today? How has the Atonement helped you or a family member through the "furnace of affliction" of sin or trials?*

12 Hearken unto me, O Jacob, and Israel my called, for I am he; I am the first, and I am also the last.

13 Mine hand hath also laid the foundation of the earth, and my right hand hath spanned the heavens. I call unto them and they stand up together.

14 All ye, assemble yourselves, and hear; who among them hath declared these things unto them? The Lord hath loved him; yea, and he will

Notes

_____

_____

_____

fulfil his word which he hath declared by them; and he will do his pleasure on Babylon, and his arm shall come upon the Chaldeans.

15 Also, saith the Lord; I the Lord, yea, I have spoken; yea, I have called him to declare, I have brought him, and he shall make his way prosperous.

16 Come ye near unto me; I have not spoken in secret; from the beginning, from the time that it was declared have I spoken; and the Lord God, and his Spirit, hath sent me.

17 And thus saith the Lord, thy Redeemer, the Holy One of Israel; I have sent him, the Lord thy God who teacheth thee to profit, who leadeth thee by the way thou shouldst go, hath done it.

18 O that thou hadst hearkened to my commandments—then had thy peace been as a river, and thy righteousness as the waves of the sea.

19 Thy seed also had been as the sand; the offspring of thy bowels like the gravel thereof; his name should not have been cut off nor destroyed from before me.

20 Go ye forth of Babylon, flee ye from the Chaldeans, with a voice of singing declare ye, tell this, utter to the end of the earth; say ye: The Lord hath redeemed his servant Jacob.

21 And they thirsted not; he led them through the deserts; he caused the waters to flow out of the rock for them; he clave the rock also and the waters gushed out.

22 And notwithstanding he hath done all this, and greater also, there is no peace, saith the Lord, unto the wicked.

vv. 18, 22 Righteous brings peace. Wickedness eliminates peace.

⚡ Write the word "RIVER" and "GUILT" on the board so the class can see it when they arrive. Ask each class member to write a word or phrase that describes each of those words. Briefly discuss some of the answers.

🔍 Look in verses 18 and 22 and find what

additional phrase we can write on the board for each word.

❓ Analyze: *How could a river be a good description of the peace that comes through keeping the commandments? How does sin remove peace?*

❓ Apply: *When have you felt the peace of righteous doing?* (You may want to quote the line from hymn #239 "Choose the Right": "Choose the right, there is peace in righteous doing . . ." and encourage class members to follow that counsel.

♥ Read the invitation in the first line of verse 20 to class members, "Go ye out of Babylon" and bear your testimony about the principle you have taught.

1 NEPHI 21

Nephi Quotes Isaiah 49
About 592 BC

1–13, The gathering of Israel is explained; 14–21, God will never forget his children; 22–26, The Gentiles are to gather in scattered Israel.

Overarching Principle: The gathering of Israel teaches that God will never abandon us.

1 And again: Hearken, O ye house of Israel, all ye that are broken off and are driven out because of the wickedness of the pastors of my people; yea, all ye that are broken off, that are scattered abroad, who are of my people, O house of Israel. Listen, O isles, unto me, and hearken ye people from far; the Lord hath called me from the womb; from the bowels of my mother hath he made mention of my name.

2 And he hath made my mouth like a sharp sword; in the shadow of his hand hath he hid me, and made me a polished shaft; in his quiver hath he hid me;

Notes

3 And said unto me: Thou art my servant, O Israel, in whom I will be glorified.

4 Then I said, I have labored in vain, I have spent my strength for naught and in vain; surely my judgment is with the Lord, and my work with my God.

5 And now, saith the Lord—that formed me from the womb that I should be his servant, to bring Jacob again to him—though Israel be not gathered, yet shall I be glorious in the eyes of the Lord, and my God shall be my strength.

6 And he said: It is a light thing that thou shouldst be my servant to raise up the tribes of Jacob, and to restore the preserved of Israel. I will also give thee for a light to the Gentiles, that thou mayest be my salvation unto the ends of the earth.

7 Thus saith the Lord, the Redeemer of Israel, his Holy One, to him whom man despiseth, to him whom the nations abhorreth, to servant of rulers: Kings shall see and arise, princes also shall worship, because of the Lord that is faithful.

8 Thus saith the Lord: In an acceptable time have I heard thee, O isles of the sea, and in a day of salvation have I helped thee; and I will preserve thee, and give thee my servant for a covenant of the people, to establish the earth, to cause to inherit the desolate heritages;

9 That thou mayest say to the prisoners: Go forth; to them that sit in darkness: Show yourselves. They shall feed in the ways, and their pastures shall be in all high places.

10 They shall not hunger nor thirst, neither shall the heat nor the sun smite them; for he that hath mercy on them shall lead them, even by the springs of water shall he guide them.

11 And I will make all my mountains a way, and my highways shall be exalted.

12 And then, O house of Israel, behold, these shall come from far; and lo, these from the north and from the west; and these from the land of Sinim.

13 Sing, O heavens; and be joyful, O earth; for the feet of those who are in the east shall be established; and break forth into singing, O mountains; for they shall be smitten no more; for the Lord hath comforted his people, and will have mercy upon his afflicted.

💡 A recurring theme in the book of Isaiah is the gathering of Israel. Isaiah uses the gathering to teach about God's longsuffering toward Israel collectively and to us individually. Considering the wickedness of Israel as described in Isaiah 48 (1 Nephi 20), the message of the gathering as found in this chapter paints a poignant picture of God's love and longsuffering.

🔍 Explain to class members that due to Israel's wickedness they will be scattered, but Isaiah promises that they will eventually be gathered. Have the following verses written on the board and ask class members to find phrases that indicate people being helped, gathered, or guided: vv. 10, 18, 22, 23. (For variety, you may assign one verse to one or more class members to read, or have the each member of the class read all the verses individually.) Invite class members to write these phrases from their assigned verse(s) on the board or assign a scribe to do so.

14 But, behold, Zion hath said: The Lord hath forsaken me, and my Lord hath forgotten me—but he will show that he hath not.

15 For can a woman forget her sucking child, that she should not have compassion on the son of her womb? Yea, they may forget, yet will I not forget thee, O house of Israel.

16 Behold, I have graven thee upon the palms of my hands; thy walls are continually before me.

vv. 14–16 God has graven us upon the palms of His hands, therefore He will never forget or abandon us.

⚡ *Do you know of anyone who, because of a trial, feels like God has forsaken them?*

Notes

Invite class members to share if it is not too personal.

🔍 *Because of their wickedness, look for what the house of Israel thinks God will do to them in verse 14.*

❓ Analyze: *Knowing how wicked and hypocritical the house of Israel has been, do you blame them for thinking like this?*

🔍 *In verses 15–16, have class members search for what Isaiah says proves God has not forgotten Israel.*

❓ Analyze:
- *When you have something important to remember, have you ever written a reminder on your hand?*
- *How has the Lord done something similar in verse 16?*
- *How has God graven His people on the palms of His hands?*
- *What is the principle that Isaiah is trying to teach us about God? (You could write an answer on the board as class members share.)*

❓ Apply: *How would this principle* (referring to what you just wrote on the board) *apply to someone who thinks they have sinned too much or too long to be able to repent?*

🗨 Jeffrey R. Holland stated, "Considering the incomprehensible cost of the Crucifixion and Atonement, I promise you He is not going to turn His back on us now. When He says to the poor in spirit, 'Come unto me,' He means He knows the way out and He knows the way up. He knows it because He has walked it. He knows the way because He *is* the way. Brothers and sisters . . . *please* don't give up and *please* don't yield to fear" (Jeffrey R. Holland, "Broken Things to Mend," *Ensign,* May 2006, 69).

❤ Before class, privately ask a class member to prepare to share their testimony of the Atonement near the end of the lesson. Give that person the opportunity now to share his or her testimony.

17 Thy children shall make haste against thy destroyers; and they that made thee waste shall go forth of thee.

18 Lift up thine eyes round about and behold; all these gather themselves together, and they shall come to thee. And as I live, saith the Lord, thou shalt surely clothe thee with them all, as with an ornament, and bind them on even as a bride.

19 For thy waste and thy desolate places, and the land of thy destruction, shall even now be too narrow by reason of the inhabitants; and they that swallowed thee up shall be far away.

20 The children whom thou shalt have, after thou hast lost the first, shall again in thine ears say: The place is too strait for me; give place to me that I may dwell.

21 Then shalt thou say in thine heart: Who hath begotten me these, seeing I have lost my children, and am desolate, a captive, and removing to and fro? And who hath brought up these? Behold, I was left alone; these, where have they been?

22 Thus saith the Lord God: Behold, I will lift up mine hand to the Gentiles, and set up my standard to the people; and they shall bring thy sons in their arms, and thy daughters shall be carried upon their shoulders.

23 And kings shall be thy nursing fathers, and their queens thy nursing mothers; they shall bow down to thee with their face towards the earth, and lick up the dust of thy feet; and thou shalt know that I am the Lord; for they shall not be ashamed that wait for me.

24 For shall the prey be taken from the mighty, or the lawful captives delivered?

25 But thus saith the Lord, even the captives of the mighty shall be taken away, and the prey of the terrible shall be delivered; for I will contend with him that contendeth with thee, and I will save thy children.

26 And I will feed them that oppress thee with their own flesh; they shall be drunken with their own blood as with sweet wine; and all flesh shall

Notes

know that I, the Lord, am thy Savior and thy Redeemer, the Mighty One of Jacob.

> **Teaching Tips from Prophets' Lips** "True conversion depends on seeking freely in faith, with great effort and some pain. Then it is the Lord who can grant, in His time, the miracle of cleansing and change. Each person starts from a different place, with a different set of experiences, and so a different need for cleansing and for change. The Lord knows that place, and so only He can set the course (Henry B. Eyring, "We must raise our sights" *Ensign*, September, 2004).

1 NEPHI 22

Destiny of Israel and the Gentiles
About 588–570 BC

1–5, Nephi states that the scattering of Israel has already begun; 6–12, The Gentiles will assist in gathering Israel through the restored gospel; 13–16, The wicked will be destroyed; 17–21, The Lord will protect his people; 22–23, Priestcraft will be destroyed when the Lord returns; 24–31, When the Lord reigns, Satan will be bound.

1 And now it came to pass that after I, Nephi, had read these things which were engraven upon the plates of brass, my brethren came unto me and said unto me: What meaneth these things which ye have read? Behold, are they to be understood according to things which are spiritual, which shall come to pass according to the spirit and not the flesh?

2 And I, Nephi, said unto them: Behold they were manifest unto the prophet by the voice of the Spirit; for by the Spirit are all things made known unto the prophets, which shall come upon the children of men according to the flesh.

3 Wherefore, the things of which I have read are things pertaining to things both temporal and spiritual; for it appears that the house of Israel, sooner or later, will be scattered upon all the face of the earth, and also among all nations.

4 And behold, there are many who are already lost from the knowledge of those who are at Jerusalem. Yea, the more part of all the tribes have been led away; and they are scattered to and fro upon the isles of the sea; and whither they are none of us knoweth, save that we know that they have been led away.

5 And since they have been led away, these things have been prophesied concerning them, and also concerning all those who shall hereafter be scattered and be confounded, because of the Holy One of Israel; for against him will they harden their hearts; wherefore, they shall be scattered among all nations and shall be hated of all men.

6 Nevertheless, after they shall be nursed by the Gentiles, and the Lord has lifted up his hand upon the Gentiles and set them up for a standard, and their children have been carried in their arms, and their daughters have been carried upon their shoulders, behold these things of which are spoken are temporal; for thus are the covenants of the Lord with our fathers; and it meaneth us in the days to come, and also all our brethren who are of the house of Israel.

7 And it meaneth that the time cometh that after all the house of Israel have been scattered and confounded, that the Lord God will raise up a mighty nation among the Gentiles, yea, even upon the face of this land; and by them shall our seed be scattered.

8 And after our seed is scattered the Lord God will proceed to do a marvelous work among the Gentiles, which shall be of great worth unto our seed; wherefore, it is likened unto their being nourished by the Gentiles and being carried in their arms and upon their shoulders.

9 And it shall also be of worth unto the Gentiles; and not only unto the Gentiles but unto all the house of Israel, unto the making known of the covenants of the Father of heaven unto Abraham,

Notes

saying: In thy seed shall all the kindreds of the earth be blessed.

vv. 6–9 The Gentiles in the United States will assist in the gathering of Israel.

🔎 Look for what the "mighty nation" is that would be raised up in verse 7.

❓ Analyze: *What nation does verse 7 refer to? What role has the United States had in scattering Lehi's seed?*

🔎 *Look for what role the Gentiles in the United State have in gathering Lehi's seed in verse 8? How do the Gentiles in the United States help the gospel spread throughout the world in verse 9?*

💬 Mark E. Peterson stated, "The preparation for the Second Coming of Christ depended largely on the restoration of the gospel. There could not be a restoration of the gospel without freedom. God provided this country as the base of his operations in these, the last days, a place where there would be freedom, where he could restore his gospel. Therefore, the United States was given and is yet to be given a great mission in respect to the Second Coming of the Lord Jesus Christ" (Fireside address given at BYU on 4 July 1976).

v. 12 People do not need to move from where they live in order to be gathered to Zion.

🔎 In verse 12, invite the class to look for what will happen when the gospel is accepted by people.

❓ Analyze: *Does this mean that everyone who joins the Church should immigrate to the United States?*

💬 Bruce R. McConkie stated, "A stake has geographical boundaries. To create a stake is like founding a City of Holiness. Every stake on earth is the gathering place for the lost sheep of Israel who live in its area. The gathering place for Peruvians is in the stakes of Zion in Peru, or in the places in which soon will become stakes. The gathering place of Chileans is Chile; for Bolivians, it is in Bolivia; for Koreans, it is in Korea; and so it goes through all the length and breadth of the earth. Scattered Israel in every nation is called to gather to the fold of Christ, to the stakes of Zion, as such are established in their nations" ("Come: Let Israel Build Zion," *Ensign*, April 1977).

❤ Explain that there are times in Church history that the Saints are commanded to gather geographically and other times they remain where they live.

10 And I would, my brethren, that ye should know that all the kindreds of the earth cannot be blessed unless he shall make bare his arm in the eyes of the nations.

11 Wherefore, the Lord God will proceed to make bare his arm in the eyes of all the nations, in bringing about his covenants and his gospel unto those who are of the house of Israel.

12 Wherefore, he will bring them again out of captivity, and they shall be gathered together to the lands of their inheritance; and they shall be brought out of obscurity and out of darkness; and they shall know that the Lord is their Savior and their Redeemer, the Mighty One of Israel.

13 And the blood of that great and abominable church, which is the whore of all the earth, shall turn upon their own heads; for they shall war among themselves, and the sword of their own hands shall fall upon their own heads, and they shall be drunken with their own blood.

14 And every nation which shall war against thee, O house of Israel, shall be turned one against another, and they shall fall into the pit which they digged to ensnare the people of the Lord. And all that fight against Zion shall be destroyed, and that great whore, who hath perverted the right ways of the Lord, yea, that great and abominable church, shall tumble to the dust and great shall be the fall of it.

Notes

15 For behold, saith the prophet, the time cometh speedily that Satan shall have no more power over the hearts of the children of men; for the day soon cometh that all the proud and they who do wickedly shall be as stubble; and the day cometh that they must be burned.

16 For the time soon cometh that the fulness of the wrath of God shall be poured out upon all the children of men; for he will not suffer that the wicked shall destroy the righteous.

17 Wherefore, he will preserve the righteous by his power, even if it so be that the fulness of his wrath must come, and the righteous be preserved, even unto the destruction of their enemies by fire. Wherefore, the righteous need not fear; for thus saith the prophet, they shall be saved, even if it so be as by fire.

18 Behold, my brethren, I say unto you, that these things must shortly come; yea, even blood, and fire, and vapor of smoke must come; and it must needs be upon the face of this earth; and it cometh unto men according to the flesh if it so be that they will harden their hearts against the Holy One of Israel.

v. 14 Very often the Lord uses the wicked to destroy the wicked.

🔎 *In verse 14, look for one way that the wicked will be destroyed before the Lord returns.*

💬 Bruce R. McConkie stated: "Israel's triumph over her enemies will occur not because her marching armies defeat their foes in battle, but because her enemies [the Gentiles, the great and abominable church, the nations that fight against God call them what you will, the meaning is the same] will be destroyed, simply because every corruptible thing will be consumed at the Second Coming. In that day the Lord will truly fight the battles of his saints, for as he descends from heaven, amid fire and burning, all the proud and they that do wickedly shall be burned as stubble" (*New Witness for the Articles of Faith*, 562–63).

🔎 *Skim verses 15–18 and look for an additional way the wicked will be destroyed. ("Burned" is mentioned once and "fire" is mentioned three times.) Through some means of fire, the Lord will protect the righteous and destroy the wicked.*

19 For behold, the righteous shall not perish; for the time surely must come that all they who fight against Zion shall be cut off.

20 And the Lord will surely prepare a way for his people, unto the fulfilling of the words of Moses, which he spake, saying: A prophet shall the Lord your God raise up unto you, like unto me; him shall ye hear in all things whatsoever he shall say unto you. And it shall come to pass that all those who will not hear that prophet shall be cut off from among the people.

21 And now I, Nephi, declare unto you, that this prophet of whom Moses spake was the Holy One of Israel; wherefore, he shall execute judgment in righteousness.

💡 Have class members look in verses 20–21 and the footnotes for the prophet who would be raised up.

22 And the righteous need not fear, for they are those who shall not be confounded. But it is the kingdom of the devil, which shall be built up among the children of men, which kingdom is established among them which are in the flesh—

23 For the time speedily shall come that all churches which are built up to get gain, and all those who are built up to get power over the flesh, and those who are built up to become popular in the eyes of the world, and those who seek the lusts of the flesh and the things of the world, and to do all manner of iniquity; yea, in fine, all those who belong to the kingdom of the devil are they who need fear, and tremble, and quake; they are those who must be brought low in the dust; they are those who must be consumed as stubble; and

Notes

this is according to the words of the prophet.

v. 23 True servants of God seek God's will and not selfish desires.

💡 Although the term "great and abominable church" is not used here, verse 23 describes many elements of false religion. Be sure to emphasize that although Nephi uses the word church, he is referring to more than one church, or rather any organization that falls under the characteristics he lists in this verse.

✋ Ask a volunteer to be a scribe at the board and have class members determine the elements of false religion listed in verse 23.

❓ Analyze: *What is the motivation of the leaders of these churches? What are the differences in the motivations listed here and the motivations of a true servant of God?*

🖊 Invite class members to write "Priestcraft, 2 Nephi 26:29 & 31" in their margins.

❤ Invite class members to always serve God with pure intentions.

24 And the time cometh speedily that the righteous must be led up as calves of the stall, and the Holy One of Israel must reign in dominion, and might, and power, and great glory.

25 And he gathereth his children from the four quarters of the earth; and he numbereth his sheep, and they know him; and there shall be one fold and one shepherd; and he shall feed his sheep, and in him they shall find pasture.

26 And because of the righteousness of his people, Satan has no power; wherefore, he cannot be loosed for the space of many years; for he hath no power over the hearts of the people, for they dwell in righteousness, and the Holy One of Israel reigneth.

v. 26 Satan has less power in our lives as we consistently follow the Savior.

⚡ *Why won't Satan have power to tempt us during the Millennium?*

🔍 *Look for why Satan will not have power over us in verse 26.*

❓ Analyze: Note with the class that Satan has no power over the righteous. Ask, *How is that applicable to us?*

27 And now behold, I, Nephi, say unto you that all these things must come according to the flesh.

28 But, behold, all nations, kindreds, tongues, and people shall dwell safely in the Holy One of Israel if it so be that they will repent.

29 And now I, Nephi, make an end; for I durst not speak further as yet concerning these things.

30 Wherefore, my brethren, I would that ye should consider that the things which have been written upon the plates of brass are true; and they testify that a man must be obedient to the commandments of God.

31 Wherefore, ye need not suppose that I and my father are the only ones that have testified, and also taught them. Wherefore, if ye shall be obedient to the commandments, and endure to the end, ye shall be saved at the last day. And thus it is. Amen.

Notes

THE SECOND BOOK OF NEPHI

2 NEPHI BOOK SUMMARY

Time Period: About 588–545 BC (43 years)

Contributors: Lehi, Nephi, Jacob, Isaiah (quoted)

Source: Small plates of Nephi

Synopsis:

Chapters 1–3: Lehi's last teachings to his family.

Chapter 4: Lehi finishes his teachings, and Nephi rededicates himself to the Lord.

Chapter 5: Nephites separate and the Lamanites are cursed.

Chapters 6–10: Jacob teaches from Isaiah 50 through 52:2.

Chapter 11: Nephi teaches the Law, testifies of Christ, and introduces Isaiah.

Chapters 12–24: Isaiah 2–14 as taken from the brass plates.

Chapters 25–30: Nephi's prophecies of the last days before Christ returns.

Chapters 31–33: Nephi teaches of Christ, baptism, repentance, and the Holy Ghost.

An account of the death of Lehi. Nephi's brethren rebel against him. The Lord warns Nephi to depart into the wilderness. His journeyings in the wilderness, and so forth.

2 NEPHI 1

Lehi's Words to Laman, Lemuel, and Zoram

About 588–570 BC

1–11, Lehi teaches his oldest sons about the promises in the Americas; 12–23, He challenges Laman and Lemuel to be men of God; 24–29, Lehi explains why Nephi has been blessed and how they too can be blessed; 30–32, Lehi's words to Zoram.

Overarching Principle: 2 Nephi 1:1–4:12 are the words of council from Lehi to his children before he dies. A theme for these sections could be "Life Lessons for Happiness and Success."

Notes

⚡ *Pretend you are a parent who has just found out that you will die in the next few days. What last words of council and advice would you give to your children?*

✎ Have class members write down a few brief lines of advice they would give their children and then invite a few to share what they wrote. Explain that most of 2 Nephi 1–4 are Lehi's words of council to his family before he dies. You can also write on the board the title, "Advice for a Happy and Successful Life." Then as you identify Lehi's advice, write it on the board. This can also be a way to review these chapters.

1 And now it came to pass that after I, Nephi, had made an end of teaching my brethren, our father, Lehi, also spake many things unto them, and rehearsed unto them, how great things the Lord had done for them in bringing them out of the land of Jerusalem.

2 And he spake unto them concerning their rebellions upon the waters, and the mercies of God in sparing their lives, that they were not swallowed up in the sea.

3 And he also spake unto them concerning the land of promise, which they had obtained—how merciful the Lord had been in warning us that we should flee out of the land of Jerusalem.

4 For, behold, said he, I have seen a vision, in which I know that Jerusalem is destroyed; and had we remained in Jerusalem we should also have perished.

5 But, said he, notwithstanding our afflictions, we have obtained a land of promise, a land which is choice above all other lands; a land which the Lord God hath covenanted with me should be a land for the inheritance of my seed. Yea, the Lord hath covenanted this land unto me, and to my children forever, and also all those who should be led out of other countries by the hand of the Lord.

6 Wherefore, I, Lehi, prophesy according to the workings of the Spirit which is in me, that there shall none come into this land save they shall be brought by the hand of the Lord.

7 Wherefore, this land is consecrated unto him whom he shall bring. And if it so be that they shall serve him according to the commandments which he hath given, it shall be a land of liberty unto them; wherefore, they shall never be brought down into captivity; if so, it shall be because of iniquity; for if iniquity shall abound cursed shall be the land for their sakes, but unto the righteous it shall be blessed forever.

8 And behold, it is wisdom that this land should be kept as yet from the knowledge of other nations; for behold, many nations would overrun the land, that there would be no place for an inheritance.

9 Wherefore, I, Lehi, have obtained a promise, that inasmuch as those whom the Lord God shall bring out of the land of Jerusalem shall keep his commandments, they shall prosper upon the face of this land; and they shall be kept from all other nations, that they may possess this land unto themselves. And if it so be that they shall keep his commandments they shall be blessed upon the face of this land, and there shall be none to molest them, nor to take away the land of their inheritance; and they shall dwell safely forever.

10 But behold, when the time cometh that they shall dwindle in unbelief, after they have received so great blessings from the hand of the Lord—having a knowledge of the creation of the earth, and all men, knowing the great and marvelous works of the Lord from the creation of the world; having power given them to do all things by faith; having all the commandments from the beginning, and having been brought by his infinite goodness into this precious land of promise—behold, I say, if the day shall come that they will reject the Holy One of Israel, the true Messiah, their Redeemer and their God, behold, the judgments of him that is just shall rest upon them.

Notes

11 Yea, he will bring other nations unto them, and he will give unto them power, and he will take away from them the lands of their possessions, and he will cause them to be scattered and smitten.

vv. 1–11 Blessings and warnings concerning the promise land.

🔍 *Why is the land called a "land of promise" in verse 5?*

✋ Write "Promises on the land" near the top of your board, then on the left-hand side write verses 5–7, 9, 11–12. Invite class members to read each of the verses looking for the promise(s) in each verse. Have a scribe write on the board what the class discovers. After this exercise, it may look like the following:

Promises on the Land

5 Choicest of lands
6 All here are led by God's hand (even today)
7 Always free if not in iniquity
8 Keep commandments; will prosper
9 Keep commandments and be in safety
11 If wicked, others will take away their possessions

❓ Analyze: *In order to have these promises, what must the people do?* (v. 9)

💜 Challenge class members to be deserving of the promises of the Lord.

12 Yea, as one generation passeth to another there shall be bloodsheds, and great visitations among them; wherefore, my sons, I would that ye would remember; yea, I would that ye would hearken unto my words.

13 O that ye would awake; awake from a deep sleep, yea, even from the sleep of hell, and shake off the awful chains by which ye are bound, which are the chains which bind the children of men, that

they are carried away captive down to the eternal gulf of misery and woe.

14 Awake! and arise from the dust, and hear the words of a trembling parent, whose limbs ye must soon lay down in the cold and silent grave, from whence no traveler can return; a few more days and I go the way of all the earth.

15 But behold, the Lord hath redeemed my soul from hell; I have beheld his glory, and I am encircled about eternally in the arms of his love.

vv. 12–15 Staying awake spiritually and avoiding Satan's chains help us to feel the Lord's love in our lives.

✏️ Explain to your class that in scripture, the prophets often teach through the use of imagery. Give each class member a small piece of paper and invite them to quickly draw what Lehi is encouraging his sons to do in verses 13–15. Review their drawings afterward and allow some to explain.

❓ Analyze:
• *Why is Lehi telling his sons to "awake" so many times?*
• *How does someone become spiritually asleep?*
• *Why would Satan want someone to be asleep?*
• *What kinds of things wake a person from spiritual sleep?*

💬 Ezra Taft Benson, speaking of the prosperity of our day, stated, "Ours then seems to be the toughest test of all, for the evils are more subtle, more clever. It all seems less menacing, and it is harder to detect. While every test of righteousness represents a struggle, this particular test seems like no test at all, no struggle, and so could be the most deceiving of all tests. Do you know what peace and prosperity can do to a people—it can put them to sleep" (Ezra Taft Benson, address to Regional Representatives, September 30, 1977).

💜 Have your class think of areas of their lives in

Notes

which they might spiritually be falling asleep. Particularly have them consider how hand-held electronic devices affect their spiritual alertness and challenge class members to awaken themselves if needed.

🔍 *Look for the two different ways Lehi describes being "encircled" in verses 13–15.*

❓ Analyze: *What does being encircled like this lead to? What are the benefits of being encircled in the arms of the Lord's love?*

💬 "The scriptures speak of His arms being open, extended, stretched out, and encircling. They are described as mighty and holy, arms of mercy, arms of safety, arms of love, lengthened out all day long. We have each felt to some extent these spiritual arms around us. We have felt His forgiveness, His love and comfort" (Neal L. Anderson, "Repent . . . That I May Heal You," *Ensign,* October 2009, 40).

💜 Ask class members to assess their own lives and determine if there are any metaphorical chains that are developing in their lives. Invite class members to take the action necessary to shake off those chains. Testify of the joy that comes from feeling God's love in your life.

16 And I desire that ye should remember to observe the statutes and the judgments of the Lord; behold, this hath been the anxiety of my soul from the beginning.

17 My heart hath been weighed down with sorrow from time to time, for I have feared, lest for the hardness of your hearts the Lord your God should come out in the fulness of his wrath upon you, that ye be cut off and destroyed forever;

18 Or, that a cursing should come upon you for the space of many generations; and ye are visited by sword, and by famine, and are hated, and are led according to the will and captivity of the devil.

19 O my sons, that these things might not come upon you, but that ye might be a choice and a favored people of the Lord. But behold, his will

be done; for his ways are righteousness forever.

20 And he hath said that: Inasmuch as ye shall keep my commandments ye shall prosper in the land; but inasmuch as ye will not keep my commandments ye shall be cut off from my presence.

21 And now that my soul might have joy in you, and that my heart might leave this world with gladness because of you, that I might not be brought down with grief and sorrow to the grave, arise from the dust, my sons, and be men, and be determined in one mind and in one heart, united in all things, that ye may not come down into captivity;

22 That ye may not be cursed with a sore cursing; and also, that ye may not incur the displeasure of a just God upon you, unto the destruction, yea, the eternal destruction of both soul and body.

23 Awake, my sons; put on the armor of righteousness. Shake off the chains with which ye are bound, and come forth out of obscurity, and arise from the dust.

24 Rebel no more against your brother, whose views have been glorious, and who hath kept the commandments from the time that we left Jerusalem; and who hath been an instrument in the hands of God, in bringing us forth into the land of promise; for were it not for him, we must have perished with hunger in the wilderness; nevertheless, ye sought to take away his life; yea, and he hath suffered much sorrow because of you.

25 And I exceedingly fear and tremble because of you, lest he shall suffer again; for behold, ye have accused him that he sought power and authority over you; but I know that he hath not sought for power nor authority over you, but he hath sought the glory of God, and your own eternal welfare.

26 And ye have murmured because he hath been plain unto you. Ye say that he hath used sharpness; ye say that he hath been angry with you; but behold, his sharpness was the sharpness of the power of the word of God, which was in him; and that which ye call anger was the truth, according to that which is in God, which he

Notes

_____

_____

_____

could not restrain, manifesting boldly concerning your iniquities.

27 And it must needs be that the power of God must be with him, even unto his commanding you that ye must obey. But behold, it was not he, but it was the Spirit of the Lord which was in him, which opened his mouth to utterance that he could not shut it.

vv. 21–27 Characteristics of a real man.

⚡ *In the world's way of thinking, at what age does a boy become a man?*

🔎 Have class members underline verse 21 where Lehi is commanding his sons to "be men." Explain to your class that in verses 21–27, Lehi is giving characteristics of what it means to be a real man. Have class members read verses 21–27 to themselves and underline characteristics of how a man of God lives his life. After they have done this, have your class share the characteristics they found in each verse. Your list might include the following:

Real men are:
Verse 21
    Determined
    Unified in good causes
Verse 23
    Spiritually awake
    Clad with the armor of God
    Not bound by the chains of sin
    Not obscure (they are willing to stand for
      righteousness)
Verse 24
    Not rebellious to God
    An instrument in God's hands
Verse 25
    Seeking God's glory
    Seeking to help others
Verse 26
    Refraining from murmuring
    Speaking clearly the word of God
Verse 27
    Speaking by the power of the Holy Ghost

♥ Have your class review the list they formulated on the board. Ask them how the list also applies to womanhood. Challenge class members to identify one area in which they can improve.

28 And now my son, Laman, and also Lemuel and Sam, and also my sons who are the sons of Ishmael, behold, if ye will hearken unto the voice of Nephi ye shall not perish. And if ye will hearken unto him I leave unto you a blessing, yea, even my first blessing.

29 But if ye will not hearken unto him I take away my first blessing, yea, even my blessing, and it shall rest upon him.

30 And now, Zoram, I speak unto you: Behold, thou art the servant of Laban; nevertheless, thou hast been brought out of the land of Jerusalem, and I know that thou art a true friend unto my son, Nephi, forever.

v. 30 Characteristics of a "true friend."

🔎 *Look for who Lehi is talking to in verse 30. How does Lehi describe Zoram?*

🖉 Write on the board: "A true friend _____." Have class members ponder how they would fill in the blank. You may want to have them write it in a journal or on a piece of paper first and then ask class members to share.

♥ Once class members have shared characteristics of a true friend, invite them to be a true friend to others.

31 Wherefore, because thou hast been faithful thy seed shall be blessed with his seed, that they dwell in prosperity long upon the face of this land; and nothing, save it shall be iniquity among them, shall harm or disturb their prosperity upon the face of this land forever.

32 Wherefore, if ye shall keep the commandments of the Lord, the Lord hath consecrated this land for the security of thy seed with the seed of my son.

Notes

Teaching Tips from Prophets' Lips "Teach your students to see with the eyes they possessed before they had a mortal body; teach them to hear with ears they possessed before they were born; teach them to push back the curtains of mortality and see into the eternities" (Boyd K. Packer, *The Great Plan of Happiness*," CES symposium on the Doctrine and Covenants/Church History, August 10, 1993, Brigham Young University, 6).

2 NEPHI 2

Lehi's Words to Jacob
About 588–570 BC

1–9, Lehi explains how Jacob will be blessed through the goodness of Christ; 10–16, The doctrine of opposition in all things; 17–25, How the Devil tempts Adam and Eve; 26–30, Man is free to act for himself in choosing between good and evil.

1 And now, Jacob, I speak unto you: Thou art my first-born in the days of my tribulation in the wilderness. And behold, in thy childhood thou hast suffered afflictions and much sorrow, because of the rudeness of thy brethren.

2 Nevertheless, Jacob, my first-born in the wilderness, thou knowest the greatness of God; and he shall consecrate thine afflictions for thy gain.

vv. 1–2 If we trust in God, He can consecrate our afflictions for our gain.

⚡ Ask class members to name some trials people often face in life. After you have listed them on the board, write the following quote: "The only difference between stumbling blocks and stepping stones is the way you use them" (American Proverb, author unknown).

🔎 Look for what this quote has to do with 2 Nephi 2:1–2.

❓ Analyze:
- *Do all afflictions lead to good?*
- *How can afflictions lead a person away from God?*
- *How can God help us turn our afflictions for our good?* Refer to the list of afflictions on the board and ask how each item listed can become an affliction that leads to good.

♥ Invite class members to turn life's stumbling blocks into stepping stones by trusting in and following God regardless of the circumstances.

3 Wherefore, thy soul shall be blessed, and thou shalt dwell safely with thy brother, Nephi; and thy days shall be spent in the service of thy God. Wherefore, I know that thou art redeemed, because of the righteousness of thy Redeemer; for thou hast beheld that in the fulness of time he cometh to bring salvation unto men.

4 And thou hast beheld in thy youth his glory; wherefore, thou art blessed even as they unto whom he shall minister in the flesh; for the Spirit is the same, yesterday, today, and forever. And the way is prepared from the fall of man, and salvation is free.

5 And men are instructed sufficiently that they know good from evil. And the law is given unto men. And by the law no flesh is justified; or, by the law men are cut off. Yea, by the temporal law they were cut off; and also, by the spiritual law they perish from that which is good, and become miserable forever.

6 Wherefore, redemption cometh in and through the Holy Messiah; for he is full of grace and truth.

7 Behold, he offereth himself a sacrifice for sin, to answer the ends of the law, unto all those who have a broken heart and a contrite spirit; and unto none else can the ends of the law be answered.

8 Wherefore, how great the importance to make these things known unto the inhabitants of the

Notes

earth, that they may know that there is no flesh that can dwell in the presence of God, save it be through the merits, and mercy, and grace of the Holy Messiah, who layeth down his life according to the flesh, and taketh it again by the power of the Spirit, that he may bring to pass the resurrection of the dead, being the first that should rise.

9 Wherefore, he is the first fruits unto God, inasmuch as he shall make intercession for all the children of men; and they that believe in him shall be saved.

vv. 3–9 Only through the merits of Christ can we be saved. He redeems those with a broken heart and contrite spirit.

⚡ Ask class members to close their scriptures. Have the following scripture written on the board or paper. Without them reading the actual verse, have class members decide which words in parenthesis are the correct words in the verse:

And men are instructed sufficiently that they know good from evil. And the law is given unto men. And by the law **(man/no flesh)** is justified; or, by the law men are **(redeemed/cut off)**. Yea, by the temporal law they were **(redeemed/cut off)**; and also, by the spiritual law they **(live to/perish from)** that which is good, and **(rejoice/become miserable)** forever (2 Nephi 2:5).

Once they have decided on the words they believe are correct, have class members look up the correct answer and discuss why it reads one way and not the other.

❓ Analyze: *Can we save ourselves? Why or why not?*

🔍 Divide your class into two parts. Invite one half of your class to:

Underline everything in verses 3–9 that shows that it is only through Christ that we are saved.

Invite the other half of the class to:

Underline everything in verses 3–9 that shows what we need to do to be saved.

After each portion of the class has shared what they found, help class members understand that it is through Christ's merits that we are saved, but He saves those who have a heart broken and contrite spirit.

❓ Analyze: *What does it mean to have a broken heart?*

❤ Challenge class members to strive to submit their will to the Lord.

10 And because of the intercession for all, all men come unto God; wherefore, they stand in the presence of him, to be judged of him according to the truth and holiness which is in him. Wherefore, the ends of the law which the Holy One hath given, unto the inflicting of the punishment which is affixed, which punishment that is affixed is in opposition to that of the happiness which is affixed, to answer the ends of the atonement—

11 For it must needs be, that there is an opposition in all things. If not so, my first-born in the wilderness, righteousness could not be brought to pass, neither wickedness, neither holiness nor misery, neither good nor bad. Wherefore, all things must needs be a compound in one; wherefore, if it should be one body it must needs remain as dead, having no life neither death, nor corruption nor incorruption, happiness nor misery, neither sense nor insensibility.

12 Wherefore, it must needs have been created for a thing of naught; wherefore there would have been no purpose in the end of its creation. Wherefore, this thing must needs destroy the wisdom of God and his eternal purposes, and also the power, and the mercy, and the justice of God.

13 And if ye shall say there is no law, ye shall also say there is no sin. If ye shall say there is no sin, ye shall also say there is no righteousness. And if there be no righteousness there be no happiness.

Notes

And if there be no righteousness nor happiness there be no punishment nor misery. And if these things are not there is no God. And if there is no God we are not, neither the earth; for there could have been no creation of things, neither to act nor to be acted upon; wherefore, all things must have vanished away.

14 And now, my sons, I speak unto you these things for your profit and learning; for there is a God, and he hath created all things, both the heavens and the earth, and all things that in them are, both things to act and things to be acted upon.

15 And to bring about his eternal purposes in the end of man, after he had created our first parents, and the beasts of the field and the fowls of the air, and in fine, all things which are created, it must needs be that there was an opposition; even the forbidden fruit in opposition to the tree of life; the one being sweet and the other bitter.

16 Wherefore, the Lord God gave unto man that he should act for himself. Wherefore, man could not act for himself save it should be that he was enticed by the one or the other.

vv. 11–16, 23 The doctrine of opposition in all things helps us to have greater knowledge and understanding.

⚡ Write the following on the board: "Think of a time you appreciated this most." List:

Food
Air conditioning
Warmth
A true friend
Health

Divide the class into five groups and assign each group one of the listed items. After they have had time to discuss times when they have appreciated their assigned topic the most, have someone in each group share their responses.

🔑 Read together verses 11–16 and 23 and look for what is the value of having opposition in all things in this earth life?

❓ Analyze:
- *Why was it not as possible in the premortal life?*
- *How do the extremes of good and evil give us knowledge and understanding?*
- *What should we learn from all the extremes of life?*

17 And I, Lehi, according to the things which I have read, must needs suppose that an angel of God, according to that which is written, had fallen from heaven; wherefore, he became a devil, having sought that which was evil before God.

18 And because he had fallen from heaven, and had become miserable forever, he sought also the misery of all mankind. Wherefore, he said unto Eve, yea, even that old serpent, who is the devil, who is the father of all lies, wherefore he said: Partake of the forbidden fruit, and ye shall not die, but ye shall be as God, knowing good and evil.

19 And after Adam and Eve had partaken of the forbidden fruit they were driven out of the garden of Eden, to till the earth.

20 And they have brought forth children; yea, even the family of all the earth.

21 And the days of the children of men were prolonged, according to the will of God, that they might repent while in the flesh; wherefore, their state became a state of probation, and their time was lengthened, according to the commandments which the Lord God gave unto the children of men. For he gave commandment that all men must repent; for he showed unto all men that they were lost, because of the transgression of their parents.

22 And now, behold, if Adam had not transgressed he would not have fallen, but he would have remained in the garden of Eden. And all things which were created must have remained in the same state in which they were after they were created; and they must have remained forever, and had no end.

Notes

23 And they would have had no children; wherefore they would have remained in a state of innocence, having no joy, for they knew no misery; doing no good, for they knew no sin.

24 But behold, all things have been done in the wisdom of him who knoweth all things.

25 Adam fell that men might be; and men are, that they might have joy.

vv. 18 & 25 We should follow God because His purpose is for us to be happy and Satan's purpose is to make us miserable.

⚡ Discuss with the class what God's purpose is for us. *What are some scriptures that show this?* (2 Nephi 2:25; Moses 1:39.)

💬 "Happiness is the object and design of our existence; and will be the end thereof, if we pursue the path that leads to it; and this path is virtue, uprightness, faithfulness, holiness, and keeping all the commandments of God" (Joseph Smith, in *History of the Church,* 5:34–35).

🔑 Look for Satan's purpose for us in verse 18.

❓ Analyze: *What tool does Satan use to make us miserable? How does he use lies to make people miserable?*

♥ Ask class members to determine some of the lies Satan uses to make people miserable. Use the *For the Strength of Youth* pamphlet as a guide. After the discussion, invite class members to follow God's directions because they bring happiness.

26 And the Messiah cometh in the fulness of time, that he may redeem the children of men from the fall. And because that they are redeemed from the fall they have become free forever, knowing good from evil; to act for themselves and not to be acted upon, save it be by the punishment of the law at the great and last day, according to the commandments which God hath given.

27 Wherefore, men are free according to the flesh;

and all things are given them which are expedient unto man. And they are free to choose liberty and eternal life, through the great Mediator of all men, or to choose captivity and death, according to the captivity and power of the devil; for he seeketh that all men might be miserable like unto himself.

v. 26–27 We should choose to live God's commandments so we can be happier.

⚡ *Why does God give commandments?*

💬 Have class members listen for why God gives commandments as you read what Joseph Smith stated about God, "He never will institute an ordinance or give a commandment to His people that is not calculated in its nature to promote that happiness which He has designed, and which will not end in the greatest amount of good and glory to those who become the recipients of his law and ordinances" (Teachings of the Presidents of the Church: Joseph Smith, 256).

✋ Have your class list all the principles they have learned so far in 2 Nephi 2 on the board. Then ask them to read verses 26–27 and search for a way that the verses relate to the other principles found in the lesson.

♥ Invite class members to make choices that will lead to happiness and not misery.

28 And now, my sons, I would that ye should look to the great Mediator, and hearken unto his great commandments; and be faithful unto his words, and choose eternal life, according to the will of his Holy Spirit;

29 And not choose eternal death, according to the will of the flesh and the evil which is therein, which giveth the spirit of the devil power to captivate, to bring you down to hell, that he may reign over you in his own kingdom.

30 I have spoken these few words unto you all, my sons, in the last days of my probation; and I have chosen the good part, according to the words of

Notes

the prophet. And I have none other object save it be the everlasting welfare of your souls. Amen.

2 NEPHI 3

Lehi's Words to Joseph
About 588–570 BC

1–4, Joseph, the son of Lehi, is a descendant of Joseph of Egypt; 5–25, Joseph of Egypt prophesies of Joseph Smith, the Book of Mormon, and the Restoration.

Overarching Principle—The Restoration of the gospel through the Prophet Joseph Smith was foretold by Joseph in Egypt and teaches us of the foreknowledge of God.

⚡ Bring a framed picture of Joseph Smith (one that can stand on its own) and place it on a table in the front of the class covered with a sheet, cloth, or other covering. Have *"Guess Who"* written on the board and explain to your class that they will discover clues in the scriptures that will help them determine the person whose picture is under the covering.

1 And now I speak unto you, Joseph, my last-born. Thou wast born in the wilderness of mine afflictions; yea, in the days of my greatest sorrow did thy mother bear thee.

2 And may the Lord consecrate also unto thee this land, which is a most precious land, for thine inheritance and the inheritance of thy seed with thy brethren, for thy security forever, if it so be that ye shall keep the commandments of the Holy One of Israel.

3 And now, Joseph, my last-born, whom I have brought out of the wilderness of mine afflictions, may the Lord bless thee forever, for thy seed shall not utterly be destroyed.

4 For behold, thou art the fruit of my loins; and I am a descendant of Joseph who was carried captive into Egypt. And great were the covenants of the Lord which he made unto Joseph.

5 Wherefore, Joseph truly saw our day. And he obtained a promise of the Lord, that out of the fruit of his loins the Lord God would raise up a righteous branch unto the house of Israel; not the Messiah, but a branch which was to be broken off, nevertheless, to be remembered in the covenants of the Lord that the Messiah should be made manifest unto them in the latter days, in the spirit of power, unto the bringing of them out of darkness unto light—yea, out of hidden darkness and out of captivity unto freedom.

vv. 1–5 Joseph of Egypt prophesies.

💡 Explain verses 1–5 in your own words to your class. (Lehi teaches that Joseph of Egypt gives a prophecy about someone who will save the house of Israel, and note the footnote in the LDS edition of the scriptures for the JST footnote in Genesis 50.) Explain that the person described in this chapter is the person whose picture is under the covering.

6 For Joseph truly testified, saying: A seer shall the Lord my God raise up, who shall be a choice seer unto the fruit of my loins.

7 Yea, Joseph truly said: Thus saith the Lord unto me: A choice seer will I raise up out of the fruit of thy loins; and he shall be esteemed highly among the fruit of thy loins. And unto him will I give commandment that he shall do a work for the fruit of thy loins, his brethren, which shall be of great worth unto them, even to the bringing of them to the knowledge of the covenants which I have made with thy fathers.

8 And I will give unto him a commandment that he shall do none other work, save the work which I shall command him. And I will make him great in mine eyes; for he shall do my work.

9 And he shall be great like unto Moses, whom I have said I would raise up unto you, to deliver my people, O house of Israel.

Notes

10 And Moses will I raise up, to deliver thy people out of the land of Egypt.

11 But a seer will I raise up out of the fruit of thy loins; and unto him will I give power to bring forth my word unto the seed of thy loins—and not to the bringing forth my word only, saith the Lord, but to the convincing them of my word, which shall have already gone forth among them.

12 Wherefore, the fruit of thy loins shall write; and the fruit of the loins of Judah shall write; and that which shall be written by the fruit of thy loins, and also that which shall be written by the fruit of the loins of Judah, shall grow together, unto the confounding of false doctrines and laying down of contentions, and establishing peace among the fruit of thy loins, and bringing them to the knowledge of their fathers in the latter days, and also to the knowledge of my covenants, saith the Lord.

13 And out of weakness he shall be made strong, in that day when my work shall commence among all my people, unto the restoring thee, O house of Israel, saith the Lord.

14 And thus prophesied Joseph, saying: Behold, that seer will the Lord bless; and they that seek to destroy him shall be confounded; for this promise, which I have obtained of the Lord, of the fruit of my loins, shall be fulfilled. Behold, I am sure of the fulfilling of this promise;

15 And his name shall be called after me; and it shall be after the name of his father. And he shall be like unto me; for the thing, which the Lord shall bring forth by his hand, by the power of the Lord shall bring my people unto salvation.

16 Yea, thus prophesied Joseph: I am sure of this thing, even as I am sure of the promise of Moses; for the Lord hath said unto me, I will preserve thy seed forever.

17 And the Lord hath said: I will raise up a Moses; and I will give power unto him in a rod; and I will give judgment unto him in writing. Yet I will not loose his tongue, that he shall speak much, for I will not make him mighty in speaking. But

I will write unto him my law, by the finger of mine own hand; and I will make a spokesman for him.

18 And the Lord said unto me also: I will raise up unto the fruit of thy loins; and I will make for him a spokesman. And I, behold, I will give unto him that he shall write the writing of the fruit of thy loins, unto the fruit of thy loins; and the spokesman of thy loins shall declare it.

19 And the words which he shall write shall be the words which are expedient in my wisdom should go forth unto the fruit of thy loins. And it shall be as if the fruit of thy loins had cried unto them from the dust; for I know their faith.

20 And they shall cry from the dust; yea, even repentance unto their brethren, even after many generations have gone by them. And it shall come to pass that their cry shall go, even according to the simpleness of their words.

21 Because of their faith their words shall proceed forth out of my mouth unto their brethren who are the fruit of thy loins; and the weakness of their words will I make strong in their faith, unto the remembering of my covenant which I made unto thy fathers.

22 And now, behold, my son Joseph, after this manner did my father of old prophesy.

23 Wherefore, because of this covenant thou art blessed; for thy seed shall not be destroyed, for they shall hearken unto the words of the book.

24 And there shall rise up one mighty among them, who shall do much good, both in word and in deed, being an instrument in the hands of God, with exceeding faith, to work mighty wonders, and do that thing which is great in the sight of God, unto the bringing to pass much restoration unto the house of Israel, and unto the seed of thy brethren.

25 And now, blessed art thou, Joseph. Behold, thou art little; wherefore hearken unto the words of thy brother, Nephi, and it shall be done unto thee even according to the words which I have

Notes

spoken. Remember the words of thy dying father. Amen.

vv. 6–25 A prophesy of Joseph Smith and the Book of Mormon.

⚡ Refer to the object lesson listed under the overarching principle at the beginning of this chapter.

✎ Either have the following written on the board or create a handout for the class to complete with the help of the following clues:

Clue 1: verse 7
Clue 2: verse 8
Clue 3: verse 9
Clue 4: verse 11
Clue 5: verse 13
Clue 6: verse 14
Clue 7: verse 15

🔍 As a class, read each verse out loud and allow class members to discover the clue found in each scripture. Then, write the clue on the board, but don't allow class members to guess who it is until all the clues are identified. The following are suggested answers for each clue:

Clue 1: The man will be esteemed highly; he will do a work of great worth and bring people to the knowledge of God's covenants.
Clue 2: He shall be made great.
Clue 3: He shall not be Moses but will be great like Moses.
Clue 4: He will bring forth God's word and convince others of God's word that has already gone forth.
Clue 5: He will be considered weak but will be made strong.
Clue 6: People will seek to kill him but will be confounded.
Clue 7: His name will be Joseph, and he will be named after his father.

The above are suggestions; you should allow class members to discover and explain in their own words what these clues describe.

When all the clues have been identified, allow your class to guess whose picture is under the covering. Once your class has guessed correctly, remove the covering to reveal the picture.

❓ Analyze: Assign each clue to various class members. *How does your clue describe Joseph Smith?* If you chose to distribute a handout, you may want to encourage your class to write these answers down. *When Joseph was translating the Book of Mormon, do you think he realized this chapter was about him?*

💬 "It was decreed in the counsels of eternity, long before the foundations of the earth were laid, that he, Joseph Smith, should be the man, in the last dispensation of this world, to bring forth the word of God to the people, and receive the fullness of the keys and power of the Priesthood of the Son of God. The Lord had His eyes upon him, and upon his father, and upon his father's father, and upon their progenitors clear back to Abraham, and from Abraham to the flood, from the flood to Enoch, and from Enoch to Adam. He has watched that family and that blood as it has circulated from its fountain to the birth of that man. He [the Prophet Joseph Smith] was fore-ordained in eternity to preside over this last dispensation" (Brigham Young, *Deseret News,* Oct. 26, 1859, 266).

💬 "I feel like shouting Hallelujah, all the time, when I think that I ever knew Joseph Smith, the Prophet whom the Lord raised up. I am bold to say that, Jesus Christ excepted, no better man ever lived or does live upon this earth. I am his witness" (*Discourses of Brigham Young,* sel. John A. Widtsoe [1954], 458–59).

❤ Read verse 24 with class members and share your testimony of the prophet Joseph Smith. As a class, you may also want to sing "Praise to the Man" as a closing hymn.

Notes

2 NEPHI 4

The Psalm of Nephi

About 588–570 BC

1–11, Lehi gives a final blessing to his posterity—He blesses Laman and Lemuel's sons that their cursing will be answered on their fathers' heads; 12–14, Lehi dies; Laman, Lemuel, and the sons of Ishmael rebel against Nephi; 15–27, Nephi acknowledges his weaknesses and blessings; 28–35, Nephi recommits himself to continually follow God.

1 And now, I, Nephi, speak concerning the prophecies of which my father hath spoken, concerning Joseph, who was carried into Egypt.

2 For behold, he truly prophesied concerning all his seed. And the prophecies which he wrote, there are not many greater. And he prophesied concerning us, and our future generations; and they are written upon the plates of brass.

3 Wherefore, after my father had made an end of speaking concerning the prophecies of Joseph, he called the children of Laman, his sons, and his daughters, and said unto them: Behold, my sons, and my daughters, who are the sons and the daughters of my first-born, I would that ye should give ear unto my words.

4 For the Lord God hath said that: Inasmuch as ye shall keep my commandments ye shall prosper in the land; and inasmuch as ye will not keep my commandments ye shall be cut off from my presence.

5 But behold, my sons and my daughters, I cannot go down to my grave save I should leave a blessing upon you; for behold, I know that if ye are brought up in the way ye should go ye will not depart from it.

6 Wherefore, if ye are cursed, behold, I leave my blessing upon you, that the cursing may be taken from you and be answered upon the heads of your parents.

7 Wherefore, because of my blessing the Lord God will not suffer that ye shall perish; wherefore, he will be merciful unto you and unto your seed forever.

8 And it came to pass that after my father had made an end of speaking to the sons and daughters of Laman, he caused the sons and daughters of Lemuel to be brought before him.

9 And he spake unto them, saying: Behold, my sons and my daughters, who are the sons and the daughters of my second son; behold I leave unto you the same blessing which I left unto the sons and daughters of Laman; wherefore, thou shalt not utterly be destroyed; but in the end thy seed shall be blessed.

10 And it came to pass that when my father had made an end of speaking unto them, behold, he spake unto the sons of Ishmael, yea, and even all his household.

11 And after he had made an end of speaking unto them, he spake unto Sam, saying: Blessed art thou, and thy seed; for thou shalt inherit the land like unto thy brother Nephi. And thy seed shall be numbered with his seed; and thou shalt be even like unto thy brother, and thy seed like unto his seed; and thou shalt be blessed in all thy days.

vv. 3–11 A father can offer priesthood blessings to his children.

Notes

_____

_____

_____

⚡ Show a picture of a family (ideally yours). Explain that according to "The Family: A Proclamation to the World," mothers are primarily responsible for the nurture of the children. Ask,

- *What is the responsibility of fathers?* Explain that part of this responsibility is to give father's blessings.
- *When have you received a father's blessing?*
- *Why did you ask for one* (if not too personal)*?*
- *How did it help you?*

🔍 *Read verses 5–11 and look for what Lehi is doing for his sons before his death.* Once class members have identified that Lehi blesses his posterity, explain that one duty of a father is to bless his children. You may want to share how this happens in your own family.

Note: Be sensitive to those in your class who may come from varying family situations. Encourage them that priesthood blessings can still be available to them through priesthood leaders and in their own future families.

💬 Encourage class members to seek a father's blessing even if their father is unworthy or inactive. Share the following quote from Boyd K. Packer: "I remember once we had been to Chicago to a servicemen's convention. . . . A young man came up to us as we were leaving and said, 'Elder Lee, I'm leaving within the week to go to Vietnam. I don't know whether I'll come back or not. I come from an inactive family. Will you give me a blessing, please?' . . . You could hardly resist the pleadings of a soldier boy. To my surprise, Elder Lee said, "My son, your father should give that blessing." . . . He said, 'Oh, my father isn't active. He wouldn't even know how. He's never given a blessing of any kind.' . . . Then Brother Lee said, 'Nevertheless, he should give you the blessing.' . . . That was the end of that conversation, and the boy went away sorrowing. That incident was out of my mind until nearly a year later when I met that young man. He reminded me of that circumstance. . . . He said, 'Do you know what happened? My father gave me the blessing. It was a marvelous thing and a strength and a protection' (CES Evening with a General Authority, February 29, 2008).

💜 Encourage class members to turn to their fathers for blessings of comfort and council.

12 And it came to pass after my father, Lehi, had spoken unto all his household, according to the feelings of his heart and the Spirit of the Lord which was in him, he waxed old. And it came to pass that he died, and was buried.

13 And it came to pass that not many days after his death, Laman and Lemuel and the sons of Ishmael were angry with me because of the admonitions of the Lord.

vv. 12–13 Lehi dies and is buried.

💡 Notice that once Lehi dies and is buried, Laman, Lemuel, and the sons of Ishmael completely rebel against Nephi and the others. In fact, by the next chapter there is a complete separation of the two groups.

14 For I, Nephi, was constrained to speak unto them, according to his word; for I had spoken many things unto them, and also my father, before his death; many of which sayings are written upon mine other plates; for a more history part are written upon mine other plates.

15 And upon these I write the things of my soul, and many of the scriptures which are engraven upon the plates of brass. For my soul delighteth in the scriptures, and my heart pondereth them, and writeth them for the learning and the profit of my children.

16 Behold, my soul delighteth in the things of the Lord; and my heart pondereth continually upon the things which I have seen and heard.

17 Nevertheless, notwithstanding the great

Notes

_____

_____

_____

goodness of the Lord, in showing me his great and marvelous works, my heart exclaimeth: O wretched man that I am! Yea, my heart sorroweth because of my flesh; my soul grieveth because of mine iniquities.

18 I am encompassed about, because of the temptations and the sins which do so easily beset me.

19 And when I desire to rejoice, my heart groaneth because of my sins; nevertheless, I know in whom I have trusted.

20 My God hath been my support; he hath led me through mine afflictions in the wilderness; and he hath preserved me upon the waters of the great deep.

21 He hath filled me with his love, even unto the consuming of my flesh.

22 He hath confounded mine enemies, unto the causing of them to quake before me.

23 Behold, he hath heard my cry by day, and he hath given me knowledge by visions in the night-time.

24 And by day have I waxed bold in mighty prayer before him; yea, my voice have I sent up on high; and angels came down and ministered unto me.

25 And upon the wings of his Spirit hath my body been carried away upon exceedingly high mountains. And mine eyes have beheld great things, yea, even too great for man; therefore I was bidden that I should not write them.

26 O then, if I have seen so great things, if the Lord in his condescension unto the children of men hath visited men in so much mercy, why should my heart weep and my soul linger in the valley of sorrow, and my flesh waste away, and my strength slacken, because of mine afflictions?

27 And why should I yield to sin, because of my flesh? Yea, why should I give way to temptations, that the evil one have place in my heart to destroy my peace and afflict my soul? Why am I angry because of mine enemy?

28 Awake, my soul! No longer droop in sin.

Rejoice, O my heart, and give place no more for the enemy of my soul.

29 Do not anger again because of mine enemies. Do not slacken my strength because of mine afflictions.

30 Rejoice, O my heart, and cry unto the Lord, and say: O Lord, I will praise thee forever; yea, my soul will rejoice in thee, my God, and the rock of my salvation.

31 O Lord, wilt thou redeem my soul? Wilt thou deliver me out of the hands of mine enemies? Wilt thou make me that I may shake at the appearance of sin?

32 May the gates of hell be shut continually before me, because that my heart is broken and my spirit is contrite! O Lord, wilt thou not shut the gates of thy righteousness before me, that I may walk in the path of the low valley, that I may be strict in the plain road!

33 O Lord, wilt thou encircle me around in the robe of thy righteousness! O Lord, wilt thou make a way for mine escape before mine enemies! Wilt thou make my path straight before me! Wilt thou not place a stumbling block in my way—but that thou wouldst clear my way before me, and hedge not up my way, but the ways of mine enemy.

34 O Lord, I have trusted in thee, and I will trust in thee forever. I will not put my trust in the arm of flesh; for I know that cursed is he that putteth his trust in the arm of flesh. Yea, cursed is he that putteth his trust in man or maketh flesh his arm.

35 Yea, I know that God will give liberally to him that asketh. Yea, my God will give me, if I ask not amiss; therefore I will lift up my voice unto thee; yea, I will cry unto thee, my God, the rock of my righteousness. Behold, my voice shall forever ascend up unto thee, my rock and mine everlasting God. Amen.

vv. 15–35 The Psalm of Nephi : "My God hath been my support. . . . Oh Lord, I will praise thee forever."

Notes

The Bible Dictionary indicates that the Hebrew word for "Psalms" can be translated as "Praises" and are generally set to music. This section of 2 Nephi 4 is often referred to as "The Psalm of Nephi" because in it Nephi offers praises to God for his abundant goodness, though there is no evidence that what Nephi wrote was ever set to music. 2 Nephi 4:15–35 may be separated into three parts.

vv. 20–25: What God has done for Nephi

vv. 17–19, 26–29: Nephi's realization of his weaknesses

vv. 30–35: Nephi's recommitment *because* of his realization

Create a handout that will allow class members to track each of the three parts of the Psalm of Nephi, or you can track it on the board.

The Psalm of Nephi
2 Nephi 4:15–35

What God has done for Nephi
(2 Nephi 4:20–25):

What God has done for me:

Nephi's realization
(2 Nephi 4:17–19, 26–29):

My own realization:

Nephi's recommitment to the Lord
(2 Nephi 4:30–35):

My personal recommitment to the Lord:

Give class members time to complete the top half of the handout and allow them to share their insights and favorite phrases.

♥ Select a phrase from each of the three sections that you would consider your favorite, or the most powerful, and create a mini-lesson based on that phrase. Encourage class members to complete the bottom half of the handout on their own.

2 NEPHI 5
"After the Manner of Happiness"
About 588–559 BC

1–4, Nephi's brethren seek to kill him; 5–8, The Lord commands Nephi to leave with those who are willing, and they settle a land they call Nephi; 9–18, The Nephites are faithful and industrious and build a temple; 19–25, The word of God is fulfilled in the cursing upon those who followed Laman; 26–34, The Nephites "lived after the manner of happiness" and keep records.

1 Behold, it came to pass that I, Nephi, did cry much unto the Lord my God, because of the anger of my brethren.

2 But behold, their anger did increase against me, insomuch that they did seek to take away my life.

3 Yea, they did murmur against me, saying: Our younger brother thinks to rule over us; and we have had much trial because of him; wherefore, now let us slay him, that we may not be afflicted more because of his words. For behold, we will not have him to be our ruler; for it belongs unto us, who are the elder brethren, to rule over this people.

♀ Note with the class that verse 3 explains why the Lamanites feel it is their right to rule over all others.

4 Now I do not write upon these plates all the words which they murmured against me. But it sufficeth me to say, that they did seek to take away my life.

5 And it came to pass that the Lord did warn me, that I, Nephi, should depart from them and flee

Notes

into the wilderness, and all those who would go with me.

6 Wherefore, it came to pass that I, Nephi, did take my family, and also Zoram and his family, and Sam, mine elder brother and his family, and Jacob and Joseph, my younger brethren, and also my sisters, and all those who would go with me. And all those who would go with me were those who believed in the warnings and the revelations of God; wherefore, they did hearken unto my words.

7 And we did take our tents and whatsoever things were possible for us, and did journey in the wilderness for the space of many days. And after we had journeyed for the space of many days we did pitch our tents.

8 And my people would that we should call the name of the place Nephi; wherefore, we did call it Nephi.

9 And all those who were with me did take upon them to call themselves the people of Nephi.

10 And we did observe to keep the judgments, and the statutes, and the commandments of the Lord in all things, according to the law of Moses.

11 And the Lord was with us; and we did prosper exceedingly; for we did sow seed, and we did reap again in abundance. And we began to raise flocks, and herds, and animals of every kind.

12 And I, Nephi, had also brought the records which were engraven upon the plates of brass; and also the ball, or compass, which was prepared for my father by the hand of the Lord, according to that which is written.

13 And it came to pass that we began to prosper exceedingly, and to multiply in the land.

14 And I, Nephi, did take the sword of Laban, and after the manner of it did make many swords, lest by any means the people who were now called Lamanites should come upon us and destroy us; for I knew their hatred towards me and my children and those who were called my people.

15 And I did teach my people to build buildings, and to work in all manner of wood, and of iron, and of copper, and of brass, and of steel, and of gold, and of silver, and of precious ores, which were in great abundance.

16 And I, Nephi, did build a temple; and I did construct it after the manner of the temple of Solomon save it were not built of so many precious things; for they were not to be found upon the land, wherefore, it could not be built like unto Solomon's temple. But the manner of the construction was like unto the temple of Solomon; and the workmanship thereof was exceedingly fine.

17 And it came to pass that I, Nephi, did cause my people to be industrious, and to labor with their hands.

18 And it came to pass that they would that I should be their king. But I, Nephi, was desirous that they should have no king; nevertheless, I did for them according to that which was in my power.

vv. 6–34 How to be happy.

⚡ Before class, write on the board, "What is the secret to happiness?" After class has started, ask class members if they have had any thoughts in answer to the question on the board and if so, have them share. Have a class member read verse 27 and ask, *What is the manner of happiness?*

🔍 Explain that embedded in this chapter are the elements of the Nephites' lifestyle that led them to be happy. On another board, have the following chart depicted. As you read each of those verses as a class, complete the squares, including personal application of those elements. Refrain from expecting class members to furnish the answer you are thinking of. Instead, let them decide what to write in the squares. The following chart offers some suggestions.

Notes

Verse	How they "lived after the manner of happiness"	How we can live after the manner of happiness
6	Follow the prophet	Follow the prophet
10	Keep the commandments	Avoid bad media
11, 17	Work hard, industrious	Provide for family
12	Value the scriptures	Read daily
13	Have children	Have children
14	Have a strong defense	Support our national defense
15	Learn skills	Attain continual education
16	Build a temple	Attend the temple
18	Seek good leaders	Be politically active; vote
26	Have Church leaders	Sustain and serve
32	Record God's hand in our lives	Keep a personal journal
33	Keep a history	Do family history work

♥ Review the list you have made on the board and ask, *How is our society doing with this list? How are you doing personally?* Invite class members to select one area in their lives to improve to attain a happier life.

19 And behold, the words of the Lord had been fulfilled unto my brethren, which he spake concerning them, that I should be their ruler and their teacher. Wherefore, I had been their ruler and their teacher, according to the commandments of the Lord, until the time they sought to take away my life.

20 Wherefore, the word of the Lord was fulfilled which he spake unto me, saying that: Inasmuch as they will not hearken unto thy words they shall be cut off from the presence of the Lord. And behold, they were cut off from his presence.

21 And he had caused the cursing to come upon them, yea, even a sore cursing, because of their iniquity. For behold, they had hardened their hearts against him, that they had become like unto a flint; wherefore, as they were white, and exceedingly fair and delightsome, that they might not be enticing unto my people the Lord God did cause a skin of blackness to come upon them.

22 And thus saith the Lord God: I will cause that they shall be loathsome unto thy people, save they shall repent of their iniquities.

23 And cursed shall be the seed of him that mixeth with their seed; for they shall be cursed even with the same cursing. And the Lord spake it, and it was done.

24 And because of their cursing which was upon them they did become an idle people, full of mischief and subtlety, and did seek in the wilderness for beasts of prey.

💡 Some people mistake the dark skin of the Lamanites as their curse. Note in verse 21, however, that the skin of blackness which came upon them was so that they would not be enticing to the Nephites.

25 And the Lord God said unto me: They shall be a scourge unto thy seed, to stir them up in remembrance of me; and inasmuch as they will not remember me, and hearken unto my words, they shall scourge them even unto destruction.

26 And it came to pass that I, Nephi, did consecrate Jacob and Joseph, that they should be priests and teachers over the land of my people.

27 And it came to pass that we lived after the manner of happiness.

28 And thirty years had passed away from the time we left Jerusalem.

29 And I, Nephi, had kept the records upon my plates, which I had made, of my people thus far.

Notes

30 And it came to pass that the Lord God said unto me: Make other plates; and thou shalt engraven many things upon them which are good in my sight, for the profit of thy people.

31 Wherefore, I, Nephi, to be obedient to the commandments of the Lord, went and made these plates upon which I have engraven these things.

32 And I engraved that which is pleasing unto God. And if my people are pleased with the things of God they will be pleased with mine engravings which are upon these plates.

33 And if my people desire to know the more particular part of the history of my people they must search mine other plates.

34 And it sufficeth me to say that forty years had passed away, and we had already had wars and contentions with our brethren.

Teaching Tips from Prophets' Lips "Far from diminishing its impact, purity and simplicity of expression allow the Holy Spirit to witness with greater certainty to the hearts of men" (Gerald Causse, "Even a Child Can Understand," *Liahona*, November 2008, 32–34).

2 NEPHI 6

Jacob's Discourse on Isaiah
About 588–559 BC

1–7, Jacob teaches Isaiah's words; 8–11, Jacob prophecies of how the Jews will receive the Messiah after the Babylonian captivity; 12–18, The role of the Gentiles in the latter-days.

1 The words of Jacob, the brother of Nephi, which he spake unto the people of Nephi:

2 Behold, my beloved brethren, I, Jacob, having been called of God, and ordained after the manner of his holy order, and having been consecrated by my brother Nephi, unto whom ye look as a king or a protector, and on whom ye depend for safety, behold ye know that I have spoken unto you exceedingly many things.

3 Nevertheless, I speak unto you again; for I am desirous for the welfare of your souls. Yea, mine anxiety is great for you; and ye yourselves know that it ever has been. For I have exhorted you with all diligence; and I have taught you the words of my father; and I have spoken unto you concerning all things which are written, from the creation of the world.

4 And now, behold, I would speak unto you concerning things which are, and which are to come; wherefore, I will read you the words of Isaiah. And they are the words which my brother has desired that I should speak unto you. And I speak unto you for your sakes, that ye may learn and glorify the name of your God.

5 And now, the words which I shall read are they which Isaiah spake concerning all the house of Israel; wherefore, they may be likened unto you, for ye are of the house of Israel. And there are many things which have been spoken by Isaiah which may be likened unto you, because ye are of the house of Israel.

vv. 1–5 Characteristics of a great leader.

⚡ *In your opinion, who was or currently is a great leader? What characteristics made or make that person a great leader?*

🔍 After a few class members have shared, explain that they will explore verses 1–5 and search for characteristics of a great leader. Some of the answers you could lead them to are:

v. 2 Called of God and set apart

v. 3 Seeks the welfare of those in stewardship

v. 4 Helps people glorify God's name

v. 5 Teaches from the scriptures and likens them

♥ Challenge class members to follow the same examples in their own church callings.

Notes

6 And now, these are the words: Thus saith the Lord God: Behold, I will lift up mine hand to the Gentiles, and set up my standard to the people; and they shall bring thy sons in their arms, and thy daughters shall be carried upon their shoulders.

7 And kings shall be thy nursing fathers, and their queens thy nursing mothers; they shall bow down to thee with their faces towards the earth, and lick up the dust of thy feet; and thou shalt know that I am the Lord; for they shall not be ashamed that wait for me.

vv. 6–7 Repetition of the words of Isaiah.

💡 Explain to class members that the Isaiah verses quoted in this chapter are found in three places throughout the scriptures: Isaiah 49:22–26, 1 Nephi 21:22–26, and here in 2 Nephi 6:6–7 and 16–18. Ask, *Why is there repetition in the scriptures?*

8 And now I, Jacob, would speak somewhat concerning these words. For behold, the Lord has shown me that those who were at Jerusalem, from whence we came, have been slain and carried away captive.

9 Nevertheless, the Lord has shown unto me that they should return again. And he also has shown unto me that the Lord God, the Holy One of Israel, should manifest himself unto them in the flesh; and after he should manifest himself they should scourge him and crucify him, according to the words of the angel who spake it unto me.

10 And after they have hardened their hearts and stiffened their necks against the Holy One of Israel, behold, the judgments of the Holy One of Israel shall come upon them. And the day cometh that they shall be smitten and afflicted.

vv. 9–10 The Jews were "smitten and afflicted" in AD 70.

💡 Explain to class members that Nephi prophesies that the Jews will be smitten and afflicted because they crucified the Savior. In AD 70, approximately 36 years after the death of Jesus, the Romans destroyed the city of Jerusalem, killed and brutalized the Jews, and destroyed the temple which has never been rebuilt.

11 Wherefore, after they are driven to and fro, for thus saith the angel, many shall be afflicted in the flesh, and shall not be suffered to perish, because of the prayers of the faithful; they shall be scattered, and smitten, and hated; nevertheless, the Lord will be merciful unto them, that when they shall come to the knowledge of their Redeemer, they shall be gathered together again to the lands of their inheritance.

12 And blessed are the Gentiles, they of whom the prophet has written; for behold, if it so be that they shall repent and fight not against Zion, and do not unite themselves to that great and abominable church, they shall be saved; for the Lord God will fulfil his covenants which he has made unto his children; and for this cause the prophet has written these things.

v. 11 The afflictions and gathering of the Jews.

💡 Ask, *As verse 11 indicates, how have the Jewish people been afflicted in the last hundred years? In what ways have the Jewish people been gathered to their inheritance?* Explain that after the Jewish people had been persecuted all over the world, culminating with the Holocaust, the United Nations helped create a Jewish state in what is today the nation of Israel. The nation of Israel was founded in 1948 after the atrocities of World War II. To study this, you can perform an Internet search on the subject.

13 Wherefore, they that fight against Zion and the covenant people of the Lord shall lick up the dust of their feet; and the people of the Lord shall not be ashamed. For the people of the Lord

Notes

are they who wait for him; for they still wait for the coming of the Messiah.

14 And behold, according to the words of the prophet, the Messiah will set himself again the second time to recover them; wherefore, he will manifest himself unto them in power and great glory, unto the destruction of their enemies, when that day cometh when they shall believe in him; and none will he destroy that believe in him.

15 And they that believe not in him shall be destroyed, both by fire, and by tempest, and by earthquakes, and by bloodsheds, and by pestilence, and by famine. And they shall know that the Lord is God, the Holy One of Israel.

16 For shall the prey be taken from the mighty, or the lawful captive delivered?

17 But thus saith the Lord: Even the captives of the mighty shall be taken away, and the prey of the terrible shall be delivered; for the Mighty God shall deliver his covenant people. For thus saith the Lord: I will contend with them that contendeth with thee—

18 And I will feed them that oppress thee, with their own flesh; and they shall be drunken with their own blood as with sweet wine; and all flesh shall know that I the Lord am thy Savior and thy Redeemer, the Mighty One of Jacob.

vv. 13–18 The Jews find their Messiah.

Doctrine and Covenants 133:46–53 gives an account of future events wherein the Jewish people will finally recognize Jesus Christ as the Messiah. You can also cross-reference Zechariah 13:6 and 14:4.

2 NEPHI 7

Jacob Quotes Isaiah 50
About 559–545 BC

1, We remove ourselves from God when we sin; 2–6, God's Omnipotence; 7–11, Isaiah recognizes that "the Lord God will help me."

1 Yea, for thus saith the Lord: Have I put thee away, or have I cast thee off forever? For thus saith the Lord: Where is the bill of your mother's divorcement? To whom have I put thee away, or to which of my creditors have I sold you? Yea, to whom have I sold you? Behold, for your iniquities have ye sold yourselves, and for your transgressions is your mother put away.

2 Wherefore, when I came, there was no man; when I called, yea, there was none to answer. O house of Israel, is my hand shortened at all that it cannot redeem, or have I no power to deliver? Behold, at my rebuke I dry up the sea, I make their rivers a wilderness and their fish to stink because the waters are dried up, and they die because of thirst.

3 I clothe the heavens with blackness, and I make sackcloth their covering.

4 The Lord God hath given me the tongue of the learned, that I should know how to speak a word in season unto thee, O house of Israel. When ye are weary he waketh morning by morning. He waketh mine ear to hear as the learned.

5 The Lord God hath opened mine ear, and I was not rebellious, neither turned away back.

6 I gave my back to the smiter, and my cheeks to them that plucked off the hair. I hid not my face from shame and spitting.

7 For the Lord God will help me, therefore shall I not be confounded. Therefore have I set my face like a flint, and I know that I shall not be ashamed.

8 And the Lord is near, and he justifieth me. Who will contend with me? Let us stand together.

Notes

Who is mine adversary? Let him come near me, and I will smite him with the strength of my mouth.

9 For the Lord God will help me. And all they who shall condemn me, behold, all they shall wax old as a garment, and the moth shall eat them up.

10 Who is among you that feareth the Lord, that obeyeth the voice of his servant, that walketh in darkness and hath no light?

11 Behold all ye that kindle fire, that compass yourselves about with sparks, walk in the light of your fire and in the sparks which ye have kindled. This shall ye have of mine hand—ye shall lie down in sorrow.

Overarching Doctrine: The nature of covenants establishes our relationship with God and allows Him to bless and comfort us despite our shortcomings. Note: 2 Nephi 7–8 are used by Jacob as one continual message, so these two chapters are best taught together.

⚡ Explain that when we make a covenant with God we bind ourselves to Him. Draw the following on the board: ∞+10= ? Ask, If you add anything to infinity, what will the answer always be? What if the equation looked like this: ∞−10= ? (The answer is still infinity. In other words, infinity is never affected by what is added to or subtracted from it.) Explain that this formula teaches, in part, the benefits of our covenant relationship with God.

✏ Explain to class members that they will learn one aspect of the nature of covenants through 2 Nephi 7–8. Create the following chart on the board or as a worksheet to help your class identify what Isaiah teaches about covenants:

The Covenant Relationship with God
Why does Jacob quote these two chapters in Isaiah?
See 2 Nephi 9:1

God's omnipotence and ability to save
2 Nephi 7:2
2 Nephi 7:6
2 Nephi 8:5
2 Nephi 8:6
2 Nephi 8:21–22

What God can do for us
2 Nephi 7:7–9
2 Nephi 8:3
2 Nephi 8:7–8
2 Nephi 8:12
2 Nephi 8:14

How do we disqualify ourselves from the covenant blessings?
2 Nephi 7:1
2 Nephi 7:11

Isaiah's Conclusion
What is Isaiah's invitation to all of us who have made a covenant with God?
See 2 Nephi 8:24–25

💡 To help you better understand the verses used in the above worksheet, the following is an explanation of each verse.

v. 1 God never separates Himself from us; we remove ourselves from Him through the choices we make ("for your iniquities have ye sold yourselves").

v. 2 God's ability to save and help us is not "shortened" (meaning "limited") by anything but our own actions. The last half of verse 2 proves this point.

v. 6 This verse has reference to the Atonement. The purpose of it being used here is to establish that the Atonement is part of God's covenant relationship with us.

vv. 7–9 Isaiah understands that through God's help he will not be confounded and will therefore "set [his] face like a flint," meaning that he will keep his part

Notes

_____

_____

_____

of the covenant despite his "adversary" or those "who shall condemn" him.

v. 11 Isaiah warns the people of Israel about the dangers of continuing in wickedness and of their eventual "sorrow." Notice that Isaiah uses the words "ye," "yourselves," and "your" to teach the doctrine of personal accountability. The fire and sparks could represent living in wickedness or "compassing yourselves about with sparks."

Teaching Tips from Prophets' Lips "The Spirit of God speaking to the spirit of man has power to impart truth with greater effect and understanding than the truth can be imparted by personal contact even with heavenly beings. Through the Holy Ghost the truth is woven into the very fiber and sinews of the body so that it cannot be forgotten" (Joseph Fielding Smith, *Doctrines of Salvation*, comp. Bruce R. McConkie, 3 vols. [1954–56], 1:47–48).

2 NEPHI 8

Jacob Quotes Isaiah 51 & 52:1–2
About 559–545 BC

1–12, God comforts His people in times of need; 13–25, Despite Israel's scattering, God will redeem them.

Note: 2 Nephi 7–8 are used by Jacob as one continual message; therefore, these two chapters are best taught together.

1 Hearken unto me, ye that follow after righteousness. Look unto the rock from whence ye are hewn, and to the hole of the pit from whence ye are digged.

2 Look unto Abraham, your father, and unto Sarah, she that bare you; for I called him alone, and blessed him.

3 For the Lord shall comfort Zion, he will comfort all her waste places; and he will make her wilderness like Eden, and her desert like the garden of the Lord. Joy and gladness shall be found therein, thanksgiving and the voice of melody.

4 Hearken unto me, my people; and give ear unto me, O my nation; for a law shall proceed from me, and I will make my judgment to rest for a light for the people.

5 My righteousness is near; my salvation is gone forth, and mine arm shall judge the people. The isles shall wait upon me, and on mine arm shall they trust.

6 Lift up your eyes to the heavens, and look upon the earth beneath; for the heavens shall vanish away like smoke, and the earth shall wax old like a garment; and they that dwell therein shall die in like manner. But my salvation shall be forever, and my righteousness shall not be abolished.

7 Hearken unto me, ye that know righteousness, the people in whose heart I have written my law, fear ye not the reproach of men, neither be ye afraid of their revilings.

8 For the moth shall eat them up like a garment, and the worm shall eat them like wool. But my righteousness shall be forever, and my salvation from generation to generation.

9 Awake, awake! Put on strength, O arm of the Lord; awake as in the ancient days. Art thou not he that hath cut Rahab, and wounded the dragon?

10 Art thou not he who hath dried the sea, the waters of the great deep; that hath made the depths of the sea a way for the ransomed to pass over?

11 Therefore, the redeemed of the Lord shall return, and come with singing unto Zion; and everlasting joy and holiness shall be upon their heads; and they shall obtain gladness and joy; sorrow and mourning shall flee away.

12 I am he; yea, I am he that comforteth you. Behold, who art thou, that thou shouldst be afraid of man, who shall die, and of the son of

Notes

man, who shall be made like unto grass?

13 And forgettest the Lord thy maker, that hath stretched forth the heavens, and laid the foundations of the earth, and hast feared continually every day, because of the fury of the oppressor, as if he were ready to destroy? And where is the fury of the oppressor?

14 The captive exile hasteneth, that he may be loosed, and that he should not die in the pit, nor that his bread should fail.

15 But I am the Lord thy God, whose waves roared; the Lord of Hosts is my name.

16 And I have put my words in thy mouth, and have covered thee in the shadow of mine hand, that I may plant the heavens and lay the foundations of the earth, and say unto Zion: Behold, thou art my people.

17 Awake, awake, stand up, O Jerusalem, which hast drunk at the hand of the Lord the cup of his fury—thou hast drunken the dregs of the cup of trembling wrung out—

18 And none to guide her among all the sons she hath brought forth; neither that taketh her by the hand, of all the sons she hath brought up.

19 These two sons are come unto thee, who shall be sorry for thee—thy desolation and destruction, and the famine and the sword—and by whom shall I comfort thee?

20 Thy sons have fainted, save these two; they lie at the head of all the streets; as a wild bull in a net, they are full of the fury of the Lord, the rebuke of thy God.

21 Therefore hear now this, thou afflicted, and drunken, and not with wine:

22 Thus saith thy Lord, the Lord and thy God pleadeth the cause of his people; behold, I have taken out of thine hand the cup of trembling, the dregs of the cup of my fury; thou shalt no more drink it again.

23 But I will put it into the hand of them that afflict thee; who have said to thy soul: Bow down, that

we may go over—and thou hast laid thy body as the ground and as the street to them that went over.

Overarching Doctrine: The nature of covenants establishes our relationship with God and allows Him to bless and comfort us despite our shortcomings.

For teaching ideas, refer to 2 Nephi 7.

To help you better understand the verses used in the worksheet from chapter 7, the following is an explanation of each verse.

v. 3 God will comfort us, our waste places, and our wilderness, meaning that God will help us despite our personal trials or sins.

v. 5 Part of God's covenant with us is to judge us in righteousness.

v. 6 God's righteousness will stand forever; therefore, we can have confidence that He will keep His promises made under covenant.

vv. 7–8 We shouldn't be concerned about the reproach or the persecutions of men because, compared to God, their opinions are irrelevant. This is evidenced by the following: "The moth shall eat them up like a garment" compared to God's righteousness which "shall be forever."

v. 12 God will comfort us; therefore, we should trust in Him and not in man, who will wither and die like the grass.

v. 14 Isaiah refers to "the captive exile" not dying in the pit meaning that God will redeem everyone, including those who feel like they are in exile because of their sins.

vv. 21–22 Through repentance, God allows us to escape drinking from the "cup of trembling"; instead, that cup is given to the Savior to drink through the Atonement.

Notes

24 Awake, awake, put on thy strength, O Zion; put on thy beautiful garments, O Jerusalem, the holy city; for henceforth there shall no more come into thee the uncircumcised and the unclean.

25 Shake thyself from the dust; arise, sit down, O Jerusalem; loose thyself from the bands of thy neck, O captive daughter of Zion.

♥ When we understand the doctrine of covenants, namely that God has done so much for us, we should be led to faith-inspired action. Read verses 24 and 25 with your class and invite them to be strong, arise from the dust, and no longer be held captive by Satan.

2 NEPHI 9

"O How Great the Plan of Our God"

About 559–545 BC

1–3, Jacob teaches of the restoration of Israel; 4–13, Through the Atonement, all are resurrected; 14–19, With a perfect knowledge all will stand before God and his saints are redeemed through God's mercy; 20, God knoweth all things; 21–26, The way is prepared for all to be saved; 27–39, Warnings concerning various sins; 40–54, Exhortations of Jacob to righteousness.

1 And now, my beloved brethren, I have read these things that ye might know concerning the covenants of the Lord that he has covenanted with all the house of Israel—

2 That he has spoken unto the Jews, by the mouth of his holy prophets, even from the beginning down, from generation to generation, until the time comes that they shall be restored to the true church and fold of God; when they shall be gathered home to the lands of their inheritance, and shall be established in all their lands of promise.

3 Behold, my beloved brethren, I speak unto you

these things that ye may rejoice, and lift up your heads forever, because of the blessings which the Lord God shall bestow upon your children.

4 For I know that ye have searched much, many of you, to know of things to come; wherefore I know that ye know that our flesh must waste away and die; nevertheless, in our bodies we shall see God.

vv. 4–24 Doctrines of the Atonement of Christ.

⚡ *Where is the best place in the scriptures to learn about the Atonement of Christ?* Share the quote below.

💬 "I think there is no place where we have a finer discussion of the plan of the Atonement than in the writings of Jacob, as found in the Book of Mormon, 2 Nephi, the ninth chapter. I therefore call it to your attention and urge you to read carefully again and again that precious explanation" (*Teachings of Presidents of the Church: Harold B. Lee*, 18).

💡 Explain to class members that after studying every few set of verses, you will be asking them to explain how those verses relate with the Atonement of Christ.

v. 4 Resurrection.

🔍 *Try to think of a scripture mastery verse in the Old Testament that is similar to verse 4.* Share Job 19:25–26 and have class members find the similarities.

❓ Analyze: *What does verse 4 have to do with the Atonement of Christ?*

5 Yea, I know that ye know that in the body he shall show himself unto those at Jerusalem, from whence we came; for it is expedient that it should be among them; for it behooveth the great Creator that he suffereth himself to become subject unto man in the flesh, and die for all men, that all men might become subject unto him.

6 For as death hath passed upon all men, to fulfil

Notes

the merciful plan of the great Creator, there must needs be a power of resurrection, and the resurrection must needs come unto man by reason of the fall; and the fall came by reason of transgression; and because man became fallen they were cut off from the presence of the Lord.

7 Wherefore, it must needs be an infinite atonement—save it should be an infinite atonement this corruption could not put on incorruption. Wherefore, the first judgment which came upon man must needs have remained to an endless duration. And if so, this flesh must have laid down to rot and to crumble to its mother earth, to rise no more.

8 O the wisdom of God, his mercy and grace! For behold, if the flesh should rise no more our spirits must become subject to that angel who fell from before the presence of the Eternal God, and became the devil, to rise no more.

9 And our spirits must have become like unto him, and we become devils, angels to a devil, to be shut out from the presence of our God, and to remain with the father of lies, in misery, like unto himself; yea, to that being who beguiled our first parents, who transformeth himself nigh unto an angel of light, and stirreth up the children of men unto secret combinations of murder and all manner of secret works of darkness.

vv. 5 & 9 Subjects to Christ or the Devil.

🔎 *Look for who we become subject to through the Atonement.*

❓ Analyze:
- *What does it mean that "all men become subject unto him"?*
- *Who holds the keys of heaven?*
- *Who holds the keys of hell? (Christ holds the keys of hell also. See Revelation 1:18)*

🔎 Search verses 8–9 to find out who we would be subject to if it were not for Christ's sacrifice for us.

❓ Analyze: *How do these verses describe what it would be like to be subject to the devil?*

vv. 7, 21 Infinite Atonement.

🔎 Look in verse 7 for a word that describes the Atonement of Christ.

❓ Analyze: *In what way was the Atonement infinite? Look in verse 21 for something He suffered infinitely.*

💬 Invite the class to look for all the ways the Atonement was infinite in the following quote from Russell M. Nelson, "His Atonement is infinite—without an end [see 2 Nephi 9:7; 2 Nephi 25:16; Alma 34:10, 12, 14]. It was also infinite in that all humankind would be saved from never-ending death. It was infinite in terms of His immense suffering. It was infinite in time, putting an end to the preceding prototype of animal sacrifice. It was infinite in scope—it was to be done once for all [see Doctrine and Covenants 76:24; Moses 1:33]. And the mercy of the Atonement extends not only to an infinite number of people, but also to an infinite number of worlds created by Him. It was infinite beyond any human scale of measurement or mortal comprehension. Jesus was the only one who could offer such an infinite atonement, since He was born of a mortal mother and an immortal Father. Because of that unique birthright, Jesus was an infinite Being" ("The Atonement," *Ensign*, November 1996, 35).

10 O how great the goodness of our God, who prepareth a way for our escape from the grasp of this awful monster; yea, that monster, death and hell, which I call the death of the body, and also the death of the spirit.

11 And because of the way of deliverance of our God, the Holy One of Israel, this death, of which I have spoken, which is the temporal, shall deliver up its dead; which death is the grave.

12 And this death of which I have spoken, which is the spiritual death, shall deliver up its dead; which spiritual death is hell; wherefore, death and hell must deliver up their dead, and hell must deliver up its captive spirits, and the grave

Notes

must deliver up its captive bodies, and the bodies and the spirits of men will be restored one to the other; and it is by the power of the resurrection of the Holy One of Israel.

13 O how great the plan of our God! For on the other hand, the paradise of God must deliver up the spirits of the righteous, and the grave deliver up the body of the righteous; and the spirit and the body is restored to itself again, and all men become incorruptible, and immortal, and they are living souls, having a perfect knowledge like unto us in the flesh, save it be that our knowledge shall be perfect.

14 Wherefore, we shall have a perfect knowledge of all our guilt, and our uncleanness, and our nakedness; and the righteous shall have a perfect knowledge of their enjoyment, and their righteousness, being clothed with purity, yea, even with the robe of righteousness.

vv. 13–14 A perfect knowledge.

♥ Bear testimony that because Christ suffered all of the pains, sorrows, and sins of this world, we have been bought by Him and are placed under His jurisdiction. Yet the Lord gives us agency to still reject Him to follow Satan.

🔎 Look for what is restored to us at the resurrection in verses 13–14.

❓ Analyze: *What does it mean we will have a perfect knowledge of all our guilt? What does it mean that we will have a perfect knowledge of our righteousness?*

15 And it shall come to pass that when all men shall have passed from this first death unto life, insomuch as they have become immortal, they must appear before the judgment-seat of the Holy One of Israel; and then cometh the judgment, and then must they be judged according to the holy judgment of God.

16 And assuredly, as the Lord liveth, for the Lord God hath spoken it, and it is his eternal word, which cannot pass away, that they who are righteous shall be righteous still, and they who are filthy shall be filthy still; wherefore, they who are filthy are the devil and his angels; and they shall go away into everlasting fire, prepared for them; and their torment is as a lake of fire and brimstone, whose flame ascendeth up forever and ever and has no end.

17 O the greatness and the justice of our God! For he executeth all his words, and they have gone forth out of his mouth, and his law must be fulfilled.

18 But, behold, the righteous, the saints of the Holy One of Israel, they who have believed in the Holy One of Israel, they who have endured the crosses of the world, and despised the shame of it, they shall inherit the kingdom of God, which was prepared for them from the foundation of the world, and their joy shall be full forever.

19 O the greatness of the mercy of our God, the Holy One of Israel! For he delivereth his saints from that awful monster the devil, and death, and hell, and that lake of fire and brimstone, which is endless torment.

20 O how great the holiness of our God! For he knoweth all things, and there is not anything save he knows it.

21 And he cometh into the world that he may save all men if they will hearken unto his voice; for behold, he suffereth the pains of all men, yea, the pains of every living creature, both men, women, and children, who belong to the family of Adam.

22 And he suffereth this that the resurrection might pass upon all men, that all might stand before him at the great and judgment day.

23 And he commandeth all men that they must repent, and be baptized in his name, having perfect faith in the Holy One of Israel, or they cannot be saved in the kingdom of God.

24 And if they will not repent and believe in his name, and be baptized in his name, and endure to the end, they must be damned; for the Lord God, the Holy One of Israel, has spoken it.

Notes

vv. 18, 21, 23, 24 Requirements for salvation.

🔎 Assign verses 18, 21, 23 and 24 to be read, and as a class, look for what requirements for salvation can be found in the verses. Write the list on the board.

♥ Review the list and ask which items might be more difficult to do. Invite class members to do accordingly.

25 Wherefore, he has given a law; and where there is no law given there is no punishment; and where there is no punishment there is no condemnation; and where there is no condemnation the mercies of the Holy One of Israel have claim upon them, because of the atonement; for they are delivered by the power of him.

26 For the atonement satisfieth the demands of his justice upon all those who have not the law given to them, that they are delivered from that awful monster, death and hell, and the devil, and the lake of fire and brimstone, which is endless torment; and they are restored to that God who gave them breath, which is the Holy One of Israel.

27 But wo unto him that has the law given, yea, that has all the commandments of God, like unto us, and that transgresseth them, and that wasteth the days of his probation, for awful is his state!

28 O that cunning plan of the evil one! O the vainness, and the frailties, and the foolishness of men! When they are learned they think they are wise, and they hearken not unto the counsel of God, for they set it aside, supposing they know of themselves, wherefore, their wisdom is foolishness and it profiteth them not. And they shall perish.

29 But to be learned is good if they hearken unto the counsels of God.

30 But wo unto the rich, who are rich as to the things of the world. For because they are rich they despise the poor, and they persecute the meek, and their hearts are upon their treasures; wherefore, their treasure is their god. And behold, their treasure shall perish with them also.

31 And wo unto the deaf that will not hear; for they shall perish.

32 Wo unto the blind that will not see; for they shall perish also.

33 Wo unto the uncircumcised of heart, for a knowledge of their iniquities shall smite them at the last day.

34 Wo unto the liar, for he shall be thrust down to hell.

35 Wo unto the murderer who deliberately killeth, for he shall die.

36 Wo unto them who commit whoredoms, for they shall be thrust down to hell.

37 Yea, wo unto those that worship idols, for the devil of all devils delighteth in them.

38 And, in fine, wo unto all those who die in their sins; for they shall return to God, and behold his face, and remain in their sins.

39 O, my beloved brethren, remember the awfulness in transgressing against that Holy God, and also the awfulness of yielding to the enticings of that cunning one. Remember, to be carnally-minded is death, and to be spiritually-minded is life eternal.

40 O, my beloved brethren, give ear to my words. Remember the greatness of the Holy One of Israel. Do not say that I have spoken hard things against you; for if ye do, ye will revile against the truth; for I have spoken the words of your Maker. I know that the words of truth are hard against all uncleanness; but the righteous fear them not, for they love the truth and are not shaken.

41 O then, my beloved brethren, come unto the Lord, the Holy One. Remember that his paths are righteous. Behold, the way for man is narrow, but it lieth in a straight course before him, and the keeper of the gate is the Holy One of Israel; and he employeth no servant there; and there is none other way save it be by the gate; for he

Notes

cannot be deceived, for the Lord God is his name.

42 And whoso knocketh, to him will he open; and the wise, and the learned, and they that are rich, who are puffed up because of their learning, and their wisdom, and their riches—yea, they are they whom he despiseth; and save they shall cast these things away, and consider themselves fools before God, and come down in the depths of humility, he will not open unto them.

43 But the things of the wise and the prudent shall be hid from them forever—yea, that happiness which is prepared for the saints.

44 O, my beloved brethren, remember my words. Behold, I take off my garments, and I shake them before you; I pray the God of my salvation that he view me with his all-searching eye; wherefore, ye shall know at the last day, when all men shall be judged of their works, that the God of Israel did witness that I shook your iniquities from my soul, and that I stand with brightness before him, and am rid of your blood.

45 O, my beloved brethren, turn away from your sins; shake off the chains of him that would bind you fast; come unto that God who is the rock of your salvation.

46 Prepare your souls for that glorious day when justice shall be administered unto the righteous, even the day of judgment, that ye may not shrink with awful fear; that ye may not remember your awful guilt in perfectness, and be constrained to exclaim: Holy, holy are thy judgments, O Lord God Almighty—but I know my guilt; I transgressed thy law, and my transgressions are mine; and the devil hath obtained me, that I am a prey to his awful misery.

47 But behold, my brethren, is it expedient that I should awake you to an awful reality of these things? Would I harrow up your souls if your minds were pure? Would I be plain unto you according to the plainness of the truth if ye were freed from sin?

48 Behold, if ye were holy I would speak unto you of holiness; but as ye are not holy, and ye look upon me as a teacher, it must needs be expedient that I teach you the consequences of sin.

49 Behold, my soul abhorreth sin, and my heart delighteth in righteousness; and I will praise the holy name of my God.

50 Come, my brethren, every one that thirsteth, come ye to the waters; and he that hath no money, come buy and eat; yea, come buy wine and milk without money and without price.

51 Wherefore, do not spend money for that which is of no worth, nor your labor for that which cannot satisfy. Hearken diligently unto me, and remember the words which I have spoken; and come unto the Holy One of Israel, and feast upon that which perisheth not, neither can be corrupted, and let your soul delight in fatness.

52 Behold, my beloved brethren, remember the words of your God; pray unto him continually by day, and give thanks unto his holy name by night. Let your hearts rejoice.

vv. 27–52 Formulating principles for life.

Have your class look for what a principle is as you read the following quote: "Principles are concentrated truths packaged for application to a wide variety of circumstances" (Richard G. Scott "Acquiring Spiritual Knowledge," *Ensign*, November 1993, 86).

Explain to your class that they will form principle statements based on their assigned verses. To help them, explain that principles usually:

• Say what we are to do
• Use personal pronouns
• Have a result

Write the following on the board to help explain the structure principles usually fall under:

Examples of Principles:

• "If I . . . then . . ."
• "We should . . . so that . . ."

Notes

- "When we . . . then . . ."
- "We need to . . . because . . ."
- "I need to . . . so that . . ."

Have the following verses written on the board, and assign them to pairs in the class (27, 28–29, 30, 31–33, 34, 35, 36, 37, 38, 39, 40, 41, 42, 45, 50, 51, 52). After class members study the verse(s), have them discover the principle and write it as one of the statement structures you wrote on the board. For example: "Wickedness never was happiness" could be placed in a principle statement to say, "I need to avoid sin, because it takes away happiness." Invite class members to share what they have learned and write the principles beside the verses in their scriptures.

♥ When the pairs present, take time to ask questions like: *How have you found that to be true in your own life? Have you had an experience that demonstrates that principle?*

53 And behold how great the covenants of the Lord, and how great his condescensions unto the children of men; and because of his greatness, and his grace and mercy, he has promised unto us that our seed shall not utterly be destroyed, according to the flesh, but that he would preserve them; and in future generations they shall become a righteous branch unto the house of Israel.

54 And now, my brethren, I would speak unto you more; but on the morrow I will declare unto you the remainder of my words. Amen.

Teaching Tips from Prophets' Lips "Power comes when a teacher has done all that he can to prepare, not just the individual lesson, but in keeping his life in tune with the Spirit. If he will learn to rely on the Spirit for inspiration, he can go before his class . . . secure in the knowledge that he can teach with inspiration" (Boyd K. Packer, *Teach Ye Diligently*, rev. ed. [1991], 358–59.)

2 NEPHI 10

Reconcile Yourselves to the Will of God
About 559–545 BC

1–9, The crucifixion of Christ and its effects on those who crucified him; 10–22, Promises on the land for Lehi's posterity; 23–24, Choose to be reconciled to God through God's Grace.

1 And now I, Jacob, speak unto you again, my beloved brethren, concerning this righteous branch of which I have spoken.

2 For behold, the promises which we have obtained are promises unto us according to the flesh; wherefore, as it has been shown unto me that many of our children shall perish in the flesh because of unbelief, nevertheless, God will be merciful unto many; and our children shall be restored, that they may come to that which will give them the true knowledge of their Redeemer.

3 Wherefore, as I said unto you, it must needs be expedient that Christ—for in the last night the angel spake unto me that this should be his name—should come among the Jews, among those who are the more wicked part of the world; and they shall crucify him—for thus it behooveth our God, and there is none other nation on earth that would crucify their God.

v. 3 The word "Christ" is used.

💡 Have class members look for the word "Christ" in verse 3 and mark it in their scriptures. Explain that this is the very first time that the title "Christ" is used in the Book of Mormon.

🗩 Ezra Taft Benson Stated: "Over one-half of all the verses in the Book of Mormon refer to our Lord. Some form of Christ's name is mentioned more frequently per verse in the Book of Mormon than even in the New Testament. He is given over one hundred different names

Notes

in the Book of Mormon. Those names have a particular significance in describing His divine nature" ("What the Book of Mormon Tells Us," *Ensign*, November 1987, 83).

v. 3 The only nation that would crucify their God.

🔍 Have class members look in verse 3 for the most wicked nation on the earth. *What makes them the most wicked? How does our world compare in wickedness to other worlds that God created?* (See Moses 7:36.)

4 For should the mighty miracles be wrought among other nations they would repent, and know that he be their God.

5 But because of priestcrafts and iniquities, they at Jerusalem will stiffen their necks against him, that he be crucified.

6 Wherefore, because of their iniquities, destructions, famines, pestilences, and bloodshed shall come upon them; and they who shall not be destroyed shall be scattered among all nations.

7 But behold, thus saith the Lord God: When the day cometh that they shall believe in me, that I am Christ, then have I covenanted with their fathers that they shall be restored in the flesh, upon the earth, unto the lands of their inheritance.

v. 7 Jews believe in Christ.

💡 Explain that when Jews come to believe in Jesus as the Messiah, they are often called, "Messianic Jews." The term Messianic is used because "Messiah" is the Hebrew word for Christ.

8 And it shall come to pass that they shall be gathered in from their long dispersion, from the isles of the sea, and from the four parts of the earth; and the nations of the Gentiles shall be great in the eyes of me, saith God, in carrying them forth to the lands of their inheritance.

9 Yea, the kings of the Gentiles shall be nursing fathers unto them, and their queens shall become nursing mothers; wherefore, the promises of the Lord are great unto the Gentiles, for he hath spoken it, and who can dispute?

10 But behold, this land, said God, shall be a land of thine inheritance, and the Gentiles shall be blessed upon the land.

11 And this land shall be a land of liberty unto the Gentiles, and there shall be no kings upon the land, who shall raise up unto the Gentiles.

12 And I will fortify this land against all other nations.

13 And he that fighteth against Zion shall perish, saith God.

14 For he that raiseth up a king against me shall perish, for I, the Lord, the king of heaven, will be their king, and I will be a light unto them forever, that hear my words.

15 Wherefore, for this cause, that my covenants may be fulfilled which I have made unto the children of men, that I will do unto them while they are in the flesh, I must needs destroy the secret works of darkness, and of murders, and of abominations.

16 Wherefore, he that fighteth against Zion, both Jew and Gentile, both bond and free, both male and female, shall perish; for they are they who are the whore of all the earth; for they who are not for me are against me, saith our God.

17 For I will fulfil my promises which I have made unto the children of men, that I will do unto them while they are in the flesh—

18 Wherefore, my beloved brethren, thus saith our God: I will afflict thy seed by the hand of the Gentiles; nevertheless, I will soften the hearts of the Gentiles, that they shall be like unto a father to them; wherefore, the Gentiles shall be blessed and numbered among the house of Israel.

19 Wherefore, I will consecrate this land unto thy seed, and them who shall be numbered among thy seed, forever, for the land of their inheritance;

Notes

for it is a choice land, saith God unto me, above all other lands, wherefore I will have all men that dwell thereon that they shall worship me, saith God.

20 And now, my beloved brethren, seeing that our merciful God has given us so great knowledge concerning these things, let us remember him, and lay aside our sins, and not hang down our heads, for we are not cast off; nevertheless, we have been driven out of the land of our inheritance; but we have been led to a better land, for the Lord has made the sea our path, and we are upon an isle of the sea.

v. 20 "We are upon an isle of the sea."

💡 Explain that the land of Israel is connected to Africa, Europe, and Asia. Other continents were unknown to them, so there was the thought that any place that was not connected to them by land was naturally an "isle of the sea."

21 But great are the promises of the Lord unto them who are upon the isles of the sea; wherefore as it says isles, there must needs be more than this, and they are inhabited also by our brethren.

22 For behold, the Lord God has led away from time to time from the house of Israel, according to his will and pleasure. And now behold, the Lord remembereth all them who have been broken off, wherefore he remembereth us also.

23 Therefore, cheer up your hearts, and remember that ye are free to act for yourselves—to choose the way of everlasting death or the way of eternal life.

24 Wherefore, my beloved brethren, reconcile yourselves to the will of God, and not to the will of the devil and the flesh; and remember, after ye are reconciled unto God, that it is only in and through the grace of God that ye are saved.

25 Wherefore, may God raise you from death by the power of the resurrection, and also from everlasting death by the power of the atonement,

that ye may be received into the eternal kingdom of God, that ye may praise him through grace divine. Amen.

vv. 23–24 We can all return to live with Heavenly Father.

⚡ Ask class members to think of something that makes them happy and be ready to share.

🔍 After they share, ask them to look for something that should make us happy in verse 23.

❓ Apply: *Why should it make us happy to know we are "free to act for [ourselves]"?*

🔍 *Look in verse 24 for what else we need in order for salvation to be within our reach.*

❤ Share your gratitude to know that we can all return to Heavenly Father through the goodness of the Lord and our righteous choices.

2 NEPHI 11

Nephi's Reasons for Quoting Isaiah
About 559–545 BC

1–3, Nephi's soul rejoices in proving to his people of the coming of Christ; 4–8, Nephi offers five reasons why he quotes Isaiah.

Note: In 2 Nephi chapters 11 and 25, Nephi offers some reasons as to why he quotes Isaiah and how we as Latter-day Saint readers can understand him. There will be a lesson outline in each of these two chapters to help you teach Nephi's prophetic reasons, and you may want to consider using some of chapter 25 here as an introduction to Isaiah before you begin teaching chapters 12–24.

1 And now, Jacob spake many more things to my people at that time; nevertheless only these things have I caused to be written, for the things which I have written sufficeth me.

2 And now I, Nephi, write more of the words of

Notes

Isaiah, for my soul delighteth in his words. For I will liken his words unto my people, and I will send them forth unto all my children, for he verily saw my Redeemer, even as I have seen him.

3 And my brother, Jacob, also has seen him as I have seen him; wherefore, I will send their words forth unto my children to prove unto them that my words are true. Wherefore, by the words of three, God hath said, I will establish my word. Nevertheless, God sendeth more witnesses, and he proveth all his words.

vv. 1–3 Since Nephi has seen God, he uses Isaiah's writings to prove the coming of Christ.

💬 Daniel H. Ludlow taught that "God has said through his prophets, 'In the mouth of two or three witnesses shall every word be established.' (2 Corinthians 13:1.) Nephi was apparently aware of this system of witnesses when he introduced three great pre-Christian witnesses of the coming of Jesus Christ: Isaiah, Nephi himself, and Nephi's brother Jacob. Nephi then continues: 'Wherefore, by the words of three, God hath said, I will establish my word' (2 Nephi 11:3)" (Ludlow, Daniel H., *A Companion to Your Study of the Book of Mormon*, [Salt Lake City: Deseret Book, 1976]).

🔎 *Nephi uses the law of witnesses to prove something to us. Look in verses 1–3 to find who the witnesses are and what he is trying to prove.*

4 Behold, my soul delighteth in proving unto my people the truth of the coming of Christ; for, for this end hath the law of Moses been given; and all things which have been given of God from the beginning of the world, unto man, are the typifying of him.

5 And also my soul delighteth in the covenants of the Lord which he hath made to our fathers; yea, my soul delighteth in his grace, and in his justice, and power, and mercy in the great and eternal plan of deliverance from death.

6 And my soul delighteth in proving unto my people that save Christ should come all men must perish.

7 For if there be no Christ there be no God; and if there be no God we are not, for there could have been no creation. But there is a God, and he is Christ, and he cometh in the fulness of his own time.

8 And now I write some of the words of Isaiah, that whoso of my people shall see these words may lift up their hearts and rejoice for all men. Now these are the words, and ye may liken them unto you and unto all men.

vv. 4–8 Nephi's five "delights".

🔎 *In verses 4–6, Nephi delights in five things. What are they?* Help class members create a list similar to the one below:

The coming of Christ
The covenants of God
His grace and mercy
His divine power
His justice

These five "delights" are found in the writings of Isaiah.

Teaching Tips from Prophets' Lips "The small changes I would look for are those which would increase the likelihood that a person I was teaching would inquire of God in faith. That will surely, every time, bring enlightenment by the Spirit. And that is the feeding we seek for those we teach. That will help us find improvements we might consider in everything we do regularly as we teach" ("The Lord Will Multiply the Harvest," *An Evening with Elder Henry B. Eyring*, February 6, 1998, 3).

Notes

2 NEPHI 12

Nephi Quotes Isaiah 2
About 559–545 BC

1–3, The Salt Lake Temple is seen and prophesied in vision by Isaiah; 4–22, Those who persist in wickedness will be brought down low in the Second Coming.

Note: Many people feel that Isaiah is hard to understand. Two possible reasons for this are 1) Isaiah's use of various literary styles that modern readers are not familiar with, and 2) the fact that Isaiah was facing issues of his day while also prophesying about our day. If we, therefore, are unfamiliar with both Jewish literary techniques and Jewish history, we may lose some of the message Isaiah is trying to teach. Notes at the beginning of some chapters will help establish some basic historical and literary context to help you better understand and teach Isaiah.

Historical Context: Isaiah is speaking to the people of Israel who have made covenants with God, though they are not keeping them. He is warning them that their continual sins will lead to destruction.

Literary Context: One literary technique Isaiah employs is the use of opposites to teach the contrast between the spiritual results of righteousness and wickedness. In this chapter, Isaiah uses the opposite directions of up and down.

1 The word that Isaiah, the son of Amoz, saw concerning Judah and Jerusalem:

2 And it shall come to pass in the last days, when the mountain of the Lord's house shall be established in the top of the mountains, and shall be exalted above the hills, and all nations shall flow unto it.

3 And many people shall go and say, Come ye, and let us go up to the mountain of the Lord, to the house of the God of Jacob; and he will teach us of his ways, and we will walk in his paths; for out of Zion shall go forth the law, and the word of the Lord from Jerusalem.

vv. 1–3 Isaiah prophesies of the Salt Lake Temple.

⚡ Invite a class member who is an artist to the front of the class. Instruct the person to draw a picture of what Isaiah describes in verses 1–3 as the class reads the verses.

🔎 Establish with the class that Isaiah is prophesying of an event that will happen "in the last days" (verse 2). Read verses 1–3 out loud as a class, pausing after each verse to allow time for your artist to draw the details of what is happening in the verses.

💬 At the dedication of the Conference Center in October 2000, Gordon B. Hinckley said, "I believe that prophecy [referring to Isaiah 2:1–3] applies to the historic and wonderful Salt Lake Temple. But I believe also that it is related to this magnificent hall [the Conference Center]. For it is from this pulpit that the law of God shall go forth, together with the word and testimony of the Lord" (Gordon B. Hinckley, October General Conference, 2000).

❓ Analyze: *Since these verses are a prophecy of the Salt Lake Temple and Conference Center, how do they fulfill the following phrases:*

"Established in the tops of the mountains"
"All nations shall flow unto it"
"He will teach us his ways"
"Out of Zion shall go forth the law"

❤ Testify of the importance of the temple and general conference for us to learn of God's ways. Ask class members if they would like to share any learning experiences they have had either at the temple or in general conference.

4 And he shall judge among the nations, and shall rebuke many people: and they shall beat their swords into plow-shares, and their spears into pruning-hooks—nation shall not lift up sword against

Notes

nation, neither shall they learn war any more.

5 O house of Jacob, come ye and let us walk in the light of the Lord; yea, come, for ye have all gone astray, every one to his wicked ways.

6 Therefore, O Lord, thou hast forsaken thy people, the house of Jacob, because they be replenished from the east, and hearken unto soothsayers like the Philistines, and they please themselves in the children of strangers.

7 Their land also is full of silver and gold, neither is there any end of their treasures; their land is also full of horses, neither is there any end of their chariots.

8 Their land is also full of idols; they worship the work of their own hands, that which their own fingers have made.

9 And the mean man boweth not down, and the great man humbleth himself not, therefore, forgive him not.

10 O ye wicked ones, enter into the rock, and hide thee in the dust, for the fear of the Lord and the glory of his majesty shall smite thee.

11 And it shall come to pass that the lofty looks of man shall be humbled, and the haughtiness of men shall be bowed down, and the Lord alone shall be exalted in that day.

12 For the day of the Lord of Hosts soon cometh upon all nations, yea, upon every one; yea, upon the proud and lofty, and upon every one who is lifted up, and he shall be brought low.

13 Yea, and the day of the Lord shall come upon all the cedars of Lebanon, for they are high and lifted up; and upon all the oaks of Bashan;

14 And upon all the high mountains, and upon all the hills, and upon all the nations which are lifted up, and upon every people;

15 And upon every high tower, and upon every fenced wall;

16 And upon all the ships of the sea, and upon all the ships of Tarshish, and upon all pleasant pictures.

17 And the loftiness of man shall be bowed down, and the haughtiness of men shall be made low; and the Lord alone shall be exalted in that day.

18 And the idols he shall utterly abolish.

19 And they shall go into the holes of the rocks, and into the caves of the earth, for the fear of the Lord shall come upon them and the glory of his majesty shall smite them, when he ariseth to shake terribly the earth.

20 In that day a man shall cast his idols of silver, and his idols of gold, which he hath made for himself to worship, to the moles and to the bats;

21 To go into the clefts of the rocks, and into the tops of the ragged rocks, for the fear of the Lord shall come upon them and the majesty of his glory shall smite them, when he ariseth to shake terribly the earth.

22 Cease ye from man, whose breath is in his nostrils; for wherein is he to be accounted of?

vv. 4–22 Living the gospel lifts us up while not keeping the commandments brings us down.

⚡ To help the class visualize the contrast that Isaiah is painting in this chapter, bring a cup filled with dirt and an action figure or a paper-man cutout small enough to bury in the dirt. In front of the class, bury the man in the dirt. Ask, *Where would you much rather be: in the dirt or standing on the dirt?* The answer is obvious, but you want the class to see it so they can clearly understand Isaiah's message. Explain the literary context of Isaiah found at the beginning of this chapter and draw an up arrow and a down arrow on the board.

🔑 *As we read the following verses, identify which direction Isaiah is talking about.* You may want to invite the class to draw an arrow next to each verse:

vv. 2–3 (up)
vv. 10–17 (down)
v. 19 (down)

Notes

❓ Analyze: Note with the class that the temple is "up" and we need to "flow" unto it. Rivers normally flow down rather than up, yet Isaiah is using an opposite to draw the contrast that hearing the word of God, walking in His ways, and leaving the world behind is hard and could be considered swimming upstream. Ask,

- *If God wants all His children to listen to His word, why do you think He would place it at the tops of the mountains where not everyone may be able to access it easily?*
- *Looking at the contrast in this chapter, what is Isaiah teaching about following after the world?*
- *Why do you think Isaiah uses the contrast he does?*

💬 Henry B. Eyring stated, "Too many of our young people want the blessings of a mission and the temple and yet fail to meet the qualifications to claim them. . . . Far too many say to themselves: 'Well, I know I may have to repent someday, and I know that a mission and temple marriage will require big changes, but I can always take care of that when the time comes. I have a testimony. I know the scriptures. I know what it takes to repent. I'll see the bishop when it's time, and I'll make the changes later. I'm only young once. For now, I'll go with the flow.' Well, the flow has become a flood and soon will be a torrent, . . . Swimming back upstream to purity against the tides of the world was never easy. It is getting harder and may soon be frighteningly difficult" ("We Must Raise Our Sights," *Ensign,* September 2004, 14).

♥ Read verse 22 with your class and look for Isaiah's concluding invitation. Help class members understand that Isaiah is inviting us to cease from worldliness. Ask, *Have there been times when you have replaced worldly activities for spiritual ones? What difference would it make in your life if you ceased from worldly music, movies, or language?*

Bear your testimony of the importance of

rising above worldly trends. Refer back to the cup of dirt with the man on top of it.

2 NEPHI 13
Nephi Quotes Isaiah 3
About 559–545 BC

1–3, The Lord removes his help and support from Israel because of their wickedness; 4–15, The consequences that come to Israel because of their wickedness; 16–26, The children of Israel are compared to the "haughty daughters of Zion."

Historical Context: Isaiah is speaking to the people of Israel who have made covenants with God, though they are not keeping them. He is warning them that their continual sins will lead to destruction.

Literary Context: One theme that Isaiah uses frequently throughout his writings is destruction and salvation, which he uses to contrast the effects of wickedness versus righteousness. In the case of 2 Nephi chapters 13–14 (Isaiah 3–4), Isaiah refers to destruction in chapter 13 with the removal of the stay and staff of bread and water and the results that follow, and he speaks of salvation in chapter 14 in referring to the glory of the millennial day.

1 For behold, the Lord, the Lord of Hosts, doth take away from Jerusalem, and from Judah, the stay and the staff, the whole staff of bread, and the whole stay of water—

2 The mighty man, and the man of war, the judge, and the prophet, and the prudent, and the ancient;

3 The captain of fifty, and the honorable man, and the counselor, and the cunning artificer, and the eloquent orator.

4 And I will give children unto them to be their princes, and babes shall rule over them.

5 And the people shall be oppressed, every one by

Notes

another, and every one by his neighbor; the child shall behave himself proudly against the ancient, and the base against the honorable.

6 When a man shall take hold of his brother of the house of his father, and shall say: Thou hast clothing, be thou our ruler, and let not this ruin come under thy hand—

7 In that day shall he swear, saying: I will not be a healer; for in my house there is neither bread nor clothing; make me not a ruler of the people.

8 For Jerusalem is ruined, and Judah is fallen, because their tongues and their doings have been against the Lord, to provoke the eyes of his glory.

9 The show of their countenance doth witness against them, and doth declare their sin to be even as Sodom, and they cannot hide it. Wo unto their souls, for they have rewarded evil unto themselves!

10 Say unto the righteous that it is well with them; for they shall eat the fruit of their doings.

11 Wo unto the wicked, for they shall perish; for the reward of their hands shall be upon them!

12 And my people, children are their oppressors, and women rule over them. O my people, they who lead thee cause thee to err and destroy the way of thy paths.

13 The Lord standeth up to plead, and standeth to judge the people.

14 The Lord will enter into judgment with the ancients of his people and the princes thereof; for ye have eaten up the vineyard and the spoil of the poor in your houses.

15 What mean ye? Ye beat my people to pieces, and grind the faces of the poor, saith the Lord God of Hosts.

vv. 1–15 The Lord removes his support from us after a prolonged time of wickedness.

⚡ To help class members understand the words "stay" and "staff," bring various paper cups or blocks with which you can build a tower.

Label one of the pieces "STAY" and one of the other "STAFF." Build the tower making sure the STAY and STAFF blocks are on the bottom and are visible because you will remove them during the lesson so the tower falls.

Discuss with the class what will happen if you remove the STAY and STAFF, then remove the two and watch the tower fall.

After the fall, explain that they will use this object lesson to define the words STAY and STAFF. Write the two words on the board and ask for possible definitions. (In Hebrew, both words can be defined as "support.")

🔍 Read verse 1 and look for how Isaiah is using these two words.

❓ Analyze: Why do you think God would remove His help and support from His people?

🔍 Read verses 8–15 and look for the results that come to the Jews once God removes the stay and the staff. Notice that Isaiah is speaking about destruction and the judgment of God.

16 Moreover, the Lord saith: Because the daughters of Zion are haughty, and walk with stretched-forth necks and wanton eyes, walking and mincing as they go, and making a tinkling with their feet—

17 Therefore the Lord will smite with a scab the crown of the head of the daughters of Zion, and the Lord will discover their secret parts.

18 In that day the Lord will take away the bravery of their tinkling ornaments, and cauls, and round tires like the moon;

19 The chains and the bracelets, and the mufflers;

20 The bonnets, and the ornaments of the legs, and the headbands, and the tablets, and the ear-rings;

21 The rings, and nose jewels;

22 The changeable suits of apparel, and the mantles, and the wimples, and the crisping-pins;

23 The glasses, and the fine linen, and hoods, and the veils.

Notes

24 And it shall come to pass, instead of sweet smell there shall be stink; and instead of a girdle, a rent; and instead of well set hair, baldness; and instead of a stomacher, a girding of sackcloth; burning instead of beauty.

25 Thy men shall fall by the sword and thy mighty in the war.

26 And her gates shall lament and mourn; and she shall be desolate, and shall sit upon the ground.

vv. 16–26 "The Haughty Daughters of Zion." Chasing after material possession will result in heartache and destruction; we should instead define ourselves by our spiritual growth.

The covenant people of God (ourselves included) are always referred to as women in the scriptures, hence the parable of the ten virgins where Jesus is the bridegroom and His covenant people are His bride. In this set of verses, Isaiah will use an analogy of girls—the daughters of Zion—who are overly concerned about their appearance, and their eventual fate is destruction. Isaiah uses this analogy as a warning to those of us who become concerned in meaningless, worldly pursuits. The contrast of their beauty with their destruction is designed to conjure in our minds the image that material pursuits will bring us nothing but heartache.

How does Isaiah describe the haughty daughters of Zion in verses 16, 19–23? You may want to assign a class member to draw some of these descriptions as the verses are read.

What will the Lord do to these haughty daughters of Zion in verses 17, 18, 24–26?

Apply: Help class members understand that these daughters of Zion will be destroyed because of their worldly ways and pursuits. *In what ways are we like these daughters of Zion? Why do you think the constant pursuit of material possessions is so damaging?*

Encourage class members to not allow worldly pursuits, no matter how fashionable or popular, to outpace their spiritual pursuits

like scripture study, missionary preparation, temple attendance, and so forth.

Teaching Tips from Prophets' Lips "As a teacher, you can prepare an environment that invites the Spirit to attend your teaching. Then the Spirit can bear witness of the truthfulness of the principles you teach" (*Teaching, No Greater Call*, 45).

2 NEPHI 14
Nephi Quotes Isaiah 4
About 559–545 BC

1–4, The Lord will cleanse the wicked, including the "haughty daughters of Zion" from the Earth to prepare it for the Millennium; 5–6, The righteous will have a dwelling place of peace and safety on Mount Zion.

Historical Context: Isaiah is speaking to the people of Israel who have made covenants with God, though they are not keeping them. He uses the Millennium as a means to encourage their righteousness.

Literary Context: One theme that Isaiah uses frequently throughout his writings is destruction and salvation, which he uses to contrast the effects of wickedness versus righteousness. Isaiah just spoke of the destruction of the wicked in 2 Nephi 13 and will now speak of the peace of the Millennium to inspire his readers to be righteous.

1 And in that day, seven women shall take hold of one man, saying: We will eat our own bread, and wear our own apparel; only let us be called by thy name to take away our reproach.

2 In that day shall the branch of the Lord be beautiful and glorious; the fruit of the earth excellent and comely to them that are escaped of Israel.

3 And it shall come to pass, they that are left in

Notes

Zion and remain in Jerusalem shall be called holy, every one that is written among the living in Jerusalem—

4 When the Lord shall have washed away the filth of the daughters of Zion, and shall have purged the blood of Jerusalem from the midst thereof by the spirit of judgment and by the spirit of burning.

5 And the Lord will create upon every dwelling-place of mount Zion, and upon her assemblies, a cloud and smoke by day and the shining of a flaming fire by night; for upon all the glory of Zion shall be a defence.

6 And there shall be a tabernacle for a shadow in the daytime from the heat, and for a place of refuge, and a covert from storm and from rain.

vv. 1–6 The Millennium will be a time of peace when we are free from wickedness.

🔍 *Read verse 2–6 and mark or highlight anything that is good about the Millennium.*

♥ Testify to class members that the Millennium will be a time of peace when Christ will reign personally upon the earth. Encourage them to be worthy for the Second Coming so they can dwell with the Savior for a thousand years. Contrast the glory of the Millennium (2 Nephi 14:5–6) with the destruction of the haughty daughters of Zion (2 Nephi 13:16–26). Encourage class members to stay faithful so they can enjoy the peace and glory of the Millennium.

2 NEPHI 15

Nephi Quotes Isaiah 5
About 559–545 BC

1–7, The parable of the vineyard; 8–25, The sins and afflictions Israel to be suffered; 26–30, An ensign to gather the Lord's people.

Historical Background: In chapters 2–5, Isaiah effectively communicates to the people of Israel the consequences that will come to them because of their wickedness. Chapter 5 is especially descriptive of that destruction.

Literary Context: Isaiah continues to use the theme of destruction and salvation. In this chapter, he uses an allegory (a story that teaches an underlying principle) of a vineyard that produces wild grapes. As you study this chapter, note the destruction that will come to Israel as a result of their wickedness, but also consider the salvation promised to Israel through the "ensign" that the Lord promises them despite their wickedness (verses 26–30).

1 And then will I sing to my well-beloved a song of my beloved, touching his vineyard. My well-beloved hath a vineyard in a very fruitful hill.

2 And he fenced it, and gathered out the stones thereof, and planted it with the choicest vine, and built a tower in the midst of it, and also made a wine-press therein; and he looked that it should bring forth grapes, and it brought forth wild grapes.

3 And now, O inhabitants of Jerusalem, and men of Judah, judge, I pray you, betwixt me and my vineyard.

4 What could have been done more to my vineyard that I have not done in it? Wherefore, when I looked that it should bring forth grapes it brought forth wild grapes.

5 And now go to; I will tell you what I will do to my vineyard—I will take away the hedge thereof, and it shall be eaten up; and I will break down the wall thereof, and it shall be trodden down;

6 And I will lay it waste; it shall not be pruned nor digged; but there shall come up briers and thorns; I will also command the clouds that they rain no rain upon it.

7 For the vineyard of the Lord of Hosts is the house of Israel, and the men of Judah his pleasant plant; and he looked for judgment, and behold, oppression; for righteousness, but behold, a cry.

Notes

vv. 1–7 God will always do what he can to save us, but we must do our part.

⚡ Show a good piece of fruit to the class. Break up your class into groups of two or three with a piece of paper for each group. Have written on the board, "The gospel is like this fruit because . . ." Allow the groups time to complete the statement, then request class members to share what they wrote. Explain to your class that the book of Isaiah is often taught through symbols or allegories.

🔑 *Read verses 1–7 and underline each symbol in the story.* After the verses are read, discuss the symbols class members found and what they could represent.

❓ Analyze:
- *What might "planted it with the choicest vine" mean?* (Israel originates from those who are faithful, like Abraham.)
- *What do the wild grapes represent?* (Apostasy of Israel.)
- *What does the first question in verse 4 teach?* (God will do what He can to save us.)
- *If God does all He can to save us, why do some people choose to not follow Him?*

♥ Challenge class members to trust God's will and keep His commandments so that they can become sweet fruit unto the Lord.

8 Wo unto them that join house to house, till there can be no place, that they may be placed alone in the midst of the earth!

9 In mine ears, said the Lord of Hosts, of a truth many houses shall be desolate, and great and fair cities without inhabitant.

10 Yea, ten acres of vineyard shall yield one bath, and the seed of a homer shall yield an ephah.

11 Wo unto them that rise up early in the morning, that they may follow strong drink, that continue until night, and wine inflame them!

12 And the harp, and the viol, the tabret, and pipe, and wine are in their feasts; but they regard not the work of the Lord, neither consider the operation of his hands.

13 Therefore, my people are gone into captivity, because they have no knowledge; and their honorable men are famished, and their multitude dried up with thirst.

14 Therefore, hell hath enlarged herself, and opened her mouth without measure; and their glory, and their multitude, and their pomp, and he that rejoiceth, shall descend into it.

15 And the mean man shall be brought down, and the mighty man shall be humbled, and the eyes of the lofty shall be humbled.

16 But the Lord of Hosts shall be exalted in judgment, and God that is holy shall be sanctified in righteousness.

17 Then shall the lambs feed after their manner, and the waste places of the fat ones shall strangers eat.

18 Wo unto them that draw iniquity with cords of vanity, and sin as it were with a cart rope;

19 That say: Let him make speed, hasten his work, that we may see it; and let the counsel of the Holy One of Israel draw nigh and come, that we may know it.

20 Wo unto them that call evil good, and good evil, that put darkness for light, and light for darkness, that put bitter for sweet, and sweet for bitter!

21 Wo unto the wise in their own eyes and prudent in their own sight!

22 Wo unto the mighty to drink wine, and men of strength to mingle strong drink;

23 Who justify the wicked for reward, and take away the righteousness of the righteous from him!

24 Therefore, as the fire devoureth the stubble, and the flame consumeth the chaff, their root shall be rottenness, and their blossoms shall go up as dust; because they have cast away the law of the Lord of Hosts, and despised the word of the Holy One of Israel.

Notes

25 Therefore, is the anger of the Lord kindled against his people, and he hath stretched forth his hand against them, and hath smitten them; and the hills did tremble, and their carcasses were torn in the midst of the streets. For all this his anger is not turned away, but his hand is stretched out still.

vv. 8–25 By avoiding sin, our lives will become sweet and fulfilling.

⚡ Continue using the fruit that you used for verses 1–7. Explain that, symbolically, sin causes the fruit to become bad.

🔎 Assign the following verses to be read out loud with the class. As class members read each verse, have them look for how the sin in that verse makes our fruit go bad.

❓ Analyze:
   Verses 11, 22—*How does wine and strong drink cause problems in life?*
   Verse 12—*What does it mean to not regard the Lord? How does that make a person prideful?*
   Verse 13—*What would cause them not to have knowledge of the gospel? What is the solution?*
   Verse 15—*What is wrong with being mean?*
   Verse 18—Look at all the footnotes in the Bible for Isaiah 5:18. *What does this have to do with additions?*
   Verse 20—*What are some examples of calling good evil and evil good?*
   Verse 21—Review 2 Nephi 9:28–29.
   Verse 23—Make sure class members read the footnote. *What is wrong with someone taking a bribe?*
   Verse 24—*What are ways that people "cast away the law of the Lord"?*

Note: Isaiah uses the allegory of the vineyard again in 2 Nephi 21 (Isaiah 11) except the tree has been chopped down, presumably because of the wickedness described here in chapter 15 (Isaiah 5).

♥ After reviewing the verses, testify of one or two of the most important ones you learned about, as directed by the Spirit. Share an example of how you have seen that principle in your life. Invite class members to do accordingly.

26 And he will lift up an ensign to the nations from far, and will hiss unto them from the end of the earth; and behold, they shall come with speed swiftly; none shall be weary nor stumble among them.

27 None shall slumber nor sleep; neither shall the girdle of their loins be loosed, nor the latchet of their shoes be broken;

28 Whose arrows shall be sharp, and all their bows bent, and their horses' hoofs shall be counted like flint, and their wheels like a whirlwind, their roaring like a lion.

29 They shall roar like young lions; yea, they shall roar, and lay hold of the prey, and shall carry away safe, and none shall deliver.

30 And in that day they shall roar against them like the roaring of the sea; and if they look unto the land, behold, darkness and sorrow, and the light is darkened in the heavens thereof.

v. 26 Our lives should be an ensign (sign) to others that we live the gospel.

⚡ Tie a white handkerchief or white fabric to a stick and wave it in front of the class. Ask, *What does this signal?*

🔎 *Look for a different signal in verse 26.* Explain that an ensign is often a flag or banner used to signal something.

❓ Analyze: *What does the ensign signal in verse 26?*

❓ Apply: *How can we help gather Israel? What can our examples signal to others? What would be an example of giving a mixed signal to those around us by the way we live?*

♥ Explain that our good example is what often plants the seeds that help others want to

Notes

learn more about the gospel. Challenge class members to always be a good example.

> **Teaching Tips from Prophets' Lips** "In discussing preparation, may I also encourage you to avoid a temptation that faces almost every teacher in the Church; at least it has certainly been my experience. That is the temptation to cover too much material, the temptation to stuff more into the hour—or more into the students—than they can possibly hold!" (Jeffrey R. Holland, "Teaching and Learning in the Church," *Ensign*, June 2007, 88–105).

2 NEPHI 16

Nephi Quotes Isaiah 6
About 559–545 BC

1–4, Isaiah sees the glory of the Lord; 5–7, His sin is purged; 8–13, Isaiah is called to preach in Israel's apostate condition.

Historical Context: Isaiah chapter 6 is widely understood to explain Isaiah's calling as prophet. It is unknown when this calling came, but it seems logical that Isaiah had this vision before he began prophesying, therefore Isaiah chapter 6 should chronologically be placed at the beginning of Isaiah.

Literary Context: Isaiah relates the vision he saw while receiving his call as a prophet. Isaiah uses imagery and symbols to convey heavenly objects and beings that would otherwise be unexplainable. For instance, the fiery coal removed from the alter and placed on Isaiah's tongue was not a literal coal; rather, it represented the atoning power of Christ and His ability to cleanse Isaiah of his imperfections.

1 In the year that king Uzziah died, I saw also the Lord sitting upon a throne, high and lifted up, and his train filled the temple.

2 Above it stood the seraphim; each one had six wings; with twain he covered his face, and with twain he covered his feet, and with twain he did fly.

3 And one cried unto another, and said: Holy, holy, holy, is the Lord of Hosts; the whole earth is full of his glory.

4 And the posts of the door moved at the voice of him that cried, and the house was filled with smoke.

5 Then said I: Wo is unto me! for I am undone; because I am a man of unclean lips; and I dwell in the midst of a people of unclean lips; for mine eyes have seen the King, the Lord of Hosts.

6 Then flew one of the seraphim unto me, having a live coal in his hand, which he had taken with the tongs from off the altar;

7 And he laid it upon my mouth, and said: Lo, this has touched thy lips; and thine iniquity is taken away, and thy sin purged.

8 Also I heard the voice of the Lord, saying: Whom shall I send, and who will go for us? Then I said: Here am I; send me.

vv. 1–8 When we have experienced the Lord's goodness, we naturally want to share it with others.

⚡ *If you just discovered the cure for cancer, what would you do? Would you keep it a secret? Why or why not? Would you only share the secret with close friends and relatives? Why or why not? How are these questions similar to sharing the gospel?* Explain to class members that in this chapter, Isaiah has an experience like this that makes him want to share the gospel.

🔍 Have class members look for how Isaiah feels when he sees the Lord in verses 3–5.

❓ Analyze: *Why isn't Isaiah happy to see the Lord? Was Isaiah a wicked man?*

🔍 Have class members look for something in verses 6–8 that completely changes how Isaiah feels in the Lord's presence.

Notes

❓ Analyze:
- *What changed his mind?*
- *What symbol was used to show Isaiah that his sins had been removed?*
- *What needs to happen to us in order to feel comfortable in God's presence?*

🔍 *Look for what Isaiah is willing to do for the Lord in verse 8.*

❓ Analyze: *What is the connection between the experiences in verse 7 and verse 8?*

❓ Apply: *What does this have to do with the desire of young men, young women, and couples to serve missions? If someone is hesitant to serve a mission, what might they need to experience before they have that same desire?*

💬 Joseph Smith stated, "A man filled with the love of God is not content with blessing his family alone, but ranges through the whole world, anxious to bless the whole human race" (Joseph Smith, *History of the Church,* 4:227).

❤ Share an experience of your own or that of someone else when sharing the gospel changed the other person's life and helped them know God's goodness. This could be an opportune time to invite the local full-time missionaries to relate experiences of their desires to bless other's lives and how they have seen lives change.

9 And he said: Go and tell this people—Hear ye indeed, but they understood not; and see ye indeed, but they perceived not.

10 Make the heart of this people fat, and make their ears heavy, and shut their eyes—lest they see with their eyes, and hear with their ears, and understand with their heart, and be converted and be healed.

vv. 9–10 The Lord only gives us the degree of knowledge we are willing to receive.

🔍 Try to determine what is being expressed in verses 9–10.

✏️ Have class members write in their margins "Matthew 13:12–13." Read those verses together and point out the Joseph Smith Translation (JST) of verse 12. Have them also write "Doctrine and Covenants 82:3" in the margin and discuss how that verse applies. Explain that the Lord will only give people the degree of knowledge that they are willing to receive.

💡 Verses 9–10 may explain why Isaiah's writings are hard to understand. It appears that the Lord is instructing Isaiah to purposefully teach in a way that makes "ears heavy, and shut[s] . . . eyes."

11 Then said I: Lord, how long? And he said: Until the cities be wasted without inhabitant, and the houses without man, and the land be utterly desolate;

12 And the Lord have removed men far away, for there shall be a great forsaking in the midst of the land.

13 But yet there shall be a tenth, and they shall return, and shall be eaten, as a teil-tree, and as an oak whose substance is in them when they cast their leaves; so the holy seed shall be the substance thereof.

2 NEPHI 17

Nephi Quotes Isaiah 7
About 559–545 BC

1–9, The word of the Lord concerning the treacherous alliance of the northern tribes against Judah; 10–16, Prophecy of the Messiah: "a virgin shall conceive"; 17–25, How the Assyrians and Egyptians will afflict the northern tribes.

Historical Context: The nation of Israel, ruled by King Pekah, and the Syrian nation, ruled by King Rezin, are spurned by King Ahaz of Judah because he would not enter into a confederacy with them. These two kings, Pekah and Rezin, unify to attack King Ahaz in Jerusalem. Fearing for his kingdom's safety, King Ahaz desires help from Assyria, which the prophet Isaiah counsels him against.

1 And it came to pass in the days of Ahaz the son of Jotham, the son of Uzziah, king of Judah, that Rezin, king of Syria, and Pekah the son of Remaliah, king of Israel, went up toward Jerusalem to war against it, but could not prevail against it.

2 And it was told the house of David, saying: Syria is confederate with Ephraim. And his heart was moved, and the heart of his people, as the trees of the wood are moved with the wind.

3 Then said the Lord unto Isaiah: Go forth now to meet Ahaz, thou and Shearjashub thy son, at the end of the conduit of the upper pool in the highway of the fuller's field;

4 And say unto him: Take heed, and be quiet; fear not, neither be faint-hearted for the two tails of these smoking firebrands, for the fierce anger of Rezin with Syria, and of the son of Remaliah.

vv. 1–4 "Smoking firebrands."

Verses 1–4 explain how the northern kingdom of Israel had formed a confederacy with the Syrians to attack the Kingdom of Judah which Isaiah was a part of. "Smoking firebrands" are when sticks have been in a fire and later are removed; they still might have hot embers, but the fire has gone out. The firebrands are Isaiah's way of describing these two armies which had combined against the kingdom of Judah. Their strength, though intimidating in the moment, would soon die out and no longer be a great danger.

5 Because Syria, Ephraim, and the son of Remaliah, have taken evil counsel against thee, saying:

6 Let us go up against Judah and vex it, and let us make a breach therein for us, and set a king in the midst of it, yea, the son of Tabeal.

7 Thus saith the Lord God: It shall not stand, neither shall it come to pass.

8 For the head of Syria is Damascus, and the head of Damascus, Rezin; and within threescore and five years shall Ephraim be broken that it be not a people.

vv. 5–8 "Ephraim be broken."

The northern kingdom of Israel was often referred to as Ephraim because they were the leading tribe of the ten tribes and the nation's capital city. Verses 5–8 explain that because of their great betrayal by conspiring with Syria against the kingdom of Judah, they would be "broken that it be not a people" (v. 8). Later the ten tribes were taken away by the Assyrians and now are described as the lost ten tribes.

9 And the head of Ephraim is Samaria, and the head of Samaria is Remaliah's son. If ye will not believe surely ye shall not be established.

10 Moreover, the Lord spake again unto Ahaz, saying:

11 Ask thee a sign of the Lord thy God; ask it either in the depths, or in the heights above.

12 But Ahaz said: I will not ask, neither will I tempt the Lord.

13 And he said: Hear ye now, O house of David; is it a small thing for you to weary men, but will ye weary my God also?

14 Therefore, the Lord himself shall give you a sign—Behold, a virgin shall conceive, and shall bear a son, and shall call his name Immanuel.

15 Butter and honey shall he eat, that he may know to refuse the evil and to choose the good.

16 For before the child shall know to refuse the evil and choose the good, the land that thou abhorrest shall be forsaken of both her kings.

vv. 14–16 Immanuel (God with us).

Look for something extremely miraculous in

Notes

_____

_____

verse 14 with this prophecy concerning Jesus Christ.

✋ Have class members write "Matthew 1:22–25" in their margins and turn there to read how this prophecy was fulfilled.

💡 Note with the class that in Matthew 1:25, that Joseph "knew [Mary] not" till after she had given birth which means that not only would a virgin conceive, but also give birth while still a virgin. Thus, this was necessary to completely fulfill the prophecy.

✏️ Have the class underline the word "Immanuel" in 2 Nephi 17:14 and write in the margin its meaning, "God with us."

❓ Analyze: *How does Jesus fulfill the title "Immanuel" with his life?* Explain that Jesus shows us the goodness of our Heavenly Father in all that He does. Jesus is the manifestation of the Father's love. Being the Son of God, Jesus can also be known as God Himself. For this reason, Jesus dwelling among men was God with man.

vv. 15–16 Footnotes.

💡 For a better understanding of verses 15–16, have class members see the footnotes in Isaiah 7:15a and 16a in the LDS edition of the scriptures.

17 The Lord shall bring upon thee, and upon thy people, and upon thy father's house, days that have not come from the day that Ephraim departed from Judah, the king of Assyria.

18 And it shall come to pass in that day that the Lord shall hiss for the fly that is in the uttermost part of Egypt, and for the bee that is in the land of Assyria.

19 And they shall come, and shall rest all of them in the desolate valleys, and in the holes of the rocks, and upon all thorns, and upon all bushes.

20 In the same day shall the Lord shave with a razor that is hired, by them beyond the river, by the king of Assyria, the head, and the hair of the feet; and it shall also consume the beard.

21 And it shall come to pass in that day, a man shall nourish a young cow and two sheep;

22 And it shall come to pass, for the abundance of milk they shall give he shall eat butter; for butter and honey shall every one eat that is left in the land.

23 And it shall come to pass in that day, every place shall be, where there were a thousand vines at a thousand silverlings, which shall be for briers and thorns.

24 With arrows and with bows shall men come thither, because all the land shall become briers and thorns.

25 And all hills that shall be digged with the mattock, there shall not come thither the fear of briers and thorns; but it shall be for the sending forth of oxen, and the treading of lesser cattle.

vv. 17–15 The ten tribes' afflictions from Assyria.

💡 Explain that verses 17–25 describe how the Assyrians would quickly take all of the ten tribes away. The shaving referred to in verse 20 was a common practice to do to the new slaves of the Assyrians. This was to humiliate them, and also make them identifiable as slaves.

💡 Explain that often the footnotes in the Isaiah chapters found in the Bible are more complete and give more explanation. Have class members read the Isaiah 7 footnotes to better understand these verses.

Teaching Tips from Prophets' Lips "If you accomplish nothing else in your relationship with your students than to help them recognize and follow the promptings of the spirit, you will bless their lives immeasurably and eternally" (Richard G. Scott, *Helping Others to Be Spiritually Led* [address to religious educators, 11 Aug. 1998], 3).

Notes

2 NEPHI 18

Nephi Quotes Isaiah 8
About 559–545 BC

1–8, How the Assyrian nation will come upon Israel; 9–18, The Lord is Israel's defense; 19–22, Counsel should be sought from God.

Historical Context: The nation of Israel, ruled by King Pekah, and the Syrian nation, ruled by King Rezin, are spurned by King Ahaz of Judah because he would not enter into a confederacy with them. These two kings, Pekah and Rezin, unify to attack King Ahaz in Jerusalem. Fearing for his kingdom's safety, King Ahaz desires help from Assyria, which the prophet Isaiah counsels him against.

1 Moreover, the word of the Lord said unto me: Take thee a great roll, and write in it with a man's pen, concerning Maher-shalal-hash-baz.

2 And I took unto me faithful witnesses to record, Uriah the priest, and Zechariah the son of Jeberechiah.

3 And I went unto the prophetess; and she conceived and bare a son. Then said the Lord to me: Call his name, Maher-shalal-hash-baz.

4 For behold, the child shall not have knowledge to cry, My father, and my mother, before the riches of Damascus and the spoil of Samaria shall be taken away before the king of Assyria.

vv. 1–4, 18 Scripture names can teach of the Lord.

⚡ Before class, search the meaning of some of the class members' names and their origin. Depending on the size of your class, you might be able to find out the meaning of each class member's name. Share your findings with the class. Ask, *Why would you want your child's name to have a specific meaning?*

🔑 *Look for what Isaiah is saying about names in verse 18.* (He is saying that his own name

and the names of his children have meanings that are to teach Israel.)

✋ Assign half of your class to look for the name of one of Isaiah's children in 2 Nephi 18:1–3, and the other half of the class to look in Isaiah 7:3. You may want to hint that they look in the footnotes. Explain that these names point to the pending crisis of the people of Judah and their need for God's help. When class members are finished with this exercise, share that Isaiah's name also has a meaning, "Jehovah saves."

5 The Lord spake also unto me again, saying:

6 Forasmuch as this people refuseth the waters of Shiloah that go softly, and rejoice in Rezin and Remaliah's son;

7 Now therefore, behold, the Lord bringeth up upon them the waters of the river, strong and many, even the king of Assyria and all his glory; and he shall come up over all his channels, and go over all his banks.

8 And he shall pass through Judah; he shall overflow and go over, he shall reach even to the neck; and the stretching out of his wings shall fill the breadth of thy land, O Immanuel.

9 Associate yourselves, O ye people, and ye shall be broken in pieces; and give ear all ye of far countries; gird yourselves, and ye shall be broken in pieces; gird yourselves, and ye shall be broken in pieces.

10 Take counsel together, and it shall come to naught; speak the word, and it shall not stand; for God is with us.

11 For the Lord spake thus to me with a strong hand, and instructed me that I should not walk in the way of this people, saying:

12 Say ye not, A confederacy, to all to whom this people shall say, A confederacy; neither fear ye their fear, nor be afraid.

13 Sanctify the Lord of Hosts himself, and let him be your fear, and let him be your dread.

Notes

14 And he shall be for a sanctuary; but for a stone of stumbling, and for a rock of offense to both the houses of Israel, for a gin and a snare to the inhabitants of Jerusalem.

💡 V. 14: Have class members cross reference Romans 9:32–33 and 1 Peter 2:7–8 in the margin and then study those references.

15 And many among them shall stumble and fall, and be broken, and be snared, and be taken.

16 Bind up the testimony, seal the law among my disciples.

17 And I will wait upon the Lord, that hideth his face from the house of Jacob, and I will look for him.

18 Behold, I and the children whom the Lord hath given me are for signs and for wonders in Israel from the Lord of Hosts, which dwelleth in Mount Zion.

19 And when they shall say unto you: Seek unto them that have familiar spirits, and unto wizards that peep and mutter— should not a people seek unto their God for the living to hear from the dead?

20 To the law and to the testimony; and if they speak not according to this word, it is because there is no light in them.

vv. 19–20 We should seek guidance from Godly sources or knowledge.

⚡ When we have questions, where should be go for guidance? Have class members list sources of guidance on the board.

🔎 Invite the class to look for other sources of guidance in verses 19–20.

💡 Explain that the people of King Ahaz are under attack from a force that he thinks will destroy him. Isaiah says to trust in God and instead Ahaz seeks help beyond Isaiah.

❓ Apply: What are some counterfeit sources of guidance that Satan tries to trick people with today?

🔎 Look for why those are bad sources in verse 20.

❓ Analyze: Even if the guidance from those sources might seem remarkable, why should we not seek guidance from them? Explain that Satan's whole purpose is to seek our misery (2 Nephi 2:27) so his guidance will lead to that destination. On the other hand, God's purpose is our happiness (2 Nephi 2:25) so He will guide us in a way that leads to success.

❤ Share an experience you have had with guidance from those spiritual sources, or invite a class member to share an experience. Encourage class members to seek spiritual guidance.

21 And they shall pass through it hardly bestead and hungry; and it shall come to pass that when they shall be hungry, they shall fret themselves, and curse their king and their God, and look upward.

22 And they shall look unto the earth and behold trouble, and darkness, dimness of anguish, and shall be driven to darkness.

2 NEPHI 19

Nephi Quotes Isaiah 9
About 559–544 BC

1–7, Isaiah prophesies of Christ; 8–21, Isaiah speaks of the wickedness of nations.

Historical Context: The strife between the nations of Judah (King Ahaz), Israel (King Pekah), and Syria (King Rezin) continue. Isaiah warns and admonishes King Ahaz of Judah of the impending destruction of the nation of Israel.

Literary Context: Isaiah speaks Messianically by prophesying of the coming of Jesus Christ. He uses Palestinian geography to teach where the Messiah

Notes

will minister. In Old Testament times, Zebulun and Naphtali shared a border in the New Testament province of Galilee (see 2 Nephi 19:1–2).

1 Nevertheless, the dimness shall not be such as was in her vexation, when at first he lightly afflicted the land of Zebulun, and the land of Naphtali, and afterwards did more grievously afflict by the way of the Red Sea beyond Jordan in Galilee of the nations.

2 The people that walked in darkness have seen a great light; they that dwell in the land of the shadow of death, upon them hath the light shined.

3 Thou hast multiplied the nation, and increased the joy—they joy before thee according to the joy in harvest, and as men rejoice when they divide the spoil.

4 For thou hast broken the yoke of his burden, and the staff of his shoulder, the rod of his oppressor.

5 For every battle of the warrior is with confused noise, and garments rolled in blood; but this shall be with burning and fuel of fire.

6 For unto us a child is born, unto us a son is given; and the government shall be upon his shoulder; and his name shall be called, Wonderful, Counselor, The Mighty God, The Everlasting Father, The Prince of Peace.

7 Of the increase of government and peace there is no end, upon the throne of David, and upon his kingdom to order it, and to establish it with judgment and with justice from henceforth, even forever. The zeal of the Lord of Hosts will perform this.

vv. 1–7 Isaiah prophesies of Christ.

🔑 Write on the board, "What will Jesus do?" and "What will Jesus be called?" Explain that Isaiah is prophesying about the coming of Jesus. Invite class members to read verses 1–7, looking for the answers to both of the questions and then write those answers on the board.

❓ Analyze with your class the answers they found.

♥ Share your testimony of the Savior.

8 The Lord sent his word unto Jacob and it hath lighted upon Israel.

9 And all the people shall know, even Ephraim and the inhabitants of Samaria, that say in the pride and stoutness of heart:

10 The bricks are fallen down, but we will build with hewn stones; the sycamores are cut down, but we will change them into cedars.

11 Therefore the Lord shall set up the adversaries of Rezin against him, and join his enemies together;

12 The Syrians before and the Philistines behind; and they shall devour Israel with open mouth. For all this his anger is not turned away, but his hand is stretched out still.

13 For the people turneth not unto him that smiteth them, neither do they seek the Lord of Hosts.

14 Therefore will the Lord cut off from Israel head and tail, branch and rush in one day.

15 The ancient, he is the head; and the prophet that teacheth lies, he is the tail.

16 For the leaders of this people cause them to err; and they that are bled of them are destroyed.

17 Therefore the Lord shall have no joy in their young men, neither shall have mercy on their fatherless and widows; for every one of them is a hypocrite and an evildoer, and every mouth speaketh folly. For all this his anger is not turned away, but his hand is stretched out still.

18 For wickedness burneth as the fire; it shall devour the briers and thorns, and shall kindle in the thickets of the forests, and they shall mount up like the lifting up of smoke.

19 Through the wrath of the Lord of Hosts is the land darkened, and the people shall be as the fuel of the fire; no man shall spare his brother.

Notes

20 And he shall snatch on the right hand and be hungry; and he shall eat on the left hand and they shall not be satisfied; they shall eat every man the flesh of his own arm—

21 Manasseh, Ephraim; and Ephraim, Manasseh; they together shall be against Judah. For all this his anger is not turned away, but his hand is stretched out still.

Teaching Tips from Prophets' Lips "We must . . . get our teachers to speak out of their hearts rather than out of their books, to communicate their love for the Lord and this precious work and somehow it will catch fire in the hearts of those they teach" (*Teachings of Gordon B. Hinckley,* 1997, 619–20).

2 NEPHI 20

Nephi Quotes Isaiah 10
About 559–544 BC

1–11, The nation of Assyria will be used to destroy the wicked nation of Israel; 12–16, The Assyrians will glory in their own might but will be destroyed; 17–34, Despite their wickedness and destruction, the Lord will gather Israel.

Historical Context: The Assyrian nation conquers Israel in a brutal manner and scatters its people.

Literary Context: The Lord, through Isaiah, speaks directly to the King of Assyria explaining why they had the power to conquer the people of Israel.

1 Wo unto them that decree unrighteous decrees, and that write grievousness which they have prescribed;

2 To turn away the needy from judgment, and to take away the right from the poor of my people, that widows may be their prey, and that they may rob the fatherless!

v. 2 God's wrath is toward societies that do not help the needy.

⚡ *How does God feel about those in need, like the fatherless and widows?* For the answer, direct your class to James 1:27. Discuss the verse with them.

🔍 *Look for who the Israelites are neglecting in 2 Nephi 20:2.*

❓ Analyze: *Why does God care so much about the fatherless and widows?* (Matthew 25:40.) *What are things we can do to help those in need?*

❤ Challenge class members to look for ways to help those in need.

3 And what will ye do in the day of visitation, and in the desolation which shall come from far? to whom will ye flee for help? and where will ye leave your glory?

4 Without me they shall bow down under the prisoners, and they shall fall under the slain. For all this his anger is not turned away, but his hand is stretched out still.

5 O Assyrian, the rod of mine anger, and the staff in their hand is their indignation.

6 I will send him against a hypocritical nation, and against the people of my wrath will I give him a charge to take the spoil, and to take the prey, and to tread them down like the mire of the streets.

7 Howbeit he meaneth not so, neither doth his heart think so; but in his heart it is to destroy and cut off nations not a few.

8 For he saith: Are not my a princes altogether kings?

9 Is not Calno as Carchemish? Is not Hamath as Arpad? Is not Samaria as Damascus?

10 As my hand hath founded the kingdoms of the idols, and whose graven images did excel them of Jerusalem and of Samaria;

11 Shall I not, as I have done unto Samaria and her idols, so do to Jerusalem and to her idols?

Notes

12 Wherefore it shall come to pass that when the Lord hath performed his whole work upon Mount Zion and upon Jerusalem, I will punish the fruit of the stout heart of the king of Assyria, and the glory of his high looks.

13 For he saith: By the strength of my hand and by my wisdom I have done these things; for I am prudent; and I have moved the borders of the people, and have robbed their treasures, and I have put down the inhabitants like a valiant man;

14 And my hand hath found as a nest the riches of the people; and as one gathereth eggs that are left have I gathered all the earth; and there was none that moved the wing, or opened the mouth, or peeped.

15 Shall the ax boast itself against him that heweth therewith? Shall the saw magnify itself against him that shaketh it? As if the rod should shake itself against them that lift it up, or as if the staff should lift up itself as if it were no wood!

v. 15 We should give credit to God for any good we do.

⚡ Before class, ask a class member with musical ability to prepare and perform some music on the piano or another musical instrument. After they have performed in class, instead of thanking the person, ignore him or her, but comment on how wonderful the musical instrument was, and what a wonderful job it did. Give enough praise to the instrument—still ignoring the performer—to the point that the class will think it is strange. Ask class members what you are doing wrong.

🔎 Look for why the Lord is upset with the Israelites in verse 15.

❓ Analyze: *What does this teach about being an instrument in God's hands? If we are instruments in God's hands, who should get the credit if we do something remarkable?*

❤ Have class members think of something they are talented with. Ask them what God had to do with that talent. Challenge class members to give credit to God the next time they are complimented on it.

16 Therefore shall the Lord, the Lord of Hosts, send among his fat ones, leanness; and under his glory he shall kindle a burning like the burning of a fire.

17 And the light of Israel shall be for a fire, and his Holy One for a flame, and shall burn and shall devour his thorns and his briers in one day;

18 And shall consume the glory of his forest, and of his fruitful field, both soul and body; and they shall be as when a standard-bearer fainteth.

19 And the rest of the trees of his forest shall be few, that a child may write them.

20 And it shall come to pass in that day, that the remnant of Israel, and such as are escaped of the house of Jacob, shall no more again stay upon him that smote them, but shall stay upon the Lord, the Holy One of Israel, in truth.

21 The remnant shall return, yea, even the remnant of Jacob, unto the mighty God.

22 For though thy people Israel be as the sand of the sea, yet a remnant of them shall return; the consumption decreed shall overflow with righteousness.

23 For the Lord God of Hosts shall make a consumption, even determined in all the land.

24 Therefore, thus saith the Lord God of Hosts: O my people that dwellest in Zion, be not afraid of the Assyrian; he shall smite thee with a rod, and shall lift up his staff against thee, after the manner of Egypt.

25 For yet a very little while, and the indignation shall cease, and mine anger in their destruction.

26 And the Lord of Hosts shall stir up a scourge for him according to the slaughter of Midian at the rock of Oreb; and as his rod was upon the sea so shall he lift it up after the manner of Egypt.

27 And it shall come to pass in that day that his

Notes

burden shall be taken away from off thy shoulder, and his yoke from off thy neck, and the yoke shall be destroyed because of the anointing.

28 He is come to Aiath, he is passed to Migron; at Michmash he hath laid up his carriages.

29 They are gone over the passage; they have taken up their lodging at Geba; Ramath is afraid; Gibeah of Saul is fled.

30 Lift up the voice, O daughter of Gallim; cause it to be heard unto Laish, O poor Anathoth.

31 Madmenah is removed; the inhabitants of Gebim gather themselves to flee.

32 As yet shall he remain at Nob that day; he shall shake his hand against the mount of the daughter of Zion, the hill of Jerusalem.

33 Behold, the Lord, the Lord of Hosts shall lop the bough with terror; and the high ones of stature shall be hewn down; and the haughty shall be humbled.

34 And he shall cut down the thickets of the forests with iron, and Lebanon shall fall by a mighty one.

2 NEPHI 21

Nephi Quotes Isaiah 11
About 559–544 BC

1–5, Isaiah prophecies of the Messiah; 6–9, He speaks of the Millennium; 10–16, The latter-day gathering is described.

Historical Context: This chapter is written during the Assyrian defeat of Israel and siege of Judah.

Literary Context: Isaiah uses dualism as a means of prophesying about two future events, the coming of the Messiah, and the restoration of the gospel in the last days. He uses the imagery of a stem (or stump) to represent the destruction and apostasy of the covenant people and a rod and branch to represent the redemption and salvation. He also uses the imagery of an ensign as a means of gathering.

1 And there shall come forth a rod out of the stem of Jesse, and a branch shall grow out of his roots.

2 And the Spirit of the Lord shall rest upon him, the spirit of wisdom and understanding, the spirit of counsel and might, the spirit of knowledge and of the fear of the Lord;

3 And shall make him of quick understanding in the fear of the Lord; and he shall not judge after the sight of his eyes, neither reprove after the hearing of his ears.

4 But with righteousness shall he judge the poor, and reprove with equity for the meek of the earth; and he shall smite the earth with the rod of his mouth, and with the breath of his lips shall he slay the wicked.

5 And righteousness shall be the girdle of his loins, and faithfulness the girdle of his reins.

vv. 1–5 We should never judge on the outward appearance.

⚡ Show a picture of Moroni appearing at Joseph Smith's bedside. Explain that when Moroni appeared, he considered one chapter so important that he quoted the whole chapter three times to Joseph Smith. Ask if anyone might know what chapter he quoted. To find out, have class members look up Joseph Smith—History 1:40 to get the answer (Isaiah 11). As class members study the chapter, ask them to look for what is so important here that Moroni would quote it.

🔎 *Look for what verse 1 teaches about Christ.*

❓ Analyze: *Why are you glad that Christ will be the judge rather than someone else?*

🔎 *Search for another reason in verses 2–4 that we should be glad it will be the Lord judging us.*

❓ Analyze: *Since we are trying to be like Jesus, what do these verses teach about the way we should judge?*

Notes

♥ Challenge class members to avoid judging others because we don't have the whole perspective. Express your gratitude that Christ will be your judge.

6 The wolf also shall dwell with the lamb, and the leopard shall lie down with the kid, and the calf and the young lion and fatling together; and a little child shall lead them.

7 And the cow and the bear shall feed; their young ones shall lie down together; and the lion shall eat straw like the ox.

8 And the sucking child shall play on the hole of the asp, and the weaned child shall put his hand on the cockatrice's den.

9 They shall not hurt nor destroy in all my holy mountain, for the earth shall be full of the knowledge of the Lord, as the waters cover the sea.

vv. 6–9 Characteristics of the Millennium.

✋ Have class members verbally list everything they know about the Millennium while a volunteer writes their responses on the board.

🔍 *Look for some things that might have been missed as we read verses 6–9.*

❓ Analyze: *What seems to be the element that causes this peace during the Millennium?* (Verse 9.)

💬 Joseph Smith taught, "Friendship is one of the grand fundamental principles of "Mormonism"; [it is designed] to revolutionize and civilize the world, and cause wars and contentions to cease and men to become friends and brothers. Even the wolf and the lamb shall dwell together; the leopard shall lie down with the kid, the calf, the young lion and the fatling; and a little child shall lead them; the bear and the cow shall lie down together, and the sucking child shall play on the hole of the asp, and the weaned child shall play on the cockatrice's den; and they shall not hurt or destroy in all my holy mountain, saith

the Lord of hosts" (*Teachings of the Prophet Joseph Smith*, sel. Joseph Fielding Smith [Salt Lake City: Deseret Book, 1938], 316).

♥ Explain that as we preach "the knowledge of the Lord," and it is accepted, the earth will grow in peace. Challenge class members to share the knowledge of the Lord with others.

10 And in that day there shall be a root of Jesse, which shall stand for an ensign of the people; to it shall the Gentiles seek; and his rest shall be glorious.

11 And it shall come to pass in that day that the Lord shall set his hand again the second time to recover the remnant of his people which shall be left, from Assyria, and from Egypt, and from Pathros, and from Cush, and from Elam, and from Shinar, and from Hamath, and from the islands of the sea.

12 And he shall set up an ensign for the nations, and shall assemble the outcasts of Israel, and gather together the dispersed of Judah from the four corners of the earth.

vv. 10 & 12 "Ensign for the nations."

💡 You may want to use the teaching idea in 2 Nephi 15:26, if you did not already use it earlier. The lesson teaches what an "ensign" is and its significance.

13 The envy of Ephraim also shall depart, and the adversaries of Judah shall be cut off; Ephraim shall not envy Judah, and Judah shall not vex Ephraim.

14 But they shall fly upon the shoulders of the Philistines towards the west; they shall spoil them of the east together; they shall lay their hand upon Edom and Moab; and the children of Ammon shall obey them.

15 And the Lord shall utterly destroy the tongue of the Egyptian sea; and with his mighty wind he shall shake his hand over the river, and shall

Notes

smite it in the seven streams, and make men go over dry shod.

16 And there shall be a highway for the remnant of his people which shall be left, from Assyria, like as it was to Israel in the day that he came up out of the land of Egypt.

> **Teaching Tips from Prophets' Lips** "Questions can encourage students to participate in discussions. They can help learners understand a principle, think about it more deeply, and relate it to their lives . . . . Ask questions that encourage thoughtful comments and help individuals truly ponder the gospel" (*Teaching, No Greater Call*, 63).

2 NEPHI 22

Nephi Quotes Isaiah 12
About 559–544 BC

1–6, The praise of the Lord in the Millennium.

Literary Context: Amid the previous messages of destruction, Isaiah offers a message of hope by prophesying of the Millennium.

1 And in that day thou shalt say: O Lord, I will praise thee; though thou wast angry with me thine anger is turned away, and thou comfortedest me.

2 Behold, God is my salvation; I will trust, and not be afraid; for the Lord Jehovah is my strength and my song; he also has become my salvation.

3 Therefore, with joy shall ye draw water out of the wells of salvation.

4 And in that day shall ye say: Praise the Lord, call upon his name, declare his doings among the people, make mention that his name is exalted.

5 Sing unto the Lord; for he hath done excellent things; this is known in all the earth.

6 Cry out and shout, thou inhabitant of Zion; for

great is the Holy One of Israel in the midst of thee.

vv. 1–6 Praising the Lord.

✋ You may want to use the teaching idea for praising that was used in 1 Nephi 1:14–15, or review it.

✎ Have class members underline all of Isaiah's reasons why we should praise the Lord in verses 1–6. Have them share what they underlined.

v. 2 Jehovah.

💡 *What is unique about the name of the Lord in verse 2?* To help class members discover the importance of the name Jehovah, have them look at the footnotes for Isaiah 12:2 and also see the Bible Dictionary for "Jehovah." Read and study those references together.

2 NEPHI 23

Nephi Quotes Isaiah 13
About 559–544 BC

1–4, The Lord will gather a great army against Babylon; 5–11, The fear of the people of Babylon; 12–22, The destruction of Babylon is prophesied.

Historical Context: Isaiah prophesies dualistically, meaning as he prophesies about one specific city or people of his day, he is also prophesying about a future event of the last days. In the case of 2 Nephi 23, Isaiah is prophesying about the destruction of Babylon but also offers warning to the people of the latter days at the time of the Second Coming.

1 The burden of Babylon, which Isaiah the son of Amoz did see.

2 Lift ye up a banner upon the high mountain, exalt the voice unto them, shake the hand, that they may go into the gates of the nobles.

Notes

3 I have commanded my sanctified ones, I have also called my mighty ones, for mine anger is not upon them that rejoice in my highness.

4 The noise of the multitude in the mountains like as of a great people, a tumultuous noise of the kingdoms of nations gathered together, the Lord of Hosts mustereth the hosts of the battle.

5 They come from a far country, from the end of heaven, yea, the Lord, and the weapons of his indignation, to destroy the whole land.

6 Howl ye, for the day of the Lord is at hand; it shall come as a destruction from the Almighty.

7 Therefore shall all hands be faint, every man's heart shall melt;

8 And they shall be afraid; pangs and sorrows shall take hold of them; they shall be amazed one at another; their faces shall be as flames.

9 Behold, the day of the Lord cometh, cruel both with wrath and fierce anger, to lay the land desolate; and he shall destroy the sinners thereof out of it.

10 For the stars of heaven and the constellations thereof shall not give their light; the sun shall be darkened in his going forth, and the moon shall not cause her light to shine.

11 And I will punish the world for evil, and the wicked for their iniquity; I will cause the arrogancy of the proud to cease, and will lay down the haughtiness of the terrible.

12 I will make a man more precious than fine gold; even a man than the golden wedge of Ophir.

13 Therefore, I will shake the heavens, and the earth shall remove out of her place, in the wrath of the Lord of Hosts, and in the day of his fierce anger.

14 And it shall be as the chased roe, and as a sheep that no man taketh up; and they shall every man turn to his own people, and flee every one into his own land.

15 Every one that is proud shall be thrust through; yea, and every one that is joined to the wicked shall fall by the sword.

16 Their children also shall be dashed to pieces before their eyes; their houses shall be spoiled and their wives ravished.

17 Behold, I will stir up the Medes against them, which shall not regard silver and gold, nor shall they delight in it.

18 Their bows shall also dash the young men to pieces; and they shall have no pity on the fruit of the womb; their eyes shall not spare children.

19 And Babylon, the glory of kingdoms, the beauty of the Chaldees' excellency, shall be as when God overthrew Sodom and Gomorrah.

20 It shall never be inhabited, neither shall it be dwelt in from generation to generation: neither shall the Arabian pitch tent there; neither shall the shepherds make their fold there.

21 But wild beasts of the desert shall lie there; and their houses shall be full of doleful creatures; and owls shall dwell there, and satyrs shall dance there.

22 And the wild beasts of the islands shall cry in their desolate houses, and dragons in their pleasant palaces; and her time is near to come, and her day shall not be prolonged. For I will destroy her speedily; yea, for I will be merciful unto my people, but the wicked shall perish.

vv. 1–22 The destruction of Babylon will be like the destruction of those in the last days who are not prepared for the Second Coming.

Read verses 4–7, 9, 15, 16, 18, and ask, *Would you like to be alive during what is described in these verses?* Explain that this is what the Second Coming will be like for those who are not prepared.

Note: To view the contrast of the peace that comes to the righteous at the time of the Second Coming, refer to 2 Nephi 24:1–3.

Teaching Tips from Prophets' Lips "Every principle God has revealed carries its own convictions of its truth to the human mind" (Brigham Young, *Journal of Discourses*, 9:149).

Notes

2 NEPHI 24

Nephi Quotes Isaiah 14
About 559–544 BC

1–11, A contrast is drawn between the destruction of the wicked (Babylon) and the protection of the righteous; 12–16, In the premortal life, Lucifer fell from heaven; 17–32, In the end, Israel will conquer Babylon.

Historical Context: The nation of Assyria falls and is conquered by the Babylonians, a wicked and idolatrous nation. He prophesies of their wickedness and depravity.

Literary Context: Isaiah personifies Lucifer and draws a connection between him and Babylon in order to define the spiritual state of Babylon.

1 For the Lord will have mercy on Jacob, and will yet choose Israel, and set them in their own land; and the strangers shall be joined with them, and they shall cleave to the house of Jacob.

2 And the people shall take them and bring them to their place; yea, from far unto the ends of the earth; and they shall return to their lands of promise. And the house of Israel shall possess them, and the land of the Lord shall be for servants and handmaids; and they shall take them captives unto whom they were captives; and they shall rule over their oppressors.

3 And it shall come to pass in that day that the Lord shall give thee rest, from thy sorrow, and from thy fear, and from the hard bondage wherein thou wast made to serve.

vv. 1–3 There is peace that comes to us if we are ready for the Second Coming.

🔑 Read verses 1–3 and contrast the message of destruction with the message of mercy, peace, and rest. Testify that there is peace that comes through preparation.

4 And it shall come to pass in that day, that thou shalt take up this proverb against the king of Babylon, and say: How hath the oppressor ceased, the golden city ceased!

5 The Lord hath broken the staff of the wicked, the scepters of the rulers.

6 He who smote the people in wrath with a continual stroke, he that ruled the nations in anger, is persecuted, and none hindereth.

7 The whole earth is at rest, and is quiet; they break forth into singing.

8 Yea, the fir-trees rejoice at thee, and also the cedars of Lebanon, saying: Since thou art laid down no feller is come up against us.

9 Hell from beneath is moved for thee to meet thee at thy coming; it stirreth up the dead for thee, even all the chief ones of the earth; it hath raised up from their thrones all the kings of the nations.

10 All they shall speak and say unto thee: Art thou also become weak as we? Art thou become like unto us?

11 Thy pomp is brought down to the grave; the noise of thy viols is not heard; the worm is spread under thee, and the worms cover thee.

12 How art thou fallen from heaven, O Lucifer, son of the morning! Art thou cut down to the ground, which did weaken the nations!

13 For thou hast said in thy heart: I will ascend into heaven, I will exalt my throne above the stars of God; I will sit also upon the mount of the congregation, in the sides of the north;

14 I will ascend above the heights of the clouds; I will be like the Most High.

15 Yet thou shalt be brought down to hell, to the sides of the pit.

16 They that see thee shall narrowly look upon thee, and shall consider thee, and shall say: Is this the man that made the earth to tremble, that did shake kingdoms?

Notes

vv. 12–16 In the premortal life, Lucifer was cast out of heaven because of his selfish interests.

⚡ Bring or wear an eye patch to class (if you don't have one then you can substitute it with a bandana or piece of gauze). As class members inquire why you have an eye patch, tell them you have an "eye problem." Once class begins, explain that Lucifer has an "I" problem. Explain that Lucifer is Satan's pre-earth name and that he was cast out of heaven because of his rebellion. Ask, *What caused Lucifer to rebel?*

🔍 Read verses 12–14 and look for Lucifer's "I" problem.

❓ Analyze: *What was Satan's "I" problem? What is wrong with his desire?* (Point out that it is not necessarily *what* Lucifer wanted—since we all have the opportunity to become "like the Most High" if we prove faithful in this life—but *why* he wanted it that was so wrong.)

💬 Joseph Smith stated, "Now in this world, mankind are naturally selfish, ambitious and striving to excel one above another; yet some are willing to build up others as well as themselves . . . And this was the case with Lucifer when he fell. He sought for things which were unlawful. Hence he was sent down, and it is said he drew many away with him" (*Teachings of the Prophet Joseph Smith*, 297).

❤ Contrast Lucifer with Jehovah, who wanted to give the glory to the Father (see Moses 4:1–4) and testify that Jesus Christ unselfishly sacrificed himself so we could succeed and return to Heavenly Father.

17 And made the world as a wilderness, and destroyed the cities thereof, and opened not the house of his prisoners?

18 All the kings of the nations, yea, all of them, lie in glory, every one of them in his own house.

19 But thou art cast out of thy grave like an abominable branch, and the remnant of those that are slain, thrust through with a sword, that go down to the stones of the pit; as a carcass trodden under feet.

20 Thou shalt not be joined with them in burial, because thou hast destroyed thy land and slain thy people; the seed of evil-doers shall never be renowned.

21 Prepare slaughter for his children for the iniquities of their fathers, that they do not rise, nor possess the land, nor fill the face of the world with cities.

22 For I will rise up against them, saith the Lord of Hosts, and cut off from Babylon the name, and remnant, and son, and nephew, saith the Lord.

23 I will also make it a possession for the bittern, and pools of water; and I will sweep it with the besom of destruction, saith the Lord of Hosts.

24 The Lord of Hosts hath sworn, saying: Surely as I have thought, so shall it come to pass; and as I have purposed, so shall it stand—

25 That I will bring the Assyrian in my land, and upon my mountains tread him under foot; then shall his yoke depart from off them, and his burden depart from off their shoulders.

26 This is the purpose that is purposed upon the whole earth; and this is the hand that is stretched out upon all nations.

27 For the Lord of Hosts hath purposed, and who shall disannul? And his hand is stretched out, and who shall turn it back?

28 In the year that king Ahaz died was this burden.

29 Rejoice not thou, whole Palestina, because the rod of him that smote thee is broken; for out of the serpent's root shall come forth a cockatrice, and his fruit shall be a fiery flying serpent.

30 And the first-born of the poor shall feed, and the needy shall lie down in safety; and I will kill thy root with famine, and he shall slay thy remnant.

31 Howl, O gate; cry, O city; thou, whole Palestina, art dissolved; for there shall come from the

Notes

north a smoke, and none shall be alone in his appointed times.

32 What shall then answer the messengers of the nations? That the Lord hath founded Zion, and the poor of his people shall trust in it.

2 NEPHI 25

"We Preach of Christ"
About 559–545 BC

1–8, Nephi speaks of why he includes Isaiah's words in his record; 9–20, The Jews will reject the Messiah, be scattered, then finally be persuaded to believe in Him; 21–30, Nephi's words are to direct all to believe in Christ.

1 Now I, Nephi, do speak somewhat concerning the words which I have written, which have been spoken by the mouth of Isaiah. For behold, Isaiah spake many things which were hard for many of my people to understand; for they know not concerning the manner of prophesying among the Jews.

2 For I, Nephi, have not taught them many things concerning the manner of the Jews; for their works were works of darkness, and their doings were doings of abominations.

3 Wherefore, I write unto my people, unto all those that shall receive hereafter these things which I write, that they may know the judgments of God, that they come upon all nations, according to the word which he hath spoken.

4 Wherefore, hearken, O my people, which are of the house of Israel, and give ear unto my words; for because the words of Isaiah are not plain unto you, nevertheless they are plain unto all those that are filled with the spirit of prophecy. But I give unto you a prophecy, according to the spirit which is in me; wherefore I shall prophesy according to the plainness which hath been with me from the time that I came out from Jerusalem

with my father; for behold, my soul delighteth in plainness unto my people, that they may learn.

5 Yea, and my soul delighteth in the words of Isaiah, for I came out from Jerusalem, and mine eyes hath beheld the things of the Jews, and I know that the Jews do understand the things of the prophets, and there is none other people that understand the things which were spoken unto the Jews like unto them, save it be that they are taught after the manner of the things of the Jews.

6 But behold, I, Nephi, have not taught my children after the manner of the Jews; but behold, I, of myself, have dwelt at Jerusalem, wherefore I know concerning the regions round about; and I have made mention unto my children concerning the judgments of God, which hath come to pass among the Jews, unto my children, according to all that which Isaiah hath spoken, and I do not write them.

7 But behold, I proceed with mine own prophecy, according to my plainness; in the which I know that no man can err; nevertheless, in the days that the prophecies of Isaiah shall be fulfilled men shall know of a surety, at the times when they shall come to pass.

8 Wherefore, they are of worth unto the children of men, and he that supposeth that they are not, unto them will I speak particularly, and confine the words unto mine own people; for I know that they shall be of great worth unto them in the last days; for in that day shall they understand them; wherefore, for their good have I written them.

vv. 1–8 How to unlock Isaiah's writings.

⚡ Bring a combination lock to class and lock it to something in the classroom. Discuss with your class that Isaiah's writings are considered very difficult to understand. Ask a class member what is needed to unlock the combination lock. Explain that just like individuals need the combination to unfasten the lock, they also need additional background information to unlock Isaiah's writings. Nephi

Notes

outlines those keys to understanding Isaiah in verses 1–6.

🔍 In verses 1, 4, 5, and 6, have class members look for the key to understanding Isaiah better. The following is a suggestion of the keys:

Verse 1 "manner of prophesying among the Jews"—The Jewish way of prophesying can be very different; for instance, they will often teach using many symbols rather than literal declarations.

Verse 4 "filled with the spirit of prophecy"—one needs the spirit of personal revelation. Revelation 19:10 is a great cross reference for this.

Verse 5 "taught after the manner of the things of the Jews"—the better you know Jewish customs and culture, the better you understand Isaiah's teachings.

Verse 6 "know concerning the regions round about"—it helps to understand the geography and locations that are referred to.

Verse 6 "judgments of God, which hath come to pass"—it helps to know Jewish history of all they have been through as a people.

✏️ Invite class members to mark in their scriptures the main idea next to each of those verses, such as Personal Revelation, Culture, Geography, History.

🔍 Look for two prophecies about Isaiah's teaching in the last days in verse 8.

❓ Analyze: Have we fulfilled those two prophecies yet? What would it take for us to fulfill them?

❤️ Give a class member the combination to the lock and have him or her unlock it. Challenge your class to fulfill those prophecies by carefully studying the words of Isaiah.

9 And as one generation hath been destroyed among the Jews because of iniquity, even so have they been destroyed from generation to generation according to their iniquities; and never hath any of them been destroyed save it were foretold them by the prophets of the Lord.

10 Wherefore, it hath been told them concerning the destruction which should come upon them, immediately after my father left Jerusalem; nevertheless, they hardened their hearts; and according to my prophecy they have been destroyed, save it be those which are carried away captive into Babylon.

11 And now this I speak because of the spirit which is in me. And notwithstanding they have been carried away they shall return again, and possess the land of Jerusalem; wherefore, they shall be restored again to the land of their inheritance.

vv. 10–11 Babylonian captivity.

💡 It is believed that it was 588 BC when Jerusalem was destroyed and taken captive into Babylon. In 538 BC, King Cyrus issued the decree allowing the Jews to return, but not until around 518 BC did they actually return, making it 70 years in Babylonian captivity.

12 But, behold, they shall have wars, and rumors of wars; and when the day cometh that the Only Begotten of the Father, yea, even the Father of heaven and of earth, shall manifest himself unto them in the flesh, behold, they will reject him, because of their iniquities, and the hardness of their hearts, and the stiffness of their necks.

13 Behold, they will crucify him; and after he is laid in a sepulchre for the space of three days he shall rise from the dead, with healing in his wings; and all those who shall believe on his name shall be saved in the kingdom of God. Wherefore, my soul delighteth to prophesy concerning him, for I have seen his day, and my heart doth magnify his holy name.

14 And behold it shall come to pass that after the Messiah hath risen from the dead, and hath manifested himself unto his people, unto

Notes

as many as will believe on his name, behold, Jerusalem shall be destroyed again; for wo unto them that fight against God and the people of his church.

15 Wherefore, the Jews shall be scattered among all nations; yea, and also Babylon shall be destroyed; wherefore, the Jews shall be scattered by other nations.

vv. 14–15 Scattering of the Jews.

💡 After Jesus was crucified (about AD 34), Jerusalem and its temple is destroyed by Nero of Rome about AD 70. The Jews were once again scattered, this time among all nations as Nephi prophesied.

16 And after they have been scattered, and the Lord God hath scourged them by other nations for the space of many generations, yea, even down from generation to generation until they shall be persuaded to believe in Christ, the Son of God, and the atonement, which is infinite for all mankind—and when that day shall come that they shall believe in Christ, and worship the Father in his name, with pure hearts and clean hands, and look not forward any more for another Messiah, then, at that time, the day will come that it must needs be expedient that they should believe these things.

v. 16 The word Messiah.

💡 Have class members look for two titles referring to the Savior in verse 16. Ask your class what is the difference between the words "Christ" and "Messiah". Explain that Messiah is the Hebrew word meaning "anointed one" and Christ is the Greek word meaning "anointed one". Because the New Testament is translated from Greek, the word Christ is used. Likewise, because the Old Testament is mostly translated from Hebrew, the word Messiah is used. See the entry "Messiah" in the Bible Dictionary.

17 And the Lord will set his hand again the second time to restore his people from their lost and fallen state. Wherefore, he will proceed to do a marvelous work and a wonder among the children of men.

18 Wherefore, he shall bring forth his words unto them, which words shall judge them at the last day, for they shall be given them for the purpose of convincing them of the true Messiah, who was rejected by them; and unto the convincing of them that they need not look forward any more for a Messiah to come, for there should not any come, save it should be a false Messiah which should deceive the people; for there is save one Messiah spoken of by the prophets, and that Messiah is he who should be rejected of the Jews.

v. 18 False Messiah.

💡 Although through the years there have been many who have claimed to be the Messiah or Christ, verse 18 teaches that there will be an especially notable one who will come to deceive.

19 For according to the words of the prophets, the Messiah cometh in six hundred years from the time that my father left Jerusalem; and according to the words of the prophets, and also the word of the angel of God, his name shall be Jesus Christ, the Son of God.

20 And now, my brethren, I have spoken plainly that ye cannot err. And as the Lord God liveth that brought Israel up out of the land of Egypt, and gave unto Moses power that he should heal the nations after they had been bitten by the poisonous serpents, if they would cast their eyes unto the serpent which he did raise up before them, and also gave him power that he should smite the rock and the water should come forth; yea, behold I say unto you, that as these things are true, and as the Lord God liveth, there is none other name given under heaven save it be this Jesus Christ, of which I have spoken, whereby man can be saved.

Notes

21 Wherefore, for this cause hath the Lord God promised unto me that these things which I write shall be kept and preserved, and handed down unto my seed, from generation to generation, that the promise may be fulfilled unto Joseph, that his seed should never perish as long as the earth should stand.

22 Wherefore, these things shall go from generation to generation as long as the earth shall stand; and they shall go according to the will and pleasure of God; and the nations who shall possess them shall be judged of them according to the words which are written.

23 For we labor diligently to write, to persuade our children, and also our brethren, to believe in Christ, and to be reconciled to God; for we know that it is by grace that we are saved, after all we can do.

24 And, notwithstanding we believe in Christ, we keep the law of Moses, and look forward with steadfastness unto Christ, until the law shall be fulfilled.

25 For, for this end was the law given; wherefore the law hath become dead unto us, and we are made alive in Christ because of our faith; yet we keep the law because of the commandments.

26 And we talk of Christ, we rejoice in Christ, we preach of Christ, we prophesy of Christ, and we write according to our prophecies, that our children may know to what source they may look for a remission of their sins.

vv. 23–26 The salvation saves me after all I can do.

✋ Have the following written on the board:

Concern # 1: "I believe that we are saved by God's grace alone and we don't need to do any good works."

Concern #2: "I don't know if you Mormons are really Christians. What part does Christ play in your religion?"

Ask class members to read the two concerns and imagine that they are approached with these questions at work or school. Have them share what they might say. You may want to consider pairing class members together and allowing them to answer these questions to each other.

🔎 *Read verses 23–26 and look for verses you could share to help resolve the person's concerns.* Afterward, have class members role-play how they would share these verses to help resolves the concerns.

27 Wherefore, we speak concerning the law that our children may know the deadness of the law; and they, by knowing the deadness of the law, may look forward unto that life which is in Christ, and know for what end the law was given. And after the law is fulfilled in Christ, that they need not harden their hearts against him when the law ought to be done away.

28 And now behold, my people, ye are a stiffnecked people; wherefore, I have spoken plainly unto you, that ye cannot misunderstand. And the words which I have spoken shall stand as a testimony against you; for they are sufficient to teach any man the right way; for the right way is to believe in Christ and deny him not; for by denying him ye also deny the prophets and the law.

29 And now behold, I say unto you that the right way is to believe in Christ, and deny him not; and Christ is the Holy One of Israel; wherefore ye must bow down before him, and worship him with all your might, mind, and strength, and your whole soul; and if ye do this ye shall in nowise be cast out.

30 And, inasmuch as it shall be expedient, ye must keep the performances and ordinances of God until the law shall be fulfilled which was given unto Moses.

v. 29 Our relationship with Christ.

💬 Brigham Young stated, "The greatest and most important of all requirements of our Father in

Notes

Heaven and of his Son Jesus Christ . . . is to believe in Jesus Christ, confess him, seek him, cling to him, make friends with him. Take a course to open a communication with your Elder Brother or file-leader—our Savior" (*Journal of Discourses*, vol. 8, 339).

Teaching Tips from Prophets' Lips "I am convinced that there is no simple formula or technique that I could give you or that you could give your students that would immediately facilitate mastering the ability to be guided by the Holy Spirit. Nor do I believe that the Lord will ever allow someone to conceive a pattern that would invariably and immediately open the channels of spiritual communication. We grow when we labor to recognize the guidance of the Holy Ghost as we struggle to communicate our needs to our Father in Heaven in moments of dire need or overflowing gratitude. Each time we do that we are taking another step in fulfilling the purpose of our being here on earth" (Richard G. Scott, "Helping Others to Be Spiritually Led," CES Symposium, August 11, 1998).

2 NEPHI 26

"For He Loveth the World"
About 559–545 BC

1–10, Nephi prophesies of the eventual destruction of the Nephites; 11–13, The Spirit of the Lord will not always strive with man, but by the Holy Ghost, the Lord will manifest himself to all who believe on Him; 14–22, In the last days, God's word will oppose the works of darkness; 23–33, The Lord invites all to receive his salvation and reject temptations.

Overarching Principle: God's way for us is salvation and Satan's way for us is destruction.

1 And after Christ shall have risen from the dead he shall show himself unto you, my children, and my beloved brethren; and the words which he shall speak unto you shall be the law which ye shall do.

2 For behold, I say unto you that I have beheld that many generations shall pass away, and there shall be great wars and contentions among my people.

3 And after the Messiah shall come there shall be signs given unto my people of his birth, and also of his death and resurrection; and great and terrible shall that day be unto the wicked, for they shall perish; and they perish because they cast out the prophets, and the saints, and stone them, and slay them; wherefore the cry of the blood of the saints shall ascend up to God from the ground against them.

4 Wherefore, all those who are proud, and that do wickedly, the day that cometh shall burn them up, saith the Lord of Hosts, for they shall be as stubble.

5 And they that kill the prophets, and the saints, the depths of the earth shall swallow them up, saith the Lord of Hosts; and mountains shall cover them, and whirlwinds shall carry them away, and buildings shall fall upon them and crush them to pieces and grind them to powder.

6 And they shall be visited with thunderings, and lightnings, and earthquakes, and all manner of destructions, for the fire of the anger of the Lord shall be kindled against them, and they shall be as stubble, and the day that cometh shall consume them, saith the Lord of Hosts.

7 O the pain, and the anguish of my soul for the loss of the slain of my people! For I, Nephi, have seen it, and it well nigh consumeth me before the presence of the Lord; but I must cry unto my God: Thy ways are just.

8 But behold, the righteous that hearken unto the words of the prophets, and destroy them not, but look forward unto Christ with steadfastness for the signs which are given, notwithstanding all persecution—behold, they are they which shall not perish.

9 But the Son of Righteousness shall appear unto

Notes

them; and he shall heal them, and they shall have peace with him, until three generations shall have passed away, and many of the fourth generation shall have passed away in righteousness.

vv. 4–9 Christ's visitation to the Nephites will be similar to Christ's Second Coming.

🔎 Explain to class members that in verses 4–9, Nephi is prophesying of what will happen in 3 Nephi just before and during Christ's visit to the Nephites. Have class members look for similarities between events leading up to Christ's coming to the Nephites, and the Second Coming. After reading each verse, stop and ask class members what similarities they have found.

10 And when these things have passed away a speedy destruction cometh unto my people; for, notwithstanding the pains of my soul, I have seen it; wherefore, I know that it shall come to pass; and they sell themselves for naught; for, for the reward of their pride and their foolishness they shall reap destruction; for because they yield unto the devil and choose works of darkness rather than light, therefore they must go down to hell.

11 For the Spirit of the Lord will not always strive with man. And when the Spirit ceaseth to strive with man then cometh speedy destruction, and this grieveth my soul.

12 And as I spake concerning the convincing of the Jews, that Jesus is the very Christ, it must needs be that the Gentiles be convinced also that Jesus is the Christ, the Eternal God;

13 And that he manifesteth himself unto all those who believe in him, by the power of the Holy Ghost; yea, unto every nation, kindred, tongue, and people, working mighty miracles, signs, and wonders, among the children of men according to their faith.

vv. 10–13 Sin destroys happiness.

🔎 Look for what verse 10 teaches about sin.

❓ Analyze:
• What does verse 10 teach about sin?
• What does the word "naught" in the verse mean?
• What does that teach about sin?
• What does Satan try to teach that people get from sin?
• How are these messages lies?

❓ Apply: When have you seen sin destroy a life? What results does a righteous life lead to?

♥ Testify to class members how sin leads to nothing of value and destroys people's lives. Challenge them to live righteous lives so that they can experience happiness.

14 But behold, I prophesy unto you concerning the last days; concerning the days when the Lord God shall bring these things forth unto the children of men.

15 After my seed and the seed of my brethren shall have dwindled in unbelief, and shall have been smitten by the Gentiles; yea, after the Lord God shall have camped against them round about, and shall have laid siege against them with a mount, and raised forts against them; and after they shall have been brought down low in the dust, even that they are not, yet the words of the righteous shall be written, and the prayers of the faithful shall be heard, and all those who have dwindled in unbelief shall not be forgotten.

16 For those who shall be destroyed shall speak unto them out of the ground, and their speech shall be low out of the dust, and their voice shall be as one that hath a familiar spirit; for the Lord God will give unto him power, that he may whisper concerning them, even as it were out of the ground; and their speech shall whisper out of the dust.

vv. 14–16 The Book of Mormon will teach the people in the Americas of those who came before.

Notes

🔍 *In verses 14–16, look for what it says will happen in the last days to those who are decedents of the Lamanites.*

❓ Analyze:
- *What do the first few lines of verse 16 mean?*
- *How is the Book of Mormon speaking out of the ground?*
- *How will the voice be "familiar" to the Lamanites?*

17 For thus saith the Lord God: They shall write the things which shall be done among them, and they shall be written and sealed up in a book, and those who have dwindled in unbelief shall not have them, for they seek to destroy the things of God.

18 Wherefore, as those who have been destroyed have been destroyed speedily; and the multitude of their terrible ones shall be as chaff that passeth away—yea, thus saith the Lord God: It shall be at an instant, suddenly—

19 And it shall come to pass, that those who have dwindled in unbelief shall be smitten by the hand of the Gentiles.

20 And the Gentiles are lifted up in the pride of their eyes, and have stumbled, because of the greatness of their stumbling block, that they have built up many churches; nevertheless, they put down the power and miracles of God, and preach up unto themselves their own wisdom and their own learning, that they may get gain and grind upon the face of the poor.

21 And there are many churches built up which cause envyings, and strifes, and malice.

22 And there are also secret combinations, even as in times of old, according to the combinations of the devil, for he is the founder of all these things; yea, the founder of murder, and works of darkness; yea, and he leadeth them by the neck with a flaxen cord, until he bindeth them with his strong cords forever.

v. 22 Satan tries to slowly bind us down in sin.

⚡ Give a single long piece of thread to a volunteer for him or her to break. Then give the volunteer two pieces to break at the same time. Continue adding more pieces of thread until he or she can no longer break all of the thread together.

🔍 *Look for what this has to do with verse 22.*

❓ Analyze: *What is the "flaxen" that is mentioned in verse 22?*

⚡ To demonstrate what flaxen is, cut off an inch of a piece of rope and unravel it to the smallest piece of fiber you can get. Usually this will be the size of flaxen thread. Have a class member stretch his or her palm so that it is tight, and then drop this small piece onto it. (If the skin is very tight, he should not be able to feel it.)

❓ Analyze: *How are Satan's temptations like this flaxen cord? According to Nephi, what is Satan's end goal?*

❤ Challenge class members to beware of even the smallest temptations, because it doesn't take much for a person to be bound down in sin.

23 For behold, my beloved brethren, I say unto you that the Lord God worketh not in darkness.

24 He doeth not anything save it be for the benefit of the world; for he loveth the world, even that he layeth down his own life that he may draw all men unto him. Wherefore, he commandeth none that they shall not partake of his salvation.

25 Behold, doth he cry unto any, saying: Depart from me? Behold, I say unto you, Nay; but he saith: Come unto me all ye ends of the earth, buy milk and honey, without money and without price.

26 Behold, hath he commanded any that they should depart out of the synagogues, or out of the houses of worship? Behold, I say unto you, Nay.

27 Hath he commanded any that they should not

Notes

partake of his salvation? Behold I say unto you, Nay; but he hath given it free for all men; and he hath commanded his people that they should persuade all men to repentance.

28 Behold, hath the Lord commanded any that they should not partake of his goodness? Behold I say unto you, Nay; but all men are privileged the one like unto the other, and none are forbidden.

vv. 24–28 God's love has no bounds.

⚡ *Why do people in the world question the goodness and love of God?* Explain to class members that verses 24–28 are foundational verses that help us understand God's unquestionable goodness.

🔑 Ask class members to silently read verses 24–28 and underline everything that shows God's love for us. Have the class share when they are done.

❓ Analyze:
• *What does it mean that he doesn't do anything "save it be for the benefit of the world"? Are even trials and tragedy for our benefit? How? (Romans 8:28).*
• *Who do you love so much you would be willing to lay down your life for?*
• *Why does he offer salvation to all?*
• *In what ways is his salvation "free" and "without price"?*

♥ Testify of God's love and that all He does is to benefit the world.

29 He commandeth that there shall be no priestcrafts; for, behold, priestcrafts are that men preach and set themselves up for a light unto the world, that they may get gain and praise of the world; but they seek not the welfare of Zion.

30 Behold, the Lord hath forbidden this thing; wherefore, the Lord God hath given a commandment that all men should have charity, which charity is love. And except they should have charity they were nothing. Wherefore, if they should have charity they would not suffer the laborer in Zion to perish.

31 But the laborer in Zion shall labor for Zion; for if they labor for money they shall perish.

32 And again, the Lord God hath commanded that men should not murder; that they should not lie; that they should not steal; that they should not take the name of the Lord their God in vain; that they should not envy; that they should not have malice; that they should not contend one with another; that they should not commit whoredoms; and that they should do none of these things; for whoso doeth them shall perish.

33 For none of these iniquities come of the Lord; for he doeth that which is good among the children of men; and he doeth nothing save it be plain unto the children of men; and he inviteth them all to come unto him and partake of his goodness; and he denieth none that come unto him, black and white, bond and free, male and female; and he remembereth the heathen; and all are alike unto God, both Jew and Gentile.

vv. 29–31 We should seek to build God's kingdom, and not our own.

⚡ Make a list on the board with the class that answers the following question: what should and should not motivate someone to perform acts of religious devotion?

🔑 *Look for a list of what priestcraft is in verse 29.* Write on the board what class members find.

❓ Analyze:
• *What does it mean when people "set themselves up for a light"?*
• *Why is it bad to try to "get gain" by doing religious acts? What does verse 31 add to this? What does this teach about motivation?*
• *What is an example of seeking the "welfare of Zion"?*
• *In the context of this verse, why is seeking praise from others bad?*

🔑 *Look in verse 30 for what should be the motivating factor in all that we do in the Church.*

Notes

_____

_____

_____

❤ Challenge class members to seek pure motives as they serve the Lord.

2 NEPHI 27

Nephi Expounds Upon Isaiah 29
About 559–544 BC

1–5, The people of Israel will be in a deep sleep because of their wickedness; 6–22, The Lord will bring forth the Book of Mormon to awake Israel from the deep sleep; 23–35, The Lord will perform a marvelous work and a wonder by restoring the gospel through the means of the Book of Mormon.

Literary Context: Isaiah uses the imagery of sleep to convey the message of the spirituality of people when they reject the prophets. He then explains how these people awaken from the sleep.

1 But, behold, in the last days, or in the days of the Gentiles—yea, behold all the nations of the Gentiles and also the Jews, both those who shall come upon this land and those who shall be upon other lands, yea, even upon all the lands of the earth, behold, they will be drunken with iniquity and all manner of abominations—

2 And when that day shall come they shall be visited of the Lord of Hosts, with thunder and with earthquake, and with a great noise, and with storm, and with tempest, and with the flame of devouring fire.

3 And all the nations that fight against Zion, and that distress her, shall be as a dream of a night vision; yea, it shall be unto them, even as unto a hungry man which dreameth, and behold he eateth but he awaketh and his soul is empty; or like unto a thirsty man which dreameth, and behold he drinketh but he awaketh and behold he is faint, and his soul hath appetite; yea, even so shall the multitude of all the nations be that fight against Mount Zion.

4 For behold, all ye that doeth iniquity, stay yourselves and wonder, for ye shall cry out, and cry; yea, ye shall be drunken but not with wine, ye shall stagger but not with strong drink.

5 For behold, the Lord hath poured out upon you the spirit of deep sleep. For behold, ye have closed your eyes, and ye have rejected the prophets; and your rulers, and the seers hath he covered because of your iniquity.

vv. 1–5 The last days will be filled with sin and wickedness.

⚡ Bring a pillow and blanket and lay them on the floor to create a bed. Discuss sleeping with class members by asking them questions like, *Why do you like sleeping?* or *Is it hard to wake up from sleeping?* Explain that they will discover how Isaiah uses the metaphor of sleep to describe the purpose of the Book of Mormon.

🔍 Read verses 1–5 as a class, and ask the class members to look for who is asleep and why they are asleep?

❓ Analyze: Analyze with class members how sins can cause us to spiritually fall asleep.

6 And it shall come to pass that the Lord God shall bring forth unto you the words of a book, and they shall be the words of them which have slumbered.

7 And behold the book shall be sealed; and in the book shall be a revelation from God, from the beginning of the world to the ending thereof.

8 Wherefore, because of the things which are sealed up, the things which are sealed shall not be delivered in the day of the wickedness and abominations of the people. Wherefore the book shall be kept from them.

9 But the book shall be delivered unto a man, and he shall deliver the words of the book, which are the words of those who have slumbered in the dust, and he shall deliver these words unto another;

Notes

10 But the words which are sealed he shall not deliver, neither shall he deliver the book. For the book shall be sealed by the power of God, and the revelation which was sealed shall be kept in the book until the own due time of the Lord, that they may come forth; for behold, they reveal all things from the foundation of the world unto the end thereof.

11 And the day cometh that the words of the book which were sealed shall be read upon the house tops; and they shall be read by the power of Christ; and all things shall be revealed unto the children of men which ever have been among the children of men, and which ever will be even unto the end of the earth.

12 Wherefore, at that day when the book shall be delivered unto the man of whom I have spoken, the book shall be hid from the eyes of the world, that the eyes of none shall behold it save it be that three witnesses shall behold it, by the power of God, besides him to whom the book shall be delivered; and they shall testify to the truth of the book and the things therein.

13 And there is none other which shall view it, save it be a few according to the will of God, to bear testimony of his word unto the children of men; for the Lord God hath said that the words of the faithful should speak as if it were from the dead.

14 Wherefore, the Lord God will proceed to bring forth the words of the book; and in the mouth of as many witnesses as seemeth him good will he establish his word; and wo be unto him that rejecteth the word of God!

15 But behold, it shall come to pass that the Lord God shall say unto him to whom he shall deliver the book: Take these words which are not sealed and deliver them to another, that he may show them unto the learned, saying: Read this, I pray thee. And the learned shall say: Bring hither the book, and I will read them.

16 And now, because of the glory of the world and to get gain will they say this, and not for the glory of God.

17 And the man shall say: I cannot bring the book, for it is sealed.

18 Then shall the learned say: I cannot read it.

19 Wherefore it shall come to pass, that the Lord God will deliver again the book and the words thereof to him that is not learned; and the man that is not learned shall say: I am not learned.

20 Then shall the Lord God say unto him: The learned shall not read them, for they have rejected them, and I am able to do mine own work; wherefore thou shalt read the words which I shall give unto thee.

21 Touch not the things which are sealed, for I will bring them forth in mine own due time; for I will show unto the children of men that I am able to do mine own work.

22 Wherefore, when thou hast read the words which I have commanded thee, and obtained the witnesses which I have promised unto thee, then shalt thou seal up the book again, and hide it up unto me, that I may preserve the words which thou hast not read, until I shall see fit in mine own wisdom to reveal all things unto the children of men.

23 For behold, I am God; and I am a God of miracles; and I will show unto the world that I am the same yesterday, today, and forever; and I work not among the children of men save it be according to their faith.

24 And again it shall come to pass that the Lord shall say unto him that shall read the words that shall be delivered him:

25 Forasmuch as this people draw near unto me with their mouth, and with their lips do honor me, but have removed their hearts far from me, and their fear towards me is taught by the precepts of men—

26 Therefore, I will proceed to do a marvelous work among this people, yea, a marvelous work and a wonder, for the wisdom of their wise and learned shall perish, and the understanding of their prudent shall be hid.

Notes

vv. 6–26 The Book of Mormon will come forth as a marvelous work and a wonder to awaken the best in people.

🔎 Read verse 6 together as a class and ask, *What does Isaiah say will wake the people up from this sleep?* Explain that Isaiah will then explain two things to us: 1) How the Book of Mormon will be brought forth (verses 7–22), and 2) Why God brings the Book of Mormon forth (verses 23–26).

✋ Break class members into groups and give each group a piece of paper. Assign them to read verses 7–22, looking for the details of how the Book of Mormon will be brought forth, and invite them to write their findings on the paper provided. Then have them search verses 23–26 looking for why God brings the Book of Mormon forth, also noting their findings on their paper. When they are finished, ask class members to share their lists, taking time to answer any questions they may have about these scriptures.

💡 Refer to Joseph Smith History 1:55–65 for details of the fulfillment of the prophecy found in 2 Nephi 27:15–20.

❤ Invite class members to write their individual testimonies of the Book of Mormon on a piece of paper and share it with someone before class meets again. Ask if a class member would like to share their testimony with the class, and consider sharing your own.

27 And wo unto them that seek deep to hide their counsel from the Lord! And their works are in the dark; and they say: Who seeth us, and who knoweth us? And they also say: Surely, your turning of things upside down shall be esteemed as the potter's clay. But behold, I will show unto them, saith the Lord of Hosts, that I know all their works. For shall the work say of him that made it, he made me not? Or shall the thing framed say of him that framed it, he had no understanding?

28 But behold, saith the Lord of Hosts: I will show unto the children of men that it is yet a very little while and Lebanon shall be turned into a fruitful field; and the fruitful field shall be esteemed as a forest.

29 And in that day shall the deaf hear the words of the book, and the eyes of the blind shall see out of obscurity and out of darkness.

30 And the meek also shall increase, and their joy shall be in the Lord, and the poor among men shall rejoice in the Holy One of Israel.

31 For assuredly as the Lord liveth they shall see that the terrible one is brought to naught, and the scorner is consumed, and all that watch for iniquity are cut off;

32 And they that make a man an offender for a word, and lay a snare for him that reproveth in the gate, and turn aside the just for a thing of naught.

33 Therefore, thus saith the Lord, who redeemed Abraham, concerning the house of Jacob: Jacob shall not now be ashamed, neither shall his face now wax pale.

34 But when he seeth his children, the work of my hands, in the midst of him, they shall sanctify my name, and sanctify the Holy One of Jacob, and shall fear the God of Israel.

35 They also that erred in spirit shall come to understanding, and they that murmured shall learn doctrine.

Teaching Tips from Prophets' Lips "I heard President Marion G. Romney say on several occasions, 'I always know when I am speaking under the inspiration of the Holy Ghost because I always learn something from what I've said'" (Boyd K. Packer, *Teach Ye Diligently* [Salt Lake City: Deseret Book, 1975], 304).

Notes

2 NEPHI 28

Precepts of God versus the Precepts of Man

About 559–544 BC

1–9, The precepts of men are to "eat, drink, and be merry for tomorrow we die"; 10–19, False churches will teach men to be proud and ignore the poor; 20–29, Satan will rage, pacify, lull, or flatter us; 30–32, The precepts of God.

Overarching Principle: Satan's strategy for our destruction is to create rage in our hearts, encourage selfish living, and pacify us— slowly dragging us down to hell. In contrast, God will help us learn line upon line.

1 And now, behold, my brethren, I have spoken unto you, according as the Spirit hath constrained me; wherefore, I know that they must surely come to pass.

2 And the things which shall be written out of the book shall be of great worth unto the children of men, and especially unto our seed, which is a remnant of the house of Israel.

3 For it shall come to pass in that day that the churches which are built up, and not unto the Lord, when the one shall say unto the other: Behold, I, I am the Lord's; and the others shall say: I, I am the Lord's; and thus shall every one say that hath built up churches, and not unto the Lord—

4 And they shall contend one with another; and their priests shall contend one with another, and they shall teach with their learning, and deny the Holy Ghost, which giveth utterance.

5 And they deny the power of God, the Holy One of Israel; and they say unto the people: Hearken unto us, and hear ye our precept; for behold there is no God today, for the Lord and the Redeemer hath done his work, and he hath given his power unto men;

6 Behold, hearken ye unto my precept; if they shall say there is a miracle wrought by the hand of the Lord, believe it not; for this day he is not a God of miracles; he hath done his work.

7 Yea, and there shall be many which shall say: Eat, drink, and be merry, for tomorrow we die; and it shall be well with us.

8 And there shall also be many which shall say: Eat, drink, and be merry; nevertheless, fear God—he will justify in committing a little sin; yea, lie a little, take the advantage of one because of his words, dig a pit for thy neighbor; there is no harm in this; and do all these things, for tomorrow we die; and if it so be that we are guilty, God will beat us with a few stripes, and at last we shall be saved in the kingdom of God.

9 Yea, and there shall be many which shall teach after this manner, false and vain and foolish doctrines, and shall be puffed up in their hearts, and shall seek deep to hide their counsels from the Lord; and their works shall be in the dark.

10 And the blood of the saints shall cry from the ground against them.

11 Yea, they have all gone out of the way; they have become corrupted.

12 Because of pride, and because of false teachers, and false doctrine, their churches have become corrupted, and their churches are lifted up; because of pride they are puffed up.

13 They rob the poor because of their fine sanctuaries; they rob the poor because of their fine clothing; and they persecute the meek and the poor in heart, because in their pride they are puffed up.

14 They wear stiff necks and high heads; yea, and because of pride, and wickedness, and abominations, and whoredoms, they have all gone astray save it be a few, who are the humble followers of Christ; nevertheless, they are led, that in many instances they do err because they are taught by the precepts of men.

15 O the wise, and the learned, and the rich, that are puffed up in the pride of their hearts, and all

Notes

those who preach false doctrines, and all those who commit whoredoms, and pervert the right way of the Lord, wo, wo, wo be unto them, saith the Lord God Almighty, for they shall be thrust down to hell!

16 Wo unto them that turn aside the just for a thing of naught and revile against that which is good, and say that it is of no worth! For the day shall come that the Lord God will speedily visit the inhabitants of the earth; and in that day that they are fully ripe in iniquity they shall perish.

17 But behold, if the inhabitants of the earth shall repent of their wickedness and abominations they shall not be destroyed, saith the Lord of Hosts.

18 But behold, that great and abominable church, the whore of all the earth, must tumble to the earth, and great must be the fall thereof.

19 For the kingdom of the devil must shake, and they which belong to it must needs be stirred up unto repentance, or the devil will grasp them with his everlasting chains, and they be stirred up to anger, and perish;

20 For behold, at that day shall he rage in the hearts of the children of men, and stir them up to anger against that which is good.

21 And others will he pacify, and lull them away into carnal security, that they will say: All is well in Zion; yea, Zion prospereth, all is well—and thus the devil cheateth their souls, and leadeth them away carefully down to hell.

22 And behold, others he flattereth away, and telleth them there is no hell; and he saith unto them: I am no devil, for there is none—and thus he whispereth in their ears, until he grasps them with his awful chains, from whence there is no deliverance.

vv. 3–22 Satan's strategies for our spiritual spoil.

⚡ Write "Precepts of God vs. Precepts of Man" on the board before class. Choose your favorite sport and use this as an analogy to teach that Satan and God have two different strategies for 'winning.' Discuss with class members different strategies people may use in their sport to prepare for their competition in an upcoming game or match. Explain that in 2 Nephi 28, Nephi will warn us about Satan's strategies to ruin us spiritually.

🔍 Have the class search the following scriptures looking for the strategies Satan will use against us: 1) vv. 3–6; 2) vv. 7–9; 3) vv. 16–20; 4) v. 21; 5) v. 22; 6) vv. 24–27.

❓ Analyze: Once you have given class members enough time to identify Satan's strategies, take time to analyze and discuss them.

❓ Apply: *What do these strategies look like today?*

💬 D. Todd Christofferson, speaking of the false teachings of our day said, "Some profess that if there is a God, He makes no real demands upon us (see Alma 18:5). Others maintain that a loving God forgives all sin based on simple confession, or if there actually is a punishment for sin, 'God will beat us with a few stripes, and at last we shall be saved in the kingdom of God' (2 Nephi 28:8). . . . Their doctrine is that values, standards, and even truth are all relative. Thus, whatever one feels is right for him or her cannot be judged by others to be wrong or sinful" ("The Divine Gift of Repentance," *Ensign,* November 2011, 38).

23 Yea, they are grasped with death, and hell; and death, and hell, and the devil, and all that have been seized therewith must stand before the throne of God, and be judged according to their works, from whence they must go into the place prepared for them, even a lake of fire and brimstone, which is endless torment.

24 Therefore, wo be unto him that is at ease in Zion!

25 Wo be unto him that crieth: All is well!

Notes

26 Yea, wo be unto him that hearkeneth unto the precepts of men, and denieth the power of God, and the gift of the Holy Ghost!

27 Yea, wo be unto him that saith: We have received, and we need no more!

28 And in fine, wo unto all those who tremble, and are angry because of the truth of God! For behold, he that is built upon the rock receiveth it with gladness; and he that is built upon a sandy foundation trembleth lest he shall fall.

29 Wo be unto him that shall say: We have received the word of God, and we need no more of the word of God, for we have enough!

30 For behold, thus saith the Lord God: I will give unto the children of men line upon line, precept upon precept, here a little and there a little; and blessed are those who hearken unto my precepts, and lend an ear unto my counsel, for they shall learn wisdom; for unto him that receiveth I will give more; and from them that shall say, We have enough, from them shall be taken away even that which they have.

31 Cursed is he that putteth his trust in man, or maketh flesh his arm, or shall hearken unto the precepts of men, save their precepts shall be given by the power of the Holy Ghost.

32 Wo be unto the Gentiles, saith the Lord God of Hosts! For notwithstanding I shall lengthen out mine arm unto them from day to day, they will deny me; nevertheless, I will be merciful unto them, saith the Lord God, if they will repent and come unto me; for mine arm is lengthened out all the day long, saith the Lord God of Hosts.

vv. 30–31 God's strategy for our salvation.

🔎 Read verses 30–31 as a class and ask, *As a contrast, what will God help us do in our fight against Satan?*

❓ Analyze: *What do you think it means that God will give us line upon line, or here a little, there a little? How would this be helpful against Satan's strategies?*

❓ Apply: *When have you felt help from God to overcome Satan's temptations?* (Encourage class members to not share specific sins or misdeeds; rather, have them share in generalities.)

❤ Help class members feel the importance of following God's precepts and not succumbing to Satan's strategies. You may want to use the Mormon Message video produced by the Church, "Stay Within the Lines" by Jeffrey R. Holland, found on lds.org, youth.lds.org, or mormonchannel.org.

2 NEPHI 29

"A Bible! A Bible!"
About 559–545 BC

1–3, Some will reject the Book of Mormon because they already have the Bible; 4–6, The Bible proceeded out of the mouth of Jews; 7–11, Some reasons it is important to have more of God's word than just the Bible; 12–14, God's word will help to gather his people.

1 But behold, there shall be many—at that day when I shall proceed to do a marvelous work among them, that I may remember my covenants which I have made unto the children of men, that I may set my hand again the second time to recover my people, which are of the house of Israel;

2 And also, that I may remember the promises which I have made unto thee, Nephi, and also unto thy father, that I would remember your seed; and that the words of your seed should proceed forth out of my mouth unto your seed; and my words shall hiss forth unto the ends of the earth, for a standard unto my people, which are of the house of Israel;

3 And because my words shall hiss forth—many of the Gentiles shall say: A Bible! A Bible! We have got a Bible, and there cannot be any more Bible.

Notes

v. 3 Reasons why the Bible is not all of God's scripture to the world.

⚡ Draw a stick figure on the board and write the name "Fred" by it. Have class members imagine that they have a good friend, Fred, that they have given a Book of Mormon to. After explaining what the book was, Fred handed back the book and said, "The Bible is the complete word of God, and I don't need anything but the Bible." Ask class members how they might kindly respond to Fred. Explain that all of chapter 29 is a masterful explanation of why the Bible is not all of God's word. The chapter will help them explain to Fred why the Bible is not all of God's word. The explanations are summarized as follows:

Verses 4–6: It is hypocrisy for the Gentiles to cherish the Bible so dearly, yet to have treated the Jewish people so poorly.
Verse 7: God created more than one nation.
Verse 8: Multiple witnesses from multiple nations help prove God's word.
Verses 9–10: God is unchanging and teaches his children through the scriptures.
Verses 11–12: All nations will be judged by the word of God they have received.

4 But thus saith the Lord God: O fools, they shall have a Bible; and it shall proceed forth from the Jews, mine ancient covenant people. And what thank they the Jews for the Bible which they receive from them? Yea, what do the Gentiles mean? Do they remember the travails, and the labors, and the pains of the Jews, and their diligence unto me, in bringing forth salvation unto the Gentiles?

5 O ye Gentiles, have ye remembered the Jews, mine ancient covenant people? Nay; but ye have cursed them, and have hated them, and have not sought to recover them. But behold, I will return all these things upon your own heads; for I the Lord have not forgotten my people.

6 Thou fool, that shall say: A Bible, we have got a Bible, and we need no more Bible. Have ye obtained a Bible save it were by the Jews?

7 Know ye not that there are more nations than one? Know ye not that I, the Lord your God, have created all men, and that I remember those who are upon the isles of the sea; and that I rule in the heavens above and in the earth beneath; and I bring forth my word unto the children of men, yea, even upon all the nations of the earth?

vv. 7, 11 God loves all nations and gives his word to those willing to receive it.

⚡ Refer back to Fred and have class members imagine how Fred would respond to the following questions:

• *Does God love all people?*
• *Does God also love all people who lived long ago?*
• *Does God love those who lived in different lands?*

🔎 Invite the class to look for how those questions relate to verses 7 and help explain why God spoke to more than just the people in the Bible.

8 Wherefore murmur ye, because that ye shall receive more of my word? Know ye not that the testimony of two nations is a witness unto you that I am God, that I remember one nation like unto another? Wherefore, I speak the same words unto one nation like unto another. And when the two nations shall run together the testimony of the two nations shall run together also.

v. 8 Two witnesses are more effective than one.

⚡ Have ready two pieces of wood, a hammer, and nails. Ask, *How many Christian churches read from the Bible? Do all of those Christians believe the same doctrine since they all use the Bible? Why not?* Hammer the two pieces of wood together in the middle with one nail.

Notes

Explain that the one nail represents the Bible. Rotate the pieces of wood around the nail. Explain that just as the wood pieces can be rotated and moved, so can the Bible be twisted to mean many things to many people. Ask, *What would I need to add to make these two pieces stay in place?* Nail in the second nail and explain that the additional nail is like the Book of Mormon—together, the Bible and Book of Mormon help clarify doctrine; they are like two witnesses.

🔎 *As you read verse 8, underline the words that bring out this point.*

9 And I do this that I may prove unto many that I am the same yesterday, today, and forever; and that I speak forth my words according to mine own pleasure. And because that I have spoken one word ye need not suppose that I cannot speak another; for my work is not yet finished; neither shall it be until the end of man, neither from that time henceforth and forever.

10 Wherefore, because that ye have a Bible ye need not suppose that it contains all my words; neither need ye suppose that I have not caused more to be written.

vv. 9–10 God's pattern is to give His word to those willing to receive it.

⚡ Referring back to "Fred" on the board, imagine asking him:

  • *Do you believe the Lord is the same yesterday, and today, and forever? (Hebrews 13:8)*
  • *Why would God stop speaking to man through prophets or apostles?*
  • *Why would God stop this pattern he had used for thousands of years?*

🔎 *As you read verses 9–10, underline the words that bring out these points.*

11 For I command all men, both in the east and in the west, and in the north, and in the south, and in the islands of the sea, that they shall write the words which I speak unto them; for out of the books which shall be written I will judge the world, every man according to their works, according to that which is written.

12 For behold, I shall speak unto the Jews and they shall write it; and I shall also speak unto the Nephites and they shall write it; and I shall also speak unto the other tribes of the house of Israel, which I have led away, and they shall write it; and I shall also speak unto all nations of the earth and they shall write it.

13 And it shall come to pass that the Jews shall have the words of the Nephites, and the Nephites shall have the words of the Jews; and the Nephites and the Jews shall have the words of the lost tribes of Israel; and the lost tribes of Israel shall have the words of the Nephites and the Jews.

v. 13 More ancient is forthcoming.

🔎 *Look for something we will receive in the future.*

💬 "We conclude from this [2 Nephi 29:13] that the Lord will eventually cause the inspired teachings He has given to His children in various nations to be brought forth for the benefit of all people. This will include accounts of the visit of the resurrected Lord to what we call the lost tribes of Israel. . . . When new writings come forth—and according to prophecy they will—we hope they will not be treated with the rejection some applied to the Book of Mormon because they already had a Bible" (Dallin H. Oaks, "All Men Everywhere," *Ensign,* May 2006, 77).

14 And it shall come to pass that my people, which are of the house of Israel, shall be gathered home unto the lands of their possessions; and my word also shall be gathered in one. And I will show unto them that fight against my word and against my people, who are of the house of Israel, that I am God, and that I covenanted with Abraham that I would remember his seed forever.

Notes

2 NEPHI 30

"A Delightsome People"
About 559–545 BC

1–8, How the Gentiles will assist in the gathering of Israel; 9–10, The division of the righteous from the wicked before the Lord's return; 11–18, Conditions of peace during the Millennium.

1 And now behold, my beloved brethren, I would speak unto you; for I, Nephi, would not suffer that ye should suppose that ye are more righteous than the Gentiles shall be. For behold, except ye shall keep the commandments of God ye shall all likewise perish; and because of the words which have been spoken ye need not suppose that the Gentiles are utterly destroyed.

2 For behold, I say unto you that as many of the Gentiles as will repent are the covenant people of the Lord; and as many of the Jews as will not repent shall be cast off; for the Lord covenanteth with none save it be with them that repent and believe in his Son, who is the Holy One of Israel.

3 And now, I would prophesy somewhat more concerning the Jews and the Gentiles. For after the book of which I have spoken shall come forth, and be written unto the Gentiles, and sealed up again unto the Lord, there shall be many which shall believe the words which are written; and they shall carry them forth unto the remnant of our seed.

v. 3 "Written unto the Gentiles."

🔎 *Look for who the Book of Mormon was written for.*

💬 Concerning the Book of Mormon, Ezra Taft Benson stated, "It was written for our day. The Nephites never had the book; neither did the Lamanites of ancient times. It was meant for us. Mormon wrote near the end of the Nephite civilization. Under the inspiration of God, who sees all things from the beginning, he abridged centuries of records, choosing the stories, speeches, and events that would be most helpful to us. Each of the major writers of the Book of Mormon testified that he wrote for future generations" ("The Book of Mormon—Keystone of Our Religion," *Ensign*, November 1986, 4).

💬 Ezra Taft Benson also stated, "The time is long overdue for a massive flooding of the earth with the Book of Mormon for the many reasons which the Lord has given. In this age of the electronic media and the mass distribution of the printed word, God will hold us accountable if we do not now move the Book of Mormon in a monumental way" ("Flooding the Earth with the Book of Mormon," *Ensign*, November 1988).

4 And then shall the remnant of our seed know concerning us, how that we came out from Jerusalem, and that they are descendants of the Jews.

5 And the gospel of Jesus Christ shall be declared among them; wherefore, they shall be restored unto the knowledge of their fathers, and also to the knowledge of Jesus Christ, which was had among their fathers.

6 And then shall they rejoice; for they shall know that it is a blessing unto them from the hand of God; and their scales of darkness shall begin to fall from their eyes; and many generations shall not pass away among them, save they shall be a pure and a delightsome people.

7 And it shall come to pass that the Jews which are scattered also shall begin to believe in Christ; and they shall begin to gather in upon the face of

Notes

the land; and as many as shall believe in Christ shall also become a delightsome people.

8 And it shall come to pass that the Lord God shall commence his work among all nations, kindreds, tongues, and people, to bring about the restoration of his people upon the earth.

9 And with righteousness shall the Lord God judge the poor, and reprove with equity for the meek of the earth. And he shall smite the earth with the rod of his mouth; and with the breath of his lips shall he slay the wicked.

10 For the time speedily cometh that the Lord God shall cause a great division among the people, and the wicked will he destroy; and he will spare his people, yea, even if it so be that he must destroy the wicked by fire.

vv. 9–10 Division, then destruction.

There is a pattern in scripture. Before the destruction of the wicked, the Lord separates the righteous from the wicked. Have class members cross-reference in their margins and read Doctrine and Covenants 63:54 and Matthew 13:24–30.

11 And righteousness shall be the girdle of his loins, and faithfulness the girdle of his reins.

12 And then shall the wolf dwell with the lamb; and the leopard shall lie down with the kid, and the calf, and the young lion, and the fatling, together; and a little child shall lead them.

13 And the cow and the bear shall feed; their young ones shall lie down together; and the lion shall eat straw like the ox.

14 And the sucking child shall play on the hole of the asp, and the weaned child shall put his hand on the cockatrice's den.

15 They shall not hurt nor destroy in all my holy mountain; for the earth shall be full of the knowledge of the Lord as the waters cover the sea.

16 Wherefore, the things of all nations shall be made known; yea, all things shall be made known unto the children of men.

17 There is nothing which is secret save it shall be revealed; there is no work of darkness save it shall be made manifest in the light; and there is nothing which is sealed upon the earth save it shall be loosed.

18 Wherefore, all things which have been revealed unto the children of men shall at that day be revealed; and Satan shall have power over the hearts of the children of men no more, for a long time. And now, my beloved brethren, I make an end of my sayings.

vv. 16–17 "All things shall be made known."

In verses 16–17, look for what will be made known when the Lord returns to the earth.

Analyze: *What would you like to know more about when all things will be revealed?*

Have class members write "Doctrine and Covenants 101:32–34" in their margins and read the verses for further clarification of what will be revealed.

2 NEPHI 31

Doctrine of Christ
About 559–545 BC

1–3, The doctrine of Christ taught plainly to men's understanding; 4–12, Follow Christ and be baptized; 13–21, After following Christ we must endure to the end to obtain eternal life.

1 And now I, Nephi, make an end of my prophesying unto you, my beloved brethren. And I cannot write but a few things, which I know must surely come to pass; neither can I write but a few of the words of my brother Jacob.

2 Wherefore, the things which I have written sufficeth me, save it be a few words which I must

Notes

speak concerning the doctrine of Christ; wherefore, I shall speak unto you plainly, according to the plainness of my prophesying.

3 For my soul delighteth in plainness; for after this manner doth the Lord God work among the children of men. For the Lord God giveth light unto the understanding; for he speaketh unto men according to their language, unto their understanding.

vv. 1–3 The doctrine of Christ is plain and according to our understanding.

⚡ Display a simple maze and one that is more complex in front of the class. Ask, *Which of these mazes best represent the doctrine or gospel of Christ? Why?*

🔑 Invite class members to look in verses 2–3 to find the best words that describe the gospel of Christ.

4 Wherefore, I would that ye should remember that I have spoken unto you concerning that prophet which the Lord showed unto me, that should baptize the Lamb of God, which should take away the sins of the world.

5 And now, if the Lamb of God, he being holy, should have need to be baptized by water, to fulfil all righteousness, O then, how much more need have we, being unholy, to be baptized, yea, even by water!

6 And now, I would ask of you, my beloved brethren, wherein the Lamb of God did fulfil all righteousness in being baptized by water?

7 Know ye not that he was holy? But notwithstanding he being holy, he showeth unto the children of men that, according to the flesh he humbleth himself before the Father, and witnesseth unto the Father that he would be obedient unto him in keeping his commandments.

8 Wherefore, after he was baptized with water the Holy Ghost descended upon him in the form of a dove.

9 And again, it showeth unto the children of men the straitness of the path, and the narrowness of the gate, by which they should enter, he having set the example before them.

10 And he said unto the children of men: Follow thou me. Wherefore, my beloved brethren, can we follow Jesus save we shall be willing to keep the commandments of the Father?

11 And the Father said: Repent ye, repent ye, and be baptized in the name of my Beloved Son.

12 And also, the voice of the Son came unto me, saying: He that is baptized in my name, to him will the Father give the Holy Ghost, like unto me; wherefore, follow me, and do the things which ye have seen me do.

13 Wherefore, my beloved brethren, I know that if ye shall follow the Son, with full purpose of heart, acting no hypocrisy and no deception before God, but with real intent, repenting of your sins, witnessing unto the Father that ye are willing to take upon you the name of Christ, by baptism—yea, by following your Lord and your Savior down into the water, according to his word, behold, then shall ye receive the Holy Ghost; yea, then cometh the baptism of fire and of the Holy Ghost; and then can ye speak with the tongue of angels, and shout praises unto the Holy One of Israel.

14 But, behold, my beloved brethren, thus came the voice of the Son unto me, saying: After ye have repented of your sins, and witnessed unto the Father that ye are willing to keep my commandments, by the baptism of water, and have received the baptism of fire and of the Holy Ghost, and can speak with a new tongue, yea, even with the tongue of angels, and after this should deny me, it would have been better for you that ye had not known me.

15 And I heard a voice from the Father, saying: Yea, the words of my Beloved are true and faithful. He that endureth to the end, the same shall be saved.

16 And now, my beloved brethren, I know by this

Notes

that unless a man shall endure to the end, in following the example of the Son of the living God, he cannot be saved.

17 Wherefore, do the things which I have told you I have seen that your Lord and your Redeemer should do; for, for this cause have they been shown unto me, that ye might know the gate by which ye should enter. For the gate by which ye should enter is repentance and baptism by water; and then cometh a remission of your sins by fire and by the Holy Ghost.

18 And then are ye in this strait and narrow path which leads to eternal life; yea, ye have entered in by the gate; ye have done according to the commandments of the Father and the Son; and ye have received the Holy Ghost, which witnesses of the Father and the Son, unto the fulfilling of the promise which he hath made, that if ye entered in by the way ye should receive.

19 And now, my beloved brethren, after ye have gotten into this strait and narrow path, I would ask if all is done? Behold, I say unto you, Nay; for ye have not come thus far save it were by the word of Christ with unshaken faith in him, relying wholly upon the merits of him who is mighty to save.

20 Wherefore, ye must press forward with a steadfastness in Christ, having a perfect brightness of hope, and a love of God and of all men. Wherefore, if ye shall press forward, feasting upon the word of Christ, and endure to the end, behold, thus saith the Father: Ye shall have eternal life.

21 And now, behold, my beloved brethren, this is the way; and there is none other way nor name given under heaven whereby man can be saved in the kingdom of God. And now, behold, this is the doctrine of Christ, and the only and true doctrine of the Father, and of the Son, and of the Holy Ghost, which is one God, without end. Amen.

vv. 4–20 Follow the Lord and Savior.

✋ Print the following phrases and put them in an envelope for groups of three or four. Have class members see if they can put the doctrines of Christ in order. (Note: many of them may be interchangeable, but ask what they think is the best order).

Repentance (v. 11)
Baptism (v. 11)
Receive the Holy Ghost (v. 12)
Follow the Son (v. 13)
Full purpose of heart (v. 13)
No hypocrisy (v. 13)
No deception (v. 13)
Real intent (v. 13)
Witnessing to God that you are willing to take upon you the name of Christ (v. 13)
Holy Ghost (v. 13)
Baptism of fire (v. 13)
Endure to the end (v. 16)
Remission of sins (v. 17)
Faith in Him (v. 19)
Relying wholly on him who is mighty to save (v. 19)
Press forward with hope and a steadfastness in Christ (v. 20)

Invite the groups to search the scriptures looking for the correct order and mark the doctrines of Christ in their scriptures. Suggest that as Nephi wrote the doctrines of Christ, he may not have intended all of them to go in any particular order. Discuss what you think is important to be in order and what is not.

❤ Invite class members to seek to understand and live the doctrine of Christ.

❤ Consider asking the following questions:

• *Why do you think the gospel of Christ is so plain and simple?*
• *Why is it hard to live the gospel if it is so plain?*
• *What keeps people from following Christ?*
• *What one doctrine taught in 2 Nephi 31 would help someone follow Christ to the waters of baptism?*

Invite all to follow Christ.

Notes

2 NEPHI 32

Ask, Show, and Tell
About 559–545 BC

1–2, After entering in at the way, we receive the Holy Ghost; 3–6, the words of Christ and the Holy Ghost will tell us all things that we should do; 7–9, The Spirit teaches us to pray always.

1 And now, behold, my beloved brethren, I suppose that ye ponder somewhat in your hearts concerning that which ye should do after ye have entered in by the way. But, behold, why do ye ponder these things in your hearts?

2 Do ye not remember that I said unto you that after ye had received the Holy Ghost ye could speak with the tongue of angels? And now, how could ye speak with the tongue of angels save it were by the Holy Ghost?

3 Angels speak by the power of the Holy Ghost; wherefore, they speak the words of Christ. Wherefore, I said unto you, feast upon the words of Christ; for behold, the words of Christ will tell you all things what ye should do.

4 Wherefore, now after I have spoken these words, if ye cannot understand them it will be because ye ask not, neither do ye knock; wherefore, ye are not brought into the light, but must perish in the dark.

5 For behold, again I say unto you that if ye will enter in by the way, and receive the Holy Ghost, it will show unto you all things what ye should do.

6 Behold, this is the doctrine of Christ, and there will be no more doctrine given until after he shall manifest himself unto you in the flesh. And when he shall manifest himself unto you in the flesh, the things which he shall say unto you shall ye observe to do.

vv. 1–6 The words of Christ and the Holy Ghost will tell us all things that we should do as we pray and ask for understanding.

⚡ Before class, select a personal item that you could show to class members. Choose something interesting that would allow them to get to know you better. Draw the chart (found following) on the board with only the words "who," "action," and "what" filled in. Then display the item in the front of the class and inform class members that you will be doing a brief "Show and Tell" activity. Quickly tell the members of your class about the item you brought, show them the item, and invite them to ask questions about it. Ask, *What are the three major elements of the activity we just participated in to get better acquainted with one another?* Write the words "Tell, Ask, Show" on the chart. Explain that those three elements are also a part of getting better acquainted with what the Lord would like us to do in our lives.

🔍 Show the chart to the class and read 2 Nephi 32:1–6, looking for who or what does the telling, asking, or showing in those verses. Then, look for what is being told, asked, or shown. Fill in the rest of the chart as class members respond with their findings.

Notes

Who?	The words of Christ	We	The Holy Ghost will
Action?	Tell (v. 3)	Ask (v. 4)	Show (v. 5)
What?	All things what we should do	To understand the words of Christ	All things what we should do

? Analyze: Direct class members toward verse 3 and ask:
- *What are some different sources where we find the words of Christ?*
- *What do you think it means that "the words of Christ will tell all things what we should do"?*
- *The word "feast" is used. Why do you think Nephi chose the word "feast" to describe studying the words of Christ?*

? Apply:
- *How does someone feast on the words of Christ?*
- *How do you know when you have really feasted on the words of Christ?*
- *What do you feel as a result of your feast?*

💬 Direct class members toward 2 Nephi 32:4 and have someone read the following quote from Boyd K. Packer: "You have your agency, and inspiration does not—perhaps cannot—flow unless you ask for it, or someone asks for you. No message in scripture is repeated more often than the invitation, even the command, to pray—to ask. Prayer is so essential a part of revelation that without it the veil may remain closed to you. Learn to pray. Pray often. Pray in your mind, in your heart. Pray on your knees" ("Personal Revelation: The Gift, the Test, and the Promise," *Ensign*, November 1994).

? Apply: *How has prayer benefited your personal scripture study? In what ways has your understanding been enhanced by asking for help from God to understand the scriptures?*

❤ Prior to class, consider your own experiences regarding the doctrine taught in 2 Nephi 32:3. Share an example from your life when the Holy Ghost has taught you what you should do to resolve an issue, overcome a challenge, or be guided toward safety, spiritually or physically. You may also consider asking a class member to prepare something to share in advance. Testify that the scriptures and the Holy Ghost can give us the answers regarding "all things what we should do."

v. 6 More doctrine.

🔍 In verse 6, look for what the Lord would bring when he would finally visit the Nephites.

💡 Explain what when Jesus came, He brought more doctrine. Invite your class to write "3 Nephi 11:30–41" in the margin and look at those verses to see what additional doctrines Jesus shared with the Nephites.

7 And now I, Nephi, cannot say more; the Spirit stoppeth mine utterance, and I am left to mourn because of the unbelief, and the wickedness, and the ignorance, and the stiffneckedness of men; for they will not search knowledge, nor understand great knowledge, when it is given unto them in plainness, even as plain as word can be.

8 And now, my beloved brethren, I perceive that ye ponder still in your hearts; and it grieveth me that I must speak concerning this thing. For if ye would hearken unto the Spirit which teacheth a man to pray, ye would know that ye must pray; for the evil spirit teacheth not a man to pray, but teacheth him that he must not pray.

9 But behold, I say unto you that ye must pray always, and not faint; that ye must not perform any thing unto the Lord save in the first place ye shall pray unto the Father in the name of Christ, that he will consecrate thy performance unto thee, that thy performance may be for the welfare of thy soul.

Notes

vv. 7–9 We must hearken unto the Spirit and pray always and not faint.

💬 Brigham Young taught, "It matters not whether you or I feel like praying, when the time comes to pray, pray. If we do not feel like it, we should pray till we do. . . . If the Devil says you cannot pray when you are angry, tell him it is none of his business, and pray until that species of insanity is dispelled and serenity is restored to the mind" ("The Communication between God and Man," *Teachings of Presidents of the Church: Brigham Young,* 41).

❓ Analyze: *In the above quote, why do you think President Young referred to the feeling that one cannot pray when angry or otherwise indisposed as a "species of insanity"? What do you know about prayer that would give support to President Young's statement?*

❤ Testify regarding the importance of frequent prayer. Invite class members to "pray always and not faint."

2 NEPHI 33

Nephi's Concluding Words
About 559–545 BC

1–5, Nephi speaks concerning his writings; 6–9, Nephi's feelings for the Lord and all people; 10–15, At the judgment bar of Christ, these words will be made known.

1 And now I, Nephi, cannot write all the things which were taught among my people; neither am I mighty in writing, like unto speaking; for when a man speaketh by the power of the Holy Ghost the power of the Holy Ghost carrieth it unto the hearts of the children of men.

2 But behold, there are many that harden their hearts against the Holy Spirit, that it hath no place in them; wherefore, they cast many things away which are written and esteem them as things of naught.

vv. 1–2 We must receive the Holy Ghost by acting in faith.

⚡ Put some type of food (grape, piece of candy) in front of each person in the class. Explain that it is a symbol of the Holy Ghost. As you read verse one, look for the role of the Holy Ghost. Ask, *If the food represents the Holy Ghost and I as your teacher speak by the power of the Holy Ghost and place the food there, what is your role?* Share the quote below by David A. Bednar and talk about how a teacher can explain, demonstrate, and so on, but ultimately the learner must take it in. Invite all class members to partake. Ask,
• *Is it possible for two people to be sitting right next to each other in a class, and one feel the Holy Ghost and the other not feel it?*
• *How is that possible?*
• *What factors might cause that?*

🔍 *Look for how it is possible as you read verses 1–2.*

💬 Speaking of this verse, Elder Bednar said, "Please notice how the power of the Spirit carries the message *unto* but not necessarily *into* the heart. A teacher can explain, demonstrate, persuade, and testify, and do so with great spiritual power and effectiveness. Ultimately, however, the content of a message and the witness of the Holy Ghost penetrate into the heart only if a receiver allows them to enter . . . A learner exercising agency by acting in accordance with correct principles opens his or her heart to the Holy Ghost—and invites His teaching, testifying power and confirming witness. Learning by faith requires spiritual, mental, and physical exertion and not just passive reception. It is in the sincerity and consistency of our faith–inspired action that we indicate to our Heavenly Father and His Son, Jesus Christ, our willingness to learn and receive instruction from the Holy Ghost" ("Seek Learning By Faith," Address to CES Religious Educators, February 3, 2006, 1, 3).

✋ Using Elder Bednar's statement, help class

Notes

members create a list of things they can do to feel the Holy Ghost in class. You may also want to discuss what class members do that might distract each other from feeling the Holy Ghost in class.

♥ Challenge class members to do these things so that the power of the Holy Ghost can help them learn.

3 But I, Nephi, have written what I have written, and I esteem it as of great worth, and especially unto my people. For I pray continually for them by day, and mine eyes water my pillow by night, because of them; and I cry unto my God in faith, and I know that he will hear my cry.

4 And I know that the Lord God will consecrate my prayers for the gain of my people. And the words which I have written in weakness will be made strong unto them; for it persuadeth them to do good; it maketh known unto them of their fathers; and it speaketh of Jesus, and persuadeth them to believe in him, and to endure to the end, which is life eternal.

5 And it speaketh harshly against sin, according to the plainness of the truth; wherefore, no man will be angry at the words which I have written save he shall be of the spirit of the devil.

6 I glory in plainness; I glory in truth; I glory in my Jesus, for he hath redeemed my soul from hell.

7 I have charity for my people, and great faith in Christ that I shall meet many souls spotless at his judgment-seat.

8 I have charity for the Jew—I say Jew, because I mean them from whence I came.

9 I also have charity for the Gentiles. But behold, for none of these can I hope except they shall be reconciled unto Christ, and enter into the narrow gate, and walk in the strait path which leads to life, and continue in the path until the end of the day of probation.

vv. 3–9 The things that really matter in life.

🔎 Have class members read verses 3–9 to themselves and underline words that show what Nephi really cares about. Then have class members list what they underlined and why.

✎ Now have class members write down the things that matter most to them. Ask them to share what they wrote and why.

10 And now, my beloved brethren, and also Jew, and all ye ends of the earth, hearken unto these words and believe in Christ; and if ye believe not in these words believe in Christ. And if ye shall believe in Christ ye will believe in these words, for they are the words of Christ, and he hath given them unto me; and they teach all men that they should do good.

11 And if they are not the words of Christ, judge ye—for Christ will show unto you, with power and great glory, that they are his words, at the last day; and you and I shall stand face to face before his bar; and ye shall know that I have been commanded of him to write these things, notwithstanding my weakness.

12 And I pray the Father in the name of Christ that many of us, if not all, may be saved in his kingdom at that great and last day.

vv. 10–12 If we truly believe in Christ, we should try to do good.

⚡ Write on the board, "The most important thing in life is to _____." Ask class members to give responses to complete the sentence.

🔎 *Look for how Nephi might fill in the blank as you read verses 10–11.*

❓ Analyze:
  • *Why might Nephi say, "believe in Christ"?*
  • *How do people act when they truly believe in Christ?*
  • *Why would it affect someone accepting the Book of Mormon or not?*

Notes

♥ Bear your testimony of the Savior and how the Book of Mormon has affected that testimony. Invite members of your class to do the same. Note: One way you could do this is to let a few of your class members know ahead of time that you will ask them to bear their testimony on how the Book of Mormon has affected their testimony of Christ. This gives class members time to formulate a response.

13 And now, my beloved brethren, all those who are of the house of Israel, and all ye ends of the earth, I speak unto you as the voice of one crying from the dust: Farewell until that great day shall come.

14 And you that will not partake of the goodness of God, and respect the words of the Jews, and also my words, and the words which shall proceed forth out of the mouth of the Lamb of God, behold, I bid you an everlasting farewell, for these words shall condemn you at the last day.

15 For what I seal on earth, shall be brought against you at the judgment bar; for thus hath the Lord commanded me, and I must obey. Amen.

Teaching Tips from Prophets' Lips "First of all, we are teaching people, not subject matter *per se*; and second, every lesson outline that I have ever seen will inevitably have more in it than we can possibly cover in the allotted time" (Jeffrey R. Holland, "Teaching and Learning in the Church," *Ensign*, June 2007, 88–105).

Notes

THE BOOK OF JACOB

JACOB BOOK SUMMARY

Time Period: About 544–482 BC (63 years)

Contributors: Jacob, Zenos

Source: Small plates of Nephi

Synopsis:

Chapter 1: Jacob prefaces his book.

Chapter 2–4: Jacob's teachings concerning the love of money, chastity, and the Lord's dealings with Israel.

Chapters 5–6: Zenos's Allegory of the Olive Trees and Jacob's further commentary.

Chapter 7: Jacob's encounter with Sherem and final words.

The Brother of Nephi

The words of his preaching unto his brethren. He confoundeth a man who seeketh to overthrow the doctrine of Christ. A few words concerning the history of the people of Nephi.

JACOB 1

"We Did Magnify Our Office"
About 544–421 BC

1–4, The charge of recording sacred events on the plates; 5–8, Jacob's desire to persuade all to come unto Christ; 9–12, The last affairs of Nephi and his death; 13–19, Jacob and others magnify their callings to teach.

1 For behold, it came to pass that fifty and five years had passed away from the time that Lehi left Jerusalem; wherefore, Nephi gave me, Jacob, a commandment concerning the small plates, upon which these things are engraven.

2 And he gave me, Jacob, a commandment that I should write upon these plates a few of the things which I considered to be most precious; that I should not touch, save it were lightly, concerning the history of this people which are called the people of Nephi.

3 For he said that the history of his people should be engraven upon his other plates, and that I should preserve these plates and hand them down unto my seed, from generation to generation.

4 And if there were preaching which was sacred,

Notes

or revelation which was great, or prophesying, that I should engraven the heads of them upon these plates, and touch upon them as much as it were possible, for Christ's sake, and for the sake of our people.

vv. 1–4 If we record our spiritual experiences, they will bless the lives of others.

⚡ Hold up the scriptures and a journal and discuss with the class what is the difference between these books and how they could be similar.

🔍 In verses 1–4, look for the most valuable things that can be written in a journal.

❓ Analyze: Why is writing down spiritual impressions often more important than writing down events that occur?

💬 Look for what Richard G. Scott taught about how to receive more direction from the Spirit: "Write down in a secure place the important things you learn from the Spirit. You will find that as you record a precious impression, often others will come that you would not have otherwise received. Also, the spiritual knowledge you gain will be available throughout your life. Always, day or night, wherever you are, whatever you are doing, seek to recognize and respond to the direction of the Spirit" ("To Learn and to Teach More Effectively," Education Week Devotional, August 21, 2007).

♥ If you have time, distribute pieces of paper and invite class members to write down when they first started to gain a testimony. Ask them if they would like to be able to read the written testimony of their parents or other faithful family members. Challenge them to record their testimonies in a personal journal so that family members can one day see what was written by them.

5 For because of faith and great anxiety, it truly had been made manifest unto us concerning our people, what things should happen unto them.

6 And we also had many revelations, and the spirit of much prophecy; wherefore, we knew of Christ and his kingdom, which should come.

7 Wherefore we labored diligently among our people, that we might persuade them to come unto Christ, and partake of the goodness of God, that they might enter into his rest, lest by any means he should swear in his wrath they should not enter in, as in the provocation in the days of temptation while the children of Israel were in the wilderness.

8 Wherefore, we would to God that we could persuade all men not to rebel against God, to provoke him to anger, but that all men would believe in Christ, and view his death, and suffer his cross and bear the shame of the world; wherefore, I, Jacob, take it upon me to fulfil the commandment of my brother Nephi.

vv. 7–8 When we come to know of Christ, we seek to persuade all to come unto Him.

👥 Explain to class members that sometimes when the phrases in the scriptures are hard to understand, it can be helpful to put the phrases into their own words. Break class members into two groups. Assign one group verse 7, and the other group verse 8. Ask class members to read their verse carefully and attempt to put it into their own words. Have them write down what they came up with and share it with a person nearby. Then ask for a volunteer in each group to share their reworded scriptures. Ask if others in the class had something different they would be willing to share.

♥ After each group has shared, ask, what is the lesson for us from your verse? Invite them to do accordingly.

9 Now Nephi began to be old, and he saw that he must soon die; wherefore, he anointed a man to be a king and a ruler over his people now, according to the reigns of the kings.

Notes

10 The people having loved Nephi exceedingly, he having been a great protector for them, having wielded the sword of Laban in their defence, and having labored in all his days for their welfare—

11 Wherefore, the people were desirous to retain in remembrance his name. And whoso should reign in his stead were called by the people, second Nephi, third Nephi, and so forth, according to the reigns of the kings; and thus they were called by the people, let them be of whatever name they would.

12 And it came to pass that Nephi died.

13 Now the people which were not Lamanites were Nephites; nevertheless, they were called Nephites, Jacobites, Josephites, Zoramites, Lamanites, Lemuelites, and Ishmaelites.

14 But I, Jacob, shall not hereafter distinguish them by these names, but I shall call them Lamanites that seek to destroy the people of Nephi, and those who are friendly to Nephi I shall call Nephites, or the people of Nephi, according to the reigns of the kings.

15 And now it came to pass that the people of Nephi, under the reign of the second king, began to grow hard in their hearts, and indulge themselves somewhat in wicked practices, such as like unto David of old desiring many wives and concubines, and also Solomon, his son.

16 Yea, and they also began to search much gold and silver, and began to be lifted up somewhat in pride.

17 Wherefore I, Jacob, gave unto them these words as I taught them in the temple, having first obtained mine errand from the Lord.

18 For I, Jacob, and my brother Joseph had been consecrated priests and teachers of this people, by the hand of Nephi.

19 And we did magnify our office unto the Lord, taking upon us the responsibility, answering the sins of the people upon our own heads if we did not teach them the word of God with all diligence; wherefore, by laboring with our might their blood might not come upon our garments; otherwise their blood would come upon our garments, and we would not be found spotless at the last day.

vv. 17–19 Magnifying your calling.

⚡ Hold up a magnifying glass and ask, *What does this have to do with good leadership?*

🔍 *Search for what the magnifying glass has to do with leadership in verses 17–19.*

❓ Analyze:
  • *What does the magnifying glass teach about leadership?*
  • *What does it mean to "magnify your calling"?*
  • *In verse 19, what did Jacob and his brother feel would happen if they minimized, instead of magnified, their responsibility?*

💬 Share the following quote by John Taylor: "If you do not magnify your calling, God will hold you responsible for those you might have saved, had you done your duty" (*Teachings of Presidents of the Church: John Taylor* [2001], 164).

❓ Analyze: *What does the phrase "having first obtained my errand from the Lord" in verse 17 add to our understanding of magnifying our callings?* Explain that as we come to know that we have been called of God and are doing his work, we will diligently magnify our calling.

♥ Ask each class member to think of someone they know who is an example of one who magnifies his or her calling, and invite a few of them to share specific examples. Challenge the class to magnify their callings like Nephi, Jacob, and the examples that have been shared.

Teaching Tips from Prophets' Lips "I beg of you, for yourselves and for the students, to have faith that they will want to read [the scriptures], not that you must drive them to it, but that it will draw them to it . . . The Lord wrote the book. He showed Nephi how to do

Notes

it in such a way that it would draw you. And, it will draw your students" (Henry B. Eyring "The Book of Mormon Will Change Your Life," CES symposium on the Book of Mormon, August 17, 1990, 2).

JACOB 2

The Destructive Nature of Riches and Immorality

About 544–421 BC

1–11, Jacob explains the weight of his calling and responsibility; 12–22, The destructive nature of riches and how to overcome; 23–35, Jacob censures the people about having more than one wife: "The Lord delights in the chastity of women."

Overarching Principle: Jacob warns his people against two evils: the destructive nature of riches and immorality.

1 The words which Jacob, the brother of Nephi, spake unto the people of Nephi, after the death of Nephi:

2 Now, my beloved brethren, I, Jacob, according to the responsibility which I am under to God, to magnify mine office with soberness, and that I might rid my garments of your sins, I come up into the temple this day that I might declare unto you the word of God.

3 And ye yourselves know that I have hitherto been diligent in the office of my calling; but I this day am weighed down with much more desire and anxiety for the welfare of your souls than I have hitherto been.

4 For behold, as yet, ye have been obedient unto the word of the Lord, which I have given unto you.

5 But behold, hearken ye unto me, and know that by the help of the all-powerful Creator of heaven and earth I can tell you concerning your

thoughts, how that ye are beginning to labor in sin, which sin appeareth very abominable unto me, yea, and abominable unto God.

6 Yea, it grieveth my soul and causeth me to shrink with shame before the presence of my Maker, that I must testify unto you concerning the wickedness of your hearts.

7 And also it grieveth me that I must use so much boldness of speech concerning you, before your wives and your children, many of whose feelings are exceedingly tender and chaste and delicate before God, which thing is pleasing unto God;

8 And it supposeth me that they have come up hither to hear the pleasing word of God, yea, the word which healeth the wounded soul.

9 Wherefore, it burdeneth my soul that I should be constrained, because of the strict commandment which I have received from God, to admonish you according to your crimes, to enlarge the wounds of those who are already wounded, instead of consoling and healing their wounds; and those who have not been wounded, instead of feasting upon the pleasing word of God have daggers placed to pierce their souls and wound their delicate minds.

10 But, notwithstanding the greatness of the task, I must do according to the strict commands of God, and tell you concerning your wickedness and abominations, in the presence of the pure in heart, and the broken heart, and under the glance of the piercing eye of the Almighty God.

11 Wherefore, I must tell you the truth according to the plainness of the word of God. For behold, as I inquired of the Lord, thus came the word unto me, saying: Jacob, get thou up into the temple on the morrow, and declare the word which I shall give thee unto this people.

vv. 2–6 Prophets care about their people.

⚡ Invite a class member who plays an organized sport to the front of class. Ask him/her what they appreciate about their coach. Ask,

Notes

Does the coach ever tell you what you are doing wrong? How does that make you feel? (The purpose of this brief discussion is to establish that prophets warn us against sins for our own benefit.)

Write on the board, "A prophet is like a coach . . ." and ask class members to come up with their own comparisons and share them.

🔎 Explain that Jacob, as their teacher and religious leader, instructs his people in Jacob chapter 2. Read verses 2–3, 6–11, *look for what Jacob's message is going to be about.*

❓ Analyze: *Why is Jacob worried? How does this reaction show his love and concern for his people?*

♥ Testify to class members that our prophets today are equally concerned for us. Share the following quote from Jeffrey R. Holland: "I feel much like Jacob of old, who said 'It grieveth me that I must use so much boldness of speech . . . before . . . many . . . whose feelings are exceedingly tender and chaste and delicate.' [Jacob 2:7] But bold we need to be" (Jeffrey R. Holland, "Place No More for the Enemy of My Soul," *Ensign,* May 2010, 44).

12 And now behold, my brethren, this is the word which I declare unto you, that many of you have begun to search for gold, and for silver, and for all manner of precious ores, in the which this land, which is a bland of promise unto you and to your seed, doth abound most plentifully.

13 And the hand of providence hath smiled upon you most pleasingly, that you have obtained many riches; and because some of you have obtained more abundantly than that of your brethren ye are lifted up in the pride of your hearts, and wear stiff necks and high heads because of the costliness of your apparel, and persecute your brethren because ye suppose that ye are better than they.

14 And now, my brethren, do ye suppose that God

justifieth you in this thing? Behold, I say unto you, Nay. But he condemneth you, and if ye persist in these things his judgments must speedily come unto you.

15 O that he would show you that he can pierce you, and with one glance of his eye he can smite you to the dust!

16 O that he would rid you from this iniquity and abomination. And, O that ye would listen unto the word of his commands, and let not this pride of your hearts destroy your souls!

17 Think of your brethren like unto yourselves, and be familiar with all and free with your substance, that they may be rich like unto you.

18 But before ye seek for riches, seek ye for the kingdom of God.

19 And after ye have obtained a hope in Christ ye shall obtain riches, if ye seek them; and ye will seek them for the intent to ado good—to clothe the naked, and to feed the hungry, and to liberate the captive, and administer relief to the sick and the afflicted.

20 And now, my brethren, I have spoken unto you concerning pride; and those of you which have afflicted your neighbor, and persecuted him because ye were proud in your hearts, of the things which God hath given you, what say ye of it?

21 Do ye not suppose that such things are abominable unto him who created all flesh? And the one being is as precious in his sight as the other. And all flesh is of the dust; and for the selfsame end hath he created them, that they should keep his commandments and glorify him forever.

vv. 12–21 Jacob's First Lesson—The pride of your hearts and desire for riches destroys your soul.

⚡ Draw a chart on the board like the one seen below. If possible, encourage class members to create their own chart to follow along on their own.

Notes

The Problem(s)	
What THEY did	What WE do
The Solution(s)	

This chart can be used to identify 1) the problem that Jacob points out to his people, 2) what "they did" to cause the problem, and 3) what Jacob's solution to the problem is. The column labeled "What we do" will allow you to discuss modern-day application of the problem and solution with the class.

🔎 *What problem are the people having in verses 12 and 16?* Read verses 13–15, 20. *What did the people do once they obtained riches?* (Write the class's answer in the 'What THEY did' column on the chart).

❓ Analyze:
- *Why do you think having costly apparel leads some people to be lifted up in pride?*
- *Why do some people persecute others because of their clothing?*
- *What does God think of people who persecute others because of their apparel?* (Look in verse 14)

❓ Apply: *What does the world do today that is similar to the problem the Nephites are having?* Write their answers in the 'What WE do' column.

🗨 Share and discuss the following quote from Ezra Taft Benson regarding pride: "Pride is a sin that can readily be seen in others but is rarely admitted in ourselves. Most of us consider pride to be a sin of those on the top, such as the rich and the learned, looking down at the rest of us. (See 2 Nephi 9:42.) There is,

however, a far more common ailment among us—and that is pride from the bottom looking up. It is manifest in so many ways, such as faultfinding, gossiping, backbiting, murmuring, living beyond our means, envying, coveting, withholding gratitude and praise that might lift another, and being unforgiving and jealous" (in Conference Report, April 1989).

🔎 *In verses 17–19, 21 what is the solution to the problem?* Write class members answers on the chart.

❓ Analyze:
- What do you think verse 18 means?
- How do we seek for the kingdom of God?
- According to Jacob, under what circumstances is it acceptable to have riches?
- *What is Jacob's point in verse 21 and how does it apply to his lesson?*

❓ Apply: *How does Jacob's solution apply to us today?*

22 And now I make an end of speaking unto you concerning this pride. And were it not that I must speak unto you concerning a grosser crime, my heart would rejoice exceedingly because of you.

23 But the word of God burdens me because of your grosser crimes. For behold, thus saith the Lord: This people begin to wax in iniquity; they understand not the scriptures, for they seek to excuse themselves in committing whoredoms, because of the things which were written concerning David, and Solomon his son.

24 Behold, David and Solomon truly had many wives and concubines, which thing was abominable before me, saith the Lord.

25 Wherefore, thus saith the Lord, I have led this people forth out of the land of Jerusalem, by the power of mine arm, that I might raise up unto me a righteous branch from the fruit of the loins of Joseph.

26 Wherefore, I the Lord God will not suffer that this people shall do like unto them of old.

Notes

27 Wherefore, my brethren, hear me, and hearken to the word of the Lord: For there shall not any man among you have save it be one wife; and concubines he shall have none;

28 For I, the Lord God, delight in the chastity of women. And whoredoms are an abomination before me; thus saith the Lord of Hosts.

29 Wherefore, this people shall keep my commandments, saith the Lord of Hosts, or cursed be the land for their sakes.

30 For if I will, saith the Lord of Hosts, raise up seed unto me, I will command my people; otherwise they shall hearken unto these things.

31 For behold, I, the Lord, have seen the sorrow, and heard the mourning of the daughters of my people in the land of Jerusalem, yea, and in all the lands of my people, because of the wickedness and abominations of their husbands.

32 And I will not suffer, saith the Lord of Hosts, that the cries of the fair daughters of this people, which I have led out of the land of Jerusalem, shall come up unto me against the men of my people, saith the Lord of Hosts.

33 For they shall not lead away captive the daughters of my people because of their tenderness, save I shall visit them with a sore curse, even unto destruction; for they shall not commit whoredoms, like unto them of old, saith the Lord of Hosts.

34 And now behold, my brethren, ye know that these commandments were given to our father, Lehi; wherefore, ye have known them before; and ye have come unto great condemnation; for ye have done these things which ye ought not to have done.

35 Behold, ye have done greater iniquities than the Lamanites, our brethren. Ye have broken the hearts of your tender wives, and lost the confidence of your children, because of your bad examples before them; and the sobbings of their hearts ascend up to God against you. And because of the strictness of the word of God,

which cometh down against you, many hearts died, pierced with deep wounds.

vv. 22–35 Jacob's Second Lesson—The Lord delights in the chastity of women.

⚡ Use the same chart and identification process as above. You can create an additional chart on the board or continue to complete the previous one.

🔍 *What does Jacob think about his second topic in verse 22?*
 • *What is their problem in verses 23–24?* Write class members answers next to "The Problem"
 • *What did the people do that was so bad in verses 31–35?* Write their answers in the column labeled "What THEY did"
 • *What is Jacob's solution to the problem in verses 27–28?* Write their answer next to "The Solution."

❓ Analyze: *What do you think "The Lord delights in the chastity of women" means? Why do you think Jacob offers this information as a solution to the peoples' immorality problems?*

❓ Apply: *How do we commit offenses today that are similar to those of the Nephites?* (Note: the Nephite problem was they were justifying their immoral practice of having many wives and concubines because of their misinterpretation of the scriptures. While we may not face an identical problem today, the world does bombard us with the message that sexual immorality is justifiable.)

💡 Notice in verse 30 that the Lord gives one example of why He may authorize plural marriage if He chooses. Joseph Smith taught, "I have constantly said no man shall have but one wife at a time, unless the Lord directs otherwise" (*Teachings of the Presidents of the Church: Joseph Smith* [Salt Lake City: The Church of Jesus Christ of Latter-day Saints, 2007], 324).

Notes

JACOB 3

"Unto You That Are Pure in Heart"
About 544–421 BC

1–4, Jacob discusses the blessings of being pure in heart; 5–11, Because the Lamanites have faithful families, they are declared "more righteous" than the Nephites; 12–14, Jacob warns his people and records his ministry on the plates.

1 But behold, I, Jacob, would speak unto you that are pure in heart. Look unto God with firmness of mind, and pray unto him with exceeding faith, and he will console you in your afflictions, and he will plead your cause, and send down justice upon those who seek your destruction.

2 O all ye that are pure in heart, lift up your heads and receive the pleasing word of God, and feast upon his love; for ye may, if your minds are firm, forever.

3 But, wo, wo, unto you that are not pure in heart, that are filthy this day before God; for except ye repent the land is cursed for your sakes; and the Lamanites, which are not filthy like unto you, nevertheless they are cursed with a sore cursing, shall scourge you even unto destruction.

4 And the time speedily cometh, that except ye repent they shall possess the land of your inheritance, and the Lord God will lead away the righteous out from among you.

vv. 1–2 The Nephites judged the Lamanites on outward appearance; the Lord judges and blesses us according to the purity of our hearts.

⚡ Prior to the lesson, obtain a drinking cup that you are not concerned about ruining (a paper or plastic cup would work well.) Before class, use a marker to scribble on the outside of the cup and smear the inside and lip of the cup with dirt or mud. Place the cup in the front of the room with a pitcher of water. At the beginning of the lesson, invite a class member to the front of the room to have a drink of water. Allow the individual to inspect the cup and ask,

- *Is there anything that concerns you about drinking from this cup?*
- *What concerns you more, the scribbling on the outside or the dirt on the inside?*
- *Why?*

Explain that the Nephites in Jacob's time judged the Lamanites on superficial outward appearance, but that the Lord used a different set of criteria—the purity of their hearts and lives.

🔍 *Look in verses 1–2 for what are several blessings given to those who are pure of heart.*

❓ Analyze: *Why is it that receiving these blessings is contingent on the purity of our hearts and not outward circumstances?*

❓ Apply: *Which of these blessings would you most like to receive? Why?*

💜 Testify that what truly matters is the condition of a person's heart, not outward circumstances. If we are pure in heart we can "feast upon his love." Explain that verses 3–4 describe the consequence of being "filthy before God," but this chapter will teach an important lesson about how to be "pure of heart." Testify that by living the teachings in this chapter, class members will qualify for the blessings promised by the Lord.

5 Behold, the Lamanites your brethren, whom ye hate because of their filthiness and the cursing which hath come upon their skins, are more righteous than you; for they have not forgotten the commandment of the Lord, which was given unto our father—that they should have save it were one wife, and concubines they should have none, and there should not be whoredoms committed among them.

6 And now, this commandment they observe to keep; wherefore, because of this observance, in keeping this commandment, the Lord God will

Notes

not destroy them, but will be merciful unto them; and one day they shall become a blessed people.

7 Behold, their husbands love their wives, and their wives love their husbands; and their husbands and their wives love their children; and their unbelief and their hatred towards you is because of the iniquity of their fathers; wherefore, how much better are you than they, in the sight of your great Creator?

8 O my brethren, I fear that unless ye shall repent of your sins that their skins will be whiter than yours, when ye shall be brought with them before the throne of God.

9 Wherefore, a commandment I give unto you, which is the word of God, that ye revile no more against them because of the darkness of their skins; neither shall ye revile against them because of their filthiness; but ye shall remember your own filthiness, and remember that their filthiness came because of their fathers.

10 Wherefore, ye shall remember your children, how that ye have grieved their hearts because of the example that ye have set before them; and also, remember that ye may, because of your filthiness, bring your children unto destruction, and their sins be heaped upon your heads at the last day.

11 O my brethren, hearken unto my words; arouse the faculties of your souls; shake yourselves that ye may awake from the slumber of death; and loose yourselves from the pains of hell that ye may not become angels to the devil, to be cast into that lake of fire and brimstone which is the second death.

vv. 5–11 The Lord is merciful to us when we strive to have faithful and loving families.

Invite class members to read verses 5–7 and 10 and look for why the Lord was more pleased with the Lamanites than with the Nephites and what He promises them.

Analyze:
- Why do you think the Lord is willing to be

merciful when we strive to be faithful and loving within our families?
- Why might one's family relationships be a good indicator of the purity of his or her heart?
- What does Jacob teach us about the long-term effects that our family life will have on our children? (Look in verses 7 and 10.)

Provide class members with copies of "The Family: A Proclamation to the World." Depending on your circumstances, read through the proclamation together in small groups or as individuals. Encourage class members to share which aspects of the Lord's plan for family life have brought them the most blessings. Ask, *How has living that principle purified your heart or the hearts of your family members?*

Challenge class members to select one principle in the proclamation to strive to live within their families.

12 And now I, Jacob, spake many more things unto the people of Nephi, warning them against fornication and lasciviousness, and every kind of sin, telling them the awful consequences of them.

13 And a hundredth part of the proceedings of this people, which now began to be numerous, cannot be written upon these plates; but many of their proceedings are written upon the larger plates, and their wars, and their contentions, and the reigns of their kings.

14 These plates are called the plates of Jacob, and they were made by the hand of Nephi. And I make an end of speaking these words.

Teaching Tips from Prophets' Lips "If you have properly prepared yourself, the Holy Ghost will enlighten and guide you as you teach. You may receive impressions about those you teach, what you should emphasize in teaching them, and how you can teach them most effectively. Your diligent efforts will be magnified as you humbly obey the whisperings of the Spirit" (*Teaching, No Greater Call*, 47).

Notes

JACOB 4

"We Knew of Christ"

About 544–421 BC

1–4, Jacob engraves the plates with the intent to testify of Christ; 5–13, Jacob discourses on the means by which we receive power and revelation through Christ; 14–18, Jacob explains why some Jews struggled to accept the Savior

1 Now behold, it came to pass that I, Jacob, having ministered much unto my people in word, (and I cannot write but a little of my words, because of the difficulty of engraving our words upon plates) and we know that the things which we write upon plates must remain;

2 But whatsoever things we write upon anything save it be upon plates must perish and vanish away; but we can write a few words upon plates, which will give our children, and also our beloved brethren, a small degree of knowledge concerning us, or concerning their fathers—

3 Now in this thing we do rejoice; and we labor diligently to engraven these words upon plates, hoping that our beloved brethren and our children will receive them with thankful hearts, and look upon them that they may learn with joy and not with sorrow, neither with contempt, concerning their first parents.

4 For, for this intent have we written these things, that they may know that we knew of Christ, and we had a hope of his glory many hundred years before his coming; and not only we ourselves had a hope of his glory, but also all the holy prophets which were before us.

vv. 1–4 When we have the love of God, we are willing to endure difficulties to share that love with others.

⚡ *What are some difficult trials or experiences people have been willing to go through in order to testify of Jesus Christ?* Encourage class members to think of examples from the scriptures, church history, or personal experiences—the discussion might include anything from missionary experiences to scriptural martyrs.

🔍 *In verses 1–4, search for the difficult task Jacob was willing to do to bear his testimony of the Savior.* Write the phrase "We Knew of Christ" on the board.

💬 "I love your soul and the souls of all men, and do all I can to bring them salvation. . . . A man filled with the love of God, is not content with blessing his family alone, but ranges through the whole world, anxious to bless the whole human race" (*Teachings of the Prophet Joseph Smith*, comp. Joseph Fielding Smith [1976], 174).

❤ Explain that this love for God and others comes from understanding important doctrines about Jesus Christ and leads individuals to have the strength to complete difficult tasks in order to share that love. When we see the difficult things people are willing to do to share what they "knew of Christ" we are able to see how important their message is. Invite class members to be willing to make sacrifices in order to share their testimony of Christ with loved ones.

5 Behold, they believed in Christ and worshiped the Father in his name, and also we worship the Father in his name. And for this intent we keep the law of Moses, it pointing our souls to him; and for this cause it is sanctified unto us for righteousness, even as it was accounted unto Abraham in the wilderness to be obedient unto the commands of God in offering up his son Isaac, which is a similitude of God and his Only Begotten Son.

6 Wherefore, we search the prophets, and we have many revelations and the spirit of prophecy; and having all these witnesses we obtain a hope, and our faith becometh unshaken, insomuch that we

Notes

truly can command in the name of Jesus and the very trees obey us, or the mountains, or the waves of the sea.

7 Nevertheless, the Lord God showeth us our weakness that we may know that it is by his grace, and his great condescensions unto the children of men, that we have power to do these things.

8 Behold, great and marvelous are the works of the Lord. How unsearchable are the depths of the mysteries of him; and it is impossible that man should find out all his ways. And no man knoweth of his ways save it be revealed unto him; wherefore, brethren, despise not the revelations of God.

9 For behold, by the power of his word man came upon the face of the earth, which earth was created by the power of his word. Wherefore, if God being able to speak and the world was, and to speak and man was created, O then, why not able to command the dearth, or the workmanship of his hands upon the face of it, according to his will and pleasure?

10 Wherefore, brethren, seek not to counsel the Lord, but to take counsel from his hand. For behold, ye yourselves know that he counseleth in wisdom, and in justice, and in great mercy, over all his works.

11 Wherefore, beloved brethren, be reconciled unto him through the atonement of Christ, his Only Begotten Son, and ye may obtain a resurrection, according to the power of the resurrection which is in Christ, and be presented as the first-fruits of Christ unto God, having faith, and obtained a good hope of glory in him before he manifesteth himself in the flesh.

12 And now, beloved, marvel not that I tell you these things; for why not speak of the atonement of Christ, and attain to a perfect knowledge of him, as to attain to the knowledge of a resurrection and the world to come?

13 Behold, my brethren, he that prophesieth, let him prophesy to the understanding of men;

for the Spirit speaketh the truth and lieth not. Wherefore, it speaketh of things as they really care, and of things as they really will be; wherefore, these things are manifested unto us plainly, for the salvation of our souls. But behold, we are not witnesses alone in these things; for God also spake them unto prophets of old.

vv. 5–13 Prophets, scriptures, and revelation teach of Christ, his power, and His Atonement.

✋ Write the words "what," "how," and "why" on the board under the phrase "We Knew of Christ." Have class members search verses 5–13 and mark any phrases that teach what Jacob knew about Christ or how he knew it. Ask class members to share what they found, writing verse numbers on the board under the "what" or "how." Allow class members to explain what they chose to mark and why.

❓ Apply: During your discussion, look for opportunities to encourage class members to bear testimony by using follow-up questions. Consider asking, *How has knowing that about Christ helped you? When have you felt the Holy Ghost teach truths "as they really are"?*

14 But behold, the Jews were a stiffnecked people; and they despised the words of plainness, and killed the prophets, and sought for things that they could not understand. Wherefore, because of their blindness, which blindness came by looking beyond the mark, they must needs fall; for God hath taken away his plainness from them, and delivered unto them many things which they cannot understand, because they desired it. And because they desired it God hath done it, that they may stumble.

15 And now I, Jacob, am led on by the Spirit unto prophesying; for I perceive by the workings of the Spirit which is in me, that by the stumbling of the Jews they will reject the stone upon which they might build and have safe foundation.

16 But behold, according to the scriptures, this stone shall become the great, and the last, and

Notes

the only sure foundation, upon which the Jews can build.

17 And now, my beloved, how is it possible that these, after having rejected the sure foundation, can ever build upon it, that it may become the head of their corner?

18 Behold, my beloved brethren, I will unfold this mystery unto you; if I do not, by any means, get shaken from my firmness in the Spirit, and stumble because of my over anxiety for you.

vv. 14–18 We must not "look beyond the mark;" Christ and His Atonement are the focal point of our worship.

⚡ Draw a target on the board with a question mark in the center.

🔎 *As you read verses 14–18, look for what caused the Jews to stumble.*

❓ Analyze: *What do you think it means to "look beyond the mark"? What do you think should be the central focus of our lives?* (Christ and His Atonement.)

❓ Apply: *What might distract us? If we are not careful, in what ways might we over-complicate our worship and lose power to overcome adversity?*

❤ Invite class members to eliminate anything from their lives that might be causing them to forget or overlook the central role of Jesus Christ in the plan of salvation.

JACOB 5

The Allegory of the Olive Tree
About 544–421 BC

1–3, Jacob quotes Zenos in which he likens the house of Israel to a tame olive tree; 4–14, To save the house of Israel, Gentiles are grafted in whereas the house of Israel is scattered (first visit, before Christ); 15–28, Both Gentiles and house of Israel bear fruit, references

to Nephites and Lamanites (second visit, time of Christ); 29–48, Both Gentiles and house of Israel are corrupted (third visit, Apostasy); 50–72, (fourth visit, house of Israel is gathered, gospel to all the world) Laborers are called to gather the house of Israel before the burning of the vineyard.

Overarching Principle: The Lord loves each of his children, and will do all that He can to save us, even though we may reject Him.

⚡ Show a picture of the Christus statue. Ask, *In what ways do people reject the Savior?* (Make a list of their responses on the board.) *How does Christ feel toward those who have rejected Him? Is it ever possible to return to Christ even though someone may have already rejected Him?* Take time to go beyond the class's first response by asking them follow-up questions such as, *Why is that? How do you know that is true?* Asking these follow-up questions will help establish a greater understanding for this allegory.

Note: The allegory of the olive tree was a response to a specific question posed by Jacob himself in Jacob 4:15–18; therefore, in order to understand this allegory, it would be helpful to review Jacob's question.

🔎 Direct your class's attention to the word "mystery" in Jacob 4:18. Ask, *What is Jacob talking about when he says* this *mystery?* Have the class look in verses 15–17 for the answer. To help them understand this mystery, have class members put Jacob 4:17 in their own words. Write on the board a result of their combined answers. The answer could read something like this, "How can we still accept the Savior even though we reject Him?" Explain to the class that Jacob 5 answers this question.

1 Behold, my brethren, do ye not remember to have read the words of the prophet Zenos, which he spake unto the house of Israel, saying:

Notes

2 Hearken, O ye house of Israel, and hear the words of me, a prophet of the Lord.

3 For behold, thus saith the Lord, I will liken thee, O house of Israel, like unto a tame olive tree, which a man took and nourished in his vineyard; and it grew, and waxed old, and began to decay.

4 And it came to pass that the master of the vineyard went forth, and he saw that his olive tree began to decay; and he said: I will prune it, and dig about it, and nourish it, that perhaps it may shoot forth young and tender branches, and it perish not.

5 And it came to pass that he pruned it, and digged about it, and nourished it according to his word.

6 And it came to pass that after many days it began to put forth somewhat a little, young and tender branches; but behold, the main atop thereof began to perish.

7 And it came to pass that the master of the vineyard saw it, and he said unto his servant: It grieveth me that I should lose this tree; wherefore, go and pluck the branches from a wild olive tree, and bring them hither unto me; and we will pluck off those main branches which are beginning to wither away, and we will cast them into the fire that they may be burned.

8 And behold, saith the Lord of the vineyard, I take away many of these young and tender branches, and I will graft them whithersoever I will; and it mattereth not that if it so be that the root of this tree will perish, I may preserve the fruit thereof unto myself; wherefore, I will take these young and tender branches, and I will graft them whithersoever I will.

9 Take thou the branches of the wild olive tree, and graft them in, in the stead thereof; and these which I have plucked off I will cast into the fire and burn them, that they may not cumber the ground of my vineyard.

10 And it came to pass that the servant of the Lord of the vineyard did according to the word of the Lord of the vineyard, and grafted in the branches of the wild olive tree.

11 And the Lord of the vineyard caused that it should be digged about, and pruned, and nourished, saying unto his servant: It grieveth me that I should lose this tree; wherefore, that perhaps I might preserve the roots thereof that they perish not, that I might preserve them unto myself, I have done this thing.

12 Wherefore, go thy way; watch the tree, and nourish it, according to my words.

13 And these will I place in the nethermost part of my vineyard, whithersoever I will, it mattereth not unto thee; and I do it that I may preserve unto myself the natural branches of the tree; and also, that I may lay up fruit thereof against the season, unto myself; for it grieveth me that I should lose this tree and the fruit thereof.

14 And it came to pass that the Lord of the vineyard went his way, and hid the natural branches of the tame olive tree in the nethermost parts of the vineyard, some in one and some in another, according to his will and pleasure.

vv. 1–14 The symbols of the allegory.

🔎 Take time to list and make comparisons to the following elements of the allegory in verses 3–13. Invite class members to write in their scriptures the meaning of each element of the allegory as you study the Lord's first visit to the vineyard.

First Visit
v. 3 "tame olive tree" (house of Israel), "it grew" (growth of Christ's church through righteousness), "began to decay" (see scriptural footnote, apostasy), "vineyard" (the earth).
v. 4 "master of the vineyard" (Jesus Christ), "prune, dig, nourish" (the master's efforts to save and preserve his vineyard)
v. 7 "servant" (one who helps the work of the Lord—prophets, apostles,

Notes

missionaries, and so forth), "wild olive tree" (see scriptural footnote for verse 10, Gentiles), "fire" (final judgment of God)

v. 8 "take away" (scriptural footnote, Scattering of Israel)

v. 13 "fruit" (works of men)

Explain that in this allegory the Lord of the vineyard will make three separate visits to assess the fruit of His trees. Each visit will teach a principle about how the Lord reacts to His people's acceptance or rejection of Him.

15 And it came to pass that a long time passed away, and the Lord of the vineyard said unto his servant: Come, let us go down into the vineyard, that we may labor in the vineyard.

16 And it came to pass that the Lord of the vineyard, and also the servant, went down into the vineyard to labor. And it came to pass that the servant said unto his master: Behold, look here; behold the tree.

17 And it came to pass that the Lord of the vineyard looked and beheld the tree in the which the wild olive branches had been grafted; and it had sprung forth and begun to bear fruit. And he beheld that it was good; and the fruit thereof was like unto the natural fruit.

18 And he said unto the servant: Behold, the branches of the wild tree have taken hold of the moisture of the root thereof, that the root thereof hath brought forth much strength; and because of the much strength of the root thereof the wild branches have brought forth tame fruit. Now, if we had not grafted in these branches, the tree thereof would have perished. And now, behold, I shall lay up much fruit, which the tree thereof hath brought forth; and the fruit thereof I shall lay up against the season, unto mine own self.

19 And it came to pass that the Lord of the vineyard said unto the servant: Come, let us go to the nethermost part of the vineyard, and behold if the natural branches of the tree have not brought forth much fruit also, that I may lay up of the fruit thereof against the season, unto mine own self.

20 And it came to pass that they went forth whither the master had hid the natural branches of the tree, and he said unto the servant: Behold these; and he beheld the first that it had brought forth much fruit; and he beheld also that it was good. And he said unto the servant: Take of the fruit thereof, and lay it up against the season, that I may preserve it unto mine own self; for behold, said he, this long time have I nourished it, and it hath brought forth much fruit.

21 And it came to pass that the servant said unto his master: How comest thou hither to plant this tree, or this branch of the tree? For behold, it was the poorest spot in all the land of thy vineyard.

22 And the Lord of the vineyard said unto him: Counsel me not; I knew that it was a poor spot of ground; wherefore, I said unto thee, I have nourished it this long time, and thou beholdest that it hath brought forth much fruit.

23 And it came to pass that the Lord of the vineyard said unto his servant: Look hither; behold I have planted another branch of the tree also; and thou knowest that this spot of ground was poorer than the first. But, behold the tree. I have nourished it this long time, and it hath brought forth much fruit; therefore, gather it, and lay it up against the season, that I may preserve it unto mine own self.

24 And it came to pass that the Lord of the vineyard said again unto his servant: Look hither, and behold another branch also, which I have planted; behold that I have nourished it also, and it hath brought forth fruit.

25 And he said unto the servant: Look hither and behold the last. Behold, this have I planted in a good spot of ground; and I have nourished it this long time, and only a part of the tree hath brought forth tame fruit, and the other part of the tree hath brought forth wild fruit; behold, I have nourished this tree like unto the others.

Notes

26 And it came to pass that the Lord of the vineyard said unto the servant: Pluck off the branches that have not brought forth good fruit, and cast them into the fire.

27 But behold, the servant said unto him: Let us prune it, and dig about it, and nourish it a little longer, that perhaps it may bring forth good fruit unto thee, that thou canst lay it up against the season.

28 And it came to pass that the Lord of the vineyard and the servant of the Lord of the vineyard did nourish all the fruit of the vineyard.

29 And it came to pass that a long time had passed away, and the Lord of the vineyard said unto his servant: Come, let us go down into the vineyard, that we may labor again in the vineyard. For behold, the time draweth near, and the end soon cometh; wherefore, I must lay up fruit against the season, unto mine own self.

30 And it came to pass that the Lord of the vineyard and the servant went down into the vineyard; and they came to the tree whose natural branches had been broken off, and the wild branches had been grafted in; and behold all sorts of fruit did cumber the tree.

31 And it came to pass that the Lord of the vineyard did taste of the fruit, every sort according to its number. And the Lord of the vineyard said: Behold, this long time have we nourished this tree, and I have laid up unto myself against the season much fruit.

32 But behold, this time it hath brought forth much fruit, and there is none of it which is good. And behold, there are all kinds of bad fruit; and it profiteth me nothing, notwithstanding all our labor; and now it grieveth me that I should lose this tree.

33 And the Lord of the vineyard said unto the servant: What shall we do unto the tree, that I may preserve again good fruit thereof unto mine own self?

34 And the servant said unto his master: Behold,

because thou didst graft in the branches of the wild olive tree they have nourished the roots, that they are alive and they have not perished; wherefore thou beholdest that they are yet good.

35 And it came to pass that the Lord of the vineyard said unto his servant: The tree profiteth me nothing, and the roots thereof profit me nothing so long as it shall bring forth evil fruit.

36 Nevertheless, I know that the roots are good, and for mine own purpose I have preserved them; and because of their much strength they have hitherto brought forth, from the wild branches, good fruit.

37 But behold, the wild branches have grown and have overrun the roots thereof; and because that the wild branches have overcome the roots thereof it hath brought forth much evil fruit; and because that it hath brought forth so much evil fruit thou beholdest that it beginneth to perish; and it will soon become ripened, that it may be cast into the fire, except we should do something for it to preserve it.

38 And it came to pass that the Lord of the vineyard said unto his servant: Let us go down into the nethermost parts of the vineyard, and behold if the natural branches have also brought forth evil fruit.

39 And it came to pass that they went down into the nethermost parts of the vineyard. And it came to pass that they beheld that the fruit of the natural branches had become corrupt also; yea, the first and the second and also the last; and they had all become corrupt.

40 And the wild fruit of the last had overcome that part of the tree which brought forth good fruit, even that the branch had withered away and died.

41 And it came to pass that the Lord of the vineyard wept, and said unto the servant: What could I have done more for my vineyard?

42 Behold, I knew that all the fruit of the vineyard, save it were these, had become corrupted. And

Notes

now these which have once brought forth good fruit have also become corrupted; and now all the trees of my vineyard are good for nothing save it be to be hewn down and cast into the fire.

43 And behold this last, whose branch hath withered away, I did plant in a good spot of ground; yea, even that which was choice unto me above all other parts of the land of my vineyard.

44 And thou beheldest that I also cut down that which cumbered this spot of ground, that I might plant this tree in the stead thereof.

45 And thou beheldest that a part thereof brought forth good fruit, and a part thereof brought forth wild fruit; and because I plucked not the branches thereof and cast them into the fire, behold, they have overcome the good branch that it hath withered away.

46 And now, behold, notwithstanding all the care which we have taken of my vineyard, the trees thereof have become corrupted, that they bring forth no good fruit; and these I had hoped to preserve, to have laid up fruit thereof against the season, unto mine own self. But, behold, they have become like unto the wild olive tree, and they are of no worth but to be hewn down and cast into the fire; and it grieveth me that I should lose them.

47 But what could I have done more in my vineyard? Have I slackened mine hand, that I have not nourished it? Nay, I have nourished it, and I have digged about it, and I have pruned it, and I have dunged it; and I have stretched forth mine hand almost all the day long, and the end draweth nigh. And it grieveth me that I should hew down all the trees of my vineyard, and cast them into the fire that they should be burned. Who is it that has corrupted my vineyard?

48 And it came to pass that the servant said unto his master: Is it not the loftiness of thy vineyard— have not the branches thereof overcome the roots which are good? And because the branches have overcome the roots thereof, behold they grew faster than the strength of the roots, taking strength unto themselves. Behold, I say, is not this the cause that the trees of thy vineyard have become corrupted?

49 And it came to pass that the Lord of the vineyard said unto the servant: Let us go to and hew down the trees of the vineyard and cast them into the fire, that they shall not cumber the ground of my vineyard, for I have done all. What could I have done more for my vineyard?

vv. 15–49 The three visits.

Divide the class into pairs and assign each of them one of the following scriptures.

Second Visit vv. 15–28
Third Visit vv. 29–49

Ask each class member to look for the three following questions within their assigned verses. Also invite each person to prepare to share the answers by marking what they find in their scriptures.

- *What is the state of the fruit?*
- *Is there a reason for why the fruit is good or bad? If so, what is the reason?*
- *What specific phrases show how the master cares about His vineyard and fruit?*

After each person has answered these questions by marking phrases in their scriptures, have class members share what they found with their assigned partner. Have a few individuals discuss with the class what they discovered. Use the questions below to drive a discussion.

Analyze: *Why do you think the Lord doesn't just give up? If the fruit is already bad, what good will it do to try and fix it?*

Apply: *What happens when we think we know better than God, like the branches taking strength unto themselves? How have you come to know that God cares for you?*

50 But, behold, the servant said unto the Lord of the vineyard: Spare it a little longer.

51 And the Lord said: Yea, I will spare it a little

longer, for it grieveth me that I should lose the trees of my vineyard.

52 Wherefore, let us take of the branches of these which I have planted in the nethermost parts of my vineyard, and let us graft them into the tree from whence they came; and let us pluck from the tree those branches whose fruit is most bitter, and graft in the natural branches of the tree in the stead thereof.

53 And this will I do that the tree may not perish, that, perhaps, I may preserve unto myself the roots thereof for mine own purpose.

54 And, behold, the roots of the natural branches of the tree which I planted whithersoever I would are yet alive; wherefore, that I may preserve them also for mine own purpose, I will take of the branches of this tree, and I will graft them in unto them. Yea, I will graft in unto them the branches of their mother tree, that I may pre- serve the roots also unto mine own self, that when they shall be sufficiently strong perhaps they may bring forth good fruit unto me, and I may yet have glory in the fruit of my vineyard.

55 And it came to pass that they took from the natural tree which had become wild, and grafted in unto the natural trees, which also had become wild.

56 And they also took of the natural trees which had become wild, and grafted into their mother tree.

57 And the Lord of the vineyard said unto the servant: Pluck not the wild branches from the trees, save it be those which are most bitter; and in them ye shall graft according to that which I have said.

58 And we will nourish again the trees of the vine- yard, and we will trim up the branches thereof; and we will pluck from the trees those branches which are ripened, that must perish, and cast them into the fire.

59 And this I do that, perhaps, the roots thereof may take strength because of their goodness; and

because of the change of the branches, that the good may overcome the evil.

60 And because that I have preserved the natural branches and the roots thereof, and that I have grafted in the natural branches again into their mother tree, and have preserved the roots of their mother tree, that, perhaps, the trees of my vine- yard may bring forth again good fruit; and that I may have joy again in the fruit of my vineyard, and, perhaps, that I may rejoice exceedingly that I have preserved the roots and the branches of the first fruit—

61 Wherefore, go to, and call servants, that we may labor diligently with our might in the vineyard, that we may prepare the way, that I may bring forth again the natural fruit, which natural fruit is good and the most precious above all other fruit.

62 Wherefore, let us go to and labor with our might this last time, for behold the end draweth nigh, and this is for the last time that I shall prune my vineyard.

63 Graft in the branches; begin at the last that they may be first, and that the first may be blast, and dig about the trees, both old and young, the first and the last; and the last and the first, that all may be nourished once again for the last time.

64 Wherefore, dig about them, and prune them, and dung them once more, for the last time, for the end draweth nigh. And if it be so that these last grafts shall grow, and bring forth the natural fruit, then shall ye prepare the way for them, that they may grow.

65 And as they begin to grow ye shall clear away the branches which bring forth bitter fruit, according to the strength of the good and the size thereof; and ye shall not clear away the bad thereof all at once, lest the roots thereof should be too strong for the graft, and the graft thereof shall perish, and I lose the trees of my vineyard.

66 For it grieveth me that I should lose the trees of my vineyard; wherefore ye shall clear away the bad according as the good shall grow, that the

Notes

root and the top may be equal in strength, until the good shall overcome the bad, and the bad be hewn down and cast into the fire, that they cumber not the ground of my vineyard; and thus will I sweep away the bad out of my vineyard.

67 And the branches of the natural tree will I graft in again into the natural tree;

68 And the branches of the natural tree will I graft into the natural branches of the tree; and thus will I bring them together again, that they shall bring forth the natural fruit, and they shall be one.

69 And the bad shall be cast away, yea, even out of all the land of my vineyard; for behold, only this once will I prune my vineyard.

70 And it came to pass that the Lord of the vineyard sent his servant; and the servant went and did as the Lord had commanded him, and brought other servants; and they were few.

71 And the Lord of the vineyard said unto them: Go to, and labor in the vineyard, with your might. For behold, this is the last time that I shall nourish my vineyard; for the end is nigh at hand, and the season speedily cometh; and if ye labor with your might with me ye shall have joy in the fruit which I shall lay up unto myself against the time which will soon come.

72 And it came to pass that the servants did go and labor with their mights; and the Lord of the vineyard labored also with them; and they did obey the commandments of the Lord of the vineyard in all things.

73 And there began to be the natural fruit again in the vineyard; and the natural branches began to grow and thrive exceedingly; and the wild branches began to be plucked off and to be cast away; and they did keep the root and the top thereof equal, according to the strength thereof.

74 And thus they labored, with all diligence, according to the commandments of the Lord of the vineyard, even until the bad had been cast away out of the vineyard, and the Lord had preserved unto himself that the trees had become again the natural fruit; and they became like unto one body; and the fruits were equal; and the Lord of the vineyard had preserved unto himself the natural fruit, which was most precious unto him from the beginning.

75 And it came to pass that when the Lord of the vineyard saw that his fruit was good, and that his vineyard was no more corrupt, he called up his servants, and said unto them: Behold, for this last time have we nourished my vineyard; and thou beholdest that I have done according to my will; and I have preserved the natural fruit, that it is good, even like as it was in the beginning. And blessed art thou; for because ye have been diligent in laboring with me in my vineyard, and have kept my commandments, and have brought unto me again the natural fruit, that my vineyard is no more corrupted, and the bad is cast away, behold ye shall have joy with me because of the fruit of my vineyard.

76 For behold, for a long time will I lay up of the fruit of my vineyard unto mine own self against the season, which speedily cometh; and for the last time have I nourished my vineyard, and pruned it, and dug about it, and dunged it; wherefore I will lay up unto mine own self of the fruit, for a long time, according to that which I have spoken.

77 And when the time cometh that evil fruit shall again come into my vineyard, then will I cause the good and the bad to be gathered; and the good will I preserve unto myself, and the bad will I cast away into its own place. And then cometh the season and the end; and my vineyard will I cause to be burned with fire.

vv. 50–77 The last visit.

🔍 As a class, read each of following verses and look for what happens during the fourth visit.

Fourth Visit

v. 52 (Gathering—see scriptural footnote)
vv. 61, 70–72 (A call for missionaries and

Notes

the joy that comes with serving the Lord)

v. 65 (Good and bad shall grow together)

v. 66 (Good will triumph over evil)

vv. 74–75 (Second Coming and Millennium)

vv. 77 (End of the world after the Millennium)

❓ Analyze: *What do each of the following verses teach us about what will happen in the last days? Which of these events give you hope and joy?*

❤ Again show the picture of the Christus and refer to the "mystery" that Jacob was unfolding. Ask, *How is it possible for someone to return to God after sinning and rejecting Christ?* You may want to refer to some of the phrases that were found by class member about how the master cares about his vineyard and the state of the fruit. For example, the Lord uses the phrase "it grieveth me" eight times in verses 7, 11, 13, 32, 46, 47, 51, 66. Add your testimony of Christ's love and mercy and His desire to have us return to Him. Additionally, testify that as we see the big picture of His plan through this allegory and rely on the Atonement of Jesus Christ, we gain an understanding that Heavenly Father will forgive us and do all He can to help us return to Him.

> **Teaching Tips from Prophets' Lips** "Never, and I mean never, give a lecture where there is no student participation. A 'talking head' is the weakest form of class instruction" (Richard G. Scott, "To Understand and Live Truth," Address to CES Religious Educators, February 4, 2005, 3).

JACOB 6

Application of the Allegory of the Olive Tree
About 544–421 BC

1–5, God is merciful in his dealings with man; 6–11, Why people reject God, despite His mercy; 12–13, "O be wise; what can I say more?"

Note: Jacob chapter 6 is Jacob's own conclusion to and application of the allegory of the olive tree from Jacob 5. If time permits, you may want to consider teaching these two chapters in the same lesson.

1 And now, behold, my brethren, as I said unto you that I would prophesy, behold, this is my prophecy—that the things which this prophet Zenos spake, concerning the house of Israel, in the which he likened them unto a tame olive tree, must surely come to pass.

2 And the day that he shall set his hand again the second time to recover his people, is the day, yea, even the last time, that the servants of the Lord shall go forth in his power, to nourish and prune his vineyard; and after that the fend soon cometh.

3 And how blessed are they who have labored diligently in his vineyard; and how cursed are they who shall be cast out into their own place! And the world shall be burned with fire.

4 And how merciful is our God unto us, for he remembereth the house of Israel, both roots and branches; and he stretches forth his hands unto them all the day long; and they are a stiffnecked and a gainsaying people; but as many as will not harden their hearts shall be saved in the kingdom of God.

5 Wherefore, my beloved brethren, I beseech of you in words of soberness that ye would repent, and come with full purpose of heart, and cleave unto God as he cleaveth unto you. And while

Notes

his arm of mercy is extended towards you in the light of the day, harden not your hearts.

6 Yea, today, if ye will hear his voice, harden not your hearts; for why will ye die?

7 For behold, after ye have been nourished by the good word of God all the day long, will ye bring forth evil fruit, that ye must be hewn down and cast into the fire?

8 Behold, will ye reject these words? Will ye reject the words of the prophets; and will ye reject all the words which have been spoken concerning Christ, after so many have spoken concerning him; and deny the good word of Christ, and the power of God, and the gift of the Holy Ghost, and quench the Holy Spirit, and make a mock of the great plan of redemption, which hath been laid for you?

9 Know ye not that if ye will do these things, that the power of the redemption and the resurrection, which is in Christ, will bring you to stand with shame and awful guilt before the bar of God?

10 And according to the power of justice, for justice cannot be denied, ye must go away into that lake of fire and brimstone, whose flames are unquenchable, and whose smoke ascendeth up forever and ever, which lake of fire and brimstone is endless torment.

11 O then, my beloved brethren, repent ye, and enter in at the strait gate, and continue in the way which is narrow, until ye shall obtain eternal life.

12 O be wise; what can I say more?

13 Finally, I bid you farewell, until I shall meet you before the pleasing bar of God, which bar striketh the wicked with awful dread and fear. Amen.

vv. 1–13 God is so abundant with His mercy toward us; we would be wise to accept it and foolish to reject it.

⚡ Create cut-outs of both a happy face and a sad face that you can display for your class, as depicted below. Write on the board "Wise or Foolish" and explain to your class that they are going to learn the difference between wisdom and foolishness. Give class members examples of things that would be considered either wise or foolish and ask them to tell you which corresponding cut-out face to hold up. (Some examples could include, "wearing a seat belt," or "inserting a metal object into an electrical outlet.") Explain that Jacob applies this idea to the lesson of the olive tree allegory from the previous chapter.

Wise   Foolish

🔍 Invite the class to read in verse 4. Ask, *How does Jacob interpret the Lord's actions in the allegory of the olive tree?* You may want to review how often he continued to nourish the olive trees despite their bad fruit from Jacob chapter 5.

🔍 In verse 5, *look for the four suggested actions Jacob encourages us to take because God is merciful. Are these actions wise or foolish?* Write Jacob's suggestions under the "Wise" category on the board.

❓ Analyze:
• *What do you think Jacob means by "cleave unto God as He cleaveth unto you"?* You may want to look up the definition of the word "cleave" and share it with class members to help them understand.
• *When or why would people want to cleave unto God?*
• *In what ways does God cleave unto us?*

Note with the class that we have to cleave unto God first. Ask, *Why should we have to cleave unto God first?*

Notes

❓ Apply: *When have you felt the need to cleave unto God? How have you felt God cleaves unto you?* (You may want to consider sharing your own experiences for this question.)

🔍 Look in verses 6–10 for the five questions Jacob asks and invite class members to mark all of the questions in their scriptures as they find them. As they identify each question, ask, *Is what Jacob is asking wise or foolish?* Summarize each question and write them on the board under the appropriate heading. (Note: All of the responses should be written on the board under the "Foolish" heading.)

❓ Analyze: Select one or two of the summarized questions from the "Foolish" column and ask, *Why is it foolish to . . . ?* or ask, *What do you think Jacob means when he says . . . ?*

❓ Analyze: Compare the "Wise" list from verse 5 with the "Foolish" list in verses 6–10. *What does Jacob teach are the final outcomes of being wise or foolish?*

🔍 *After sharing the allegory of the olive tree in chapter 5 and explaining how it applies to us in chapter 6, what is Jacob's conclusion in verse 12?*

💬 "[Jacob] had taught them as clearly as he could and with all the energy of his soul. He warned them in no uncertain terms what would happen if they chose to not 'enter at the strait gate, and continue in the way which is narrow (Jacob 6:11). He couldn't think of anything else to say to warn, to urge, to inspire, to motivate. And so he, simply and profoundly, said, 'O be wise; what can I say more?'" (M. Russell Ballard, "O Be Wise," *Ensign,* November 2006, 17).

❤ With your class, contrast the difference between cleaving to God (v. 5) or rejecting him in spite of his efforts to save us (vv. 7–8). Encourage class members to be wise and accept God's help.

JACOB 7
"Sherem the Anti-Christ"
About 544–421 BC

1–4, Sherem the anti-Christ seeks to lead away the church; 5–12, Sherem contends with Jacob and seeks to shake him from the faith; 13–19, Sherem demands a sign, is smitten, and confesses his sins to the people; 20–25, Sherem dies, peace and the love of God are restored among the people; 26–27, Jacob hands down the plates to his son Enos and bids farewell.

1 And now it came to pass after some years had passed away, there came a man among the people of Nephi, whose name was Sherem.

2 And it came to pass that he began to preach among the people, and to declare unto them that there should be no Christ. And he preached many things which were flattering unto the people; and this he did that he might overthrow the doctrine of Christ.

3 And he labored diligently that he might lead away the hearts of the people, insomuch that he did lead away many hearts; and he knowing that I, Jacob, had faith in Christ who should come, he sought much opportunity that he might come unto me.

4 And he was learned, that he had a perfect knowledge of the language of the people; wherefore, he could use much flattery, and much power of speech, according to the power of the devil.

5 And he had hope to shake me from the faith, notwithstanding the many revelations and the many things which I had seen concerning these things; for I truly had seen angels, and they had ministered unto me. And also, I had heard the voice of the Lord speaking unto me in very word, from time to time; wherefore, I could not be shaken.

6 And it came to pass that he came unto me, and on this wise did he speak unto me, saying: Brother Jacob, I have sought much opportunity that I might speak unto you; for I have heard and

also know that thou goest about much, preaching that which ye call the gospel, or the doctrine of Christ.

7 And ye have led away much of this people that they pervert the right way of God, and keep not the law of Moses which is the right way; and convert the law of Moses into the worship of a being which ye say shall come many hundred years hence. And now behold, I, Sherem, declare unto you that this is blasphemy; for no man knoweth of such things; for he cannot tell of things to come. And after this manner did Sherem contend against me.

8 But behold, the Lord God poured in his Spirit into my soul, insomuch that I did confound him in all his words.

9 And I said unto him: Deniest thou the Christ who shall come? And he said: If there should be a Christ, I would not deny him; but I know that there is no Christ, neither has been, nor ever will be.

10 And I said unto him: Believest thou the scriptures? And he said, Yea.

11 And I said unto him: Then ye do not understand them; for they truly testify of Christ. Behold, I say unto you that none of the prophets have written, nor prophesied, save they have spoken concerning this Christ.

12 And this is not all—it has been made manifest unto me, for I have heard and seen; and it also has been made manifest unto me by the power of the Holy Ghost; wherefore, I know if there should be no atonement made all mankind must be lost.

13 And it came to pass that he said unto me: Show me a sign by this power of the Holy Ghost, in the which ye know so much.

14 And I said unto him: What am I that I should tempt God to show unto thee a sign in the thing which thou knowest to be true? Yet thou wilt deny it, because thou art of the devil. Nevertheless, not my will be done; but if God shall smite thee, let that be a sign unto thee that he

has power, both in heaven and in earth; and also, that Christ shall come. And thy will, O Lord, be done, and not mine.

15 And it came to pass that when I, Jacob, had spoken these words, the power of the Lord came upon him, insomuch that he fell to the earth. And it came to pass that he was nourished for the space of many days.

16 And it came to pass that he said unto the people: Gather together on the morrow, for I shall die; wherefore, I desire to speak unto the people before I shall die.

17 And it came to pass that on the morrow the multitude were gathered together; and he spake plainly unto them and denied the things which he had taught them, and confessed the Christ, and the power of the Holy Ghost, and the ministering of angels.

18 And he spake plainly unto them, that he had been deceived by the power of the devil. And he spake of hell, and of eternity, and of eternal punishment.

19 And he said: I fear lest I have committed the unpardonable sin, for I have lied unto God; for I denied the Christ, and said that I believed the scriptures; and they truly testify of him. And because I have thus lied unto God I greatly fear lest my case shall be awful; but I confess unto God.

20 And it came to pass that when he had said these words he could say no more, and he gave up the ghost.

21 And when the multitude had witnessed that he spake these things as he was about to give up the ghost, they were astonished exceedingly; insomuch that the power of God came down upon them, and they were overcome that they fell to the earth.

22 Now, this thing was pleasing unto me, Jacob, for I had requested it of my Father who was in heaven; for he had heard my cry and answered my prayer.

Notes

23 And it came to pass that peace and the love of God was restored again among the people; and they searched the scriptures, and hearkened no more to the words of this wicked man.

24 And it came to pass that many means were devised to reclaim and restore the Lamanites to the knowledge of the truth; but it all was vain, for they delighted in wars and bloodshed, and they had an eternal hatred against us, their brethren. And they sought by the power of their arms to destroy us continually.

25 Wherefore, the people of Nephi did fortify against them with their arms, and with all their might, trusting in the God and rock of their salvation; wherefore, they became as yet, conquerors of their enemies.

26 And it came to pass that I, Jacob, began to be old; and the record of this people being kept on the other plates of Nephi, wherefore, I conclude this record, declaring that I have written according to the best of my knowledge, by saying that the time passed away with us, and also our lives passed away like as it were unto us a dream, we being a lonesome and a solemn people, wanderers, cast out from Jerusalem, born in tribulation, in a wilderness, and hated of our brethren, which caused wars and contentions; wherefore, we did mourn out our days.

27 And I, Jacob, saw that I must soon go down to my grave; wherefore, I said unto my son Enos: Take these plates. And I told him the things which my brother Nephi had commanded me, and he promised obedience unto the commands. And I make an end of my writing upon these plates, which writing has been small; and to the reader I bid farewell, hoping that many of my brethren may read my words. Brethren, adieu.

vv. 1–27 A testimony must be built on the scriptures, the prophets, and the Holy Ghost in order to withstand those who would shake it.

⚡ Discuss times in the class members' lives when they have been confronted about their testimony or some aspect of the Church. Ask, *what do you think helped you the most as you defended what you know is true?* Explain that this lesson outlines a similar situation of someone challenging a prophet's faith.

💡 In order to understand that in the last days we will be confronted by false Christs and false prophets, invite class members to read Joseph Smith—Matthew 1:22 in the Pearl of Great Price. Explain that Jesus Christ is telling his ancient apostles what will happen in the last days before the Second Coming.

❓ Analyze: *What does the phrase mean when it says, "the very elect, who are the elect according to the covenant?" What does a false Christ and a false prophet look like in our day?* Explain that a false Christ and a false prophet is more than someone posing as Christ, it is all those who teach false doctrine to persuade you away from Christ.

🔍 Look for how Jacob was able to defend himself against false teachings. Write the following two questions at the top of the board (side by side) with room to give answers underneath: *What methods did Sherem use to destroy the church?* and *What are the teachings of Satan taught by Sherem?* Have class members work in pairs; have one partner read and look for the answers to one question, and the other person look for answers to the other question. Then let them share with each other. If there is time, you may want them to mark all of Sherem's methods with one color and all of Satan's teachings with another color. (If you chose to have them mark in their scriptures, invite them to make some type of key at the beginning of the chapter.)

❓ Apply: *Why are the teachings of Satan appealing? What did you learn as you looked for the teachings and methods of Satan?*

💬 Sheldon F. Child stated, "Jacob points out three sources of truth—the scriptures, the prophets, and the Holy Ghost—that testify of Christ. They will help us build 'upon the rock

Notes

of our Redeemer, who is Christ, the Son of God'" ("A Sure Foundation," *Ensign*, November 2003).

❓ Apply: *From your own experiences, how have the things mentioned by Elder Child (scriptures, prophets, Holy Ghost) helped you as you have defended yourselves against the false teachings?*

🔍 As you have class members read verses 13–25 together or individually, consider asking the following questions as you read about Sherems's death.

- *In contrast to Jacob, what was Sherem's "testimony" based on?*
- *Why do you think Sherem asked for a sign?*
- *What did Sherem finally confess?*
- *What effect did that have on the people?*

❤ Share the following by Sheldon F. Child:

"Several years ago a severe storm hit the area in which we were living. It began with a torrential downpour, followed by a devastating easterly wind. When the storm was over, damages were assessed—power lines were down, property had been damaged, and many of the beautiful trees that grew in the area had been uprooted. A few days later I was talking to a friend who had lost several of the trees in his yard. The trees on one side of his home were standing straight and tall. They had weathered the storm well, while the trees that were in what I considered the prime spot on his property had not been able to withstand the heavy winds. He pointed out to me that the trees that survived the storm were planted on firm ground; their roots had to sink deep into the soil to receive nourishment. The trees he had lost were planted near a small stream, where nourishment was readily available. The roots were shallow. They were not anchored deeply enough to protect them from the storm. Our testimonies, like those trees, must be built on a sure foundation, deeply rooted in the gospel of Jesus Christ, so that when the winds and rains come into our lives, as they surely will, we will be strong enough to weather the storms that rage about us" ("A Sure Foundation," *Ensign*, November 2003). Invite class members to build their testimonies on Christ so that when false teachings are taught in the last days, they will not fall.

Teaching Tips from Prophets' Lips "Part of your work as a gospel teacher is to help learners understand and feel Heavenly Father's love for them. This cannot be done with words alone. It requires reaching out to individuals—those you see often, those you see occasionally, and those you would not see without making special effort" (*Teaching, No Greater Call,* 35).

Notes

THE BOOK OF ENOS

ENOS BOOK SUMMARY

Time Period: About 544–420 BC (124 years)

Contributors: Enos

Source: Small Plates of Nephi

ENOS

"My Soul Did Hunger"
About 544–420 BC

1–8, Enos seeks the Lord in prayer and receives a remission of sins; 9–18, Enos seeks the welfare of his brethren the Nephites and the Lamanites; 19–27, Enos recounts his ministry among the Nephites.

1 Behold, it came to pass that I, Enos, knowing my father that he was a just man—for he taught me in his language, and also in the nurture and admonition of the Lord—and blessed be the name of my God for it—

2 And I will tell you of the wrestle which I had before God, before I received a remission of my sins.

3 Behold, I went to hunt beasts in the forests; and the words which I had often heard my father speak concerning eternal life, and the joy of the saints, sunk deep into my heart.

4 And my soul hungered; and I kneeled down before my Maker, and I cried unto him in mighty prayer and supplication for mine own soul; and all the day long did I cry unto him; yea, and when the night came I did still raise my voice high that it reached the heavens.

5 And there came a voice unto me, saying: Enos, thy sins are forgiven thee, and thou shalt be blessed.

6 And I, Enos, knew that God could not lie; wherefore, my guilt was swept away.

7 And I said: Lord, how is it done?

8 And he said unto me: Because of thy faith in Christ, whom thou hast never before heard nor seen. And many years pass away before he shall manifest himself in the flesh; wherefore, go to, thy faith hath made thee whole.

vv. 1–8 A remission of sins comes as we gain a desire for the things of God, and then seek for forgiveness with faith in Christ.

⚡ Put a blank formula on the board similar to the following:

_____ + _____ divided by _____ x _____ = "thy sins are

Notes

forgiven" Invite class members to read verses 1–8 and write a formula for how Enos received a remission of his sins. Explain that the formula does not necessarily need to exactly replicate the example above but it should include all the applicable elements found in the scriptures. After a few minutes, allow class members to share what formula they have written down.

💬 Share the following quote about Robert D. Hales's formula in regard to Enos's experience:

"Let us review some of the elements of Enos' profound, faith-building experience: First, Enos heard the gospel truths from his father, just as you are hearing them in your families and in this conference. Second, he let his father's teachings about 'eternal life, and the joy of the saints' [Enos 1:3] sink deep into his heart. Third, he was filled with a desire to know for himself whether these teachings were true and where he himself stood before his Maker. To use Enos' words, 'My soul hungered.' [Enos 1:4] By this intense spiritual appetite, Enos qualified himself to receive the Savior's promise: 'Blessed are all they who do hunger and thirst after righteousness, for they shall be filled with the Holy Ghost.' [3 Ne. 12:6] Fourth, Enos obeyed the commandments of God, which enabled him to be receptive to the Spirit of the Holy Ghost. Fifth, Enos records, 'I kneeled down before my Maker, and I cried unto him in mighty prayer and supplication for mine own soul; and all the day long did I cry unto him; yea, and when the night came I did still raise my voice high that it reached the heavens.' [Enos 1:4] It wasn't easy. Faith did not come quickly. In fact, Enos characterized his experience in prayer as a 'wrestle which [he] had before God.' [Enos 1:2] But faith did come. By the power of the Holy Ghost, he did receive a witness for himself" ("Finding Faith in the Lord Jesus Christ," *Ensign,* November 2004).

❓ Apply: *What step of this formula was a turning point for Enos? Which step of this formula have you found to be most effective as you have sought remission for your sins?*

9 Now, it came to pass that when I had heard these words I began to feel a desire for the welfare of my brethren, the Nephites; wherefore, I did pour out my whole soul unto God for them.

10 And while I was thus struggling in the spirit, behold, the voice of the Lord came into my mind again, saying: I will visit thy brethren according to their diligence in keeping my commandments. I have given unto them this land, and it is a holy land; and I curse it not save it be for the cause of iniquity; wherefore, I will visit thy brethren according as I have said; and their transgressions will I bring down with sorrow upon their own heads.

11 And after I, Enos, had heard these words, my faith began to be unshaken in the Lord; and I prayed unto him with many long strugglings for my brethren, the Lamanites.

12 And it came to pass that after I had prayed and labored with all diligence, the Lord said unto me: I will grant unto thee according to thy desires, because of thy faith.

13 And now behold, this was the desire which I desired of him—that if it should so be, that my people, the Nephites, should fall into transgression, and by any means be destroyed, and the Lamanites should not be destroyed, that the Lord God would preserve a record of my people, the Nephites; even if it so be by the power of his holy arm, that it might be brought forth at some future day unto the Lamanites, that, perhaps, they might be brought unto salvation—

14 For at the present our strugglings were vain in restoring them to the true faith. And they swore in their wrath that, if it were possible, they would destroy our records and us, and also all the traditions of our fathers.

15 Wherefore, I knowing that the Lord God was able to preserve our records, I cried unto him

Notes

continually, for he had said unto me: Whatsoever thing ye shall ask in faith, believing that ye shall receive in the name of Christ, ye shall receive it.

16 And I had faith, and I did cry unto God that he would preserve the records; and he covenanted with me that he would bring them forth unto the Lamanites in his own due time.

17 And I, Enos, knew it would be according to the covenant which he had made; wherefore my soul did rest.

18 And the Lord said unto me: Thy fathers have also required of me this thing; and it shall be done unto them according to their faith; for their faith was like unto thine.

vv. 9–18 When we become truly converted, we seek the salvation of others.

⚡ Write the above principle on the board. Invite class members to give examples of stories in the scriptures where this principle is applied.

🔍 Invite the class to read verses 9–18 to see whose salvation Enos seeks first. Ask, *Whose welfare does he seek after that?*

❓ Analyze: *Why is it that those who have been converted have a natural desire to share the gospel with everyone?*

♥ *If we do not feel that desire, does that mean that we are not converted?* Share an experience where you felt a desire to share the gospel with someone. Invite class members to first seek the Lord for forgiveness and then share with everyone the goodness of the Lord's gospel.

19 And now it came to pass that I, Enos, went about among the people of Nephi, prophesying of things to come, and testifying of the things which I had heard and seen.

20 And I bear record that the people of Nephi did seek diligently to restore the Lamanites unto the true faith in God. But our labors were vain;

their hatred was fixed, and they were led by their evil nature that they became wild, and ferocious, and a blood-thirsty people, full of idolatry and filthiness; feeding upon beasts of prey; dwelling in tents, and wandering about in the wilderness with a short skin girdle about their loins and their heads shaven; and their skill was in the bow, and in the cimeter, and the ax. And many of them did eat nothing save it was raw meat; and they were continually seeking to destroy us.

21 And it came to pass that the people of Nephi did till the land, and raise all manner of grain, and of fruit, and flocks of herds, and flocks of all manner of cattle of every kind, and goats, and wild goats, and also many horses.

22 And there were exceedingly many prophets among us. And the people were a stiffnecked people, hard to understand.

23 And there was nothing save it was exceeding harshness, preaching and prophesying of wars, and contentions, and destructions, and continually reminding them of death, and the duration of eternity, and the judgments and the power of God, and all these things—stirring them up continually to keep them in the fear of the Lord. I say there was nothing short of these things, and exceedingly great plainness of speech, would keep them from going down speedily to destruction. And after this manner do I write concerning them.

24 And I saw wars between the Nephites and Lamanites in the course of my days.

25 And it came to pass that I began to be old, and an hundred and seventy and nine years had passed away from the time that our father Lehi left Jerusalem.

26 And I saw that I must soon go down to my grave, having been wrought upon by the power of God that I must preach and prophesy unto this people, and declare the word according to the truth which is in Christ. And I have declared it in all my days, and have rejoiced in it above that of the world.

Notes

27 And I soon go to the place of my rest, which is with my Redeemer; for I know that in him I shall rest. And I rejoice in the day when my mortal shall put on immortality, and shall stand before him; then shall I see his face with pleasure, and he will say unto me: Come unto me, ye blessed, there is a place prepared for you in the mansions of my Father. Amen.

vv. 22–27 We should be motivated by the love of God rather than the fear of punishment.

⚡ Discuss with the class what motivates them: desire for reward and success, or fear of failure and consequences? Ask, *What are the best reasons to do things?*

🔍 *Read verses 23–27 and look for the different types of motivations in those verses.*

❓ Analyze:
  • *What way did Enos often have to motivate his fellow Nephites in verse 23?*

  • *What words in verses 26–27 show a different motivation?*
  • *Which is better and why?*
  • *What does it show about a person's conversion?*

❤ Encourage class members to seek that higher motivation when someone wants to please God and enjoy his Spirit. Invite them to come unto to the Savior by following the formula given by Enos.

Teaching Tips from Prophets' Lips "If you want to be an effective teacher of the gospel, you have to live the principles that you propose to teach. The more perfectly you live the gospel, the more perfectly you will be able to teach the gospel" (Harold B. Lee, *The Teachings of Harold B. Lee: Eleventh President of The Church of Jesus Christ of Latter-day Saints*, ed. Clyde J. Williams [Salt Lake City: Bookcraft, 1996], 459).

Notes

THE BOOK OF JAROM

JAROM BOOK SUMMARY

Time Period: About 399–361 BC (38 years)

Contributors: Jarom

Source: Small plates of Nephi

JAROM

The Righteous Prosper in the Land
About 399–361 BC

1–2, Jarom explains the intent of his writings; 3–5, Despite their pride, many Nephites remain righteous and are blessed; 6–9, Though outnumbered, the Nephites defend themselves against Lamanite aggression by industry and righteous living; 10–13, The prophets teach the people to look toward the coming Messiah and repent; 14–15, Jarom finishes his record and delivers the plates to Omni.

1 Now behold, I, Jarom, write a few words according to the commandment of my father, Enos, that our genealogy may be kept.

2 And as these plates are small, and as these things are written for the intent of the benefit of our brethren the Lamanites, wherefore, it must needs be that I write a little; but I shall not write the things of my prophesying, nor of my revelations. For what could I write more than my fathers have written? For have not they revealed the plan of salvation? I say unto you, Yea; and this sufficeth me.

vv. 1–2 The Book of Mormon teaches the plan of salvation.

🔍 Have class members read Jarom 1:1–2. *Look for what Jarom says his ancestors have already revealed in their writings.*

❓ Analyze: *Do you think Jarom's statement is accurate? How has the plan of salvation been revealed at this point in the Book of Mormon?*

Discuss class members' answers. Tell them that you will now ask several rhetorical questions to get them thinking about what Jarom said.

• *Have we read about the premortal life or the council in heaven yet?*
• *What about temple work and the redemption of the dead?*
• *Is there anything written about the kingdoms of glory, or exaltation and eternal progression?*

Explain that many of these details that we generally consider to be part of the plan of salvation have not been discussed by Lehi, Nephi, Jacob, or Enos. Ask, *What, then, is the plan of salvation?*

Notes

💬 "In the great council in heaven, God's plan was presented: the plan of salvation, the plan of redemption, the great plan of happiness. The plan provides for a proving; all must choose between good and evil. His plan provides for a Redeemer, an atonement, the Resurrection, and, if we obey, our return to the presence of God" (Boyd K. Packer, in Conference Report, October 1993). *What are the essential elements of the plan of salvation according to this quote?*

👥 Divide the class into small groups or partnerships. Invite class members to reflect on what has been taught in the Book of Mormon from 1 Nephi through Jarom regarding the plan of salvation and find examples of when it has been taught in its simplicity. Refer to the quote above for specific elements of the plan to look for. Invite groups or partnerships to share and testify of what they find with the rest of the class.

❤ Bear your testimony regarding the simplicity of the plan of salvation as taught in the Book of Mormon.

3 Behold, it is expedient that much should be done among this people, because of the hardness of their hearts, and the deafness of their ears, and the blindness of their minds, and the stiffness of their necks; nevertheless, God is exceedingly merciful unto them, and has not as yet swept them off from the face of the land.

4 And there are many among us who have many revelations, for they are not all stiffnecked. And as many as are not stiffnecked and have faith, have communion with the Holy Spirit, which maketh manifest unto the children of men, according to their faith.

5 And now, behold, two hundred years had passed away, and the people of Nephi had waxed strong in the land. They observed to keep the law of Moses and the sabbath day holy unto the Lord. And they profaned not; neither did they blaspheme. And the laws of the land were exceedingly strict.

6 And they were scattered upon much of the face of the land, and the Lamanites also. And they were exceedingly more numerous than were they of the Nephites; and they loved murder and would drink the blood of beasts.

7 And it came to pass that they came many times against us, the Nephites, to battle. But our kings and our leaders were mighty men in the faith of the Lord; and they taught the people the ways of the Lord; wherefore, we withstood the Lamanites and swept them away out of our lands, and began to fortify our cities, or whatsoever place of our inheritance.

8 And we multiplied exceedingly, and spread upon the face of the land, and became exceedingly rich in gold, and in silver, and in precious things, and in fine workmanship of wood, in buildings, and in machinery, and also in iron and copper, and brass and steel, making all manner of tools of every kind to till the ground, and weapons of war—yea, the sharp pointed arrow, and the quiver, and the dart, and the javelin, and all preparations for war.

9 And thus being prepared to meet the Lamanites, they did not prosper against us. But the word of the Lord was verified, which he spake unto our fathers, saying that: Inasmuch as ye will keep my commandments ye shall prosper in the land.

vv. 3–9 "Inasmuch as ye will keep my commandments ye shall prosper in the land."

⚡ Write the following on the board: "Keep commandments and Prosper in the Land"

🔎 Invite class members to read verses 3–9. Ask half of the class to look for ways the Nephites kept the commandments and ask the other half of the class to look for ways the Lord caused the Nephites to prosper.

❓ Analyze: *What are a few reasons why the Lord follows the pattern of blessing those who keep his commandments?*

❓ Apply: *Have you seen the Lord's promise*

Notes

fulfilled where those who keep his commandments are blessed?

10 And it came to pass that the prophets of the Lord did threaten the people of Nephi, according to the word of God, that if they did not keep the commandments, but should fall into transgression, they should be destroyed from off the face of the land.

11 Wherefore, the prophets, and the priests, and the teachers, did labor diligently, exhorting with all long-suffering the people to diligence; teaching the law of Moses, and the intent for which it was given; persuading them to look forward unto the Messiah, and believe in him to come as though he already was. And after this manner did they teach them.

12 And it came to pass that by so doing they kept them from being destroyed upon the face of the land; for they did prick their hearts with the word, continually stirring them up unto repentance.

13 And it came to pass that two hundred and thirty and eight years had passed away—after the manner of wars, and contentions, and dissensions, for the space of much of the time.

14 And I, Jarom, do not write more, for the plates are small. But behold, my brethren, ye can go to the bother plates of Nephi; for behold, upon them the records of our wars are engraven, according to the writings of the kings, or those which they caused to be written.

15 And I deliver these plates into the hands of my son Omni, that they may be kept according to the commandments of my fathers.

vv. 10–15 Prophets labor diligently to bring the Lord's people to repentance.

✋ Invite class members to mark the action phrases that describe the work of the prophets in verses 10–12. Ask them to share and discuss the significance of the phrases they mark as you write them on the board. (Consider selecting a class member to act as scribe.)

💡 The word "threaten" in Jarom 1:10 may seem to be an unusual description of the role of prophets. However, Noah Webster's 1828 *American Dictionary of the English Language*, which was published during the time the Book of Mormon was translated, offers the following alternate definition for the word *threaten*: "To exhibit the appearance of something evil or unpleasant approaching." This definition may help to better communicate Jarom's intent to the members of your class. He wasn't saying the prophets were speaking threats against the people; rather, they were forewarning of "unpleasant" things to come.

❓ Analyze: (When a class member gives an answer, ask why he or she selected that phrase.)
• *Which phrase do you think best describes what a prophet should do?*
• *Why do you think the Lord has such high expectations regarding a prophet's diligence?*
• *What are some examples of modern prophets fulfilling similar responsibilities today?*

💬 Share the following quote from Thomas S. Monson's first general conference address as President of the Church: "I pledge my life, my strength—all that I have to offer—in serving Him and in directing the affairs of His Church in accordance with His will and by His inspiration" (Thomas S. Monson, in Conference Report, April 2008).

❤ Testify of the diligence of prophets, ancient and modern, in bringing those they serve closer to Jesus Christ.

Teaching Tips from Prophets' Lips "As gospel instructors, you and I are not in the business of distributing fish; rather, our work is to help individuals learn to 'fish' and to become spiritually self-reliant. This important objective is best accomplished as we encourage and facilitate learners acting in accordance with correct principles—as we help them to learn by doing" (David A. Bednar, "Seek Learning by Faith," address to CES religious educators, February 3, 2006, 4).

Notes

THE BOOK OF OMNI

OMNI BOOK SUMMARY

Time Period: About 323–130 BC (194 years)

Contributors: Omni, Amaron, Chemish, Abinadom, Amaleki

Source: Small plates of Nephi

OMNI

A Brief History
About 323–130 BC

1–3, Omni son of Jarom writes; 4–8, Amaron son of Omni writes; 9, Chemish brother of Amaron writes; 10–11, Abinadom son of Chemish writes; 12–13, Amaleki son of Chemish writes concerning King Mosiah fleeing with his people from the Land of Nephi to Zarahemla; 14–19, the people of Zarahemla (Mulekites) are discovered and join Mosiah's people; 20–22, Discovery of the last Jaredite Coriantumr; 23–25, Amaleki gives the small slates to King Benjamin and exhorts all to come unto Christ; 26–30, The return of Zeniff and his followers to the land of Nephi is mentioned.

1 Behold, it came to pass that I, Omni, being commanded by my father, Jarom, that I should write somewhat upon these plates, to preserve our genealogy—

2 Wherefore, in my days, I would that ye should know that I fought much with the sword to preserve my people, the Nephites, from falling into the hands of their enemies, the Lamanites. But behold, I of myself am a wicked man, and I have not kept the statutes and the commandments of the Lord as I ought to have done.

3 And it came to pass that two hundred and seventy and six years had passed away, and we had many seasons of peace; and we had many seasons of serious war and bloodshed. Yea, and in fine, two hundred and eighty and two years had passed away, and I had kept these plates according to the commandments of my fathers; and I conferred them upon my son Amaron. And I make an end.

4 And now I, Amaron, write the things whatsoever I write, which are few, in the book of my father.

5 Behold, it came to pass that three hundred and twenty years had passed away, and the more wicked part of the Nephites were destroyed.

6 For the Lord would not suffer, after he had led them out of the land of Jerusalem and kept and preserved them from falling into the hands of their enemies, yea, he would not suffer that the words should not be verified, which he spake unto our fathers, saying that: Inasmuch as ye

will not keep my commandments ye shall not prosper in the land.

7 Wherefore, the Lord did visit them in great judgment; nevertheless, he did spare the righteous that they should not perish, but did deliver them out of the hands of their enemies.

8 And it came to pass that I did deliver the plates unto my brother Chemish.

9 Now I, Chemish, write what few things I write, in the same book with my brother; for behold, I saw the last which he wrote, that he wrote it with his own hand; and he wrote it in the day that he delivered them unto me. And after this manner we keep the records, for it is according to the commandments of our fathers. And I make an end.

10 Behold, I, Abinadom, am the son of Chemish. Behold, it came to pass that I saw much war and contention between my people, the Nephites, and the Lamanites; and I, with my own sword, have taken the lives of many of the Lamanites in the defence of my brethren.

11 And behold, the record of this people is engraven upon plates which is had by the kings, according to the generations; and I know of no revelation save that which has been written, neither prophecy; wherefore, that which is sufficient is written. And I make an end.

vv. 1–11 Effective journal writing will be a blessing to others.

✋ List the names of the five record keepers in Omni on the left side of the chalk board with the verse numbers next to them: Omni (vv. 1–3), Amaron (vv. 4–8), Chemish (v. 9), Abinadom (vv. 12–13), and Amaleki (vv. 14–30). Divide the class into four groups and give each group one of the first four record keepers. Give the group one minute to study what that writer wrote in his verses, and one minute to send a representative to the chalk board and summarize important information from that writer.

❓ Analyze: *Why did these record keepers write so much less than Enos, Jacob, and Nephi? Do you feel it would have been better if they wrote more?*

❓ Apply: *What are excuses for why people don't write more often in their journals? How might our descendants feel about us not writing anything about our lives?*

💬 Spencer W. Kimball stated, "Get a notebook, a journal that will last through all time, and maybe the angels may quote from it for eternity. Begin today and write in it your goings and comings, your deepest thoughts, your achievements and your failures, your associations and your triumphs, your impressions and your testimonies. Remember, the Savior chastised those who failed to record important events" (Spencer W. Kimball, *New Era*, October 1975).

12 Behold, I am Amaleki, the son of Abinadom. Behold, I will speak unto you somewhat concerning Mosiah, who was made king over the land of Zarahemla; for behold, he being warned of the Lord that he should flee out of the land of Nephi, and as many as would hearken unto the voice of the Lord should also depart out of the land with him, into the wilderness—

13 And it came to pass that he did according as the Lord had commanded him. And they departed out of the land into the wilderness, as many as would hearken unto the voice of the Lord; and they were led by many preachings and prophesyings. And they were admonished continually by the word of God; and they were led by the power of his arm, through the wilderness until they came down into the land which is called the bland of Zarahemla.

vv. 11–13 We need to recognize that we live in exciting times in the history of the world.

⚡ Discuss with the class the amount of revelation we receive from our prophet in our day. Ask, *How does the amount of revelation we*

Notes

receive compare to other times throughout history?

🔍 Have the class look for and underline a significant contrast between verses 11 and 13. ❓ Analyze: *Why did one say they have few manifestations of God's direction while the next writer says they had many? How could it be a matter of perspective?*

💬 Joseph Smith taught, "The building up of Zion is a cause that has interested the people of God in every age; it is a theme upon which prophets, priests and kings have dwelt with peculiar delight; they have looked forward with joyful anticipation to the day in which we live; and fired with heavenly and joyful anticipations they have sung and written and prophesied of this our day; but they died without the sight; we are the favored people that God has made choice of to bring about the latter-day glory; it is left for us to see, participate in and help to roll forward the latter-day glory, 'the dispensation of the fullness of times, when God will gather together all things that are in heaven, and all things that are upon the earth' " (*History of the Church,* 4:609–10).

💜 Challenge class members to do their part in these exciting times before the return of the Savior to the earth.

14 And they discovered a people, who were called the people of Zarahemla. Now, there was great rejoicing among the people of Zarahemla; and also Zarahemla did rejoice exceedingly, because the Lord had sent the people of Mosiah with the plates of brass which contained the record of the Jews.

15 Behold, it came to pass that Mosiah discovered that the people of Zarahemla came out from Jerusalem at the time that Zedekiah, king of Judah, was carried away captive into Babylon.

16 And they journeyed in the wilderness, and were brought by the hand of the Lord across the great waters, into the land where Mosiah discovered them; and they had dwelt there from that time forth.

17 And at the time that Mosiah discovered them, they had become exceedingly numerous. Nevertheless, they had had many wars and serious contentions, and had fallen by the sword from time to time; and their language had become corrupted; and they had brought no records with them; and they denied the being of their Creator; and Mosiah, nor the people of Mosiah, could understand them.

vv. 14–17 If we leave the scriptures out of our lives, we may stop believing in God.

🔍 Explain that verses 14–17 tell us about the people of Zarahemla, who were also called the Mulekites. In those verses, have your class look for one thing that may have led to other problems they had.

❓ Analyze:
- *How could not having records lead to "serious contentions" and their language becoming corrupt?*
- *What caused these people to deny the being of their Creator?*
- *Why would not having the scriptures affect their belief in God?*

❓ Apply: *How might something similar happen today? If a person chooses to stop learning from the scriptures, what effect might transpire in the person's life?*

💜 Challenge class members to study the scriptures daily so that their faith in God will increase.

18 But it came to pass that Mosiah caused that they should be taught in his language. And it came to pass that after they were taught in the language of Mosiah, Zarahemla gave a genealogy of his fathers, according to his memory; and they are written, but not in these plates.

19 And it came to pass that the people of Zarahemla, and of Mosiah, did unite together; and

Notes

Mosiah was appointed to be their king.

20 And it came to pass in the days of Mosiah, there was a large stone brought unto him with engravings on it; and he did interpret the engravings by the gift and power of God.

21 And they gave an account of one Coriantumr, and the slain of his people. And Coriantumr was discovered by the people of Zarahemla; and he dwelt with them for the space of nine moons.

22 It also spake a few words concerning his fathers. And his first parents came out from the tower, at the time the Lord confounded the language of the people; and the severity of the Lord fell upon them according to his judgments, which are just; and their bones lay scattered in the land northward.

23 Behold, I, Amaleki, was born in the days of Mosiah; and I have lived to see his death; and Benjamin, his son, reigneth in his stead.

24 And behold, I have seen, in the days of king Benjamin, a serious war and much bloodshed between the Nephites and the Lamanites. But behold, the Nephites did obtain much advantage over them; yea, insomuch that king Benjamin did drive them out of the land of Zarahemla.

25 And it came to pass that I began to be old; and, having no seed, and knowing king Benjamin to be a just man before the Lord, wherefore, I shall deliver up these plates unto him, exhorting all men to come unto God, the Holy One of Israel, and believe in prophesying, and in revelations, and in the ministering of angels, and in the gift of speaking with tongues, and in the gift of interpreting languages, and in all things which are good; for there is nothing which is good save it comes from the Lord: and that which is evil cometh from the devil.

26 And now, my beloved brethren, I would that ye should come unto Christ, who is the Holy One of Israel, and partake of his salvation, and the power of his redemption. Yea, come unto him, and offer your whole souls as an offering unto him, and continue in fasting and praying, and

endure to the end; and as the Lord liveth ye will be saved.

v. 26 We should completely consecrate ourselves to God.

To help your class gain a basic understanding of verses 18–26, you may want to summarize what happens in those verses.

In verse 26, search for what the Lord wants us to give as an offering to Him.

Analyze: *To a person living in Old Testament times, what did giving an offering generally refer to? What does the symbolism of animal sacrifice teach us in verse 26?*

While sacrifices in the Law of Moses varied, the first sacrifice described in the book of Leviticus is sometimes referred to as the "whole burnt offering" because the entire animal, except for the hide, was consumed on the altar (see Leviticus 1:3–17).

Neal A. Maxwell stated, "So it is that real, personal sacrifice never was placing an animal on the altar. Instead, it is a willingness to put the animal in us upon the altar and letting it be consumed! Such is the 'sacrifice unto the Lord . . . of a broken heart and a contrite spirit,' (Doctrine and Covenants 59:8), a prerequisite to taking up the cross, while giving 'away all [our] sins' in order to 'know God' (Alma 22:18) for the denial of self precedes the full acceptance of Him" (Neal A. Maxwell, "Deny Yourselves of All Ungodliness," *Ensign*, May 1995, 68).

As a class, list on the board ways we give ourselves over to God. Challenge class members to do likewise.

27 And now I would speak somewhat concerning a certain number who went up into the wilderness to return to the land of Nephi; for there was a large number who were desirous to possess the land of their inheritance.

28 Wherefore, they went up into the wilderness.

Notes

And their leader being a strong and mighty man, and a stiffnecked man, wherefore he caused a contention among them; and they were all slain, save fifty, in the wilderness, and they returned again to the land of Zarahemla.

29 And it came to pass that they also took others to a considerable number, and took their journey again into the wilderness.

30 And I, Amaleki, had a brother, who also went with them; and I have not since known concerning them. And I am about to lie down in my grave; and these plates are full. And I make an end of my speaking.

💡 Note with the class that there are various time frames and groups of people in the Book of Mormon. Write the following groupings of verses on the board and read them as a class to visualize the timeline.

vv. 1–13 *After the Nephites split from the Lamanites and move to the land of Zarahemla.*

vv. 14–17 *Where the people of Zarahemla (Mulekites) came from.*

vv. 18–22 *The Jaredites and their end.*

vv. 27–30 *Zeniff and his people return to the land of Nephi.*

Teaching Tips from Prophets' Lips "Teaching that is nourishing to the soul uplifts others, builds their faith, and gives them confidence to meet life's challenges. It motivates them to forsake sin and to come to Christ, call on His name, obey His commandments, and abide in His Love" (*Teaching, No Greater Call*, 5).

Notes

THE WORDS OF MORMON

THE WORDS OF MORMON

For a Wise Purpose
About AD 385

1–2, Mormon mentions that the Nephites are almost destroyed in his time; 3–7, Mormon combines the small plates with his abridgment of the large plates of Nephi; 8–11, The plates were given to King Benjamin and handed down until they were given to Mormon; 12–18, King Benjamin's reign is summarized.

1 And now I, Mormon, being about to deliver up the record which I have been making into the hands of my son Moroni, behold I have witnessed almost all the destruction of my people, the Nephites.

2 And it is many hundred years after the coming of Christ that I deliver these records into the hands of my son; and it supposeth me that he will witness the entire destruction of my people. But may God grant that he may survive them, that he may write somewhat concerning them, and somewhat concerning Christ, that perhaps some day it may profit them.

💡 Refer to a Nephite historical chronology. Have class members read verses 1–2 and determine where the Words of Mormon would fit on the chronology. Explain that Mormon inserts some words here to explain the combining of the small plates of Nephi with the large plates of Nephi that Mormon has been abridging (condensing) for the golden plates Joseph Smith would receive.

3 And now, I speak somewhat concerning that which I have written; for after I had made an abridgment from the plates of Nephi, down to the reign of this king Benjamin, of whom Amaleki spake, I searched among the records which had been delivered into my hands, and I found these plates, which contained this small account of the prophets, from Jacob down to the reign of this king Benjamin, and also many of the words of Nephi.

4 And the things which are upon these plates pleasing me, because of the prophecies of the coming of Christ; and my fathers knowing that many of them have been fulfilled; yea, and I also know that as many things as have been prophesied concerning us down to this day have been fulfilled, and as many as go beyond this day must surely come to pass—

5 Wherefore, I chose these things, to finish my record upon them, which remainder of my record I shall take from the plates of Nephi; and I cannot write the hundredth part of the things of my people.

vv. 3–5 The Book of Mormon is the "best of the best" of all the records of the Nephites.

Notes

⚡ *Were there other records made concerning the people in America besides those that Joseph Smith translated?*

💬 Ask class members to listen for how many records there were as you read the following quote from Brigham Young, "Oliver Cowdery went with the Prophet Joseph when he deposited these plates. Joseph did not translate all of the plates . . . Oliver says that when Joseph and Oliver went there, the hill opened, and they walked into a cave, in which there was a large and spacious room. He says he did not think, at the time, whether they had the light of the sun or artificial light; but that it was just as light as day. They laid the plates on a table; it was a large table that stood in the room. Under this table there was a pile of plates as much as two feet high, and there were altogether in this room more plates than probably many wagon loads; they were piled up in the corners and along the walls. The first time they went there the sword of Laban hung upon the wall; but when they went again it had been taken down and laid upon the table across the gold plates; it was unsheathed, and on it was written these words: "This sword will never be sheathed again until the kingdoms of this world become the kingdom of our God and his Christ" (*Journal of Discourses* 19:38).

🔍 *Read verses 3–5 and try to determine how many more records there were in addition to the golden plates.*

❓ Analyze:
- *How many records were there besides the golden plates Mormon abridged?*
- *What verse also indicates this?*
- *What does this teach about the portion of the Book of Mormon we do have?*

❤ Bear your testimony of the how precious the Book of Mormon is to you.

6 But behold, I shall take these plates, which contain these prophesyings and revelations, and put them with the remainder of my record, for they are choice unto me; and I know they will be choice unto my brethren.

7 And I do this for a wise purpose; for thus it whispereth me, according to the workings of the Spirit of the Lord which is in me. And now, I do not know all things; but the Lord knoweth all things which are to come; wherefore, he worketh in me to do according to his will.

✏ Next to verse 7, you may want to invite class members cross-reference 2 Nephi 9 and Doctrine and Covenants 3. In those verses, we see why Nephi needed to make two histories and the wise purpose God had behind it.

8 And my prayer to God is concerning my brethren, that they may once again come to the knowledge of God, yea, the redemption of Christ; that they may once again be a delightsome people.

9 And now I, Mormon, proceed to finish out my record, which I take from the plates of Nephi; and I make it according to the knowledge and the understanding which God has given me.

10 Wherefore, it came to pass that after Amaleki had delivered up these plates into the hands of king Benjamin, he took them and put them with the other plates, which contained records which had been handed down by the kings, from generation to generation until the days of king Benjamin.

11 And they were handed down from king Benjamin, from generation to generation until they have fallen into my hands. And I, Mormon, pray to God that they may be preserved from this time henceforth. And I know that they will be preserved; for there are great things written upon them, out of which my people and their brethren shall be judged at the great and last day, according to the word of God which is written.

12 And now, concerning this king Benjamin—he had somewhat of contentions among his own people.

Notes

13 And it came to pass also that the armies of the Lamanites came down out of the land of Nephi, to battle against his people. But behold, king Benjamin gathered together his armies, and he did stand against them; and he did fight with the strength of his own arm, with the sword of Laban.

14 And in the strength of the Lord they did contend against their enemies, until they had slain many thousands of the Lamanites. And it came to pass that they did contend against the Lamanites until they had driven them out of all the lands of their inheritance.

15 And it came to pass that after there had been false Christs, and their mouths had been shut, and they punished according to their crimes;

16 And after there had been false prophets, and false preachers and teachers among the people, and all these having been punished according to their crimes; and after there having been much contention and many dissensions away unto the Lamanites, behold, it came to pass that king Benjamin, with the assistance of the holy prophets who were among his people—

17 For behold, king Benjamin was a holy man, and he did reign over his people in righteousness; and there were many holy men in the land, and they did speak the word of God with power and with authority; and they did use much sharpness because of the stiffneckedness of the people—

18 Wherefore, with the help of these, king Benjamin, by laboring with all the might of his body and the faculty of his whole soul, and also the prophets, did once more establish peace in the land.

vv. 13–18 Principles of life.

✋ Divide class members into groups of three. Have one person in each group read verses 12–14 and summarize the verses in five words or less. Have the second person in each group do the same for verses 15–16, and have the third person with 17–18. Have class members share with each other. Then ask all those who were assigned verses 15–16, *How is that similar to today?* Then ask the same question for the other two groups.

Teaching Tips from Prophets' Lips "How do you personally use the scriptures? Do you mark your copy? Do you put notes in the margin to remember a moment of spiritual guidance or an experience that has taught you a profound lesson?" (Richard G. Scott, "The Power of Scripture," *Ensign*, November 2011).

Notes

THE BOOK OF MOSIAH

MOSIAH BOOK SUMMARY

Time Period: About 160–91 BC (70 years)

Contributors: King Benjamin (chapters 1–5), Mosiah (chapter 27, 29), Alma (chapters 18–19, 23–26), Abinadi (chapters 12–17), Zeniff (chapter 11)

Source: Large plates of Nephi

Abridged by: Mormon

Synopsis:

Chapters 1–5: King Benjamin's preparations and address to his people

Chapter 6: The names of the converted are recorded

Chapters 7–8: The people of Limhi are found

Chapters 9–22: The recount of Zeniff, King Noah, Abinadi, Alma's conversion, and Limhi.

Chapters 23–24: Alma and his people's time in the wilderness

Chapters 25–26: The affairs of the Nephite nation

Chapters 27–28: Alma the younger's conversion with the four sons of Mosiah

Chapter 29: A judicial form of government is chosen

MOSIAH 1

"Were It Not for These Plates"
About 130–124 BC

1–8, King Benjamin teaches his sons that the messages in their records have preserved and prospered them; 9–14, Mosiah will be proclaimed as the new king to the diligent people; 15–18, Mosiah is entrusted with the records and other sacred items, and prepares the kingdom for his father's address.

1 And now there was no more contention in all the land of Zarahemla, among all the people who belonged to king Benjamin, so that king Benjamin had continual peace all the remainder of his days.

2 And it came to pass that he had three sons; and he called their names Mosiah, and Helorum, and Helaman. And he caused that they should be taught in all the language of his fathers, that thereby they might become men of understanding; and that they might know concerning

Notes

the prophecies which had been spoken by the mouths of their fathers, which were delivered them by the hand of the Lord.

💡 Ask a class member to explain the differences between first, second, and third person voice. Then ask your class to compare the voice of Mosiah 1:1 and 1 Nephi 1:1. Ask, *Why is Mosiah 1:1 in third person voice?* (Because Mormon is abridging what was written on the large plates of Nephi.) Explain that Mosiah through 4 Nephi is an abridgment (summary) by Mormon, so it is written in his words. 1 Nephi through Omni was in first person without any abridgment by a secondary author.

3 And he also taught them concerning the records which were engraven on the plates of brass, saying: My sons, I would that ye should remember that were it not for these plates, which contain these records and these commandments, we must have suffered in ignorance, even at this present time, not knowing the mysteries of God.

4 For it were not possible that our father, Lehi, could have remembered all these things, to have taught them to his children, except it were for the help of these plates; for he having been taught in the language of the Egyptians therefore he could read these engravings, and teach them to his children, that thereby they could teach them to their children, and so fulfilling the commandments of God, even down to this present time.

5 I say unto you, my sons, were it not for these things, which have been kept and preserved by the hand of God, that we might read and understand of his mysteries, and have his commandments always before our eyes, that even our fathers would have dwindled in unbelief, and we should have been like unto our brethren, the Lamanites, who know nothing concerning these things, or even do not believe them when they are taught them, because of the traditions of their fathers, which are not correct.

6 O my sons, I would that ye should remember that

these sayings are true, and also that these records are true. And behold, also the plates of Nephi, which contain the records and the sayings of our fathers from the time they left Jerusalem until now, and they are true; and we can know of their surety because we have them before our eyes.

7 And now, my sons, I would that ye should remember to search them diligently, that ye may profit thereby; and I would that ye should keep the commandments of God, that ye may prosper in the land according to the promises which the Lord made unto our fathers.

vv. 3–7 Learning (secular and spiritual) helps us prosper and succeed.

⚡ Write on the board, "Ignorance is bliss." Ask class members if they have ever heard this phrase. (Depending on the age of class members, you may need to explain the phrase.) Ask, *Is this true?*

🔎 *Read verse 3 and underline any words that disagree with the idea that "Ignorance is bliss."*

🔎 *What word does verse 3 associate with ignorance?* On the board, erase the word "bliss" and replace it with "suffering."

❓ Analyze:
  • *What does it mean to be ignorant?*
  • *How could ignorance lead to suffering?*
  • *What would make someone ignorant?*
  • *How does neglecting a spiritual education lead to suffering?*

🔎 *Look for how neglecting a spiritual education leads to suffering in verses 4–6.*

⚡ Write "Prophet" and "Profit" on the board and ask a member of the class to explain the difference. Make sure they understand that profit is to get more out of something than is put into it. Ask, *Do the scriptures explain much about the second word?*

🔎 *Look for how we can profit in verse 7.*

❓ Apply: *How can you get more out of scripture study than you put into it?*

Notes

❤ Testify to class members that studying the scriptures is a great blessing because the benefits are even greater than the sacrifice put into studying them. Challenge them to make scripture study a constant habit.

8 And many more things did king Benjamin teach his sons, which are not written in this book.

9 And it came to pass that after king Benjamin had made an end of teaching his sons, that he waxed old, and he saw that he must very soon go the way of all the earth; therefore, he thought it expedient that he should confer the kingdom upon one of his sons.

10 Therefore, he had Mosiah brought before him; and these are the words which he spake unto him, saying: My son, I would that ye should make a proclamation throughout all this land among all this people, or the people of Zarahemla, and the people of Mosiah who dwell in the land, that thereby they may be gathered together; for on the morrow I shall proclaim unto this my people out of mine own mouth that thou art a king and a ruler over this people, whom the Lord our God hath given us.

💡 Explain that the phrase "on the morrow" suggests that Benjamin's people were not spread out very much because he was able to let everyone know of the proclamation in a single day. Mosiah 2:2 explains that there were a lot of people in that fairly small area.

11 And moreover, I shall give this people a name, that thereby they may be distinguished above all the people which the Lord God hath brought out of the land of Jerusalem; and this I do because they have been a diligent people in keeping the commandments of the Lord.

12 And I give unto them a name that never shall be blotted out, except it be through transgression.

💡 *What is the name King Benjamin gives his*

people in verses 11–12? Have class members refer to Mosiah 5:8–12. You may want to return to these verses when you teach Mosiah 5.

13 Yea, and moreover I say unto you, that if this highly favored people of the Lord should fall into transgression, and become a wicked and an adulterous people, that the Lord will deliver them up, that thereby they become weak like unto their brethren; and he will no more preserve them by his matchless and marvelous power, as he has hitherto preserved our fathers.

14 For I say unto you, that if he had not extended his arm in the preservation of our fathers they must have fallen into the hands of the Lamanites, and become victims to their hatred.

15 And it came to pass that after king Benjamin had made an end of these sayings to his son, that he gave him charge concerning all the affairs of the kingdom.

16 And moreover, he also gave him charge concerning the records which were engraven on the plates of brass; and also the plates of Nephi; and also, the sword of Laban, and the ball or director, which led our fathers through the wilderness, which was prepared by the hand of the Lord that thereby they might be led, every one according to the heed and diligence which they gave unto him.

17 Therefore, as they were unfaithful they did not prosper nor progress in their journey, but were driven back, and incurred the displeasure of God upon them; and therefore they were smitten with famine and sore afflictions, to stir them up in remembrance of their duty.

18 And now, it came to pass that Mosiah went and did as his father had commanded him, and proclaimed unto all the people who were in the land of Zarahemla that thereby they might gather themselves together, to go up to the temple to hear the words which his father should speak unto them.

Notes

MOSIAH 2

King Benjamin's Sermon: Our Dependence on the Lord

About 124 BC

1–8, Events preceding King Benjamin's sermon; 9–17, King Benjamin reviews his humble service as king; 18–26, We are all completely indebted to God; 27–30, Mosiah will be the new king; 31–41, The awfulness of rebellion against God and the blessedness of obedience.

1 And it came to pass that after Mosiah had done as his father had commanded him, and had made a proclamation throughout all the land, that the people gathered themselves together throughout all the land, that they might go up to the temple to hear the words which king Benjamin should speak unto them.

2 And there were a great number, even so many that they did not number them; for they had multiplied exceedingly and waxed great in the land.

3 And they also took of the firstlings of their flocks, that they might offer sacrifice and burnt offerings according to the law of Moses;

4 And also that they might give thanks to the Lord their God, who had brought them out of the land of Jerusalem, and who had delivered them out of the hands of their enemies, and had appointed just men to be their teachers, and also a just man to be their king, who had established peace in the land of Zarahemla, and who had

taught them to keep the commandments of God, that they might rejoice and be filled with love towards God and all men.

5 And it came to pass that when they came up to the temple, they pitched their tents round about, every man according to his family, consisting of his wife, and his sons, and his daughters, and their sons, and their daughters, from the eldest down to the youngest, every family being separate one from another.

6 And they pitched their tents round about the temple, every man having his tent with the door thereof towards the temple, that thereby they might remain in their tents and hear the words which king Benjamin should speak unto them;

7 For the multitude being so great that king Benjamin could not teach them all within the walls of the temple, therefore he caused a tower to be erected, that thereby his people might hear the words which he should speak unto them.

8 And it came to pass that he began to speak to his people from the tower; and they could not all hear his words because of the greatness of the multitude; therefore he caused that the words which he spake should be written and sent forth among those that were not under the sound of his voice, that they might also receive his words.

9 And these are the words which he spake and caused to be written, saying: My brethren, all ye that have assembled yourselves together, you that can hear my words which I shall speak unto you this day; for I have not commanded you to come up hither to trifle with the words which I shall speak, but that you should hearken unto me, and open your ears that ye may hear, and your hearts that ye may understand, and your minds that the mysteries of God may be unfolded to your view.

vv. 1–9 There are certain things we should do to take advantage of general conference.

⚡ Ask class members to share a favorite memory from the most recent general conference. Ask, *What event in the Book of Mormon is*

Notes

very similar to general conference?

👥 Give groups of three or four class members each a piece of paper. Have them read verses 1–9 looking for and writing down as many similarities between these verses and modern-day general conference as possible. Have the groups share and compare. Some comparisons could include:

v. 1 Announcements for general conference
v. 1 Near the temple (like the Conference Center)
v. 2 Vast numbers participating
v. 5 Attend as families (and watching separately)
v. 7 Tower to allow more to hear (like communication towers)
v. 8 Words written down (show a copy of the most recent conference Ensign)
v. 9 We are not to trifle with the words spoken

❤ When the list is made, ask class members how they can make the most of general conference. Ask, *How might people trifle with the word in general conference? How can people metaphorically "pitch their tents round about" for general conference?* Invite class members to learn from general conference.

10 I have not commanded you to come up hither that ye should fear me, or that ye should think that I of myself am more than a mortal man.

11 But I am like as yourselves, subject to all manner of infirmities in body and mind; yet I have been chosen by this people, and consecrated by my father, and was suffered by the hand of the Lord that I should be a ruler and a king over this people; and have been kept and preserved by his matchless power, to serve you with all the might, mind and strength which the Lord hath granted unto me.

12 I say unto you that as I have been suffered to spend my days in your service, even up to this time, and have not sought gold nor silver nor any manner of riches of you;

13 Neither have I suffered that ye should be confined in dungeons, nor that ye should make slaves one of another, nor that ye should murder, or plunder, or steal, or commit adultery; nor even have I suffered that ye should commit any manner of wickedness, and have taught you that ye should keep the commandments of the Lord, in all things which he hath commanded you—

14 And even I, myself, have labored with mine own hands that I might serve you, and that ye should not be laden with taxes, and that there should nothing come upon you which was grievous to be borne—and of all these things which I have spoken, ye yourselves are witnesses this day.

15 Yet, my brethren, I have not done these things that I might boast, neither do I tell these things that thereby I might accuse you; but I tell you these things that ye may know that I can answer a clear conscience before God this day.

16 Behold, I say unto you that because I said unto you that I had spent my days in your service, I do not desire to boast, for I have only been in the service of God.

17 And behold, I tell you these things that ye may learn wisdom; that ye may learn that when ye are in the service of your fellow beings ye are only in the service of your God.

vv. 10–17 Qualities of great civic leaders.

⚡ Ask class members to think of and name various political leaders that they feel are/were great. Have them share.

✋ Explain that, in small groups, they will search verses 10–17 to look for and list elements of a great leader. Some answers could include:

v. 10 Refrains from trying to get people to think they are better than everyone else.
v. 11 Recognizes God's hand in their lives.
v. 12 Refrains from serving in order to get rich.
v. 13 Seeks to promote virtuous living.
v. 14 Supports own self financially

Notes

vv. 15–16 Knows that it is really God they are serving.

♥ Challenge class members to vote for and support people they feel would be good leaders in civil government.

17 And behold, I tell you these things that ye may learn wisdom; that ye may learn that when ye are in the service of your fellow beings ye are only in the service of your God.

v. 17 When we are serving our fellow men, we are serving God.

💬 Thomas S. Monson taught, "This is the service that counts, the service to which all of us have been called: the service of the Lord Jesus Christ. Along your pathway of life you will observe that you are not the only traveler. There are others who need your help. There are feet to steady, hands to grasp, minds to encourage, hearts to inspire, and souls to save" (Thomas S. Monson, *Ensign*, October 2006).

✏ Ask class members what a cross-reference to this scripture might be. One is Matthew 25:40. Invite them to write that cross-reference in the margins of their scriptures.

18 Behold, ye have called me your king; and if I, whom ye call your king, do labor to serve you, then ought not ye to labor to serve one another?

19 And behold also, if I, whom ye call your king, who has spent his days in your service, and yet has been in the service of God, do merit any thanks from you, O how you ought to thank your heavenly King!

20 I say unto you, my brethren, that if you should render all the thanks and praise which your whole soul has power to possess, to that God who has created you, and has kept and preserved you, and has caused that ye should rejoice, and has granted that ye should live in peace one with another—

21 I say unto you that if ye should serve him who has created you from the beginning, and is preserving you from day to day, by lending you breath, that ye may live and move and do according to your own will, and even supporting you from one moment to another—I say, if ye should serve him with all your whole souls yet ye would be unprofitable servants.

22 And behold, all that he requires of you is to keep his commandments; and he has promised you that if ye would keep his commandments ye should prosper in the land; and he never doth vary from that which he hath said; therefore, if ye do keep his commandments he doth bless you and prosper you.

23 And now, in the first place, he hath created you, and granted unto you your lives, for which ye are indebted unto him.

24 And secondly, he doth require that ye should do as he hath commanded you; for which if ye do, he doth immediately bless you; and therefore he hath paid you. And ye are still indebted unto him, and are, and will be, forever and ever; therefore, of what have ye to boast?

25 And now I ask, can ye say aught of yourselves? I answer you, Nay. Ye cannot say that ye are even as much as the dust of the earth; yet ye were created of the dust of the earth; but behold, it belongeth to him who created you.

26 And I, even I, whom ye call your king, am no better than ye yourselves are; for I am also of the dust. And ye behold that I am old, and am about to yield up this mortal frame to its mother earth.

vv. 19–26 We need to recognize our dependence on God.

⚡ Write on the board, "Profitable is when income is greater than expenses" and "Unprofitable is when expenses are greater than income." Determine whether or not class members understand these ideas and give examples of a small business if they are not sure. You could also bring fake money from a board

Notes

game and demonstrate the idea of profit. Ask, *Are we profitable or unprofitable to the Lord?*

🔍 Have class members look for whether or not we are profitable or unprofitable to the Lord in verses 20–21.

❓ Analyze:
- *What does Benjamin mean when he refers to an unprofitable servant?*
- *Does that mean we are bad investments?*
- *If we are unprofitable, why did the Lord suffer and die for us?*

🔍 Have class members look for other words that would describe how unprofitable we are in verses 23–26.

❓ Analyze: *Why do you think King Benjamin is speaking of his people in these disparaging terms?* (See the principle at the top of the lesson idea.)

27 Therefore, as I said unto you that I had served you, walking with a clear conscience before God, even so I at this time have caused that ye should assemble yourselves together, that I might be found blameless, and that your blood should not come upon me, when I shall stand to be judged of God of the things whereof he hath commanded me concerning you.

28 I say unto you that I have caused that ye should assemble yourselves together that I might rid my garments of your blood, at this period of time when I am about to go down to my grave, that I might go down in peace, and my immortal spirit may join the choirs above in singing the praises of a just God.

💡 Compare King Benjamin's expectation at the end of verse 28 with Enos's expectation in Enos 1:27. Ask, *Why were they so sure of their fate?*

29 And moreover, I say unto you that I have caused that ye should assemble yourselves together, that I might declare unto you that I can no longer be your teacher, nor your king;

30 For even at this time, my whole frame doth tremble exceedingly while attempting to speak unto you; but the Lord God doth support me, and hath suffered me that I should speak unto you, and hath commanded me that I should declare unto you this day, that my son Mosiah is a king and a ruler over you.

31 And now, my brethren, I would that ye should do as ye have hitherto done. As ye have kept my commandments, and also the commandments of my father, and have prospered, and have been kept from falling into the hands of your enemies, even so if ye shall keep the commandments of my son, or the commandments of God which shall be delivered unto you by him, ye shall prosper in the land, and your enemies shall have no power over you.

32 But, O my people, beware lest there shall arise contentions among you, and ye list to obey the evil spirit, which was spoken of by my father Mosiah.

33 For behold, there is a wo pronounced upon him who listeth to obey that spirit; for if he listeth to obey him, and remaineth and dieth in his sins, the same drinketh damnation to his own soul; for he receiveth for his wages an everlasting punishment, having transgressed the law of God contrary to his own knowledge.

34 I say unto you, that there are not any among you, except it be your little children that have not been taught concerning these things, but what knoweth that ye are eternally indebted to your heavenly Father, to render to him all that you have and are; and also have been taught concerning the records which contain the prophecies which have been spoken by the holy prophets, even down to the time our father, Lehi, left Jerusalem;

35 And also, all that has been spoken by our fathers until now. And behold, also, they spake that which was commanded them of the Lord; therefore, they are just and true.

Notes

36 And now, I say unto you, my brethren, that after ye have known and have been taught all these things, if ye should transgress and go contrary to that which has been spoken, that ye do withdraw yourselves from the Spirit of the Lord, that it may have no place in you to guide you in wisdom's paths that ye may be blessed, prospered, and preserved—

37 I say unto you, that the man that doeth this, the same cometh out in open rebellion against God; therefore he listeth to obey the evil spirit, and becometh an enemy to all righteousness; therefore, the Lord has no place in him, for he dwelleth not in unholy temples.

38 Therefore if that man repenteth not, and remaineth and dieth an enemy to God, the demands of divine justice do awaken his immortal soul to a lively sense of his own guilt, which doth cause him to shrink from the presence of the Lord, and doth fill his breast with guilt, and pain, and anguish, which is like an unquenchable fire, whose flame ascendeth up forever and ever.

39 And now I say unto you, that mercy hath no claim on that man; therefore his final doom is to endure a never-ending torment.

40 O, all ye old men, and also ye young men, and you little children who can understand my words, for I have spoken plainly unto you that ye might understand, I pray that ye should awake to a remembrance of the awful situation of those that have fallen into transgression.

vv. 32–40 When we sin intentionally we withdraw ourselves from the spirit of the Lord.

⚡ Discuss with class members what the difference is between sinning intentionally and sinning because we are imperfect. Ask, *Which is worse?*

🔍 *Look for and identify words that convey rebellion as you read verses 32–42.*

✏️ Next to verse 37, invite class members to write "1 Samuel 15:23." Read that verse together and discuss why rebellion is such an awful sin.

❤️ *In our day, give examples of when it might be common to rebelliously sin?* Invite class members to always choose the right.

41 And moreover, I would desire that ye should consider on the blessed and happy state of those that keep the commandments of God. For behold, they are blessed in all things, both temporal and spiritual; and if they hold out faithful to the end they are received into heaven, that thereby they may dwell with God in a state of never-ending happiness. O remember, remember that these things are true; for the Lord God hath spoken it.

v. 41 Following God and keeping His commandments leads to happiness.

⚡ Ask class members to think of people they know who are striving diligently to follow the Lord.

❓ Analyze: Read verse 41 and ask,
• *Why are people who are trying to follow the Lord generally happier than those who don't?*
• *What is the connection between happiness and keeping the commandments?*
• *How does Alma 41:10 relate with this principle?* (Read it and invite class members to write the cross-reference to the side.)

Contrast verses 32–40 to the happiness referred to in verse 41.

💬 Ask class members to listen for the connection between commandments and happiness in the following quote by Joseph Smith: "In obedience there is joy and peace unspotted, unalloyed; and as God has designed our happiness . . . He never has—He never will institute an ordinance or give a commandment to His people that is not calculated in its nature to promote that happiness which He has designed, and which will not end in the greatest amount of good and glory to

Notes

those who become the recipients of his law and ordinances" (*Teachings of the Prophet Joseph Smith,* comp. Joseph Fielding Smith [1976], 256–57).

❤ Testify to class members of the happiness that has come to you as you have tried to live the commandments. Challenge them to constantly strive to keep the commandments so they can always be happy.

MOSIAH 3

King Benjamin's Sermon: Discourse on the Atonement
About 124 BC

1–4, King Benjamin is visited by an angel and told about the earthly ministry of Christ; 5–10, Jesus Christ will experience all the pains and temptations of mortal life, be crucified, and resurrect in order to bring salvation to us; 11–18, Salvation is not for those who rebel against God; 19–27, The natural man is an enemy to God.

Overarching Principle: "There shall be no other name given . . . whereby salvation can come unto the children of men, only in and through the name of Christ" (Mosiah 3:17).

⚡ Display a picture of the Savior at the front of the classroom and write on the board near the picture, "Who is Jesus Christ, and what has he done for us?" Ask class members how they would answer that question if asked by someone who is not a member of the Church.

🔑 Invite class members to look for a very simple doctrine in Mosiah 3:17 that would help a missionary give an explanation to the question on the board. Once identified, explain to your class that they will learn basic doctrine about the Savior and His Atonement in Mosiah 3.

1 And again my brethren, I would call your attention, for I have somewhat more to speak unto you; for behold, I have things to tell you concerning that which is to come.

2 And the things which I shall tell you are made known unto me by an angel from God. And he said unto me: Awake; and I awoke, and behold he stood before me.

3 And he said unto me: Awake, and hear the words which I shall tell thee; for behold, I am come to declare unto you the glad tidings of great joy.

4 For the Lord hath heard thy prayers, and hath judged of thy righteousness, and hath sent me to declare unto thee that thou mayest rejoice; and that thou mayest declare unto thy people, that they may also be filled with joy.

5 For behold, the time cometh, and is not far distant, that with power, the Lord Omnipotent who reigneth, who was, and is from all eternity to all eternity, shall come down from heaven among the children of men, and shall dwell in a tabernacle of clay, and shall go forth amongst men, working mighty miracles, such as healing the sick, raising the dead, causing the lame to walk, the blind to receive their sight, and the deaf to hear, and curing all manner of diseases.

6 And he shall cast out devils, or the evil spirits which dwell in the hearts of the children of men.

7 And lo, he shall suffer temptations, and pain of body, hunger, thirst, and fatigue, even more than man can suffer, except it be unto death; for behold, blood cometh from every pore, so great shall be his anguish for the wickedness and the abominations of his people.

8 And he shall be called Jesus Christ, the Son of God, the Father of heaven and earth, the Creator of all things from the beginning; and his mother shall be called Mary.

9 And lo, he cometh unto his own, that salvation might come unto the children of men even through faith on his name; and even after all this they shall consider him a man, and say that he

Notes

hath a devil, and shall scourge him, and shall crucify him.

10 And he shall rise the third day from the dead; and behold, he standeth to judge the world; and behold, all these things are done that a righteous judgment might come upon the children of men.

11 For behold, and also his blood atoneth for the sins of those who have fallen by the transgression of Adam, who have died not knowing the will of God concerning them, or who have ignorantly sinned.

12 But wo, wo unto him who knoweth that he rebelleth against God! For salvation cometh to none such except it be through repentance and faith on the Lord Jesus Christ.

13 And the Lord God hath sent his holy prophets among all the children of men, to declare these things to every kindred, nation, and tongue, that thereby whosoever should believe that Christ should come, the same might receive remission of their sins, and rejoice with exceedingly great joy, even as though he had already come among them.

14 Yet the Lord God saw that his people were a stiffnecked people, and he appointed unto them a law, even the law of Moses.

15 And many signs, and wonders, and types, and shadows showed he unto them, concerning his coming; and also holy prophets spake unto them concerning his coming; and yet they hardened their hearts, and understood not that the law of Moses availeth nothing except it were through the atonement of his blood.

16 And even if it were possible that little children could sin they could not be saved; but I say unto you they are blessed; for behold, as in Adam, or by nature, they fall, even so the blood of Christ atoneth for their sins.

17 And moreover, I say unto you, that there shall be no other name given nor any other way nor means whereby salvation can come unto the children of men, only in and through the name of Christ, the Lord Omnipotent.

18 For behold he judgeth, and his judgment is just; and the infant perisheth not that dieth in his infancy; but men drink damnation to their own souls except they humble themselves and become as little children, and believe that salvation was, and is, and is to come, in and through the atoning blood of Christ, the Lord Omnipotent.

19 For the natural man is an enemy to God, and has been from the fall of Adam, and will be, forever and ever, unless he yields to the enticings of the Holy Spirit, and putteth off the natural man and becometh a saint through the atonement of Christ the Lord, and becometh as a child, submissive, meek, humble, patient, full of love, willing to submit to all things which the Lord seeth fit to inflict upon him, even as a child doth submit to his father.

vv. 5–19 In order to accept the Atonement, I must put off the natural man and become as a child.

✎ Have the following chart written on the board:

Salvation through the Savior

What did Jesus do to bring salvation?
(Mosiah 3:5–10)

Who can be saved?
(Mosiah 3:11–12, 16–18)

How do we use the Atonement?
(Mosiah 3:19)

Invite class members to complete this chart on their own. Depending on the size of your class, you may want to pair class members into groups of two or three. Once they have completed their charts, ask someone in the class to be scribe at the board and encourage class members to share and explain

Notes

what they completed in each column while the scribe writes it on the board.

⚡ Spend some time discussing with your class what is written in each column. To help class members understand verses 5–10, you may want to consider showing a short Church-produced film that depicts the Atonement of the Jesus Christ. The Bible videos found on lds.org are a good resource you could use.

❓ Analyze:
  • *What do you think it means to ignorantly sin? (vv. 11–12)*
  • *What does it mean to be a natural man? (v. 19)*
  • *Why do you think a natural man is an enemy to God?*

❓ Apply: *How are we like a natural man? When have you felt you have put off the natural man, and became changed through the Atonement?*

♥ Encourage class members to think of ways they find themselves being a natural man or woman. Invite them to repent and put off that natural man to become a saint through the Atonement of Jesus Christ.

v. 16 Little children are not capable of committing sin.

💡 Point out the doctrine from this verse that little children are not capable of sinning and are therefore saved by the Atonement. You may want to cross-reference Moroni 8:8 and Doctrine and Covenants 29:47.

20 And moreover, I say unto you, that the time shall come when the knowledge of a Savior shall spread throughout every nation, kindred, tongue, and people.

21 And behold, when that time cometh, none shall be found blameless before God, except it be little children, only through repentance and faith on the name of the Lord God Omnipotent.

22 And even at this time, when thou shalt have taught thy people the things which the Lord thy God hath commanded thee, even then are they found no more blameless in the sight of God, only according to the words which I have spoken unto thee.

23 And now I have spoken the words which the Lord God hath commanded me.

24 And thus saith the Lord: They shall stand as a bright testimony against this people, at the judgment day; whereof they shall be judged, every man according to his works, whether they be good, or whether they be evil.

25 And if they be evil they are consigned to an awful view of their own guilt and abominations, which doth cause them to shrink from the presence of the Lord into a state of misery and endless torment, from whence they can no more return; therefore they have drunk damnation to their own souls.

26 Therefore, they have drunk out of the cup of the wrath of God, which justice could no more deny unto them than it could deny that Adam should fall because of his partaking of the forbidden fruit; therefore, mercy could have claim on them no more forever.

27 And their torment is as a lake of fire and brimstone, whose flames are unquenchable, and whose smoke ascendeth up forever and ever. Thus hath the Lord commanded me. Amen.

vv. 21, 24–27 The result of being a natural man is to drink out of the cup of the wrath of God. We should therefore repent and have faith on the name of the Lord.

🔍 Read verses 24–27 as a class and look for the result of a person who persists in being a natural man. Then read verse 21. Ask, *Look for how we can avoid that suffering.* You may also want to cross reference Alma 12:14.

♥ Express to your class the importance of repenting and encourage them to do so. Bear your testimony of the reality of the Atonement and of the truth of verse 17.

Notes

MOSIAH 4

King Benjamin's Sermon: Discourse on the Atonement

About 124 BC

1–3, The people fall to the earth and call upon the Lord; 4–7, Benjamin testifies of the atonement; 8–11, He testifies of God and his glory; 12–16, The remission of sins leads to good works; 17–26, Benjamin exhorts his people to be merciful unto the poor; 27–30, He extols order and admonishes against all sin.

1 And now, it came to pass that when king Benjamin had made an end of speaking the words which had been delivered unto him by the angel of the Lord, that he cast his eyes round about on the multitude, and behold they had fallen to the earth, for the fear of the Lord had come upon them.

2 And they had viewed themselves in their own carnal state, even less than the dust of the earth. And they all cried aloud with one voice, saying: O have mercy, and apply the atoning blood of Christ that we may receive forgiveness of our sins, and our hearts may be purified; for we believe in Jesus Christ, the Son of God, who created heaven and earth, and all things; who shall come down among the children of men.

3 And it came to pass that after they had spoken these words the Spirit of the Lord came upon them, and they were filled with joy, having received a remission of their sins, and having peace of conscience, because of the exceeding faith which they had in Jesus Christ who should come, according to the words which king Benjamin had spoken unto them.

4 And king Benjamin again opened his mouth and began to speak unto them, saying: My friends and my brethren, my kindred and my people, I would again call your attention, that ye may hear and understand the remainder of my words which I shall speak unto you.

5 For behold, if the knowledge of the goodness of God at this time has awakened you to a sense of your nothingness, and your worthless and fallen state—

6 I say unto you, if ye have come to a knowledge of the goodness of God, and his matchless power, and his wisdom, and his patience, and his long-suffering towards the children of men; and also, the atonement which has been prepared from the foundation of the world, that thereby salvation might come to him that should put his trust in the Lord, and should be diligent in keeping his commandments, and continue in the faith even unto the end of his life, I mean the life of the mortal body—

7 I say, that this is the man who receiveth salvation, through the atonement which was prepared from the foundation of the world for all mankind, which ever were since the fall of Adam, or who are, or who ever shall be, even unto the end of the world.

8 And this is the means whereby salvation cometh. And there is none other salvation save this which hath been spoken of; neither are there any conditions whereby man can be saved except the conditions which I have told you.

9 Believe in God; believe that he is, and that he created all things, both in heaven and in earth; believe that he has all wisdom, and all power, both in heaven and in earth; believe that man doth not comprehend all the things which the Lord can comprehend.

Notes

10 And again, believe that ye must repent of your sins and forsake them, and humble yourselves before God; and ask in sincerity of heart that he would forgive you; and now, if you believe all these things see that ye do them.

11 And again I say unto you as I have said before, that as ye have come to the knowledge of the glory of God, or if ye have known of his goodness and have tasted of his love, and have received a remission of your sins, which causeth such exceedingly great joy in your souls, even so I would that ye should remember, and always retain in remembrance, the greatness of God, and your own nothingness, and his goodness and long-suffering towards you, unworthy creatures, and humble yourselves even in the depths of humility, calling on the name of the Lord daily, and standing steadfastly in the faith of that which is to come, which was spoken by the mouth of the angel.

12 And behold, I say unto you that if ye do this ye shall always rejoice, and be filled with the love of God, and always retain a remission of your sins; and ye shall grow in the knowledge of the glory of him that created you, or in the knowledge of that which is just and true.

13 And ye will not have a mind to injure one another, but to live peaceably, and to render to every man according to that which is his due.

14 And ye will not suffer your children that they go hungry, or naked; neither will ye suffer that they transgress the laws of God, and fight and quarrel one with another, and serve the devil, who is the master of sin, or who is the devil spirit which hath been spoken of by our fathers, he being an enemy to all righteousness.

15 But ye will teach them to walk in the ways of truth and soberness; ye will teach them to love one another, and to serve one another.

16 And also, ye yourselves will succor those that stand in need of your succor; ye will administer of your substance unto him that standeth in need; and ye will not suffer that the beggar putteth up his petition to you in vain, and turn him out to perish.

vv. 1–16 As we experience the Atonement of Christ in our lives, our hearts are changed and we are motivated to do good works.

⚡ *Many people in the world say that it is impossible for a person to change his or her weaknesses and imperfections. What do you think? What kinds of experiences can lead people to change?* Have a class member read Mosiah 5:1–2 and verse 7. Explain that by the end of King Benjamin's address, the people have experienced a mighty change. Mosiah chapter 4 explains how that was possible.

💬 "The Lord works from the inside out. The world works from the outside in. The world would take people out of the slums. Christ takes the slums out of people, and then they take themselves out of the slums. The world would mold men by changing their environment. Christ changes men, who then change their environment. The world would shape human behavior, but Christ can change human nature. . . . Yes, Christ changes men, and changed men can change the world. Men changed for Christ will be captained by Christ. Like Paul they will be asking, 'Lord, what wilt thou have me to do?' (Acts 9:6.) Peter stated they will 'follow his steps.' (1 Peter 2:21.) John said they will 'walk, even as he walked.' (1 John 2:6.)" (Ezra Taft Benson, "Born of God," *Ensign,* July 1989).

✋ Explain that we all need to be changed by Christ if we want to inherit eternal life, but it is often difficult to know how to change. Invite class members, as individuals or in groups, to read Mosiah 4:1–16, looking for how the people prepared themselves to be changed by the Savior. Invite them to compile a list or mark each of their findings in their scriptures. Discuss their findings as a class.

🔎 *Read verses 13–16 and look for specific actions that result from the change that*

Notes

occurs in a person's life after they have experienced the Atonement.

? Analyze:
- *Why does the Atonement produce the desire to do good works?*
- *What do you think happens to an individual as he or she gives the actions in verses 13–16?*
- *What about receiving them?*

? Apply: *How have you experienced the love of Christ by either doing good works or receiving good works from another? How have you been changed by such Christ-centered actions?*

♥ After the activity, ask class members to describe a personal experience they have witnessed where the principles discussed have led someone to be changed by Christ. Bear testimony of the personal change that has come to your life through the power of the Atonement.

17 Perhaps thou shalt say: The man has brought upon himself his misery; therefore I will stay my hand, and will not give unto him of my food, nor impart unto him of my substance that he may not suffer, for his punishments are just—

18 But I say unto you, O man, whosoever doeth this the same hath great cause to repent; and except he repenteth of that which he hath done he perisheth forever, and hath no interest in the kingdom of God.

19 For behold, are we not all beggars? Do we not all depend upon the same Being, even God, for all the substance which we have, for both food and raiment, and for gold, and for silver, and for all the riches which we have of every kind?

20 And behold, even at this time, ye have been calling on his name, and begging for a remission of your sins. And has he suffered that ye have begged in vain? Nay; he has poured out his Spirit upon you, and has caused that your hearts should be filled with joy, and has caused that

your mouths should be stopped that ye could not find utterance, so exceedingly great was your joy.

21 And now, if God, who has created you, on whom you are dependent for your lives and for all that ye have and are, doth grant unto you whatsoever ye ask that is right, in faith, believing that ye shall receive, O then, how ye ought to impart of the substance that ye have one to another.

22 And if ye judge the man who putteth up his petition to you for your substance that he perish not, and condemn him, how much more just will be your condemnation for withholding your substance, which doth not belong to you but to God, to whom also your life belongeth; and yet ye put up no petition, nor repent of the thing which thou hast done.

23 I say unto you, wo be unto that man, for his substance shall perish with him; and now, I say these things unto those who are rich as pertaining to the things of this world.

24 And again, I say unto the poor, ye who have not and yet have sufficient, that ye remain from day to day; I mean all you who deny the beggar, because ye have not; I would that ye say in your hearts that: I give not because I have not, but if I had I would give.

25 And now, if ye say this in your hearts ye remain guiltless, otherwise ye are condemned; and your condemnation is just for ye covet that which ye have not received.

26 And now, for the sake of these things which I have spoken unto you—that is, for the sake of retaining a remission of your sins from day to day, that ye may walk guiltless before God—I would that ye should impart of your substance to the poor, every man according to that which he hath, such as feeding the hungry, clothing the naked, visiting the sick and administering to their relief, both spiritually and temporally, according to their wants.

27 And see that all these things are done in wisdom and order; for it is not requisite that a man should run faster than he has strength. And again, it is

Notes

expedient that he should be diligent, that thereby he might win the prize; therefore, all things must be done in order.

vv. 17–27 Because Christ has blessed me when spiritually poor, I can bless others when they are temporally poor.

⚡ Consider creating a cardboard sign. On one side of the sign write, "Poor and Hungry. Please help with food or money." On the reverse, write, "Imperfect and Sinful. Please help with mercy or grace." Display the sign in the front of the room with "Poor and Hungry" showing. Ask, *Have you ever seen a sign like this? What are some of your impressions when you do?* (Be careful to keep discussion brief and to the point. If the discussion goes further than you like, consider saying something like, *This can be an opinionated topic. Let's see what the scriptures say about it.*)

❓ Analyze: Have a class member read verses 16–17 out loud. *Why do you think King Benjamin is so harsh toward those unwilling to give to the poor?* Have the same class member read verses 19–21, then flip around the sign you have displayed. *How are we considered "beggars" before the Lord?*

❓ Apply: *In what ways could the Lord rightfully say we have brought it upon ourselves (v. 17) and stay his hand from blessing us? What does it teach you about the Lord?*

✏️ Have class members read verse 26 silently and write the principle taught here in their own words. Invite them to share with a neighbor or the entire class.

27 And see that all these things are done in wisdom and order; for it is not requisite that a man should run faster than he has strength. And again, it is expedient that he should be diligent, that thereby he might win the prize; therefore, all things must be done in order.

28 And I would that ye should remember, that whosoever among you borroweth of his neighbor should return the thing that he borroweth, according as he doth agree, or else thou shalt commit sin; and perhaps thou shalt cause thy neighbor to commit sin also.

29 And finally, I cannot tell you all the things whereby ye may commit sin; for there are divers ways and means, even so many that I cannot number them.

30 But this much I can tell you, that if ye do not watch yourselves, and your thoughts, and your words, and your deeds, and observe the commandments of God, and continue in the faith of what ye have heard concerning the coming of our Lord, even unto the end of your lives, ye must perish. And now, O man, remember, and perish not.

vv. 27–30 The righteous must be orderly and diligent in gospel living.

❓ Have class members read verses 27, 29–30. *How are these verses a kind of balancing act? How have you been able to live as diligently as possible but also not push yourself beyond your abilities? What role does the Atonement of Christ play in that balance?*

MOSIAH 5

The Children of Christ
About 124 BC

1–5, Benjamin's people enter into a covenant with God; 4–7, The people receive a new name—the children of Christ; 13–15, The people are admonished to always retain the name in remembrance through faith and good works.

1 And now, it came to pass that when king Benjamin had thus spoken to his people, he sent among them, desiring to know of his people if they believed the words which he had spoken unto them.

Notes

2 And they all cried with one voice, saying: Yea, we believe all the words which thou hast spoken unto us; and also, we know of their surety and truth, because of the Spirit of the Lord Omnipotent, which has wrought a mighty change in us, or in our hearts, that we have no more disposition to do evil, but to do good continually.

3 And we, ourselves, also, through the infinite goodness of God, and the manifestations of his Spirit, have great views of that which is to come; and were it expedient, we could prophesy of all things.

4 And it is the faith which we have had on the things which our king has spoken unto us that has brought us to this great knowledge, whereby we do rejoice with such exceedingly great joy.

5 And we are willing to enter into a covenant with our God to do his will, and to be obedient to his commandments in all things that he shall command us, all the remainder of our days, that we may not bring upon ourselves a never-ending torment, as has been spoken by the angel, that we may not drink out of the cup of the wrath of God.

6 And now, these are the words which king Benjamin desired of them; and therefore he said unto them: Ye have spoken the words that I desired; and the covenant which ye have made is a righteous covenant.

7 And now, because of the covenant which ye have made ye shall be called the children of Christ, his sons, and his daughters; for behold, this day he hath spiritually begotten you; for ye say that your hearts are changed through faith on his name; therefore, ye are born of him and have become his sons and his daughters.

8 And under this head ye are made free, and there is no other head whereby ye can be made free. There is no other name given whereby salvation cometh; therefore, I would that ye should take upon you the name of Christ, all you that have entered into the covenant with God that ye should be obedient unto the end of your lives.

9 And it shall come to pass that whosoever doeth this shall be found at the right hand of God, for he shall know the name by which he is called; for he shall be called by the name of Christ.

10 And now it shall come to pass, that whosoever shall not take upon him the name of Christ must be called by some other name; therefore, he findeth himself on the left hand of God.

11 And I would that ye should remember also, that this is the name that I said I should give unto you that never should be blotted out, except it be through transgression; therefore, take heed that ye do not transgress, that the name be not blotted out of your hearts.

12 I say unto you, I would that ye should remember to retain the name written always in your hearts, that ye are not found on the left hand of God, but that ye hear and know the voice by which ye shall be called, and also, the name by which he shall call you.

13 For how knoweth a man the master whom he has not served, and who is a stranger unto him, and is far from the thoughts and intents of his heart?

14 And again, doth a man take an ass which belongeth to his neighbor, and keep him? I say unto you, Nay; he will not even suffer that he shall feed among his flocks, but will drive him away, and cast him out. I say unto you, that even so shall it be among you if ye know not the name by which ye are called.

15 Therefore, I would that ye should be steadfast and immovable, always abounding in good works, that Christ, the Lord God Omnipotent, may seal you his, that you may be brought to heaven, that ye may have everlasting salvation and eternal life, through the wisdom, and power, and justice, and mercy of him who created all things, in heaven and in earth, who is God above all. Amen.

vv. 1–2, 7 Our hearts are changed through faith on his name.

🔎 *Read verses 2 and 7 and find the words that*

Notes

describe by what means we are "changed."

❓ Analyze:
- *What does 'changed through faith on his name' mean?*
- *What are the two parts to the change?*
- *Why does it require change by the spirit and by faith on his name?*

❤ *What does being changed by Christ really mean? How do you know if you have been changed by Christ?* Extend invitations to class members to speak from their hearts.

vv. 1–15 Through sacred covenants, we can become the children of Christ and take His name upon us.

⚡ Ask one or two class members to write their full names on the board. Ask them to explain how they received their names, the significance of them, and what it means to them to be called by those names. Point out that in Mosiah 1:11, at the beginning of his address, King Benjamin said he would give the people a name by which they may be distinguished above all the people.

🔍 Have class members read verses 2–11 to themselves and look for what name the people received and what they did to receive it. As you read, you could look for and mark the word "name."

❓ Analyze:
- *How is taking upon us the name of Christ similar to the family names that we take upon us?*
- *How can we be considered the sons and daughters of Christ? (v. 7)*
- *How is taking upon the name of Christ more significant than taking on a family name?*

❓ Apply:
- *In what ways do we take upon us the name of Christ today?*
- *What does it mean to you to be called by His name?*
- *How does being called by His name affect your choices and actions?*

❤ Read verse 15 to the class. Summarize some of the lessons learned from Benjamin's address and testify that the truths in verse 15 will become a part our lives as we are changed by Christ, do His works, and take His name upon us. If prompted, ask class members to share testimony of what they have learned as well.

Teaching Tips from Prophets' Lips "Every teacher needs to remember that we have to 'nourish by the good word of God.' We can be fed too—that can be part of the fun of it—but the significance of teaching is nourishment anchored in the word of God" (Jeffrey R. Holland, "Teaching and Learning in the Church," *Ensign*, June 2007, 88–105).

MOSIAH 6

King Benjamin's Final Words
About 124–121 BC

1–3, King Benjamin records the names of those who entered the covenant, consecrates Mosiah as king, and appoints priests; 4–7, King Mosiah walks in the ways of the Lord; he and his people till the earth.

1 And now, king Benjamin thought it was expedient, after having finished speaking to the people, that he should take the names of all those who had entered into a covenant with God to keep his commandments.

2 And it came to pass that there was not one soul, except it were little children, but who had entered into the covenant and had taken upon them the name of Christ.

3 And again, it came to pass that when king Benjamin had made an end of all these things, and had consecrated his son Mosiah to be a ruler and a king over his people, and had given him all the charges concerning the kingdom, and also had appointed priests to teach the people, that thereby they might hear and know the

commandments of God, and to stir them up in remembrance of the oath which they had made, he dismissed the multitude, and they returned, every one, according to their families, to their own houses.

4 And Mosiah began to reign in his father's stead. And he began to reign in the thirtieth year of his age, making in the whole, about four hundred and seventy-six years from the time that Lehi left Jerusalem.

5 And king Benjamin lived three years and he died.

6 And it came to pass that king Mosiah did walk in the ways of the Lord, and did observe his judgments and his statutes, and did keep his commandments in all things whatsoever he commanded him.

7 And king Mosiah did cause his people that they should till the earth. And he also, himself, did till the earth, that thereby he might not become burdensome to his people, that he might do according to that which his father had done in all things. And there was no contention among all his people for the space of three years.

vv. 1–7 I must be continually nourished by the word of God in order to stay on the correct path and remember Him.

⚡ Draw or show a picture of a plant. *What would you need to do if you moved this plant to a different location in your yard?* Make a list of class members' responses. *How is caring for a newly transplanted plant similar to caring for someone who has just been converted to the Gospel?*

✋ Explain that in every dispensation, prophets have had a desire for new converts to stay converted to the gospel. Ask class members to compare the words of the following three prophets and look for what converts need in order for them to remain converted. Write the following two references and quote on the board for class members with the above instructions.

King Benjamin—Mosiah 6:1–3
Moroni—Moroni 6:4–6

President Gordon B. Hinckley—"With the ever-increasing number of converts, we must make an increasingly substantial effort to assist them as they find their way. Every one of them needs three things: a friend, a responsibility, and nurturing with 'the good word of God (Moroni 6:4)'" (Gordon B. Hinckley, "Converts and Young Men," *Ensign*, May 1997).

❓ Analyze:
• *What did these three prophets teach us that we must do in order to stay converted after we have come to know the gospel?*
• *What aspect did all three of them mention?*
• *How is it that the word of God keeps us converted to the gospel?*

💗 Before class, give the following question to three class members and let them know that you will ask this question of them during the lesson. *How has the word of God (reading the scriptures and hearing the gospel) helped you stay converted to the gospel?* Have them share their responses at this point in the lesson. Invite class members to always take the opportunity, in both a class setting and as an individual, to be nourished by the word of God.

MOSIAH 7
King Limhi and His People Are Found
About 121 BC

1–4, Ammon leads a group to find the descendants of those who left with Zeniff; 5–16, They are found and Ammon is brought before King Limhi; 17–24, Limhi gathers his people and details the afflictions they have suffered; 25–33, Limhi tells of their past wickedness for which they have been afflicted.

Notes

1 And now, it came to pass that after king Mosiah had had continual peace for the space of three years, he was desirous to know concerning the people who went up to dwell in the land of Lehi-Nephi, or in the city of Lehi-Nephi; for his people had heard nothing from them from the time they left the land of Zarahemla; therefore, they wearied him with their teasings.

2 And it came to pass that king Mosiah granted that sixteen of their strong men might go up to the land of Lehi-Nephi, to inquire concerning their brethren.

3 And it came to pass that on the morrow they started to go up, having with them one Ammon, he being a strong and mighty man, and a descendant of Zarahemla; and he was also their leader.

4 And now, they knew not the course they should travel in the wilderness to go up to the land of Lehi-Nephi; therefore they wandered many days in the wilderness, even forty days did they wander.

5 And when they had wandered forty days they came to a hill, which is north of the land of Shilom, and there they pitched their tents.

6 And Ammon took three of his brethren, and their names were Amaleki, Helem, and Hem, and they went down into the land of Nephi.

7 And behold, they met the king of the people who were in the land of Nephi, and in the land of Shilom; and they were surrounded by the king's guard, and were taken, and were bound, and were committed to prison.

8 And it came to pass when they had been in prison two days they were again brought before the king, and their bands were loosed; and they stood before the king, and were permitted, or rather commanded, that they should answer the questions which he should ask them.

⚡ As you approach the story line that begins in Mosiah 7 and concludes in Mosiah 24, it may be helpful to visually outline the various journeys, groups, and events. This will allow class members to frequently review what has been discussed in previous lessons, understand what is happening in the current lesson, and gain an overall perspective of one of the more complicated story lines of the Book of Mormon. The following chart and explanation is one possibility. Consider displaying the entire chart at the beginning of chapter 7 and giving a brief overview of what will occur. Then as you move through the upcoming chapters, refer back to the illustration and explain the details of each event.

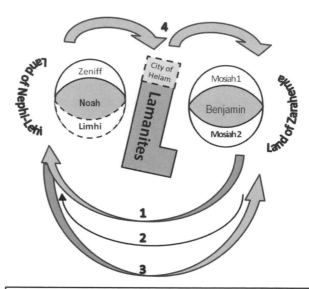

1) **Zeniff's Colonization** - Omni 1:27-30; Mosiah 9:1-8
2) **Ammon's Expedition** - Mosiah 7:2-4
3) **Gideon's Rescue** - Mosiah 22:1-3, 11-16
4) **Alma's Escape** - Mosiah 23:1-4,19-20

"Facing" Nephite History

The face's left eye represents the three kings of the Nephites in the land of Zarahemla (left ear) during this time period.

The face's right eye represents the three kings of Zeniff's people in the land of Nephi-Lehi (right ear) during the same time period.

Notes

The nose represents the separation of the two major groups of Nephites by Lamanite-inhabited regions.

The arrows making up the mouth represent (1) Zeniff's original colonization, (2) Ammon's expedition, and (3) Gideon's rescue.

The eyebrows (4) represent Alma's exodus, stay in the city of Helaman, and escape from Amulon's bondage.

The dotted lines represent captivity.

vv. 1–33 Tic-Tac-Toe.

✋ This lesson idea is meant to help your class learn the story line of what happens in chapter 7. Divide the class into two teams and draw a large tic-tac-toe grid on the board. Explain that they need to study the chapter carefully so that they can answer the true/false questions you will ask them without referring to their scriptures. If they answer it correctly, they get to mark their symbol on the grid; if they are incorrect, the other team gets to put their mark in the square. Remember to always pause and discuss when an important principle is found in the scriptures.

T / F King Mosiah had many people teasing him. (v. 1)

T / F Ammon was a descendant of Nephi. (v. 3)

T / F Ammon took forty men with him. (v. 2)

T / F Ammon and his brethren were captured and put in prison. (v. 7)

T / F They were interrogated by the king himself. (v. 8)

Once you have finished these questions, have them read the next set of verses and continue the game throughout the chapter.

9 And he said unto them: Behold, I am Limhi, the son of Noah, who was the son of Zeniff, who came up out of the land of Zarahemla to inherit this land, which was the land of their fathers, who was made a king by the voice of the people.

10 And now, I desire to know the cause whereby ye were so bold as to come near the walls of the city, when I, myself, was with my guards without the gate?

11 And now, for this cause have I suffered that ye should be preserved, that I might inquire of you, or else I should have caused that my guards should have put you to death. Ye are permitted to speak.

12 And now, when Ammon saw that he was permitted to speak, he went forth and bowed himself before the king; and rising again he said: O king, I am very thankful before God this day that I am yet alive, and am permitted to speak; and I will endeavor to speak with boldness;

13 For I am assured that if ye had known me ye would not have suffered that I should have worn these bands. For I am Ammon, and am a descendant of Zarahemla, and have come up out of the land of Zarahemla to inquire concerning our brethren, whom Zeniff brought up out of that land.

14 And now, it came to pass that after Limhi had heard the words of Ammon, he was exceedingly glad, and said: Now, I know of a surety that my brethren who were in the land of Zarahemla are yet alive. And now, I will rejoice; and on the morrow I will cause that my people shall rejoice also.

15 For behold, we are in bondage to the Lamanites, and are taxed with a tax which is grievous to be borne. And now, behold, our brethren will deliver us out of our bondage, or out of the hands of the Lamanites, and we will be their slaves; for it is better that we be slaves to the Nephites than to pay tribute to the king of the Lamanites.

16 And now, king Limhi commanded his guards that they should no more bind Ammon nor his brethren, but caused that they should go to the hill which was north of Shilom, and bring their brethren into the city, that thereby they might eat, and drink, and rest themselves from the labors of their journey; for they had suffered many things; they had suffered hunger, thirst, and fatigue.

Notes

vv. 9–16

T / F Limhi's father was Zeniff. (v. 9)

T / F Limhi was always firm but kind to Ammon. (v. 11)

T / F Limhi was thrilled to learn that they were from Zarahemla. (v. 14)

T / F Limhi thought that the people in Zarahemla might have perished. (v. 14)

T / F Limhi considered slavery under the Nephites. (v. 15)

17 And now, it came to pass on the morrow that king Limhi sent a proclamation among all his people, that thereby they might gather themselves together to the temple, to hear the words which he should speak unto them.

18 And it came to pass that when they had gathered themselves together that he spake unto them in this wise, saying: O ye, my people, lift up your heads and be comforted; for behold, the time is at hand, or is not far distant, when we shall no longer be in subjection to our enemies, notwithstanding our many strugglings, which have been in vain; yet I trust there remaineth an effectual struggle to be made.

19 Therefore, lift up your heads, and rejoice, and put your trust in God, in that God who was the God of Abraham, and Isaac, and Jacob; and also, that God who brought the children of Israel out of the land of Egypt, and caused that they should walk through the Red Sea on dry ground, and fed them with manna that they might not perish in the wilderness; and many more things did he do for them.

20 And again, that same God has brought our fathers out of the land of Jerusalem, and has kept and preserved his people even until now; and behold, it is because of our iniquities and abominations that he has brought us into bondage.

21 And ye all are witnesses this day, that Zeniff, who was made king over this people, he being over-zealous to inherit the land of his fathers, therefore being deceived by the cunning and craftiness of king Laman, who having entered into a treaty with king Zeniff, and having yielded up into his hands the possessions of a part of the land, or even the city of Lehi-Nephi, and the city of Shilom; and the land round about—

22 And all this he did, for the sole purpose of bringing this people into subjection or into bondage. And behold, we at this time do pay tribute to the king of the Lamanites, to the amount of one half of our corn, and our barley, and even all our grain of every kind, and one half of the increase of our flocks and our herds; and even one half of all we have or possess the king of the Lamanites doth exact of us, or our lives.

23 And now, is not this grievous to be borne? And is not this, our affliction, great? Now behold, how great reason we have to mourn.

24 Yea, I say unto you, great are the reasons which we have to mourn; for behold how many of our brethren have been slain, and their blood has been spilt in vain, and all because of iniquity.

vv. 17–24

T / F The people were gathered together at the palace of the king. (v. 17)

T / F King Limhi figured things would be much easier from then on. (v. 18)

T / F Limhi was sure their afflictions were because of the wickedness of the Lamanites. (v. 20)

T / F The king of the Lamanites tricked Zeniff's people by giving them low tax rates. (v. 21)

25 For if this people had not fallen into transgression the Lord would not have suffered that this great evil should come upon them. But behold, they would not hearken unto his words; but there arose contentions among them, even so much that they did shed blood among themselves.

26 And a prophet of the Lord have they slain; yea, a chosen man of God, who told them of their wickedness and abominations, and prophesied

Notes

of many things which are to come, yea, even the coming of Christ.

27 And because he said unto them that Christ was the God, the Father of all things, and said that he should take upon him the image of man, and it should be the image after which man was created in the beginning; or in other words, he said that man was created after the image of God, and that God should come down among the children of men, and take upon him flesh and blood, and go forth upon the face of the earth—

28 And now, because he said this, they did put him to death; and many more things did they do which brought down the wrath of God upon them. Therefore, who wondereth that they are in bondage, and that they are smitten with sore afflictions?

29 For behold, the Lord hath said: I will not succor my people in the day of their transgression; but I will hedge up their ways that they prosper not; and their doings shall be as a stumbling block before them.

30 And again, he saith: If my people shall sow filthiness they shall reap the chaff thereof in the whirlwind; and the effect thereof is poison.

31 And again he saith: If my people shall sow filthiness they shall reap the east wind, which bringeth immediate destruction.

32 And now, behold, the promise of the Lord is fulfilled, and ye are smitten and afflicted.

33 But if ye will turn to the Lord with full purpose of heart, and put your trust in him, and serve him with all diligence of mind, if ye do this, he will, according to his own will and pleasure, deliver you out of bondage.

vv. 25–33

T / F Limhi said they had been guilty of contentions and murder. (vv. 25–26)

T / F Abinadi taught that God should come down among the children of men. (v. 27)

T / F God said that his doings would be a stumbling block for them. (v. 29)

T / F Limhi taught that if they would turn to the Lord, he would immediately deliver them. (v. 33)

♥ Consider highlighting v. 33 as an overarching theme of chapters 7–24. Invite class members to look for how the Lord will do this over and over again as the people turn to the Lord.

Teaching Tips from Prophets' Lips "When you touch the life of a young person to make the choices which lead to touch them to go towards eternal life, you reach a multitude. Every hour you spend in careful preparation, in teaching, and then in wondering how you could have done it better has the potential for good so large that it will be worth all the prices you pay. And I know those prices are high" (Elder Henry B. Eyring, Comments given at *An Evening with Elder L. Tom Perry*, 2 February 1996).

MOSIAH 8

The Gift of Seership
About 121 BC

1–6, Ammon relates King Benjamin's sermon to the people of Limhi and also reads the record of Limhi's people; 7–12, Limhi relates the discovery of the twenty-four plates of the Jaredites; 13–21, Ammon explains the gift of seership to Limhi.

1 And it came to pass that after king Limhi had made an end of speaking to his people, for he spake many things unto them and only a few of them have I written in this book, he told his people all the things concerning their brethren who were in the land of Zarahemla.

2 And he caused that Ammon should stand up before the multitude, and rehearse unto them all that had happened unto their brethren from the

Notes

time that Zeniff went up out of the land even until the time that he himself came up out of the land.

3 And he also rehearsed unto them the last words which king Benjamin had taught them, and explained them to the people of king Limhi, so that they might understand all the words which he spake.

4 And it came to pass that after he had done all this, that king Limhi dismissed the multitude, and caused that they should return every one unto his own house.

5 And it came to pass that he caused that the plates which contained the record of his people from the time that they left the land of Zarahemla, should be brought before Ammon, that he might read them.

6 Now, as soon as Ammon had read the record, the king inquired of him to know if he could interpret languages, and Ammon told him that he could not.

7 And the king said unto him: Being grieved for the afflictions of my people, I caused that forty and three of my people should take a journey into the wilderness, that thereby they might find the land of Zarahemla, that we might appeal unto our brethren to deliver us out of bondage.

8 And they were lost in the wilderness for the space of many days, yet they were diligent, and found not the land of Zarahemla but returned to this land, having traveled in a land among many waters, having discovered a land which was covered with bones of men, and of beasts, and was also covered with ruins of buildings of every kind, having discovered a land which had been peopled with a people who were as numerous as the hosts of Israel.

9 And for a testimony that the things that they had said are true they have brought twenty-four plates which are filled with engravings, and they are of pure gold.

10 And behold, also, they have brought breastplates, which are large, and they are of brass and of copper, and are perfectly sound.

11 And again, they have brought swords, the hilts thereof have perished, and the blades thereof were cankered with rust; and there is no one in the land that is able to interpret the language or the engravings that are on the plates. Therefore I said unto thee: Canst thou translate?

12 And I say unto thee again: Knowest thou of any one that can translate? For I am desirous that these records should be translated into our language; for, perhaps, they will give us a knowledge of a remnant of the people who have been destroyed, from whence these records came; or, perhaps, they will give us a knowledge of this very people who have been destroyed; and I am desirous to know the cause of their destruction.

vv. 7–12 Adventures of the lost Nephites—King Limhi discovers the Jaredite ruins.

King Limhi sends people to find the land of Zarahemla in hopes of obtaining assistance from them. Read verses 7–12 as a class to see what these men discover instead of Zarahemla.

Explain that the plates these people discover are the record of the Jaredite people and will be translated into the book of Ether (see Mosiah 28:11–19 and Ether 1:1–2).

13 Now Ammon said unto him: I can assuredly tell thee, O king, of a man that can translate the records; for he has wherewith that he can look, and translate all records that are of ancient date; and it is a gift from God. And the things are called interpreters, and no man can look in them except he be commanded, lest he should look for that he ought not and he should perish. And whosoever is commanded to look in them, the same is called seer.

14 And behold, the king of the people who are in the land of Zarahemla is the man that is

Notes

commanded to do these things, and who has this high gift from God.

15 And the king said that a seer is greater than a prophet.

16 And Ammon said that a seer is a revelator and a prophet also; and a gift which is greater can no man have, except he should possess the power of God, which no man can; yet a man may have great power given him from God.

17 But a seer can know of things which are past, and also of things which are to come, and by them shall all things be revealed, or, rather, shall secret things be made manifest, and hidden things shall come to light, and things which are not known shall be made known by them, and also things shall be made known by them which otherwise could not be known.

18 Thus God has provided a means that man, through faith, might work mighty miracles; therefore he becometh a great benefit to his fellow beings.

vv. 13–18 A seer is a revelator and a prophet. God calls seers to be of great benefit to us when we apply their teachings.

⚡ Bring either a pair of glasses, binoculars, or a telescope, and display it in the front of class. Discuss with the class how this object aids in seeing. Ask, *If you couldn't see far, how would these help you? Imagine that we all were having trouble seeing something and only one person had this* (referring to the glasses, binoculars, or telescope). *Why do you think we should listen to and respect what he or she says? What might some consequences be if we didn't listen to that person?*

🔍 As you read verse 13 as a class, look for what we are to call a person who has the ability to "see." Write that title on the board. Then have the class read verses 13 and 16–18 looking for what a seer does. Write class members' responses on the board. The following are suggested answers:

v. 13—Translates records

v. 16—Provides revelation

v. 17—Knows of things past, present, and future

v. 18—Works mighty miracles

💡 Notice that in verses 15–16, Limhi concludes that a seer is greater than a prophet, and Ammon corrects him by saying that a seer *is* a prophet.

🔍 Look for Ammon's concluding comment about a seer in verse 18.

❓ Analyze: *Why do you think it is beneficial to have a seer?* (Refer to the list on the board.)

❓ Apply: Display a picture of Joseph Smith. *In what ways was Joseph a seer?* Encourage the class to think of examples for each of the duties of a seer listed on the board. Next, display a picture of the current prophet. *In what ways is our prophet a seer? In what ways does a prophet reveal knowledge?*

❤ Help class members to understand the importance of the role of a seer. *When have you followed counsel from general conference? What happened? How did it bless your life?* Consider sharing an example from your own experience.

19 And now, when Ammon had made an end of speaking these words the king rejoiced exceedingly, and gave thanks to God, saying: Doubtless a great mystery is contained within these plates, and these interpreters were doubtless prepared for the purpose of unfolding all such mysteries to the children of men.

20 O how marvelous are the works of the Lord, and how long doth he suffer with his people; yea, and how blind and impenetrable are the understandings of the children of men; for they will not seek wisdom, neither do they desire that she should rule over them!

21 Yea, they are as a wild flock which fleeth from the shepherd, and scattereth, and are driven, and are devoured by the beasts of the forest.

Notes

MOSIAH 9

Zeniff Obtains Land from the Lamanites
About 200–187 BC

1–2, Zeniff's first attempt at obtaining the land of inheritance fails; 3–9, Zeniff returns and obtains land from the Lamanites and begins to create a city; 10–19, the Lamanites attack the people of Zeniff but they are protected because of the Lord.

1 I, Zeniff, having been taught in all the language of the Nephites, and having had a knowledge of the land of Nephi, or of the land of our fathers' first inheritance, and having been sent as a spy among the Lamanites that I might spy out their forces, that our army might come upon them and destroy them—but when I saw that which was good among them I was desirous that they should not be destroyed.

2 Therefore, I contended with my brethren in the wilderness, for I would that our ruler should make a treaty with them; but he being an austere and a blood-thirsty man commanded that I should be slain; but I was rescued by the shedding of much blood; for father fought against father, and brother against brother, until the greater number of our army was destroyed in the wilderness; and we returned, those of us that were spared, to the land of Zarahemla, to relate that tale to their wives and their children.

vv. 1–2 Zeniff's first attempt at returning to the land of the Nephites' first inheritance.

🔎 Read verses 1–2 as a class to get a sense of the storyline and why Zeniff wants to return to the land of their first inheritance.

3 And yet, I being over-zealous to inherit the land of our fathers, collected as many as were desirous to go up to possess the land, and started again on our journey into the wilderness to go up to the land; but we were smitten with famine and sore afflictions; for we were slow to remember the Lord our God.

4 Nevertheless, after many days' wandering in the wilderness we pitched our tents in the place where our brethren were slain, which was near to the land of our fathers.

5 And it came to pass that I went again with four of my men into the city, in unto the king, that I might know of the disposition of the king, and that I might know if I might go in with my people and possess the land in peace.

6 And I went in unto the king, and he covenanted with me that I might possess the land of Lehi-Nephi, and the land of Shilom.

7 And he also commanded that his people should depart out of the land, and I and my people went into the land that we might possess it.

8 And we began to build buildings, and to repair the walls of the city, yea, even the walls of the city of Lehi-Nephi, and the city of Shilom.

9 And we began to till the ground, yea, even with all manner of seeds, with seeds of corn, and of wheat, and of barley, and with neas, and with sheum, and with seeds of all manner of fruits; and we did begin to multiply and prosper in the land.

vv. 3–9 Zeniff obtains land from the Lamanites.

💡 Explain that on their second attempt, Zeniff does obtain land from the king of the Lamanites (v. 6), and this small group of Nephites begins to build a city.

10 Now it was the cunning and the craftiness of king Laman, to bring my people into bondage, that he yielded up the land that we might possess it.

11 Therefore it came to pass, that after we had dwelt in the land for the space of twelve years that king Laman began to grow uneasy, lest by any means my people should wax strong in the

Notes

land, and that they could not overpower them and bring them into bondage.

12 Now they were a lazy and an idolatrous people; therefore they were desirous to bring us into bondage, that they might glut themselves with the labors of our hands; yea, that they might feast themselves upon the flocks of our fields.

13 Therefore it came to pass that king Laman began to stir up his people that they should contend with my people; therefore there began to be wars and contentions in the land.

14 For, in the thirteenth year of my reign in the land of Nephi, away on the south of the land of Shilom, when my people were watering and feeding their flocks, and tilling their lands, a numerous host of Lamanites came upon them and began to slay them, and to take off their flocks, and the corn of their fields.

15 Yea, and it came to pass that they fled, all that were not overtaken, even into the city of Nephi, and did call upon me for protection.

16 And it came to pass that I did arm them with bows, and with arrows, with swords, and with cimeters, and with clubs, and with slings, and with all manner of weapons which we could invent, and I and my people did go forth against the Lamanites to battle.

17 Yea, in the strength of the Lord did we go forth to battle against the Lamanites; for I and my people did cry mightily to the Lord that he would deliver us out of the hands of our enemies, for we were awakened to a remembrance of the deliverance of our fathers.

18 And God did hear our cries and did answer our prayers; and we did go forth in his might; yea, we did go forth against the Lamanites, and in one day and a night we did slay three thousand and forty-three; we did slay them even until we had driven them out of our land.

19 And I, myself, with mine own hands, did help to bury their dead. And behold, to our great sorrow

and lamentation, two hundred and seventy-nine of our brethren were slain.

vv. 10–19 The Lamanites attack.

🔍 In verse 11, look for what the Lamanite plan was for this small civilization of Nephites.

🔍 Explain that the Lamanites come to war against Zeniff's people. *How did the people of Zeniff react to the war in verses 17–19?* Emphasize the importance of turning to the Lord during struggles.

Teaching Tips from Prophets' Lips "The eyes of the alert teacher move constantly back and forth across the class, taking in each movement, recording each expression, responding quickly to disinterest or confusion. They read immediately a puzzled expression or sense at once when learning has taken place" (Boyd K Packer, *Teach Ye Diligently*, 138–39).

MOSIAH 10
In the Strength of the Lord
About 124 BC

1–5, Zeniff leads his people to be industrious, diligent, and prepared; 6–9, The Lamanites prepare for battle; 10–12, Zeniff and his people meet them in the strength of the Lord; 13–18, Incorrect traditions lead the Lamanites to be wroth and vengeful toward the Nephites; 19–22, Zeniff's people are successful in battle due to their trust in the Lord.

1 And it came to pass that we again began to establish the kingdom and we again began to possess the land in peace. And I caused that there should be weapons of war made of every kind, that thereby I might have weapons for my people against the time the Lamanites should come up again to war against my people.

2 And I set guards round about the land, that

Notes

the Lamanites might not come upon us again unawares and destroy us; and thus I did guard my people and my flocks, and keep them from falling into the hands of our enemies.

3 And it came to pass that we did inherit the land of our fathers for many years, yea, for the space of twenty and two years.

4 And I did cause that the men should till the ground, and raise all manner of grain and all manner of fruit of every kind.

5 And I did cause that the women should spin, and toil, and work, and work all manner of fine linen, yea, and cloth of every kind, that we might clothe our nakedness; and thus we did prosper in the land—thus we did have continual peace in the land for the space of twenty and two years.

6 And it came to pass that king Laman died, and his son began to reign in his stead. And he began to stir his people up in rebellion against my people; therefore they began to prepare for war, and to come up to battle against my people.

7 But I had sent my spies out round about the land of Shemlon, that I might discover their preparations, that I might guard against them, that they might not come upon my people and destroy them.

8 And it came to pass that they came up upon the north of the land of Shilom, with their numerous hosts, men armed with bows, and with arrows, and with swords, and with cimeters, and with stones, and with slings; and they had their heads shaved that they were naked; and they were girded with a leathern girdle about their loins.

9 And it came to pass that I caused that the women and children of my people should be hid in the wilderness; and I also caused that all my old men that could bear arms, and also all my young men that were able to bear arms, should gather themselves together to go to battle against the Lamanites; and I did place them in their ranks, every man according to his age.

10 And it came to pass that we did go up to battle against the Lamanites; and I, even I, in my old age, did go up to battle against the Lamanites. And it came to pass that we did go up in the strength of the Lord to battle.

11 Now, the Lamanites knew nothing concerning the Lord, nor the strength of the Lord, therefore they depended upon their own strength. Yet they were a strong people, as to the strength of men.

vv. 1–11 In the strength of the Lord, I can overcome all things.

⚡ *What would you consider the most important aspect of winning a battle? Why?* After a brief discussion, write "Mosiah 10:1–9, 12" on the board and "Lamanites vs. Zeniff's People".

🔍 *Read Mosiah 10:1–9, 12 and look for what advantages, disadvantages, and preparations both the Lamanites and Zeniff's people faced for the approaching battle.* Make a list on the board under the respective group heading (Lamanites or Zeniff's people) of what class members find.

❓ Analyze:
- *Based solely on what you found in those verses, which group do you think has a better chance at victory?*
- *Why might the Lamanites feel very confident going into battle?*
- *Why might Zeniff's people be anxious or fearful?*

Have a class member read Mosiah 10:10–11.

- *What other advantage did Zeniff's people have? How might that affect the outcome of the battle?*
- *How would you define "the strength of the Lord" in your own terms?*
- *Why were the Lamanites forced to rely upon their own strength?*

❓ Apply:
- *What causes us to rely on our own strength during our trials?*
- *What types of activities can increase our reliance on the Lord?*
- *How can we overcome our tendency to rely*

Notes

on our own strength and instead strive to have "the strength of the Lord" during hard times?

❓ Elder David A. Bednar shared the following experience in his first general conference talk as newly ordained apostle. Elder Bednar and his associates were involved with the challenging and daunting task of transitioning Rick's College to BYU–Idaho. He said, "As we walked out of the building that night, one of my colleagues asked, 'President, are you scared?' As best as I can recall, I answered something like this: 'If I thought we had to execute this transition relying exclusively upon our own experience and our own judgment, then I would be terrified. But we will have help from heaven. Because we know who is in charge and that we are not alone, then no, I am not scared.' And we who serve at BYU–Idaho unitedly testify that there has been help from heaven, miracles have occurred, revelations have been received, doors have been opened, and we have been greatly blessed as individuals and as an institution."

Elder Bednar then continued, "I will go where the Lord and the leaders of His Church want me to go, I will do what they want me to do, I will teach what they want me to teach, and I will strive to become what I should and must become. In the strength of the Lord and through His grace, I know that you and I can be blessed to accomplish all things" (David A. Bednar, *Ensign*, November 2004).

♥ Have class members look ahead to Mosiah 10:19–20 to see the end result of the battle. Testify that if we can embrace the principle in the last paragraph of the quote above, we will overcome all things in the end through the "strength of the Lord."

12 They were a wild, and ferocious, and a bloodthirsty people, believing in the tradition of their fathers, which is this—Believing that they were driven out of the land of Jerusalem because of the iniquities of their fathers, and that they were wronged in the wilderness by their brethren, and they were also wronged while crossing the sea;

13 And again, that they were wronged while in the land of their first inheritance, after they had crossed the sea, and all this because that Nephi was more faithful in keeping the commandments of the Lord—therefore he was favored of the Lord, for the Lord heard his prayers and answered them, and he took the lead of their journey in the wilderness.

14 And his brethren were wroth with him because they understood not the dealings of the Lord; they were also wroth with him upon the waters because they hardened their hearts against the Lord.

15 And again, they were wroth with him when they had arrived in the promised land, because they said that he had taken the ruling of the people out of their hands; and they sought to kill him.

16 And again, they were wroth with him because he departed into the wilderness as the Lord had commanded him, and took the records which were engraven on the plates of brass, for they said that he robbed them.

17 And thus they have taught their children that they should hate them, and that they should murder them, and that they should rob and plunder them, and do all they could to destroy them; therefore they have an eternal hatred towards the children of Nephi.

18 For this very cause has king Laman, by his cunning, and lying craftiness, and his fair promises, deceived me, that I have brought this my people up into this land, that they may destroy them; yea, and we have suffered these many years in the land.

19 And now I, Zeniff, after having told all these things unto my people concerning the Lamanites, I did stimulate them to go to battle with their might, putting their trust in the Lord; therefore, we did contend with them, face to face.

Notes

20 And it came to pass that we did drive them again out of our land; and we slew them with a great slaughter, even so many that we did not number them.

21 And it came to pass that we returned again to our own land, and my people again began to tend their flocks, and to till their ground.

22 And now I, being old, did confer the kingdom upon one of my sons; therefore, I say no more. And may the Lord bless my people. Amen.

vv. 12–22 Relying on false traditions and dwelling on perceived injustices leads to feelings of bitterness, anger, and hatred. Trusting in the Lord leads to protection and peace.

⚡ Announce to the class that today they will get a rare glimpse into Lamanite education. Or if it fits with your personal style, you may consider pretending to be a Lamanite teacher. You could say something like, "Welcome to today's lecture, my Lamanite friends. Today we will be studying some fundamental elements of our nation's history and traditions." Write on the board in large letters:

Lamanite History 101
$W^3=W^4$
. . . It doesn't add up

🔑 *Read Mosiah 10:12–16 and look for three occurrences of a word that starts with "w" that leads to the four occurrences of an emotion that starts with "w."* After giving them a chance to look silently, you may consider reading the verses aloud and asking class members to raise a hand, stomp on the ground, or do some other action every time they hear the words they have found. This may work well if you are using the "Lamanite teacher" idea above.

❓ Analyze:
- *What are some major differences between what you read about Lamanite traditions and what the scriptures teach about their history?*

- *Why would the Lamanites reinterpret the past to find injustices and times they were "wronged"?*
- *Read Mosiah 10:17–18. How did dwelling on past conflicts—real or exaggerated—affect the Lamanites' emotions? Their actions? Their spirituality?*

✏️ Have class members write 1 Nephi 7:16–20 in the margin of their scriptures. Briefly explain the context and have someone read 1 Nephi 7:20 to the class. In that verse, ask them to underline what they see as the difference between Nephi's views of past injustices when contrasted with the Lamanite viewpoint. Then have them turn back to Mosiah 10 and write a summary statement in the margin of their scriptures explaining what they learned and why Lamanite history "doesn't add up." Invite class members to share what they marked and wrote.

❓ Apply:
- *What are some of the ways the Lord would have us respond to offenses and injustices?*
- *How have you overcome the negative feelings of being "wronged" or mistreated?*
- *What if someone really has been wronged in their life? How can they overcome hurt or negative feelings?*

💬 The prophet Joseph Smith taught, "I am glad I have the privilege of communicating to you some things which, if grasped closely, will be a help to you when earthquakes bellow, the clouds gather, the lightnings flash, and the storms are ready to burst upon you like peals of thunder. . . . What can [these disasters] do? Nothing. All your losses will be made up to you in the resurrection provided you continue faithful" (*Teachings of Presidents of the Church: Joseph Smith* [The Church of Jesus Christ of Latter-day Saints, 2007], 51).

❤️ Testify that because of Christ's Atonement and resurrection, any wrong can be made right, any wound can be healed, and all negative feelings can be overcome and replaced with peace. Invite class members to come unto the Savior for peace.

Notes

MOSIAH 11

"Except This People Repent"
About 160–150 BC

1–15, The wickedness of King Noah; 16–19, The wickedness and pride of King Noah's people; 20–29, Abinadi cries repentance but the people harden their hearts and seek to kill him.

1 And now it came to pass that Zeniff conferred the kingdom upon Noah, one of his sons; therefore Noah began to reign in his stead; and he did not walk in the ways of his father.

2 For behold, he did not keep the commandments of God, but he did walk after the desires of his own heart. And he had many wives and concubines. And he did cause his people to commit sin, and do that which was abominable in the sight of the Lord. Yea, and they did commit whoredoms and all manner of wickedness.

3 And he laid a tax of one fifth part of all they possessed, a fifth part of their gold and of their silver, and a fifth part of their ziff, and of their copper, and of their brass and their iron; and a fifth part of their fatlings; and also a fifth part of all their grain.

4 And all this did he take to support himself, and his wives and his concubines; and also his priests, and their wives and their concubines; thus he had changed the affairs of the kingdom.

5 For he put down all the priests that had been consecrated by his father, and consecrated new ones in their stead, such as were lifted up in the pride of their hearts.

6 Yea, and thus they were supported in their laziness, and in their idolatry, and in their whoredoms, by the taxes which king Noah had put upon his people; thus did the people labor exceedingly to support iniquity.

7 Yea, and they also became idolatrous, because they were deceived by the vain and flattering words of the king and priests; for they did speak flattering things unto them.

8 And it came to pass that king Noah built many elegant and spacious buildings; and he ornamented them with fine work of wood, and of all manner of precious things, of gold, and of silver, and of iron, and of brass, and of ziff, and of copper;

9 And he also built him a spacious palace, and a throne in the midst thereof, all of which was of fine wood and was ornamented with gold and silver and with precious things.

10 And he also caused that his workmen should work all manner of fine work within the walls of the temple, of fine wood, and of copper, and of brass.

11 And the seats which were set apart for the high priests, which were above all the other seats, he did ornament with pure gold; and he caused a breastwork to be built before them, that they might rest their bodies and their arms upon while they should speak lying and vain words to his people.

12 And it came to pass that he built a tower near the temple; yea, a very high tower, even so high that he could stand upon the top thereof and overlook the land of Shilom, and also the land of Shemlon, which was possessed by the Lamanites; and he could even look over all the land round about.

13 And it came to pass that he caused many buildings to be built in the land Shilom; and he caused a great tower to be built on the hill north of the land Shilom, which had been a resort for the children of Nephi at the time they fled out of the land; and thus he did do with the riches which he obtained by the taxation of his people.

14 And it came to pass that he placed his heart upon his riches, and he spent his time in riotous living with his wives and his concubines; and so did also his priests spend their time with harlots.

15 And it came to pass that he planted vineyards round about in the land; and he built

Notes

wine-presses, and made wine in abundance; and therefore he became a wine-bibber, and also his people.

16 And it came to pass that the Lamanites began to come in upon his people, upon small numbers, and to slay them in their fields, and while they were tending their flocks.

17 And king Noah sent guards round about the land to keep them off; but he did not send a sufficient number, and the Lamanites came upon them and killed them, and drove many of their flocks out of the land; thus the Lamanites began to destroy them, and to exercise their hatred upon them.

18 And it came to pass that king Noah sent his armies against them, and they were driven back, or they drove them back for a time; therefore, they returned rejoicing in their spoil.

19 And now, because of this great victory they were lifted up in the pride of their hearts; they did boast in their own strength, saying that their fifty could stand against thousands of the Lamanites; and thus they did boast, and did delight in blood, and the shedding of the blood of their brethren, and this because of the wickedness of their king and priests.

Overarching Theme: Prophets denounce sin and warn of its consequence.

vv. 1–11

⚡ Bring some type of a red flag to class or draw one on the board. Show the flag to the class and ask what a red flag means. Explain that one of the meanings of a red flag, according to the United States National Weather Service, is as follows: "A red-flag warning is issued when the combination of dry fuels and weather conditions support extreme fire danger." This warning is to highlight the increased fire danger. Explain that just as a red flag is a warning of potential fire conditions, scriptures and prophets warn us of

potential conditions that could lead to tragedy if we do not repent.

🔍 As a class or individually, have class members read Mosiah verses 1–15 and instruct them to note any description of the wickedness of King Noah or his people.

❓ Analyze: *As you look at all the sins of King Noah and his people, which ones do you think could lead to tragedy? How do King Noah's sins lead to the wickedness of his people (v. 19)? If you knew these people were heading toward danger, what would you do to try and help them?*

20 And it came to pass that there was a man among them whose name was Abinadi; and he went forth among them, and began to prophesy, saying: Behold, thus saith the Lord, and thus hath he commanded me, saying, Go forth, and say unto this people, thus saith the Lord—Wo be unto this people, for I have seen their abominations, and their wickedness, and their whoredoms; and except they repent I will visit them in mine anger.

21 And except they repent and turn to the Lord their God, behold, I will deliver them into the hands of their enemies; yea, and they shall be brought into bondage; and they shall be afflicted by the hand of their enemies.

22 And it shall come to pass that they shall know that I am the Lord their God, and am a jealous God, visiting the iniquities of my people.

23 And it shall come to pass that except this people repent and turn unto the Lord their God, they shall be brought into bondage; and none shall deliver them, except it be the Lord the Almighty God.

24 Yea, and it shall come to pass that when they shall cry unto me I will be slow to hear their cries; yea, and I will suffer them that they be smitten by their enemies.

25 And except they repent in sackcloth and ashes, and cry mightily to the Lord their God, I will

Notes

not hear their prayers, neither will I deliver them out of their afflictions; and thus saith the Lord, and thus hath he commanded me.

26 Now it came to pass that when Abinadi had spoken these words unto them they were wroth with him, and sought to take away his life; but the Lord delivered him out of their hands.

27 Now when king Noah had heard of the words which Abinadi had spoken unto the people, he was also wroth; and he said: Who is Abinadi, that I and my people should be judged of him, or who is the Lord, that shall bring upon my people such great affliction?

28 I command you to bring Abinadi hither, that I may slay him, for he has said these things that he might astir up my people to anger one with another, and to raise contentions among my people; therefore I will slay him.

29 Now the eyes of the people were blinded; therefore they hardened their hearts against the words of Abinadi, and they sought from that time forward to take him. And king Noah hardened his heart against the word of the Lord, and he did not repent of his evil doings.

vv. 20–25

Write the following phrase on the board: "Except this people repent . . ." Invite the class to help you finish this phrase according to the prophet's Abinadi's words as found in verses 20–25. Write all of the responses on the board so class members can clearly see and understand what would happen if the people did not listen to the Lord through the words of His prophet. Additionally, point out that as they continue to study the rest of the book of Mosiah they should look for and recognize how each of these prophecies were fulfilled. If the class has a substantial knowledge of the book of Mosiah, you could have them help you identify what events took place that fulfilled all of Abinadi's words.

Analyze:

- What is the role of a prophet according to these verses?
- Why do you think the Lord does not just destroy the people because of their wickedness?
- Why do you think He warns them first?

Look for how the people respond to Abinadi's warnings in verse 29.

Help class members understand the importance of following a prophet's warning by explaining that how we respond to a prophet's voice will determine our future blessings or tragedies. Ask, *What has the prophet warned us about that is plaguing our society and families?*

Invite class members to ponder on the following questions. You may consider having class members write down responses to these questions if they are too personal to share. Ask, *What are some "red flags" or indications in your life that, if left unchanged, could lead to tragedy? Have you and I listened to His voice or hardened our hearts?*

Invite class members to follow the promptings and warnings of the Spirit as they study these words.

Teaching Tips from Prophets' Lips "Teach them. And, above all, testify to them. Love them. Bear your witness from the depths of your soul. It will be the most important thing you say to them in the entire hour, and it may save someone's spiritual life" (Jeffrey R. Holland, "Teaching and Learning in the Church," *Ensign*, June 2007, 88–105).

MOSIAH 12

Apply Your Heart to Understanding
About 148 BC

1–8, Abinadi returns and testifies of the consequence of their sins; 9–16, He is taken by the people and

Notes

delivered to King Noah; 17–37, He is questioned by King Noah and his priests and rebukes them for their hypocrisy.

1 And it came to pass that after the space of two years that Abinadi came among them in disguise, that they knew him not, and began to prophesy among them, saying: Thus has the Lord commanded me, saying—Abinadi, go and prophesy unto this my people, for they have hardened their hearts against my words; they have repented not of their evil doings; therefore, I will visit them in my anger, yea, in my fierce anger will I visit them in their iniquities and abominations.

2 Yea, wo be unto this generation! And the Lord said unto me: Stretch forth thy hand and prophesy, saying: Thus saith the Lord, it shall come to pass that this generation, because of their iniquities, shall be brought into bondage, and shall be smitten on the cheek; yea, and shall be driven by men, and shall be slain; and the vultures of the air, and the dogs, yea, and the wild beasts, shall devour their flesh.

3 And it shall come to pass that the life of king Noah shall be valued even as a garment in a hot furnace; for he shall know that I am the Lord.

4 And it shall come to pass that I will smite this my people with sore afflictions, yea, with famine and with pestilence; and I will cause that they shall howl all the day long.

5 Yea, and I will cause that they shall have burdens lashed upon their backs; and they shall be driven before like a dumb ass.

6 And it shall come to pass that I will send forth hail among them, and it shall smite them; and they shall also be smitten with the beast wind; and insects shall pester their land also, and devour their grain.

7 And they shall be smitten with a great pestilence—and all this will I do because of their iniquities and abominations.

8 And it shall come to pass that except they repent I will utterly destroy them from off the face of the earth; yet they shall leave a record behind them, and I will preserve them for other nations which shall possess the land; yea, even this will I do that I may discover the abominations of this people to other nations. And many things did Abinadi prophesy against this people.

vv. 2–8 Sin leads to destruction.

⚡ Discuss natural consequences by having the class complete the blanks of if—then statements (IF _____, THEN _____. For example, IF you touch fire, THEN you will get burned.) You may also want to fill in the IF and allow the class to decide the THEN. Write one or two of the phrases on the board.

🔍 Invite class members to read verse 1 to find out what the spiritual condition of the people was. Then have the class read verses 2–8 and look for the consequences that would come to them as a result.

❓ Analyze: *Why are there consequences to wrongdoing?* Take time to explain that the consequences of sin will always lead to destruction. *What is the role of a prophet in this process?*

9 And it came to pass that they were angry with him; and they took him and carried him bound before the king, and said unto the king: Behold, we have brought a man before thee who has prophesied evil concerning thy people, and saith that God will destroy them.

10 And he also prophesieth evil concerning thy life, and saith that thy life shall be as a garment in a furnace of fire.

11 And again, he saith that thou shalt be as a stalk, even as a dry stalk of the field, which is run over by the beasts and trodden under foot.

12 And again, he saith thou shalt be as the blossoms of a thistle, which, when it is fully ripe, if the wind bloweth, it is driven forth upon the face of the land. And he pretendeth the Lord hath

Notes

_____

_____

_____

spoken it. And he saith all this shall come upon thee except thou repent, and this because of thine iniquities.

3 And now, O king, what great evil hast thou done, or what great sins have thy people committed, that we should be condemned of God or judged of this man?

14 And now, O king, behold, we are guiltless, and thou, O king, hast not sinned; therefore, this man has lied concerning you, and he has prophesied in vain.

15 And behold, we are strong, we shall not come into bondage, or be taken captive by our enemies; yea, and thou hast prospered in the land, and thou shalt also prosper.

16 Behold, here is the man, we deliver him into thy hands; thou mayest do with him as seemeth thee good.

17 And it came to pass that king Noah caused that Abinadi should be cast into prison; and he commanded that the priests should gather themselves together that he might hold a council with them what he should do with him.

18 And it came to pass that they said unto the king: Bring him hither that we may question him; and the king commanded that he should be brought before them.

19 And they began to question him, that they might cross him, that thereby they might have wherewith to accuse him; but he answered them boldly, and withstood all their questions, yea, to their astonishment; for he did withstand them in all their questions, and did confound them in all their words.

20 And it came to pass that one of them said unto him: What meaneth the words which are written, and which have been taught by our fathers, saying:

21 How beautiful upon the mountains are the feet of him that bringeth good tidings; that publisheth peace; that bringeth good tidings of good; that publisheth salvation; that saith unto Zion, Thy God reigneth;

22 Thy watchmen shall lift up the voice; with the voice together shall they sing; for they shall see eye to eye when the Lord shall bring again Zion;

23 Break forth into joy; sing together ye waste places of Jerusalem; for the Lord hath comforted his people, he hath redeemed Jerusalem;

24 The Lord hath made bare his holy arm in the eyes of all the nations, and all the ends of the earth shall see the salvation of our God?

25 And now Abinadi said unto them: Are you priests, and pretend to teach this people, and to understand the spirit of prophesying, and yet desire to know of me what these things mean?

26 I say unto you, wo be unto you for perverting the ways of the Lord! For if ye understand these things ye have not taught them; therefore, ye have perverted the ways of the Lord.

27 Ye have not applied your hearts to understanding; therefore, ye have not been wise. Therefore, what teach ye this people?

28 And they said: We teach the law of Moses.

29 And again he said unto them: If ye teach the law of Moses why do ye not keep it? Why do ye set your hearts upon riches? Why do ye commit whoredoms and spend your strength with harlots, yea, and cause this people to commit sin, that the Lord has cause to send me to prophesy against this people, yea, even a great evil against this people?

30 Know ye not that I speak the truth? Yea, ye know that I speak the truth; and you ought to tremble before God.

31 And it shall come to pass that ye shall be smitten for your iniquities, for ye have said that ye teach the law of Moses. And what know ye concerning the law of Moses? Doth salvation come by the law of Moses? What say ye?

32 And they answered and said that salvation did come by the law of Moses.

33 But now Abinadi said unto them: I know if ye keep the commandments of God ye shall be

Notes

saved; yea, if ye keep the commandments which the Lord delivered unto Moses in the mount of Sinai, saying:

34 I am the Lord thy God, who hath brought thee out of the land of Egypt, out of the house of bondage.

35 Thou shalt have no other God before me.

36 Thou shalt not make unto thee any graven image, or any likeness of any thing in heaven above, or things which are in the earth beneath.

37 Now Abinadi said unto them, Have ye done all this? I say unto you, Nay, ye have not. And have ye taught this people that they should do all these things? I say unto you, Nay, ye have not.

vv. 9–37 Being wise is "applying your heart to understanding."

⚡ Draw the outline of a person from the waist up on the board. Ask, *What is the definition of the word "wise"?* Write down some of the class members' definitions and then look in verse 27 for Abinadi's definition. On the outline of the person, draw a line from the head to the heart and indicate that wisdom can mean applying to our heart what we know in our head. Additionally, teach that at least all of the adults in this time grew up with the gospel but had fallen away because of their sins and the sins of King Noah.

✋ Assign three different groups the following verses and ask them to find in the verses something that the priests of King Noah thought in their heads but did not understand in their hearts. Have the groups read the verses individually first, and then come together to collaborate with a final response that can be shared with the class.

vv. 13–15 (Suggested answer) They thought that they prospered because of their own strength.

vv. 25–29 (Suggested answer) They thought that you can teach one thing and do another.

vv. 31–32 (Suggested answer) They thought that salvation came from the law of Moses.

❓ Analyze: *How is it possible for someone to know something in their head but not live it?*

♥ Refer again to the outline of the person on the board and indicate that with each of these verses there was a disconnect between knowing and doing.

💬 Share the following quote from Elder Melvin J. Hammond. "Many years ago, a returned missionary stood boldly in a sacrament meeting and proclaimed aloud that he knew from his study of the scriptures that the gospel was true and that he would give his life for the Lord and His Church. Two weeks later he stood before the bishop of his student ward, humiliated and frightened, as he confessed that in a moment of weakness he had lost his virtue. Somehow his proclaimed devotion to the Savior had been forgotten in the whirl of his passion. Although a student of the word of God, he had not linked his study with the practical application of everyday, down-to-earth, Christlike living. A beautiful girl worked her way through all the requirements to achieve the Young Womanhood Recognition. Her personal goals were thoughtfully written and carefully placed in her book of remembrance. Adamantly, she wrote that she would date only worthy young men and find that special one that would take her to the temple. When she was eighteen, her goals were forgotten; she eloped with a boy who was not a member of the Church. Many tears were shed by those who loved her most—her parents, teachers, and friends. She had fallen into the awful void between the requirements of the law and the reality of true discipleship. You see, the challenge that we face is to eliminate the void between information and application" ("Eliminating the Void Between Information and Application," CES Satellite Training Broadcast, August 2003).

♥ One of the keys to being wise is turning the knowledge of the scriptures into righteous

Notes

_____

_____

_____

living. Ask, *How does someone know the scriptures and yet not live righteously? What can we do to make sure we live according to our knowledge?* Invite the class to live righteously.

MOSIAH 13

Abinadi: Preaches the Ten Commandments

About 148 BC

1–10, Filled with God's power, Abinadi rebuffs the king's attempt to capture and slay him; 11–24, Abinadi continues his teaching of the Ten Commandments; 25–35, The commandments themselves do not save except it be through the Atonement of Christ.

1 And now when the king had heard these words, he said unto his priests: Away with this fellow, and slay him; for what have we to do with him, for he is mad.

2 And they stood forth and attempted to lay their hands on him; but he withstood them, and said unto them:

3 Touch me not, for God shall smite you if ye lay your hands upon me, for I have not delivered the message which the Lord sent me to deliver; neither have I told you that which ye requested that I should tell; therefore, God will not suffer that I shall be destroyed at this time.

4 But I must fulfil the commandments wherewith God has commanded me; and because I have told you the truth ye are angry with me. And again, because I have spoken the word of God ye have judged me that I am mad.

5 Now it came to pass after Abinadi had spoken these words that the people of king Noah durst not lay their hands on him, for the Spirit of the Lord was upon him; and his face shone with exceeding luster, even as Moses' did while in the mount of Sinai, while speaking with the Lord.

6 And he spake with power and authority from God; and he continued his words, saying:

7 Ye see that ye have not power to slay me, therefore I finish my message. Yea, and I perceive that it cuts you to your hearts because I tell you the truth concerning your iniquities.

8 Yea, and my words fill you with wonder and amazement, and with anger.

9 But I finish my message; and then it matters not whither I go, if it so be that I am saved.

10 But this much I tell you, what you do with me, after this, shall be as a type and a shadow of things which are to come.

vv. 1–10 Abinadi stands before King Noah.

Note: If you feel like you need variety when you read the scriptures as a class, you could suggest for a class member to read the dialogue found in the verses as if he were the one speaking.

11 And now I read unto you the remainder of the commandments of God, for I perceive that they are not written in your hearts; I perceive that ye have studied and taught iniquity the most part of your lives.

12 And now, ye remember that I said unto you: Thou shalt not make unto thee any graven image, or any likeness of things which are in heaven above, or which are in the earth beneath, or which are in the water under the earth.

13 And again: Thou shalt not bow down thyself unto them, nor serve them; for I the Lord thy God am a jealous God, visiting the iniquities of the fathers upon the children, unto the third and fourth generations of them that hate me;

14 And showing mercy unto thousands of them that love me and keep my commandments.

15 Thou shalt not take the name of the Lord thy God in vain; for the Lord will not hold him guiltless that taketh his name in vain.

16 Remember the sabbath day, to keep it holy.

Notes

17 Six days shalt thou labor, and do all thy work;

18 But the seventh day, the sabbath of the Lord thy God, thou shalt not do any work, thou, nor thy son, nor thy daughter, thy man-servant, nor thy maid-servant, nor thy cattle, nor thy stranger that is within thy gates;

19 For in six days the Lord made heaven and earth, and the sea, and all that in them is; wherefore the Lord blessed the sabbath day, and hallowed it.

20 Honor thy father and thy mother, that thy days may be long upon the land which the Lord thy God giveth thee.

21 Thou shalt not kill.

22 Thou shalt not commit adultery. Thou shalt not steal.

23 Thou shalt not bear false witness against thy neighbor.

24 Thou shalt not covet thy neighbor's house, thou shalt not covet thy neighbor's wife, nor his man-servant, nor his maid-servant, nor his ox, nor his ass, nor anything that is thy neighbor's.

vv. 11–24 Principles from the Ten Commandments.

⚡ Give class members 30 seconds to list the Ten Commandments.

✏ Have class members write #1 through #10 next to each of the verses where the Ten Commandments are listed. After reading the verses carefully, read those that give additional insight to that commandment and ask, *What is an additional lesson Abinadi teaches from the commandment?* In the Book of Mormon, they are found in:

- #1 (Mosiah 12:35) See also Doctrine and Covenants 59:5
- #2 (12:36 and 13:12–14) See also Doctrine and Covenants 1:15–16
- #3 (13:15) See also Doctrine and Covenants 63:61–62
- #4 (13:16–19) See also Doctrine and Covenants 59:9–13
- #5 (13:20) See also Ephesians 6:1–3
- #6 (13:21) See also Matthew 5:21–26
- #7 (13:22) See also Doctrine and Covenants 42:22–26
- #8 (13:22) See also Doctrine and Covenants 59:6
- #9 (13:23) See also Doctrine and Covenants 42:21, 27
- #10 (13:24) See also Doctrine and Covenants 19:25–26

❤ Invite class members to write down one way they want to live one of the Ten Commandments more fully and invite them to act accordingly.

25 And it came to pass that after Abinadi had made an end of these sayings that he said unto them: Have ye taught this people that they should observe to do all these things for to keep these commandments?

26 I say unto you, Nay; for if ye had, the Lord would not have caused me to come forth and to prophesy evil concerning this people.

27 And now ye have said that salvation cometh by the law of Moses. I say unto you that it is expedient that ye should keep the law of Moses as yet; but I say unto you, that the time shall come when it shall no more be expedient to keep the law of Moses.

28 And moreover, I say unto you, that salvation doth not come by the law alone; and were it not for the atonement, which God himself shall make for the sins and iniquities of his people, that they must unavoidably perish, notwithstanding the law of Moses.

29 And now I say unto you that it was expedient that there should be a law given to the children of Israel, yea, even a very strict law; for they were a stiffnecked people, quick to do iniquity, and slow to remember the Lord their God;

30 Therefore there was a law given them, yea, a law of performances and of ordinances, a law which they were to observe strictly from day to day, to

Notes

keep them in remembrance of God and their duty towards him.

31 But behold, I say unto you, that all these things were types of things to come.

32 And now, did they understand the law? I say unto you, Nay, they did not all understand the law; and this because of the hardness of their hearts; for they understood not that there could not any man be saved except it were through the redemption of God.

33 For behold, did not Moses prophesy unto them concerning the coming of the Messiah, and that God should redeem his people? Yea, and even all the prophets who have prophesied ever since the world began—have they not spoken more or less concerning these things?

34 Have they not said that God himself should come down among the children of men, and take upon him the form of man, and go forth in mighty power upon the face of the earth?

35 Yea, and have they not said also that he should bring to pass the resurrection of the dead, and that he, himself, should be oppressed and afflicted?

vv. 27–28, 32–33 The commandments alone can't save people. Christ saves those who strive to follow Him by keeping His commandments.

⚡ Ask, *If you learn to keep the Ten Commandments, will that save you? Can we save ourselves by learning to keep the commandments perfectly?*

🔎 *Look in verses 27–28 and 32–33 to determine whether or not the commandments can save a person.*

Teaching Tips from Prophets' Lips "Participation allows individuals to *experience* being led by the Spirit" (Elder Richard G. Scott, "Helping Others to Be Spiritually Led," CES Symposium, August 11, 1998, 3).

MOSIAH 14

Abinadi Quotes Isaiah 53
About 148 BC

1–3, The Messiah is "despised and rejected of men;" 4–9, He vicariously suffers the pains, sorrows, and sins of man and dies; 10–12, He "shall see his seed" and intercedes for the transgressors.

1 Yea, even doth not Isaiah say: Who hath believed our report, and to whom is the arm of the Lord revealed?

2 For he shall grow up before him as a tender plant, and as a root out of dry ground; he hath no form nor comeliness; and when we shall see him there is no beauty that we should desire him.

3 He is despised and rejected of men; a man of sorrows, and acquainted with grief; and we hid as it were our faces from him; he was despised, and we esteemed him not.

vv. 1–3 Jesus was despised and rejected.

✋ Prior to teaching this principle, write on the board, "It's new to me." Explain to class members that you want them to read verses 1–3 and be ready to share something they learn that is new to them. After they share, ask how those thoughts broaden their understanding of the Savior's life.

4 Surely he has borne our griefs, and carried our sorrows; yet we did esteem him stricken, smitten of God, and afflicted.

5 But he was wounded for our transgressions, he was bruised for our iniquities; the chastisement of our peace was upon him; and with his stripes we are healed.

6 All we, like sheep, have gone astray; we have turned every one to his own way; and the Lord hath laid on him the iniquities of us all.

7 He was oppressed, and he was afflicted, yet he opened not his mouth; he is brought as a lamb to

Notes

the slaughter, and as a sheep before her shearers is dumb so he opened not his mouth.

8 He was taken from prison and from judgment; and who shall declare his generation? For he was cut off out of the land of the living; for the transgressions of my people was he stricken.

9 And he made his grave with the wicked, and with the rich in his death; because he had done no evil, neither was any deceit in his mouth.

10 Yet it pleased the Lord to bruise him; he hath put him to grief; when thou shalt make his soul an offering for sin he shall see his seed, he shall prolong his days, and the pleasure of the Lord shall prosper in his hand.

11 He shall see the travail of his soul, and shall be satisfied; by his knowledge shall my righteous servant justify many; for he shall bear their iniquities.

12 Therefore will I divide him a portion with the great, and he shall divide the spoil with the strong; because he hath poured out his soul unto death; and he was numbered with the transgressors; and he bore the sins of many, and made intercession for the transgressors.

vv. 4–6, 11–12 Christ's Atonement can heal us from more than just sin.

🔍 Explain that in verses 4–6 and 11–12, Isaiah is referring to Jesus's suffering during the Atonement. Invite class members to underline anything in those verses that describe what Jesus experienced during that process.

❓ Analyze: Ask class members to share what they underlined. Select one or two phrases that can be analyzed further and ask questions that allow your class to ponder and discuss those verses together.

💬 Consider sharing this quote by Neal A. Maxwell: "Since not all human sorrow and pain is connected to sin, the full intensiveness of the Atonement involved bearing our pains, infirmities, and sicknesses, as well as our sins. Whatever our sufferings, we can safely cast our care upon him; for he careth for [us]" (1 Peter 5:7). Jesus is a fully comprehending Christ" (Neal A. Maxwell, *Not My Will, But Thine*, Salt Lake City, UT: Deseret Book, 2008).

💬 "The Savior, as a member of the Godhead, knows each of us personally. Isaiah and the prophet Abinadi said that when Christ would 'make his soul an offering for sin, he shall see his seed' (Isaiah 53:10; compare Mosiah 15:10). Abinadi explains that 'his seed' are the righteous, those who follow the prophets (see Mosiah 15:11). In the garden and on the cross, Jesus saw each of us and not only bore our sins, but also experienced our deepest feelings so that he would know how to comfort and strengthen us. . . . The Savior's atonement in the garden and on the cross is intimate as well as infinite. Infinite in that it spans the eternities. Intimate in that the Savior felt each person's pains, sufferings, and sicknesses. Consequently, he knows how to carry our sorrows and relieve our burdens that we might be healed from within, made whole persons, and receive everlasting joy in his kingdom. May our faith in the Father and the Son help each of us to become whole" (Merrill J. Bateman, "The Power to Heal from Within," *Ensign*, May 1995).

❤ Invite class members to write down one thing they would want to have the Savior heal in their life. Explain that, despite the Atonement, we still have our agency so He can only heal us as we allow Him to and in His way. Express your gratitude for the Savior for healing you from sin and also the sins of others.

Notes

MOSIAH 15

Abinadi: Teachings on the Atonement

About 148 BC

1–4, Doctrine of the unity of the Godhead; 3–7, Details of the Atonement; 8–20, Explanation of the doctrine of the Atonement; 21–25, The first resurrection; 26–31, "The Lord redeemeth none such that rebel against him and die in their sins."

Note: This is a continuation of Abinadi's words to King Noah and his priests. You may want to consider how his message from previous chapters (Mosiah 12–14) corresponds with what he is teaching in this chapter.

Overarching Principle: The Atonement of Jesus Christ allows the Savior to stand between us and judgment, and it redeems us from death through the resurrection.

⚡ Before class, draw the following diagram on the board (leave the listed answers blank, and fill them in as the class discovers the doctrine from Abinadi's teachings), which will help you teach the doctrine of the Atonement found throughout the entire chapter. Note that there is an object lesson idea for verses 5–9 that will also use the diagram, so plan accordingly.

The Atonement of Jesus Christ

What does the Atonement accomplish? vv 8–9

- Break the bands of death
- Have bowels filled with mercy and compassion
- Stands between the sinner and justice by taking our sins upon him

How does the Atonement accomplish the "what"? vv. 5–7, 10–13, 19–20

- Through Jesus's death and resurrection vv. 19–20
- When His soul has been made an offering for sin, He shall see His seed v. 10
- Jesus suffered the will of the Father through His suffering

1 And now Abinadi said unto them: I would that ye should understand that God himself shall come down among the children of men, and shall redeem his people.

2 And because he dwelleth in flesh he shall be called the Son of God, and having subjected the flesh to the will of the Father, being the Father and the Son—

3 The Father, because he was conceived by the power of God; and the Son, because of the flesh; thus becoming the Father and Son—

4 And they are one God, yea, the very Eternal Father of heaven and of earth.

vv. 1–4 The Godhead consists of three separate beings. The title of Father can be applied to Jesus Christ.

💡 Explain to class members the doctrine of the Godhead as taught by The Church of Jesus Christ of Latter-day Saints, namely that God the Father, Jesus Christ, and the Holy Ghost are three distinct beings (see Doctrine and Covenants 130:22–23). Though separate beings, they are one in purpose.

🔎 *Read verses 1–4 and look for what Abinadi says might seem contradictory to the doctrine that Heavenly Father and Jesus Christ are separate beings.*

💬 Joseph Fielding Smith stated, "What is a father? One who begets or gives life. What did our Savior do? He begot us, or gave us life from death. . . . He became a father to us because he gave us immortality or eternal life through his death and sacrifice upon the cross. I think we have a perfect right to speak of him as a Father" (Conference report, October 1962, 20–22). Cross-reference Mosiah 5:7.

💡 Explain to class members that Abinadi uses this as an introductory doctrine to prove that Jesus Christ was obedient to the will of the Father though His death.

5 And thus the flesh becoming subject to the Spirit, or the Son to the Father, being one God, suffereth temptation, and yieldeth not to the temptation, but suffereth himself to be mocked, and scourged, and cast out, and disowned by his people.

6 And after all this, after working many mighty miracles among the children of men, he shall be led, yea, even as Isaiah said, as a sheep before the shearer is dumb, so he opened not his mouth.

7 Yea, even so he shall be led, crucified, and slain, the flesh becoming subject even unto death, the will of the Son being swallowed up in the will of the Father.

8 And thus God breaketh the bands of death, having gained the victory over death; giving the Son power to make intercession for the children of men—

9 Having ascended into heaven, having the bowels of mercy; being filled with compassion towards the children of men; standing betwixt them and justice; having broken the bands of death, taken upon himself their iniquity and their transgressions, having redeemed them, and satisfied the demands of justice.

vv. 5–9 The Atonement gives Jesus the ability to stand between His people and justice because He took their iniquity upon Himself.

⚡ To help establish with your class the importance of this principle, draw a target on the board and label it "Judgment for our sins." In addition, bring a toy dart gun (with plastic or foam darts) to shoot at the target. Label the dart gun "Justice." Note: if a toy dart gun is not available, you can use other soft items as a means of shooting at the target. Explain to your class that this target represents the judgment we receive from our actions on earth; the dart gun represents justice exacting judgment upon us because of our mistakes. Depending on the age of class members and the amount of time you have, you may want to allow them ample time to shoot at the target.

🔎 *What does this object lesson have to do with the Atonement?* Look in verses 8–9 to find the answer. Abinadi uses the phrase "standing betwixt them and justice." Refer back to the object lesson and point out that Jesus would stand in front of the target to ensure that we are not exposed to the full weight of justice.

✏️ Have class members list the aspects that the Atonement of Jesus Christ covers from verses 8–9. Invite them to identify those aspects and write them on the board in the "What does the Atonement accomplish" column (see the ⚡ underneath the overarching principle.)

❓ Analyze: Make sure you take some time here to ensure that class members understand what each of the identified phrases mean. You may want to ask questions to check for understanding.

Notes

🔍 Look in verses 5–7 to find out how the Atonement accomplishes the list you just created. Write class members' responses in the "How" column.

10 And now I say unto you, who shall declare his generation? Behold, I say unto you, that when his soul has been made an offering for sin he shall see his seed. And now what say ye? And who shall be his seed?

11 Behold I say unto you, that whosoever has heard the words of the prophets, yea, all the holy prophets who have prophesied concerning the coming of the Lord—I say unto you, that all those who have hearkened unto their words, and believed that the Lord would redeem his people, and have looked forward to that day for a remission of their sins, I say unto you, that these are his seed, or they are the heirs of the kingdom of God.

12 For these are they whose sins he has borne; these are they for whom he has died, to redeem them from their transgressions. And now, are they not his seed?

13 Yea, and are not the prophets, every one that has opened his mouth to prophesy, that has not fallen into transgression, I mean all the holy prophets ever since the world began? I say unto you that they are his seed.

14 And these are they who have published peace, who have brought good tidings of good, who have published salvation; and said unto Zion: Thy God reigneth!

15 And O how beautiful upon the mountains were their feet!

16 And again, how beautiful upon the mountains are the feet of those that are still publishing peace!

17 And again, how beautiful upon the mountains are the feet of those who shall hereafter publish peace, yea, from this time henceforth and forever!

18 And behold, I say unto you, this is not all. For

O how beautiful upon the mountains are the feet of him that bringeth good tidings, that is the founder of peace, yea, even the Lord, who has redeemed his people; yea, him who has granted salvation unto his people;

vv. 10–13 Jesus Christ has compassion for us individually because he suffered for us individually.

💡 Refer to the chart on the board to indicate that one of the aspects of the Atonement is that it allows Jesus to be compassionate.

🔍 Read verse 10 as a class. Ask, *During the agony of the Atonement, "when Jesus made himself an offering for sin" who does He see in the process?*

❓ Analyze: Ask class members the same question Abinadi asks, *"Who is his seed?"*

🔍 *Read verses 11–12 and look for who is counted as "his seed".*

❓ Analyze: *Therefore, who did Jesus see during the agonizing time of the Atonement?*

🗨 "The Savior, as a member of the Godhead, knows each of us personally. Isaiah and the prophet Abinadi said that when Christ would 'make his soul an offering for sin, he shall see his seed' (Isaiah 53:10; compare Mosiah 15:10). Abinadi explains that 'his seed' are the righteous, those who follow the prophets (see Mosiah 15:11). In the garden and on the cross, Jesus saw each of us and not only bore our sins but also experienced our deepest feelings so He would know how to comfort and strengthen us" (Merrill J. Bateman, "The Power to Heal from Within," *Ensign*, May 1995).

💜 Bear testimony of the Savior's individual compassion toward us because of his individual suffering.

19 For were it not for the redemption which he hath made for his people, which was prepared from the foundation of the world, I say unto you, were

Notes

it not for this, all mankind must have perished.

20 But behold, the bands of death shall be broken, and the Son reigneth, and hath power over the dead; therefore, he bringeth to pass the resurrection of the dead.

vv. 19–20 Christ breaks the bands of death, making resurrection possible.

🔍 *Look for how Jesus makes our resurrection from the dead possible in verses 19–20.*

💜 Help class members understand that were it not for the resurrection, we would not be able to live again.

21 And there cometh a resurrection, even a first resurrection; yea, even a resurrection of those that have been, and who are, and who shall be, even until the resurrection of Christ—for so shall he be called.

22 And now, the resurrection of all the prophets, and all those that have believed in their words, or all those that have kept the commandments of God, shall come forth in the first resurrection; therefore, they are the first resurrection.

23 They are raised to dwell with God who has redeemed them; thus they have eternal life through Christ, who has broken the bands of death.

24 And these are those who have part in the first resurrection; and these are they that have died before Christ came, in their ignorance, not having salvation declared unto them. And thus the Lord bringeth about the restoration of these; and they have a part in the first resurrection, or have eternal life, being redeemed by the Lord.

25 And little children also have eternal life.

26 But behold, and fear, and tremble before God, for ye ought to tremble; for the Lord redeemeth none such that rebel against him and die in their sins; yea, even all those that have perished in their sins ever since the world began, that have wilfully rebelled against God, that have known

the commandments of God, and would not keep them; these are they that have no part in the first resurrection.

27 Therefore ought ye not to tremble? For salvation cometh to none such; for the Lord hath redeemed none such; yea, neither can the Lord redeem such; for he cannot deny himself; for he cannot deny justice when it has its claim.

28 And now I say unto you that the time shall come that the salvation of the Lord shall be declared to every nation, kindred, tongue, and people.

29 Yea, Lord, thy watchmen shall lift up their voice; with the voice together shall they sing; for they shall see eye to eye, when the Lord shall bring again Zion.

30 Break forth into joy, sing together, ye waste places of Jerusalem; for the Lord hath comforted his people, he hath redeemed Jerusalem.

31 The Lord hath made bare his holy arm in the eyes of all the nations; and all the ends of the earth shall see the salvation of our God.

vv. 26–27 The Savior does not save anyone who willfully rebels against Him.

🔍 Refer to the chart on the board and explain and testify that because Jesus has done so much for us, He expects us to follow Him. Write the following next to the diagram: 1) "What will happen if we accept all of this?" Allow class members to answer, writing their responses on the board. You can also refer back to the target object lesson. 2) "What will happen if we reject all of this?" Look in verses 26–27 to see how Abinadi answers that question.

💜 Encourage class members to accept the power of the Atonement.

Teaching Tips from Prophets' Lips "Understanding, as the word is used in the scriptures, does not refer solely or even primarily to intellectual or cognitive comprehension. Rather, understanding occurs when what we know in

Notes

our minds is confirmed as true in our hearts by the witness of the Holy Ghost" (David A. Bednar, "A Reservoir of Living Water," CES Fireside, February 4, 2007).

MOSIAH 16

Abinadi: Redemption from the Fall
About 148 BC

1–5, Men will be judged for their carnal and devilish actions; 6–12, Christ's resurrection redeems men from the fall and brings them before God to be judged; 13–15, Redemption comes by Christ, not simply by the law of Moses.

1 And now, it came to pass that after Abinadi had spoken these words he stretched forth his hand and said: The time shall come when all shall see the salvation of the Lord; when every nation, kindred, tongue, and people shall see eye to eye and shall confess before God that his judgments are just.

2 And then shall the wicked be cast out, and they shall have cause to howl, and weep, and wail, and gnash their teeth; and this because they would not hearken unto the voice of the Lord; therefore the Lord redeemeth them not.

3 For they are carnal and devilish, and the devil has power over them; yea, even that old serpent that did beguile our first parents, which was the cause of their fall; which was the cause of all mankind becoming carnal, sensual, devilish, knowing evil from good, subjecting themselves to the devil.

4 Thus all mankind were lost; and behold, they would have been endlessly lost were it not that God redeemed his people from their lost and fallen state.

5 But remember that he that persists in his own carnal nature, and goes on in the ways of sin and rebellion against God, remaineth in his fallen state and the devil hath all power over him.

Therefore he is as though there was no redemption made, being an enemy to God; and also is the devil an enemy to God.

6 And now if Christ had not come into the world, speaking of things to come as though they had already come, there could have been no redemption.

7 And if Christ had not risen from the dead, or have broken the bands of death that the grave should have no victory, and that death should have no sting, there could have been no resurrection.

8 But there is a resurrection, therefore the grave hath no victory, and the sting of death is swallowed up in Christ.

9 He is the light and the life of the world; yea, a light that is endless, that can never be darkened; yea, and also a life which is endless, that there can be no more death.

10 Even this mortal shall put on immortality, and this corruption shall put on incorruption, and shall be brought to stand before the bar of God, to be judged of him according to their works whether they be good or whether they be evil—

11 If they be good, to the resurrection of endless life and happiness; and if they be evil, to the resurrection of endless damnation, being delivered up to the devil, who hath subjected them, which is damnation—

12 Having gone according to their own carnal wills and desires; having never called upon the Lord while the arms of mercy were extended towards them; for the arms of mercy were extended towards them, and they would not; they being warned of their iniquities and yet they would not depart from them; and they were commanded to repent and yet they would not repent.

13 And now, ought ye not to tremble and repent of your sins, and remember that only in and through Christ ye can be saved?

14 Therefore, if ye teach the law of Moses, also teach that it is a shadow of those things which are to come—

Notes

15 Teach them that redemption cometh through Christ the Lord, who is the very Eternal Father. Amen.

vv. 1–15 Through the resurrection and redemption of Jesus Christ, I can overcome the results of the Fall and be prepared to stand before God at the final judgment.

⚡ Prior to class write the following words on the board: "The Fall," "Judgment," and "Resurrection." Explain that these three doctrines are pivotal aspects of the plan of salvation.

✋ Class members may participate in this activity individually or in small groups. Ask class members to read chapter 16 and organize each verse under one of the three doctrines on the board. Depending on the ages of class members, you may need to help define words or phrases like "carnal," "sensual," "corruption," "incorruption," and so forth. This will help them understand what Abinadi is saying. From the list they create, ask them to choose the verse that they think best explains these basic doctrines. After giving them time, ask class members to indicate where they placed each verse, which verses they chose to best explain the doctrines, and why they did so.

❤ Testify that every individual in the room will stand before the Father because of Christ's redemption. Testify that Christ can redeem them from the effects of the fall and prepare them for the final judgment if they choose to follow Him.

MOSIAH 17

Abinadi's Martyrdom
About 148 BC

1–4, Alma pleads for Abinadi's life, is threatened with death, and escapes from the king; 5–8, Noah's priests conspire to take Abinadi's life; 9–10, Facing death, Abinadi further testifies; 11–12, Noah considers releasing Abinadi but is dissuaded by the priests; 13–20, Abinadi further prophesies and suffers death by fire.

1 And now it came to pass that when Abinadi had finished these sayings, that the king commanded that the priests should take him and cause that he should be put to death.

2 But there was one among them whose name was Alma, he also being a descendant of Nephi. And he was a young man, and he believed the words which Abinadi had spoken, for he knew concerning the iniquity which Abinadi had testified against them; therefore he began to plead with the king that he would not be angry with Abinadi, but suffer that he might depart in peace.

3 But the king was more wroth, and caused that Alma should be cast out from among them, and sent his servants after him that they might slay him.

4 But he fled from before them and hid himself that they found him not. And he being concealed for many days did write all the words which Abinadi had spoken.

vv. 1–4 We may not see the results of our missionary labors until much later, but bringing a single soul to Christ is cause for joy.

⚡ Display an apple at the front of class. Ask, *How many seeds do you think are in this apple?* If you have time, consider slicing the apple horizontally and allowing a class member to count the number of seeds. Hold a single seed in your hand and ask, *How many apples do you think are in this seed?* Write on the board, "You can count the number of seeds in an apple, but you cannot count the number of apples in a seed."

🔍 As a class member reads verses 1–4, give the rest of the class the following prompt: *Look for the name of the person who is the only evidence that Abinadi's words made an impact on Noah's court.*

Notes

❓ Analyze:

- *How might Abinadi have felt when he saw only one person who cared about his message?*
- Have class members read Mosiah 18:16, 35. Then ask, *What do you learn about the success of Abinadi's single convert from these verses?*
- *What lesson does the phrase about the apple teach concerning Abinadi's success as a missionary?*

💬 Share the following story from President James E. Faust: "Those of us who have served missions have seen the miracle in the lives of some we have taught as they have come to realize that they are sons and daughters of God. Many years ago, an elder who served a mission in the British Isles said at the end of his labors, 'I think my mission has been a failure. I have labored all my days as a missionary here and I have only baptized one dirty little Irish kid. That is all I baptized.'

"Years later, after his return to his home in Montana, he had a visitor come to his home who asked, 'Are you the elder who served a mission in the British Isles in 1873?'

'Yes.'

"Then the man went on, 'And do you remember having said that you thought your mission was a failure because you had only baptized one dirty little Irish kid?'

"He said, 'Yes.'

"The visitor put out his hand and said, 'I would like to shake hands with you. My name is Charles A. Callis, of the Council of the Twelve of The Church of Jesus Christ of Latter-day Saints. I am that dirty little Irish kid that you baptized on your mission' (see Clyde J. Williams, *The Teachings of Harold B. Lee*, 1996, 602–3).

"That little Irish boy came to a knowledge of his potential as a son of God. Elder Callis left a lasting legacy for his large family. Serving as a mission president for 25 years and in his apostolic ministry for 13 years, he blessed the lives of literally thousands"

(James E. Faust, "Them That Honour Me I Will Honour," *Ensign*, May 2001, 46–47).

💙 Testify that every effort to share the gospel can be successful, but it takes time to see the results of our actions. Invite class members to share the gospel with others.

5 And it came to pass that the king caused that his guards should surround Abinadi and take him; and they bound him and cast him into prison.

6 And after three days, having counseled with his priests, he caused that he should again be brought before him.

7 And he said unto him: Abinadi, we have found an accusation against thee, and thou art worthy of death.

8 For thou hast said that God himself should come down among the children of men; and now, for this cause thou shalt be put to death unless thou wilt recall all the words which thou hast spoken evil concerning me and my people.

9 Now Abinadi said unto him: I say unto you, I will not recall the words which I have spoken unto you concerning this people, for they are true; and that ye may know of their surety I have suffered myself that I have fallen into your hands.

10 Yea, and I will suffer even until death, and I will not recall my words, and they shall stand as a testimony against you. And if ye slay me ye will shed innocent blood, and this shall also stand as a testimony against you at the last day.

11 And now king Noah was about to release him, for he feared his word; for he feared that the judgments of God would come upon him.

12 But the priests lifted up their voices against him, and began to accuse him, saying: He has reviled the king. Therefore the king was stirred up in anger against him, and he delivered him up that he might be slain.

13 And it came to pass that they took him and bound him, and scourged his skin with faggots, yea, even unto death.

Notes

14 And now when the flames began to scorch him, he cried unto them, saying:

15 Behold, even as ye have done unto me, so shall it come to pass that thy seed shall cause that many shall suffer the pains that I do suffer, even the pains of death by fire; and this because they believe in the salvation of the Lord their God.

16 And it will come to pass that ye shall be afflicted with all manner of diseases because of your iniquities.

17 Yea, and ye shall be smitten on every hand, and shall be driven and scattered to and fro, even as a wild flock is driven by wild and ferocious beasts.

18 And in that day ye shall be hunted, and ye shall be taken by the hand of your enemies, and then ye shall suffer, as I suffer, the pains of death by fire.

19 Thus God executeth vengeance upon those that destroy his people. O God, receive my soul.

20 And now, when Abinadi had said these words, he fell, having suffered death by fire; yea, having been put to death because he would not deny the commandments of God, having sealed the truth of his words by his death.

vv. 5–20 True disciples of Jesus Christ stand for the truth despite the wicked influence of those around them.

⚡ *Have you ever had an experience when you had to stand up for what was right in the face of great opposition?* Invite class members to share appropriate examples from their lives. Ask, *Why was it a difficult thing to do? What did you learn about yourself or those around you? What was it that gave you the strength you needed to stand up for the right?*

🔑 Explain that both King Noah and Abinadi have the chance to stand up for what they know is right, but they respond differently. Invite class members to read Mosiah 17:5–12. *Look for and contrast how Abinadi and King Noah respond to the influences of evil around them.*

❓ Analyze: *What caused King Noah to choose evil over good? What do you think gave Abinadi the strength to stand up despite the opposition?*

💡 Note that Abinadi ended up dying because of his choice. Sometimes individuals assume that making correct choices always leads to immediate temporal blessings, when in reality we may wait until the next life to receive our reward. If you have time to discuss this concept, consider discussing with class members which truths from Mosiah 16 might have made Abinadi's choice easier to make.

💬 President Monson said, "May we ever be courageous and prepared to stand for what we believe, and if we must stand alone in the process, may we do so courageously, strengthened by the knowledge that in reality we are never alone when we stand with our Father in Heaven" ("Dare to Stand Alone," *Ensign,* November 2011).

❤ Summarize the death of Abinadi in the last few verses of the chapter, choosing some phrases or verses to read verbatim. Express gratitude for the strength Abinadi had to stand up for the truth. Invite class members to stand for the right with similar courage.

> **Teaching Tips from Prophets' Lips** "Questions that can be answered *yes* or *no* have limited use in gospel instruction. . . . Some questions encourage learners to think deeply about the meaning of scripture passages and gospel principles. These questions often begin with the words *what, how,* or *why.* They cannot be answered with *yes* or *no,* and they usually have more than one right answer (*Teaching, No Greater Call*, 68).

Notes

MOSIAH 18

"Bear One Another's Burdens That They May Be Light"
About 147–145 BC

1–6, Many believe on the words of Alma; 7–11, Qualifications and blessings of the covenant of baptism; 12–16, Many are baptized at the waters of Mormon; 17–30, Alma ordains priests and organizes the church of Christ; 31–34, Alma and the people of God depart into the wilderness.

1 And now, it came to pass that Alma, who had fled from the servants of king Noah, repented of his sins and iniquities, and went about privately among the people, and began to teach the words of Abinadi—

2 Yea, concerning that which was to come, and also concerning the resurrection of the dead, and the redemption of the people, which was to be brought to pass through the power, and sufferings, and death of Christ, and his resurrection and ascension into heaven.

3 And as many as would hear his word he did teach. And he taught them privately, that it might not come to the knowledge of the king. And many did believe his words.

4 And it came to pass that as many as did believe him did go forth to a place which was called Mormon, having received its name from the king, being in the borders of the land having been infested, by times or at seasons, by wild beasts.

5 Now, there was in Mormon a fountain of pure water, and Alma resorted thither, there being near the water a thicket of small trees, where he did hide himself in the daytime from the searches of the king.

6 And it came to pass that as many as believed him went thither to hear his words.

vv. 1–6 Speed Read.

✋ Invite class members to attempt speed-reading verses 1–6 in 30 seconds. After the 30 seconds, ask someone to summarize what happened. Invite others to add information the other person may have left out of their summary. This activity will give the context to be able to teach the rest of the chapter.

7 And it came to pass after many days there were a goodly number gathered together at the place of Mormon, to hear the words of Alma. Yea, all were gathered together that believed on his word, to hear him. And he did teach them, and did preach unto them repentance, and redemption, and faith on the Lord.

8 And it came to pass that he said unto them: Behold, here are the waters of Mormon (for thus were they called) and now, as ye are desirous to come into the fold of God, and to be called his people, and are willing to bear one another's burdens, that they may be light;

9 Yea, and are willing to mourn with those that mourn; yea, and comfort those that stand in need of comfort, and to stand as witnesses of God at all times and in all things, and in all places that ye may be in, even until death, that ye may be redeemed of God, and be numbered with those of the first resurrection, that ye may have eternal life—

10 Now I say unto you, if this be the desire of your hearts, what have you against being baptized in the name of the Lord, as a witness before him that ye have entered into a covenant with him, that ye will serve him and keep his commandments, that he may pour out his Spirit more abundantly upon you?

11 And now when the people had heard these words, they clapped their hands for joy, and exclaimed: This is the desire of our hearts.

12 And now it came to pass that Alma took Helam, he being one of the first, and went and stood forth in the water, and cried, saying: O Lord, pour out thy Spirit upon thy servant, that he may

Notes

do this work with holiness of heart.

13 And when he had said these words, the Spirit of the Lord was upon him, and he said: Helam, I baptize thee, having authority from the Almighty God, as a testimony that ye have entered into a covenant to serve him until you are dead as to the mortal body; and may the Spirit of the Lord be poured out upon you; and may he grant unto you eternal life, through the redemption of Christ, whom he has prepared from the foundation of the world.

14 And after Alma had said these words, both Alma and Helam were buried in the water; and they arose and came forth out of the water rejoicing, being filled with the Spirit.

15 And again, Alma took another, and went forth a second time into the water, and baptized him according to the first, only he did not bury himself again in the water.

16 And after this manner he did baptize every one that went forth to the place of Mormon; and they were in number about two hundred and four souls; yea, and they were baptized in the waters of Mormon, and were filled with the grace of God.

17 And they were called the church of God, or the church of Christ, from that time forward. And it came to pass that whosoever was baptized by the power and authority of God was added to his church.

18 And it came to pass that Alma, having authority from God, ordained priests; even one priest to every fifty of their number did he ordain to preach unto them, and to teach them concerning the things pertaining to the kingdom of God.

19 And he commanded them that they should teach nothing save it were the things which he had taught, and which had been spoken by the mouth of the holy prophets.

20 Yea, even he commanded them that they should preach nothing save it were repentance and faith on the Lord, who had redeemed his people.

21 And he commanded them that there should be no contention one with another, but that they should look forward with bone eye, having one faith and one baptism, having their hearts knit together in unity and in love one towards another.

22 And thus he commanded them to preach. And thus they became the children of God.

23 And he commanded them that they should observe the sabbath day, and keep it holy, and also every day they should give thanks to the Lord their God.

24 And he also commanded them that the priests whom he had ordained should labor with their own hands for their support.

25 And there was one day in every week that was set apart that they should gather themselves together to teach the people, and to worship the Lord their God, and also, as often as it was in their power, to assemble themselves together.

26 And the priests were not to depend upon the people for their support; but for their labor they were to receive the grace of God, that they might wax strong in the Spirit, having the knowledge of God, that they might teach with power and authority from God.

27 And again Alma commanded that the people of the church should impart of their substance, every one according to that which he had; if he have more abundantly he should impart more abundantly; and of him that had but little, but little should be required; and to him that had not should be given.

28 And thus they should impart of their substance of their own free will and good desires towards God, and to those priests that stood in need, yea, and to every needy, naked soul.

29 And this he said unto them, having been commanded of God; and they did walk uprightly before God, imparting to one another both temporally and spiritually according to their needs and their wants.

Notes

vv. 7–29 As I honor my baptismal covenants, God will pour out His spirit upon me.

⚡ Invite class members to share with someone next to them what covenants they made at baptism and the promised blessings of those covenants. Do not give them the answers yet, but explain that they will be doing an activity that will help them begin to understand an aspect of their baptismal covenants. Bring to class many heavy objects that, when combined, are difficult for one person to hold, perhaps a backpack full of rocks. Have a class member see how long they can hold the heavy items in their arms. (Make sure the items are heavy enough that it becomes difficult after 1–2 minutes.) Give the person the instruction that they must not let any of the items touch the ground. After the first class member is given a chance to try, invite another member of the class to see if they can do better. This time, however, as he or she is struggling at the front of the class, go around the room and invite different individuals to remove one rock out of the bag and hold it for the individual. Do this until there are several class members holding the items in their hands and the load is easy for all to carry.

🔑 *Search verses 7–9 to see what this activity has to do with baptismal covenants.* Write class members' responses on the board under the following headings: "Covenants" and "Promised Blessings." You may want to explain that the Lord often uses the word "that" to help us understand that each aspect of the covenant has an associated blessing. Write under the appropriate heading what class members find in each of these verses.

✏️ Ask class members to choose one of the aspects of covenants and its associated blessing and write down a time when they have seen this in action in their wards or families. You may want to begin with an example to help class members understand what you are looking for. When they are done, refer to the list and point to each covenant and ask,

Who wrote an example of this part of the covenant? Choose one or two individuals to share what they wrote down for each aspect. As class members share, ask follow-up questions and seek to help the class understand the importance of their baptismal covenants.

💬 President Monson stated, "When we can work together cooperatively to lift the level of life for so many people, we can accomplish anything. When we do so, we eliminate the weakness of one person standing alone and substitute the strength of many serving together. While we may not be able to do everything, we can and must do something" ("Our Brothers' Keepers," *Ensign*, June 1998, 33, 38).

🔑 Write the following verses on the board: 10, 20, 21, 23–25, 27–29. Invite class members to read on their own and find what else we must do as part of our baptismal covenants and what their associated blessings are. As a class, add to the list that has already been made on the board and choose a few of these aspects. Point out each aspect and ask, *What does this say we should be doing as Latter-day Saints?*

❤️ Invite class members to once again share with the person next to them the covenants they made at baptism and the promised blessings of those covenants. Invite class members to honor their covenants, and then testify of the blessings that can be theirs as they do so. Invite one class member to testify of how he has been blessed because of his baptismal covenants.

30 And now it came to pass that all this was done in Mormon, yea, by the waters of Mormon, in the forest that was near the waters of Mormon; yea, the place of Mormon, the waters of Mormon, the forest of Mormon, how beautiful are they to the eyes of them who there came to the knowledge of their Redeemer; yea, and how blessed are they, for they shall sing to his praise forever.

31 And these things were done in the borders of the

Notes

land, that they might not come to the knowledge of the king.

32 But behold, it came to pass that the king, having discovered a movement among the people, sent his servants to watch them. Therefore on the day that they were assembling themselves together to hear the word of the Lord they were discovered unto the king.

33 And now the king said that Alma was stirring up the people to rebellion against him; therefore he sent his army to destroy them.

34 And it came to pass that Alma and the people of the Lord were apprised of the coming of the king's army; therefore they took their tents and their families and departed into the wilderness.

35 And they were in number about four hundred and fifty souls.

vv. 30–35 Speed Read.

✋ Invite the class to speed read verses 30–35 (as they did with verses 1–6) and summarize for the class what happened in the final verses of the chapter.

MOSIAH 19
The Death of King Noah
About 145–121 BC

1–6, King Noah faces rebellions in his kingdom; 7–15, Lamanites invade the land and exact a tax of one half of all that the people possess; 16–23, Limhi learns of the death of his father, King Noah, by fire and of the escape of the wicked priests; 24–29, Limhi reins under Lamanite control.

vv. 1–6 Rebellions begin in the kingdom of Noah; Gideon fights King Noah.

1 And it came to pass that the army of the king returned, having searched in vain for the people of the Lord.

2 And now behold, the forces of the king were small, having been reduced, and there began to be a division among the remainder of the people.

3 And the lesser part began to breathe out threatenings against the king, and there began to be a great contention among them.

4 And now there was a man among them whose name was Gideon, and he being a strong man and an enemy to the king, therefore he drew his sword, and swore in his wrath that he would slay the king.

5 And it came to pass that he fought with the king; and when the king saw that he was about to overpower him, he fled and ran and got upon the tower which was near the temple.

6 And Gideon pursued after him and was about to get upon the tower to slay the king, and the king cast his eyes round about towards the land of Shemlon, and behold, the army of the Lamanites were within the borders of the land.

vv. 7–15 King Noah appeals to Gideon to spare his life in order to save his people from the ensuing Lamanites. King Noah abandons his people to flee into the wilderness. The remainder plead for mercy and agree to give up one half of all they have.

7 And now the king cried out in the anguish of his soul, saying: Gideon, spare me, for the Lamanites are upon us, and they will destroy us; yea, they will destroy my people.

8 And now the king was not so much concerned about his people as he was about his own life; nevertheless, Gideon did spare his life.

9 And the king commanded the people that they should flee before the Lamanites, and he himself did go before them, and they did flee into the wilderness, with their women and their children.

10 And it came to pass that the Lamanites did pursue them, and did overtake them, and began to slay them.

11 Now it came to pass that the king commanded

Notes

them that all the men should leave their wives and their children, and flee before the Lamanites.

12 Now there were many that would not leave them, but had rather stay and perish with them. And the rest left their wives and their children and fled.

13 And it came to pass that those who tarried with their wives and their children caused that their fair daughters should stand forth and plead with the Lamanites that they would not slay them.

14 And it came to pass that the Lamanites had compassion on them, for they were charmed with the beauty of their women.

15 Therefore the Lamanites did spare their lives, and took them captives and carried them back to the land of Nephi, and granted unto them that they might possess the land, under the conditions that they would deliver up king Noah into the hands of the Lamanites, and deliver up their property, even one half of all they possessed, one half of their gold, and their silver, and all their precious things, and thus they should pay tribute to the king of the Lamanites from year to year.

vv. 16–23 Those who fled return and explain how King Noah was put to death by fire and that the wicked priests ran off.

16 And now there was one of the sons of the king among those that were taken captive, whose name was Limhi.

17 And now Limhi was desirous that his father should not be destroyed; nevertheless, Limhi was not ignorant of the iniquities of his father, he himself being a just man.

18 And it came to pass that Gideon sent men into the wilderness secretly, to search for the king and those that were with him. And it came to pass that they met the people in the wilderness, all save the king and his priests.

19 Now they had sworn in their hearts that they would return to the land of Nephi, and if their wives and their children were slain, and also those that had tarried with them, that they would seek revenge, and also perish with them.

20 And the king commanded them that they should not return; and they were angry with the king, and caused that he should suffer, even unto death by fire.

21 And they were about to take the priests also and put them to death, and they fled before them.

22 And it came to pass that they were about to return to the land of Nephi, and they met the men of Gideon. And the men of Gideon told them of all that had happened to their wives and their children; and that the Lamanites had granted unto them that they might possess the land by paying a tribute to the Lamanites of one half of all they possessed.

23 And the people told the men of Gideon that they had slain the king, and his priests had fled from them farther into the wilderness.

vv. 24–29 Limhi becomes king and his people continue to pay tribute to the Lamanites.

24 And it came to pass that after they had ended the ceremony, that they returned to the land of Nephi, rejoicing, because their wives and their children were not slain; and they told Gideon what they had done to the king.

25 And it came to pass that the king of the Lamanites made an oath unto them, that his people should not slay them.

26 And also Limhi, being the son of the king, having the kingdom conferred upon him by the people, made oath unto the king of the Lamanites that his people should pay tribute unto him, even one half of all they possessed.

27 And it came to pass that Limhi began to establish the kingdom and to establish peace among his people.

28 And the king of the Lamanites set guards round about the land, that he might keep the people of Limhi in the land, that they might not depart into the wilderness; and he did support his

Notes

guards out of the tribute which he did receive from the Nephites.

29 And now king Limhi did have continual peace in his kingdom for the space of two years, that the Lamanites did not molest them nor seek to destroy them.

vv. 1–29 Learning the story line of Mosiah 19.

✋ Explain to your class that they will read the storyline of Mosiah 19 and then in groups will pantomime (no speaking or sounds) sets of verses from the story to allow the rest of the class to guess what part of the story is being acted out. Give the class five minutes to briefly skim chapter 19. After they are done reading, write on the board the following sets of verses: (4–8), (9–11), (12–15), (19–21). Divide the class into four groups. Hand each group a piece of paper with one of the sets of verses written on it and give them time to quietly discuss how they will pantomime the verses. For smaller class sizes, break them into two groups and have them do the pantomiming twice.

Teaching Tips from Prophets' Lips "As you seek spiritual knowledge, search for principles. Carefully separate them from the detail used to explain them. Principles are concentrated truth, packaged for application to a wide variety of circumstances. A true principle makes decisions clear even under the most confusing and compelling circumstances. It is worth great effort to organize the truth we gather to simple statements of principle" (Richard G. Scott, "Acquiring Spiritual Knowledge," *Ensign*, November 1993, 86).

MOSIAH 20

Lamanite Daughters Abducted
About 145–123 BC

1–5, Fugitive priests of King Noah abduct some Lamanite daughters; 6–16, The Lamanites blame the people of Limhi for the loss of their daughters and attack them; 17–26, The two groups make peace with each other.

✋ Consider using the lesson activity found in Mosiah 19 to teach this chapter. Mosiah 20 continues the storyline about the escape of the wicked priests of King Noah. The verses for this chapter are summarized in bolded text.

vv. 1–5 Ashamed to return to their people, the fugitive priests of King Noah abduct some daughters of the Lamanites, whom they eventually marry (see also Mosiah 23:32–33).

1 Now there was a place in Shemlon where the daughters of the Lamanites did gather themselves together to sing, and to dance, and to make themselves merry.

2 And it came to pass that there was one day a small number of them gathered together to sing and to dance.

3 And now the priests of king Noah, being ashamed to return to the city of Nephi, yea, and also fearing that the people would slay them, therefore they durst not return to their wives and their children.

4 And having tarried in the wilderness, and having discovered the daughters of the Lamanites, they laid and watched them;

5 And when there were but few of them gathered together to dance, they came forth out of their secret places and took them and carried them into the wilderness; yea, twenty and four of the daughters of the Lamanites they carried into the wilderness.

Notes

vv. 6–16 The Lamanites blame the people of Limhi for the loss of their daughters and attack them. The king of the Lamanites is badly wounded and recovered by the people of King Limhi.

6 And it came to pass that when the Lamanites found that their daughters had been missing, they were angry with the people of Limhi, for they thought it was the people of Limhi.

7 Therefore they sent their armies forth; yea, even the king himself went before his people; and they went up to the land of Nephi to destroy the people of Limhi.

8 And now Limhi had discovered them from the tower, even all their preparations for war did he discover; therefore he gathered his people together, and laid wait for them in the fields and in the forests.

9 And it came to pass that when the Lamanites had come up, that the people of Limhi began to fall upon them from their waiting places, and began to slay them.

10 And it came to pass that the battle became exceedingly sore, for they fought like lions for their prey.

11 And it came to pass that the people of Limhi began to drive the Lamanites before them; yet they were not half so numerous as the Lamanites. But they fought for their lives, and for their wives, and for their children; therefore they exerted themselves and like dragons did they fight.

12 And it came to pass that they found the king of the Lamanites among the number of their dead; yet he was not dead, having been wounded and left upon the ground, so speedy was the flight of his people.

13 And they took him and bound up his wounds, and brought him before Limhi, and said: Behold, here is the king of the Lamanites; he having received a wound has fallen among their dead, and they have left him; and behold, we have brought him before you; and now let us slay him.

14 But Limhi said unto them: Ye shall not slay him, but bring him hither that I may see him. And they brought him. And Limhi said unto him: What cause have ye to come up to war against my people? Behold, my people have not broken the oath that I made unto you; therefore, why should ye break the oath which ye made unto my people?

15 And now the king said: I have broken the oath because thy people did carry away the daughters of my people; therefore, in my anger I did cause my people to come up to war against thy people.

16 And now Limhi had heard nothing concerning this matter; therefore he said: I will search among my people and whosoever has done this thing shall perish. Therefore he caused a search to be made among his people.

vv. 17–26 Limhi explains about the priests of King Noah to the king of the Lamanites and they agree to stop fighting, swearing an oath to not return to war again.

17 Now when Gideon had heard these things, he being the king's captain, he went forth and said unto the king: I pray thee forbear, and do not search this people, and lay not this thing to their charge.

18 For do ye not remember the priests of thy father, whom this people sought to destroy? And are they not in the wilderness? And are not they the ones who have stolen the daughters of the Lamanites?

19 And now, behold, and tell the king of these things, that he may tell his people that they may be pacified towards us; for behold they are already preparing to come against us; and behold also there are but few of us.

20 And behold, they come with their numerous hosts; and except the king doth pacify them towards us we must perish.

21 For are not the words of Abinadi fulfilled, which

Notes

he prophesied against us—and all this because we would not hearken unto the words of the Lord, and turn from our iniquities?

22 And now let us pacify the king, and we fulfil the oath which we have made unto him; for it is better that we should be in bondage than that we should lose our lives; therefore, let us put a stop to the shedding of so much blood.

23 And now Limhi told the king all the things concerning his father, and the priests that had fled into the wilderness, and attributed the carrying away of their daughters to them.

24 And it came to pass that the king was pacified towards his people; and he said unto them: Let us go forth to meet my people, without arms; and I swear unto you with an oath that my people shall not slay thy people.

25 And it came to pass that they followed the king, and went forth without arms to meet the Lamanites. And it came to pass that they did meet the Lamanites; and the king of the Lamanites did bow himself down before them, and did plead in behalf of the people of Limhi.

26 And when the Lamanites saw the people of Limhi, that they were without arms, they had compassion on them and were pacified towards them, and returned with their king in peace to their own land.

MOSIAH 21

"Slow to Hear Their Cries"
About 122–121 BC

1–19, The people of Limhi go to war three more times against the Lamanites and are defeated each time; 20–36, Ammon is discovered in the wilderness by the guards of Limhi and taken captive. Plans to escape the bondage of the Lamanites are discussed.

Note: The continual story of the liberation of the people of King Limhi and the people of Alma is taught over the next few chapters of Mosiah. Though each chapter will have its own lesson outline, it may be helpful to review and teach these stories together to find an overarching theme among the stories.

1 And it came to pass that Limhi and his people returned to the city of Nephi, and began to dwell in the land again in peace.

2 And it came to pass that after many days the Lamanites began again to be stirred up in anger against the Nephites, and they began to come into the borders of the land round about.

3 Now they durst not slay them, because of the oath which their king had made unto Limhi; but they would smite them on their cheeks, and exercise authority over them; and began to put heavy burdens upon their backs, and drive them as they would a dumb ass—

4 Yea, all this was done that the word of the Lord might be fulfilled.

5 And now the afflictions of the Nephites were great, and there was no way that they could deliver themselves out of their hands, for the Lamanites had surrounded them on every side.

6 And it came to pass that the people began to murmur with the king because of their afflictions; and they began to be desirous to go against them to battle. And they did afflict the king sorely with their complaints; therefore he granted unto them that they should do according to their desires.

7 And they gathered themselves together again, and put on their armor, and went forth against the Lamanites to drive them out of their land.

8 And it came to pass that the Lamanites did beat them, and drove them back, and slew many of them.

9 And now there was a great mourning and lamentation among the people of Limhi, the widow mourning for her husband, the son and the daughter mourning for their father, and the brothers for their brethren.

Notes

10 Now there were a great many widows in the land, and they did cry mightily from day to day, for a great fear of the Lamanites had come upon them.

11 And it came to pass that their continual cries did stir up the remainder of the people of Limhi to anger against the Lamanites; and they went again to battle, but they were driven back again, suffering much loss.

12 Yea, they went again even the third time, and suffered in the like manner; and those that were not slain returned again to the city of Nephi.

13 And they did humble themselves even to the dust, subjecting themselves to the yoke of bondage, submitting themselves to be smitten, and to be driven to and fro, and burdened, according to the desires of their enemies.

14 And they did humble themselves even in the depths of humility; and they did cry mightily to God; yea, even all the day long did they cry unto their God that he would deliver them out of their afflictions.

vv. 1–14 God allows us to suffer natural consequences so that we learn.

⚡ Use the concept of natural consequences to help teach the suffering and bondage of the people of Limhi, despite their repentance. Write the phrase, "Natural Consequence" on the board. Hold up an object and ask, *What is the natural consequence that will occur if I drop this object?* Allow class members to answer, then drop the object. Based on responses, write a definition of "Natural Consequence" on the board.

🔎 Read verses 1–6 as a class and look for and discuss what life was like for the people of Limhi. Have class members look for what the people of Limhi do next in verses 7–10. Then explain that they went to war against the Lamanites two other times, being defeated each time.

💡 Refer class members to verse 4 and point out

that all of this happened as a natural consequence of their wickedness. You may want to cross-reference Mosiah 11:21–24.

❓ Analyze:
- *What are some common sins in society?*
- *What are some examples of natural consequences of those sins?*
- *How can a person avoid those consequences?*

🔎 *Now that the people of Limhi have been beaten and oppressed, what do they do next in verse 14?*

❓ Analyze: *Knowing how wicked they have been, why do you think this is an odd or ironic request?*

15 And now the Lord was slow to hear their cry because of their iniquities; nevertheless the Lord did hear their cries, and began to soften the hearts of the Lamanites that they began to ease their burdens; yet the Lord did not see fit to deliver them out of bondage.

16 And it came to pass that they began to prosper by degrees in the land, and began to raise grain more abundantly, and flocks, and herds, that they did not suffer with hunger.

vv. 15–16 The Lord allows us to suffer natural consequences for our actions but is still willing to bless us despite our wickedness.

🔎 Explain that the people of Limhi cry unto the Lord to be released from bondage, yet the Lord does not answer their prayers at first. *Look for three things that the Lord does for the people despite the fact that He does not release them from bondage.*

❓ Analyze: *Why do you think that even though the Lord won't release the people from bondage, He is still willing to help and bless them?*

♥ Refer back to the definition of natural consequences and help class members understand that God allows us to suffer the consequences of our choices, yet He willingly

Notes

blesses us despite our unworthiness.

vv. 17–32 Limhi keeps guards outside of the city to watch for and catch the priests of King Noah. Instead they discover Ammon, who had come from Zarahemla in search of them.

17 Now there was a great number of women, more than there was of men; therefore king Limhi commanded that every man should impart to the support of the widows and their children, that they might not perish with hunger; and this they did because of the greatness of their number that had been slain.

18 Now the people of Limhi kept together in a body as much as it was possible, and secured their grain and their flocks;

19 And the king himself did not trust his person without the walls of the city, unless he took his guards with him, fearing that he might by some means fall into the hands of the Lamanites.

20 And he caused that his people should watch the land round about, that by some means they might take those priests that fled into the wilderness, who had stolen the daughters of the Lamanites, and that had caused such a great destruction to come upon them.

21 For they were desirous to take them that they might punish them; for they had come into the land of Nephi by night, and carried off their grain and many of their precious things; therefore they laid wait for them.

22 And it came to pass that there was no more disturbance between the Lamanites and the people of Limhi, even until the time that Ammon and his brethren came into the land.

23 And the king having been without the gates of the city with his guard, discovered Ammon and his brethren; and supposing them to be priests of Noah therefore he caused that they should be taken, and bound, and cast into prison. And had they been the priests of Noah he would have caused that they should be put to death.

24 But when he found that they were not, but that they were his brethren, and had come from the land of Zarahemla, he was filled with exceedingly great joy.

25 Now king Limhi had sent, previous to the coming of Ammon, a small number of men to search for the land of Zarahemla; but they could not find it, and they were lost in the wilderness.

26 Nevertheless, they did find a land which had been peopled; yea, a land which was covered with dry bones; yea, a land which had been peopled and which had been destroyed; and they, having supposed it to be the land of Zarahemla, returned to the land of Nephi, having arrived in the borders of the land not many days before the coming of Ammon.

27 And they brought a record with them, even a record of the people whose bones they had found; and it was engraven on plates of ore.

28 And now Limhi was again filled with joy on learning from the mouth of Ammon that king Mosiah had a gift from God, whereby he could interpret such engravings; yea, and Ammon also did rejoice.

29 Yet Ammon and his brethren were filled with sorrow because so many of their brethren had been slain;

30 And also that king Noah and his priests had caused the people to commit so many sins and iniquities against God; and they also did mourn for the death of Abinadi; and also for the departure of Alma and the people that went with him, who had formed a church of God through the strength and power of God, and faith on the words which had been spoken by Abinadi.

31 Yea, they did mourn for their departure, for they knew not whither they had fled. Now they would have gladly joined with them, for they themselves had entered into a covenant with God to serve him and keep his commandments.

32 And now since the coming of Ammon, king Limhi had also entered into a covenant with

Notes

God, and also many of his people, to serve him and keep his commandments.

33 And it came to pass that king Limhi and many of his people were desirous to be baptized; but there was none in the land that had authority from God. And Ammon declined doing this thing, considering himself an unworthy servant.

v. 33 Priesthood holders should always be worthy to exercise their priesthood.

🔍 Explain that the people of Limhi desired Ammon to baptize them since no one in the land had the proper authority. *Read verse 33 and look for why Ammon declines.*

♥ Depending on the ages of class members, consider how this scripture applies to them. For example, in teaching young men, help them understand that as a holder of the priesthood, they should be ready and worthy at all times to use it. The Church produced a Mormon Message video that may help teach this principle. The video is entitled "Sanctify Yourselves" by Jeffrey R. Holland (September 8, 2011) and can be found on lds.org, youth.lds.org, or mormonchannel.org.

34 Therefore they did not at that time form themselves into a church, waiting upon the Spirit of the Lord. Now they were desirous to become even as Alma and his brethren, who had fled into the wilderness.

35 They were desirous to be baptized as a witness and a testimony that they were willing to serve God with all their hearts; nevertheless they did prolong the time; and an account of their baptism shall be given hereafter.

36 And now all the study of Ammon and his people, and king Limhi and his people, was to deliver themselves out of the hands of the Lamanites and from bondage.

Teaching Tips from Prophets' Lips "Some questions invite inspiration. Great teachers ask those. That may take just a small change of words, an inflection in the voice . . . . 'When have you felt that you were in the presence of a prophet?' That will invite individuals to search their memories for feelings. After asking, we might wisely wait for a moment before calling on someone to respond. Even those who do not speak will be thinking of spiritual experiences. That will invite the Holy Ghost. Then, even if no one should speak, they will be ready for you to bear quiet testimony of your witness that we are blessed to live when God has called prophets to guide and teach us" ("The Lord Will Multiply the Harvest," *An Evening with Elder Henry B. Eyring*, February 6, 1998, 6).

MOSIAH 22

Escape Versus Deliverance
About 121–120 BC

1–9, Gideon proposes a plan of escape for Limhi's people; 10–13, The people escape at night while the guards are drunken; 14–16, After many days in the wilderness the people are received with joy in Zarahemla.

1 And now it came to pass that Ammon and king Limhi began to consult with the people how they should deliver themselves out of bondage; and even they did cause that all the people should gather themselves together; and this they did that they might have the voice of the people concerning the matter.

2 And it came to pass that they could find no way to deliver themselves out of bondage, except it were to take their women and children, and their flocks, and their herds, and their tents, and depart into the wilderness; for the Lamanites being so numerous, it was impossible for the people of Limhi to contend with them, thinking to deliver themselves out of bondage by the sword.

Notes

3 Now it came to pass that Gideon went forth and stood before the king, and said unto him: Now O king, thou hast hitherto hearkened unto my words many times when we have been contending with our brethren, the Lamanites.

4 And now O king, if thou hast not found me to be an unprofitable servant, or if thou hast hitherto listened to my words in any degree, and they have been of service to thee, even so I desire that thou wouldst listen to my words at this time, and I will be thy servant and deliver this people out of bondage.

5 And the king granted unto him that he might speak. And Gideon said unto him:

6 Behold the back pass, through the back wall, on the back side of the city. The Lamanites, or the guards of the Lamanites, by night are drunken; therefore let us send a proclamation among all this people that they gather together their flocks and herds, that they may drive them into the wilderness by night.

7 And I will go according to thy command and pay the last tribute of wine to the Lamanites, and they will be drunken; and we will pass through the secret pass on the left of their camp when they are drunken and asleep.

8 Thus we will depart with our women and our children, our flocks, and our herds into the wilderness; and we will travel around the land of Shilom.

9 And it came to pass that the king hearkened unto the words of Gideon.

10 And king Limhi caused that his people should gather their flocks together; and he sent the tribute of wine to the Lamanites; and he also sent more wine, as a present unto them; and they did drink freely of the wine which king Limhi did send unto them.

11 And it came to pass that the people of king Limhi did depart by night into the wilderness with their flocks and their herds, and they went round about the land of Shilom in the wilderness, and bent their course towards the land of Zarahemla, being led by Ammon and his brethren.

12 And they had taken all their gold, and silver, and their precious things, which they could carry, and also their provisions with them, into the wilderness; and they pursued their journey.

13 And after being many days in the wilderness they arrived in the land of Zarahemla, and joined Mosiah's people, and became his subjects.

14 And it came to pass that Mosiah received them with joy; and he also received their records, and also the records which had been found by the people of Limhi.

15 And now it came to pass when the Lamanites had found that the people of Limhi had departed out of the land by night, that they sent an army into the wilderness to pursue them;

16 And after they had pursued them two days, they could no longer follow their tracks; therefore they were lost in the wilderness.

vv. 1–15 The Lord has the power to deliver us when we have faith in Him; our deliverance may be slowed if we rely on the arm of the flesh.

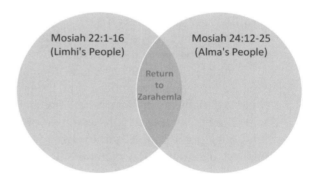

Note: Consider teaching this principle chronologically with the account of Alma's people in Mosiah 23–24.

⚡ Draw a diagram on the board like the one provided. Explain that in this lesson, class

Notes

members will see two stories with similar endings (each group will escape bondage and return to Zarahemla); however, one account will demonstrate full reliance on the Lord while the other will show the results of relying on personal abilities rather than trusting in the Lord's wisdom.

✋ Divide class members into two groups. Assign one group to silently study Mosiah 22:1–16; ask the other group to study Mosiah 24:12–25. Invite class members to summarize and share the basic elements of the two accounts. List the main points in the appropriate circle of the diagram on the board.

❓ Analyze:
- If you had to summarize the major differences between the two stories in one statement, what would you say?
- If both groups successfully achieved their goal of escape, why do you think it is important to rely on the Lord?
- Compare and contrast the overall experiences of Alma's and Limhi's people from the time they entered bondage until the time of their escapes to Zarahemla. With which group would you rather have been involved?

💡 Review the history of the Alma's and Limhi's people. Point out that all of the people were in bondage because of their rejection of Abinadi's first visit (see Mosiah 11:20; 12:2–5), but Alma's people repented quickly and did not have to experience the punishment foretold in Abinadi's second visit (see Mosiah 12:8). Remind class members that Limhi's people lost many loved ones in wars and battles as they continued to fight with their own might, but Alma's people had their burden's lightened. Instruct class members to read and contrast Mosiah 22:12–13 and Mosiah 24:23–25.

❓ Analyze:
- What differences in time or methods do you see between the two escapes?
- Why might that be significant? (Limhi's people relied on their own strength and

wealth and had to journey many days, while Alma and his people relied on the Lord and only had to journey for twelve days.)
- How could the difference between those small verses be representative of the overall principle taught in these accounts?

❓ Apply: How can an individual learn to better rely on the Lord for help through trials? When have you seen the benefits of trusting in the Lord's strength in your own life?

❤ Testify that although relying on the Lord will not eliminate all trials and struggles in our lives, it will give us greater strength to weather those trials and perhaps shorten them and limit their negative impact. Invite class members to turn to the Lord when faced with trials.

MOSIAH 23

"The Lord Seeth Fit to Chasten His People"
About 145–121 BC

1–5, The people of Alma build a beautiful city; 6–20, Alma refuses to be king, but as high priest he consecrates priests and teachers; 21–30, The Lord chastens the people of Alma as they are put into bondage under the Lamanites; 31–39, The priests of Noah are found, they join the Lamanites, and Amulon becomes king over the people of Alma.

1 Now Alma, having been warned of the Lord that the armies of king Noah would come upon them, and having made it known to his people, therefore they gathered together their flocks, and took of their grain, and departed into the wilderness before the armies of king Noah.

2 And the Lord did strengthen them, that the people of king Noah could not overtake them to destroy them.

3 And they fled eight days' journey into the wilderness.

Notes

4 And they came to a land, yea, even a very beautiful and pleasant land, a land of pure water.

5 And they pitched their tents, and began to till the ground, and began to build buildings; yea, they were industrious, and did labor exceedingly.

6 And the people were desirous that Alma should be their king, for he was beloved by his people.

7 But he said unto them: Behold, it is not expedient that we should have a king; for thus saith the Lord: Ye shall not esteem one flesh above another, or one man shall not think himself above another; therefore I say unto you it is not expedient that ye should have a king.

8 Nevertheless, if it were possible that ye could always have just men to be your kings it would be well for you to have a king.

9 But remember the iniquity of king Noah and his priests; and I myself was caught in a snare, and did many things which were abominable in the sight of the Lord, which caused me sore repentance;

10 Nevertheless, after much tribulation, the Lord did hear my cries, and did answer my prayers, and has made me an instrument in his hands in bringing so many of you to a knowledge of his truth.

11 Nevertheless, in this I do not glory, for I am unworthy to glory of myself.

12 And now I say unto you, ye have been oppressed by king Noah, and have been in bondage to him and his priests, and have been brought into iniquity by them; therefore ye were bound with the bands of iniquity.

13 And now as ye have been delivered by the power of God out of these bonds; yea, even out of the hands of king Noah and his people, and also from the bonds of iniquity, even so I desire that ye should stand fast in this liberty wherewith ye have been made free, and that ye trust no man to be a king over you.

14 And also trust no one to be your teacher nor your minister, except he be a man of God, walking in his ways and keeping his commandments.

15 Thus did Alma teach his people, that every man should love his neighbor as himself, that there should be no contention among them.

16 And now, Alma was their high priest, he being the founder of their church.

17 And it came to pass that none received authority to preach or to teach except it were by him from God. Therefore he consecrated all their priests and all their teachers; and none were consecrated except they were just men.

18 Therefore they did watch over their people, and did nourish them with things pertaining to righteousness.

19 And it came to pass that they began to prosper exceedingly in the land; and they called the land Helam.

20 And it came to pass that they did multiply and prosper exceedingly in the land of Helam; and they built a city, which they called the city of Helam.

vv. 1–20 Trust no man to be a king over you.

⚡ Bring or draw on the board a pictures of a king and a prophet. Show the pictures to the class and ask, *What are the similarities and differences between a king and a prophet?*

🔍 *As you read verses 6–13, look for the reasons Alma discouraged the people from having a king.* You may want to compare and contrast the description of a king (v. 12) with the description of a prophet/priest (v. 18).

❤ Invite class members to seek men of God to be their teachers and leaders.

21 Nevertheless the Lord seeth fit to chasten his people; yea, he trieth their patience and their faith.

22 Nevertheless—whosoever putteth his trust in him the same shall be lifted up at the last day. Yea, and thus it was with this people.

Notes

23 For behold, I will show unto you that they were brought into bondage, and none could deliver them but the Lord their God, yea, even the God of Abraham and Isaac and of Jacob.

24 And it came to pass that he did deliver them, and he did show forth his mighty power unto them, and great were their rejoicings.

25 For behold, it came to pass that while they were in the land of Helam, yea, in the city of Helam, while tilling the land round about, behold an army of the Lamanites was in the borders of the land.

26 Now it came to pass that the brethren of Alma fled from their fields, and gathered themselves together in the city of Helam; and they were much frightened because of the appearance of the Lamanites.

27 But Alma went forth and stood among them, and exhorted them that they should not be frightened, but that they should remember the Lord their God and he would deliver them.

28 Therefore they hushed their fears, and began to cry unto the Lord that he would soften the hearts of the Lamanites, that they would spare them, and their wives, and their children.

29 And it came to pass that the Lord did soften the hearts of the Lamanites. And Alma and his brethren went forth and delivered themselves up into their hands; and the Lamanites took possession of the land of Helam.

30 Now the armies of the Lamanites, which had followed after the people of king Limhi, had been lost in the wilderness for many days.

31 And behold, they had found those priests of king Noah, in a place which they called Amulon; and they had begun to possess the land of Amulon and had begun to till the ground.

32 Now the name of the leader of those priests was Amulon.

33 And it came to pass that Amulon did plead with the Lamanites; and he also sent forth their wives, who were the daughters of the Lamanites, to plead with their brethren, that they should not destroy their husbands.

34 And the Lamanites had compassion on Amulon and his brethren, and did not destroy them, because of their wives.

35 And Amulon and his brethren did join the Lamanites, and they were traveling in the wilderness in search of the land of Nephi when they discovered the land of Helam, which was possessed by Alma and his brethren.

36 And it came to pass that the Lamanites promised unto Alma and his brethren, that if they would show them the way which led to the land of Nephi that they would grant unto them their lives and their liberty.

37 But after Alma had shown them the way that led to the land of Nephi the Lamanites would not keep their promise; but they set guards round about the land of Helam, over Alma and his brethren.

38 And the remainder of them went to the land of Nephi; and a part of them returned to the land of Helam, and also brought with them the wives and the children of the guards who had been left in the land.

39 And the king of the Lamanites had granted unto Amulon that he should be a king and a ruler over his people, who were in the land of Helam; nevertheless he should have no power to do anything contrary to the will of the king of the Lamanites.

vv. 21–39 Whosoever putteth his trust in Him, the same shall be lifted up in the last day.

❤ Bring a small stick to class and ask a class member to come to the front of the room and pick up the stick. Invite them to only pick up one side of the stick. Discuss the concept of consequences; explain that while we can choose our actions we cannot choose the consequences to our actions, just like if you choose to pick up one end of the stick, you automatically pick up the other end.

Notes

🔍 *Read verses 25–29 to understand what is happening to the people of Alma.*

❓ Analyze: *Which choice(s) did the people of Alma make in the past that resulted in this consequence?* (You may want to turn to the prophesying of Abinadi in Mosiah 11:21 and 12:2.)

❓ Apply:
- *Even after we fully repent, do we still have to live with the consequences of our past choices?* Follow up with appropriate questions such as, *Why? How does that work?*
- *Can you share a story where you or someone you know had to live with a consequence even after they had repented and been forgiven?*
- *Can those consequences ever be overcome?*

🔍 Have class members search in verses 21–24 for what the people of Alma do in order to overcome the consequences of their choices.

💜 Invite class members to write down what they learned and what the Spirit taught them about the consequences of sin. After class members have had some time to write, invite a few to share what they learned. Conclude with your testimony of our ability to overcome the consequences of our choices as we trust in the Lord.

Teaching Tips from Prophets' Lips "Many topics are interesting, important, and even relevant to life and yet not nourishing to the soul. It is not our commission to teach such topics. . . . Teaching that stimulates the intellect without speaking to the spirit cannot nourish. Nor can anything that raises doubts about the truth of the restored gospel or the need to commit ourselves to it with all our heart, might, mind, and strength" (*Teaching, No Greater Call*, 5).

MOSIAH 24

Burdens Made Light
About 145–121 BC

1–10, Amulon begins to exercise authority and great afflictions on the people of Alma; 11–15, The people of Alma cry to the Lord, and He makes their burdens light; 16–25, The Lord delivers the people of Alma and leads them to Zarahemla.

💡 Notice that there is a lesson idea in Mosiah 22 that also helps teach Mosiah 24. It compares the escape of Zeniff's people to the escape of Alma's people.

1 And it came to pass that Amulon did gain favor in the eyes of the king of the Lamanites; therefore, the king of the Lamanites granted unto him and his brethren that they should be appointed teachers over his people, yea, even over the people who were in the land of Shemlon, and in the land of Shilom, and in the land of Amulon.

2 For the Lamanites had taken possession of all these lands; therefore, the king of the Lamanites had appointed kings over all these lands.

3 And now the name of the king of the Lamanites was Laman, being called after the name of his father; and therefore he was called king Laman. And he was king over a numerous people.

4 And he appointed teachers of the brethren of Amulon in every land which was possessed by his people; and thus the language of Nephi began to be taught among all the people of the Lamanites.

5 And they were a people friendly one with another; nevertheless they knew not God; neither did the brethren of Amulon teach them anything concerning the Lord their God, neither the law of Moses; nor did they teach them the words of Abinadi;

6 But they taught them that they should keep their record, and that they might write one to another.

7 And thus the Lamanites began to increase in riches, and began to trade one with another and

wax great, and began to be a cunning and a wise people, as to the wisdom of the world, yea, a very cunning people, delighting in all manner of wickedness and plunder, except it were among their own brethren.

8 And now it came to pass that Amulon began to exercise authority over Alma and his brethren, and began to persecute him, and cause that his children should persecute their children.

9 For Amulon knew Alma, that he had been one of the king's priests, and that it was he that believed the words of Abinadi and was driven out before the king, and therefore he was wroth with him; for he was subject to king Laman, yet he exercised authority over them, and put tasks upon them, and put task-masters over them.

10 And it came to pass that so great were their afflictions that they began to cry mightily to God.

11 And Amulon commanded them that they should stop their cries; and he put guards over them to watch them, that whosoever should be found calling upon God should be put to death.

12 And Alma and his people did not raise their voices to the Lord their God, but did pour out their hearts to him; and he did know the thoughts of their hearts.

vv. 10–12 Prayer blesses our lives.

⚡ Ask, *Is it better to pray in our heart and mind or out loud? When was the last time you prayed out loud? Has there been a time when it may have been more appropriate to pray in your heart?*

🔍 Have class members browse Mosiah 24 and ask, *What situation in Mosiah chapter 24 requires the people of Alma to pray in their hearts?*

❓ Analyze: *In verse 12 it states that "they did pour out their hearts unto God." Why do you think it is written that way?*

❓ Apply: *What can we learn about prayer from that phrase?*

❤ Testify of the power of prayer and that the Lord knows the thoughts of our hearts.

13 And it came to pass that the voice of the Lord came to them in their afflictions, saying: Lift up your heads and be of good comfort, for I know of the covenant which ye have made unto me; and I will covenant with my people and deliver them out of bondage.

14 And I will also ease the burdens which are put upon your shoulders, that even you cannot feel them upon your backs, even while you are in bondage; and this will I do that ye may stand as witnesses for me hereafter, and that ye may know of a surety that I, the Lord God, do visit my people in their afflictions.

15 And now it came to pass that the burdens which were laid upon Alma and his brethren were made light; yea, the Lord did strengthen them that they could bear up their burdens with ease, and they did submit cheerfully and with patience to all the will of the Lord.

16 And it came to pass that so great was their faith and their patience that the voice of the Lord came unto them again, saying: Be of good comfort, for on the morrow I will deliver you out of bondage.

17 And he said unto Alma: Thou shalt go before this people, and I will go with thee and deliver this people out of bondage.

18 Now it came to pass that Alma and his people in the night-time gathered their flocks together, and also of their grain; yea, even all the night-time were they gathering their flocks together.

19 And in the morning the Lord caused a deep sleep to come upon the Lamanites, yea, and all their task-masters were in a profound sleep.

20 And Alma and his people departed into the wilderness; and when they had traveled all day they pitched their tents in a valley, and they called the valley Alma, because he led their way in the wilderness.

Notes

21 Yea, and in the valley of Alma they poured out their thanks to God because he had been merciful unto them, and eased their burdens, and had delivered them out of bondage; for they were in bondage, and none could deliver them except it were the Lord their God.

22 And they gave thanks to God, yea, all their men and all their women and all their children that could speak lifted their voices in the praises of their God.

23 And now the Lord said unto Alma: Haste thee and get thou and this people out of this land, for the Lamanites have awakened and do pursue thee; therefore get thee out of this land, and I will stop the Lamanites in this valley that they come no further in pursuit of this people.

24 And it came to pass that they departed out of the valley, and took their journey into the wilderness.

25 And after they had been in the wilderness twelve days they arrived in the land of Zarahemla; and king Mosiah did also receive them with joy.

MOSIAH 25

The Nephites Organize Politically and Spiritually
About 120 BC

1–3, The people of Zarahemla become one with the Nephites; 4–13, All the people hear the record of Zeniff and his people; 14–24, Alma preaches, baptizes, and organizes the church.

1 And now king Mosiah caused that all the people should be gathered together.

2 Now there were not so many of the children of Nephi, or so many of those who were descendants of Nephi, as there were of the people of Zarahemla, who was a descendant of Mulek, and those who came with him into the wilderness.

3 And there were not so many of the people of Nephi and of the people of Zarahemla as there were of the Lamanites; yea, they were not half so numerous.

4 And now all the people of Nephi were assembled together, and also all the people of Zarahemla, and they were gathered together in two bodies.

5 And it came to pass that Mosiah did read, and caused to be read, the records of Zeniff to his people; yea, he read the records of the people of Zeniff, from the time they left the land of Zarahemla until they returned again.

6 And he also read the account of Alma and his brethren, and all their afflictions, from the time they left the land of Zarahemla until the time they returned again.

7 And now, when Mosiah had made an end of reading the records, his people who tarried in the land were struck with wonder and amazement.

8 For they knew not what to think; for when they beheld those that had been delivered out of bondage they were filled with exceedingly great joy.

9 And again, when they thought of their brethren who had been slain by the Lamanites they were filled with sorrow, and even shed many tears of sorrow.

10 And again, when they thought of the immediate goodness of God, and his power in delivering Alma and his brethren out of the hands of the Lamanites and of bondage, they did raise their voices and give thanks to God.

11 And again, when they thought upon the Lamanites, who were their brethren, of their sinful and polluted state, they were filled with pain and anguish for the welfare of their souls.

vv. 4–11 Review of events from Zeniff's people leaving until their descendants return.

Notes

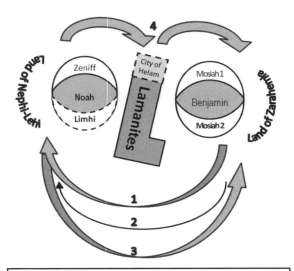

1) **Zeniff's Colonization** - Omni 1:27-30; Mosiah 9:1-8
2) **Ammon's Expedition** - Mosiah 7:2-4
3) **Gideon's Rescue** - Mosiah 22:1-3, 11-16
4) **Alma's Escape** - Mosiah 23:1-4,19-20

In verses 4–11, Mosiah recounts to his people the events from Zeniff's people leaving until their descendants' return. You may consider using the following chart, which is explained in the discussion of Mosiah 7:1–8 and charts the groups and events visually. This can be used as a review tool.

Break class members into five groups and assign each group one of the following verses: 7, 8, 9, 10, 11. Have them look for an emotion expressed in those verses. Then have them reflect on the events that were just reviewed and look for a story that could cause the emotions described in their assigned verse. Have a person in each group share what they found.

12 And it came to pass that those who were the children of Amulon and his brethren, who had taken to wife the daughters of the Lamanites, were displeased with the conduct of their fathers, and they would no longer be called by the names of their fathers, therefore they took upon themselves the name of Nephi, that they might be called the children of Nephi and be numbered

among those who were called Nephites.

13 And now all the people of Zarahemla were numbered with the Nephites, and this because the kingdom had been conferred upon none but those who were descendants of Nephi.

vv. 12–13 Who are the "children of Amulon"?

Amulon was the leader of the wicked priests of King Noah (Mosiah 23:32). He and the other wicked priests abandoned their families to flee with King Noah and were ashamed to return. Later they kidnapped and married the Lamanite daughters. The "children of Amulon" mentioned in Mosiah 25 are those abandoned children of the wicked priest who were conceived before the priests left into the wilderness. Because their fathers had abandoned them and their mothers to start new families with the Lamanite daughters, they no longer wanted to be called by their father's names and "took upon themselves the name of Nephi" (v. 12). These people are not to be confused with the Amulonites who remained in the land of Nephi, retained the name of their fathers, and are the descendants of the wicked priests through the kidnapped Lamanite daughters (Alma 21:3–4; 25:5–9).

14 And now it came to pass that when Mosiah had made an end of speaking and reading to the people, he desired that Alma should also speak to the people.

15 And Alma did speak unto them, when they were assembled together in large bodies, and he went from one body to another, preaching unto the people repentance and faith on the Lord.

16 And he did exhort the people of Limhi and his brethren, all those that had been delivered out of bondage, that they should remember that it was the Lord that did deliver them.

17 And it came to pass that after Alma had taught the people many things, and had made an end of speaking to them, that king Limhi was desirous

Notes

that he might be baptized; and all his people were desirous that they might be baptized also.

18 Therefore, Alma did go forth into the water and did baptize them; yea, he did baptize them after the manner he did his brethren in the waters of Mormon; yea, and as many as he did baptize did belong to the church of God; and this because of their belief on the words of Alma.

19 And it came to pass that king Mosiah granted unto Alma that he might establish churches throughout all the land of Zarahemla; and gave him power to ordain priests and teachers over every church.

20 Now this was done because there were so many people that they could not all be governed by one teacher; neither could they all hear the word of God in one assembly;

21 Therefore they did assemble themselves together in different bodies, being called churches; every church having their priests and their teachers, and every priest preaching the word according as it was delivered to him by the mouth of Alma.

22 And thus, notwithstanding there being many churches they were all one church, yea, even the church of God; for there was nothing preached in all the churches except it were repentance and faith in God.

23 And now there were seven churches in the land of Zarahemla. And it came to pass that whosoever were desirous to take upon them the name of Christ, or of God, they did join the churches of God;

24 And they were called the people of God. And the Lord did pour out his Spirit upon them, and they were blessed, and prospered in the land.

vv. 18–24 Everything taught in the Church is an extension of faith and repentance.

Quickly read verses 18–24 to yourselves and underline everything in their church that is similar to the Church today. Have class members share similarities and comparisons they

found. Similarities might include baptism, separate congregations but united in their teachings, priests and teachers called, and so forth.

In verse 22, look for the only topics that were preached in their churches.

Ask, How is it possible that they could only teach two topics, week after week? Ask class members to think of at least two topics that were taught the previous Sunday at church, and to raise their hands when they have thought of two. Ask them to share some of those topics and write them on the board. Then ask, How can each of those topics be thought of as either an extension of faith or repentance? Put an "F" by the topics that can be thought of as an extension of faith, and an "R" for repentance. You may need to remind the class that the root of the word repentance is change (see Bible Dictionary on "Repentance").

Have class members look at the list of topics on the board and decide on one area in which they will try to have greater faith or in which they have a need for repentance. Have them record it on a piece of paper or in their journals.

Teaching Tips from Prophets' Lips "Teaching by the spirit requires first that we keep the commandments and be clean before God so his Spirit can dwell in our personal temples" ("Teaching and Learning by the Spirit," *Ensign,* March 1997, 9).

MOSIAH 26

Discipline in the Church
About 120–100 BC

1–5, Many of the rising generation do not believe and separate themselves from believers; 6–13, Alma studies what to do with those who sin; 14–32, The Lord teaches what to do with those who fall into sin;

33–39, Alma institutes church discipline and the church prospers.

1 Now it came to pass that there were many of the rising generation that could not understand the words of king Benjamin, being little children at the time he spake unto his people; and they did not believe the tradition of their fathers.

2 They did not believe what had been said concerning the resurrection of the dead, neither did they believe concerning the coming of Christ.

3 And now because of their unbelief they could not understand the word of God; and their hearts were hardened.

4 And they would not be baptized; neither would they join the church. And they were a separate people as to their faith, and remained so ever after, even in their carnal and sinful state; for they would not call upon the Lord their God.

5 And now in the reign of Mosiah they were not half so numerous as the people of God; but because of the dissensions among the brethren they became more numerous.

vv. 1–5 We must teach the youth, or the Church will falter.

⚡ Before class, write on the board, "The church in Mosiah's time was experiencing a significant problem. What was it?" Explain to the class that they will discover what the problem was and if it is applicable in our day.

🔎 *Read verses 1–5 and make a list of what problem the church is facing.*

❓ Analyze: *Why do you think the adult leaders were so concerned about the youth?* Note with the class the reason for the youths' disbelief in verses 1–3. Ask, *Why is it significant to understand in order to believe?*

✋ Write the following on the board, "The Church has always been one _____ away from extinction." Have class members guess what the answer might be.

💬 Share the following quote: "The young people

of the Church . . . hold the future in their hands. The Church has always been one generation away from extinction. If a whole generation were lost, which will not happen, we would lose the Church. But even a single individual lost to the gospel of Jesus Christ closes doors for generations of descendants, unless the Lord reaches out to bring some of them back" ("We Must Raise Our Sights," Church Educational System Conference on the Book of Mormon, Aug. 14, 2001).

❓ Apply:
• *In what ways could we be facing a similar problem today?*
• *What are we encouraged to do as families to help strengthen the rising generation?*
• *What can we do to help the youth understand doctrine so that they are not faced with a similar problem as those in Mosiah's time?*

6 For it came to pass that they did deceive many with their flattering words, who were in the church, and did cause them to commit many sins; therefore it became expedient that those who committed sin, that were in the church, should be admonished by the church.

7 And it came to pass that they were brought before the priests, and delivered up unto the priests by the teachers; and the priests brought them before Alma, who was the high priest.

8 Now king Mosiah had given Alma the authority over the church.

9 And it came to pass that Alma did not know concerning them; but there were many witnesses against them; yea, the people stood and testified of their iniquity in abundance.

10 Now there had not any such thing happened before in the church; therefore Alma was troubled in his spirit, and he caused that they should be brought before the king.

11 And he said unto the king: Behold, here are many whom we have brought before thee, who are accused of their brethren; yea, and they

Notes

have been taken in divers iniquities. And they do not repent of their iniquities; therefore we have brought them before thee, that thou mayest judge them according to their crimes.

12 But king Mosiah said unto Alma: Behold, I judge them not; therefore I deliver them into thy hands to be judged.

13 And now the spirit of Alma was again troubled; and he went and inquired of the Lord what he should do concerning this matter, for he feared that he should do wrong in the sight of God.

vv. 6–39 A pattern for how to solve problems.

⚡ Explain to class members that Mosiah chapter 26 can be thought of as a pattern for how to solve problems. Ask them to list general steps of problem solving.

🔍 *What is the problem that Alma tries to solve in verses 7–14?*

❓ Analyze: *Why do you think involving the Lord is the best way to solve a problem?*

🔍 Invite class members to look in verses 15–32 for the Lord's solution to the problem.

❓ Analyze: *Does the Lord's solution seem fair? Why or why not?*

🔍 Invite class members to look for what the result of the Lord's instructions was.

❓ Apply: *In what ways could we use a similar pattern in problem solving today?*

♥ Challenge class members to use this same process the next time they are faced with a difficult situation.

14 And it came to pass that after he had poured out his whole soul to God, the voice of the Lord came to him, saying:

15 Blessed art thou, Alma, and blessed are they who were baptized in the waters of Mormon. Thou art blessed because of thy exceeding faith in the words alone of my servant Abinadi.

16 And blessed are they because of their exceeding faith in the words alone which thou hast spoken unto them.

17 And blessed art thou because thou hast established a church among this people; and they shall be established, and they shall be my people.

18 Yea, blessed is this people who are willing to bear my name; for in my name shall they be called; and they are mine.

19 And because thou hast inquired of me concerning the transgressor, thou art blessed.

vv. 19, 29–30 God still loves and seeks to help those who transgress.

🔍 *Look for what verses 19 and 29–30 teach about how God feels about those who sin.*

❓ Analyze:
- *How does the Lord feel about those who sin?*
- *How does this verse teach that God still loves those who sin?*
- *Why should this verse give us joy?*
- *What does this verse teach about we should be doing?*

♥ Bear your testimony of God's love for us even when we make mistakes. Challenge class members to continue to love those who have made mistakes and fallen away from Church activity.

20 Thou art my servant; and I covenant with thee that thou shalt have eternal life; and thou shalt serve me and go forth in my name, and shalt gather together my sheep.

21 And he that will hear my voice shall be my sheep; and him shall ye receive into the church, and him will I also receive.

22 For behold, this is my church; whosoever is baptized shall be baptized unto repentance. And whomsoever ye receive shall believe in my name; and him will I freely forgive.

23 For it is I that taketh upon me the sins of the world; for it is I that hath created them; and it is

Notes

I that granteth unto him that believeth unto the end a place at my right hand.

24 For behold, in my name are they called; and if they know me they shall come forth, and shall have a place eternally at my right hand.

25 And it shall come to pass that when the second trump shall sound then shall they that never knew me come forth and shall stand before me.

26 And then shall they know that I am the Lord their God, that I am their Redeemer; but they would not be redeemed.

27 And then I will confess unto them that I never knew them; and they shall depart into everlasting fire prepared for the devil and his angels.

28 Therefore I say unto you, that he that will not hear my voice, the same shall ye not receive into my church, for him I will not receive at the last day.

29 Therefore I say unto you, Go; and whosoever transgresseth against me, him shall ye judge according to the sins which he has committed; and if he confess his sins before thee and me, and repenteth in the sincerity of his heart, him shall ye forgive, and I will forgive him also.

30 Yea, and as often as my people repent will I forgive them their trespasses against me.

31 And ye shall also forgive one another your trespasses; for verily I say unto you, he that forgiveth not his neighbor's trespasses when he says that he repents, the same hath brought himself under condemnation.

32 Now I say unto you, Go; and whosoever will not repent of his sins the same shall not be numbered among my people; and this shall be observed from this time forward.

33 And it came to pass when Alma had heard these words he wrote them down that he might have them, and that he might judge the people of that church according to the commandments of God.

v. 33 If we will record impressions from the Spirit, we will receive further impressions.

⚡ Explain and summarize what the Lord revealed to Alma, then ask, *What should Alma do immediately after receiving such a revelation?*

🔎 *Look for what Alma did immediately after receiving the revelation in verse 33.*

❓ Analyze:
• *What does verse 33 say was the reason to write it down?*
• *Does timing matter with writing it down? Why?*
• *Why would it be important to have those things you wrote later?*

💬 Share the following statement from Elder Richard G. Scott: "Knowledge carefully recorded is knowledge available in time of need. Spiritually sensitive information should be kept in a sacred place that communicates to the Lord how you treasure it. That practice enhances the likelihood of your receiving further light" (Richard G. Scott, "Acquiring Spiritual Knowledge," *Ensign*, November 1993, 86).

💜 Challenge class members to record impressions they receive from the Spirit so that they will have those in the future and receive further inspiration.

34 And it came to pass that Alma went and judged those that had been taken in iniquity, according to the word of the Lord.

35 And whosoever repented of their sins and did confess them, them he did number among the people of the church;

36 And those that would not confess their sins and repent of their iniquity, the same were not numbered among the people of the church, and their names were blotted out.

37 And it came to pass that Alma did regulate all the affairs of the church; and they began again to have peace and to prosper exceedingly in the affairs of the church, walking circumspectly before God, receiving many, and baptizing many.

38 And now all these things did Alma and his

Notes

fellow laborers do who were over the church, walking in all diligence, teaching the word of God in all things, suffering all manner of afflictions, being persecuted by all those who did not belong to the church of God.

39 And they did admonish their brethren; and they were also admonished, every one by the word of God, according to his sins, or to the sins which he had committed, being commanded of God to pray without ceasing, and to give thanks in all things.

MOSIAH 27

The Conversion of Alma the Younger

About 100–92 BC

1–7, King Mosiah encourages his subjects to not persecute anyone because of their belief; 8–17, Alma the younger and the four sons of Mosiah go about persecuting the church and are visited by an angel; Alma falls to the earth, losing his strength; 18–31, Alma is without strength for a period of time during which he repents of his sins; 32–37, Alma and the four sons of Mosiah seek to repair the damage they caused and preach the gospel.

Overarching Principle: Repentance is changing from our natural, carnal, fallen, and sinful state to a state of righteousness, "being redeemed of God." As we accept the Atonement, we will be freed from the pain and anguish of sin and can "behold the marvelous light of God."

Note: This chapter teaches two aspects of repentance: 1) *why* we should repent, and 2) *how* to repent.

⚡ To introduce the overarching principle, bring one or two apples and set them in the front of the class. Explain that the apple represents

each of us in our current mortal condition. Depending on how many apples you bring, invite a class member to the front of the room and ask him or her to take a few bites from the apple. Explain that the bites will represent sin. (The exposed parts of the apple will quickly turn brown during the course of the lesson which will help teach the effects that sin has upon us.) Use this object lesson at the beginning of class so that when you are near the end of class the apple will be visually unappealing to eat.

1 And now it came to pass that the persecutions which were inflicted on the church by the unbelievers became so great that the church began to murmur, and complain to their leaders concerning the matter; and they did complain to Alma. And Alma laid the case before their king, Mosiah. And Mosiah consulted with his priests.

2 And it came to pass that king Mosiah sent a proclamation throughout the land round about that there should not any unbeliever persecute any of those who belonged to the church of God.

3 And there was a strict command throughout all the churches that there should be no persecutions among them, that there should be an equality among all men;

4 That they should let no pride nor haughtiness disturb their peace; that every man should esteem his neighbor as himself, laboring with their own hands for their support.

5 Yea, and all their priests and teachers should labor with their own hands for their support, in all cases save it were in sickness, or in much

want; and doing these things, they did abound in the grace of God.

6 And there began to be much peace again in the land; and the people began to be very numerous, and began to scatter abroad upon the face of the earth, yea, on the north and on the south, on the east and on the west, building large cities and villages in all quarters of the land.

7 And the Lord did visit them and prosper them, and they became a large and wealthy people.

vv. 1–7 Members of the Church should never persecute others; rather, we should esteem all people as our neighbors.

🔍 *What conflict is happening in verse 1? How does King Mosiah resolve this conflict in verses 2–7?*

❓ Analyze: *Why is it important to not persecute others for their beliefs?*

❓ Apply: *Have you ever been persecuted for your beliefs, and if so, what did you do about it?*

8 Now the sons of Mosiah were numbered among the unbelievers; and also one of the sons of Alma was numbered among them, he being called Alma, after his father; nevertheless, he became a very wicked and an idolatrous man. And he was a man of many words, and did speak much flattery to the people; therefore he led many of the people to do after the manner of his iniquities.

9 And he became a great hinderment to the prosperity of the church of God; stealing away the hearts of the people; causing much dissension among the people; giving a chance for the enemy of God to exercise his power over them.

vv. 8–9 The rebellion of Alma the younger and the four sons of Mosiah.

⚡ Use the apple object lesson as suggested at the beginning of this chapter to teach the overarching principle. Note: the storyline in

this chapter must be understood in order for class members to understand the principle that will be taught by Alma at the end of the chapter. To help lay out the storyline, the verses are broken into smaller sets. Depending on the ages of class members and your teaching preference, you may choose to have class members act out portions of the storyline, have someone summarize the story in their own words, or read the story out loud as a class.

vv. 10–12 The appearance of the angel.

10 And now it came to pass that while he was going about to destroy the church of God, for he did go about secretly with the sons of Mosiah seeking to destroy the church, and to lead astray the people of the Lord, contrary to the commandments of God, or even the king—

11 And as I said unto you, as they were going about rebelling against God, behold, the angel of the Lord appeared unto them; and he descended as it were in a cloud; and he spake as it were with a voice of thunder, which caused the earth to shake upon which they stood;

12 And so great was their astonishment, that they fell to the earth, and understood not the words which he spake unto them.

vv. 13–17 The angel's words to Alma.

13 Nevertheless he cried again, saying: Alma, arise and stand forth, for why persecutest thou the church of God? For the Lord hath said: This is my church, and I will establish it; and nothing shall overthrow it, save it is the transgression of my people.

14 And again, the angel said: Behold, the Lord hath heard the prayers of his people, and also the prayers of his servant, Alma, who is thy father; for he has prayed with much faith concerning thee that thou mightest be brought to the knowledge of the truth; therefore, for this purpose have I come to convince thee of the power and

Notes

authority of God, that the prayers of his servants might be answered according to their faith.

15 And now behold, can ye dispute the power of God? For behold, doth not my voice shake the earth? And can ye not also behold me before you? And I am sent from God.

16 Now I say unto thee: Go, and remember the captivity of thy fathers in the land of Helam, and in the land of Nephi; and remember how great things he has done for them; for they were in bondage, and he has delivered them. And now I say unto thee, Alma, go thy way, and seek to destroy the church no more, that their prayers may be answered, and this even if thou wilt of thyself be cast off.

17 And now it came to pass that these were the last words which the angel spake unto Alma, and he departed.

vv. 18–24 Alma loses his strength and is unconscious for a time, but eventually wakes and declares he has repented.

18 And now Alma and those that were with him fell again to the earth, for great was their astonishment; for with their own eyes they had beheld an angel of the Lord; and his voice was as thunder, which shook the earth; and they knew that there was nothing save the power of God that could shake the earth and cause it to tremble as though it would part asunder.

19 And now the astonishment of Alma was so great that he became dumb, that he could not open his mouth; yea, and he became weak, even that he could not move his hands; therefore he was taken by those that were with him, and carried helpless, even until he was laid before his father.

20 And they rehearsed unto his father all that had happened unto them; and his father rejoiced, for he knew that it was the power of God.

21 And he caused that a multitude should be gathered together that they might witness what the Lord had done for his son, and also for those that were with him.

22 And he caused that the priests should assemble themselves together; and they began to fast, and to pray to the Lord their God that he would open the mouth of Alma, that he might speak, and also that his limbs might receive their strength—that the eyes of the people might be opened to see and know of the goodness and glory of God.

23 And it came to pass after they had fasted and prayed for the space of two days and two nights, the limbs of Alma received their strength, and he stood up and began to speak unto them, bidding them to be of good comfort:

24 For, said he, I have repented of my sins, and have been redeemed of the Lord; behold I am born of the Spirit.

25 And the Lord said unto me: Marvel not that all mankind, yea, men and women, all nations, kindreds, tongues and people, must be born again; yea, born of God, changed from their carnal and fallen state, to a state of righteousness, being redeemed of God, becoming his sons and daughters;

26 And thus they become new creatures; and unless they do this, they can in nowise inherit the kingdom of God.

27 I say unto you, unless this be the case, they must be cast off; and this I know, because I was like to be cast off.

28 Nevertheless, after wading through much tribulation, repenting nigh unto death, the Lord in mercy hath seen fit to snatch me out of an everlasting burning, and I am born of God.

29 My soul hath been redeemed from the gall of bitterness and bonds of iniquity. I was in the darkest abyss; but now I behold the marvelous light of God. My soul was cracked with eternal torment; but I am snatched, and my soul is pained no more.

30 I rejected my Redeemer, and denied that which had been spoken of by our fathers; but now that

Notes

they may foresee that he will come, and that he remembereth every creature of his creating, he will make himself manifest unto all.

31 Yea, every knee shall bow, and every tongue confess before him. Yea, even at the last day, when all men shall stand to be judged of him, then shall they confess that he is God; then shall they confess, who live without God in the world, that the judgment of an everlasting punishment is just upon them; and they shall quake, and tremble, and shrink beneath the glance of his all-searching eye.

vv. 25–31 Repentance is changing from our natural, carnal, fallen, and sinful state to a state of righteousness, "being redeemed of God."

⚡ Refer back to the eaten apple and discuss what has happened to it over the course of the class. Ask, *Is there any way for this apple to return to how it was originally?*

🔎 *In verses 25–26, what is the first thing that Alma tells the people when he wakes up?*

❓ Analyze: *What do you think Alma means when he says to "become new creatures"? What do you think it means to change from a carnal and fallen state to a state of righteousness? (Depending on the ages of class members, you may want to define the word "carnal.")*

❓ Apply: *How is it possible to change from a sinful state to a state of righteousness?*

Testify that when we repent, we change from our sinful state to a state of righteousness.

🔎 *In verses 27–30, search for what is the result of that change for Alma. How does the result of his sins make him feel compared to the feeling of forgiveness from God?*

❤ Refer back to the apple and discuss that through the Atonement of Jesus Christ, we are able to repent and be restored to a state of righteousness and happiness—free from guilt, pain, and anguish. You may want to throw away the brown, eaten apple and replace it with a new, uneaten one.

32 And now it came to pass that Alma began from this time forward to teach the people, and those who were with Alma at the time the angel appeared unto them, traveling round about through all the land, publishing to all the people the things which they had heard and seen, and preaching the word of God in much tribulation, being greatly persecuted by those who were unbelievers, being smitten by many of them.

33 But notwithstanding all this, they did impart much consolation to the church, confirming their faith, and exhorting them with long-suffering and much travail to keep the commandments of God.

34 And four of them were the sons of Mosiah; and their names were Ammon, and Aaron, and Omner, and Himni; these were the names of the sons of Mosiah.

35 And they traveled throughout all the land of Zarahemla, and among all the people who were under the reign of king Mosiah, zealously striving to repair all the injuries which they had done to the church, confessing all their sins, and publishing all the things which they had seen, and explaining the prophecies and the scriptures to all who desired to hear them.

36 And thus they were instruments in the hands of God in bringing many to the knowledge of the truth, yea, to the knowledge of their Redeemer.

37 And how blessed are they! For they did publish peace; they did publish good tidings of good; and they did declare unto the people that the Lord reigneth.

vv. 32–37 After we repent, we should zealously strive to repair the damage we caused by sinning.

⚡ Display a printed picture to the class and give the impression that it depicts a very special and cherished memory for you. Ask the class if anyone would like to hold this really important picture. Prearrange with a class member to come to the front of the room and tear the

Notes

picture. Use this object lesson to teach what a repentant individual must do to repair the damage caused by sinning. In the case of the object lesson, the class member should repair the picture. (Depending on time, you may want to bring tape and allow him or her to tape the picture.)

🔍 *In verse 10, look for what rebellious acts Alma did that were so wrong. Look in verses 32–37 and notice what he and the sons of Mosiah do to try and repair the damage they have caused.*

❓ Analyze: *Why do you think that repairing what we do wrong is part of the repentance process?*

❓ Apply: Ask for examples of the kinds of sins we are faced with today and write them on the board. *What can we do to repair the damage caused by these sins?* Note with class members that the sins that are more serious are harder to repair, such as murder.

💜 Invite class members to repent as we see Alma the younger doing by accepting the Atonement and striving to repair the damage we cause.

Teaching Tips from Prophets' Lips "When preparing lessons, don't ask 'What shall I do in class today?' but ask, 'What will my students do in class today?' not, 'What will I teach today?' but rather, 'How will I help my students discover what they need to know?'" (*Teaching, No Greater Call*, 61).

MOSIAH 28

Desires to Preach to the Lamanites
About 92 BC

1–5, The sons of Mosiah desire to preach among the Lamanites in order to bring them salvation and peace; 6–9, King Mosiah inquires of the Lord concerning his sons' mission; 10–20, After his sons leave to preach,

Mosiah translates the Jaredite records by means of the interpreters.

1 Now it came to pass that after the sons of Mosiah had done all these things, they took a small number with them and returned to their father, the king, and desired of him that he would grant unto them that they might, with these whom they had selected, go up to the land of Nephi that they might preach the things which they had heard, and that they might impart the word of God to their brethren, the Lamanites—

2 That perhaps they might bring them to the knowledge of the Lord their God, and convince them of the iniquity of their fathers; and that perhaps they might cure them of their hatred towards the Nephites, that they might also be brought to rejoice in the Lord their God, that they might become friendly to one another, and that there should be no more contentions in all the land which the Lord their God had given them.

3 Now they were desirous that salvation should be declared to every creature, for they could not bear that any human soul should perish; yea, even the very thoughts that any soul should endure endless torment did cause them to quake and tremble.

4 And thus did the Spirit of the Lord work upon them, for they were the very vilest of sinners. And the Lord saw fit in his infinite mercy to spare them; nevertheless they suffered much anguish of soul because of their iniquities, suffering much and fearing that they should be cast off forever.

5 And it came to pass that they did plead with their father many days that they might go up to the land of Nephi.

6 And king Mosiah went and inquired of the Lord if he should let his sons go up among the Lamanites to preach the word.

7 And the Lord said unto Mosiah: Let them go up, for many shall believe on their words, and they

shall have eternal life; and I will deliver thy sons out of the hands of the Lamanites.

8 And it came to pass that Mosiah granted that they might go and do according to their request.

9 And they took their journey into the wilderness to go up to preach the word among the Lamanites; and I shall give an account of their proceedings hereafter.

vv. 1–9 True conversion leads to a desire to bring others unto Christ.

⚡ *Imagine you have just seen a really good movie, heard a fantastic new song, or tried a delicious food for the first time. What would probably be one of the first things you would do after experiencing any of those three things? Would you keep it a secret? Would you avoid talking about it with your friends and family?*

🔑 Ask a class member to read Mosiah 28:1–5 and have the class look for what the sons of Mosiah wanted to do after being converted to the gospel.

❓ Analyze: Ask, *Which phrases or ideas impress you about the way the sons of Mosiah feel about the Lamanites? Why do you think the sons of Mosiah had such strong feelings about preaching the gospel?*

💬 President Henry B. Eyring, explaining the missionary zeal of some members of the Church, has taught, "First, they feel that they are the beloved children of a loving Heavenly Father. Because of that, they turn to Him easily and often in prayer. They expect to receive His personal direction. They obey in meekness and humility, as the children of a perfect parent. He is close to them. Second, they are the grateful disciples of the resurrected Jesus Christ. They know for themselves that the Atonement is real and necessary for all. They have felt cleansed through baptism by those in authority and the receipt of the Holy Ghost for themselves. And because of the peace they have experienced, they are like

the sons of Mosiah, 'desirous that salvation should be declared to every creature, for they could not bear that any human soul should perish; yea, even the very thoughts that any soul should endure endless torment did cause them to quake and tremble' " (Henry B. Eyring, "A Child and a Disciple," *Ensign,* May 2003).

❤ Encourage class members to express gratitude for their personal salvation by teaching others about the Atonement, gospel, and Church of Jesus Christ, so that they may experience the same blessings in their lives.

10 Now king Mosiah had no one to confer the kingdom upon, for there was not any of his sons who would accept of the kingdom.

11 Therefore he took the records which were engraven on the plates of brass, and also the plates of Nephi, and all the things which he had kept and preserved according to the commandments of God, after having translated and caused to be written the records which were on the plates of gold which had been found by the people of Limhi, which were delivered to him by the hand of Limhi;

12 And this he did because of the great anxiety of his people; for they were desirous beyond measure to know concerning those people who had been destroyed.

13 And now he translated them by the means of those two stones which were fastened into the two rims of a bow.

14 Now these things were prepared from the beginning, and were handed down from generation to generation, for the purpose of interpreting languages;

15 And they have been kept and preserved by the hand of the Lord, that he should discover to every creature who should possess the land the iniquities and abominations of his people;

16 And whosoever has these things is called seer, after the manner of old times.

Notes

17 Now after Mosiah had finished translating these records, behold, it gave an account of the people who were destroyed, from the time that they were destroyed back to the building of the great tower, at the time the Lord confounded the language of the people and they were scattered abroad upon the face of all the earth, yea, and even from that time back until the creation of Adam.

18 Now this account did cause the people of Mosiah to mourn exceedingly, yea, they were filled with sorrow; nevertheless it gave them much knowledge, in the which they did rejoice.

19 And this account shall be written hereafter; for behold, it is expedient that all people should know the things which are written in this account.

20 And now, as I said unto you, that after king Mosiah had done these things, he took the plates of brass, and all the things which he had kept, and conferred them upon Alma, who was the son of Alma; yea, all the records, and also the interpreters, and conferred them upon him, and commanded him that he should keep and preserve them, and also keep a record of the people, handing them down from one generation to another, even as they had been handed down from the time that Lehi left Jerusalem.

vv. 10–20 The Lord prepares means by which His prophets can bring forth scripture.

⚡ Tell class members that you will be reading a few facts about a historical figure. Ask them to raise their hand when they think they know who you are describing. The individual is King Mosiah, but many class members will likely assume the answer is Joseph Smith until the last two facts.

- *He was a prophet* (v. 10).
- *He received plates of gold* (v. 11).
- *He translated a record about a people who had been destroyed* (v. 12).
- *He used two stones to translate the record* (v. 13).
- *He received the stones from earlier prophets* (v. 14).

- *He was called a seer* (v. 16).
- *The people who received his translation mourned when they read it* (v. 18).
- *He gave the stones and records to a prophet named Alma* (v. 20).

Ask class members if they know who you were describing. Help them understand why the correct answer is King Mosiah from verses 10–20.

❤ Testify that the Lord operates in similar ways throughout all dispensations. Express your gratitude for the consistency of the Lord in calling prophets and revealing scriptures for our benefit.

MOSIAH 29
Judges Instead of Kings
About 92–91 BC

1–3, Mosiah's people desire that Aaron should be king after him; 4–9, Mosiah shares with his people how becoming king can corrupt people; 10–11, He proposes that judges be appointed instead of a king; 12–23, He speaks of the iniquity that can come from a wicked king; 24–36, Mosiah gives some details of governing through judges and why; 37–47, The people accept and choose Alma the younger as their first chief judge, and Mosiah dies.

1 Now when Mosiah had done this he sent out throughout all the land, among all the people, desiring to know their will concerning who should be their king.

2 And it came to pass that the voice of the people came, saying: We are desirous that Aaron thy son should be our king and our ruler.

3 Now Aaron had gone up to the land of Nephi, therefore the king could not confer the kingdom upon him; neither would Aaron take upon him the kingdom; neither were any of the sons of Mosiah willing to take upon them the kingdom.

Notes

4 Therefore king Mosiah sent again among the people; yea, even a written word sent he among the people. And these were the words that were written, saying:

5 Behold, O ye my people, or my brethren, for I esteem you as such, I desire that ye should consider the cause which ye are called to consider—for ye are desirous to have a king.

6 Now I declare unto you that he to whom the kingdom doth rightly belong has declined, and will not take upon him the kingdom.

7 And now if there should be another appointed in his stead, behold I fear there would rise contentions among you. And who knoweth but what my son, to whom the kingdom doth belong, should turn to be angry and draw away a part of this people after him, which would cause wars and contentions among you, which would be the cause of shedding much blood and perverting the way of the Lord, yea, and destroy the souls of many people.

8 Now I say unto you let us be wise and consider these things, for we have no right to destroy my son, neither should we have any right to destroy another if he should be appointed in his stead.

9 And if my son should turn again to his pride and vain things he would recall the things which he had said, and claim his right to the kingdom, which would cause him and also this people to commit much sin.

vv. 7–9 Beware of power because of its tendency to corrupt.

⚡ Before class, write on the board, "Power corrupts, and absolute power corrupts absolutely."—Lord Acton. Invite class members to expound on how this is true and to give examples of it.

🔍 *Look for how the quote on the board is true as you read verses 7–9.*

❓ Apply: *According to those verses and from your own experiences, what should we be careful of when we are given positions of responsibility?*

✏️ Invite class members to write "Doctrine and Covenants 121:39–44" to the side of the verses in Mosiah. After turning to the reference, have them look for what leaders can do to avoid being corrupted by their own power.

❤️ Invite class members to write the quote on the board in the margin of their scriptures. Challenge them to strive to be good leaders.

10 And now let us be wise and look forward to these things, and do that which will make for the peace of this people.

v. 10 The purpose of government.

💡 Have class members look for a purpose of government in verse 10.

💬 Have your class listen for other purposes of government in the Preamble of the United States Constitution: "We the people of the United States, in order to form a more perfect union, establish justice, insure domestic tranquility, provide for the common defense, promote the general welfare, and secure the blessings of liberty to ourselves and our posterity, do ordain and establish this Constitution for the United States of America."

11 Therefore I will be your king the remainder of my days; nevertheless, let us appoint judges, to judge this people according to our law; and we will newly arrange the affairs of this people, for we will appoint wise men to be judges, that will judge this people according to the commandments of God.

12 Now it is better that a man should be judged of God than of man, for the judgments of God are always just, but the judgments of man are not always just.

13 Therefore, if it were possible that you could have just men to be your kings, who would establish the laws of God, and judge this people according

Notes

to his commandments, yea, if ye could have men for your kings who would do even as my father Benjamin did for this people—I say unto you, if this could always be the case then it would be expedient that ye should always have kings to rule over you.

14 And even I myself have labored with all the power and faculties which I have possessed, to teach you the commandments of God, and to establish peace throughout the land, that there should be no wars nor contentions, no stealing, nor plundering, nor murdering, nor any manner of iniquity;

15 And whosoever has committed iniquity, him have I punished according to the crime which he has committed, according to the law which has been given to us by our fathers.

16 Now I say unto you, that because all men are not just it is not expedient that ye should have a king or kings to rule over you.

vv. 11–16 The best forms of government.

Note that since the people of Lehi came out of Jerusalem, they brought with them the culture of kings. The first Nephite king was Nephi; yet in this chapter, King Mosiah will abandon the monarchy as a means of leadership and establish a new form of government.

Look for some advantages and disadvantages of having a king in verses 11–16.

"In the Church of Christ where the government is that of the Kingdom of Heaven, neither autocracy nor democracy obtains, but government by Common Consent. That is to say, the initiative in all that pertains to the government of the Church rests with the Head of the Church, even our Lord Jesus Christ, and He exercises this sovereign function through His authorized servants, upon whom He has bestowed the Holy Priesthood; but it is the privilege of the people to accept, or reject, His laws and ordinances, for God has given every individual free agency. Obedience

must be voluntary. The government of the Church has been called a Theodemocracy. It is the form of government that will be general during the Millennium" (Hyrum M. Smith and Janne M. Sjodahl, *The Doctrine and Covenants Commentary*, 131–32).

17 For behold, how much iniquity doth one wicked king cause to be committed, yea, and what great destruction!

18 Yea, remember king Noah, his wickedness and his abominations, and also the wickedness and abominations of his people. Behold what great destruction did come upon them; and also because of their iniquities they were brought into bondage.

19 And were it not for the interposition of their all-wise Creator, and this because of their sincere repentance, they must unavoidably remain in bondage until now.

20 But behold, he did deliver them because they did humble themselves before him; and because they cried mightily unto him he did deliver them out of bondage; and thus doth the Lord work with his power in all cases among the children of men, extending the arm of mercy towards them that put their trust in him.

21 And behold, now I say unto you, ye cannot dethrone an iniquitous king save it be through much contention, and the shedding of much blood.

22 For behold, he has his friends in iniquity, and he keepeth his guards about him; and he teareth up the laws of those who have reigned in righteousness before him; and he trampleth under his feet the commandments of God;

23 And he enacteth laws, and sendeth them forth among his people, yea, laws after the manner of his own wickedness; and whosoever doth not obey his laws he causeth to be destroyed; and whosoever doth rebel against him he will send his armies against them to war, and if he can he will destroy them; and thus an unrighteous king

Notes

doth pervert the ways of all righteousness.

24 And now behold I say unto you, it is not expedient that such abominations should come upon you.

25 Therefore, choose you by the voice of this people, judges, that ye may be judged according to the laws which have been given you by our fathers, which are correct, and which were given them by the hand of the Lord.

26 Now it is not common that the voice of the people desireth anything contrary to that which is right; but it is common for the lesser part of the people to desire that which is not right; therefore this shall ye observe and make it your law—to do your business by the voice of the people.

27 And if the time comes that the voice of the people doth choose iniquity, then is the time that the judgments of God will come upon you; yea, then is the time he will visit you with great destruction even as he has hitherto visited this land.

vv. 25–27 We must support effective leaders in order to have a prosperous society.

🔎 *In verses 25–27, look for what role the Nephite citizens will play in their new government.*

❓ Analyze: *Why is it important for citizens to vote? Why do you think Mosiah would establish the government this way rather than continuing with a king?*

🔎 *Look for one disadvantage to this new form of government.*

💬 "Democracy is the recurrent suspicion that more than half of the people are right more than half the time" (E. B. White, *New Yorker*, July 3, 1944).

💜 Challenge class members to play an active role in government, and discuss how they can do this.

28 And now if ye have judges, and they do not judge you according to the law which has been given, ye can cause that they may be judged of a higher judge.

29 If your higher judges do not judge righteous judgments, ye shall cause that a small number of your lower judges should be gathered together, and they shall judge your higher judges, according to the voice of the people.

30 And I command you to do these things in the fear of the Lord; and I command you to do these things, and that ye have no king; that if these people commit sins and iniquities they shall be answered upon their own heads.

31 For behold I say unto you, the sins of many people have been caused by the iniquities of their kings; therefore their iniquities are answered upon the heads of their kings.

32 And now I desire that this inequality should be no more in this land, especially among this my people; but I desire that this land be a land of liberty, and every man may enjoy his rights and privileges alike, so long as the Lord sees fit that we may live and inherit the land, yea, even as long as any of our posterity remains upon the face of the land.

33 And many more things did king Mosiah write unto them, unfolding unto them all the trials and troubles of a righteous king, yea, all the travails of soul for their people, and also all the murmurings of the people to their king; and he explained it all unto them.

34 And he told them that these things ought not to be; but that the burden should come upon all the people, that every man might bear his part.

35 And he also unfolded unto them all the disadvantages they labored under, by having an unrighteous king to rule over them;

36 Yea, all his iniquities and abominations, and all the wars, and contentions, and bloodshed, and the stealing, and the plundering, and the committing of whoredoms, and all manner of iniquities which cannot be enumerated—telling them that these things ought not to be, that they were

Notes

expressly repugnant to the commandments of God.

37 And now it came to pass, after king Mosiah had sent these things forth among the people they were convinced of the truth of his words.

38 Therefore they relinquished their desires for a king, and became exceedingly anxious that every man should have an equal chance throughout all the land; yea, and every man expressed a willingness to answer for his own sins.

39 Therefore, it came to pass that they assembled themselves together in bodies throughout the land, to cast in their voices concerning who should be their judges, to judge them according to the law which had been given them; and they were exceedingly rejoiced because of the liberty which had been granted unto them.

vv. 28–39 The new Nephite government.

In verses 28–39, have class members look for the details of how the Nephites would structure their government, and compare it to our government today.

40 And they did wax strong in love towards Mosiah; yea, they did esteem him more than any other man; for they did not look upon him as a tyrant who was seeking for gain, yea, for that lucre which doth corrupt the soul; for he had not exacted riches of them, neither had he delighted in the shedding of blood; but he had established peace in the land, and he had granted unto his people that they should be delivered from all manner of bondage; therefore they did esteem him, yea, exceedingly, beyond measure.

41 And it came to pass that they did appoint judges to rule over them, or to judge them according to the law; and this they did throughout all the land.

42 And it came to pass that Alma was appointed to be the first chief judge, he being also the high priest, his father having conferred the office upon him, and having given him the charge concerning all the affairs of the church.

43 And now it came to pass that Alma did walk in the ways of the Lord, and he did keep his commandments, and he did judge righteous judgments; and there was continual peace through the land.

44 And thus commenced the reign of the judges throughout all the land of Zarahemla, among all the people who were called the Nephites; and Alma was the first and chief judge.

45 And now it came to pass that his father died, being eighty and two years old, having lived to fulfil the commandments of God.

46 And it came to pass that Mosiah died also, in the thirty and third year of his reign, being sixty and three years old; making in the whole, five hundred and nine years from the time Lehi left Jerusalem.

47 And thus ended the reign of the kings over the people of Nephi; and thus ended the days of Alma, who was the founder of their church.

Teaching Tips from Prophets' Lips "A gospel teacher should always teach with love for the students. . . . Love of God and love of His children is the highest reason for service. Those who teach out of love will be magnified as instruments in the hands of Him whom they serve" (Dallin H. Oaks, "Teaching and Learning by the Spirit," *Ensign*, March 1997, 7).

Notes

THE BOOK OF ALMA

ALMA BOOK SUMMARY

Time Period: About 91–53 BC (39 years)

Major Contributors: Moroni, Alma the Younger, Amulek, Ammon, Aaron, Zenos, Zenock

Source: Large plates of Nephi

Abridged by: Mormon

Synopsis:

Chapters 1–4: Alma's time in the judgment seat

Chapters 5–6: Alma's ministry in the land of Zarahemla

Chapter 7: Alma's ministry in Gideon

Chapters 8–14: Alma and Amulek's ministry, persecutions and deliverance in Ammonihah

Chapters 15–16: Church affairs are set in order

Chapters 17–28: The missions of the sons of Mosiah to the Lamanites: their preachings, sufferings, deliverance, and the affairs concerning the people of Ammon

Chapter 29: A psalm of Ammon

Chapter 30: An account of Korihor, an antichrist

Chapters 31–35: The mission to the Zoramites

Chapters 36–42: The commandments of Alma to his sons

Chapters 43–62: The wars and political unrest between the Nephites and Lamanites

Chapter 63: Hagoth builds and sails ships; the sacred records are passed to Helaman

The account of Alma, who was the son of Alma, the first and chief judge over the people of Nephi, and also the high priest over the Church. An account of the reign of the judges, and the wars and contentions among the people. And also an account of a war between the Nephites and the Lamanites, according to the record of Alma, the first and chief judge.

Notes

ALMA 1

Priestcraft Introduced among the People
About 91–88 BC

1–6, Priestcraft is introduced by Nehor; 7–15, Nehor slays Gideon and is condemned to death; 16–33, Priestcraft continues among the people but is countered by the righteousness of those who belong to the church.

1 Now it came to pass that in the first year of the reign of the judges over the people of Nephi, from this time forward, king Mosiah having gone the way of all the earth, having warred a good warfare, walking uprightly before God, leaving none to reign in his stead; nevertheless he had established laws, and they were acknowledged by the people; therefore they were obliged to abide by the laws which he had made.

2 And it came to pass that in the first year of the reign of Alma in the judgment-seat, there was a man brought before him to be judged, a man who was large, and was noted for his much strength.

3 And he had gone about among the people, preaching to them that which he termed to be the word of God, bearing down against the church; declaring unto the people that every priest and teacher ought to become popular; and they ought not to labor with their hands, but that they ought to be supported by the people.

4 And he also testified unto the people that all mankind should be saved at the last day, and that they need not fear nor tremble, but that they might lift up their heads and rejoice; for the Lord had created all men, and had also redeemed all men; and, in the end, all men should have eternal life.

5 And it came to pass that he did teach these things so much that many did believe on his words, even so many that they began to support him and give him money.

6 And he began to be lifted up in the pride of his heart, and to wear very costly apparel, yea, and even began to establish a church after the manner of his preaching.

7 And it came to pass as he was going, to preach to those who believed on his word, he met a man who belonged to the church of God, yea, even one of their teachers; and he began to contend with him sharply, that he might lead away the people of the church; but the man withstood him, admonishing him with the words of God.

8 Now the name of the man was Gideon; and it was he who was an instrument in the hands of God in delivering the people of Limhi out of bondage.

9 Now, because Gideon withstood him with the words of God he was wroth with Gideon, and drew his sword and began to smite him. Now Gideon being stricken with many years, therefore he was not able to withstand his blows, therefore he was slain by the sword.

10 And the man who slew him was taken by the people of the church, and was brought before Alma, to be judged according to the crimes which he had committed.

11 And it came to pass that he stood before Alma and pled for himself with much boldness.

12 But Alma said unto him: Behold, this is the first time that priestcraft has been introduced among this people. And behold, thou art not only guilty of priestcraft, but hast endeavored to enforce it by the sword; and were priestcraft to be enforced among this people it would prove their entire destruction.

13 And thou hast shed the blood of a righteous man, yea, a man who has done much good among this people; and were we to spare thee his blood would come upon us for vengeance.

14 Therefore thou art condemned to die, according to the law which has been given us by Mosiah, our last king; and it has been acknowledged by this people; therefore this people must abide by the law.

Notes

15 And it came to pass that they took him; and his name was Nehor; and they carried him upon the top of the hill Manti, and there he was caused, or rather did acknowledge, between the heavens and the earth, that what he had taught to the people was contrary to the word of God; and there he suffered an ignominious death.

Overarching Principle: The practice of priestcraft destroys individuals and then the nation.

vv. 1–15 The practice of priestcraft leads an individual to destruction.

⚡ Ask, *What is priestcraft?* If the class is unable to answer this question, encourage them to look in the Topical Guide to discover the definition. Have the class refer to 2 Nephi 26:29 for a more complete definition of priestcraft.

🔎 Invite class members to search Alma 1:2–6 and highlight all of the characteristics of priestcraft. Write on the board the characteristics that were found in the scriptures. Encourage them to write the word "priestcraft" in their scripture margin.

❓ Analyze: *Why do you think the church members started to support Nehor?*

✋ To help summarize verses 7–15, write the following words on the board: "Contend, wroth, smite, pleaded, condemned, acknowledged, and suffered." Invite class members to find one of these words in these verses and have them share further details that they discovered with the class. Help them understand what happened to Nehor and what led to his death.

🔎 Ask, *What is Alma's warning about priestcraft in verse 12?*

❓ Analyze: *Why would priestcraft prove the entire destruction of the people? How did it destroy Nehor?*

♥ Invite class members to ponder the following questions: *Do Latter-day Saints struggle with priestcraft? What aspect or teaching of priestcraft do you think Latter-day Saints struggle with the most and why?* Invite class members to seek to have no part of priestcraft.

16 Nevertheless, this did not put an end to the spreading of priestcraft through the land; for there were many who loved the vain things of the world, and they went forth preaching false doctrines; and this they did for the sake of riches and honor.

17 Nevertheless, they durst not lie, if it were known, for fear of the law, for liars were punished; therefore they pretended to preach according to their belief; and now the law could have no power on any man for his belief.

18 And they durst not steal, for fear of the law, for such were punished; neither durst they rob, nor murder, for he that murdered was punished unto death.

19 But it came to pass that whosoever did not belong to the church of God began to persecute those that did belong to the church of God, and had taken upon them the name of Christ.

20 Yea, they did persecute them, and afflict them with all manner of words, and this because of their humility; because they were not proud in their own eyes, and because they did impart the word of God, one with another, without money and without price.

21 Now there was a strict law among the people of the church, that there should not any man, belonging to the church, arise and persecute those that did not belong to the church, and that there should be no persecution among themselves.

22 Nevertheless, there were many among them who began to be proud, and began to contend warmly with their adversaries, even unto blows; yea, they would smite one another with their fists.

23 Now this was in the second year of the reign of

Notes

Alma, and it was a cause of much affliction to the church; yea, it was the cause of much trial with the church.

24 For the hearts of many were hardened, and their names were blotted out, that they were remembered no more among the people of God. And also many withdrew themselves from among them.

25 Now this was a great trial to those that did stand fast in the faith; nevertheless, they were steadfast and immovable in keeping the commandments of God, and they bore with patience the persecution which was heaped upon them.

26 And when the priests left their labor to impart the word of God unto the people, the people also left their labors to hear the word of God. And when the priest had imparted unto them the word of God they all returned again diligently unto their labors; and the priest, not esteeming himself above his hearers, for the preacher was no better than the hearer, neither was the teacher any better than the learner; and thus they were all equal, and they did all labor, every man according to his strength.

27 And they did impart of their substance, every man according to that which he had, to the poor, and the needy, and the sick, and the afflicted; and they did not wear costly apparel, yet they were neat and comely.

28 And thus they did establish the affairs of the church; and thus they began to have continual peace again, notwithstanding all their persecutions.

29 And now, because of the steadiness of the church they began to be exceedingly rich, having abundance of all things whatsoever they stood in need—an abundance of flocks and herds, and fatlings of every kind, and also abundance of grain, and of gold, and of silver, and of precious things, and abundance of silk and fine-twined linen, and all manner of good homely cloth.

30 And thus, in their prosperous circumstances, they did not send away any who were naked, or that were hungry, or that were athirst, or that were sick, or that had not been nourished; and they did not set their hearts upon riches; therefore they were liberal to all, both old and young, both bond and free, both male and female, whether out of the church or in the church, having no respect to persons as to those who stood in need.

31 And thus they did prosper and become far more wealthy than those who did not belong to their church.

32 For those who did not belong to their church did indulge themselves in sorceries, and in idolatry or idleness, and in babblings, and in envyings and strife; wearing costly apparel; being lifted up in the pride of their own eyes; persecuting, lying, thieving, robbing, committing whoredoms, and murdering, and all manner of wickedness; nevertheless, the law was put in force upon all those who did transgress it, inasmuch as it was possible.

33 And it came to pass that by thus exercising the law upon them, every man suffering according to that which he had done, they became more still, and durst not commit any wickedness if it were known; therefore, there was much peace among the people of Nephi until the fifth year of the reign of the judges.

vv. 16–33 The practice of priestcraft leads a nation to destruction.

✋ Contrast the following sets of verses and have class members look for how the Lord's way differs from the world's way. Depending on the size of your class, you may consider having class members work in groups.

v. 16 contrast v. 26
v. 19 contrast vv. 27–28
v. 20 contrast v. 21
v. 24 contrast v. 25
vv. 29–31 contrast v. 32

Have the class mark the key differences in their scriptures or write on the board a list of differences as they are found. Take time to

Notes

discuss each difference and how the Lord's way brings contentment and happiness.

💬 Use this quote from Elder Dallin H. Oaks when you feel it is appropriate during the lesson, "Focusing on the needs of the students, a gospel teacher will never obscure their view of the Master by standing in the way or by shadowing the lesson with self-promotion or self-interest. This means that a gospel teacher must never indulge in priest-crafts, which are 'that men preach and set themselves up for a light unto the world, that they may get gain and praise of the world.' A gospel teacher does not preach 'to become popular' or 'for the sake of riches and honor.' He or she follows the marvelous Book of Mormon example in which 'the preacher was no better than the hearer, neither was the teacher any better than the learner.' Both will always look to the Master" (Dallin H. Oaks, "Gospel Teaching," *Ensign*, November 1999, 79).

♥ Invite class members to seek out and be teachers who follow the light, rather than trying to be the light to follow. Additionally, testify of the happiness that can come as we follow the Lord's way and the destruction to ourselves and our nation as we follow those who practice priestcraft.

Teaching Tips from Prophets' Lips "A gospel teacher does not focus on himself or herself. One who understands that principle will not look upon his or her calling as 'giving or presenting a lesson,' because that definition views teaching from the standpoint of the teacher, not the student" (Dallin H. Oaks, "Gospel Teaching," *Ensign*, November 1999, 78).

ALMA 2

The Amlicites Rebel
About 87 BC

1–8, Amlici strives to become king, but the majority reject him; 9–19, He gathers his followers, who make him king, and battles against the Nephites; 20–26, The Amlicites join forces with the Lamanites; 27–38, The Nephites are strengthened; Alma slays Amlici, and the enemy is driven out of the land.

vv. 1–38 "Stump the Teacher" teaching activity.

✋ To teach this chapter, have your class play a game called "Stump the Teacher." In this game, they will read sets of verses and ask questions to stump you that come from the content of those verses. For example, they can't ask, "What is the seventh word is the second verse?" Give them a limited period of time to study the set of verses and come up with a question. Only allow one question per member of the class for each set of verses. The set of verses could be verses 1–8, then verses 9–19, verses 20–26, and verses 27–38. Be sure to pause the game to talk about important doctrines and principles as they are addressed. There are also quotes and insights below that go with some of the verses.

1 And it came to pass in the commencement of the fifth year of their reign there began to be a contention among the people; for a certain man, being called Amlici, he being a very cunning man, yea, a wise man as to the wisdom of the world, he being after the order of the man that slew Gideon by the sword, who was executed according to the law—

2 Now this Amlici had, by his cunning, drawn away much people after him; even so much that they began to be very powerful; and they began to endeavor to establish Amlici to be a king over the people.

3 Now this was alarming to the people of the church, and also to all those who had not been drawn away after the persuasions of Amlici; for they knew that according to their law that such things must be established by the voice of the people.

4 Therefore, if it were possible that Amlici should gain the voice of the people, he, being a wicked man, would deprive them of their rights and privileges of the church; for it was his intent to destroy the church of God.

5 And it came to pass that the people assembled themselves together throughout all the land, every man according to his mind, whether it were for or against Amlici, in separate bodies, having much dispute and wonderful contentions one with another.

6 And thus they did assemble themselves together to cast in their voices concerning the matter; and they were laid before the judges.

7 And it came to pass that the voice of the people came against Amlici, that he was not made king over the people.

8 Now this did cause much joy in the hearts of those who were against him; but Amlici did stir up those who were in his favor to anger against those who were not in his favor.

9 And it came to pass that they gathered themselves together, and did consecrate Amlici to be their king.

10 Now when Amlici was made king over them he commanded them that they should take up arms against their brethren; and this he did that he might subject them to him.

11 Now the people of Amlici were distinguished by the name of Amlici, being called Amlicites; and the remainder were called Nephites, or the people of God.

12 Therefore the people of the Nephites were aware of the intent of the Amlicites, and therefore they did prepare to meet them; yea, they did arm themselves with swords, and with cimeters, and with bows, and with arrows, and with stones, and with slings, and with all manner of weapons of war, of every kind.

13 And thus they were prepared to meet the Amlicites at the time of their coming. And there were appointed captains, and higher captains, and chief captains, according to their numbers.

14 And it came to pass that Amlici did arm his men with all manner of weapons of war of every kind; and he also appointed rulers and leaders over his people, to lead them to war against their brethren.

15 And it came to pass that the Amlicites came upon the hill Amnihu, which was east of the river Sidon, which ran by the land of Zarahemla, and there they began to make war with the Nephites.

16 Now Alma, being the chief judge and the governor of the people of Nephi, therefore he went up with his people, yea, with his captains, and chief captains, yea, at the head of his armies, against the Amlicites to battle.

17 And they began to slay the Amlicites upon the hill east of Sidon. And the Amlicites did contend with the Nephites with great strength, insomuch that many of the Nephites did fall before the Amlicites.

18 Nevertheless the Lord did strengthen the hand of the Nephites, that they slew the Amlicites with great slaughter, that they began to flee before them.

19 And it came to pass that the Nephites did pursue the Amlicites all that day, and did slay them with much slaughter, insomuch that there were slain of the Amlicites twelve thousand five hundred thirty and two souls; and there were slain of the Nephites six thousand five hundred sixty and two souls.

v. 19 Casualties.

♀ Have class members write the numbers of casualties in the margin next to verse 19 and calculate the ratio of Amlicites to Nephites.

Notes

_____

_____

_____

20 And it came to pass that when Alma could pursue the Amlicites no longer he caused that his people should pitch their tents in the valley of Gideon, the valley being called after that Gideon who was slain by the hand of Nehor with the sword; and in this valley the Nephites did pitch their tents for the night.

21 And Alma sent spies to follow the remnant of the Amlicites, that he might know of their plans and their plots, whereby he might guard himself against them, that he might preserve his people from being destroyed.

22 Now those whom he had sent out to watch the camp of the Amlicites were called Zeram, and Amnor, and Manti, and Limher; these were they who went out with their men to watch the camp of the Amlicites.

23 And it came to pass that on the morrow they returned into the camp of the Nephites in great haste, being greatly astonished, and struck with much fear, saying:

24 Behold, we followed the camp of the Amlicites, and to our great astonishment, in the land of Minon, above the land of Zarahemla, in the course of the land of Nephi, we saw a numerous host of the Lamanites; and behold, the Amlicites have joined them;

25 And they are upon our brethren in that land; and they are fleeing before them with their flocks, and their wives, and their children, towards our city; and except we make haste they obtain possession of our city, and our fathers, and our wives, and our children be slain.

26 And it came to pass that the people of Nephi took their tents, and departed out of the valley of Gideon towards their city, which was the city of Zarahemla.

27 And behold, as they were crossing the river Sidon, the Lamanites and the Amlicites, being as numerous almost, as it were, as the sands of the sea, came upon them to destroy them.

28 Nevertheless, the Nephites being strengthened by the hand of the Lord, having prayed mightily to him that he would deliver them out of the hands of their enemies, therefore the Lord did hear their cries, and did strengthen them, and the Lamanites and the Amlicites did fall before them.

29 And it came to pass that Alma fought with Amlici with the sword, face to face; and they did contend mightily, one with another.

30 And it came to pass that Alma, being a man of God, being exercised with much faith, cried, saying: O Lord, have mercy and spare my life, that I may be an instrument in thy hands to save and preserve this people.

31 Now when Alma had said these words he contended again with Amlici; and he was strengthened, insomuch that he slew Amlici with the sword.

vv. 28–31 Prayer can strengthen us in times of need.

In verses 28–30, search for what the Nephites did to overcome the enemy who was much greater than they were.

Analyze: Why does God help those who pray for help?

Ask class members to think of a time that prayer strengthened them. Give them time to write their thoughts in their journals or on a piece of paper. Share a time prayer strengthened you, and then give class members time to share their experiences as well.

32 And he also contended with the king of the Lamanites; but the king of the Lamanites fled back from before Alma and sent his guards to contend with Alma.

33 But Alma, with his guards, contended with the guards of the king of the Lamanites until he slew and drove them back.

34 And thus he cleared the ground, or rather the bank, which was on the west of the river Sidon,

Notes

throwing the bodies of the Lamanites who had been slain into the waters of Sidon, that thereby his people might have room to cross and contend with the Lamanites and the Amlicites on the west side of the river Sidon.

35 And it came to pass that when they had all crossed the river Sidon that the Lamanites and the Amlicites began to flee before them, notwithstanding they were so numerous that they could not be numbered.

36 And they fled before the Nephites towards the wilderness which was west and north, away beyond the borders of the land; and the Nephites did pursue them with their might, and did slay them.

37 Yea, they were met on every hand, and slain and driven, until they were scattered on the west, and on the north, until they had reached the wilderness, which was called Hermounts; and it was that part of the wilderness which was infested by wild and ravenous beasts.

38 And it came to pass that many died in the wilderness of their wounds, and were devoured by those beasts and also the vultures of the air; and their bones have been found, and have been heaped up on the earth.

ALMA 3

The Amlicite Condemnation
About 87–86 BC

1–5, The Amlicites had marked themselves after the manner of the Lamanites; 6–12, The Lamanite curse is reviewed; 13–18, the Amlicite marking is a fulfillment of prophecy; 19–27, man brings upon himself his own condemnation.

1 And it came to pass that the Nephites who were not slain by the weapons of war, after having buried those who had been slain—now the number of the slain were not numbered, because

of the greatness of their number—after they had finished burying their dead they all returned to their lands, and to their houses, and their wives, and their children.

2 Now many women and children had been slain with the sword, and also many of their flocks and their herds; and also many of their fields of grain were destroyed, for they were trodden down by the hosts of men.

3 And now as many of the Lamanites and the Amlicites who had been slain upon the bank of the river Sidon were cast into the waters of Sidon; and behold their bones are in the depths of the sea, and they are many.

4 And the Amlicites were distinguished from the Nephites, for they had marked themselves with red in their foreheads after the manner of the Lamanites; nevertheless they had not shorn their heads like unto the Lamanites.

5 Now the heads of the Lamanites were shorn; and they were naked, save it were skin which was girded about their loins, and also their armor, which was girded about them, and their bows, and their arrows, and their stones, and their slings, and so forth.

vv. 4–5 We should not "mark ourselves" after the manner of the world.

Note with the class that the Amlicites, who were Nephites, intentionally marked themselves to appear as Lamanites. That act brought a curse upon them which led to their destruction. Consider with the class how this example of the Amlicites could apply to us today.

Gordon B. Hinckley has stated, "Now comes the craze of tattooing one's body. I cannot understand why any young man—or young woman, for that matter—would wish to undergo the painful process of disfiguring the skin with various multicolored representations of people, animals, and various symbols. With tattoos, the process is permanent,

Notes

unless there is another painful and costly undertaking to remove it. . . . A tattoo is graffiti on the temple of the body.

"Likewise the piercing of the body for multiple rings in the ears, in the nose, even in the tongue. Can they possibly think that is beautiful? It is a passing fancy, but its effects can be permanent. Some have gone to such extremes that the ring had to be removed by surgery. The First Presidency and the Quorum of the Twelve have declared that we discourage tattoos and also 'the piercing of the body for other than medical purposes.' We do not, however, take any position 'on the minimal piercing of the ears by women for one pair of earrings'" (*Ensign*, November 2000, 52).

♥ Encourage class members to avoid marking themselves after the manner of the world.

6 And the skins of the Lamanites were dark, according to the mark which was set upon their fathers, which was a curse upon them because of their transgression and their rebellion against their brethren, who consisted of Nephi, Jacob, and Joseph, and Sam, who were just and holy men.

7 And their brethren sought to destroy them, therefore they were cursed; and the Lord God set a mark upon them, yea, upon Laman and Lemuel, and also the sons of Ishmael, and Ishmaelitish women.

8 And this was done that their seed might be distinguished from the seed of their brethren, that thereby the Lord God might preserve his people, that they might not mix and believe in incorrect traditions which would prove their destruction.

9 And it came to pass that whosoever did mingle his seed with that of the Lamanites did bring the same curse upon his seed.

10 Therefore, whosoever suffered himself to be led away by the Lamanites was called under that head, and there was a mark set upon him.

11 And it came to pass that whosoever would not believe in the tradition of the Lamanites, but believed those records which were brought out of the land of Jerusalem, and also in the tradition of their fathers, which were correct, who believed in the commandments of God and kept them, were called the Nephites, or the people of Nephi, from that time forth—

12 And it is they who have kept the records which are true of their people, and also of the people of the Lamanites.

13 Now we will return again to the Amlicites, for they also had a mark set upon them; yea, they set the mark upon themselves, yea, even a mark of red upon their foreheads.

14 Thus the word of God is fulfilled, for these are the words which he said to Nephi: Behold, the Lamanites have I cursed, and I will set a mark on them that they and their seed may be separated from thee and thy seed, from this time henceforth and forever, except they repent of their wickedness and turn to me that I may have mercy upon them.

15 And again: I will set a mark upon him that mingleth his seed with thy brethren, that they may be cursed also.

16 And again: I will set a mark upon him that fighteth against thee and thy seed.

17 And again, I say he that departeth from thee shall no more be called thy seed; and I will bless thee, and whomsoever shall be called thy seed, henceforth and forever; and these were the promises of the Lord unto Nephi and to his seed.

18 Now the Amlicites knew not that they were fulfilling the words of God when they began to mark themselves in their foreheads; nevertheless they had come out in open rebellion against God; therefore it was expedient that the curse should fall upon them.

19 Now I would that ye should see that they brought upon themselves the curse; and even so doth every man that is cursed bring upon himself his own condemnation.

Notes

20 Now it came to pass that not many days after the battle which was fought in the land of Zarahemla, by the Lamanites and the Amlicites, that there was another army of the Lamanites came in upon the people of Nephi, in the same place where the first army met the Amlicites.

21 And it came to pass that there was an army sent to drive them out of their land.

22 Now Alma himself being afflicted with a wound did not go up to battle at this time against the Lamanites;

23 But he sent up a numerous army against them; and they went up and slew many of the Lamanites, and drove the remainder of them out of the borders of their land.

24 And then they returned again and began to establish peace in the land, being troubled no more for a time with their enemies.

25 Now all these things were done, yea, all these wars and contentions were commenced and ended in the fifth year of the reign of the judges.

26 And in one year were thousands and tens of thousands of souls sent to the eternal world, that they might reap their rewards according to their works, whether they were good or whether they were bad, to reap eternal happiness or eternal misery, according to the spirit which they listed to obey, whether it be a good spirit or a bad one.

27 For every man receiveth wages of him whom he listeth to obey, and this according to the words of the spirit of prophecy; therefore let it be according to the truth. And thus endeth the fifth year of the reign of the judges.

vv. 19–27 We bring upon ourselves our own condemnation because of our foolish choices.

⚡ Bring a donut or a similar treat to class and ask for a volunteer. Entice the volunteer to eat the treat you brought. Allow him or her to eat it and then explain that you put something harmful in the treat (of course, don't actually put anything harmful in it), and await their

reaction. Ask, *If this was actually harmful, whose fault was it that he/she ate this treat?* Use this object lesson to teach the importance of one's own choices and their resulting consequences.

💬 "There is also an age-old excuse: 'The devil made me do it.' Not so! He can deceive you and mislead you, but he does not have the power to force you or anyone else to transgress or to keep you in transgression" (President Boyd K. Packer, "Cleansing the Inner Vessel," *Ensign,* November, 2010, 74).

🔍 *Look in verse 19 to see how the object lesson and the quote apply together.* Note: The class would need to understand the context of the Amlicite rebellion from chapters 2 and 3 to fully understand this principle.

❓ Analyze: *Why do you think we can't blame others for our choices?*

🔍 *What is Mormon's concluding point of the Amlicite story in verses 26–27?*

❓ Analyze: *What do you think it means to receive wages from him who you obey?*

❓ Apply: *When have you seen righteous choices bring happiness? When has a bad choice brought misery?*

❤ Encourage class members to not allow things or people to entice them to make foolish choices. When foolish choices are made, repentance is available.

Teaching Tips from Prophets' Lips "The calling of the gospel teacher is one of the noblest in the world. The good teacher can make all the difference in inspiring boys and girls and men and women to change their lives and fulfill their highest destiny. The importance of the teacher has been beautifully

Notes

described by Daniel Webster when he said, 'If we work upon marble, it will perish; if we work upon brass, time will efface it; but if we work upon immortal minds, if we imbue them with principles and the just fear of God and love of our fellowman, we engrave upon those tablets something that will brighten through all eternity" (Clyde J. Williams, *The Teachings of Harold B. Lee*, Bookcraft: 1996, 461).

ALMA 4

The Iniquity of the Church Members
About 86–83 BC

1–5, The people were humbled because of the wars and many were baptized as a result; 6–14, Church members become prideful, wicked, and lead many astray because of their example; 15–20, Alma delivers the judgment seat to Nephihah and confines himself to teaching the word of God.

1 Now it came to pass in the sixth year of the reign of the judges over the people of Nephi, there were no contentions nor wars in the land of Zarahemla;

2 But the people were afflicted, yea, greatly afflicted for the loss of their brethren, and also for the loss of their flocks and herds, and also for the loss of their fields of grain, which were trodden under foot and destroyed by the Lamanites.

3 And so great were their afflictions that every soul had cause to mourn; and they believed that it was the judgments of God sent upon them because of their wickedness and their abominations; therefore they were awakened to a remembrance of their duty.

4 And they began to establish the church more fully; yea, and many were baptized in the waters of Sidon and were joined to the church of God; yea, they were baptized by the hand of Alma, who had been consecrated the high priest over the people of the church, by the hand of his father Alma.

5 And it came to pass in the seventh year of the reign of the judges there were about three thousand five hundred souls that united themselves to the church of God and were baptized. And thus ended the seventh year of the reign of the judges over the people of Nephi; and there was continual peace in all that time.

6 And it came to pass in the eighth year of the reign of the judges, that the people of the church began to wax proud, because of their exceeding riches, and their fine silks, and their fine-twined linen, and because of their many flocks and herds, and their gold and their silver, and all manner of precious things, which they had obtained by their industry; and in all these things were they lifted up in the pride of their eyes, for they began to wear very costly apparel.

7 Now this was the cause of much affliction to Alma, yea, and to many of the people whom Alma had consecrated to be teachers, and priests, and elders over the church; yea, many of them were sorely grieved for the wickedness which they saw had begun to be among their people.

8 For they saw and beheld with great sorrow that the people of the church began to be lifted up in the pride of their eyes, and to set their hearts upon riches and upon the vain things of the world, that they began to be scornful, one towards another, and they began to persecute those that did not believe according to their own will and pleasure.

9 And thus, in this eighth year of the reign of the judges, there began to be great contentions among the people of the church; yea, there were envyings, and strife, and malice, and persecutions, and pride, even to exceed the pride of those who did not belong to the church of God.

10 And thus ended the eighth year of the reign of the judges; and the wickedness of the church was a great stumbling-block to those who did not

Notes

belong to the church; and thus the church began to fail in its progress.

11 And it came to pass in the commencement of the ninth year, Alma saw the wickedness of the church, and he saw also that the example of the church began to lead those who were unbelievers on from one piece of iniquity to another, thus bringing on the destruction of the people.

12 Yea, he saw great inequality among the people, some lifting themselves up with their pride, despising others, turning their backs upon the needy and the naked and those who were hungry, and those who were athirst, and those who were sick and afflicted.

vv. 6–12 Riches and pride may prevent progress, while helping the poor perpetuates humility and kindness.

⚡ Bring some weeds to class and place them somewhere where everyone can see them as they enter. After class begins, discuss weeds and why they are so troublesome. Explain that they are going to look for a weed that the Nephites lived with and that we live with today. If we are not careful, this weed can overpower our lives.

✎ Have the following chart written on the board:

What Happens within Four Years?

2nd to 4th years of the reign of the judges Alma 1:26–30	8th and 9th years of the reign of the judges Alma 4:6–11

What is the Weed?

🔍 Use this chart to look for what the members of the church are doing in both columns. Once both columns are completed, ask the class to identify what the weed in the church is.

❓ Analyze: *Why do you think the wearing of costly apparel can lead people to be prideful? How does helping the poor keep people humble?*

♥ Discuss potential local service activities class members can do in your area. Invite your class to do some acts of service during the week, and encourage them to report back to you.

13 Now this was a great cause for lamentations among the people, while others were abasing themselves, succoring those who stood in need of their succor, such as imparting their substance to the poor and the needy, feeding the hungry, and suffering all manner of afflictions, for Christ's sake, who should come according to the spirit of prophecy;

14 Looking forward to that day, thus retaining a remission of their sins; being filled with great joy because of the resurrection of the dead, according to the will and power and deliverance of Jesus Christ from the bands of death.

15 And now it came to pass that Alma, having seen the afflictions of the humble followers of God, and the persecutions which were heaped upon them by the remainder of his people, and seeing all their inequality, began to be very sorrowful; nevertheless the Spirit of the Lord did not fail him.

16 And he selected a wise man who was among the elders of the church, and gave him power according to the voice of the people, that he might have power to enact laws according to the laws which had been given, and to put them in force according to the wickedness and the crimes of the people.

17 Now this man's name was Nephihah, and he was appointed chief judge; and he sat in the judgment-seat to judge and to govern the people.

18 Now Alma did not grant unto him the office of

Notes

being high priest over the church, but he retained the office of high priest unto himself; but he delivered the judgment-seat unto Nephihah.

19 And this he did that he himself might go forth among his people, or among the people of Nephi, that he might preach the word of God unto them, to stir them up in remembrance of their duty, and that he might pull down, by the word of God, all the pride and craftiness and all the contentions which were among his people, seeing no way that he might reclaim them save it were in bearing down in pure testimony against them.

20 And thus in the commencement of the ninth year of the reign of the judges over the people of Nephi, Alma delivered up the judgment-seat to Nephihah, and confined himself wholly to the high priesthood of the holy order of God, to the testimony of the word, according to the spirit of revelation and prophecy.

vv. 15–20 Prophets' teachings will "pull down pride and craftiness" among us and help us become better.

✎ Write, "The Role of a Prophet" on the board and, using the following teaching suggestion, define the role of a prophet with class members.

🔎 Explain that Alma, who is the chief judge of the land, is going to give up his position to teach the people full time. Read verses 15–20 as a class to look for 1) why Alma wants to teach, and 2) what he hopes to accomplish. Write their answers on the board underneath "The Role of a Prophet."

💡 The rest of Alma's life, comprising Alma 5–45, is spent teaching the people throughout the land of the Nephites.

❓ Analyze: *Why do you think Alma was willing to give up so much to teach the people?*

❓ Apply: *In what ways does a prophet do the same thing in our day?*

♥ Help class members understand the importance of the prophet's calling and of his desire to help us return to our Heavenly Father. You may want to review current general conference messages to find modern-day examples of a prophet's teaching.

ALMA 5

"Have You Been Spiritually Born of God?"
About 83 BC

1–13, Alma recounts the temporal and spiritual history of his fathers; 14–17, Alma asks questions regarding the mighty change of heart and personal conversion; 18–26, If man does not repent, he will stand guilty before God with a knowledge of his sins; 27–32, Alma asks concerning specific sins and encourages repentance; 33–42, The Lord is calling for the repentant as the good shepherd calls after his sheep; 43–52, Alma speaks according to his personal testimony, given by the Spirit of the Lord; 53–63, A final invitation to repentance with the promise of eternal life.

1 Now it came to pass that Alma began to deliver the word of God unto the people, first in the land of Zarahemla, and from thence throughout all the land.

2 And these are the words which he spake to the people in the church which was established in the city of Zarahemla, according to his own record, saying:

3 I, Alma, having been consecrated by my father, Alma, to be a high priest over the church of God, he having power and authority from God to do these things, behold, I say unto you that he began to establish a church in the land which was in the borders of Nephi; yea, the land which was called the land of Mormon; yea, and he did baptize his brethren in the waters of Mormon.

4 And behold, I say unto you, they were delivered

Notes

out of the hands of the people of king Noah, by the mercy and power of God.

5 And behold, after that, they were brought into bondage by the hands of the Lamanites in the wilderness; yea, I say unto you, they were in captivity, and again the Lord did deliver them out of bondage by the power of his word; and we were brought into this land, and here we began to establish the church of God throughout this land also.

6 And now behold, I say unto you, my brethren, you that belong to this church, have you sufficiently retained in remembrance the captivity of your fathers? Yea, and have you sufficiently retained in remembrance his mercy and long-suffering towards them? And moreover, have ye sufficiently retained in remembrance that he has delivered their souls from hell?

7 Behold, he changed their hearts; yea, he awakened them out of a deep sleep, and they awoke unto God. Behold, they were in the midst of darkness; nevertheless, their souls were illuminated by the light of the everlasting word; yea, they were encircled about by the bands of death, and the chains of hell, and an everlasting destruction did await them.

8 And now I ask of you, my brethren, were they destroyed? Behold, I say unto you, Nay, they were not.

9 And again I ask, were the bands of death broken, and the chains of hell which encircled them about, were they loosed? I say unto you, Yea, they were loosed, and their souls did expand, and they did sing redeeming love. And I say unto you that they are saved.

10 And now I ask of you on what conditions are they saved? Yea, what grounds had they to hope for salvation? What is the cause of their being loosed from the bands of death, yea, and also the chains of hell?

11 Behold, I can tell you—did not my father Alma believe in the words which were delivered by the mouth of Abinadi? And was he not a holy prophet? Did he not speak the words of God, and my father Alma believe them?

12 And according to his faith there was a mighty change wrought in his heart. Behold I say unto you that this is all true.

13 And behold, he preached the word unto your fathers, and a mighty change was also wrought in their hearts, and they humbled themselves and put their trust in the true and living God. And behold, they were faithful until the end; therefore they were saved.

14 And now behold, I ask of you, my brethren of the church, have ye spiritually been born of God? Have ye received his image in your countenances? Have ye experienced this mighty change in your hearts?

15 Do ye exercise faith in the redemption of him who created you? Do you look forward with an eye of faith, and view this mortal body raised in immortality, and this corruption raised in incorruption, to stand before God to be judged according to the deeds which have been done in the mortal body?

16 I say unto you, can you imagine to yourselves that ye hear the voice of the Lord, saying unto you, in that day: Come unto me ye blessed, for behold, your works have been the works of righteousness upon the face of the earth?

17 Or do ye imagine to yourselves that ye can lie unto the Lord in that day, and say—Lord, our works have been righteous works upon the face of the earth—and that he will save you?

18 Or otherwise, can ye imagine yourselves brought before the tribunal of God with your souls filled with guilt and remorse, having a remembrance of all your guilt, yea, a perfect remembrance of all your wickedness, yea, a remembrance that ye have set at defiance the commandments of God?

19 I say unto you, can ye look up to God at that day with a pure heart and clean hands? I say unto you, can you look up, having the image of God engraven upon your countenances?

Notes

vv. 1–19 All must be born of God and experience a mighty change of heart.

⚡ Ask class members, *How many of you are converts to the Church?* After gathering a response, write "Conversion" on the board. Explain that conversion must be a part of every member of the Church, regardless of when he or she was baptized.

🔍 Ask class members to read Alma 5:1–19 and find as many phrases as they can that are synonymous with "conversion." (Possibilities include "a mighty change of heart," "spiritually born of God," and more.) Discuss the phrases they choose, asking why those particular phrases stood out to them and what each phrase might add to or emphasize about the conversion process.

💬 President Ezra Taft Benson taught, "When we have undergone this mighty change, which is brought about only through faith in Jesus Christ and through the operation of the Spirit upon us, it is as though we have become a new person. Thus, the change is likened to a new birth. Thousands of you have experienced this change. You have forsaken lives of sin, sometimes deep and offensive sin, and through applying the blood of Christ in your lives, have become clean. You have no more disposition to return to your old ways. You are in reality a new person. This is what is meant by a change of heart" (Ezra Taft Benson, "A Mighty Change of Heart," *Ensign*, October 1989).

❤ Being sensitive of becoming overly personal, ask a few class members to share their experiences about conversion. Ask them concerning the circumstances leading to their conversion, what they may have been feeling, how long the conversion process took, and whether it ever ended. Invite class members who feel they have not received a mighty change of heart to seek it.

15 Do ye exercise faith in the redemption of him who created you? Do you look forward with an eye of faith, and view this mortal body raised in immortality, and this corruption raised in incorruption, to stand before God to be judged according to the deeds which have been done in the mortal body?

16 I say unto you, can you imagine to yourselves that ye hear the voice of the Lord, saying unto you, in that day: Come unto me ye blessed, for behold, your works have been the works of righteousness upon the face of the earth?

17 Or do ye imagine to yourselves that ye can lie unto the Lord in that day, and say—Lord, our works have been righteous works upon the face of the earth—and that he will save you?

18 Or otherwise, can ye imagine yourselves brought before the tribunal of God with your souls filled with guilt and remorse, having a remembrance of all your guilt, yea, a perfect remembrance of all your wickedness, yea, a remembrance that ye have set at defiance the commandments of God?

19 I say unto you, can ye look up to God at that day with a pure heart and clean hands? I say unto you, can you look up, having the image of God engraven upon your countenances?

20 I say unto you, can ye think of being saved when you have yielded yourselves to become subjects to the devil?

21 I say unto you, ye will know at that day that ye cannot be saved; for there can no man be saved except his garments are washed white; yea, his garments must be purified until they are cleansed from all stain, through the blood of him of whom it has been spoken by our fathers, who should come to redeem his people from their sins.

22 And now I ask of you, my brethren, how will any of you feel, if ye shall stand before the bar of God, having your garments stained with blood and all manner of filthiness? Behold, what will these things testify against you?

23 Behold will they not testify that ye are murderers,

Notes

yea, and also that ye are guilty of all manner of wickedness?

24 Behold, my brethren, do ye suppose that such an one can have a place to sit down in the kingdom of God, with Abraham, with Isaac, and with Jacob, and also all the holy prophets, whose garments are cleansed and are spotless, pure and white?

25 I say unto you, Nay; except ye make our Creator a liar from the beginning, or suppose that he is a liar from the beginning, ye cannot suppose that such can have place in the kingdom of heaven; but they shall be cast out for they are the children of the kingdom of the devil.

26 And now behold, I say unto you, my brethren, if ye have experienced a change of heart, and if ye have felt to sing the song of redeeming love, I would ask, can ye feel so now?

27 Have ye walked, keeping yourselves blameless before God? Could ye say, if ye were called to die at this time, within yourselves, that ye have been sufficiently humble? That your garments have been cleansed and made white through the blood of Christ, who will come to redeem his people from their sins?

28 Behold, are ye stripped of pride? I say unto you, if ye are not ye are not prepared to meet God. Behold ye must prepare quickly; for the kingdom of heaven is soon at hand, and such an one hath not eternal life.

29 Behold, I say, is there one among you who is not stripped of envy? I say unto you that such an one is not prepared; and I would that he should prepare quickly, for the hour is close at hand, and he knoweth not when the time shall come; for such an one is not found guiltless.

30 And again I say unto you, is there one among you that doth make a mock of his brother, or that heapeth upon him persecutions?

31 Wo unto such an one, for he is not prepared, and the time is at hand that he must repent or he cannot be saved!

32 Yea, even wo unto all ye workers of iniquity; repent, repent, for the Lord God hath spoken it!

33 Behold, he sendeth an invitation unto all men, for the arms of mercy are extended towards them, and he saith: Repent, and I will receive you.

34 Yea, he saith: Come unto me and ye shall partake of the fruit of the tree of life; yea, ye shall eat and drink of the bread and the waters of life freely;

35 Yea, come unto me and bring forth works of righteousness, and ye shall not be hewn down and cast into the fire—

36 For behold, the time is at hand that whosoever bringeth forth not good fruit, or whosoever doeth not the works of righteousness, the same have cause to wail and mourn.

37 O ye workers of iniquity; ye that are puffed up in the vain things of the world, ye that have professed to have known the ways of righteousness nevertheless have gone astray, as sheep having no shepherd, notwithstanding a shepherd hath called after you and is still calling after you, but ye will not hearken unto his voice!

38 Behold, I say unto you, that the good shepherd doth call you; yea, and in his own name he doth call you, which is the name of Christ; and if ye will not hearken unto the voice of the good shepherd, to the name by which ye are called, behold, ye are not the sheep of the good shepherd.

39 And now if ye are not the sheep of the good shepherd, of what fold are ye? Behold, I say unto you, that the devil is your shepherd, and ye are of his fold; and now, who can deny this? Behold, I say unto you, whosoever denieth this is a liar and a child of the devil.

40 For I say unto you that whatsoever is good cometh from God, and whatsoever is evil cometh from the devil.

41 Therefore, if a man bringeth forth good works he hearkeneth unto the voice of the good shepherd, and he doth follow him; but whosoever bringeth forth evil works, the same becometh

Notes

a child of the devil, for he hearkeneth unto his voice, and doth follow him.

42 And whosoever doeth this must receive his wages of him; therefore, for his wages he receiveth death, as to things pertaining unto righteousness, being dead unto all good works.

43 And now, my brethren, I would that ye should hear me, for I speak in the energy of my soul; for behold, I have spoken unto you plainly that ye cannot err, or have spoken according to the commandments of God.

44 For I am called to speak after this manner, according to the holy order of God, which is in Christ Jesus; yea, I am commanded to stand and testify unto this people the things which have been spoken by our fathers concerning the things which are to come.

45 And this is not all. Do ye not suppose that I know of these things myself? Behold, I testify unto you that I do know that these things whereof I have spoken are true. And how do ye suppose that I know of their surety?

46 Behold, I say unto you they are made known unto me by the Holy Spirit of God. Behold, I have fasted and prayed many days that I might know these things of myself. And now I do know of myself that they are true; for the Lord God hath made them manifest unto me by his Holy Spirit; and this is the spirit of revelation which is in me.

47 And moreover, I say unto you that it has thus been revealed unto me, that the words which have been spoken by our fathers are true, even so according to the spirit of prophecy which is in me, which is also by the manifestation of the Spirit of God.

48 I say unto you, that I know of myself that whatsoever I shall say unto you, concerning that which is to come, is true; and I say unto you, that I know that Jesus Christ shall come, yea, the Son, the Only Begotten of the Father, full of grace, and mercy, and truth. And behold, it is he that cometh to take away the sins of the world, yea, the sins of every man who steadfastly believeth on his name.

49 And now I say unto you that this is the order after which I am called, yea, to preach unto my beloved brethren, yea, and every one that dwelleth in the land; yea, to preach unto all, both old and young, both bond and free; yea, I say unto you the aged, and also the middle aged, and the rising generation; yea, to cry unto them that they must repent and be born again.

50 Yea, thus saith the Spirit: Repent, all ye ends of the earth, for the kingdom of heaven is soon at hand; yea, the Son of God cometh in his glory, in his might, majesty, power, and dominion. Yea, my beloved brethren, I say unto you, that the Spirit saith: Behold the glory of the King of all the earth; and also the King of heaven shall very soon shine forth among all the children of men.

51 And also the Spirit saith unto me, yea, crieth unto me with a mighty voice, saying: Go forth and say unto this people—Repent, for except ye repent ye can in nowise inherit the kingdom of heaven.

52 And again I say unto you, the Spirit saith: Behold, the ax is laid at the root of the tree; therefore every tree that bringeth not forth good fruit shall be hewn down and cast into the fire, yea, a fire which cannot be consumed, even an unquenchable fire. Behold, and remember, the Holy One hath spoken it.

53 And now my beloved brethren, I say unto you, can ye withstand these sayings; yea, can ye lay aside these things, and trample the Holy One under your feet; yea, can ye be puffed up in the pride of your hearts; yea, will ye still persist in the wearing of costly apparel and setting your hearts upon the vain things of the world, upon your riches?

54 Yea, will ye persist in supposing that ye are better one than another; yea, will ye persist in the persecution of your brethren, who humble themselves and do walk after the holy order of God, wherewith they have been brought into

Notes

this church, having been sanctified by the Holy Spirit, and they do bring forth works which are meet for repentance—

55 Yea, and will you persist in turning your backs upon the poor, and the needy, and in withholding your substance from them?

56 And finally, all ye that will persist in your wickedness, I say unto you that these are they who shall be hewn down and cast into the fire except they speedily repent.

57 And now I say unto you, all you that are desirous to follow the voice of the good shepherd, come ye out from the wicked, and be ye separate, and touch not their unclean things; and behold, their names shall be blotted out, that the names of the wicked shall not be numbered among the names of the righteous, that the word of God may be fulfilled, which saith: The names of the wicked shall not be mingled with the names of my people;

58 For the names of the righteous shall be written in the book of life, and unto them will I grant an inheritance at my right hand. And now, my brethren, what have ye to say against this? I say unto you, if ye speak against it, it matters not, for the word of God must be fulfilled.

59 For what shepherd is there among you having many sheep doth not watch over them, that the wolves enter not and devour his flock? And behold, if a wolf enter his flock doth he not drive him out? Yea, and at the last, if he can, he will destroy him.

60 And now I say unto you that the good shepherd doth call after you; and if you will hearken unto his voice he will bring you into his fold, and ye are his sheep; and he commandeth you that ye suffer no ravenous wolf to enter among you, that ye may not be destroyed.

61 And now I, Alma, do command you in the language of him who hath commanded me, that ye observe to do the words which I have spoken unto you.

62 I speak by way of command unto you that belong to the church; and unto those who do not belong to the church I speak by way of invitation, saying: Come and be baptized unto repentance, that ye also may be partakers of the fruit of the tree of life.

vv. 1–62 We should examine ourselves and consider the level of our personal conversion.

⚡ Inform class members that you will give them two or three minutes to circle as many questions marks as they can find in Alma 5. (For your information, there are 42 questions asked by Alma in this chapter—that means that two-thirds of the verses contain a question.)

❓ Analyze:
- *Why do you think Alma would ask so many questions in this chapter? What do you think his purpose for asking them is?*
- *Look at a few of the questions. What kinds of questions are being asked? Are they personal or general? Why?*
- *Which questions do you think would be the hardest to answer? Why?* Ask the members of your class to write "2 Corinthians 13:5" somewhere in their margin, and have a class member read the verse aloud. Explain that the Lord wants us to frequently examine ourselves to determine how we are doing spiritually. This is the purpose of Alma's questions.

✏️ Invite class members to take several minutes to think deeply about three or four of Alma's questions. If applicable, ask them to do the following in their journals. You may also consider writing these instructions on the board or preparing a handout:

Choose at least three questions from Alma 5 that stand out to you.

Think about what the questions mean. Check footnotes and surrounding verses to better understand the questions.

Rewrite the questions in your own words.

Notes

Answer the questions as honestly as possible.

Write how you feel about the answers you were able to give.

💬 Many of Alma's questions center around what he calls a "mighty change of heart," or conversion. Elder David A Bednar taught the following: "Conversion is an enlarging, a deepening, and a broadening of the undergirding base of testimony. It is the result of revelation from God, accompanied by individual repentance, obedience, and diligence. Any honest seeker of truth can become converted by experiencing the mighty change of heart and being spiritually born of God. As we honor the ordinances and covenants of salvation and exaltation, "press forward with a steadfastness in Christ," and endure in faith to the end, we become new creatures in Christ. Conversion is an offering of self, of love, and of loyalty we give to God in gratitude for the gift of testimony" (David A. Bednar, "Converted unto the Lord," *Ensign*, November 2012).

♥ Consider preparing some comments on a few of Alma's questions that are personally meaningful to you. Do not be afraid to share your own testimony and opinions. There is often great power in the testimony and words of a faithful teacher. Invite class members to act upon what the Spirit has prompted them to do as they have pondered Alma's questions. Testify that each one of them can have a mighty change of heart and retain a remission of their sins through the atonement of Jesus Christ.

Teaching Tips from Prophets' Lips "Teachers who are commanded to teach 'the principles of [the] gospel' and 'the doctrine of the kingdom' should generally forgo teaching specific rules or applications. For example, they would not teach any rules for determining what is a full tithing, and they would not provide a list of *do's* and *don'ts* for keeping the Sabbath day holy. Once a teacher has taught the doctrine and the associated principles from the scriptures and the living prophets, such specific applications or rules are generally the responsibility of individuals and families" (Dallin H. Oaks, "Gospel Teaching," *Ensign*, November 1999, 78).

ALMA 6
"The Word of God Was Liberal unto All"
About 83 BC

1–6, Alma sets the church in order in Zarahemla; 7–8, Alma preaches in Gideon.

1 And now it came to pass that after Alma had made an end of speaking unto the people of the church, which was established in the city of Zarahemla, he ordained priests and elders, by laying on his hands according to the order of God, to preside and watch over the church.

2 And it came to pass that whosoever did not belong to the church who repented of their sins were baptized unto repentance, and were received into the church.

3 And it also came to pass that whosoever did belong to the church that did not repent of their wickedness and humble themselves before God—I mean those who were lifted up in the pride of their hearts—the same were rejected, and their names were blotted out, that their names were not numbered among those of the righteous.

4 And thus they began to establish the order of the church in the city of Zarahemla.

5 Now I would that ye should understand that the word of God was liberal unto all, that none were deprived of the privilege of assembling themselves together to hear the word of God.

6 Nevertheless the children of God were commanded that they should gather themselves together oft, and join in fasting and mighty

Notes

prayer in behalf of the welfare of the souls of those who knew not God.

7 And now it came to pass that when Alma had made these regulations he departed from them, yea, from the church which was in the city of Zarahemla, and went over upon the east of the river Sidon, into the valley of Gideon, there having been a city built, which was called the city of Gideon, which was in the valley that was called Gideon, being called after the man who was slain by the hand of Nehor with the sword.

8 And Alma went and began to declare the word of God unto the church which was established in the valley of Gideon, according to the revelation of the truth of the word which had been spoken by his fathers, and according to the spirit of prophecy which was in him, according to the testimony of Jesus Christ, the Son of God, who should come to redeem his people from their sins, and the holy order by which he was called. And thus it is written. Amen.

vv. 1–6, United fasting and prayer can bring souls to God.

⚡ Ask class members to respond to the following question, *Have you fasted and prayed for someone to join the Church?* If someone has, invite that person to share their experience.

🔑 Put the phrase "United fasting and prayer can bring souls to God" on the board and invite class members to find which verse in Alma chapter 6 teaches this phrase. Once class members have discovered verse 6, invite them to search the other verses and answer the following question, *How else did the church prepare to bring souls unto God?* (v. 1, ordained priests; v. 3, cleansed the church of those who did not believe; v. 5, allowed all the privilege of hearing the word of God.)

💬 Russell M. Nelson stated, "In gospel-sharing homes we pray for guidance for ourselves, and we pray for the physical and spiritual well-being of others. We pray for the people the missionaries are teaching, for our acquaintances, and for those not of our faith. In the gospel-sharing homes of Alma's time, the people would 'join in fasting and mighty prayer in behalf of the welfare of the souls of those who knew not God' " ("Lessons from the Lord's Prayer," *Ensign,* May 2009, 48).

❤ After sharing the above quote, invite class members to ponder and write down the name of a person that they could fast and pray for. Testify of the power of fasting and prayer in bringing souls to God. Additionally, refer to the experiences of those who answered the first question of this lesson as you end this portion of the lesson.

ALMA 7
Rely on the Atonement of Christ
About 83 BC

1–6, Alma preaches in Gideon in hopes of finding the people firm in the faith; 7–13, Christ shall come among his people to loose the bands of death and take away the sins of the world; 14–16, All must repent and be born again to inherit the kingdom of God; 17–27, All must be spotless to enter the kingdom of God.

1 Behold my beloved brethren, seeing that I have been permitted to come unto you, therefore I attempt to address you in my language; yea, by my own mouth, seeing that it is the first time that I have spoken unto you by the words of my mouth, I having been wholly confined to the judgment-seat, having had much business that I could not come unto you.

2 And even I could not have come now at this time were it not that the judgment-seat hath been given to another, to reign in my stead; and the Lord in much mercy hath granted that I should come unto you.

3 And behold, I have come having great hopes and much desire that I should find that ye had

Notes

humbled yourselves before God, and that ye had continued in the supplicating of his grace, that I should find that ye were blameless before him, that I should find that ye were not in the awful dilemma that our brethren were in at Zarahemla.

4 But blessed be the name of God, that he hath given me to know, yea, hath given unto me the exceedingly great joy of knowing that they are established again in the way of his righteousness.

5 And I trust, according to the Spirit of God which is in me, that I shall also have joy over you; nevertheless I do not desire that my joy over you should come by the cause of so much afflictions and sorrow which I have had for the brethren at Zarahemla, for behold, my joy cometh over them after wading through much affliction and sorrow.

6 But behold, I trust that ye are not in a state of so much unbelief as were your brethren; I trust that ye are not lifted up in the pride of your hearts; yea, I trust that ye have not set your hearts upon riches and the vain things of the world; yea, I trust that you do not worship idols, but that ye do worship the true and the living God, and that ye look forward for the remission of your sins, with an everlasting faith, which is to come.

7 For behold, I say unto you there be many things to come; and behold, there is one thing which is of more importance than they all—for behold, the time is not far distant that the Redeemer liveth and cometh among his people.

8 Behold, I do not say that he will come among us at the time of his dwelling in his mortal tabernacle; for behold, the Spirit hath not said unto me that this should be the case. Now as to this thing I do not know; but this much I do know, that the Lord God hath power to do all things which are according to his word.

9 But behold, the Spirit hath said this much unto me, saying: Cry unto this people, saying—Repent ye, and prepare the way of the Lord, and walk in his paths, which are straight; for behold, the kingdom of heaven is at hand, and the Son of God cometh upon the face of the earth.

10 And behold, he shall be born of Mary, at Jerusalem which is the land of our forefathers, she being a virgin, a precious and chosen vessel, who shall be overshadowed and conceive by the power of the Holy Ghost, and bring forth a son, yea, even the Son of God.

11 And he shall go forth, suffering pains and afflictions and temptations of every kind; and this that the word might be fulfilled which saith he will take upon him the pains and the sicknesses of his people.

12 And he will take upon him death, that he may loose the bands of death which bind his people; and he will take upon him their infirmities, that his bowels may be filled with mercy, according to the flesh, that he may know according to the flesh how to succor his people according to their infirmities.

13 Now the Spirit knoweth all things; nevertheless the Son of God suffereth according to the flesh that he might take upon him the sins of his people, that he might blot out their transgressions according to the power of his deliverance; and now behold, this is the testimony which is in me.

14 Now I say unto you that ye must repent, and be born again; for the Spirit saith if ye are not born again ye cannot inherit the kingdom of heaven; therefore come and be baptized unto repentance, that ye may be washed from your sins, that ye may have faith on the Lamb of God, who taketh away the sins of the world, who is mighty to save and to cleanse from all unrighteousness.

15 Yea, I say unto you come and fear not, and lay aside every sin, which easily doth beset you, which doth bind you down to destruction, yea, come and go forth, and show unto your God that ye are willing to repent of your sins and enter into a covenant with him to keep his commandments, and witness it unto him this day by going into the waters of baptism.

16 And whosoever doeth this, and keepeth the

Notes

commandments of God from thenceforth, the same will remember that I say unto him, yea, he will remember that I have said unto him, he shall have eternal life, according to the testimony of the Holy Spirit, which testifieth in me.

vv. 7–16 We can be clean and born again as we rely on the Atonement of Christ.

⚡ Display four or five pictures of Christ in front of the class. Have class members list as many things that the Savior has done for them as they can. Write the list on the board.

🔍 Have class members read verses 10–13 and add to the list of what the Savior does for us.

✋ Invite class members to reread verses 10–13 and prepare to ask a question about something they do not understand or have questions about the Atonement of Christ. Be prepared to discuss that "succor" means help, relief, aid, and assistance.

🔍 After discussing the Savior's role, ask the class members to look in verses 14–16 for our part in accepting the Atonement of Christ. List our role on the board next to the role of the Savior.

❓ Analyze: *What does it mean to be born again?* Refer to the quote below to discuss what this means.

💬 D. Todd Christofferson stated, "With faith in the merciful Redeemer and His power, potential despair turns to hope. One's very heart and desires change, and the once-appealing sin becomes increasingly abhorrent. A resolve to abandon and forsake the sin and to repair, as fully as one possibly can, the damage he or she has caused now forms in that new heart. This resolve soon matures into a covenant of obedience to God. With that covenant in place, the Holy Ghost, the messenger of divine grace, will bring relief and forgiveness" (The Divine Gift of Repentance," *Ensign,* November 2011).

❤ Invite class members to think about and write down what they learned about the Atonement

of Christ and something they can do to accept it in their lives. Invite all to rely on the Atonement of Christ.

17 And now my beloved brethren, do you believe these things? Behold, I say unto you, yea, I know that ye believe them; and the way that I know that ye believe them is by the manifestation of the Spirit which is in me. And now because your faith is strong concerning that, yea, concerning the things which I have spoken, great is my joy.

18 For as I said unto you from the beginning, that I had much desire that ye were not in the state of dilemma like your brethren, even so I have found that my desires have been gratified.

19 For I perceive that ye are in the paths of righteousness; I perceive that ye are in the path which leads to the kingdom of God; yea, I perceive that ye are making his paths straight.

20 I perceive that it has been made known unto you, by the testimony of his word, that he cannot walk in crooked paths; neither doth he vary from that which he hath said; neither hath he a shadow of turning from the right to the left, or from that which is right to that which is wrong; therefore, his course is one eternal round.

21 And he doth not dwell in unholy temples; neither can filthiness or anything which is unclean be received into the kingdom of God; therefore I say unto you the time shall come, yea, and it shall be at the last day, that he who is filthy shall remain in his filthiness.

22 And now my beloved brethren, I have said these things unto you that I might awaken you to a sense of your duty to God, that ye may walk blameless before him, that ye may walk after the holy order of God, after which ye have been received.

vv. 17–22 We must be spotless in order to enter the kingdom of God.

⚡ Bring to class two items, one that is clean and one that is dirty. Have the class read verse

Notes

_____

_____

_____

21 and ask which item it describes. Have the class mark words in that scripture describing that which is unclean. Next, have the class read verse 25 and mark words describing that which is clean.

🔍 Invite class members to look within verses 21 and 25 in order to see the process of becoming clean. Have them mark what words show how to become clean.

❤ Invite class members to read over the things that they have marked in order to be clean, and choose one in which they can do better. Invite them to work on this one attribute to prepare themselves to one day enter into the kingdom of God.

23 And now I would that ye should be humble, and be submissive and gentle; easy to be entreated; full of patience and long-suffering; being temperate in all things; being diligent in keeping the commandments of God at all times; asking for whatsoever things ye stand in need, both spiritual and temporal; always returning thanks unto God for whatsoever things ye do receive.

24 And see that ye have faith, hope, and charity, and then ye will always abound in good works.

25 And may the Lord bless you, and keep your garments spotless, that ye may at last be brought to sit down with Abraham, Isaac, and Jacob, and the holy prophets who have been ever since the world began, having your garments spotless even as their garments are spotless, in the kingdom of heaven to go no more out.

26 And now my beloved brethren, I have spoken these words unto you according to the Spirit which testifieth in me; and my soul doth exceedingly rejoice, because of the exceeding diligence and heed which ye have given unto my word.

27 And now, may the peace of God rest upon you, and upon your houses and lands, and upon your flocks and herds, and all that you possess, your women and your children, according to your faith and good works, from this time forth and

forever. And thus I have spoken. Amen.

Teaching Tips from Prophets' Lips "If you have properly prepared yourself, the Holy Ghost will enlighten and guide you as you teach. You may receive impressions about those you teach what you should emphasize in teaching them, and how you can teach them most effectively. Your diligent efforts will be magnified as you humbly obey the whisperings of the Spirit" (Teaching, No Greater Call, 47).

ALMA 8

Alma Goes to Ammonihah
About 82 BC

1–5, Alma returns from Gideon, rests, teaches, and baptizes in Melek; 6–13, He is reviled and cast out of Ammonihah; 14–17, An angel commands Alma to return and preach; 18–31, Alma meets Amulek who is also called to teach the people.

vv. 1–32 Scripture Headlines.

⚡ One way to help class members become familiar with the context of the chapter is to divide class members into groups and have them create a newspaper headline for particular sets of verses you give them. Allow them enough time to study the verse and write a headline. Then have each group present and explain their headline. The verse groupings could be as follows: 3–5, 6–13, 14–17, 18–27, 28–32.

1 And now it came to pass that Alma returned from the land of Gideon, after having taught the people of Gideon many things which cannot be written, having established the order of the church, according as he had before done in the land of Zarahemla, yea, he returned to his own house at Zarahemla to rest himself from the labors which he had performed.

Notes

2 And thus ended the ninth year of the reign of the judges over the people of Nephi.

3 And it came to pass in the commencement of the tenth year of the reign of the judges over the people of Nephi, that Alma departed from thence and took his journey over into the land of Melek, on the west of the river Sidon, on the west by the borders of the wilderness.

4 And he began to teach the people in the land of Melek according to the holy order of God, by which he had been called; and he began to teach the people throughout all the land of Melek.

5 And it came to pass that the people came to him throughout all the borders of the land which was by the wilderness side. And they were baptized throughout all the land;

6 So that when he had finished his work at Melek he departed thence, and traveled three days' journey on the north of the land of Melek; and he came to a city which was called Ammonihah.

7 Now it was the custom of the people of Nephi to call their lands, and their cities, and their villages, yea, even all their small villages, after the name of him who first possessed them; and thus it was with the land of Ammonihah.

8 And it came to pass that when Alma had come to the city of Ammonihah he began to preach the word of God unto them.

9 Now Satan had gotten great hold upon the hearts of the people of the city of Ammonihah; therefore they would not hearken unto the words of Alma.

10 Nevertheless Alma labored much in the spirit, wrestling with God in mighty prayer, that he would pour out his Spirit upon the people who were in the city; that he would also grant that he might baptize them unto repentance.

v. 10 The Spirit converts and changes people.

⚡ *If you were going on a mission, what is one thing you might want to pray for in order to have success?* Have class members share their answers.

🔑 Divide your class in half and have one half of your class read verse 10 looking for a principle of prayer, and the other half read the same verse, looking for a principle about the Spirit. Ask some class members to share what they found.

💬 President Ezra Taft Benson stated, "If there is one message I have repeated to my brethren of the Twelve, it is that it's the Spirit that counts. It is the Spirit that matters. I do not know how often I have said this, but I never tire of saying it—it is the Spirit that matters most" (Ezra Taft Benson, Mission Presidents' Seminar, April 3, 1985).

❤ Ask class members to take a few moments to think of someone whose heart they would like to have the Spirit touch and write the response in their journals. Challenge them to pray as Alma did that the Lord my pour His Spirit upon them.

11 Nevertheless, they hardened their hearts, saying unto him: Behold, we know that thou art Alma; and we know that thou art high priest over the church which thou hast established in many parts of the land, according to your tradition; and we are not of thy church, and we do not believe in such foolish traditions.

12 And now we know that because we are not of thy church we know that thou hast no power over us; and thou hast delivered up the judgment-seat unto Nephihah; therefore thou art not the chief judge over us.

13 Now when the people had said this, and withstood all his words, and reviled him, and spit upon him, and caused that he should be cast out of their city, he departed thence and took his journey towards the city which was called Aaron.

14 And it came to pass that while he was journeying thither, being weighed down with sorrow, wading through much tribulation and anguish of soul, because of the wickedness of the people who were in the city of Ammonihah, it came to

Notes

pass while Alma was thus weighed down with sorrow, behold an angel of the Lord appeared unto him, saying:

vv. 11–14 We should feel sorrow for people's wickedness.

🔎 As you read verses 11–13, have class members think of a single word that describes how they would feel after those events. After you have read the verses, have them share the one word they thought of. Afterward, have class members underline words in verse 14 that describe what feelings Alma experienced after being rejected.

❓ Analyze: *What does this teach about Alma as a missionary? Why would it be easy to give up on people if they treated you this way?*

❓ Apply: *How would Alma's example apply to missionaries today?*

❤ Challenge class members to try to be more like Alma and feel sorrow for other people's wrong choices.

15 Blessed art thou, Alma; therefore, lift up thy head and rejoice, for thou hast great cause to rejoice; for thou hast been faithful in keeping the commandments of God from the time which thou receivedst thy first message from him. Behold, I am he that delivered it unto you.

16 And behold, I am sent to command thee that thou return to the city of Ammonihah, and preach again unto the people of the city; yea, preach unto them. Yea, say unto them, except they repent the Lord God will destroy them.

17 For behold, they do study at this time that they may destroy the liberty of thy people, (for thus saith the Lord) which is contrary to the statutes, and judgments, and commandments which he has given unto his people.

18 Now it came to pass that after Alma had received his message from the angel of the Lord he returned speedily to the land of Ammonihah. And he entered the city by another way, yea, by the way which is on the south of the city of Ammonihah.

19 And as he entered the city he was an hungered, and he said to a man: Will ye give to an humble servant of God something to eat?

20 And the man said unto him: I am a Nephite, and I know that thou art a holy prophet of God, for thou art the man whom an angel said in a vision: Thou shalt receive. Therefore, go with me into my house and I will impart unto thee of my food; and I know that thou wilt be a blessing unto me and my house.

vv. 18–20 As we are on the Lord's errand, He will send His angels before us.

🔎 *Look for what the Lord did to help Alma in verses 18–20.*

❓ Analyze: *What does this teach about the role of "angels" when we are on the Lord's errand?*

🔎 In verses 21–27, have class members look for how Amulek was also an angel to Alma, and how Alma was an angel to Amulek and his family.

21 And it came to pass that the man received him into his house; and the man was called Amulek; and he brought forth bread and meat and set before Alma.

22 And it came to pass that Alma ate bread and was filled; and he blessed Amulek and his house, and he gave thanks unto God.

23 And after he had eaten and was filled he said unto Amulek: I am Alma, and am the high priest over the church of God throughout the land.

24 And behold, I have been called to preach the word of God among all this people, according to the spirit of revelation and prophecy; and I was in this land and they would not receive me, but they cast me out and I was about to set my back towards this land forever.

25 But behold, I have been commanded that I should turn again and prophesy unto this people,

Notes

yea, and to testify against them concerning their iniquities.

26 And now, Amulek, because thou hast fed me and taken me in, thou art blessed; for I was an hungered, for I had fasted many days.

27 And Alma tarried many days with Amulek before he began to preach unto the people.

28 And it came to pass that the people did wax more gross in their iniquities.

29 And the word came to Alma, saying: Go; and also say unto my servant Amulek, go forth and prophesy unto this people, saying—Repent ye, for thus saith the Lord, except ye repent I will visit this people in mine anger; yea, and I will not turn my fierce anger away.

30 And Alma went forth, and also Amulek, among the people, to declare the words of God unto them; and they were filled with the Holy Ghost.

31 And they had power given unto them, insomuch that they could not be confined in dungeons; neither was it possible that any man could slay them; nevertheless they did not exercise their power until they were bound in bands and cast into prison. Now, this was done that the Lord might show forth his power in them.

32 And it came to pass that they went forth and began to preach and to prophesy unto the people, according to the spirit and power which the Lord had given them.

ALMA 9

Alma Teaches in Ammonihah
About 82 BC

1–6, The words of the people against Alma; 7–13, Alma teaches that they must repent or be destroyed; 14–25, He contrasts the sins of the Lamanites to the Nephites; 26–30, The Son of God will come and judge all men; 31–34, The people's reaction to Alma's words.

1 And again, I, Alma, having been commanded of God that I should take Amulek and go forth and preach again unto this people, or the people who were in the city of Ammonihah, it came to pass as I began to preach unto them, they began to contend with me, saying:

2 Who art thou? Suppose ye that we shall believe the testimony of one man, although he should preach unto us that the earth should pass away?

3 Now they understood not the words which they spake; for they knew not that the earth should pass away.

4 And they said also: We will not believe thy words if thou shouldst prophesy that this great city should be destroyed in one day.

v. 4 The wicked prophesy their own destruction.

💡 Ask, *Was the city of Ammonihah ever destroyed? How long do you think it took?* Have class members write "Alma 16:9–10" to the side of verse 4 and turn there to see how long it took. Notice that the wicked people were allowed to prophecy of their own destruction.

5 Now they knew not that God could do such marvelous works, for they were a hard-hearted and a stiffnecked people.

6 And they said: Who is God, that sendeth no more authority than one man among this people, to declare unto them the truth of such great and marvelous things?

7 And they stood forth to lay their hands on me; but behold, they did not. And I stood with boldness to declare unto them, yea, I did boldly testify unto them, saying:

8 Behold, O ye wicked and perverse generation, how have ye forgotten the tradition of your fathers; yea, how soon ye have forgotten the commandments of God.

9 Do ye not remember that our father, Lehi, was brought out of Jerusalem by the hand of God?

Notes

Do ye not remember that they were all led by him through the wilderness?

10 And have ye forgotten so soon how many times he delivered our fathers out of the hands of their enemies, and preserved them from being destroyed, even by the hands of their own brethren?

11 Yea, and if it had not been for his matchless power, and his mercy, and his along-suffering towards us, we should unavoidably have been cut off from the face of the earth long before this period of time, and perhaps been consigned to a state of endless misery and woe.

12 Behold, now I say unto you that he commandeth you to repent; and except ye repent, ye can in nowise inherit the kingdom of God. But behold, this is not all—he has commanded you to repent, or he will utterly destroy you from off the face of the earth; yea, he will visit you in his anger, and in his fierce anger he will not turn away.

13 Behold, do ye not remember the words which he spake unto Lehi, saying that: Inasmuch as ye shall keep my commandments, ye shall prosper in the land? And again it is said that: Inasmuch as ye will not keep my commandments ye shall be cut off from the presence of the Lord.

vv. 8–13 We should learn history because history always repeats itself.

🔎 *In verses 8–11, look for what teaching technique Alma uses.* He reflects on history to demonstrate what needs to be done. This is a common pattern that Alma and many other prophets use.

❓ Analyze: *Why is it good to reflect on history?*

💬 "If history repeats itself, and the unexpected always happens, how incapable must Man be of learning from experience." —George Bernard Shaw

❤ Have class members read verse 13 and look for a conclusion we can gain from history. Have your class reflect on scriptural history or world history in the last hundred years and try to identify this pattern found in verse 13.

14 Now I would that ye should remember, that inasmuch as the Lamanites have not kept the commandments of God, they have been cut off from the presence of the Lord. Now we see that the word of the Lord has been verified in this thing, and the Lamanites have been cut off from his presence, from the beginning of their transgressions in the land.

15 Nevertheless I say unto you, that it shall be more tolerable for them in the day of judgment than for you, if ye remain in your sins, yea, and even more tolerable for them in this life than for you, except ye repent.

16 For there are many promises which are extended to the Lamanites; for it is because of the traditions of their fathers that caused them to remain in their state of ignorance; therefore the Lord will be merciful unto them and prolong their existence in the land.

17 And at some period of time they will be brought to believe in his word, and to know of the incorrectness of the traditions of their fathers; and many of them will be saved, for the Lord will be merciful unto all who call on his name.

18 But behold, I say unto you that if ye persist in your wickedness that your days shall not be prolonged in the land, for the Lamanites shall be sent upon you; and if ye repent not they shall come in a time when you know not, and ye shall be visited with utter destruction; and it shall be according to the fierce anger of the Lord.

19 For he will not suffer you that ye shall live in your iniquities, to destroy his people. I say unto you, Nay; he would rather suffer that the Lamanites might destroy all his people who are called the people of Nephi, if it were possible that they could fall into sins and transgressions, after having had so much light and so much knowledge given unto them of the Lord their God;

20 Yea, after having been such a highly favored people of the Lord; yea, after having been favored

Notes

above every other nation, kindred, tongue, or people; after having had all things made known unto them, according to their desires, and their faith, and prayers, of that which has been, and which is, and which is to come;

21 Having been visited by the Spirit of God; having conversed with angels, and having been spoken unto by the voice of the Lord; and having the spirit of prophecy, and the spirit of revelation, and also many gifts, the gift of speaking with tongues, and the gift of preaching, and the gift of the Holy Ghost, and the gift of translation;

22 Yea, and after having been delivered of God out of the land of Jerusalem, by the hand of the Lord; having been saved from famine, and from sickness, and all manner of diseases of every kind; and they having waxed strong in battle, that they might not be destroyed; having been brought out of bondage time after time, and having been kept and preserved until now; and they have been prospered until they are rich in all manner of things—

23 And now behold I say unto you, that if this people, who have received so many blessings from the hand of the Lord, should transgress contrary to the light and knowledge which they do have, I say unto you that if this be the case, that if they should fall into transgression, it would be far more tolerable for the Lamanites than for them.

24 For behold, the promises of the Lord are extended to the Lamanites, but they are not unto you if ye transgress; for has not the Lord expressly promised and firmly decreed, that if ye will rebel against him that ye shall utterly be destroyed from off the face of the earth?

vv. 14–24 Where much is given, much is required.

✋ Ask class members if anyone knows and/or can quote what Doctrine and Covenants 82:3 reads.

❓ Analyze: Turn to the verse, read it, and ask,

What did this verse have to do with the Nephites and Lamanites? Does it say why the Nephites were destroyed but not the Lamanites?

🔎 Invite class members to skim verses 14–24 and mark parts that teach this principle about "where much is given, much is required."

❤ *What does this have to do with our society today? What does it say we need to do as a people?*

25 And now for this cause, that ye may not be destroyed, the Lord has sent his angel to visit many of his people, declaring unto them that they must go forth and cry mightily unto this people, saying: Repent ye, for the kingdom of heaven is nigh at hand;

26 And not many days hence the Son of God shall come in his glory; and his glory shall be the glory of the Only Begotten of the Father, full of grace, equity, and truth, full of patience, mercy, and long-suffering, quick to hear the cries of his people and to answer their prayers.

v. 26 The Lord wants us to be ready for His Second Coming.

🔎 *Look for how soon Alma said the Savior would come in verse 26.*

❓ Analyze: *How long until the Lord was born into the world from when Alma said that? (Have class members look at the time marker at the bottom of their scripture page: 82 BC.)*

❓ Apply: *Who believes the Lord probably will return in their life time? Why can it be good for people to believe that the Lord will come in their lifetime?*

💬 Boyd K. Packer stated, "Teenagers also sometimes think, 'What's the use? The world will soon be blown all apart and come to an end.' That feeling comes from fear, not from faith. No one knows the hour or the day (see Doctrine and Covenants 49:7), but the end cannot come until all of the purposes of the Lord are

Notes

fulfilled. Everything that I have learned from the revelations and from life convinces me that there is time and to spare for you to carefully prepare for a long life. One day you will cope with teenage children of your own. That will serve you right. Later, you will spoil your grandchildren, and they in turn spoil theirs. If an earlier end should happen to come to one, that is more reason to do things right" (Boyd K. Packer, "To Young Women and Men," *Ensign*, May 1989).

♥ Invite class members to always be ready for the Lord's return

27 And behold, he cometh to redeem those who will be baptized unto repentance, through faith on his name.

28 Therefore, prepare ye the way of the Lord, for the time is at hand that all men shall reap a reward of their works, according to that which they have been—if they have been righteous they shall reap the salvation of their souls, according to the power and deliverance of Jesus Christ; and if they have been evil they shall reap the damnation of their souls, according to the power and captivation of the devil.

29 Now behold, this is the voice of the angel, crying unto the people.

30 And now, my beloved brethren, for ye are my brethren, and ye ought to be beloved, and ye ought to bring forth works which are meet for repentance, seeing that your hearts have been grossly hardened against the word of God, and seeing that ye are a lost and a fallen people.

31 Now it came to pass that when I, Alma, had spoken these words, behold, the people were wroth with me because I said unto them that they were a hard-hearted and a stiffnecked people.

32 And also because I said unto them that they were a lost and a fallen people they were angry with me, and sought to lay their hands upon me, that they might cast me into prison.

33 But it came to pass that the Lord did not suffer them that they should take me at that time and cast me into prison.

34 And it came to pass that Amulek went and stood forth, and began to preach unto them also. And now the words of Amulek are not all written, nevertheless a part of his words are written in this book.

Teaching Tips from Prophets' Lips "Please encourage your students to . . . read more slowly and more carefully and with more questions in mind. Help them to ponder, to examine every word, every scriptural gem. Teach them to hold it up to the light, and turn it, look and see what's reflected and refracted there. For some student, on a given day with a given need, such an examination may unearth a treasure hidden in a field: a pearl of great price; a pearl beyond price" (Elder Jeffrey R. Holland, "Students need teachers to guide them," CES Satellite Broadcast, June 29, 1992, 4).

ALMA 10

Amulek Begins Preaching
About 82 BC

1–4, Amulek gives his lineage and biography; he is a descendant of Lehi, who is a descendant of Manasseh; 5–9, Amulek recounts his conversion and experience with an angel and Alma; 10–21, Amulek contends with lawyers; 22–23, the prayers of the righteous spare the wicked from destruction; 24–32, Zeezrom steps forward to contend with Amulek.

1 Now these are the words which Amulek preached unto the people who were in the land of Ammonihah, saying:

2 I am Amulek; I am the son of Giddonah, who was the son of Ishmael, who was a descendant of Aminadi; and it was that same Aminadi who interpreted the writing which was upon the wall of the temple, which was written by the finger of God.

Notes

3 And Aminadi was a descendant of Nephi, who was the son of Lehi, who came out of the land of Jerusalem, who was a descendant of Manasseh, who was the son of Joseph who was sold into Egypt by the hands of his brethren.

4 And behold, I am also a man of no small reputation among all those who know me; yea, and behold, I have many kindreds and friends, and I have also acquired much riches by the hand of my industry.

5 Nevertheless, after all this, I never have known much of the ways of the Lord, and his mysteries and marvelous power. I said I never had known much of these things; but behold, I mistake, for I have seen much of his mysteries and his marvelous power; yea, even in the preservation of the lives of this people.

6 Nevertheless, I did harden my heart, for I was called many times and I would not hear; therefore I knew concerning these things, yet I would not know; therefore I went on rebelling against God, in the wickedness of my heart, even until the fourth day of this seventh month, which is in the tenth year of the reign of the judges.

vv. 1–6 "I was called many times and I would not hear."

⚡ Before class, write on the board this question, *Have you ever received a phone call, knew who it was, and ignored it?* In addition, draw a picture frame on the board with a question mark within the frame, and beneath the picture frame write, "Biography of Amulek" You will use this to teach about Amulek and his conversion. Ask the class the question on the board and allow them to discuss and encourage them to give specific answers as to why they would not answer the phone. Write their answers on the board.

Have you ever received a phone call, knew who it was, and ignored it?

Biography of Amulek

🔍 Read verses 1–6 with your class and invite them to look for every detail about Amulek's life, writing their answers on the board underneath the picture frame. Take time to ensure the class understands what each of these details teaches about Amulek, his life, and his character.

❓ Analyze: Note with the class that Amulek was called many times but would not hear. Make a column on the board directly to the right of the list of Amulek's traits and label it "Distractions". Refer to your list of details about Amulek on the board and ask, *What from this list on the board would serve as a distraction to Amulek which would cause him to not want to 'hear' when the Lord called? Why is it a distraction?* As class members comment, write their answers on the board in the "Distractions" column.

❓ Apply: Explain that the Lord calls us many times through personal revelation or inspiration, yet sometimes we do not hear. Ask, *In what ways does the list of Amulek's distractions apply to us today? How can those distractions get in the way of our hearing the Lord?*

💬 "Casual members are usually very busy with the cares and the things of the world—much as honorable Amulek once was. Called many times, he would not hear. He really knew concerning the truths of the gospel, but Amulek would not acknowledge that he knew" (Neal A. Maxwell, "Settle This in Your Hearts," *Ensign,* November 1992, 66).

Notes

♥ You may want to consider sharing an experience (if not too personal) when you felt you received personal inspiration or direction. You may want to ask class members, *When have you followed a prompting and it blessed someone's life?* You may want to cross-reference Doctrine and Covenants 121:34–35. Encourage class members to not ignore the call of the Lord when it comes.

7 As I was journeying to see a very near kindred, behold an angel of the Lord appeared unto me and said: Amulek, return to thine own house, for thou shalt feed a prophet of the Lord; yea, a holy man, who is a chosen man of God; for he has fasted many days because of the sins of this people, and he is an hungered, and thou shalt receive him into thy house and feed him, and he shall bless thee and thy house; and the blessing of the Lord shall rest upon thee and thy house.

8 And it came to pass that I obeyed the voice of the angel, and returned towards my house. And as I was going thither I found the man whom the angel said unto me: Thou shalt receive into thy house—and behold it was this same man who has been speaking unto you concerning the things of God.

9 And the angel said unto me he is a holy man; wherefore I know he is a holy man because it was said by an angel of God.

10 And again, I know that the things whereof he hath testified are true; for behold I say unto you, that as the Lord liveth, even so has he sent his angel to make these things manifest unto me; and this he has done while this Alma hath dwelt at my house.

11 For behold, he hath blessed mine house, he hath blessed me, and my women, and my children, and my father and my kinsfolk; yea, even all my kindred hath he blessed, and the blessing of the Lord hath rested upon us according to the words which he spake.

vv. 7–11 Amulek relates his experience with Alma.

It is important for your class to understand the story line of this chapter. You may want to paraphrase the rest of the chapter, or read selected verses so the class understands what is transpiring.

12 And now, when Amulek had spoken these words the people began to be astonished, seeing there was more than one witness who testified of the things whereof they were accused, and also of the things which were to come, according to the spirit of prophecy which was in them.

13 Nevertheless, there were some among them who thought to question them, that by their cunning devices they might catch them in their words, that they might find witness against them, that they might deliver them to their judges that they might be judged according to the law, and that they might be slain or cast into prison, according to the crime which they could make appear or witness against them.

14 Now it was those men who sought to destroy them, who were lawyers, who were hired or appointed by the people to administer the law at their times of trials, or at the trials of the crimes of the people before the judges.

15 Now these lawyers were learned in all the arts and cunning of the people; and this was to enable them that they might be skilful in their profession.

16 And it came to pass that they began to question Amulek, that thereby they might make him cross his words, or contradict the words which he should speak.

17 Now they knew not that Amulek could know of their designs. But it came to pass as they began to question him, he perceived their thoughts, and he said unto them: O ye wicked and perverse generation, ye lawyers and hypocrites, for ye are laying the foundations of the devil; for ye are laying traps and snares to catch the holy ones of God.

Notes

18 Ye are laying plans to pervert the ways of the righteous, and to bring down the wrath of God upon your heads, even to the utter destruction of this people.

19 Yea, well did Mosiah say, who was our last king, when he was about to deliver up the kingdom, having no one to confer it upon, causing that this people should be governed by their own voices—yea, well did he say that if the time should come that the voice of this people should choose iniquity, that is, if the time should come that this people should fall into transgression, they would be ripe for destruction.

20 And now I say unto you that well doth the Lord judge of your iniquities; well doth he cry unto this people, by the voice of his angels: Repent ye, repent, for the kingdom of heaven is at hand.

21 Yea, well doth he cry, by the voice of his angels that: I will come down among my people, with equity and justice in my hands.

vv. 12–21 Amulek contends with the lawyers of Ammonihah.

22 Yea, and I say unto you that if it were not for the prayers of the righteous, who are now in the land, that ye would even now be visited with utter destruction; yet it would not be by flood, as were the people in the days of Noah, but it would be by famine, and by pestilence, and the sword.

23 But it is by the prayers of the righteous that ye are spared; now therefore, if ye will cast out the righteous from among you then will not the Lord stay his hand; but in his fierce anger he will come out against you; then ye shall be smitten by famine, and by pestilence, and by the sword; and the time is soon at hand except ye repent.

vv. 22–23 The prayers of the righteous sometimes spare the wicked from physical destruction.

24 And now it came to pass that the people were more angry with Amulek, and they cried out, saying: This man doth revile against our laws which are just, and our wise lawyers whom we have selected.

25 But Amulek stretched forth his hand, and cried the mightier unto them, saying: O ye wicked and perverse generation, why hath Satan got such great hold upon your hearts? Why will ye yield yourselves unto him that he may have power over you, to blind your eyes, that ye will not understand the words which are spoken, according to their truth?

26 For behold, have I testified against your law? Ye do not understand; ye say that I have spoken against your law; but I have not, but I have spoken in favor of your law, to your condemnation.

27 And now behold, I say unto you, that the foundation of the destruction of this people is beginning to be laid by the unrighteousness of your lawyers and your judges.

28 And now it came to pass that when Amulek had spoken these words the people cried out against him, saying: Now we know that this man is a child of the devil, for he hath lied unto us; for he hath spoken against our law. And now he says that he has not spoken against it.

29 And again, he has reviled against our lawyers, and our judges.

30 And it came to pass that the lawyers put it into their hearts that they should remember these things against him.

31 And there was one among them whose name was Zeezrom. Now he was the foremost to accuse Amulek and Alma, he being one of the most expert among them, having much business to do among the people.

32 Now the object of these lawyers was to get gain; and they got gain according to their employ.

Notes

ALMA 11

"Ye Cannot Be Saved in Your Sins"
About 82 BC

1–20, Mormon offers a description of Nephite measurements and wages; 21–25, Zeezrom, a lawyer, questions and tempts Amulek with money; 26–37, Christ will not save men in their sins; 38–46, The resurrection overcomes the bands of death and brings men into the presence of the Father to be judged of their works.

1 Now it was in the law of Mosiah that every man who was a judge of the law, or those who were appointed to be judges, should receive wages according to the time which they labored to judge those who were brought before them to be judged.

2 Now if a man owed another, and he would not pay that which he did owe, he was complained of to the judge; and the judge executed authority, and sent forth officers that the man should be brought before him; and he judged the man according to the law and the evidences which were brought against him, and thus the man was compelled to pay that which he owed, or be stripped, or be cast out from among the people as a thief and a robber.

3 And the judge received for his wages according to his time—a senine of gold for a day, or a senum of silver, which is equal to a senine of gold; and this is according to the law which was given.

4 Now these are the names of the different pieces of their gold, and of their silver, according to their value. And the names are given by the Nephites, for they did not reckon after the manner of the Jews who were at Jerusalem; neither did they measure after the manner of the Jews; but they altered their reckoning and their measure, according to the minds and the circumstances of the people, in every generation, until the reign of the judges, they having been established by king Mosiah.

5 Now the reckoning is thus—a senine of gold, a seon of gold, a shum of gold, and a limnah of gold.

6 A senum of silver, an amnor of silver, an ezrom of silver, and an onti of silver.

7 A senum of silver was equal to a senine of gold, and either for a measure of barley, and also for a measure of every kind of grain.

8 Now the amount of a seon of gold was twice the value of a senine.

9 And a shum of gold was twice the value of a seon.

10 And a limnah of gold was the value of them all.

11 And an amnor of silver was as great as two senums.

12 And an ezrom of silver was as great as four senums.

13 And an onti was as great as them all.

14 Now this is the value of the lesser numbers of their reckoning—

15 A shiblon is half of a senum; therefore, a shiblon for half a measure of barley.

16 And a shiblum is a half of a shiblon.

17 And a leah is the half of a shiblum.

18 Now this is their number, according to their reckoning.

19 Now an antion of gold is equal to three shiblons.

20 Now, it was for the sole purpose to get again, because they received their wages according to their employ, therefore, they did stir up the people to riotings, and all manner of disturbances and wickedness, that they might have more employ, that they might get money according to the suits which were brought before them; therefore they did stir up the people against Alma and Amulek.

vv. 1–20 Interesting details regarding Nephite civilization.

The opening twenty verses of Alma 11 provide a fascinating look at Nephite weights,

Notes

measures, and wages. If there is adequate time, many discussions could be enjoyable, such as the complexity of Nephite civilization, the intricate details of the Book of Mormon society and economy, or evidence of ancient origins for Book of Mormon authorship. However, these verses provide the most insight when used as context for the principles taught in verses immediately following the description.

21 And this Zeezrom began to question Amulek, saying: Will ye answer me a few questions which I shall ask you? Now Zeezrom was a man who was expert in the devices of the devil, that he might destroy that which was good; therefore, he said unto Amulek: Will ye answer the questions which I shall put unto you?

22 And Amulek said unto him: Yea, if it be according to the Spirit of the Lord, which is in me; for I shall say nothing which is contrary to the Spirit of the Lord. And Zeezrom said unto him: Behold, here are six onties of silver, and all these will I give thee if thou wilt deny the existence of a Supreme Being.

23 Now Amulek said: O thou child of hell, why tempt ye me? Knowest thou that the righteous yieldeth to no such temptations?

24 Believest thou that there is no God? I say unto you, Nay, thou knowest that there is a God, but thou lovest that lucre more than him.

25 And now thou hast lied before God unto me. Thou saidst unto me—Behold these six onties, which are of great worth, I will give unto thee—when thou hadst it in thy heart to retain them from me; and it was only thy desire that I should deny the true and living God, that thou mightest have cause to destroy me. And now behold, for this great evil thou shalt have thy reward.

vv. 21–25 The righteous do not yield to worldly temptations, for they love God more than riches.

⚡ Prepare a glass of water and a small candy bar prior to the lesson. When you are ready to begin the lesson, invite a class member to the front of the room. Ask the individual if they would be willing to allow you to dump the cup of water over their head. When he or she seems hesitant, offer the candy to him or her if you are allowed to dump the water on the person's head. Regardless of the response, give the class member the candy and allow him or her to sit down without pouring the water. Ask the class member if the offer made a difference in their willingness to get wet. Ask the entire class, *What would you do for candy or money, and what wouldn't you do? Where would you draw the line?*

🔍 Invite a class member to read Alma 11:22. As he or she reads, ask the class to look for the deal Zeezrom tries to make with Amulek.

❓ Analyze: After reading ask, *How much does Zeezrom offer for Amulek to deny his testimony?*

💬 Have class members quickly scan verses 1–20 and help summarize the information. Then invite someone to read the following quote: "At this juncture, a reader naturally asks, what are "six onties of silver," and how large was the offered bribe? It seems that the Nephite record keepers anticipated these sorts of questions from readers and therefore listed the relative values of the weights and measures used by the Nephites at that time to calculate wealth. Zeezrom's bribe was an impressive sum. A judge earned one onti of silver for seven days of work. Hence, six onties of silver would equal a judge's salary for 42 days of work; or if seven judges were involved in a case, enough to pay them all for a six-day trial" (John W. Welch "Weighing and Measuring in the Worlds of the Book of Mormon," *Journal of Book of Mormon Studies* 8:2 [Provo, UT: Maxwell Institute, 1999] 36–45). Invite class members to consider what 42 days (approximately a month and a half) of their own employment would yield

Notes

monetarily (be sensitive not to ask individuals or have members of the class reveal this information).

❓ Analyze: *Why do you think this would or wouldn't be a challenge for Amulek? Why would Zeezrom offer so much for a denial from Amulek? (See v. 20)* Invite a class member to read verses 23–25 and ask, *What impresses you about Amulek's response? How do you think Amulek had become strong enough to resist such an offer? (See v. 22)*

❓ Apply: *Besides money, in what ways might you or I be tempted to deny something we know for something of the world? What are some ways we can gain strength not to deny what we know by word or action?*

♥ Testify that the Lord will give us strength to be true to our testimonies as we rely on the Holy Ghost and strive to reject the offers of the world.

26 And Zeezrom said unto him: Thou sayest there is a true and living God?

27 And Amulek said: Yea, there is a true and living God.

28 Now Zeezrom said: Is there more than one God?

29 And he answered, No.

30 Now Zeezrom said unto him again: How knowest thou these things?

31 And he said: An angel hath made them known unto me.

32 And Zeezrom said again: Who is he that shall come? Is it the Son of God?

33 And he said unto him, Yea.

34 And Zeezrom said again: Shall he save his people in their sins? And Amulek answered and said unto him: I say unto you he shall not, for it is impossible for him to deny his word.

35 Now Zeezrom said unto the people: See that ye remember these things; for he said there is

but one God; yet he saith that the Son of God shall come, but he shall not save his people—as though he had authority to command God.

36 Now Amulek saith again unto him: Behold thou hast lied, for thou sayest that I spake as though I had authority to command God because I said he shall not save his people in their sins.

37 And I say unto you again that he cannot save them in their sins; for I cannot deny his word, and he hath said that no unclean thing can inherit the kingdom of heaven; therefore, how can ye be saved, except ye inherit the kingdom of heaven? Therefore, ye cannot be saved in your sins.

vv. 26–37 We cannot be saved *in* our sins, but Christ can save us *from* our sins.

⚡ Ask, *Has anyone ever tried to ask you tricky questions to prove you wrong? Has anyone attempted to use your own words against you?*

✋ Invite two class members to play the roles of Amulek and Zeezrom. Consider printing their words out on a separate piece of paper and giving them time before the lesson to prepare and get into character. As they act out verses 26–37, invite the other class members to follow along and listen for the tricky nature of Zeezrom's questions.

❓ Analyze: *Why does Amulek answer the way he does in verse 34? If Christ came to save us, what was the problem with Zeezrom's question?*

✏ Invite class members to circle the word "in" the three times it appears in verses 34 and 37. Then have them circle footnote 34a (Helaman 5:10). Ask a volunteer to read Helaman 5:10. Invite class members to write in the margin of Alma 11, "Christ cannot save us IN our sins, but he will save us FROM our sins if we repent."

♥ Ask class members, *What is the difference between being saved* in *one's sins and* from one's sins? What does it mean to you personally that Christ can save you from your sins? Testify that Christ has the power to save all those who are willing to repent by confessing and forsaking their sins.

38 Now Zeezrom saith again unto him: Is the Son of God the very Eternal Father?

39 And Amulek said unto him: Yea, he is the very Eternal Father of heaven and of earth, and all things which in them are; he is the beginning and the end, the first and the last;

40 And he shall come into the world to redeem his people; and he shall take upon him the transgressions of those who believe on his name; and these are they that shall have eternal life, and salvation cometh to none else.

41 Therefore the wicked remain as though there had been no redemption made, except it be the loosing of the bands of death; for behold, the day cometh that all shall rise from the dead and stand before God, and be judged according to their works.

42 Now, there is a death which is called a temporal death; and the death of Christ shall loose the bands of this temporal death, that all shall be raised from this temporal death.

43 The spirit and the body shall be reunited again in its perfect form; both limb and joint shall be restored to its proper frame, even as we now are at this time; and we shall be brought to stand before God, knowing even as we know now, and have a bright recollection of all our guilt.

44 Now, this restoration shall come to all, both old and young, both bond and free, both male and female, both the wicked and the righteous; and even there shall not so much as a hair of their heads be lost; but every thing shall be restored to its perfect frame, as it is now, or in the body, and shall be brought and be arraigned before the bar of Christ the Son, and God the Father, and the Holy Spirit, which is one Eternal God, to be judged according to their works,

whether they be good or whether they be evil.

45 Now, behold, I have spoken unto you concerning the death of the mortal body, and also concerning the resurrection of the mortal body. I say unto you that this mortal body is raised to an immortal body, that is from death, even from the first death unto life, that they can die no more; their spirits uniting with their bodies, never to be divided; thus the whole becoming spiritual and immortal, that they can no more see corruption.

46 Now, when Amulek had finished these words the people began again to be astonished, and also Zeezrom began to tremble. And thus ended the words of Amulek, or this is all that I have written.

vv. 38–46 We will stand before God in our bodies to be judged according to our works.

👥 Read Alma 11:46 together as a class and ask, *What might have Amulek said to make the arrogant Zeezrom begin to tremble?* Invite class members to pair up with someone next to them, read verses 38–46, and find the doctrine(s) that might have caused Zeezrom to regret his wicked choices and begin to desire repentance.

❓ Analyze: *In verse 43, what do you think the phrase "bright recollection of all our guilt" means? What must we do to soothe the pain of that recollection?*

♥ Testify that every class member will stand before the Father and the Son in their resurrected bodies to be judged for their works in this life. Testify that this could be an event at which we will tremble if unprepared, but if we repent and turn to Jesus Christ we will be ready to meet the Lord.

Teaching Tips from Prophets' Lips "The things of God are of deep import; and time, and experience, and careful and ponderous and solemn thoughts can only find them out" (Joseph Smith, *Teachings of the Prophet Joseph Smith*, 137).

Notes

ALMA 12

The Plan of Redemption
About 82 BC

*1–7, Alma continues Amulek's discussion with Zeez-
rom; 8–19, Zeezrom continues his questions, and
Alma preaches concerning resurrection and the second
death; 20–27, Alma discusses questions regarding the
fall, death, and the plan of redemption; 28–37, The
Lord gave men knowledge and commandments to
bring about repentance and redemption through the
mercy of the Only Begotten.*

1 Now Alma, seeing that the words of Amulek had
silenced Zeezrom, for he beheld that Amulek had
caught him in his lying and deceiving to destroy
him, and seeing that he began to tremble under
a consciousness of his guilt, he opened his mouth
and began to speak unto him, and to establish
the words of Amulek, and to explain things
beyond, or to unfold the scriptures beyond that
which Amulek had done.

2 Now the words that Alma spake unto Zeezrom
were heard by the people round about; for the
multitude was great, and he spake on this wise:

3 Now Zeezrom, seeing that thou hast been taken
in thy lying and craftiness, for thou hast not lied
unto men only but thou hast lied unto God; for
behold, he knows all thy thoughts, and thou
seest that thy thoughts are made known unto us
by his Spirit;

4 And thou seest that we know that thy plan was
a very subtle plan, as to the subtlety of the devil,
for to lie and to deceive this people that thou
mightest set them against us, to revile us and to
cast us out—

5 Now this was a plan of thine adversary, and he
hath exercised his power in thee. Now I would
that ye should remember that what I say unto
thee I say unto all.

6 And behold I say unto you all that this was a
snare of the adversary, which he has laid to catch

this people, that he might bring you into subjection unto him, that he might encircle you about
with his chains, that he might chain you down to
everlasting destruction, according to the power
of his captivity.

7 Now when Alma had spoken these words, Zeezrom began to tremble more exceedingly, for he
was convinced more and more of the power of
God; and he was also convinced that Alma and
Amulek had a knowledge of him, for he was convinced that they knew the thoughts and intents
of his heart; for power was given unto them that
they might know of these things according to
the spirit of prophecy.

8 And Zeezrom began to inquire of them diligently,
that he might know more concerning the kingdom of God. And he said unto Alma: What does
this mean which Amulek hath spoken concerning the resurrection of the dead, that all shall rise
from the dead, both the just and the unjust, and
are brought to stand before God to be judged
according to their works?

9 And now Alma began to expound these things
unto him, saying: It is given unto many to know
the mysteries of God; nevertheless they are laid
under a strict command that they shall not
impart only according to the portion of his word
which he doth grant unto the children of men,
according to the heed and diligence which they
give unto him.

10 And therefore, he that will harden his heart, the
same receiveth the lesser portion of the word;
and he that will not harden his heart, to him is
given the greater portion of the word, until it is
given unto him to know the mysteries of God
until he know them in full.

11 And they that will harden their hearts, to them
is given the lesser portion of the word until they
know nothing concerning his mysteries; and
then they are taken captive by the devil, and
led by his will down to destruction. Now this is
what is meant by the chains of hell.

12 And Amulek hath spoken plainly concerning

Notes

death, and being raised from this mortality to a state of immortality, and being brought before the bar of God, to be judged according to our works.

13 Then if our hearts have been hardened, yea, if we have hardened our hearts against the word, insomuch that it has not been found in us, then will our state be awful, for then we shall be condemned.

14 For our words will condemn us, yea, all our works will condemn us; we shall not be found spotless; and our thoughts will also condemn us; and in this awful state we shall not dare to look up to our God; and we would fain be glad if we could command the rocks and the mountains to fall upon us to hide us from his presence.

15 But this cannot be; we must come forth and stand before him in his glory, and in his power, and in his might, majesty, and dominion, and acknowledge to our everlasting shame that all his judgments are just; that he is just in all his works, and that he is merciful unto the children of men, and that he has all power to save every man that believeth on his name and bringeth forth fruit meet for repentance.

16 And now behold, I say unto you then cometh a death, even a second death, which is a spiritual death; then is a time that whosoever dieth in his sins, as to a temporal death, shall also die a spiritual death; yea, he shall die as to things pertaining unto righteousness.

17 Then is the time when their torments shall be as a lake of fire and brimstone, whose flame ascendeth up forever and ever; and then is the time that they shall be chained down to an everlasting destruction, according to the power and captivity of Satan, he having subjected them according to his will.

18 Then, I say unto you, they shall be as though there had been no redemption made; for they cannot be redeemed according to God's justice; and they cannot die, seeing there is no more corruption.

19 Now it came to pass that when Alma had made an end of speaking these words, the people began to be more astonished;

vv. 1–19 The Lord can reveal the plans of the wicked unto the righteous for their protection and benefit.

Analyze: Have a class member read Alma 12:3–7. Ask, *How do you think Alma was able to know of the adversary's plan to deceive the people? What effect did Alma's discernment have on Zeezrom?* (See also v. 8 for Zeezrom's change of questioning.)

Explain that Alma's ability to know these things is a spiritual gift called the gift of discernment. President James E. Faust described the benefits of that gift as follows: "Satan has had great success with this gullible generation. As a consequence, literally hosts of people have been victimized by him and his angels. There is, however, an ample shield against the power of Lucifer and his hosts. This protection lies in the spirit of discernment through the gift of the Holy Ghost. This gift comes undeviatingly by personal revelation to those who strive to obey the commandments of the Lord and to follow the counsel of the living prophets. This personal revelation will surely come to all whose eyes are single to the glory of God, for it is promised that their bodies will be "filled with light, and there shall be no darkness" in them. Satan's efforts can be thwarted by all who come unto Christ by obedience to the covenants and ordinances of the gospel. The humble followers of the divine Master need not be deceived by the devil. Satan does not sustain and uplift and bless. He leaves those he has grasped in shame and misery. The spirit of God is a sustaining and uplifting influence" (James E. Faust, "Serving the Lord and Resisting the Devil," *Ensign*, September 1995, 6–7).

Bear testimony that the Lord can reveal whatever it takes for His servants to be protected and have success as far the agency of their

Notes

listeners will allow them. Invite class members to pray for the gift of discernment to know the Spirit of God from all others.

20 But there was one Antionah, who was a chief ruler among them, came forth and said unto him: What is this that thou hast said, that man should rise from the dead and be changed from this mortal to an immortal state, that the soul can never die?

21 What does the scripture mean, which saith that God placed cherubim and a flaming sword on the east of the garden of Eden, lest our first parents should enter and partake of the fruit of the tree of life, and live forever? And thus we see that there was no possible chance that they should live forever.

22 Now Alma said unto him: This is the thing which I was about to explain. Now we see that Adam did fall by the partaking of the forbidden fruit, according to the word of God; and thus we see, that by his fall, all mankind became a lost and fallen people.

23 And now behold, I say unto you that if it had been possible for Adam to have partaken of the fruit of the tree of life at that time, there would have been no death, and the word would have been void, making God a liar, for he said: If thou eat thou shalt surely die.

24 And we see that death comes upon mankind, yea, the death which has been spoken of by Amulek, which is the temporal death; nevertheless there was a space granted unto man in which he might repent; therefore this life became a probationary state; a time to prepare to meet God; a time to prepare for that endless state which has been spoken of by us, which is after the resurrection of the dead.

25 Now, if it had not been for the plan of redemption, which was laid from the foundation of the world, there could have been no resurrection of the dead; but there was a plan of redemption laid, which shall bring to pass the resurrection of the dead, of which has been spoken.

26 And now behold, if it were possible that our first parents could have gone forth and partaken of the tree of life they would have been forever miserable, having no preparatory state; and thus the plan of redemption would have been frustrated, and the word of God would have been void, taking none effect.

27 But behold, it was not so; but it was appointed unto men that they must die; and after death, they must come to judgment, even that same judgment of which we have spoken, which is the end.

28 And after God had appointed that these things should come unto man, behold, then he saw that it was expedient that man should know concerning the things whereof he had appointed unto them;

29 Therefore he sent angels to converse with them, who caused men to behold of his glory.

30 And they began from that time forth to call on his name; therefore God conversed with men, and made known unto them the plan of redemption, which had been prepared from the foundation of the world; and this he made known unto them according to their faith and repentance and their holy works.

31 Wherefore, he gave commandments unto men, they having first transgressed the first commandments as to things which were temporal, and becoming as gods, knowing good from evil, placing themselves in a state to act, or being placed in a state to act according to their wills and pleasures, whether to do evil or to do good—

32 Therefore God gave unto them commandments, after having made known unto them the plan of redemption, that they should not do evil, the penalty thereof being a second death, which was an everlasting death as to things pertaining unto righteousness; for on such the plan of redemption could have no power, for the works of justice could not be destroyed, according to the supreme goodness of God.

Notes

33 But God did call on men, in the name of his Son, (this being the plan of redemption which was laid) saying: If ye will repent, and harden not your hearts, then will I have mercy upon you, through mine Only Begotten Son;

34 Therefore, whosoever repenteth, and hardeneth not his heart, he shall have claim on mercy through mine Only Begotten Son, unto a remission of his sins; and these shall enter into my rest.

35 And whosoever will harden his heart and will do iniquity, behold, I swear in my wrath that he shall not enter into my rest.

36 And now, my brethren, behold I say unto you, that if ye will harden your hearts ye shall not enter into the rest of the Lord; therefore your iniquity provoketh him that he sendeth down his wrath upon you as in the first provocation, yea, according to his word in the last provocation as well as the first, to the everlasting destruction of your souls; therefore, according to his word, unto the last death, as well as the first.

37 And now, my brethren, seeing we know these things, and they are true, let us repent, and harden not our hearts, that we provoke not the Lord our God to pull down his wrath upon us in these his second commandments which he has given unto us; but let us enter into the rest of God, which is prepared according to his word.

vv. 20–37 The plan of redemption provides answers to many of life's questions.

⚡ Prior to class, write the following questions on the board:

Why is death part of the plan of redemption?

Why is life on earth part of the plan of redemption?

Why were Adam and Eve asked to leave the Garden?

Why does God give commandments to us during this life?

Why is Jesus Christ so important to the plan?

Explain to the class that Alma 12 provides some of the answers to these questions.

👥 Have class members divide into small groups or partnerships. Instruct the class to study Alma 12:20–37 looking for the answers to these questions. Let them know it is more important to understand two or three questions well than to get to every question. Encourage them to keep track of which verses answer which questions. Invite them to be ready to share what they have learned after an allotted time period. Note: Many of these verses are slightly complicated. If teaching a less-experienced class, you will need to take time to instruct class members on these important doctrines.

ALMA 13

Enter into His Rest
About 82 BC

1–9, The priesthood is eternal; those called into the priesthood were called and prepared before the foundation of the earth; 10–20, Many high priests, including Melchizedek, have entered into the rest of the Lord; 21–31, Repent and prepare for the coming of the Lord.

1 And again, my brethren, I would cite your minds forward to the time when the Lord God gave these commandments unto his children; and I would that ye should remember that the Lord God ordained priests, after his holy order, which was after the order of his Son, to teach these things unto the people.

2 And those priests were ordained after the order of his Son, in a manner that thereby the people might know in what manner to look forward to his Son for redemption.

3 And this is the manner after which they were ordained—being called and prepared from the foundation of the world according to the

Notes

foreknowledge of God, on account of their exceeding faith and good works; in the first place being left to choose good or evil; therefore they having chosen good, and exercising exceedingly great faith, are called with a holy calling, yea, with that holy calling which was prepared with, and according to, a preparatory redemption for such.

4 And thus they have been called to this holy calling on account of their faith, while others would reject the Spirit of God on account of the hardness of their hearts and blindness of their minds, while, if it had not been for this they might have had as great privilege as their brethren.

5 Or in fine, in the first place they were on the same standing with their brethren; thus this holy calling being prepared from the foundation of the world for such as would not harden their hearts, being in and through the atonement of the Only Begotten Son, who was prepared—

6 And thus being called by this holy calling, and ordained unto the high priesthood of the holy order of God, to teach his commandments unto the children of men, that they also might enter into his rest—

7 This high priesthood being after the order of his Son, which order was from the foundation of the world; or in other words, being without beginning of days or end of years, being prepared from eternity to all eternity, according to his foreknowledge of all things—

8 Now they were ordained after this manner— being called with a holy calling, and ordained with a holy ordinance, and taking upon them the high priesthood of the holy order, which calling, and ordinance, and high priesthood, is without beginning or end—

9 Thus they become high priests forever, after the order of the Son, the Only Begotten of the Father, who is without beginning of days or end of years, who is full of grace, equity, and truth. And thus it is. Amen.

vv. 1–9 Brethren were foreordained for priesthood responsibilities.

Invite the class to take a true/false test about the priesthood. Do not allow them to use their scriptures until they have answered all of the questions. Read or write down each question and have class members write down their answers on a piece of paper.

1. The role of the high priest is to help the people know how to look forward to the Son for redemption. (v. 2)

2. Those who have the priesthood were called and prepared from the foundation of the world. (v. 3)

3. We had agency in the premortal life. (v. 3)

4. Some rejected the Spirit of God in the premortal life; therefore, they were not given the privilege of bearing the priesthood. (v. 4).

5. In the premortal life, all had the same opportunity to bear the priesthood on this earth. (v. 5)

6. The role of the priesthood is to teach the commandments so that all may enter into His rest. (v. 6)

7. The priesthood is without beginning or end. (v. 7)

8. The priesthood calling is without beginning or end. (vv. 8–9)

Answer each question by turning to the associated verse. Allow class members to learn the doctrine through the scriptures. All of the answers are true; however, use the scriptures to answer each of the questions before revealing this to the class.

Ask, *Which of these doctrines of the gospel most compel you to be an honorable priesthood holder or help you sustain priesthood holders*? Invite class members to share what they will do in the coming weeks to live according to the doctrines taught in Alma 13.

Notes

10 Now, as I said concerning the holy order, or this high priesthood, there were many who were ordained and became high priests of God; and it was on account of their exceeding faith and repentance, and their righteousness before God, they choosing to repent and work righteousness rather than to perish;

11 Therefore they were called after this holy order, and were sanctified, and their garments were washed white through the blood of the Lamb.

12 Now they, after being sanctified by the Holy Ghost, having their garments made white, being pure and spotless before God, could not look upon sin save it were with abhorrence; and there were many, exceedingly great many, who were made pure and entered into the rest of the Lord their God.

13 And now, my brethren, I would that ye should humble yourselves before God, and bring forth fruit meet for repentance, that ye may also enter into that rest.

14 Yea, humble yourselves even as the people in the days of Melchizedek, who was also a high priest after this same order which I have spoken, who also took upon him the high priesthood forever.

15 And it was this same Melchizedek to whom Abraham paid tithes; yea, even our father Abraham paid tithes of one-tenth part of all he possessed.

16 Now these ordinances were given after this manner, that thereby the people might look forward on the Son of God, it being a type of his order, or it being his order, and this that they might look forward to him for a remission of their sins, that they might enter into the rest of the Lord.

17 Now this Melchizedek was a king over the land of Salem; and his people had waxed strong in iniquity and abomination; yea, they had all gone astray; they were full of all manner of wickedness;

18 But Melchizedek having exercised mighty faith, and received the office of the high priesthood according to the holy order of God, did preach repentance unto his people. And behold, they did repent; and Melchizedek did establish peace in the land in his days; therefore he was called the prince of peace, for he was the king of Salem; and he did reign under his father.

19 Now, there were many before him, and also there were many afterwards, but none were greater; therefore, of him they have more particularly made mention.

20 Now I need not rehearse the matter; what I have said may suffice. Behold, the scriptures are before you; if ye will wrest them it shall be to your own destruction.

vv. 10–20 None were greater than Melchizedek.

⚡ Ask, *Who was Melchizedek?* If the class does not know how to answer this question, allow them time to look up the name in the Bible Dictionary. Help them find the answer on their own rather than simply giving the answer to them.

🔍 Read verse 19 regarding the greatness of Melchizedek. Have class members search verses 14–18 to find out why Melchizedek was regarded so highly. Invite them to find the one thing that made him so great.

♥ Invite class members who are priesthood holders to pattern their priesthood service after Melchizedek. If time allows, ask them, *What would Melchizedek do if he were fulfilling priesthood responsibilities in our day?*

21 And now it came to pass that when Alma had said these words unto them, he stretched forth his hand unto them and cried with a mighty voice, saying: Now is the time to repent, for the day of salvation draweth nigh;

22 Yea, and the voice of the Lord, by the mouth of angels, doth declare it unto all nations; yea, doth declare it, that they may have glad tidings of great joy; yea, and he doth sound these glad tidings among all his people, yea, even to them

Notes

that are scattered abroad upon the face of the earth; wherefore they have come unto us.

23 And they are made known unto us in plain terms, that we may understand, that we cannot err; and this because of our being wanderers in a strange land; therefore, we are thus highly favored, for we have these glad tidings declared unto us in all parts of our vineyard.

24 For behold, angels are declaring it unto many at this time in our land; and this is for the purpose of preparing the hearts of the children of men to receive his word at the time of his coming in his glory.

25 And now we only wait to hear the joyful news declared unto us by the mouth of angels, of his coming; for the time cometh, we know not how soon. Would to God that it might be in my day; but let it be sooner or later, in it I will rejoice.

26 And it shall be made known unto just and holy men, by the mouth of angels, at the time of his coming, that the words of our fathers may be fulfilled, according to that which they have spoken concerning him, which was according to the spirit of prophecy which was in them.

27 And now, my brethren, I wish from the inmost part of my heart, yea, with great anxiety even unto pain, that ye would hearken unto my words, and cast off your sins, and not procrastinate the day of your repentance;

28 But that ye would humble yourselves before the Lord, and call on his holy name, and watch and pray continually, that ye may not be tempted above that which ye can bear, and thus be led by the Holy Spirit, becoming humble, meek, submissive, patient, full of love and all long-suffering;

29 Having faith on the Lord; having a hope that ye shall receive eternal life; having the love of God always in your hearts, that ye may be lifted up at the last day and enter into his rest.

30 And may the Lord grant unto you repentance, that ye may not bring down his wrath upon you, that ye may not be bound down by the chains of hell, that ye may not suffer the second death.

31 And Alma spake many more words unto the people, which are not written in this book.

vv. 21–31 Now is the time to repent.

🔍 Write the following instructions on the board: "Read verses 21–31 and determine why Alma has talked at such great length about the doctrine of the priesthood and the example of Melchizedek. What does he want the people to learn or do?"

❓ Analyze: *How is repentance connected with the Priesthood?*

❤ The priesthood provides the ordinances that allow us to be baptized and return to live with our Heavenly Father and enter His rest. Invite all class members to receive the necessary ordinances through the priesthood to enter into His rest. Ask two or three individuals how the ordinances of the priesthood have allowed them to feel more prepared to return to the Father.

Teaching Tips from Prophets' Lips "[Class members'] decision to participate is an exercise in agency that permits the Holy Ghost to communicate a personalized message suited to their individual needs. Creating an atmosphere of participation enhances the probability that the Spirit will teach more important lessons than you can communicate" (Elder Richard G. Scott, "Helping Others to Be Spiritually Led," CES Symposium, August 11, 1998, 3).

ALMA 14
When Bad Things Happen to Good People
About 82–81 BC

1–5, The people are angry with Alma and Amulek because of their words; 6–7, Zeezrom regrets his

Notes

_____

_____

_____

opposition and pleads for Alma and Amulek; 8–13, Alma and Amulek are forced to watch the martyrdom of the believers; 14–23, They are taken, bound, and mistreated for many days; 24–29, Through their faith, they are miraculously delivered from bondage when the prison walls tumble down.

1 And it came to pass after he had made an end of speaking unto the people many of them did believe on his words, and began to repent, and to search the scriptures.

2 But the more part of them were desirous that they might destroy Alma and Amulek; for they were angry with Alma, because of the plainness of his words unto Zeezrom; and they also said that Amulek had lied unto them, and had reviled against their law and also against their lawyers and judges.

3 And they were also angry with Alma and Amulek; and because they had testified so plainly against their wickedness, they sought to put them away privily.

4 But it came to pass that they did not; but they took them and bound them with strong cords, and took them before the chief judge of the land.

5 And the people went forth and witnessed against them—testifying that they had reviled against the law, and their lawyers and judges of the land, and also of all the people that were in the land; and also testified that there was but one God, and that he should send his Son among the people, but he should not save them; and many such things did the people testify against Alma and Amulek. Now this was done before the chief judge of the land.

6 And it came to pass that Zeezrom was astonished at the words which had been spoken; and he also knew concerning the blindness of the minds, which he had caused among the people by his lying words; and his soul began to be harrowed up under a consciousness of his own guilt; yea, he began to be encircled about by the pains of hell.

7 And it came to pass that he began to cry unto the people, saying: Behold, I am guilty, and these men are spotless before God. And he began to plead for them from that time forth; but they reviled him, saying: Art thou also possessed with the devil? And they spit upon him, and cast him out from among them, and also all those who believed in the words which had been spoken by Alma and Amulek; and they cast them out, and sent men to cast stones at them.

8 And they brought their wives and children together, and whosoever believed or had been taught to believe in the word of God they caused that they should be cast into the fire; and they also brought forth their records which contained the holy scriptures, and cast them into the fire also, that they might be burned and destroyed by fire.

9 And it came to pass that they took Alma and Amulek, and carried them forth to the place of martyrdom, that they might witness the destruction of those who were consumed by fire.

10 And when Amulek saw the pains of the women and children who were consuming in the fire, he also was pained; and he said unto Alma: How can we witness this awful scene? Therefore let us stretch forth our hands, and exercise the power of God which is in us, and save them from the flames.

11 But Alma said unto him: The Spirit constraineth me that I must not stretch forth mine hand; for behold the Lord receiveth them up unto himself, in glory; and he doth suffer that they may do this thing, or that the people may do this thing unto them, according to the hardness of their hearts, that the judgments which he shall exercise upon them in his wrath may be just; and the blood of the innocent shall stand as a witness against them, yea, and cry mightily against them at the last day.

12 Now Amulek said unto Alma: Behold, perhaps they will burn us also.

13 And Alma said: Be it according to the will of

Notes

the Lord. But, behold, our work is not finished; therefore they burn us not.

vv. 1–13 Trials happen for many reasons; God allows the innocent to suffer in order to bring justice upon the wicked.

⚡ Write "Why do bad things happen to good people?" on the board. Ask class members to raise their hands if they have ever heard this question before. Ask, *Keep your answer to yourself, but do you feel like you could give a good answer to the questioner?* Explain that there are many possible answers to this question, but today we will just look at one or two.

🔍 *Skim Alma 14:1–5 and look for the reaction of the people toward Alma's and Amulek's teaching. Ask, What are some of the things the people did or said that show they had rejected Alma's message?*

❓ Analyze: Invite a class member to read verses 6–7.
- *What do you think about Zeezrom's reaction?*
- *What kind of attitude does it show?*
- *What do you think shows that Zeezrom's repentance is legitimate?*
- *If Zeezrom has repented, why are these terrible things happening to him?*

Under the question on the board write, "God allows for the natural consequences of our actions." Explain that even though Zeezrom had begun the repentance process, God could not rescind all of the consequences of his actions or his guilt. He had been stirring up the people for some time against Alma, Amulek, and the believers—much of the damage was already done. Ask class members to read verses 8–13 to themselves, then ask the following:

- *Why does God allow so many innocent women and children to go through such terrible trials?*
- *Why do you think would God constrain Alma from acting by the Spirit?*
- *Why can this story be considered just? What evidence is there in the verses that God is being both just and merciful?*

Write on the board, "Sometimes God allows the innocent to suffer so that justice can come upon the wicked. The innocent are received into glory."

❤ Acknowledge that watching innocent or good people suffer can be extremely difficult. It was difficult for Alma and Amulek to watch, and it is difficult for the Lord to watch. Explain that God cannot restrict the agency of man and must allow for consequences to occur. Testify that God is perfectly just and merciful and that all will be worked out by Him in the next life.

14 Now it came to pass that when the bodies of those who had been cast into the fire were consumed, and also the records which were cast in with them, the chief judge of the land came and stood before Alma and Amulek, as they were bound; and he smote them with his hand upon their cheeks, and said unto them: After what ye have seen, will ye preach again unto this people, that they shall be cast into a lake of fire and brimstone?

15 Behold, ye see that ye had not power to save those who had been cast into the fire; neither has God saved them because they were of thy faith. And the judge smote them again upon their cheeks, and asked: What say ye for yourselves?

16 Now this judge was after the order and faith of Nehor, who slew Gideon.

17 And it came to pass that Alma and Amulek answered him nothing; and he smote them again, and delivered them to the officers to be cast into prison.

18 And when they had been cast into prison three days, there came many lawyers, and judges, and priests, and teachers, who were of the profession of Nehor; and they came in unto the prison to see them, and they questioned them about many words; but they answered them nothing.

Notes

19 And it came to pass that the judge stood before them, and said: Why do ye not answer the words of this people? Know ye not that I have power to deliver you up unto the flames? And he commanded them to speak; but they answered nothing.

20 And it came to pass that they departed and went their ways, but came again on the morrow; and the judge also smote them again on their cheeks. And many came forth also, and smote them, saying: Will ye stand again and judge this people, and condemn our law? If ye have such great power why do ye not deliver yourselves?

21 And many such things did they say unto them, gnashing their teeth upon them, and spitting upon them, and saying: How shall we look when we are damned?

22 And many such things, yea, all manner of such things did they say unto them; and thus they did mock them for many days. And they did withhold food from them that they might hunger, and water that they might thirst; and they also did take from them their clothes that they were naked; and thus they were bound with strong cords, and confined in prison.

23 And it came to pass after they had thus suffered for many days, (and it was on the twelfth day, in the tenth month, in the tenth year of the reign of the judges over the people of Nephi) that the chief judge over the land of Ammonihah and many of their teachers and their lawyers went in unto the prison where Alma and Amulek were bound with cords.

24 And the chief judge stood before them, and smote them again, and said unto them: If ye have the power of God deliver yourselves from these bands, and then we will believe that the Lord will destroy this people according to your words.

25 And it came to pass that they all went forth and smote them, saying the same words, even until the last; and when the last had spoken unto them the power of God was upon Alma and Amulek, and they rose and stood upon their feet.

26 And Alma cried, saying: How long shall we suffer these great afflictions, O Lord? O Lord, give us strength according to our faith which is in Christ, even unto deliverance. And they broke the cords with which they were bound; and when the people saw this, they began to flee, for the fear of destruction had come upon them.

27 And it came to pass that so great was their fear that they fell to the earth, and did not obtain the outer door of the prison; and the earth shook mightily, and the walls of the prison were rent in twain, so that they fell to the earth; and the chief judge, and the lawyers, and priests, and teachers, who smote upon Alma and Amulek, were slain by the fall thereof.

28 And Alma and Amulek came forth out of the prison, and they were not hurt; for the Lord had granted unto them power, according to their faith which was in Christ. And they straightway came forth out of the prison; and they were loosed from their bands; and the prison had fallen to the earth, and every soul within the walls thereof, save it were Alma and Amulek, was slain; and they straightway came forth into the city.

29 Now the people having heard a great noise came running together by multitudes to know the cause of it; and when they saw Alma and Amulek coming forth out of the prison, and the walls thereof had fallen to the earth, they were struck with great fear, and fled from the presence of Alma and Amulek even as a goat fleeth with her young from two lions; and thus they did flee from the presence of Alma and Amulek.

vv. 14–29 God will not abandon His servants. The righteous who remain faithful and patient will eventually triumph.

Invite class members to take turns reading verses 14–29 out loud. You may choose to go down rows, around in a circle, or however best fits your setting. This is a powerful story. Follow the promptings of the Spirit to stop and discuss verses, ask questions,

Notes

and allow class members to share what they think about what they are reading.

❤ Testify that though trials and tribulation may seem long, the Lord never leaves His servants. All of God's children who stay faithful to Him will eventually triumph over any difficulty that might face them. Invite class members to share personal examples or testify of these principles.

ALMA 15

"Thou Canst Be Healed"
About 81 BC

1–12, Alma and Amulek go to Sidom to heal and baptize Zeezrom; 13–19, The church is established in Sidom, Alma and Amulek return to Zarahemla.

1 And it came to pass that Alma and Amulek were commanded to depart out of that city; and they departed, and came out even into the land of Sidom; and behold, there they found all the people who had departed out of the land of Ammonihah, who had been cast out and stoned, because they believed in the words of Alma.

2 And they related unto them all that had happened unto their wives and children, and also concerning themselves, and of their power of deliverance.

3 And also Zeezrom lay sick at Sidom, with a burning fever, which was caused by the great tribulations of his mind on account of his wickedness, for he supposed that Alma and Amulek were no more; and he supposed that they had been slain because of his iniquity. And this great sin, and his many other sins, did harrow up his mind until it did become exceedingly sore, having no deliverance; therefore he began to be scorched with a burning heat.

4 Now, when he heard that Alma and Amulek were in the land of Sidom, his heart began to

take courage; and he sent a message immediately unto them, desiring them to come unto him.

5 And it came to pass that they went immediately, obeying the message which he had sent unto them; and they went in unto the house unto Zeezrom; and they found him upon his bed, sick, being very low with a burning fever; and his mind also was exceedingly sore because of his iniquities; and when he saw them he stretched forth his hand, and besought them that they would heal him.

6 And it came to pass that Alma said unto him, taking him by the hand: Believest thou in the power of Christ unto salvation?

7 And he answered and said: Yea, I believe all the words that thou hast taught.

8 And Alma said: If thou believest in the redemption of Christ thou canst be healed.

9 And he said: Yea, I believe according to thy words.

10 And then Alma cried unto the Lord, saying: O Lord our God, have mercy on this man, and heal him according to his faith which is in Christ.

11 And when Alma had said these words, Zeezrom leaped upon his feet, and began to walk; and this was done to the great astonishment of all the people; and the knowledge of this went forth throughout all the land of Sidom.

12 And Alma baptized Zeezrom unto the Lord; and he began from that time forth to preach unto the people.

vv. 1–12 If you believe in Christ, you can be healed.

✋ Invite class members to read verses 3–12 and be prepared to share the lesson they learned with the class. Before the class members begin, remind them of who Zeezrom was, what he had done, and how he was removed from the city where Alma and Amulek were preaching. Possible lessons include but are not limited to: "Our sins can cause physical illness" (v. 3 "burning heat"); "If you believe

Notes

in Christ, you can be healed" (v. 8); and "We can repent and return to God." Encourage class members to share their own insights.

❓ Analyze: To help further the discussion and increase their understanding, ask class members follow-up questions based on their answers.

- *Why is it that Zeezrom was scorched by a burning heat? Can our sins affect our physical health?*
- *There are many instances where an individual has faith in Christ but is not healed of a physical illness. Why is that the case? Was Zeezrom's illness physical or spiritual?*
- *What does this experience teach us about repentance and the power of the Atonement?*

♥ After class members have shared the lessons they have learned, invite all to write down what the Spirit taught them.

13 And Alma established a church in the land of Sidom, and consecrated priests and teachers in the land, to baptize unto the Lord whosoever were desirous to be baptized.

14 And it came to pass that they were many; for they did flock in from all the region round about Sidom, and were baptized.

15 But as to the people that were in the land of Ammonihah, they yet remained a hard-hearted and a stiffnecked people; and they repented not of their sins, ascribing all the power of Alma and Amulek to the devil; for they were of the profession of Nehor, and did not believe in the repentance of their sins.

16 And it came to pass that Alma and Amulek, Amulek having forsaken all his gold, and silver, and his precious things, which were in the land of Ammonihah, for the word of God, he being rejected by those who were once his friends and also by his father and his kindred;

17 Therefore, after Alma having established the church at Sidom, seeing a great check, yea, seeing that the people were checked as to the pride of their hearts, and began to humble themselves before God, and began to assemble themselves together at their sanctuaries to worship God before the altar, watching and praying continually, that they might be delivered from Satan, and from death, and from destruction—

18 Now as I said, Alma having seen all these things, therefore he took Amulek and came over to the land of Zarahemla, and took him to his own house, and did administer unto him in his tribulations, and strengthened him in the Lord.

19 And thus ended the tenth year of the reign of the judges over the people of Nephi.

vv. 16–19 A disciple of Christ is willing to sacrifice, even if the blessings are not seen immediately.

🔎 Read verses 16–18 and look for what Amulek gave up for the gospel of Jesus Christ.

❓ Analyze:
- *Why do you think Amulek needs to be administered to?*
- *Do these verses give any indication of the blessings that Amulek received because he gave up all that he had to follow the Lord?*
- *What does Amulek teach us about being a disciple of Christ?*

♥ *When have you seen someone serve the Lord even though it was not convenient or easy? How has that strengthened your resolve to follow Christ?* Invite class members to follow the Lord, even when the blessings are not seen immediately.

Teaching Tips from Prophets' Lips "It is wise to fear that our own skills are inadequate to meet the charge we have to nourish the faith of others. Our own abilities, however great, will not be enough. But that realistic view of our limitations creates a humility which can lead to dependence on the Spirit and thus to power" (Henry B. Eyring, "Feed My Lambs," *Ensign*, November 1997, 82–83).

Notes

ALMA 16

The Wicked Destroy the Wicked
About 81–77 BC

1–3, Lamanites destroy the people of Ammonihah; 4–12, Nephites retaliate and are victorious over the Lamanites; 13–21, The word of God is preached throughout the land, and the Lord pours His blessings on the people.

1 And it came to pass in the eleventh year of the reign of the judges over the people of Nephi, on the fifth day of the second month, there having been much peace in the land of Zarahemla, there having been no wars nor contentions for a certain number of years, even until the fifth day of the second month in the eleventh year, there was a cry of war heard throughout the land.

2 For behold, the armies of the Lamanites had come in upon the wilderness side, into the borders of the land, even into the city of Ammonihah, and began to slay the people and destroy the city.

3 And now it came to pass, before the Nephites could raise a sufficient army to drive them out of the land, they had destroyed the people who were in the city of Ammonihah, and also some around the borders of Noah, and taken others captive into the wilderness.

4 Now it came to pass that the Nephites were desirous to obtain those who had been carried away captive into the wilderness.

5 Therefore, he that had been appointed chief captain over the armies of the Nephites, (and his name was Zoram, and he had two sons, Lehi and Aha)—now Zoram and his two sons, knowing that Alma was high priest over the church, and having heard that he had the spirit of prophecy, therefore they went unto him and desired of him to know whither the Lord would that they should go into the wilderness in search of their brethren, who had been taken captive by the Lamanites.

6 And it came to pass that Alma inquired of the Lord concerning the matter. And Alma returned and said unto them: Behold, the Lamanites will cross the river Sidon in the south wilderness, away up beyond the borders of the land of Manti. And behold there shall ye meet them, on the east of the river Sidon, and there the Lord will deliver unto thee thy brethren who have been taken captive by the Lamanites.

7 And it came to pass that Zoram and his sons crossed over the river Sidon, with their armies, and marched away beyond the borders of Manti into the south wilderness, which was on the east side of the river Sidon.

8 And they came upon the armies of the Lamanites, and the Lamanites were scattered and driven into the wilderness; and they took their brethren who had been taken captive by the Lamanites, and there was not one soul of them had been lost that were taken captive. And they were brought by their brethren to possess their own lands.

9 And thus ended the eleventh year of the judges, the Lamanites having been driven out of the land, and the people of Ammonihah were destroyed; yea, every living soul of the Ammonihahites was destroyed, and also their great city, which they said God could not destroy, because of its greatness.

10 But behold, in one day it was left desolate; and the carcasses were mangled by dogs and wild beasts of the wilderness.

11 Nevertheless, after many days their dead bodies were heaped up upon the face of the earth, and they were covered with a shallow covering. And now so great was the scent thereof that the people did not go in to possess the land of Ammonihah for many years. And it was called Desolation of Nehors; for they were of the profession of Nehor, who were slain; and their lands remained desolate.

12 And the Lamanites did not come again to war against the Nephites until the fourteenth year of the reign of the judges over the people of Nephi. And thus for three years did the people of Nephi

Notes

have continual peace in all the land.

vv. 1–3, 9–11 The judgments of God will overtake the wicked.

⚡ Invite class members to turn to Mormon 4:5 and highlight the three principles that are taught by Mormon: 1) The judgments of God will overtake the wicked. 2) It is by the wicked that the wicked are punished. 3) It is the wicked who stir up the hearts of the children of men unto bloodshed.

👥 Divide the class into groups and have each group read verses 1–3 and 9–11. Invite each group to discuss which of the teachings of Mormon highlighted above best fits the assigned scriptures. Have each group share their thoughts and discoveries.

♥ As each group highlights why these truths are applicable and meaningful, invite them to understand that the wicked will always be punished, even if it is not how or when we think they deserve it.

13 And Alma and Amulek went forth preaching repentance to the people in their temples, and in their sanctuaries, and also in their synagogues, which were built after the manner of the Jews.

14 And as many as would hear their words, unto them they did impart the word of God, without any respect of persons, continually.

15 And thus did Alma and Amulek go forth, and also many more who had been chosen for the work, to preach the word throughout all the land. And the establishment of the church became general throughout the land, in all the region round about, among all the people of the Nephites.

16 And there was no inequality among them; the Lord did pour out his Spirit on all the face of the land to prepare the minds of the children of men, or to prepare their hearts to receive the word which should be taught among them at the time of his coming—

17 That they might not be hardened against the word, that they might not be unbelieving, and go on to destruction, but that they might receive the word with joy, and as a branch be grafted into the true vine, that they might enter into the rest of the Lord their God.

18 Now those priests who did go forth among the people did preach against all lyings, and deceivings, and envyings, and strifes, and malice, and revilings, and stealing, robbing, plundering, murdering, committing adultery, and all manner of lasciviousness, crying that these things ought not so to be—

19 Holding forth things which must shortly come; yea, holding forth the coming of the Son of God, his sufferings and death, and also the resurrection of the dead.

20 And many of the people did inquire concerning the place where the Son of God should come; and they were taught that he would appear unto them after his resurrection; and this the people did hear with great joy and gladness.

21 And now after the church had been established throughout all the land—having got the victory over the devil, and the word of God being preached in its purity in all the land, and the Lord pouring out his blessings upon the people—thus ended the fourteenth year of the reign of the judges over the people of Nephi.

vv. 13–21 The word of God, taught in purity, is key to building the kingdom of God.

⚡ Bring or write on the board the following items: Scriptures, a car, a companion, name tag, *Preach My Gospel*, and Missionary Handbook (the rules of a mission). Ask, *Which item is most useful on a mission and why?* After the class members respond, testify of the power of the word of God in missionary work.

🔑 Invite class members to scan verses 14–21, highlighting the words "word" or "word of God."

Notes

❓ Analyze: *According to the scriptures, what are the conditions needed for anyone to receive the word of God?* Invite class members to look in their scriptures where they have highlighted "word" or "word of God" to find the answer. Possible answers include:

> v. 14 The learner must be willing to hear the words.
>
> v. 14 It must be taught without any respect to persons.
>
> v. 14 It must be taught continually.
>
> vv. 16–17 The Lord's spirit must prepare the heart to receive the word with joy.
>
> v. 21 The word must be taught in purity.

Write these responses on the board.

❓ Analyze: *Are one of these conditions more important than the other? Is there one of them that is not necessary?*

❓ Apply: *What do you learn about the importance and power of the word of God?*

♥ Share or invite a class member to share a time when the word of God brought someone to the Lord and His church. Testify of the power of the word of God taught in purity.

Notes

_____

_____

_____

APPENDIX

Chapters that can be combined into one lesson

1 NEPHI 12–15

Nephi's Vision

This activity will permit you to effectively cover much of the content of Nephi's vision in a short amount of time while focusing on keeping class members engaged. The activity does not teach chapter 11, which you could teach separately as an introduction to the vision. As it is particularly suited for youth and young adults, make sure to appropriately adapt the activity for the age group you are teaching.

• Invite class members to get into groups of two or three, but no larger.

• Prior to class, make several copies of the accompanying questions and cut them into strips. Plan to have enough sets of question strips to allow each partnership to have the same question at the same time. (For example, if there are thirty members of your class, you may have 15 groups, make sure you have 15 copies of question strip #1, 15 copies of question strip #2, etc.)

• Explain to the class that each partnership will start with question strip #1 and they will be required to search 1 Nephi chapters 12–15 for the answer. The question strips will not always provided the exact location of the answer, but they will give at least a general location. The answers will be found in the order they appear in the chapters allowing participants to focus their search.

• When partnerships have determined the correct response for the question slip, one participant will need to come to the front of the room and verbally give you the answer. If they are correct in answering, give them the next question slip for which they will then return to their seat to find the answer. Once they have determined the next answer, the other partner will approach you to answer. If they are incorrect in answering, they should return to their seat and search again. Give plenty of hints and help as needed. Class members unfamiliar with scriptural language may need additional assistant. Repeat this process for each of the question slips.

• Consider having a master copy of question answers available to speed the checking process. Avoid being overly competitive; however, encouraging a quick moving environment can be fun for class members.

• For the final question slip, ask several students to share their answers so as to enable deeper class discussion and testimony on selected principles.

Question Slips:

1. What does Nephi see in 1 Nephi 12:6 (see footnotes)? Where in the Book of Mormon can its fulfillment be found?

2. Who will judge the twelve tribes of Israel? (1 Nephi 12)

3. What blinds the eyes and hardens the hearts of the children of men? (1 Nephi 12)

4. Who is the group that will dwindle in unbelief and become full of idleness and abominations? (1 Nephi 12)

5. An historical figure is described in 1 Nephi 13:12. Who do you think he might be?

6. What historical event is described in 1 Nephi 13:16–19? What additional detail does the Book of Mormon give that history books don't?

7. What book is described in 1 Nephi 13:20–23?

8. Read 1 Nephi 13:24–29? How did the Bible change over time? Give an example.

9. What event is 1 Nephi 13:35–36 referring to?

10. Which verse describes the 'other books' that will come forth? (1 Nephi 13)

11. According to the next verse, name at least two purposes of the other books.(1 Nephi 13)

12. In addition to being called the Lamb, Jesus is also referred to in this chapter by another name—it is related to lambs. What is it? (1 Nephi 13)

13. Read 1 Nephi 14:10. What word could you replace "churches" with that would help you understand this verse better?

14. Give an example you have seen of 1 Nephi 14:14?

15. Nephi wanted to write about this and he couldn't . . . but John in the New Testament could and did. What is it? And what Book is it written in? (1 Nephi 14:18–30)

16. When Laman and Lemuel don't "inquire of the Lord" what do they end up doing with each other? How might inquiring of the Lord have helped them avoid it? (1 Nephi 15)

17. Read 1 Nephi 15:7–11. What formula does Nephi give for personal revelation?

18. What promise is given to you in 1 Nephi 15:23–24? How is this promise obtained?

19. How does Nephi describe his attempts to get Laman and Lemuel to "give heed to the word of God' and keep the commandments? (1 Nephi 15)

20. Prepare a summary of your favorite insights to share with the class.

Answers to Question Slips:

1. Jesus Christ's visit to the Americas—3 Nephi 11

2. The Twelve Apostles—1 Nephi 12:9

3. The mists of darkness or temptations of the devil—1 Nephi 12:17

4. The descendants of Laman and Lemuel—1 Nephi 12:20–23

5. Columbus

6. The American Revolution in which the Lord aided the American victory.

7. The Bible

8. Plain and precious parts were removed like the nature of the Godhead, the necessity for baptism by immersion, priesthood ordinances and conferral, etc.

9. The coming forth of the Book of Mormon

10. Verse 39

11. Establish the truth of the first (Book of Mormon), restore lost plain and precious truths, and testify that salvation comes through Christ

12. Shepherd over all the earth—1 Nephi 13:41

13. Groups, organizations, choices, plans, etc.

14. Gift of the Holy Ghost, missionary work, temple ordinances, other personal experiences

15. The end of the world—1 Nephi 14:22

16. Disputing one with another

17. Harden not your hearts, ask in faith, believe that ye shall receive, keep the commandments

18. Never perish or be overcome by temptation—holding fast to the word of God

19. "I did exhort them with all the energies of my soul, and with all the faculty which I possessed"

20. Class sharing

2 NEPHI 11–25

"For he verily saw my Redeemer"

⚡ Ask, *If you could pick anyone to teach you about Jesus Christ, whom would you choose? What qualifications would be preferable in a teacher?* Allow class members to discuss their responses.

🔍 Have class members read 2 Nephi 11:1–3 and look for whom Nephi chooses to teach about the Savior and why he thinks they are qualified. Write on the board, "Isaiah saw Jesus Christ."

❓ Ask, *How many of you have heard that Isaiah is difficult to understand? Why do you think it can be difficult to understand?* Explain that Nephi gives us a tip about understanding Isaiah in 2 Nephi 25:4. Read the verse and ask, *What does Nephi say one needs to understand the words of Isaiah?* Write on the board, "Isaiah is plain to those with the spirit of prophecy."

✏️ Invite class members to write Revelation 19:10 in the margin on 2 Nephi 25:4. Have a class member read the verse while the rest of the class listens for the definition of "the spirit of prophecy". Write on the board, "The testimony of Jesus is the Spirit of Prophecy."

❓ Point out that you have written the following on the board:

Isaiah saw Jesus Christ (2 Nephi 11:1–3)

Isaiah is plain to those with the spirit of prophecy (2 Nephi 25:4)

The testimony of Jesus is the spirit of prophecy (Revelation 19:10)

Ask, *Knowing what we have learned, how should someone approach the Isaiah chapters to gain the greatest spiritual prospective?* Explain that while much studying is required to gain knowledge concerning everything Isaiah teaches about the Savior, in this lesson we will be able to quickly discern powerful teachings by concentrating on what Isaiah directly spoke concerning Christ.

✋ The accompanying handout will allow you to cover seven sets of verses that focus on the Savior in the Isaiah chapters. You may distribute the handout to your class and have them work on it individually or in small groups. Be sure to monitor the class and assess how much help will be required for class members to complete the activity. Take time after the activity to discuss what class members have learned. If your circumstances require, you may also choose to work through the handout together as a class.

Worksheet for 2 Nephi 11–25

The following verses are examples of Isaiah's focus on Jesus Christ. Read the verses from Isaiah the answer the complete the corresponding questions or activities.

1. **2 Nephi 14:4–6** What could these verses teach about repentance through Christ's atonement? What might the storm represent? The place of refuge?

   _____
   _____
   _____

2. **2 Nephi 16:1–8** What similarities can you see between Isaiah's vision and renewing our covenants with Christ through the ordinance of the sacrament? Who might the angels and the live coal represent (see footnotes)? What or who has the power to cleanse you?

   _____
   _____
   _____

3. **2 Nephi 17:14** The name Immanuel means "God with us" in Hebrew. Why is this a good name for Jesus in regards to his birth? Why would the Father choose this type of birth for his son?

   _____
   _____
   _____

4. **2 Nephi 18:13–14** How can the Savior be considered both a sanctuary and a 'stone of stumbling'? How can you make sure that he is a sanctuary for you and your family?

   _____
   _____
   _____

5. **2 Nephi 19:6–7** This is another prophecy concerning the birth of Christ and his future. There are 5 descriptive titles for the Lord in this verse (wonderful, counselor, etc). Which is your favorite? In your own life, how have you seen Him act in that regard?

   _____
   _____
   _____

6. **Nephi 21:1–10** Read the chapter heading and Doctrine and Covenants 113:1–2 to help understand this passage about the millennial reign of Christ. What phrase is the most powerful to you? Why? 2 Nephi 22

   _____
   _____
   _____

7. **2 Nephi 22** Read this chapter. Think about Isaiah's words. How would you express the same feelings that Isaiah is expressing? What would you say?

   _____
   _____
   _____

MOSIAH 2–5
A Manual for Discipleship

⚡ Bring with you to class a manual of some type (owner's manual, how-to book, directions to electronics or appliances, etc.). Show it to the class and ask, *What is the purpose of this document? Why is it beneficial to have? What becomes more difficult if you don't have it?* Write on the board, "A Manual Discipleship." Explain that the scriptures provide us a manual for following Christ. Elder Neal A. Maxwell specifically called King Benjamin's Sermon (Mosiah 2–5) "a manual for discipleship" ("King Benjamin's Speech: That Ye May Learn Wisdom" [Provo, UT: Foundation for Ancient and Modern Research and Mormon Studies, 1998], 1–21).

👥 Explain that you would like you class to create an abridged version of King Benjamin's Manual for Discipleship.

Divide that class into four groups (if your class is large you can ask class members to get in pairs within the larger four groups).

Assign each of the four groups a chapter from Mosiah 2–5.

Invite the groups to study their assigned chapters looking for ways to complete the following sentence: "In order to be a true disciple of Jesus, I must . . ." Ask class members to come up with 3 or 4 ways to complete the phrase and to keep track of the verses they used in their sentences.

After the groups have come up with their sentences, ask them to decide on a section title for their part of the Manual for Discipleship. This will require the groups to provide a basic summary of overall message of their chapter in Mosiah.

Invite the groups to share what they have learned, pointing the class to specific verses from the scriptures. If time permits have class members or a class scribe write what the groups share on the board.

❓ *As you look at the different principles of discipleship from these chapters, can you think of any examples of people in your life that live them?*

- *What effect have those individuals had on you and others around them?*
- *What would the world around you be like if everyone lived according to these principles?"*

❤ Prior to class pick something from King Benjamin's sermon that has had an influence in your life. Bear testimony of the blessing of discipleship for those who follow Jesus Christ.

INDEX

A

Abinadi
Mosiah 11–17

Abrahamic Covenant
1 Nephi 15:18, 1 Nephi 17:40, 2 Nephi 29:14

Adam's transgression
2 Nephi 2, Mosiah 3:11–19

agency
2 Nephi 2, 2 Nephi 10:23, 2 Nephi 26:10, Mosiah 2:21, Mosiah 5:1–8, Alma 12:31–34

Alma the Elder
Mosiah 21–29

Alma the Elder, conversion of
Mosiah 17:1–4, Mosiah 18:1–7

Alma the Younger
Alma 1:11–15

Alma the Younger, conversion of
Mosiah 27:8–25

Ammon, conversion of
Mosiah 27:8–25,

Amulek
Alma 8:20–32, Alma 10:1–31

Amulek, teachings of
Alma 11

Apostasy of individuals
1 Nephi 8:23–28, Jacob 2–3

Apostasy of the church
1 Nephi 13: 5–9, 2 Nephi 28, Mosiah 11:1–7, Alma 4:6–12, Jacob 4:15–18, Jacob 5

Atonement
1 Nephi 21:14–16, 2 Nephi 9, Mosiah 14, Mosiah 15:5–13, Jacob 4:5–13

Atonement, change through
Mosiah 3:19, Mosiah 4:1–16

Atonement, crucifixion
2 Nephi 10:3–7

Atonement, redeems from sin
2 Nephi 16:1–8, Mosiah 27:25–31, Alma 7:7–16, Alma 11:26–37, Enos 1:1–8

Atonement, salvation through
2 Nephi 2:3–9, 2 Nephi 25:23–26, Mosiah 3:5–19, Mosiah 13:27–28, 32–33

B

baptism
2 Nephi 9:23, 2 Nephi 31:4–20, Mosiah 18:7–29, Alma 5:58–62, Alma 9:27

belief or believe
1 Nephi 2:11–18, 1 Nephi 11:1–5, 2 Nephi 33:10–12, Mosiah 26:1–5, Alma 15:1–12

Bible, missing books
1 Nephi 19:10

Bible, plain and precious parts
1 Nephi 13:24–29, 2 Nephi 29:3–7

Book of Mormon
Words of Mormon 1: 3–5, 2 Nephi 26:14–16, 2 Nephi 27:6–26, 2 Nephi 29:8–10

C

calling
Jacob 1:19, Jacob 2:3, Alma 13:3–8

charity
2 Nephi 26:30, 2 Nephi 33:7–9, Alma 7:24

comfort
2 Nephi 8:12, Mosiah 18:9

commandments, keeping
1 Nephi 3:7, 1 Nephi 17: 2 Nephi 2:26–27, 2 Nephi 12:4–22, Mosiah 13:12–24, Jacob 6

commandments lead to happiness
2 Nephi 2:26–27, 2 Nephi 5:6–34, Jarom 1:3–9, Mosiah 2:41

consequences
1 Nephi 14:1–7, 1 Nephi 20:18, 2 Nephi 13:1–15, Mosiah 12:2–8, Mosiah 15:26–27, Mosiah 21:1–16, Alma 3:19–27

conversion
1 Nephi 2:11–16, Enos 1:1–5, Mosiah 28:1–9, Alma 5:1–19, Alma 7:7–16, Enos 1:9–18

covenant
1 Nephi 20:1–4, 2 Nephi 7–8, Mosiah 5:1–15

covenant, baptismal
Mosiah 18:7–29

curse
1 Nephi 2:23, 2 Nephi 1:7, 2 Nephi 4:6, 2 Nephi 5:21–24

D

death, physical
2 Nephi 9:1–12, Mosiah 15:8, Mosiah 16:8–9, Alma 12:23–24

death, spiritual
2 Nephi 9:10–12, Alma 5:7, Alma 12:16–32

devil
1 Nephi 12:17–20, 2 Nephi 2:17–22, 2 Nephi 28:20–23

E

Enos
Enos 1

F

faith
1 Nephi 7:16–18, Enos 1:8, Mosiah 5:1–2, 7, Mosiah 22:1–15, Mosiah 25:18–24

faith, acting in
1 Nephi 4:1–6, Mosiah 17:5–20

faithful
1 Nephi 3:16, 1 Nephi 14:9–17

Fall, effects of
1 Nephi 10:4–6, 2 Nephi 2:1–4, 2 Nephi 2:25, 2 Nephi 9:6–12, Mosiah 2:32–40, Mosiah 3:19–21, Mosiah 16:1–15

forgiveness
1 Nephi 7:19–21, Mosiah 27:25–31

G

God, be faithful to
1 Nephi 7:6–12, Omni 1:26, Mosiah 10:12–22

God, dependence on
Mosiah 2:19–26

God, gratitude toward
2 Nephi 4:15–35,

God, help through trials
1 Nephi 3, Mosiah 10:1–11, Mosiah 23:21–29, Alma 14:1–13, Jacob 4:1–4

God, love of
1 Nephi 11:8–33

God, tender mercies of
1 Nephi 1:20

Godhead
Mosiah 15:1–4

grace
2 Nephi 10:24, 2 Nephi 25:23

H

heart
1 Nephi 2:11–16, 2 Nephi 2:3–9, Jacob 3:1–2

Holy Ghost
1 Nephi 16:27–29, 1 Nephi 17:45–55, 2 Nephi 31:4–20, 2 Nephi 32:7–9, 2 Nephi 33:1–3, Jacob 7:1–27

I

Israel, gathering of
1 Nephi 15:12–20, 1 Nephi 21, 1 Nephi 22:6–9

J

Jesus Christ, Atonement.
see Atonement

Jesus Christ, come unto Him
1 Nephi 6: 4, 1 Nephi 13:40–42, 2 Nephi 2:8–10, 2 Nephi 26:33, Jacob 1:7–8, Jacob 6:5, Alma 5:16–34

Jesus Christ, prophecies of
2 Nephi 17:14–16, 2 Nephi 19:1–7, 2 Nephi 22:2, 2 Nephi 25:16

Jews
1 Nephi 10:1–3, 2 Nephi 6:9–18, 2 Nephi 10:7, 2 Nephi 25:14–15

journal
1 Nephi 6:1–6

joy
2 Nephi 2:25

K

King Benjamin
Omni 1:23–30, Mosiah 1–5

knowledge
2 Nephi 2:11–23, 2 Nephi 9:13–14, 2 Nephi 16:9–10, 2 Nephi 18:19–20

L

liahona
1 Nephi 16:10, 1 Nephi 18:12–14

liberty
2 Nephi 2:26–27

M

marriage
1 Nephi 7:1–5

missionary work
1 Nephi 1:18, Mosiah 17:1–4, Alma 8:18–20, Alma 16:13–21, Jacob 5:50–77

O

obedience
1 Nephi 4:10–18, Mosiah 2:41

opposition
2 Nephi 2:11–23

P

parents
1 Nephi 1:1, 1 Nephi 8:35–37

peace
1 Nephi 20:18–22, 2 Nephi 14:1–6, 2 Nephi 24:1–3, Mosiah 10:12–22

plan of salvation
Jarom 1:1–2, Alma 20:20–37, 2 Nephi 31:4–20

plates, brass
1 Nephi 3:3, 1 Nephi 4:16, 1 Nephi 5:10–16

plates, small and large
1 Nephi 6:3, 1 Nephi 9, Words of Mormon 1

prayer
1 Nephi 2:11–18, 1 Nephi 10:17–19, 1 Nephi 11:1–12, 1 Nephi 15:1–20, Mosiah 24:10–12, Alma 2:28–31, Alma 6:1–6

pride
1 Nephi 11:34–36, 2 Nephi 24:12–16, Alma 4:6–12, Jacob 2:12–21

priestcraft
Alma 1:1–33

priesthood
Alma 13:1–20

prophet, role of
2 Nephi 11:1–8, Jarom 1:10–15, Mosiah 2:1–9, Mosiah 8:13–18, Mosiah 28:10–20, Jacob 2:2–6

R

repentance
Mosiah 11:1–11, Mosiah 25:18–24, Mosiah

27:25–31, Alma 10:1–6, Alma 13:21–31, Alma 15:1–12, Enos 1:1–8

Restoration, of the gospel
1 Nephi 13, 2 Nephi 3, 2 Nephi 21:10–12, 2 Nephi 27:6–26, Jacob 5:66–77

Resurrection
2 Nephi 9:4–14, Mosiah 15:19–20, Mosiah 16:1–15, Alma 11:38–46, Alma 12:1–19

revelation, personal
1 Nephi 10:17–19, 1 Nephi 11:1–5, 1 Nephi 15:1–11, 1 Nephi 16:10–16

S

sacrifice, personal
1 Nephi 2:1–4, Mosiah 4:17–27

scripture study
1 Nephi 5:19–22, 1 Nephi 8:21–30, 1 Nephi 19:23, 2 Nephi 32:1–6, Omni 1:14–17, Mosiah 6:1–7

service
Mosiah 2:17

sin, consequences of
1 Nephi 10:4–6, 1 Nephi 20:18–22, 2 Nephi 9:27–52, 2 Nephi 26:10–13, 2 Nephi

27:1–5, Mosiah 2:33–34, Mosiah 11:1–11, Mosiah 12:2–8, Alma 11:26–37

T

temple
2 Nephi 5:15–17, 2 Nephi 12:1–3

temptations
1 Nephi 12:18–19, 2 Nephi 26:22, 2 Nephi 28:3–22

testimony, how to gain your own
1 Nephi 2:1–24, 1 Nephi 5:8–9, Jacob 7:1–27

testimony, sharing of
1 Nephi 2:18–18

trials
2 Nephi 2:2

U

understand
1 Nephi 9:5–6, 1 Nephi 15:1–11, 2 Nephi 2:11–23, 2 Nephi 31:1–3, 2 Nephi 32:1–6, Mosiah 12:9–37

ABOUT THE AUTHORS

JOHN S. BUSHMAN is proud to be the father of five, the son of two, and the husband of one. He grew up in Tempe, Arizona, and served a mission in the Philippines. Later he got his bachelor's degree in psychology and his master's in instructional technology from ASU.

He worked as a full-time seminary instructor for the Church's Seminaries and Institutes for ten years in Saint George, Utah. Now he teaches institute and coordinates the seminary program in NW Washington. Second to the Lord and his family, his greatest love is teaching and studying the scriptures with the youth of the Church.

One of his other passions is writing. He is the author of *Impractical Grace,* which is a story about how God's grace can heal any wound in life. He has recently coauthored a book with his wife, *Table Talk,* which is hundreds of questions and quotes to get family discussing the issues that matter most in life. Both of these books are published with Cedar Fort.

REED ROMNEY was born in Mesa, Arizona, and grew up in various cities including Philadelphia, Baltimore, Atlanta, Las Vegas, and even London. He served his mission in the Washington Spokane Spanish-speaking mission. He and his wife have been married for ten years and are the parents of three children. Reed currently lives in St. George, Utah, where he enjoys road biking nearly year-round.

Reed attended Brigham Young University and later earned a bachelor's degree from the University of Nevada, Las Vegas, in business finance, graduating *cum laude.* He then obtained a master's degree in business administration from Southern Utah University. Reed is a full-time teacher for the Seminaries and Institutes program of the Church of Jesus Christ of Latter-day Saints. He also owns and operates two businesses.

JOHN R. MANIS, or Jack as he is known to friends, was born to goodly parents in Las Vegas, Nevada. When he was twelve years old he found a book giving life sketches of each of the major characters of the Book of Mormon. Since that day, he has been determined to understand as much as possible from the Book of Mormon and the truth it contains. Jack currently teaches LDS seminary in St. George, Utah, with the support and companionship of his wonderful wife, three little boys, and his dog, Charlemagne.

CURT WAKEFIELD was born and raised in Idaho. He served a mission to Southern Italy, and then attended BYU-Idaho, where he received his bachelor's degree in recreational leadership. He has a master's degree in professional communication from SUU and is currently pursuing a doctorate degree in educational psychology at UNLV. He currently lives in St. George, Utah, where he has been a seminary teacher for eight years. He and his amazing wife, Shawna, are the parents of four children. He loves to learn about learning and teaching, which is why he was so excited to be a part of this book.